INTERNATIONAL HANDBOOK ON THE ECONOMICS OF TOURISM

International Handbook on the Economics of Tourism

Edited by

Larry Dwyer

*Qantas Professor of Travel and Tourism Economics,
University of New South Wales, Australia*

Peter Forsyth

Professor of Economics, Monash University, Australia

Edward Elgar
Cheltenham, UK • Northampton, MA, USA

Published by
Edward Elgar Publishing Limited
Glensanda House
Montpellier Parade
Cheltenham
Glos GL50 1UA
UK

Edward Elgar Publishing, Inc.
136 West Street
Suite 202
Northampton
Massachusetts 01060
USA

A catalogue record for this book
is available from the British Library

ISBN-13: 978 1 84376 104 4
ISBN-10: 1 84376 104 1

Printed and bound in Great Britain by MPG Books Ltd, Bodmin, Cornwall

Contents

Contributor biographies

Adam Blake is Lecturer in Tourism in the Christel DeHaan Tourism and Travel Research Institute, Nottingham University Business School, UK. He is an international expert on the computable general equilibrium modelling of tourism and related policies, for example modelling the effects of foot and mouth disease on tourism in the UK and September 11 on tourism in the USA. The results from his research on the effects of FMD on tourism were cited by the Minister of Tourism and in the House of Lords. He has published in a range of economics and tourism journals and has also written research reports for numerous governmental bodies in the UK as well as in other countries.

Adrian O. Bull is Associate Professor of Tourism at the University of Lincoln in England. Previously he had experience in both tour operation and the hospitality industry, and taught at Southern Cross University in NSW, Australia. He completed his PhD (on hedonic pricing in hotel markets) in 1998 at Griffith University in Brisbane. He is the author of the best-selling international textbook *The Economics of Travel and Tourism* (Longman, 1995), and has researched and published in a number of tourism and hospitality-related areas, relating to markets and pricing, ocean and coastal tourism, impacts and management. His current interests include studies of market definition in tourism, strategies for overcoming seasonality issues in coastal tourism, and the integration of tourism variables into bioeconomic ocean modelling.

Nevenka Čavlek is Professor and faculty member of the Department of Tourism at the Faculty of Economics, University of Zagreb, Croatia. She joined the Faculty after nine years experience working in the field of the tour operating business. As a result she has published a large number of articles and papers on the topic of tour operators, and received the First Mijo Mirkovič Award for the book *Tour Operators and International Tourism* – published in Croatian. She is also editor of the scientific journal *Acta Turistica*, and editorial review board member for East and Central Europe of the *Journal of Transnational Management Development*. She is a member of AIEST (International Association of Scientific Experts in Tourism) and IMDA (International Management Development Association), and a member of the Scientific Council for Tourism of the Croatian Academy of Sciences and Arts. Her discipline and expertise include: tourism economics, management of travel and tourism intermediaries and multinational corporations in tourism.

Geoffrey I. Crouch is Chair of Marketing in the School of Business, La Trobe University, Melbourne, Australia. Before joining La Trobe University, he held positions in the World Tourism Education and Research Centre at the University of Calgary, Canada, and the Graduate School of Management at Monash University, Australia. His research interests broadly fall into the area of tourism marketing. Topics of particular interest include destination marketing and competitiveness, tourist choice modelling, tourism psychology and consumer behaviour, space tourism and marketing research. He was also an elected member of the Board of Directors of the Calgary Convention and Visitors Bureau. Professor Crouch serves on a number of editorial review boards of scholarly journals and is co-editor-in-chief of the journal, *Tourism Analysis*. He has published numerous academic articles in leading journals including the *Journal of Travel Research*, *Tourism Management*, *Annals of Tourism Research* and the *Journal of Business Research*. He is an elected Distinguished Fellow of the International Academy for the Study of Tourism. He is also a co-author (with J.R. Brent Ritchie) of the book, *The Competitive Destination: A Sustainable Tourism Perspective* (CAB International, 2003).

Brian Davies is a Senior Lecturer at Staffordshire University Business School, Stoke on Trent, UK, and has a keen interest in the economics of tourism. As well as a number of joint publications on the travel and tour operator industry he has also published work on qualitative methods and the economics of the hotel industry. Additional areas of interest include the economics of rugby league and the triangulation of qualitative and quantitative methods.

Frédéric Dimanche is Marketing Professor and founding director of the Center for Tourism Management at CERAM Sophia Antipolis European School of Business (French Riviera), where he has led a Master of Science degree in strategic tourism management since 2001. He obtained his PhD at the University of Oregon, and then worked in the College of Business Administration at the University of New Orleans, USA. Dr Dimanche has published numerous tourism research articles and has been an active consultant, working for private companies and national or regional tourism organisations in the USA and abroad. In 1994, he received the National Tour Association (USA) Visiting Scholar Award for services to the tourism industry. He is a board member of the Travel and Tourism Research Association Europe and an associate editor of the *Journal of Travel*

Research. He is also a member of the International Association of Scientific Experts in Tourism.

Paul Downward is a Senior Lecturer in Sport and Leisure Policy and Management at Loughborough University, UK. His research interests cover methodology and substantive research in the sports, recreation and tourism sectors. The focus of his methodological research aims at exploring the match between methods of analysis and the material that they interrogate. He has recently published an edited book that addresses these issues, and has run two ESRC-funded training workshops for PhD students seeking to research and apply 'interdisciplinary' economic research. Dr Downward's interest in the sports, recreation and tourism sectors are wide ranging. He has recently focused upon both professional and non-professional sports, and both recreational tourism and the industrial organisation of tourism. In relation to the former he has published a book on *The Economics of Professional Team Sports* (with A. Dawson, Routledge, 2000), but has published widely in all of these areas. He is currently working with Sport England exploring participation in sports and leisure in the UK and SUSTRANS exploring the profile and economic impact of cycle tourism.

Larry Dwyer has a PhD and is Qantas Professor of Travel and Tourism Economics at the University of New South Wales, Australia. He publishes widely in the areas of tourism economics, tourism management and event management, with over 150 publications in international journals, government reports, chapters in books and monographs. He maintains strong links with the tourism industry at international, national, state and local levels, and has undertaken an extensive number of consultancies for public and private sector tourism organisations within Australia as well as consulting work overseas for international agencies, including the World Tourism Organisation. He is Head of the Sustainable Destinations Research Program of the Sustainable Tourism Cooperative Research Centre in Australia. He is on the editorial board of nine international tourism journals.

John Fletcher is an economist and Professor of Tourism and Head of the International Centre for Tourism and Hospitality Research at Bournemouth University, UK. He is also Head of Bournemouth University Graduate School. He has written numerous articles and book chapters on tourism's economic impact and the methodologies used to estimate such impacts. He has also pioneered the development of interactive economic and environmental impact software having undertaken studies for national governments and international agencies in more than 70 countries. He is editor-in-chief of the *International Journal of Tourism Research*, special adviser to the editorial board of the *Journal of Tourism Economics* and co-author of the leading textbook *Tourism Principles and Practices*, now in its third edition (Prentice Hall, 2004). He is a reviewer for a number of journals and funding bodies, a Fellow of the Tourism Society and a member of the International Academy for the Study of Tourism.

Peter Forsyth has been Professor of Economics at Monash University, Australia, since 1997. Most of his research has been on applied microeconomics, with particular reference to the economics of air transport, tourism economics and the economics of regulation. He has done extensive research on air transport, including on international aviation regulation and Australian domestic air transport. He also works on regulatory economics, and is the joint editor of a book on airport regulation (*The Economic Regulation of Airports: Recent Developments in Australasia, North America and Europe*, Ashgate, 2004). He has also done substantial research on tourism economics and policy. This has covered measurement of the benefits of tourism, assessment of international price competitiveness of tourism industries, foreign investment in tourism and taxation of tourism. Recent work has involved using computable general equilibrium models to assess the economic impacts of tourism, including events, and in analysing tourism and aviation policy issues.

Jonathan Gillham is a researcher at the Christel DeHaan Tourism and Travel Research Institute, Nottingham University Business School, UK. He has undertaken in-depth research on computable general equilibrium (CGE) modelling of tourism using static and dynamic frameworks, at the national, regional and multi-regional levels. He has considerable experience of tourism modelling, analysis and policy formulation in the UK, including analysis of tax-related issues and analysis of London's 2012 Olympic bid.

Dominique Jolly is a faculty member of CERAM Sophia Antipolis (France). He teaches strategic management and technological management. He is a regular speaker at company programmes and a guest lecturer in several French and foreign business and engineering schools. As visiting professor he has taught in several countries including the United Kingdom, Switzerland, Denmark, China, Mexico, Indonesia, Yugoslavia, Turkey, Iran, Moldova and Senegal. His articles have been published in more than ten different academic journals, including: *R&D Management*, the *International Journal of Technology Management*, *Technovation*, *Innovation: Management, Policy & Practice*, the *European Management Journal*, the

European Business Forum, the *Asia Pacific Business Review*, the *International Journal of Human Resources Development and Management* and *Management Decision*. He is a member of the executive council of the International Association for the Management of Technology (IAMOT), a founding member of the International Association for Chinese Management Research (IACMR), and a member of the European Academy of Management (EURAM).

Christine Lim is Professor of Tourism Management at the University of Waikato, New Zealand. She obtained her PhD from the University of Western Australia. Her research is of an applied nature in tourism demand modelling, which combines time-series modelling, tourism economics and management. She has been invited as a visiting scholar to prestigious universities in Japan (the Institute for Economic Research, Kyoto University, and the Osaka School of International Public Policy, Osaka University), and research institutes in Europe (the Centre for Economic Research at Tilburg University and the Tinbergen Institute at Erasmus University, Rotterdam). She is a resource editor of *Annals of Tourism Research*, an associate editor of the *Journal of Hospitality and Tourism*, and has served as an executive committee member of the Modelling and Simulation Society of Australia and New Zealand from 1999 to 2004.

Kreg Lindberg is an Associate Professor in the Department of Forest Resources and head of the Outdoor Recreation Leadership and Tourism (ORLT) program at Oregon State University, USA. He previously held positions in the Colorado State University Department of Natural Resource Recreation and Tourism and at universities in Australia and Norway. He has a PhD in forest social science with a minor in economics from Oregon State University. His professional interest areas include pricing, economic impact analysis and inter-visitor conflict in outdoor recreation and tourism, as well as the social impacts of tourism development in rural communities. He was lead editor for both volumes of the book *Ecotourism: A Guide for Planners & Managers* (Ecotourism Society, 1998), is on the editorial board of the *Journal of Sustainable Tourism and Journal of Ecotourism*, and serves on various professional committees.

John Loomis is a Professor in the Department of Agricultural and Resource Economics at Colorado State University, USA. He is also a Distinguished Scholar of the Western Agricultural Economics Association. Dr Loomis has published more than 100 articles on the valuation of recreation and other non-marketed natural resources such as endangered species, wetlands and wilderness. His research emphasis is the application of non-market valuation to improving the efficiency of public land management. The articles have served as the basis for his three books, *Recreation Economic Decisions* (with Richard Walsh, Venture Publishing, 1997), *Environmental Policy Analysis for Decision Making* (with Gloria Helfand, Kluwer, Academic Publishers, 2001) and *Integrated Public Lands Management* (Columbia University Press, 2002).

James Mak received his PhD in economics from Purdue University, USA, in 1970 and is currently Professor of Economics at the University of Hawaii at Manoa. His research interests focus on the economics of travel and tourism, public finance and microeconomic policy. He serves on the editorial boards of the University of Hawaii Press and the *Journal of Travel Research*. In 2001, he was co-winner of the Charles R. Goeldner Article of Excellence Award presented by the Travel and Tourism Research Association (TTRA). His latest book on travel and tourism is entitled, *Tourism and the Economy, Understanding the Economics of Tourism*, (University of Hawaii Press, 2004).

Clive L. Morley is Professor of Quantitative Analysis and a former Head of the School of Management at RMIT University. He gained his PhD with a thesis on tourism demand modelling from the University of Melbourne. He has taught analysis, modelling and strategy subjects on RMIT MBA programmes since 1989 and also currently teaches a Techniques of Strategic Analysis course in the Doctor of Business Administration programme, and a research methods course in the Master of Professional Accounting. He has worked as a statistical consultant for many companies. His expertise lies in the areas of applied data analysis, tourism economics, forecasting and strategic analysis techniques. In the tourism area, he has published articles on demand theory, modelling methodologies and practice, tourism pricing, the impacts of airline alliances and strategy in *Annals of Tourism Research*, the *Journal of Travel Research*, *Tourism Management*, *Tourism Economics* and the *Asia Pacific Journal of Tourism Research*.

Andreas Papatheodorou is an Assistant Professor in Industrial Economics with emphasis on Tourism in the School of Business Administration, University of the Aegean, Greece. He studied economics at Athens University of Economics and Business (BA) and at the University of Oxford (MPhil) specialising in international economics and industrial organisation. He subsequently received a DPhil in Geography from the University of Oxford for his thesis on evolutionary patterns in tourist resorts. Dr Papatheodorou is actively engaged in tourism research, focusing on issues such as consumer choice, competition, pricing and corporate strategy in air transport and travel distribution. He has acted as an advisor to the Greek government on tourism policy making and development and participates in education programmes in the Middle East. He speaks four languages and holds a professional degree in classical guitar.

Vicente Ramos is Associate Professor and Assistant Director of the Master and PhD program in Tourism and Environmental Economics in the Department of Applied Economics at Universitat de les Illes Balears (UIB). With a PhD in economics from UIB, devoted to the analysis of the tourism labour market in the Balearic Islands, mainly on the topics of education and training and on the analysis of gender labour market discrimination. He has published several scientific articles in national and international journals related to tourism and labour market topics which appeared in *Annals of Tourism Research* (Spanish version), and the *International Journal of Manpower*. He has worked on several competitive national and international scientific projects. He is also a member of the associated research group IMEDEA (CSIC-UIB). Dr Ramos's fields of interest are labour economics and tourism economics.

Javier Rey-Maquieira is Vice Dean of the Economics Faculty, Associate Professor in the Department of Applied Economics at Universitat de les Illes Balears (UIB) and member of the Master in Tourism Environmental Economics' program committee (Master and PhD program in tourism and environmental economics). He received his PhD in economics from the Universidad de Barcelona. He has published several scientific articles in national and international journals, and book chapters. Some of these related to tourism and environmental economics topics have appeared in *Water Resources Research*, *Annals of Tourism Research* (Spanish version), the *International Journal of Manpower* and in *The Economics of Tourism and Sustainable Development* (Edward Elgar, 2005). He has worked and has been director in several competitive national and international scientific projects related to tourism and environmental economics. He is also a member of the associated research group IMEDEA (CSIC-UIB). Dr Rey-Maquieira's fields of interest are macroeconomics, international trade, and tourism and environmental economics.

J.R. Brent Ritchie, whose research and professional interests are in the field of travel and tourism, is Professor of Tourism Management in the Haskayne School of Business at the University of Calgary, Canada. He also serves as Chair of the University's World Tourism Education and Research Centre. He was elected as the Founding Chair of the World Tourism Organization's Tourism Education Council in 2001. In 2004, he was awarded the WTO Ulysses Prize for 'his scientific contributions to the theory and practice of Tourism Policy, as well as his leadership over the past 25 years in the area of tourism education and research'. Dr Ritchie also has extensive professional and industry relationships. He served as President of the Travel & Tourism Research Association; President of the Travel Industry Association of Alberta; as Chair of the Calgary Convention & Visitors Bureau; and as a member of the National Task Force for the Study of the Banff Bow Valley Region.

Mondher Sahli is a Senior Lecturer at Victoria University of Wellington in New Zealand. He pursued his doctoral studies at the University of Paris I-Panthéon Sorbonne, within the CED programme (Centre d'Études du Développement), where he obtained both a Masters degree and a PhD in economics. He has an extensive teaching experience in Europe, North Africa and the Middle East. His publication output includes book chapters and refereed articles in international academic journals with a major focus on the economic impacts of tourism in developing countries and small island tourism economies. He has also worked with the United Nations Conference on Trade and Development (UNCTAD) as a coordinator of a new training programme on sustainable tourism for development.

Marcia Sakai is the founding Dean of the College of Business and Economics, University of Hawaii at Hilo, and holds the rank of Professor in Tourism and Economics. In teaching and research, her principal areas of interest include strategic planning for tourism, sustainable tourism development, destination marketing, economics of travel decision making, and government finance. She has conducted studies and published papers and book chapters on a range of topics, including Japanese international travel, business travel, tourism program evaluation, and foreign direct investment. She is a contributor to three books on Hawaii, *The Price of Paradise* (Mutual Publishing, 1992), *Politics and Public Policy in Hawaii* (Suny Press, 1992) and the *Atlas of Hawaii* (University of Hawaii, 1999). She is currently working on a book on tourism public policy in Hawaii. She is a Fulbright Fellow and was invited to teach at the University of Innsbruck. She has served as commissioner for the 1995–1997 Hawaii State Tax Review Commission, policy analyst for the State Department of Taxation, economist for the State Public Utilities Commission and consultant to the Office of State Planning and private corporations. She holds a PhD and an MA in economics and a BA and an MA in mathematics from the University of Hawaii. She has been at the University of Hawaii at Hilo since 1991.

Pauline J. Sheldon holds a PhD and is Professor of Tourism at the School of Travel Industry Management, University of Hawaii at Manoa, USA where she teaches and researches in the areas of international tourism policy, sustainable tourism, tourism economics and information technology in the travel industry. She has published widely in the tourism journals and is the author of three books in the field. She co-founded the international tourism researchers' electronic bulletin board called TRINET (Tourism Research Information Network), which links almost 1000 tourism researchers worldwide. She serves on the editorial boards of seven international academic journals, has won outstanding teaching awards, and is a member of the International Academy for the Study of Tourism. She is active in the international professional community and has served as chair of Business Enterprises for Sustainable Tourism Education Network, on the boards of the International Federation of Information Technology and Tourism, the Travel and Tourism Research Association and the Society of Travel and Tourism Educators. She has consulted for the World Tourism Organization, the World Bank and the Asia-Pacific Economic Cooperation (APEC) International Center for Sustainable Tourism.

M. Thea Sinclair is Professor of Economics of Tourism and Director of the Christel DeHaan Tourism and Travel Research Institute, Nottingham University Business School, UK. She has published extensively on the economics of tourism. Her books include *The Economics of Tourism* (Routledge, 1997), *The Tourism Industry: An International Analysis* (CAB International, 1997) and *Gender, Work and Tourism* (Routledge, 1997). In addition, she has published numerous journal articles and chapters. She regularly speaks at international conferences and is on the editorial boards of *Tourism Economics, Tourism and Hospitality Planning and Development* and the *Journal of Hospitality and Tourism Management*. She has directed studies for the World Bank, the United Nations Centre on Transnational Corporations, the British Council and for government organisations in the UK, Scotland, Cyprus, Malta, the Canary Islands and Brazil.

Haiyan Song holds the Chair in Tourism at the Hong Kong Polytechnic University. His main research area is tourism economics with a particular focus on tourism demand modelling and forecasting. Over the years he has been involved in a number of projects related to tourism demand forecasting in Hong Kong, Macau and other Asian countries such as Korea and Thailand. Two of his co-authored books on tourism forecasting have been well received by both researchers and practitioners. Professor Song has written extensively on tourism forecasting methodologies and much of his work has appeared in academic journals such as the *Journal of Applied Economics*, the *International Journal of Forecasting*, the *Journal of Transport and Economic Policy*, the *Journal of Travel Research*, the *International*

Journal of Hospitality Management, Tourism Economics and the *Journal of Travel and Tourism Marketing.*

Ray Spurr is Senior Research Fellow for the Sustainable Tourism Cooperative Research Centre (STCRC) Sustainable Destinations research programme. He is located at the University of New South Wales (UNSW) in Sydney, Australia, where he was formerly Director of the Centre for Tourism Policy Studies and Head of the Tourism and Hospitality Management Unit. Prior to moving to the university he was First Assistant Secretary of the Australian Department of Tourism. Other current appointments include Policy Adviser Asia/Pacific to the World Travel and Tourism Council (WTTC) and member of the World Tourism Organisation's Leadership Forum of Advisers. His research interests include tourism economics and public policy. He currently leads a research programme funded by STCRC which is applying computable general equilibrium modelling to estimating the economic impacts of tourism and the effects of tourism-related policy changes.

Clem Tisdell is Professor Emeritus in Economics at the University of Queensland, Brisbane, Australia. He is a prolific author. Recent books include *Economic Globalisation* (with R.K. Sen, 2004); *Tourism Economics, the Environment and Development* (2001); and *Ecological and Environmental Economics,* (2003). *The Economics of Environmental Conservation,* second edition was published in 2005 with Edward Elgar. *The Economics of Leisure* is nearing completion and should be published in 2006 in Edward Elgar's series (edited by Mark Blaug), The International Library of Critical Writings in Economics, to which Tisdell contributed *The Economics of Tourism* in 2000.

Maria Tugores is Associate Professor and Assistant Director in the Department of Applied Economics at Universitat de les Illes Balears (UIB) with a PhD in economics from the Universidad Carlos III de Madrid, devoted to the analysis of the determinants and effects of training in the Spanish labour market. She has published several scientific articles in national and international journals, some of which, related to tourism and labour market topics, have appeared in the *Annals of Tourism Research* (Spanish version), the *Annals of Tourism Research* (English version) and the *International Journal of Manpower.* She is responsible for two periodical studies that analyse the Balearics labour market, *Conjuntura* and *Informe Econòmic i Social,* published by the CRE (Research Economic Centre). She has worked in several competitive national and international scientific projects. She is also a member of the associated research group

IMEDEA (CSIC-UIB). Dr Tugores's fields of interest are industrial economics, labour economics and tourism economics.

Lindsay Turner is an internationally recognised researcher and a specialist in tourism forecasting and tourism economics. He is Professor of Econometrics and Head of School of Applied Economics, Victoria University, Melbourne, Australia. His major research interests include econometric modelling of international tourism demand, risk management strategies in international trade and cross-cultural tourism. He is also joint editor-in-chief of the journal *Tourism, Culture and Communication* and joint author of the annual Pacific Asia Tourism Association publication *Asia Pacific Tourism Forecasts*, which provides forecasts of tourist arrivals to 40 countries in the Asia Pacific region.

John Westlake is a Professor of Tourism Management in the School of Services Management at Bournemouth University, UK. John is involved in the teaching of Masters students and supervising Doctoral students. He is active in undertaking research and publishing in academic journals and is on the Editorial Board of the journals *Tourism Economics* and the *International Journal of Tourism Research*. His interests are in planning for tourism, transport for tourism and tourism and hospitality education where he has been active in publishing and undertaking project work in these areas. John has undertaken work for the World Tourism Organization and has been involved in European Union funded projects. He is widely traveled in the Asia Pacific region and maintains close contact with institutions and academic practitioners in that part of the world.

Preface

There is a large literature on tourism economics and so one is entitled to ask: 'why another publication?'. The answer is that there has been a need for a book which provides readers with 'state of the art thinking' on the major topics of tourism economics. To this end we invited leading tourism economists to contribute to the volume. For each topic we asked the authors to address the following issues: importance of topic; overview of main contributions/themes; critical evaluation of existing literature; state of art thinking on the topic; issues for further research (conceptual and applied).

Our aim has been to produce a volume that will be regarded as reflecting 'leading edge' thinking on major topics of tourism economics, by highly reputed scholars. This aim has been achieved. We would expect the book's contents to be widely referenced in the journal literature over the coming years, and 'required reading' for instructors and students of tourism economics, internationally.

We would like to thank the authors who have contributed to the volume. Thanks are also due to the staff at Edward Elgar who have guided its production. Undoubtedly, the biggest vote of thanks must go to our families (Libby Carroll, Eve Carroll-Dwyer and Joan Forsyth) for their support and understanding of the time demands of our research activity. Where we have been inconsiderate in neglecting their needs at times we unreservedly apologize.

Larry Dwyer and Peter Forsyth

Editors' introduction: contemporary issues in tourism economics

Larry Dwyer and Peter Forsyth

Tourism economics has been a rapidly expanding subject over the past decade or so – this is partly a reflection of the increasing interest in tourism research generally. Tourism papers are published in tourism and in economics journals, and there is now a specialist journal, *Tourism Economics*, devoted to it. There are several texts on the subject as well. What specific contribution is tourism economics making?

Tourism economics is not so much a new branch of economics, but rather it is an industry- or sector-based area of work which draws on, and applies, developments in general economics. In this respect, it is like transport or energy economics. As with these areas, there are some aspects of tourism economics which have been, or are becoming, of particular importance, in the way that choice modelling is a characteristic and important aspect of transport economics. Tourism economics draws on several, mainly micro-economic, branches of economics and econometrics, such as demand modelling, taxation theory, environmental economics, human capital theory and industrial organisation. More recently, it has been drawing on trade theory and general equilibrium modelling.

Recent developments in tourism economics have taken one of a number of forms. There are some areas which have been part of the traditional content of tourism economics which are being made more rigorous. Perhaps the best example of this is in demand analysis and forecasting. This has long been an important aspect of the subject, with many contributions, with a distinct emphasis on obtaining practical empirical results. Research in this field has been made more rigorous, and results made more reliable, by the use of advanced econometric specification and testing. This is illustrated in the two chapters by Lim and by Song and Turner. Taxing and pricing issues have also formed part of the content of the subject, and these have been informed by developments in taxation theory, pricing and infrastructure analysis, as the chapters by Mak, Sakai and Loomis and Lindberg show. So far, the analysis of the supply side of tourism has not attracted as much attention as the demand side – as Davies and Downward indicate, there is ample scope for greater application of new industrial organisation theory in this field.

By contrast, some fields of tourism economics are relatively new, or have taken a rather different turn. One of these concerns the measurement of economic impacts of tourism, for example the impacts of additional tourism into an economy, policy changes, such as in taxation or promotion, which influences tourism flows, or events or crises which affect tourism. Until about a decade ago, the prevailing approach to impact measurement was one using input–output multipliers – this approach normally produced an estimate of the impact on output which was a multiple, often about two, or the original change in tourism spending. Recently there has been a trend towards the use of computable general equilibrium (CGE) models. These are models which try to capture the overall structure of the economy, and reflect the interaction of markets and the presence of resource constraints. These models are now used extensively in the USA, the UK and Australia to assess the economic impacts of policy, for example on GDP, employment, tax receipts and industry structure. While their use in other areas, such as tax policy, trade policy and investment evaluation, is commonplace, they have only recently been used to explore tourism policy questions. Typically, these models come out with much smaller impacts on the key economic variables than do the input–output-based approaches, because they allow for crowding-out effects in other parts of the economy. They are now being used to explore a whole range of tourism policy questions, such as the impacts of taxes and promotion, the impacts of crises and growth in tourism flows – these are covered in Blake, Gillham and Sinclair. These models can also be used to analyse the impacts of special events, as Dwyer, Forsyth and Spurr show. Significantly, these models give very different perspectives on impacts of tourism changes from those generated by the earlier techniques, which are still in extensive use.

Another aspect of tourism economics which has been given more attention of late has been international trade in tourism. Tourism is a major traded service, and for many countries, it represents the largest single export and import. Thus there is a new emphasis on looking at tourism as a traded service. This is reflected in the analysis of tourism competitiveness (see Crouch and Ritchie), and in the use of competitiveness and other variables to explain the patterns of trade in tourism (Sahli). Exposure to trade in turn has implications for the structure of the tourism industry, and Fletcher and Westlake show how globalisation is impacting on the industry.

Part One addresses tourism demand and modelling issues. One of the aspects of tourism economics which attracts consistent interest is forecasting of demand. There are good reasons for this. The tourism product is perishable, but many of the costs incurred in providing for tourists are sunk. Thus there are substantial benefits from getting forecasts right. To do this, the demand function needs to be understood.

A good deal of interest surrounds demand elasticity estimates, such as estimates of price, cross-price and income elasticities. This is so for at least two reasons. Good elasticity estimates enable good demand forecasts. Second, much policy analysis relies on elasticity estimates. To estimate the impact of tax increases on tourism, or the effects of promotion on inbound tourism, a fall in air fares as a result of more competition from low cost carriers, or the impact of changes in competitiveness, it is necessary to have a good handle on the relevant elasticities. Papatheodoru examines the micro foundations of tourism demand. It is with knowledge of these that we are able to derive accurate specifications of demand to test econometrically. Lim pays attention to the specification and testing of demand models. It is evident in the studies which she reviews that there have been significant improvements in modelling of demand, though best practice is not universal. Song and Turner recognise the econometric issues involved in tourism demand forecasting, but also the relevance of aspects which are less easily captured, such as industry assessments.

In Chapter 1, 'A survey of tourism demand modelling practice: issues and implications', Christine Lim analyses 124 empirical studies of international tourism demand. She provides a detailed classification according to the decade of publication, type of data used, model specifications and alternative functional forms, the number and choice of dependent and explanatory variables used in demand studies. Past tourism studies have focused primarily on the economic variables affecting tourism demand. These factors are predominantly exogenous variables over which destination or tourist-receiving countries have little control. Most of the studies undertaken have been published in the 1980s, have used annual data, and have been based on estimation of log-linear single-equation models. Tourist arrivals/departures and tourist expenditure/receipts have been the most frequently used dependent variables. Lim concludes that the major factors influencing international tourism demand include income, relative tourism prices, transportation costs and a myriad of other factors. Although there have been a proliferation of studies since the 1960s on the relationship between tourism demand and its determinants, specific areas still remain underresearched, particularly those related to marketing and non-economic factors. The chapter also includes an econometric review of these studies to examine the method of estimation and diagnostic tests used.

Over time, tourism demand modelling practice has gone from using simple to state-of-the-art statistical and econometric techniques. As Lim indicates, the use of unit root tests and statistical analysis for non-stationary processes through the use of cointegration methods has revolutionised the understanding of tourism and macroeconomic time-series data. These developments permit both long- and short-run tourism demand models to be estimated and tested. However, there are many unanswered questions regarding the plethora of test procedures now available, particularly regarding their small sample properties. Lim's conclusion is that future research to evaluate and extend existing procedures for modelling tourism and tourism-related macroeconomic time-series data through the use of Monte Carlo numerical experiments is imperative.

In Chapter 2, 'Microfoundations of tourism choice', Andreas Papatheodorou emphasises that knowledge of the formation mechanisms and determinant factors of tourist choice is of primary importance for all tourism stakeholders. Tourists need to know themselves better, become more informed about the process of decision making and choose destinations and tourist activities that will hopefully increase their attractiveness, competitiveness and prosperity. His contribution first discusses the foundations of tourist choice in the context of the mainstream classical microeconomic theory – the standard benchmark in consumer demand analysis upon which other approaches are presented and evaluated. Despite some advantages, the classical theory fails to address essential issues including separability of preferences, discreteness in choice and product differentiation. As a valid alternative, therefore, Papatheodorou analyses the characteristics theory and its application in tourism economics. This is an interesting framework that deals successfully with many of the classical theory caveats. The chapter also discusses information issues and developments from a dynamic perspective before proposing areas for further research.

Papatheodorou emphasises the policy implications of this study. From the supply side, the deciphering of tourism choice can help service providers and destination policy makers to design appropriate marketing and advertising campaigns for specific consumer target groups. It can also assist them to manage the quality of their product integrally and face periods of crisis in tourism successfully. Similarly, researchers need to understand tourist choice factors to produce robust econometric models and forecasts that can facilitate destination management and long-term projection and decision planning.

As Papatheodorou acknowledges, it is not surprising that tourism choice and its microfoundations have received substantial attention by researchers in social sciences from both a theoretical and an empirical perspective. As in most cases with tourism, researchers are predominantly interested in applying the principles of their discipline to explain tourist choices. The economists would mainly focus on rational behaviour and utility maximisation issues, the geographers would examine tourist flows in space, the psychologists would discuss motivation while other social scientists would highlight socio-cultural factors. Likewise, researchers in marketing and advertising would study how tourist choice can be affected in favour of a targeted product or destination. To understand tourist choice in full it is important to integrate the above approaches and produce a creative, interdisciplinary amalgam. Such a task, however, is beyond the scope of Papatheodorou's chapter, which essentially explains how economics has treated the issue.

Chapter 3, 'Tourism demand forecasting', by Haiyan Song and Lindsay Turner, demonstrates that the forecasting of tourism demand has taken numerous turns in regard to methodology over the past twenty years. In the history of this development the methods have been variously assessed, compared and used in different contexts. This makes it increasingly difficult to follow the methodological history and to understand the current front line, and where the next steps are likely to take research. This chapter attempts to clarify both the historical development since 1990 of tourism demand forecasting, assess the various new developments and provide a view of current research directions.

Song and Turner point out that tourism researchers and practitioners are interested in tourism demand forecasting for several reasons. First, tourism demand is the foundation on which all tourism-related business decisions ultimately rest. The success of many businesses depends largely or totally on the state of tourism demand, and ultimate management failure is quite often due to the failure to meet market demand. Accurate forecasts of tourism demand are essential for efficient planning by tourism-related businesses, particularly given the perishable nature of the tourism product. Second, tourism investment, especially investment in destination infrastructures requires long-term financial commitments and thus the prediction of long-term demand for tourism-related infrastructure often forms an important part of project appraisal. Third, government macroeconomic policies largely depend on the relative importance of individual sectors within a destination. Hence, accurate forecasts of demand in the tourism sector of the economy will help destination governments in formulating and implementing appropriate medium- to long-term tourism strategies.

Song and Turner show that tourism forecasts may be generated by either quantitative or qualitative approaches, but they focus on quantitative forecasting methods, especially econometric approaches. Their review of the literature on the recent published studies of tourism forecasting suggests that several issues deserve more attention. First, although some researchers have used modern econometric techniques, such as cointegration and error correction mechanisms, in modelling and forecasting tourism demand, more effort needs to be made to follow continuously new developments in econometrics. The cointegration and error correction approach to modelling has now become a standard research methodology in applied econometrics and forecasting but tourism researchers have been slow to adopt state-of-the-art forecasting methods. Second, more research needs to be done to evaluate forecasting performance in tourism between modern econometric techniques and traditional time-series models in order to reach some agreement in this area. Third, very little attention has been paid to the issue of directional analysis in the tourism literature, but for certain strategic business decisions it may be more important to forecast correctly the direction of change in either tourism demand or the rate of growth of tourism demand, rather than to minimise error magnitude. Failure to predict major downturns or upswings in tourism demand could have serious financial consequences. Further research is also needed to examine whether the empirical results obtained on relative forecasting performance, in terms of directional change, still hold when more destination and origin country pairs, more modern time-series methods and different forecasting horizons are involved. Fourth, more research is needed into examining the nature and breadth of economic determinants used. As tourism becomes a more universal, social activity, undertaken for a wider range of reasons, by more diverse cultures, so the causal determinants of tourist flows may also change. Fifth, since one cannot expect to obtain a single model that consistently outperforms all other models in all situations, and researchers, policy makers and practitioners have a different interest in the ways in which the forecasting models are used, combining forecasts generated from different models would benefit all stakeholders. However, forecast combination is not a straightforward process and can include non-quantitative methods such as expert opinion; also, there are different ways in which the forecasts can be combined, all of which calls for serious research to be undertaken in the area of tourism forecasting.

Part Two explores 'Tourism supply'. The supply side tends to be relatively neglected in tourism economics. This may be partly due to the fact that the industry, being composed of many disparate individual industries like accommodation, retail and airlines, is difficult to characterise or summarise. This said, as Davies and Downward show, there is ample scope of the economics of industrial organisation to be used to analyse supply issues in the industry.

Information technology, and the rapid advances in it, is a recurring theme when tourism supply is being considered. IT is leading to substantial changes in the structures of some industries such as travel agents. The general issue of IT in tourism is considered in Part 6 by Pauline Sheldon, and its relevance to different aspects of supply is recognised by Čavlek, in looking at distribution, and by Bull, who considers the use of the internet by the industry more generally. Another aspect of supply concerns firm ownership and behaviour. Not all tourism suppliers can be characterised as profit-maximising private firms. Bull notes that many tourism firms may have objectives other than profit maximisation, and that this will condition their actions. Loomis and Lindberg examine the pricing behaviour of tourism suppliers which are government owned. Much of tourism supply comes from government-owned bodies, such as national parks, infrastructure suppliers like roads and airports, and some transport industries.

In Chapter 4, 'Structure conduct performance and industrial organisation in tourism', Brian Davies and Paul Downward argue that economic investigations into tourism supply and especially the nature of interfirm relationships remains underdeveloped territory. These authors are concerned to investigate supply-side economics as related to the tourism industry concentrating on the competitive environment. Davies and Downward argue that from a microeconomic perspective, the supply of tourism can be understood in terms of the models and concepts developed and refined in the structure conduct and performance paradigm (SCP) and, relatedly, the new industrial organisation (IO) literatures. Davies and Downward draw upon their previous research in the travel agency/tour operations business and hotels to highlight key issues that need further investigation and refinement, and which could have application to other tourism sectors. The authors first indicate the scale and economic importance of tourism, its definition, and how regulators implicitly draw upon SCP–IO concepts in terms of competition policy. They then outline the key concepts and links between the SCP and IO literature. There then follows a critical review of the existing tourism literature on travel and tourism and hotels. Existing work in the area has concentrated on oligopoly in supply being purely theoretical or drawing on descriptive features of the market, and is often contradictory. Davies and Downward have pioneered the use of econometric methods consistent with the methodological roots of SCP–IO literature. Yet, there are important conceptual and methodological issues to address if SCP–IO analysis of tourism is to advance. Descriptive case study research has a role here as does the triangulation of qualitative and quantitative methods. Davies and Downward highlight the processes actually at work in the business environment and explore links to statistically defended predictions of models. The potential of this approach is illustrated with some recent results on the behaviour of UK small-scale package tour companies. Davies and Downward conclude that an econometric strategy combined with insights from descriptive analysis will provide more robust industry insights. Further, academic primary research can help qualify the more formal quantitative analysis required of the SCP–IO literature, thus better informing public policy. Ultimately, this requires refinement of existing approaches together with a broader research methodology. Such frameworks will improve our understanding of not just SCP and IO but of the tourism industry. Greater understanding of business behaviour, hotels, tour operators, travel agents and the tourism business will result.

In Chapter 5, 'Industrial economics and pricing issues within tourism enterprises and markets', Adrian Bull begins with the claim that the majority of products traded within travel and tourism markets involve special characteristics such as intangibility, heterogeneity, a shared experience, simultaneous production and consumption, perishability, high fixed or sunk costs and cyclical demand. There are, moreover, often fixed capacity constraints facing tourism firms and multiple market segments with different elasticities of demand. Tourism involves a huge range of products, only some of which are substitutable, and therefore the 'market' for tourism is in fact fragmented into markets for many products. Suppliers in these markets therefore face unusual conditions involving market structure and price/output decisions. Some of the key problems identified are 'market definitions', which are challenging and vital for competition policy; 'market structures', which are heavily influenced by product differentiation and contestability issues; and the possible 'competitive and pricing strategies' that suppliers may then employ. These problems may also be complicated by non-profit objectives and the question of how to define tourism products.

A number of issues are coming to the fore in current research and Bull discusses some of these. First, the development of the internet is having a profound impact not only on the marketing of tourism products but also on the markets themselves, providing an open information source that is changing the asymmetric nature of market knowledge, and providing more consumer information to redress the historic problem of tourism being only an experience product. Research is moving from analysing the effectiveness of the internet as a marketing tool to more sophisticated applications such as its ability to create potential monopsonist or buying power tourist groups through on-line communities or for product and price information to become more readily available for analysis by competitors. The internet also helps to permit customisation as the offspring of product differentiation as suppliers with an investment in database marketing, or with the ability to unbundle and create bespoke travel and tourism products, are able to reposition themselves into a different market structure where the neoclassical rules of oligopoly or imperfect competition may not apply so readily. Second, many suppliers in tourism face a situation of competition to sell a core product, but then provide additional products under monopolistic conditions to tourists that buy the core product from them. For example, low-cost airlines may face a highly competitive market in selling air trips, but once the passengers are on board the airline can act as a monopoly supplier of food and beverages, duty-free goods and so on. Under these conditions, suppliers may select a non profit-optimal strategy for their core product, but one that maximises sales volume in order to maximise the captive market to which they can sell monopoly products at high profit. Current research in this area is utilising the economics of competitive clubs as a theoretical framework of analysis. Third, the issue of defining market boundaries more exactly is receiving increased attention, largely due to an emphasis on the actioning of competition policy in the EU and a number of countries including the USA, Australia and New Zealand. Market definition is becoming an object of demand- rather than supply-side study in many cases, since consumers can be more accurately surveyed to determine potential substitutability where products are complex as in tourism, rather than relying on official industrial classifications that in many cases do not serve tourism at all well. Fourth, researchers are finding new uses for methodologies such as hedonic pricing. This technique has been used to demonstrate how tour operators, supposedly under oligopolistic conditions, operate with market share objectives for market power. It has also been used to show how inefficient pricing by resort hotels in undervaluing or overvaluing their attributes compared with those of competitors can quickly lose demand in a local market.

There are a number of challenges to researchers concerning industrial organisation at the local or destination level, and that at the interdestinational level. Bull highlights the fact that there is currently no good analytical framework to deal with the paradox between the need for tourism businesses, especially small ones, to undertake cooperative promotion and other marketing to gain external economies of scale, and competition between these selfsame suppliers. This problem arises in the convention sector, for example. The 'economics of alliances' between partners whose activities are rarely competitive with each other is an insufficient tool for dealing with competitive cases. Bull argues that researchers have attempted to analyse the supply side of economic activity using standard economic and econometric tools derived from market structure and industrial structure analysis. However, the complexity of market definition and product definition means that it is perfectly possible to adjust slightly the specification of a 'product' or 'supplier' from a parametric perspective and yield completely different results from an analysis. For example, Davies and Downward (see their contribution to this volume) note the contradictory findings from analyses of the UK tour operating sector by other researchers and themselves. Clearly, the specification of 'competing suppliers' in sectors with such fuzzy boundaries as many of those in tourism is a continuing problem for analysis, and particularly for competition regulation authorities. Some authorities such as the EU are turning to consumer studies to identify and specify market boundaries, and there is clearly a need for research using, for example, tourism consumption systems methods to help to develop demand-side specifications.

Bull argues that it is important to establish to what extent suppliers are operating with objectives other than profit maximisation. Several articles in the research literature produce contradictory results since empirically many firms are not operating with the expected profit-maximising strategy. What impact do market share maximisation or personal 'concealing performance' objectives have on market structure and performance, given that they could well be common objectives for many suppliers within travel and tourism?

In Chapter 6, 'Travel and tourism intermediaries', Nevenka Čavlek discusses the key issues in travel and tourism intermediation. She emphasises that the business environment within which travel and tourism intermediaries operate has undergone radical changes and thus that travel and tourism intermediaries need to undertake necessary changes too. Čavlek focuses on the current role that travel agencies and tour operators play in the market, on the business environment of the largest tourism-generating markets, on the economics of travel agencies, and on the main commercial risks faced by agencies and operators. In order to show how the worldwide distribution network differs, the structures of sales items in Europe and the USA are compared and an illustration of retailing operating accounts is analysed. The complexity of the tour operating business is shown in the light of the principle of economies of scale and enlarged scopes of operations. However, since many risks are connected with these large-scale operations, the importance and complexity of yield management in the tour operating business is also discussed. Some predict that travel intermediaries do not have a future, because the need for intermediaries will disappear with better educated and more travel-experienced customers, as well as with the new possibilities that modern information technology offers.

Čavlek acknowledges that the possibilities offered by new information and communication technologies might be seen as a threat to traditional travel and tourism intermediaries, but claims that only by accepting modern technology as a partner can traditional intermediaries find themselves in a better position to secure their future in the market. This means that travel and tourism intermediaries need to undertake some changes in their core businesses. Another challenge to tour operators comes from the rise of low-cost ('no-frills') airlines, and the possibility of direct bookings of flights and accommodation through the internet. Existing internet portals can already combine accommodation services from hotel data systems and flights from airline computer reservation systems to create a package at daily prices. In response to this challenge, Čavlek points out that many tour operators have developed their own websites, and some are also already able to perform 'dynamic packaging' at daily prices. Moreover, vertically integrated tour operators have started their own low-cost flight operations, and are offering city-breaks using low-cost carriers. She argues that as long as tour operators can add value to their products, save time and money for their clients, and ensure their protection, they can secure their competitiveness in the long term. Since the business environment in which these companies operate is becoming increasingly competitive, and since the risks of their operation are very high, travel and tourism intermediaries are constantly seeking better organisational forms. There will consequently be an increasing need in the future to put more emphasis on the economics of their business.

Čavlek argues that the trend of consolidation that has taken place among travel and tourism intermediaries in the European market is slowly moving to the American market. At the same time there are visible signs of disintegration among European leisure travel concerns. The new organisational structures require new management models, but above all they require well-educated staff who will be able to lead the development of the industry. She concludes that, in general, the modern business of travel and tourism intermediaries is increasingly characterised by integration and cooperation as well as by the use of modern technology. Over time the market is likely to be more polarised between vertically integrated concerns and 'small players'. Small companies will be able to survive the competition of vertically integrated concerns only if they are able to offer products of high quality standards for clients with specific requirements, and in the long term foster high quality management and innovative activity. This is particularly important since large companies, which may have at their disposal high technology and which possess the capital for optimal development, cannot respond as quickly to changes as small companies. Large vertically integrated concerns will try to develop yield management techniques applicable to this very complex and risky business. One business function in particular that will gain in importance, no matter what the size of the company, will be risk management.

In Chapter 7, 'Pricing principles for natural and cultural attractions in tourism', by John Loomis and Kreg Lindberg, the basic thesis is that pricing plays many more roles in recreation and tourism management than might be imagined. Loomis and Lindberg begin with the claim that natural and cultural attractions in tourism often are owned by the government or non-governmental organisations, and this leads to pricing objectives and strategies that may differ from those in the private sector. The authors note that the very decision to retain these attractions in public ownership suggests that profit maximising pricing such as a private firm would pursue may not meet the objectives of public ownership. Public pricing goals often involve recovery of at least some of the management costs, while keeping sites affordable to allow for public exposure to the natural or cultural heritage. Thus a wider range of factors may affect the pricing decision in public agencies and non-profit organisations than in the private sector. Loomis and Lindberg describe economic approaches to pricing, and then describe alternative approaches that are driven by economic (for example, decreasing production costs) or non-economic (for example, revenue requirements, social equity) considerations. Even when non-economic goals affect the pricing decision, economic principles can guide the decision. Thus, if pricing is used to reduce negative ecological or congestion impacts, it is necessary to know the price responsiveness of demand to calculate the magnitude of a price increase needed to reduce visitation levels to a target amount. Also there are economic and recreation management consequences of pricing policies sensitive to social equity concerns. For example, low prices may lead to overuse or excess demand, necessitating supplemental non-pricing rationing.

The authors draw upon the relevant portions of the general public sector pricing literature and tailor general principles to the specifics of outdoor recreation and cultural sites. The principle of marginal cost pricing is introduced, and the cases of constant, decreasing and increasing costs of production are discussed. Strategies for peak load and differential pricing across products to manage visitor flows are presented, as is price discrimination across submarkets. The relationships between pricing and objectives such as maximising total revenue or achieving public goals such as equity across visitor groups are also described. The chapter stresses that economics plays an important role in the pricing of such attractions even when they are not profit-maximising private firms. Loomis and Lindberg acknowledge that the implementation of the types of pricing principles they discuss requires knowledge of visitor demand and price elasticity. This requires systematic research on a wide variety of tourist opportunities to understand the likely range of elasticities for typical tourist sites, facilities as well as different types of users and their region of origin.

Part Three covers 'Tourism transport', with particular emphasis on airlines. The links between tourism and transport are obvious, though there has been relatively little discussion of the two together in the literature. The role of aviation in tourism has been increasing rapidly over the past four decades, and within the aviation sector there have been developments which have important implications for tourism. One of these has been the moves by airlines, to form strategic alliances. The nature of these, and their impacts, is discussed by Dimanche and Jolly, and by Morley. Aviation has long been a controversial area for governments, which have been pressured by airlines' interests to implement restrictive regulations and by tourism and consumer interests to liberalise. The dominant trend has been one towards liberalisation, and this has facilitated the increasing role of aviation in tourism, as documented by Forsyth. These developments continue, with the boom in low-cost carriers leading to shifts in the patterns of tourism flows.

Business alliances represent a growing trend, particularly in the tourism sector. In Chapter 8, 'The evolution of alliances in the airline industry', Frédéric Dimanche and Dominique Jolly explore the nature of these business alliances, the effect of pulling resources together, and the types of benefits expected by the respective partners. After reviewing the existing literature on strategic alliances, Dimanche and Jolly employ a new typology of alliances that they illustrate in the context of tourism and, more specifically, airlines. The two types of inter-firm alliances are endogamy and exogamy. Endogamy occurs when partners share related profiles, whereas exogamy appears when allies exhibit unrelated profiles. The usefulness of this typology is that it enables the researcher to use resource-based approaches so as to suggest a dichotomy between alliances generating opposite results and representing very different stakes and risks. For practitioners, this typology allows the distinction between two classes that call for significantly different managerial approaches. Dimanche and Jolly propose the use of this original alliance typology to cast a new light on the evolution of strategic alliances in the airline sector.

Dimanche and Jolly claim that the nature of inter-firm alliances in the airline industry has changed dramatically over the last decade. The change has been from alliances being 'endogamic' to becoming 'exogamic' partnerships. The split between these two types of cooperation stems from the relatedness between allies' profiles. When two allies operate similar value chains in the same environment, they are likely to bring similar resources in the alliance; this opens the door to the accumulation of undifferentiated resources. In contrast, when allies operate different value chains or come from unrelated environments, they are likely to bring differentiated resources that they will try to combine. As a consequence, endogamies generate quantitative complementarities related to size effects, while exogamies produce qualitative complementarities. As endogamies, the aim was to gain some quantitative complementarities related to size effects including gaining joint economies of scale, increasing market power, cost sharing, reaching a critical mass, and so on. Airlines have since tended to reduce their involvement in these cooperation agreements to form new partnerships. Global alliances, for example Star Alliance, Oneworld and SkyTeam, are built between airlines to benefit from their differentiated profiles. These are exogamic partnerships. Because each partner operates a network different from that of its counterpart, together they are able to benefit from geographical and market complementarities. As the size of the networks increase, so do the strategic and managerial challenges. Whatever the research issue, Dimanche and Jolly suggest that an understanding of the evolution of alliances from endogamic to exogamic, should shed increasing light on the nature and the consequences of those alliances.

International airline alliances have become an important and growing feature of the airline industry. While these alliances are not stable, they are likely to continue to be a feature of the airline industry. In Chapter 9, 'Airline alliances and tourism', Clive Morley argues that alliances can affect both the demand and supply sides of tourism. Airlines are generally believed to benefit from lower costs, improved market access, coordination of services with partners improving productivity and reducing competition, and higher barriers to entry. Travellers are expected to benefit from the better service aspects and reduced fares as a consequence of reduced costs for the airlines. The balance of outcomes for tourists of improved efficiency of airlines versus a lessening of competitive forces needs to be determined empirically. Tourism demand could conceivably be greatly affected by the changes in the airline industry and airline operations that result from airline alliances.

Morley argues that the strong growth of alliances of international airlines raises two key issues for further consideration. The first is: are alliances likely to persist as an important feature of the airline industry? The second issue is consequential: if airline alliances will persist, what are the likely impacts on tourism?

The empirical evidence is that alliances have led to both lower costs for airlines and lower fares. However, it is not clear that the impact on tourism has been as marked. There is a need for future research to use better and more specific data, and thus generate focused and particular estimates of the impacts of alliances on tourism. As Morley notes, most of the studies carried out to date have been broad and general in their conclusions, giving average and overall results. For example, estimates of profit, productivity and fare impacts of alliances, while based in sophisticated theoretical economic models, are derived from data at a high level of aggregation (such as productivity indices rather than specific measures) and, as regression coefficients, are, in a sense, averages over time and airlines. For policy and planning purposes they give an indication rather than a precise figure for use in any particular case. There is a need for more focused data and estimates.

As Morley points out, most modelling of alliance impacts assumes that the air fares before the alliances are sustainable and appropriate, so that any reduction is an efficiency gain from the alliance. He argues that the situation can be more complex, and there could be an element of correcting unsustainably high prevailing fares. Many studies of airline alliances' effects have proceeded on the basis of an event study form of model. This has meant the formulation of a model and the incorporation into it of a dummy variable representing the presence of an alliance. However, the effects of airline mergers can be distorted in such modelling, as alliances may not be independent of existing features of a route (say) such as the previous fare levels, and as effects can take some time to become fully apparent. Thus, the straightforward use of dummy variables in econometric models to indicate the presence of an alliance, and other simple alliance indicators, can be misleading in the results they give.

Morley identifies some key weaknesses in the research literature to date that provide opportunities for further work. Important among these are the derivation of the elasticities used in most models, which assume that elasticities are constant in respect of other important variables such as incomes (that is, are constant over important market segments) and over time. Both of these assumptions are likely to be invalid and tests have confirmed this. It is thus necessary for accuracy that elasticities be continually re-estimated on up-to-date data. This is a matter of importance for tourism demand analysis in general, and of importance for such areas as assessing the effects of airline alliances where such elasticities are relied upon. The lack of sound estimates of cross-price elasticities is another aspect of this issue.

More particular to the studies of airline alliances, Morley highlights the use of posted, representative or average fares. Tourism flows, and much of the actual travel decisions of air travellers more widely, are often driven by discount, special or group fares. Alliances may not have a great impact on such fares, which are already very competitive and set by demand, rather than determined by cost considerations. The fares used in studies may not be a real representation of fares actually considered by tourists, and thus the impacts can be distorted. Additionally, the impacts of alliances on marketing, and the flow-on effects on tourism, are asserted but not well tested or estimated.

Morley concludes that models that include some of the features of alliances (such as lower fares, reduced stopovers, through ticketing and so on) as explanatory variables would be a step in advance of current models. Data for such variables might be obtained from specifically designed and conducted surveys. This would enable the estimation of the impacts on tourism numbers of the component aspects of alliances.

In Chapter 10, 'Aviation and tourism', Peter Forsyth demonstrates that these concepts are closely linked – for many tourists, especially international tourists, air transport is the preferred or only effective means of transport. The growth of tourism in the past fifty years has been greatly stimulated by developments in aviation. While there is now a substantial literature on both tourism economics and the economics of aviation, there have been relatively few contributions which explore the connections.

For many journeys, the services of the air transport and the tourism industries must be consumed jointly. As a consequence, there are many ways in which the two industries impact on one another. Changes in the industry structure of one, such as those which came about due to liberalisation of air transport, have resulted in the stimulation of growth in the other, such as long-haul tourism. Technical progress in aviation has resulted in lower fares, which have stimulated tourism growth. Government policies imposed on one industry, such as taxation of tourism, have impacted on the other.

Forsyth acknowledges that there are conflicts of interest between tourism and aviation sectors – lower air fares stimulate tourism, but put pressure on airline profits – and that this has posed policy dilemmas for governments. Over time, however, governments have chosen to implement less restrictive regulation of air transport, and this has led to more competition, lower fares and more travel. Forsyth argues that this trend towards liberalisation has reflected the recognition that overall gains are made by having a liberal environment, even if some interests are adversely affected. It reflects a greater understanding of the economic and other benefits tourism can bring to a country, and it reflects a more articulate tourism industry in many countries. While there has been some cost in terms of airline profits and staff remuneration, countries see gain in encouraging tourism through more efficient and lower-cost airlines.

There have been several phases in these developments which have been critical, such as the development of charter markets in Europe, US domestic airline deregulation and the emergence of low-cost carriers. Improvements in aviation technology have also impacted on tourism, notably by lowering costs, and they have also impacted on patterns of tourism. Taxation is one area in which the links between aviation and tourism are important – governments can tax air transport, tourism products or both, and they need to determine the balance between these taxes. In spite of the links, there is not much by way of integration at the firm level between aviation and tourism, though there are some exceptions to this. Important exceptions include tour companies which operate charter airlines, and airlines which invest in travel agents.

There are challenges that require additional research. The impacts of aviation changes on tourism, and the measurement of the economic benefits from consequent changes in tourism have been under-researched. This is something which is now being factored into aviation policy making, though explicit measurement of benefits is still in its infancy. Related to this is the need for a better understanding of the determinants of tourism demand. Tourism demand modelling is becoming more sophisticated (see the chapter by Lim in this volume), and some models explicitly include aviation (for example, air fare) and ground component (for example, ground component prices) variable as determinants of tourism demand. Both types of variable are significant, and they influence demand in different, though related, ways. They will influence not only total visitor flows, but also duration of trips, and expenditure in total, and per night. As Forsyth emphasises, more detailed evidence on how aviation changes, such as falls in fares, impact on these variables will enable more accurate measures of the impact of aviation changes on tourism economic benefits.

A final aspect of the aviation–tourism connection that Forsyth examines concerns aviation and tourism taxes. The impacts that taxes on one level can have on the other can easily be understood. However, policy makers rarely put all the pieces of the jigsaw together. Does a country wish to encourage tourism, and maximise economic benefits of tourism, by keeping taxes, on both aviation and ground tourism, low? Or does it wish to make use of its market power, and use foreign tourists as a source of revenue? Whichever of these options it chooses, it will need to determine at which level – aviation or ground tourism – such taxes are best levied. Furthermore, if there is already general taxation of tourism and aviation services, it will need to determine how best to counteract these if it wishes to keep taxes low. Aviation and tourism taxation need to be considered jointly – though often they are not.

Part Four concerns 'Tourism taxation and infrastructure'. Governments both support tourism, by providing infrastructure for it, and take advantage of it, by taxing it. The tax issue is a particularly important one for the tourism industry, because tourism taxes are one of the few taxes which, from the perspective of an individual country or region, might be exportable, an issue which Mak considers. This poses a policy dilemma for governments – additional taxes on tourism exports are mainly paid by non-residents of the country – however, they do discourage tourism, and lessen the economic impacts and benefits that tourism expenditure might bring (considered in Part Five, below). Taxes can also be used to fund infrastructure provision, as considered by Sakai, and can encourage tourism in this way. Given these conflicts, it is not surprising that different countries choose different approaches – some keep taxes low to maximise the benefits from additional tourism expenditure, while others prefer to export their taxes, at some cost to the size of their tourism industries.

In Chapter 11, 'Taxation of travel and tourism', James Mak begins with the observation that tourism development is not a free good. Like residents, tourists and their suppliers demand public services which have to be paid for through taxes and user charges. The production of tourism goods and services requires resources which must be diverted from other economic uses. The net benefit from tourism development depends critically on how a destination designs its public finance/revenue system to tax travel and tourism. Taxing tourism is one way for tourist destinations to reap the economic gains from tourism development and, since the 1980s, taxes levied on travel and tourism have proliferated around the world. Destinations tax tourism for at least four reasons: to expand and diversify their tax base; to export taxes to non-resident tourists; to tax away excess profits or economic rents from tourism to benefit residents; and to correct for market failure. Mak argues that the growth of tourism has provided destinations with an excellent opportunity to broaden their tax base and export taxes to tourists. Tax exporting is not unique to tourism. Some explain that politically it is easier to tax tourists rather than residents because tourists are not constituents. Evidence, however, indicates that where tourism is an important contributor to the local economic base, tourism suppliers constitute powerful political interest groups which are quite capable of defeating or delaying efforts to impose new or increase existing tourist taxes.

Mak notes that, by the early 1990s, the travel industry became quite alarmed by the proliferation of taxes levied on tourism. The fundamental question that must be addressed by both the industry and policy makers is: 'What are the impacts of a growing tax burden on the world's largest industry?'. In response, Mak attempts to answer four questions: (i) What is a tourist tax? (ii) What are the economic reasons for taxing travel and tourism? (iii) Who ultimately bears the burden of tourist taxes? (iv) Is it economically 'efficient' and 'fair' when goods and services that are largely purchased by tourists are more heavily taxed? Within the tourist industry, it is widely believed that the industry and tourists are being unfairly singled out for taxation to the detriment of both tourism and destination residents. Mak argues that there are sound economic reasons for taxing tourism beyond simply collecting revenues to pay for public services that benefit tourists and tourism suppliers. A well-designed system of tourist taxation can benefit the residents of destinations in a number of ways: it can broaden and increase the revenue elasticity of the destination's tax base, extract economic rents, and protect the environment (which also benefits tourism). It can also benefit tourism by making more money available for tourism promotion and for the construction and operation of convention centres. Mak also argues that levying higher taxes on goods and services that are largely purchased by tourists does not necessarily reduce economic efficiency or equity.

Mak concludes with a brief discussion of user charges in tourism. Unlike taxes which are paid under coercion, user charges, like prices in private markets, are 'voluntary' payments in that only those who choose to use those services are required to pay. User charges are most appropriately used to finance public services when most or all of the benefits go to identifiable users, and those who do not pay can be denied use at a reasonable cost.

Mak points out that more research needs to be done on the direct impacts of travel and tourist taxes on the demand for travel. As well, we need to know more about the incidence and exportability (*ex post*) of tourist taxes. We also need to know more about how to tax and collect revenues from multinational tourism businesses given that their activities take place in different countries and tax juridictions. A topic which has not received much attention is the effect of tax incentives on tourism investment. To date, studies of the tourism's tax impacts have relied on static partial equilbrium analysis. In the future the greatest value added would undoubtedly come from examining the impacts of tourism taxation from a general equilibrium perspective using computable general equilibrium modelling techniques. (See the contributions in this volume by Blake, Gillham and Sinclair, and by Dwyer, Forsyth and Spurr.)

In Chapter 12, 'Public sector investment in tourism infrastructure', Marcia Sakai claims that tourism infrastructure provides an important foundation for tourism development, perhaps second in importance only to a destination's attraction resource base, because infrastructure is vital to the commerce of tourism. While infrastructure may be defined to include public safety, mail and freight services, medical systems, financial systems, education systems, national defence, and other services that support both resident and tourism demand, such as retail and shopping, Sakai defines infrastructure as capital-intensive, long-lived physical assets that provide benefits to the general public or to promote economic development.

Sakai argues that infrastructure increases the efficiency of privately producing and distributing tourism services, and in certain cases, such as tourism enclaves or remote destinations, makes possible the supply of tourism services. Tourists, in particular, travel to destinations in other countries or to other regions within their own country, thus making passenger transportation infrastructure a key element. Whether travel is by land, air or sea, the supporting airport and harbour transportation nodes, as well as railway, road, bridge and tunnel networks, are required. Tourists, moreover, add to the effective population of a destination, requiring the same basic services that are ordinarily consumed by residents. The demand for infrastructure services of water supply and waste disposal, communication and electricity is thereby increased.

Public investment in infrastructure that serves the needs of tourism is common, because it serves both tourists and residents. From an economic perspective, public investment is rationalised when private markets fail to produce an efficient amount. Sakai regards the provision of tourism infrastructure as of particular importance in the long-term environment of

tourism growth. Expanded facilities are needed to accommodate anticipated growth and to maintain a relatively uninterrupted service level. At the
same time, environmental changes in the technology that supports the
various infrastructure networks, geo-political changes that affect oil
resources heavily used in modern transportation, and socio-political
changes that affect government ability to finance tourism infrastructure are
anticipated to affect the look of tourism infrastructure finance for the future.

Sakai argues that the primary public finance issue is whether public
investment is commensurate with marginal public benefits and costs. This
may be characterised alternatively as determining whether the incremental
addition of infrastructure yields only private benefits. This issue is highlighted by greater efforts to increase the level of private investment and
funding through user charges and by the trend to privatisation or
public–private partnerships. Public policy decisions would be better
informed by research that establishes the marginal benefit and marginal
cost of public infrastructure investment, as well as the distribution of these
benefits and costs. This analysis is needed for deciding how to finance the
investment itself, as well as how to finance operations. Opportunity costs
need to be assessed, including the costs of externalities. And the long-lived
nature of the infrastructure asset requires an analysis that takes into
account benefits and costs over time. Besides the traditional static partial
equilibrium or input–output analyses (criticised in Blake et al. and Dwyer
et al. in this volume), dynamic general equilibrium analysis has significant
promise to better assess infrastructure projects and their public finance.

Part Five covers 'Evaluation for policy making'. The measurement of the
size, contribution and impacts on the economy of tourism have been areas
of major development in tourism economics over the past decade or so. An
area which has seen extensive empirical work has been the measurement of
the size of the tourism industry by means of tourism satellite accounts
(TSAs). Several countries have now incorporated these as part of their
national accounts. The measurement problem stems from the tourism
industry really being parts of other industries, rather than a single defined
industry in itself. As Spurr shows, in the past it has not even been clear how
large the tourism industry in a country was. TSAs are of interest in themselves, but they also provide data for further developments, such as productivity analysis and construction of CGE models.

While the TSA is essentially a static set of accounts, CGE models make it
possible to assess how changes in tourism impact on the economy. CGE
models are models of the whole economy, and they incorporate the interactions between sectors, and reflect resource limitations. They embody an
input–output structure, and incorporate a TSA. They enable estimates to be
made of how a change in tourism, such as additional tourism encouraged by

promotion, or reduced tourism due to a crisis, will impact on key economic variables, such as GDP, which is an overall measure of output, employment, tax receipts and exports. They also enable one to determine how other industries are affected by tourism changes. Blake et al. survey the developments in applying CGE models in tourism, and discuss specific applications such as modelling crises and tax changes. CGE models can be used to estimate the economic impacts of special events, as Dwyer et al. show. Special events are often promoted on the grounds that they encourage economic activity, and the economic impacts have, in the past, been estimated using input–output techniques. Dwyer et al. show how CGE models can be used to evaluate events, and indicate how the results of such evaluations will differ from those using the earlier techniques. Typically, much smaller economic impacts will emerge. With governments now paying particular attention to the economic impacts of their policies towards the tourism industry, CGE modelling is likely to have a growing role in informing policy making.

In Chapter 13, 'Tourism Satellite Accounts', TSAs are discussed by Ray Spurr. A TSA is a statistical tool for measuring the total economic and employment significance of tourism in a national economy. It sits alongside the main tables in the System of National Accounts and is conceptually consistent with them. To do this the TSA needs to be based on a consistent and authoritative set of definitions and methodological approach. These have been broadly agreed through international negotiations held under the auspices of the World Tourism Organization. The benefits of a TSA include that it provides an integrated set of data within accepted national accounting principles which identify a clear position and importance of tourism within the economy. It also provides an improved and more credible data and a common methodological base for further analysis to support government and industry decision making and strategic planning. TSAs can be expected to be taken up by an increasing number of countries and will contribute to enhanced understanding of tourism and recognition of its economic importance. There remains potential for a growing range of applications. For researchers, TSAs represent a valuable and, as yet, barely tapped resource.

In Chapter 14, 'CGE tourism analysis and policy modelling', Adam Blake, Jonathan Gillham and M. Thea Sinclair argue that CGE models are particularly suited to tourism analysis and policy. In contrast to partial equilibrium approaches, CGE models can take account of the interrelationships among tourism, other sectors in the domestic economy and foreign producers and consumers. The modelling can be tailored to alternative conditions, such as flexible or fixed prices, alternative exchange rate regimes, differences in the degree of mobility of factors of production and different types of competition. CGE tourism models are particularly helpful to policy makers, who can use them to provide guidance about a wide variety of 'What if?' questions, concerning the range of domestic or international shocks or policy scenarios that can arise.

CGE models are based on the recognition of the economy as a general equilibrium system. There are four types of equation: equilibrium conditions for each market ensure that supply is equal to demand for each good, service, factor of production and foreign currency; income–expenditure identities ensure that the economic model is a closed system; behavioural relationships give economic agents' reactions to changes in prices and incomes, determining consumers' demand for each good and service; production functions determine how much is produced for any given level of factor utilisation.

The authors document the main contributions that CGE modelling has made to tourism analysis, initially outlining the theory that underlies the models and subsequently providing an overview of the empirical studies that have been undertaken in the tourism field. They review the application of CGE models to tourism in a range of countries including Australia, the UK, the USA and Indonesia. The CGE modelling framework is sufficiently flexible to allow for the incorporation of different sets of assumptions concerning consumption and production relationships, in accordance with the empirical circumstances or scenarios under consideration. Although the assumptions of fixed prices and fixed coefficients may be valid within some empirical contexts, in cases where the assumptions do not hold, input–output (I–O) models provide overestimates of economic impacts. The implication is that policy makers should use the more widely encompassing framework of CGE modelling, within which the I–O model is but one of a set of alternative models. The development of CGE models designed specifically for tourism has been geared mainly towards examining the economic impact of changes in tourism demand on the macro economy and the different economic sectors within it. Subsequent studies have examined alternative tourism-related policy options that the government can follow.

The use of CGE models has been facilitated by the development of Tourism Satellite Accounts, which have provided substantial increases in the quantity and quality of the data that can be used in the models (see the chapter by Spurr). TSAs provide an ideal basis for CGE models that can examine the analytical and policy-related questions that the more descriptive TSAs are not designed to answer. It is within the context of further and more geographically widespread TSA development that the use of CGE tourism models throughout the world is taking off.

The authors examine CGE models in the context of their theoretical framework and applications to tourism analysis and policy making. The discussion explains the ways in which the general equilibrium framework of the models is evolving to incorporate imperfect competition and dynamic analysis, each of which contributes further insights into the nature of the interrelationships between tourism and other sectors of the economy. The models have provided information relevant to the formation of policies for dealing with events as diverse as shocks resulting from foot and mouth disease or terrorism or changes in different types of tourism taxation. CGE models can also be used to examine such issues as the implications for tourism and other economic sectors of membership of the European Union or other trade associations. Further research should concentrate on further development of models incorporating imperfect competition and dynamic analysis, extending the models to take account of more microeconomic information and undertaking further policy analysis, complementary to the information provided by TSAs.

Blake et al. claim that future research on CGE tourism analysis is likely to focus on three main areas. The first involves further research on dynamic CGE analysis. This is currently at the frontier of developments in tourism modelling, in terms of both theoretical and empirical contributions. The second area concerns the incorporation of more microeconomic information into CGE models of tourism. This is an area that is in the forefront of research on CGE modelling. The incorporation of detailed information at the level of individual households' consumption and firms' production behaviour and their interactions with the macroeconomic representations of economic behaviour characterised by CGE models would improve the quality, accuracy and insights available from the analysis. It would also provide interesting results about the distributional implications of tourism shocks or tourism-related policies. This type of information is a prerequisite for effective strategies to enable tourism development to contribute effectively to poverty alleviation. Such developments in CGE tourism modelling should not be considered in isolation but should complement developments in econometric modelling. The latter can provide more accurate estimates of the parameter values that are included in CGE models, relating to more disaggregated levels of analysis, providing improved means of policy formulation. Thus, the future of CGE tourism analysis depends upon both improvements in modelling and the provision of a superior quantity and quality of data. In the context of tourism modelling, such improvements should encompass the provision of a more disaggregated range of data for different types of tourism production and consumption, such as business tourism, short breaks, educational tourism and adventure tourism. Improved data at the regional and local levels would also assist more effective policy formulation, along with better coordination of policy making at the local, regional, national and international levels.

The third area concerns policy analysis. CGE modelling can show the ways in which tourism impacts and policies are integral to wider macroeconomic events and policy making, demonstrating the ways in which shocks or policies that affect one sector of the economy impact upon others. The modelling can shed specific light on a wide range of issues, including foreign direct investment in tourism, tourism productivity and competitiveness, fiscal policies for tourism, policies within wider international groupings such as the European Union, policies for transportation, the environment and related externalities. The future for CGE modelling of tourism is bright, particularly given the context of ongoing development of TSAs for countries across the world. Clearly, TSAs provide the means of describing and quantifying tourism's contribution to different economies. However, they must be complemented by tourism modelling if they are to provide businesspeople and governments with effective guidance for dealing with the range of events and policy decisions that have to be made on an ongoing basis. CGE tourism modelling provides a versatile and effective means of examining the wide range of scenarios that can occur.

Special events are typically regarded as major generators of economic activity and jobs. While there may be other perceived benefits from events, such as 'putting a city on the map', facilitating business networking and civic pride, much of the public justification of events funding centres around the perceived positive economic impacts of events. In Chapter 15, 'Economic evaluation of special events', Larry Dwyer, Peter Forsyth and Ray Spurr argue that the economic impacts and benefits of events, if rigorously assessed, are very much lower than those invariably claimed, implying a misallocation of events funding generally, and excessive overall spending in promoting events. Input–output models estimate the positive economic impacts on spending brought about by changes such as special events; however, they do not measure the equally real negative economic impacts. An event brings additional demand to the economy – as this demand is met, additional output and jobs are created. However, the process does not end with the positive effects. I–O analysis essentially assumes that all resources and inputs are provided freely, and that no resource constraints exist. In real-life economies, when more resources are required in one area of the economy, they are drawn away, at least in part, from productive activities elsewhere in the economy. Prices of inputs and wages get bid up, and other activity is discouraged. The net impact on output and jobs from a boom in demand, such as would be created by a special event, is much less than the initial injection of spending. Despite its continued use in event assessment, I–O analysis has been rejected in other areas of economic impact evaluation. In industrial countries at least, much economic policy discussion of the impacts of shocks to different industries now relies on the much more rigorous evaluation technique of CGE analysis, which recognises resource constraints and the inter-industry effects of demand shocks.

An issue neglected to date concerns the interests of the different levels of governments involved in the event assessment process. To make informed decisions about events policy, governments need to know the answers to the following questions: (i) How much will the event add to economic activity and jobs after accounting for inter-industry effects? (ii) Is the event likely to produce net economic benefits, and if so, how much is it worth subsidising? (iii) To what extent do the benefits of the event come at a cost to other jurisdictions? Such questions cannot be answered within the I–O approach. It needs to be emphasised that the perspectives on an event from the local, state and national levels will be quite different. An event may be highly attractive to a rural city, though only of marginal or negative benefit to a state. Notwithstanding this, a state government may be prepared to subsidise the event, even though it is basically shifting, rather than creating, economic activity and jobs. This could be so if a region is depressed, and the state government wishes to give it some stimulus. For this to be worthwhile, the event must be assessed in comparison with other forms of stimulus – there may be ways in which the same funds could generate a greater impact on local economic activity, or a similar impact without as large a negative impact on other parts of the state. If so, it would be more effective to subsidise these alternatives rather than the event. And such decisions should be taken in full awareness of who the winners and losers within the state will be, both in regional and industry terms. The losers might well be other depressed regions, or industries, within the state. An I–O analysis will provide no information on this. Where an event receives financial support from the state government, assessment of the statewide effects is critical.

Dwyer et al. estimate the economic impacts of a selected event on the New South Wales and Australian economies, and on the economy of the rest of Australia using both a CGE and an I–O model. The I–O model is that contained within the CGE model which they have developed for the Australian Sustainable Tourism Cooperative Research Centre. The comparison reveals substantial differences between the techniques with respect to estimates of the economic impacts. Specifically, I–O modelling projects a much greater impact on real output, value added and employment on both New South Wales and Australia, as compared to CGE modelling. In contrast to the I–O model, which projects a positive (or zero) change in output in each industry sector in the state, the CGE model projects reduced output and employment in several industries.

The authors discuss, and reject, arguments that continue to be advanced by advocates of I–O modelling of event impacts. Several types of (inter-related) claims are often made for continuing to use I–O models to estimate the multiplier effects of event. These are: the choice of model depends on the size of the event; the choice of model depends on the location of the event; the choice of model does not matter since adjustments can be made to I–O results to make them more realistic; CGE models are required to make too many assumptions making them too complex to use; and CGE models are costly, and often unavailable. On the basis of such arguments, I–O analysis continues to receive support in some quarters as the preferred technique of event assessment. The authors consider carefully the nature of each claim and the qualifications that must be made to each.

The distinction must be made also between the impacts and net benefits of events, a distinction which many researchers have failed to appreciate. Economic impacts, such as the change in GDP resulting from an event, are not the same thing as the economic benefits which arise. The impact on GDP is a *gross* measure of the change in value of output as a result of an event. This addition to output normally requires additional inputs, of land, labour and capital, to enable it to be produced. These inputs have a cost, and this cost must be deducted from the change in value of gross output if a measure of the net economic gain is to be made. Standard CGE models can be adapted to produce, as part of their output, an estimate of net benefits – the cost of additional inputs is subtracted from the value of the additional output.

A rational events strategy involves funding events at a level which is appropriate given the benefits they create, and which reflects the benefits which could be obtained by using the funds elsewhere. It also involves allocating the funds available to the events which create the greatest net benefits. Achieving this requires at least two things to happen. First, there needs to be rigorous economic evaluation of events, implying a move away from the current practice of exaggerating economic impacts. Second, there needs to be an institutional framework under which there is the incentive for this to happen.

Part Six includes applications of economic theory to resolve problems in the tourism industry. At its core, it deals with aspects and determinants of economic performance of the tourism industry. Tisdell deals with the environmental performance – how environmental impacts can be valued in economic terms, and how they can be handled efficiently using economic instruments. Two key inputs to tourism are labour and IT. Rey-Maquieira, Tugores and Ramos examine labour, and more specifically, human capital issues in so far as they affect tourism and its performance. Sheldon documents the increasing role of IT in the industry, and how it is changing structures and performance.

International dimensions of performance are considered in the last three chapters. Crouch and Ritchie discuss tourism competitiveness in broad terms, highlighting non-economic as well as economic dimensions to destination competitiveness. Sahli looks at competitiveness and trade patterns in tourism. Competitiveness, along with other factors, influences how countries trade in tourism services. Trade in tourism services, in turn, is having impacts on countries' tourism industries. Globalisation, which encompasses trade and other aspects, is considered by Fletcher and Westlake. Aspects of globalisation, such as the formation of multinational enterprises, are having an impact on home tourism industries, for example by putting pressure on small and medium-sized enterprises, which have formed the basis of many sectors of the tourism industries up to now.

In Chapter 16, 'Valuation of tourism's natural resources', Clem Tisdell discusses the implications of the economic valuation of natural resources used for tourism. Much tourism depends on the environment(s) at the destination(s) of tourists. Such environments may be natural, cultural, or partly man-made and partly natural. Considerable progress has been made since the early 1960s in developing and applying techniques for the economic valuation of environmental/natural resources. However, as far as tourism and recreation are concerned, these developments have concentrated on estimating the use value of natural sites or resources for this purpose. While this emphasis has its relevance, this chapter emphasises the risk of neglecting non-use economic values. Taking these values into account may strengthen the economic case for conserving a natural area used by tourists and recreationists.

Since access to many environmental goods, such as beaches, national parks and other open-air recreational facilities are either not priced or only partially priced, there is a danger of their not being valued (when they are economically valuable) or of their being undervalued from an economic point of view. As Tisdell notes, this can distort economic resource allocation. Land areas which would be best left in a relatively natural state for tourism and other purposes may, for example, be developed for uses such as agriculture or housing. From an economics perspective, rational decisions about resource use or allocation require appropriate economic valuations to be made about their alternative uses. From an operational viewpoint, economic valuation might be best based on monetary values. Money enables economic values to be expressed in a single unit of measurement and facilitates the comparison of economic values. Tisdell notes that this is the basis of social cost–benefit analysis. According to this approach, the aim of economic valuation of a natural resource or an area of land is to determine its social economic value for all of its alternative uses in monetary terms. The use with the highest net monetary value (determined by social cost–benefit analysis) constitutes the best economic use of the natural resource. This may involve its preservation in a relatively natural state, with tourism being one of its uses.

Measures of consumers' surplus have typically been the basis for assigning monetary economic values to possible alternative states for environmental resources. Willingness to pay by stakeholders for a particular state of a natural resource has been most frequently used as the indicator of the economic value of the resource in that particular state. This involves the *independent* estimation of the willingness to pay of each individual stakeholder for this particular environmental state and the *addition* of all these amounts to determine an aggregate economic valuation. An alternative approach is to consider the aggregate monetary sum that individuals would have to be paid to compensate them for the loss of an environmental asset. Empirically it has been found that the willingness to accept compensation for the loss of an environmental resource usually exceeds the willingness to pay for its retention. The difference is often considerable. That raises the question of which of the two approaches is to be preferred. The first alternative allocates property rights or entitlements in favour of those who want to retain the environmental or natural resource. The second alternative assigns property rights or entitlements in favour of those who may want to exploit the natural resources. As Tisdell notes, the choice of the technique, therefore, involves a question of distributional justice. According to 'new welfare economics', the choice cannot be resolved without a value judgement. Despite this problem, Tisdell acknowledges that there can be a large number of cases in which both approaches (willingness to pay and willingness to accept compensation) lead to the same conclusion about optimal resource use, and that this strengthens any economic policy prescription based on this type of social cost–benefit analysis.

According to the theory of total economic valuation, the economic value of a natural resource may be assessed by taking into account its total economic value consisting of its use value plus its non-use value. The benefit of using net total economic benefit is that it takes into account both market values and non-market values. Tisdell argues that total economic valuations can play a useful role in determining the economically optimal allocation of resources. While the economic value of natural resources for tourism can provide a strong case for their conservation, this case can often be bolstered if account is also taken of off-site non-tourism values of a natural site. Hence, those who want the site conserved for tourism purposes rather than developed would find it worthwhile not only to stress the tourism value of the natural site but also its other economic values as well. Conversely those who want the site preserved primarily for its ecological or off-site values would do well not to ignore its value for tourism purposes. In real political situations, all these sets of economic values can make a difference in influencing political decisions about whether a natural area is conserved. Most attempts by economists to measure the value of outdoor natural assets used by tourists or visitors concentrate on their value for recreation. In doing so, their focus is on a particular aspect of use value. For some resources, this may be their complete or prime source of economic value. However, for other resources used for tourism and recreation, their source of economic value is mixed and only partially accounted for by their tourism or recreational value. The passive or non-use value of many natural areas is considerable and measurement solely of their tourism and recreational value is liable to understate significantly the economic value of conserving such areas. On the other hand, some sites (such as recreational parks surrounding some man-made reservoirs) may have little or no passive use value.

Tisdell reviews various techniques, such as the travel cost method and contingent valuation method (CVM) in relation to tourism's natural resources, and then considers the relevance of a more recent development, choice modelling, to this subject, and refinements of the CVM. Travel cost methods do not measure non-use values, and applied choice models to date have not done so either, as Tisdell points out. Tisdell's view is that the real test of the choice experiment method, however, may lie in its ability to address non-use economic values such as preservation and existence. It is possible for applications of CVM to measure total economic value. However, this depends on the questions asked and the population surveyed. He notes that the various evaluation techniques all involve application costs and the accuracy of most varies with sample sizes. More attention needs to be given to assessing the net operational benefits of using the different available techniques, desirable sample size and so on. This would be a useful step towards optimally imperfect decision making in this area.

Tisdell raises the possibility that developments in economic valuation by economists have been restricted by the existing theory of economic welfare. This focus is too narrow for many policy applications. One approach of increasing interest to policy makers is to somehow combine environmental cost–benefit analysis with multi-criteria analysis and with participatory approaches, such as citizen juries. Whether and how this can be done is an important area for future research. Of course this shifts the focus of research to the exploration of methods of social conflict resolution. It involves an interdisciplinary search for 'socially optimal methods' of conflict resolution subject to political and institutional constraints. The definitions of social optimality in such cases could, therefore, be different from those used traditionally in welfare economics, as Tisdell notes, and thus one might consider such approaches as complements rather than substitutes for existing economic approaches to optimal resource use. Further research might consider the attributes of different natural resources used by tourists or recreationists in assessing the value of those resources and the possible economic impacts of a variation in these attributes. Choice experiments provide useful insights in this regard, but are subject to the limitation that the utility function in relation to the characteristics taken into account is usually assumed to be linear; no multiplicative effects on utility of the attributes is allowed. While linear relationships can be used to approximate nonlinear ones as a rule over a range, linearity remains a restriction. As Tisdell points out, the appropriateness of this assumption will depend operationally on whether it promotes optimally imperfect decision making in this subject area.

In Chapter 17, 'Implications of human capital analysis in tourism', Javier Rey-Maquieira, Maria Tugores and Vicente Ramos begin by noting that economic theory has improved its understanding of the role of human capital in economic development, with implications for tourism economics. The authors review how human capital issues have been tackled in the tourism literature and critically evaluate the main contributions, specially relating to curriculum planning and career paths, to training incidence and training needs of workers, as well as to the evaluation of private and public education and training activities. They present some general considerations on the state of the art in human capital research, specifying the topics that could be further developed in the tourism field.

An important part of the economic growth literature has focused on the effects of human capital on productivity and some of the relevant questions about human capital in the tourism sector coincide with general issues in the wider economic literature. However, the importance of personal services in this industry, where the customer is directly in contact with the worker, makes it necessary to study some other specific topics such as the relationship between quality of the product and the employee's education. The authors claim that, for an industry accounting for about 194 million jobs directly and indirectly worldwide in 2003, the role of human capital in tourism is essential for at least two reasons. First, one of the main unsolved problems in the economics of growth literature is the link between sectoral composition and development. The second reason has to do with the role of human capital within the sector. Logically, the problem of delimitation of the tourism sector makes it difficult to analyse training and education needs as well as individuals' demand for education. The authors argue that some relevant questions about human capital in the tourism sector coincide with general issues of the economic analysis: what is the contribution of educated labour to productivity? Which are the strategic sectors of an economy? What is the role of sectoral policies? However, other questions stem from specific tourism characteristics: Is tourism a sector with a low level of productivity? How can productivity be measured in this sector? Which are the education and training needs of the sector? What is the role of general and specific training? What is the relationship between education, training and the quality of the product supplied? What is the role of human capital in the innovation decisions of the tourism industry? Could it be the driving force of the sector? What is the relationship between investment in human capital and earnings?

The authors note that most of the relevant issues related to the role of human capital have already been studied in depth in the manufacturing or service sectors as a whole. Some of these general topics that can be further applied to the tourism industry are: the substitution possibilities between educated labour and other inputs, the demand for education, the relationship between qualifications and productivity, the role of training, the policy implications, or the relationship between migrations and qualifications, among others. Moreover, the importance of personal services in the tourism sector, where the customer is directly in contact with the worker makes it necessary to study some other specific topics such as the relationship between quality of the product and employees' education. As some see it, only a properly educated workforce would be able to sustain the high level of friendly, efficient and professional service, which is a major ingredient in ensuring satisfied customers and continued growth. However, labour conditions in the sector are very poor, with low salaries, high rates of turnover, high seasonality, unsocial working hours, a lack of a career path design, constituting a significant proportion of the informal sector. All make the acquisition of skills and, therefore, the improvement of the final service, difficult.

The authors claim that the existing literature on the role of human capital in tourism suffers from several shortcomings that limit its scope and open possibilities of new research on the topic. First, most of the human capital studies are limited to specific segments of the tourism sector, mainly hotels and restaurants, or have focused on the analysis of the tourism education system or the training needs in a specific region or country. More effort should be made to make geographical comparisons and to compare the characteristics of the different segments of the tourism sector. Second, there is imprecision in the definition and measurement of human capital. On the one hand, when the role of formal education is evaluated, a variety of medium- and high-level studies (such as university degrees, tourism management qualifications, or vocational school courses, among others) are analysed without any distinction. On the other hand, educational and training needs may differ with the job hierarchy and the department in which the employee is actually working. And yet, most of the studies do not disaggregate jobs, and the few that do have only differentiated the role of education for managers. Third, a similar problem arises when analysing the incidence and consequences of on-the-job training. In many cases, the definition of training is based on the fulfilment of formal or informal courses, the place where the training has been provided, the instructors, or the institution that pays for the courses. This situation creates a wide range of classifications that makes it difficult to compare training activities through different papers. Fourth, the nature of the existing tourism literature is mainly empirical and based on descriptive analysis. Most of the studies have been conducted through questionnaires addressed to managers or experts in the sector, and sometimes to customers, which reflect their opinion or quantify some particular actions. However, little attention has been paid to the direct measurement of human capital investment effects on salaries, productivity, or turnover, based on workers' responses. Moreover, there are serious shortcomings in the use of modern econometric techniques and the availability of large representative samples.

Another important gap in the literature which the authors identify is the lack of theoretical support for the empirical research. There has been little attempt to test human capital theoretical models in the tourism sector. As the authors see it, this is because most of the topics have been analysed from a management, marketing, or sociological perspective. Two other topics are considered to be especially relevant for future research. One is the lack of literature on innovation in the tourism sector. This is relevant since human capital is a complementary factor to innovations and is necessary for the adoption of existing innovations or the production of new innovations. Also, there needs to be serious reflection on whether human capital policies require an improvement in the conditions of the workforce in order to break the vicious circle of low qualifications and poor labour conditions.

Information technology is an important and growing contributor to the field of tourism, in both the private and public sectors. In Chapter 18, 'Tourism information technology', Pauline Sheldon argues that many factors, including tourism's reliance on, and production of, information, and the intangible nature of the tourism product are partly responsible for this. The tourism industry is both a service industry and an experience industry, requiring unique applications of IT. Since many models of technological development are in the production industries, as such tourism is a leader in the types of technologies that are being applied to service industries.

Sheldon argues that the IT field represents a strong driving force in tourism development, bringing with it business changes and new structures as well as new technologies and applications. New types of firms are emerging and existing firms are restructuring themselves as a result of the available technologies. Fundamental changes are occurring in the area of human resources and the automation of jobs, travel distribution channels, consumer behaviour, competitive strategies and the production function of travel firms. IT and knowledge are important resources that need to be considered together with land, labour and capital in the firm's decisions. She also highlights the fact that IT is also being used at a higher level for strategic decision making with the use of expert systems, knowledge management systems, intelligent agents, neural networks, artificial intelligence, and even virtual reality. Although these developments are still in their infancy as far as commercial implementation is concerned, they hold great promise for future applications. Mobile technologies, which are also still in the growth phase, are becoming increasingly important for travellers en route and for those navigating unfamiliar and foreign destinations. In general, the need for IT applications will be greater in the future as the desire for travel and the need for electronic connectivity grow.

The success of IT in the tourism industry is due to the many benefits that it brings to private firms, tourism destinations and to travellers. Even though there is a cost (often significant) with the installation and maintenance of good computer systems, and the necessary training, there are many benefits that accrue to those making the investment. Areas of benefits include: service differentiation; creating innovative product; building competitive intelligence by collaboration and better resource acquisition; cost reductions by re-engineering the business process; yielding optimal revenue; reaching customer intimacy; facilitating business transformation by expending intellectual capital; increasing business value; and customer focus. Cost efficiencies are perhaps the most often expected benefit. These efficiencies can be realised in many operational situations such as the reservations function, the accounting and financial functions, market analysis and information retrieval. The technology facilitates transactions and communications between customers and businesses (B2C) and between businesses and other businesses (B2B). Importantly, IT allows for the real-location of the human resources in a travel firm. With the automation of mundane data-processing tasks, staff are often assigned to provide improved service to the customer, or trained to perform higher-level functions; alternatively the human resource expenditures of the firm can be diminished. Processes such as ordering from suppliers, dealing with customer complaints and preferences, and tracking historical performance are all made more efficient with the use of IT.

Large corporations with many branches experience economies of scale in the design and installation of systems. They also typically experience benefits from centralised knowledge management and record keeping that can assist with such functions as financial reporting and customer relationship management. Economies of scope from implementing IT are occurring as a result of the electronic networks that are in place. Airlines, for example are able to offer additional services as a result of their huge computer reservation networks. Strategic alliances and partnerships between firms in different sectors, so critical to success in the travel industry, are also facilitated by the electronic networks that are in place.

Sheldon notes that the distribution of any travel product is facilitated by computer reservation systems, the internet and other computerised marketing channels. Smaller firms that in the past have found it cost-prohibitive to compete with large international corporations can be more competitive as the technology, particularly the internet, has levelled the playing field. Companies that have chosen to have a more virtual presence are also reducing their cost structure by having employees telecommute, thereby reducing high rental costs. All sectors of the travel industry are experiencing these benefits.

Sheldon discusses the themes that have developed in chronological order: application of IT to enhance operations in travel firms; special considerations for small and medium-sized enterprises; destination management systems; IT applications to strategic management and decision making; the travel distribution system, travel advising and trip planning systems; marketing and marketing research applications; internet, intranet and extranet; and mobile technologies.

Some critical areas that need further attention by researchers are highlighted by Sheldon. She claims that there has been perhaps too much attention on the commercial and marketing implications of the technology rather than on other important areas for study and development. The literature on consumer access to information, for example, would be well augmented by the introduction of experiential studies of consumer behaviour, in addition to the reportage through surveys using questionnaires, and would add more robustness. Additionally, the use of the World Wide Web for destination management organisation advertising and the need for tourism organisations to be flexible and open to change in the new economy is a fruitful area for more research.

Sheldon also notes that most research on IT usage tends to focus on applications or issues in the individual country or region in which the researcher works. More studies examining the comparative adoption of IT systems across international boundaries would add to the global understanding of the topic. Such comparative analysis can be synthesised to generate more conceptual understandings of the field. The differential between developed and developing countries in their use of technology, and models to assist the developing countries would also be of value, recognising that different political systems and different information and telecommunications environments may lead to different scenarios. She claims that this is particularly relevant as discussions of standards for systems and communications become important in the global economy.

Another area of potential research involves the documentation of the changing structure of the industry and its various sectors. Change is happening at a rapid rate with dramatic impacts on the competitive environment, on the consumer, and on the changing nature of firms in the travel industry. Barriers to entry and exit are changing, regulations are changing, and competition is not only becoming more fierce, but in some cases is also becoming 'co-opetition' instead, where competitors find ways to cooperate for mutual advantage. These changes have been addressed in part, but large-scale studies examining structural changes in the industry are more difficult to perform and are lacking. A few studies have provided insight into the changes in various sectors (airlines, travel agencies, hotels and so on), however, many sectors are still to be examined, as is the industry as a whole. Sheldon considers that the models and theories from industrial economics could assist in researching these shifts and trends in a rigorous manner.

An area for further development that Sheldon highlights is the application of IT to issues of environmental protection and cultural sustainability. Tourism today cannot be successful without the consideration of these two issues, and yet the overlay of IT with them has received little attention. There are many potential ways that IT can assist in the development of those goals. The application of global positioning systems and geographic information systems has much to offer destinations in regard to the management of natural resources such as national parks, wildlife reserves, culturally and environmentally sensitive areas and so on. More websites are including information of cultures, cultural resources and cultural interpretations of destinations, but it is often demand rather than supply driven. There is, however, a need for more of this type of information and focus in the future and this will require close collaboration between the public sector and the vendors of these technologies, in addition to the suppliers of tourism services in the private sector.

Sheldon identifies the cutting edge of the research in tourism information technology is that which examines the use of increasingly intelligent systems. This involves studies on the applications of neural network technologies, intelligent query management, data-mining and data-warehousing systems, multi-media information and virtual reality. When collaboration occurs between the system developers, funding sources and the destinations, the opportunities to further enhance the visitor industry using technology are endless. Firms will benefit economically by applying systems at the operational level by increased efficiency, productivity, customer relationship management, and reach to global markets. At the strategic level they can benefit by becoming more competitive, by developing new products and new market segments, and by creating knowledge warehouses as a basis for strategic decision making. Destinations can benefit in similar ways to firms, but they can also harness technology to facilitate planning and policy making, to improve their transportation and other infrastructure systems, and to improve their sustainability and the overall economic benefit to the destination.

Sheldon concludes that more theories and paradigms are needed to form strong pillars for the field to move forward. This may require the use of concepts, theories and methods from other disciplines, or the creation of new methodologies within the area of tourism information technology. Tourism is an interdisciplinary field of study, and IT is the realm of computer scientists, management scientists and psychologists to name a few. Cross-fertilisation between these disciplines and collaboration across sectors will be necessary to ensure the richest development of research in the field. It is a critical success factor for the tourism industry in general that researchers, educators and practitioners alike collaborate to examine how IT in all its forms can enhance all aspects of tourism, including the travellers and the host community.

A conceptual model of destination competitiveness can contribute to sustainable tourism development policies and practices. Economic factors, although often important, are not the only consideration and indeed in some instances the goal might be to restrain, reduce, or shift tourism demand such that the type of tourism that develops, and its economic, socio-cultural and environmental impacts, are congruent with the aspirations of the destination's local community. In Chapter 19, 'Destination competitive-ness', Geoffrey Crouch and Brent Ritchie argue that competitiveness in tourism at the level of the destination is more complex and multifaceted than is the case when one considers competitiveness at the level of the individual enterprise or product and that tourism destinations are also driven to compete for a much broader range of goals or motives. They observe that as the tourism industry matures, and ever more tourism experiences and destinations seek to compete, the quest to understand destination competitive-ness and to use this knowledge in destination marketing and management programmes and activities has grown considerably. In response to the various changes taking place globally, on both the demand and supply sides of the industry, Crouch and Ritchie note that many destinations are seeking solutions to the question of how to become or remain competitive. In doing so, numerous questions often arise. For example, how important are convention facilities; should the airport be expanded; would the construction of a landmark help to enhance the image of the destination by providing it with a recognisable icon; would it be better to concentrate resources on the promotion of the destination; should a hotel room tax be introduced to fund increased destination marketing; should there be more municipal government revenues spent on developing or improving visitor-friendly infrastructure/services; are residents sufficiently visitor friendly; would the hosting of a special event like a cultural festival, World Expo, or Olympic Games help; would efforts to reduce crime have much impact given the media hysteria over isolated events; and so on. To answer such questions, the elements of destination competitiveness need to be fully understood.

The authors argue that the concepts of comparative and competitive advantage provide a theoretically sound basis for the development of a model of destination competitiveness, but that no single general trade theory will provide the necessary insight or cover the most appropriate determinants from among the many variables possible. The conceptual model of destination competitiveness that is presented is one that Crouch and Ritchie have developed over the past decade. The model emphasises the two cornerstones of competitiveness; namely, 'comparative advantage' (consisting of endowed resources) and 'competitive advantage' (consisting of aspects of resource deployment). The main part of the model, then, illustrates how we see these two cornerstones being operationalised with respect to destination competitiveness.

Crouch and Ritchie emphasise that destinations operate within an environment. The 'global (macro) environment' consists of a vast array of phenomena which broadly impact all human activities and which are therefore not specific to the travel and tourism industry in their effect. Global forces can alter a destination's attractiveness to tourists, shift the pattern of wealth to create new emerging origin markets, adjust the relative costs of travel to different destinations, and disrupt relations between cultures and nations, among many others. The authors emphasise that these forces present a given destination with a number of special concerns, problems, or issues that it must either adapt to, or overcome, if it is to remain competitive, while also providing destinations with a whole new spectrum of opportunities for innovation and market exploitation. By comparison, the 'competitive (micro) environment' is part of the tourism system because it concerns the actions and activities of entities in the tourism system which directly affects the goals of each member of the system whether they are individual companies or a collection of organisations constituting a destination. In the model, a destination's competitive (micro) environment is made up of organisations, influences and forces that lie within the destination's immediate arena of tourism activities and competition. The authors emphasise that these 'close-in' elements of the environment tend to have a more direct and immediate impact than do elements of the global (macro) environment, as a general rule. The micro environment, nevertheless, because of its proximity and greater sense of immediacy, often occupies the attention of managers due to the ramifications for the destination's ability to serve visitors and remain competitive.

A destination's core resources and attractors describe the primary elements of destination appeal. It is these factors that are the key motivators for visitation to a destination. Crouch and Ritchie acknowledge that while other components are essential for success and profitability, it is the core resources and attractors that are the fundamental reasons why prospective visitors choose one destination over another. Whereas the core resources and attractors of a destination constitute the primary motivations for inbound tourism, supporting factors and resources provide a foundation upon which a successful tourism industry can be established. A destination with an abundance of core resources and attractors but a dearth of supporting factors and resources, may find it very difficult to develop its tourism industry, at least in the short term, until some attention is paid to those things that are lacking. A strategic or policy-driven framework for the planning and development of the destination results from the factors shown in the model under destination policy, planning and development. With particular economic, social and other societal goals as the intended outcome, these factors can provide a guiding hand to the direction, form and structure of tourism development. Such a framework can help to ensure that the tourism development that does occur promotes a competitive and sustainable destination while meeting the quality-of-life aspirations of those who reside in the destination.

The destination management component of the model focuses on those activities which implement the policy and planning framework established under destination policy, planning and development, enhance the appeal of the core resources and attractors, strengthen the quality and effectiveness of the supporting factors and resources, and adapt best to the constraints or opportunities imposed or presented by the qualifying and amplifying determinants. Crouch and Ritchie argue that these activities represent the greatest scope for managing a destination's competitiveness as they include programmes, structures, systems and processes which are highly actionable and manageable by individuals, organisations and through collective action.

The potential competitiveness of a destination is conditioned or limited by a number of factors which fall outside the scope of the preceding four groups of determinants. This final group of factors, which Crouch and Ritchie call 'qualifying and amplifying determinants', represents factors whose affect on the competitiveness of a tourist destination is to define its scale, limit or potential. These qualifiers and amplifiers moderate or magnify destination competitiveness by filtering the influence of the other three groups of factors. They may be so important as to represent a ceiling to tourism demand and potential, but are largely beyond the control or influence of the tourism sector alone to do anything about.

Crouch and Ritchie develop a speculative research agenda. First, research to examine the relative importance of the factors of destination competitiveness as a function of the competitive environment, target markets and competitor characteristics. Without this information, destinations will find it difficult to apply these conceptual models. Second, processes and principles for auditing destination competitiveness and performance. Mounting anecdotal evidence indicates that destination stakeholders are demanding reliable and valid assessments of a destination's competitive position and the suitability of its strategic response. More specifically, on the premise that one cannot manage what one cannot measure, Crouch and Ritchie advocate the development of indices, metrics and diagnostic tools for measuring destination competitiveness. They also claim that it would be very helpful to have a better understanding of the factors that deter the achievement of competitiveness once we know what its determinants are. Destinations have always sought to understand and improve their competitiveness. In good times, during periods of growth, tourism destinations have been able to prosper with little difficulty. But in these more difficult times, experiencing declining or stagnating global travel and tourism, destinations have had demonstrated the need to take a more serious look at their competitive positions. Research which helps them do so will be critical.

Chapter 20, 'Tourism destination specialisation', by Mondher Sahli, presents findings and conclusions from an examination of the competitiveness of 19 OECD destination countries. Tourism and travel-related services are still strongly dominated by OECD countries. The main sources remain Europe and the USA, with some new influx from East Asia and the Pacific. Almost half of international tourists come from six OECD countries which are also among the world's top ten tourism earners/spenders. Some of these destinations appear to be coping with increased competition quite well, whereas others are struggling.

The authors examine the concepts of external competitiveness and comparative advantage in terms of its application to tourism destinations. They regard competitiveness as a general concept that encompasses price differentials, coupled with exchange rate movements, productivity levels of various components of the tourism industry (transport, accommodation, tour services, restaurants, entertainment and so on) and qualitative factors affecting the attractiveness of a destination. The external competitiveness of country j's tourism industry i (TC_{ti}) is defined as that country's competitive ability to retain or increase its market share of tourism export in terms of ground and travel components. This phenomenon is illustrated graphically by the authors by simultaneous analysis of the degree of commitment to exporting in the tourism industry and of net performance in tourism. A country is regarded as competitive in the tourism industry when it has a growing commitment to exporting (market share) and a high net performance (coverage ratio).

Once measures of overall external competitiveness have been developed, it is useful to know where a destination's competitive position is changing. Empirical analysis of tourism in OECD countries provides a comprehensive overview of two aspects of the various countries' competitiveness. First, the authors argue that a well-known size effect makes the large OECD countries major players in terms of tourism market shares, as for international trade. Short-term competitiveness effects show a certain degree of similarity with trade in goods. On the basis of econometric estimation, it is established that the real exchange rate is one of the key determinants of competitiveness in tourism. This confirms the role of foreign currency holdings, that is, money balances held by tourists to undertake travel activity. Intuitively these monetary holdings must respond to changes in exchange rates as the real value of these balances increases (decreases) in response to devaluation (appreciation) of the foreign exchange rate. Second, even if tourism remains to a large extent governed by the existence of certain resources (sea, sun, mountains and cultural heritage), other factors also play an important role. These include technological factors, which serve to differentiate the nature of tourism comparative advantages, as well as the social dimension, the destination's degree of maturity, the level of domestic demand for tourism (Linder effect), and the price competitiveness and dominance of the transport segment. The econometric analysis of panel data demonstrated the relevance and relative importance of these last factors. Moreover, it revealed that their impact differs depending on the level of development of a country's tourism industry.

The authors examine the role of several variables on the tourism comparative advantage in 19 OECD countries. The variables that determine tourism specialisation are: per capita income; real exchange rate; revealed comparative advantage in international passenger transport; the hotel function; and the tourism intensity rate. The empirical findings on specialisation in tourism show that a good number of these hypotheses can be verified. They indicate, first, that specialisation in tourism is not unrelated to a country's economic structure and, second, that the quality and dynamic of that specialisation differ from one country to the next (or from one subgroup to the next). Moreover, the econometric results indicate that tourism does not evolve in the same way in all countries. Its evolution depends on price competitiveness, the degree of specialisation in passenger transportation, the level of domestic demand for tourist services and the destination's degree of maturity. Tourism specialisation creates pressures on the natural and cultural environment, and hence on resources, social structures, economic activities and land use. It is then in the interest of all players to cooperate in forming the direction of their tourism policies and actions.

Globalisation is a process that involves economic, political and cultural forces in such a way that they extend the reach of companies and shrink the economic distance between suppliers and consumers. In Chapter 21, 'Globalisation', John Fletcher and John Westlake emphasise that globalisation is not a single phenomenon – rather it is a collection of forces that tend to change the way that the economic, political and cultural worlds operate. Globalisation may be regarded as a process in which the geographical distance between economic factors, producers and consumers becomes a factor of diminishing significance as a result of faster and more efficient forms of travel, communication and finance. The concentration of capital has served to reinforce the capability of those involved in driving forward the globalisation process. Fletcher and Westlake emphasise that it can be seen as a beneficial process whereby the most efficient use can be made of scarce resources and homogeneity in supply can be achieved irrespective of location. In contrast, it can also be viewed as a predatory process whereby global forces face local economic factors and producers with unfair competitive advantages.

Fletcher and Westlake list a number of key drivers that fuel the process of globalisation. Technological progress brings innovations that facilitate and encourage (directly and/or indirectly) trade between nations. The two most important technological factors that provide the driving force behind economic globalisation are increased specialisation in production, forming one of the principal bases for international trade and advances in communications technology. Economic changes are another driver. The widespread liberalisation of current and capital account transactions and the development of international financial markets have enhanced the process of globalisation. Cultural and demographic trends are also important. Increasing global population combined with increased flows of information has acted like a catalyst to open up trading opportunities. Further encouragement has come from cultural exposure, through the 'demonstration effect' and via media sources that set in place a move towards homogenisation. Political stability is also a crucial factor in underpinning the willingness and ability of nations to trade. A major characteristic of the past 50 years has been the cooperative international efforts to reduce state-imposed barriers to trade such as those implemented through the World Trade Organisation (WTO) that is, GATT and GATS. The liberalisation of trade and investment has been influenced by the expansion and intensification of regional integration efforts. In fact, it may be suggested that globalisation, internationalisation and regionalisation are together a cyclical process of amorphous dimensions that feed and consume off each other.

Fletcher and Westlake observe that the globalisation of the world economy is a process that has been embraced by tourism which has been a pioneer in terms of both liberalisation and global expansion. Its importance as a service industry makes it vital that the globalisation process is successful not only from an industry and company perspective, but also from the point of view of the destinations and the tourists that consume the services. The process of globalisation means that the multinational corporations have had to adjust their management and control systems to be able to enjoy the significant economies of large-scale production that are available, and yet provide sufficient flexibility within their operational structure to allow local delivery of services in a satisfactory manner. They claim that this is true for all aspects of the tourism industry but particularly so for the airlines, the cruise ship companies and the multinational hotel companies. They then explore globalisation issues within the key sectors of tourism drawing upon examples to demonstrate its influence on tourism development.

Fletcher and Westlake admit that the plight of small and medium-sized enterprises (SMEs), the most dominant form of business in the tourism industry, is less easily identified. If effective alliances can be formed at the local and regional levels then there are huge opportunities for such businesses to compete in an expanding market. However, globalisation puts enormous pressures on SMEs which are already disadvantaged by being subject to higher unit costs than their multinational counterparts. The challenge for the future is for SMEs to be able to embrace fully the technology that provides them with access to the new markets and to be able to invest in that technology and train their employees in its effective operation.

Fletcher and Westlake stress the need for greater understanding of the true costs of globalisation. To some extent those costs can be seen in the transfer of power away from national government control and in favour of multinational corporations. The latter demands that these multinational corporations have to take on a greater sense of responsibility in the operation of their companies if other global objectives are to be achieved such as the sustainability of the tourism industry. There is also a greater need to understand the ways that SMEs can not only withstand the pressures of competing in a globalised economy but also take advantage of the enormous economies that can be derived from forming alliances and cooperative systems.

From a human resource management point of view, there are, as Fletcher and Westlake note, many unanswered questions. These range from issues relating to the concentration of intellectual capital through the human resource policies and practices that will hold the workforce in place, to the issues relating to centralisation or decentralisation. In terms of training and education, there are clear signs that globalisation is affecting the way that tourism programmes and curricula are structured.

PART ONE

TOURISM DEMAND
AND FORECASTING

1 A survey of tourism demand modelling practice: issues and implications
Christine Lim

Introduction

Tourism exports have become an important sector in many countries as a growing source of foreign exchange earnings. This has arisen through the rapid expansion of international tourism, which is mainly attributed to high growth rates of income in developed and newly industrialised countries, shorter working hours and the substantial decrease in real transportation costs between countries. Besides generating foreign exchange earnings and alleviating the balance of payments problems encountered in many countries, international tourism also creates employment. Most tourism businesses are small and/or medium-sized enterprises. As a labour-intensive industry, it absorbs an increasing percentage of the labour force released from agriculture and the manufacturing industries, and prevents large-scale unemployment. For instance, it is estimated that the tourism industry employed more than 550 000 people and generated AU$17 billion per annum in export earnings in Australia in 2001–02. Other benefits contributed by international tourism include increasing income, savings, investment and economic growth. Tourism has also contributed significantly to regional economic development, rejuvenation and sustainability in Australia.

Tourism development and growth have undoubtedly taken place at considerable cost in some destination countries. Unlike other industrial activities, both tourism production and consumption take place in the destination. The provision of tourism infrastructure requires capital investment, and land acquisition for tourism projects can distort the housing market. These activities may in turn give rise to inflation as they compete for the country's scarce resources. Although destinations try to preserve and capitalise on their environment to attract tourists, the impact of tourism activities and tourism growth has arguably been detrimental to the environmental quality of countries. Pollution, waste, overcrowding, crime and intensive use of certain geographical areas, are some of the adverse impacts of tourism on the natural, social–cultural and physical environment of a destination. Without paying necessary attention to the environment, tourism growth is not sustainable in the long run.

Given the importance of tourism to economic development and trade performance, government as well as the tourism industry are interested in the factors that influence tourist flows to a particular destination and the responsiveness of tourism demand to these factors. Such knowledge is useful for making accurate predictions of tourism demand, the planning of infrastructure and facilities for tourists, and the development of sensible tourism policies. Appropriate policy measures taken by the private and public sectors to stimulate tourism need to be underpinned by analytical research. A review of past empirical tourism studies undertaken in the area will not only foster our understanding of the determinants of tourism demand for a range of destinations, but will help us identify some crucial issues regarding the practice of tourism demand modelling, and to evaluate the empirical performance of these models.

The plan of the chapter is as follows. A comparison of the world top destinations' performance in terms of tourism exports/imports, tourist arrivals and tourism receipts is given in the next section. An analytical review of 124 empirical studies on the major factors influencing tourism demand and their estimated elasticity values is presented in the third section, where data used in the empirical literature, model specifications and alternative functional forms, the choice of dependent variable, and the number and choice of explanatory variables are analysed. The next two sections focus on the implications of the estimation methods and diagnostic tests used in these studies. Some concluding remarks are given in the final section.

World top destinations
Table 1.1 shows the value of credits, debits and surpluses on the international tourism services account of the top ten countries in 2000, measured in millions of US dollars. Travel credits and debits do not include inbound tourist payments to national carriers and outbound tourist payments to foreign carriers, respectively, for international transport which tourists pay in advance of their journeys. The International Monetary Fund (IMF) classifies international fare receipts and expenditures separately. All the countries shown in Table 1.1 are industrial countries, with the exception of China and Greece. Of the top ten countries in international credits, China has performed remarkably well. In 1990 and 1996, it was ranked twenty-sixth and eighth, respectively, and in 2000, it surpassed Canada, Austria and Greece in tourism exports. In terms of travel surplus, China ranked ninth in the world, as indicated in the last column of the table.

The contributions of travel receipts to total exports range between 2.5 per cent for Germany and 25.4 per cent for Greece. For some developing countries like the small island economies of Cyprus, Jamaica and the

Table 1.1   *Top ten countries in travel services exports and imports in 2000 (US $m)*

Major destinations	Travel credit	Major origins	Travel debit	Major countries	Travel surplus
USA	97 820	USA	67 670	USA	30 150
Spain	30 978	Germany	47 502	Spain	25 502
France	30 925	UK	38 262	France	13 002
Italy	27 493	Japan	31 884	Italy	11 808
UK	21 769	France	17 923	Turkey	5 923
Germany	18 404	Italy	15 685	Thailand	4711
China	16 231	China	13 114	Greece	4661
Canada	10 847	Hong Kong	12 502	Egypt	3273
Austria	9998	Canada	12 352	China	3117
Greece	9219	Netherlands	12 191	Portugal	3015

Source: International Monetary Fund, *Balance of Payments Statistics Yearbook*, 2002.

Table 1.2   *Share of world travel exports and imports in 1995 and 2000 (%)*

Country	Credit		Debit	
	1995	2000	1995	2000
Industrial countries	69.9	67.3	75.4	72.3
United States	19.1	21.0	12.8	15.7

Source: International Monetary Fund, *Balance of Payments Statistics Yearbook*, 2002.

Maldives, the importance of tourism as a percentage of total exports is approximately 37, 33 and 52 per cent, respectively.

The US ranked first in international travel credit, debit and surplus in 2000. Although the US travel debit is very large by world standards, it has also experienced a large surplus on international travel services. Its share of the world travel credit and debit has increased from 1995 to 2000 (see Table 1.2).

Gray (1967) argues that 'actual' imports (exports) of travel services, defined as international tourism expenditures (receipts) of outbound (inbound) tourists plus transportation costs paid to foreign (national) carriers, are a better measure of foreign travel imports (exports) than the travel account itself, in which international fare expenditures (receipts) are excluded. In other words, the United Nations measure of international travel exports and imports is preferred to that of the IMF.

Table 1.3   World's top ten tourism destinations in 2000 by international tourist arrivals

Country	% share of arrivals worldwide	Average annual growth rate 1990–1999 (%)
France	10.8	3.79
United States	7.3	2.48
Spain	6.9	4.04
Italy	5.9	3.64
China	4.5	11.47
United Kingdom	3.6	4.02
Russian Federation	3.0	0.35
Mexico	3.0	14.47
Canada	2.9	2.82
Germany	2.7	0.19

Source: World Tourism Organization, 2002.

According to the World Tourism Organization (WTO) and the Organisation for Economic Cooperation and Development (OECD) Tourism Committee, an international tourist is a person who makes temporary visits across international borders, resides there for at least 24 hours to less than a year, and for a purpose other than establishing residence. Tourist-generating and tourist-receiving countries are also known as origins and destinations, respectively. Hence, the definition of tourist excludes same-day visitors or excursionists, that is, visitors who do not spend a night in the destination country.

France was the most popular tourist destination in 2000, measured in terms of international tourist arrivals, followed by the United States (WTO 2002). Six of the top ten destinations were in Europe and they accounted for almost a third of international tourist arrivals worldwide in 2000 (see Table 1.3). Mexico and China experienced impressive double digit average annual growth rates in international tourist arrivals in the 1990s.

Table 1.4 presents the world's top ten tourism earners in terms of tourism receipts, excluding receipts from international transport. Thus, the information is quite similar to that in Table 1.1, which is obtained from the IMF. Although Australia's share of world international tourism receipts is small, accounting for 1.8 per cent in 2000, its share has steadily increased and has thereby positioned the country in the world's top twenty tourism earners (Australia ranked eleventh in 2000). France, Italy and Spain accounted for 18.6 per cent of international tourism receipts in 2000. These three countries have been the dominant players in tourism worldwide since the 1960s.

*Table 1.4   World's top ten tourism earners in 2000 by international
tourism receipts*

Country	% share of receipts worldwide
United States	17.9
Spain	6.5
France	6.3
Italy	5.8
United Kingdom	4.1
Germany	3.7
China	3.4
Austria	2.4
Canada	2.3
Greece	1.9

Source: World Tourism Organization, 2002.

Various classification criteria have been proposed, with inbound tourists categorised as follows: recreation (or holiday), business, visiting friends and relatives, and other motives, including studying, shopping, employment on a working visa and so on. Most short-term tourists indicate that their main purpose in visiting a destination is for holiday and recreation (including tourists accompanying business travellers). Business tourists also include overseas visitors attending conferences or conventions in a destination. Undoubtedly, there would be considerable overlap between holiday and visiting friends/relatives when overseas visitors nominate their main purpose of trip, as these activities are usually related.

Factors affecting international tourism demand
The general international tourism demand model typically estimated (and occasionally tested) is:

$$DT_{ij} = f(Y_j, TC_{ij}, RP_{ij}, ER_{ij}, QF_i) \qquad (1.1)$$

where

DT_{ij} = demand for international travel services by origin j for destination i;

Y_j = income of origin j;

TC_{ij} = transportation cost between destination i and origin j;

RP_{ij} = relative prices (that is, the ratio of prices in destination i to prices in origin j and in alternative destinations);

ER_{ij} = currency exchange rate, measured as units of destination i's currency per unit of origin j's currency;

QF_i = qualitative factors in destination i.

A detailed discussion and analysis of these factors (and the proxy variables used) are undertaken in the fourth section.

Data description
Most published tourism studies have used time-series data to determine the quantity of tourism demanded. Few studies have used cross-section or pooled data which combines time-series data for a number of origins or destinations to estimate international tourism demand in a single equation. In time-series samples, as Klein (1962, p. 53) states succinctly: 'we estimate fundamental parameters on the basis of time variation, from period to period, of economic quantities for an individual economic unit or an aggregate of units and for an individual good or an aggregate of goods'. In estimating the parameters from time-series samples, homogeneity across time periods is assumed. This implies that the jth individual associating x_{jt_0} (the observed explanatory variable for individual j at time 0) with y_{jt_0} (the observed dependent variable for individual j at time 0) would behave like the kth individual in associating x_{kt_0} with y_{kt_0}.

The major advantage of time-series analysis is that deterministic and stochastic time trends, representing changes in travel tastes, can be included in the tourism model, which can be useful in forecasting international tourism demand for a particular country or region. A cross-section is a sample of inter-individual differences. Unlike time-series studies which examine changes in tourism over time, cross-section studies explain the determinants of tourism demand within a country or across countries during a fixed time period. Cross-section data are usually obtained from specially designed surveys which sample individual economic units, such as households or firms. The advantage of using cross-section data is the availability of large samples which are essential for studying certain characteristics and behaviour of tourists. Homogeneity among individuals is assumed. This implies, for instance, that the jth individual would spend as much on international travel as the kth individual, given identical income levels. As the individual moves from one income level to another, the propensity to travel changes to what is typical at the new income level. Attempts have also been made in tourism studies to pool statistical information from both time series and cross-section samples to estimate tourism demand parameters in a single equation. The 'pooled' approach involves relating differences in demand between origin/destination pairs to differences in explanatory variables over time and across individuals.

Table 1.5   Classification by type of data used

Decades of publication	Annual	Cross-section	Pooled	Other	Total
1961–69	2	2	0	0	4
1970–79	11	1	4	10	26
1980–89	30	3	4	13	50
1990–99	22	3	1	13	39
2000–2003	2	0	0	3	5
Total	67	9	9	39	124

Common sources of tourism data include the national tourist offices, international organisations such as the IMF, the OECD, and the WTO, ABC/OAG World Airways Guide, survey data and bank foreign exchange records. The unavailability or poor quality of data, and differences in definitions and measurement methods used for tourism demand, have been persistent problems encountered in tourism studies. It would seem to be imperative to standardise the techniques for collecting data for tourism studies in order for meaningful international comparisons of travel demand to be made.

In Table 1.5, the 124 studies are classified according to the decade of publication. Overall, 40 per cent of these papers were published in the 1980s, and 31 per cent in the 1990s. The four broad classifications of data used are annual, cross-section, pooled and other. A majority of the tourism studies have used annual data to determine the quantity of tourism demanded. Sixty-seven studies used only annual data, and 73 in total used annual data. There were nine studies which each used cross-section and pooled data in their models. The last category ('Other') includes 39 entries, with 14 using quarterly data, eight survey data, six monthly data, two annual and quarterly data, one annual and cross-section data, one annual and monthly data, one quarterly and pooled data, two annual, cross-section and pooled data, one monthly and survey data, one pooled and cross-section data, and two undisclosed.

Table 1.6 shows the number of sample observations in the 67 studies that used only annual data, which includes two studies that did not state explicitly whether they used annual data. Fourteen of these 67 studies used more than one sample size, in which case the maximum number of observations is reported for these studies. The number of annual observations ranges from a low of five to a high of 34, with frequencies varying between one and seven; the modal number of observations is 20, and the median and mean numbers are 18 and 17.5, respectively. It is obvious that the sample sizes of

Table 1.6   Classification by number of annual observations

Number of observations	Frequency
5	1
6	1
8	1
9	3
10	1
11	5
12	2
13	3
14	3
15	6
16	5
17	2
18	4
19	5
20	7
21	3
22	1
23	3
24	1
25	1
28	4
30	1
33	1
34	1
Not available	2
Total	67

studies using annual data are typically very small. This is a serious concern because it is generally not easy to obtain meaningful regression estimates in such circumstances, and this could cast doubt on the reliability of the estimation results. To circumvent the problem related to the unavailability of long time-series of annual data, some studies used monthly, quarterly, cross-section, and pooled annual and cross-section data, or some combination of the above.

Model specification
Most econometric analyses of tourism demand have used single-equation models. Relatively few studies have used a complete demand system to describe the allocation of travel expenditures among various categories

of goods in a particular destination, or among various groups of destinations/holiday types by a particular tourist market (O'Hagan and Harrison 1984a, 1984b; Fujii et al. 1985, 1987; White 1985; Pyo et al. 1991; Divisekera 1993, 1994; Syriopoulos and Sinclair 1993; Papatheodorou 1999; Smeral et al. 1992).

In empirical economics, computational convenience and the ease of interpretation of (functions of) parameters are typically paramount in the determination of a specific functional form for purposes of estimation and testing. Key focuses of interpretation of economic models are short- and long-run marginal effects (that is, first derivatives or slopes of functions) and elasticities (that is, percentage responsiveness). Two functional forms which provide such useful information are the linear and log-linear (or double-logarithmic) regression models (see Lim 1997c). According to McAleer (1994) and Franses and McAleer (1998), the key features of such models are as follows:

1. Log-linear model:
    (a) both the dependent variable and the set (or a subset) of explanatory variables are expressed in logarithms;
    (b) has variable marginal effects and constant elasticities;
    (c) yields a steady-state growth path;
    (d) permits straightforward testing of whether the dependent variable should be expressed in nominal or real values;
    (e) imposes non-negative restrictions upon variables; and
    (f) permits the random errors in the equation to be normally distributed.
2. Linear model:
    (a) both the dependent variable and the set (or a subset) of explanatory variables are expressed in levels;
    (b) has constant marginal effects and variable elasticities;
    (c) is computationally straightforward when there is temporal aggregation of the dependent variable; and
    (d) does not permit the random errors in the equation to be normally distributed.

In Figure 1.1, the classification is by model specification. Six categories are considered, namely only log-linear single equations, only linear single equations, both linear and log-linear single equations, system of equations, other (including 12 entries for log-linear single equations and system of equations, two entries for translog utility function, one entry for each of probit and unstated model), and none. It is interesting to note that 65 studies used only log-linear single equations, while 92 (= 65 + 15 + 12)

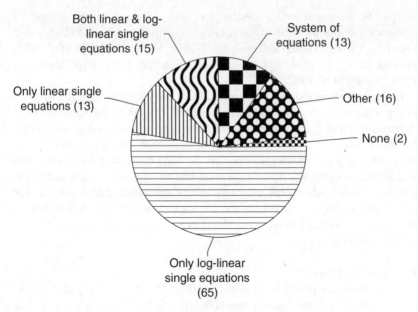

Figure 1.1   Classification by type of model used

used log-linear models, usually in conjunction with linear single equations. Where an explanation was provided regarding the choice of log-linear specification, the reason was invariably the ease of interpretation of the coefficients as estimated elasticities. Thirteen studies used only linear single equations, while both linear and log-linear single equations were used in 15 studies, system of equations were used in 13, and two did not use any model at all.

Dependent variable
International tourism demand (dependent variable) can be measured in terms of tourist arrivals and/or departures, tourist expenditures and/or receipts, travel exports and/or imports, tourist length of stay, nights spent at tourist accommodation, and other. Some studies have used more than one dependent variable. Figure 1.2 shows that tourist arrivals and/or departures are the most frequently used dependent variable. It includes: the number of visits or trips; tourist or visitor flows; the number of tourists or holiday visitors (per capita) on independent travel (scheduled flights), on package tours (charter flights) and by surface travel; share of tourist arrivals; proportion of tourists to a particular destination; visit rate; total departures of citizens less non-returning citizens; and the

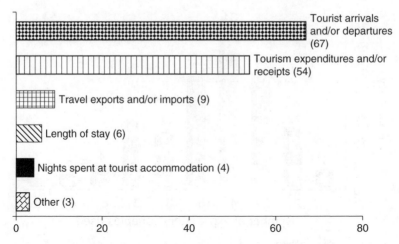

Figure 1.2   Classification by type of dependent variable used

number or proportion of recreational and business tourists, separately from total tourists. Only one study used conference tourist attendance as the dependent variable (Witt et al. 1992).

Tourist expenditures and/or receipts are also frequently used to measure demand for international tourism. Tourism receipts are regarded as the most appropriate dependent variable given that their changes reflect fluctuations in tourism consumption patterns which have a direct impact on the generation of income and foreign exchange earnings in a destination. This dependent variable is expressed in nominal or real terms, per head of origin population, and per visitor or per diem. It also includes real monthly sales tax receipts, the share of total expenditure on airfares, expenditure shares, nominal and real share in the travel market. Fujii et al. (1985, 1987), White (1985) and Pyo et al. (1991) used systems of equations to classify real per capita expenditure budget shares under aggregated headings such as food, clothing, lodging, transport, entertainment and other, in the destination. Besides using total tourist expenditures, Stronge and Redman (1982) also disaggregated tourist expenditure in the border and interior areas of Mexico.

The number of nights spent at tourist accommodation also includes tourist arrivals at hotels, and hotel expenditure. Number of nights spent at tourist accommodation is argued to be superior to using other proxies (Bakkal and Scaperlanda 1991) because it accounts for the length of stay, and excludes stays with friends and relatives. The number of nights spent in the destination, and visitor days, are included in the length-of-stay

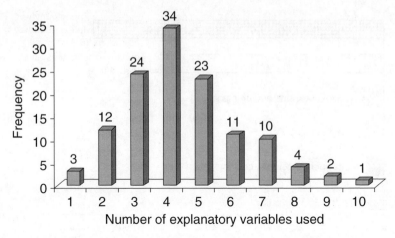

Figure 1.3   Classification by number of explanatory variables used

dependent variable. Only two studies classified under 'other' used the probability of tourists using a travel agent (Mak and Moncur 1980), and the
odds of selecting package tours over independent travel (Sheldon and Mak
1987), as the dependent variable.

Choice of explanatory variables
As the availability of time-series data for tourism studies is severely limited,
this means that the number of explanatory variables that can be investigated is restricted. Figure 1.3 shows the number of explanatory variables
used in each of the published papers. Some studies used more than one
qualitative factor or other variables. The number of explanatory variables
used ranges from one to ten, with frequencies varying between one and 34.
The mean is 4.4, the median and mode are five and four, respectively, with
three studies using as few as one explanatory variable and one study using
as many as ten explanatory variables.

   In Figure 1.4, the classification is by type of explanatory variable used.
The range of factors affecting the demand for international tourism is
undoubtedly very large, the most prominent including the level of income
which affects the ability to pay for overseas travel, relative prices of goods
and services purchased by tourists in the destination compared with the
origin and competing destinations, transportation cost, exchange rates
between the currencies of origin and destination, dynamics, trend and qualitative factors. The assumption of no money illusion is imposed, which
means that a proportional increase in all prices and money incomes would
leave demand for tourism unchanged.

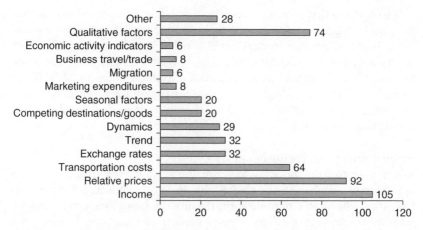

Figure 1.4 Classification by type of explanatory variable used

Income

Income in the origin country is the most frequently used explanatory variable in the 124 published tourism studies. Overseas travel (especially recreational travel) is expensive and is generally regarded as a luxury good, in which case the discretionary income of origin country (or income remaining after expenditure on necessities) would be an appropriate income variable. However, discretionary income is a subjective variable and is not precisely measurable. Hence, most researchers have relied on nominal or real (per capita) personal, disposable, or national income, and GDP or GNP as measures (or proxies) for income in the origin. Less frequently used proxies include: real per capita consumption or recreational expenditure, foreign travel budget, destination budget share, supernumerary income, permanent income (a weighted average of current and lagged personal income), real average wage per employee, and production or industrial production index to estimate income elasticities. Edwards (1976, 1979) used real disposable income less expenditure on food, housing, fuel and light, or beverages and tobacco. A number of studies have included household average, net annual or real disposable income, disaggregated into wage and non-wage incomes. Lim and McAleer (2001) have also used real private consumption services and consumption expenditures on non-durables. Stronge and Redman (1982) is the only study that uses both total personal income and border states' (namely, California, Arizona, New Mexico and Texas) share of US total personal income concurrently. Large income differentials between adjacent states are expected to generate more 'border travel'.

It is expected that tourism demand will be influenced not only by current, but also by lagged income in the origin, since changes in income may take some time to affect tourism demand. When both current and lagged income are used in a study, the latter would be classified as reflecting dynamics. However, if only lagged income is used (for example, lagged real GDP per capita), it will be regarded as a measure (or proxy) for income. The same reasoning applies to all other variables when current and/or lagged explanatory variables are used.

Relative prices and tourism prices
Relative or tourism prices, which are the second most frequently used explanatory variables in the studies, are costs of goods and services that tourists are likely to pay while at the destination (such as accommodation, local transportation, food and entertainment). In measuring relative price movements in the origin and destination, it is desirable to have indices constructed using a basket of goods purchased by tourists. Since tourist price indices (TPIs) are typically unavailable, the consumer price indices (CPIs) of the origin and destination are used as proxies to reflect the relative prices of foreign travel goods and services. The CPI ratio is often adjusted for differences in exchange rates between the currencies of the origin and destination countries. When the exchange rate-adjusted CPI ratio (also known as 'real exchange rate', as in Rosensweig 1986) is used to measure the effective prices of goods and services in the destination, the impacts of inflation and exchange rate movements are measured through one variable, namely:

$$RP_{it} = (CPI_{it}/CPI_{jt}) * ER_{it} \qquad (1.2)$$

where:

RP_{it} = relative price variable in destination i in period t;
CPI_{it} = consumer price index in destination i in period t;
CPI_{jt} = consumer price index in origin j in period t;
ER_{it} = an index of the price of origin currency in terms of destination i currency in period t.

A rise in RP means that purchases in destination i are relatively more expensive for tourists from j, which could be due either to a higher inflation rate in the destination compared with the origin, or the destination currency having become more expensive in terms of the origin currency.

The above relative price variable captures the tourist cost of living in the destination relative to the origin, as measured by the CPI. This method assumes that the goods and services purchased by tourists are similar to those of a representative household for which the CPI is constructed. However, the CPI of the origin and destination may not reflect the prices of goods which tourists actually purchase, because the expenditure pattern of a tourist is quite different from that of the average household. Since there are likely to be substantial measurement errors associated with the use of the CPI as a proxy for relative tourism prices, some researchers have preferred to use a specific tourist cost of living variable, such as drink and tobacco price indices, shopping/meals/entertainment and hotel price indices, or weighted prices of food, accommodation, transport, entertainment and other variables, as proxies, or the average spending on travel goods and services as the composite tourism price. Blackwell (1970), Kwack (1972) and Kliman (1981) use the implicit consumer expenditure deflator to measure the disparity between the origin, destination and competing destinations' prices. The costs of package tours have been used in some studies as proxies for tourism prices (Jorgenson and Solvoll 1996; Kulendran 1996; Kulendran and King 1997).

Transportation costs
This refers to the cost of round-trip travel between the origin and destination countries. Unlike other goods, the consumer (tourist) has to be transported to the product (destination) rather than the reverse. Hence, the demand for transportation in international travel is a derived demand, namely to purchase tourism services. However, only 51 per cent of the published papers included this important explanatory variable in their studies. Although the theoretical justification for the inclusion of transportation costs is not disputed, many past tourism studies have excluded this variable mainly because of the unavailability of such data. Another reason often cited is the potential problem with multicollinearity in ordinary least squares (OLS) regression.

Transportation costs are usually measured by the price of air travel. However, the problem of measuring the effective transportation cost arises, namely, the actual costs borne by tourists. This problem is caused mainly by the pricing practices of airlines, which have resulted in two main categories of passenger fares on scheduled airline services, namely 'normal' (unrestricted) fares and 'special' fares. Normal fares are available for first, business and economy class, whereas special fares are only available for economy class, which includes excursion and promotional fares. The most widely offered type of special fares is the excursion fare.

Proxies for the transportation cost variable include the real economy airfare, real air travel cost, real average airfare, excursion airfare, cheapest airfare, distance, exchange rate-adjusted airfare and real revenue per passenger-kilometre/mile of scheduled airfares. Smith and Tom (1978) use an equivalent fare, which incorporates differences or changes in the level of services attached to the ticket, such as restrictions on stopovers, trip duration and booking constraints. Private gasoline costs between the origin and major destination cities (plus ferry costs) are often used as proxies for surface travel.

Exchange rates

Exchange rates are often introduced into tourism demand models in addition to, and separately from, the relative price variable. Such studies specifically examine the influence of nominal exchange rates on international tourism demand. Data on exchange rates are readily available because they are widely published and are reasonably accurate. Some researchers argue that tourists respond to exchange rate movements but not to changes in relative inflation rates when they make their decision to travel, because of imperfect knowledge. Tourists are well-informed of changes in exchange rates, whereas information on price changes in destinations is generally not known in advance (Gray 1966; Artus 1970). However, the inclusion of both exchange rates and relative prices as explanatory variables may lead to multicollinearity because the exchange rate is also a measure of relative prices.

Other factors

Secular changes in tourist tastes for foreign travel may be captured by the time trend variable, as in Barry and O'Hagan (1972, p. 147):

> population increase and changes in the age structure of population; the increase in the degree of urbanisation and the concomitant increase in the desire of people to get into open spaces; the increase in the length of paid holidays; the increase in the level of education giving people greater interest in travelling abroad and learning about other people first-hand . . .

Besides these temporal influences, a time trend may also be included to capture the steady change in the tourist mix (Fujii et al. 1985, 1987). Dynamics may also be included to account for lagged effects, such as the previous values of income, relative prices, exchange rates and foreign investment. Competing destinations/goods include location, travel costs, relative prices and cross-elasticities of competing destination(s), and prices of other consumer goods. Substitution of foreign travel for domestic travel, or for an alternative foreign destination, could be expected when transportation costs or costs of goods and services in a particular destination rise relative to domestic travel costs, or costs associated with alternative overseas destinations.

Dummy variables may be used to capture seasonal variations in travel demand. Seasonal patterns in tourist flows and expenditures are well-known characteristics of international tourism demand, but only 19 studies have tried to account for seasonality in modelling tourism demand. Although marketing expenditures by private or national agencies are vital for promoting the country as a tourist destination, especially where tourism makes significant contributions to the economy, it is somewhat strange that very few tourism studies (only 18 of the 124 studies) have included this variable in the tourism demand models. For policy purposes, it is valuable to investigate the significance of marketing/promotional expenditures, namely the absolute effectiveness of promotional activity and the relative effectiveness in various origin markets. The choice of destination is also influenced by ethnic and migration factors, which capture the idea of tourists' visiting friends and relatives in the various destinations (Smith and Tom 1978; Qiu and Zhang 1995). Very few tourism studies (only eight of the 124 studies) attempt to measure business travel, and have used proxies such as trade or trade volume, direct foreign investment or capital outflows. However, given its magnitude, international business activity and spending could be an important source of foreign exchange earnings. Only six studies include economic activity indicators, such as the unemployment rate, real assets, government budget forecast of change in private consumption, change in income and income distribution.

There are a large number of qualitative factors which influence the decision to demand international travel, including: tourists' attributes (gender, age, education level and employment/profession), which may affect leisure time availability or similar constraints; household size (composition of household and child/children age); population or population change in the origin; trip motive or frequency; destination attractiveness (climate, culture, history and natural environment); political, social and sporting events in a destination (threat of terrorism, political unrest, grounding aircraft strike, energy crises affecting gasoline availability and price, Expo, Olympic Games, historical commemorations and World Fairs). Qualitative factors are typically accommodated with the use of dummy variables.

The 'Other' category includes real tourist expenditure, supply/capacity constraints on tourist accommodation, exchange rate reforms or foreign exchange restrictions, cross-price elasticities of vacation goods, the average propensity to consume tourism goods, summer weather index and destination preference index.

Demand for international travel to a particular destination is expected to be positively related to income in the origin, marketing/promotion and migration, and negatively related to both relative tourism prices and transportation costs. Demand for overseas travel is expected to be positively related to exchange rate if the latter is measured as units of destination's currency per unit of origin's currency. However, if an increase in exchange

Table 1.7　Elasticity estimates for various explanatory variables

Explanatory variable	Elasticity estimate	Source
Income	0.033 to 14.32	Ffrench (1972)
	(3.35) (4.77)	Lee, Var and Blaine (1996)
Tourism prices	−0.15 to −7.01	Divisekera (1995)
	(2.68) (4.5)	Lee, Var and Blaine (1996)
Transportation costs	−0.07 to −2.372	Arbel and Ravid (1985)
	(2.8) (3.47)	Hultkrantz (1995)
Exchange rate	−0.34 to −12.01	BTCE (1988)
	(2.73) (4.5)	Webber (2001)
Marketing/promotion	0.279 to 1.611	Papadopoulos (1987)
	(3.64) (5.39)	
Migration	0.017 to 0.601	Qiu and Zhang (1995)
	(2.44) (3.25)	

rate represents a depreciation in origin's currency, the demand for international travel is expected to be negatively related to exchange rate. Based on the 124 studies reviewed in this chapter, the lowest and the highest significant elasticity estimates of these explanatory variables with the correct sign are selected. The elasticity estimates of income, tourism prices, transportation costs, exchange rate, marketing and migration are reported in Table 1.7 (with absolute *t*-ratios in parentheses). As shown in the table, the income and migration variables have the largest and smallest range of elasticity values of 14.29 and 0.58, respectively.

Lim (1999, p. 273) argues that 'variability in the measures, types of data, model specifications used, and the number of variables used, serve to confound the integration of results and the interpretation of findings'. The author has reviewed and integrated the research findings of 100 studies in the area using meta-analysis and based on the test statistic data derived from these studies.

Method of estimation
In order to evaluate the significance of empirical tourism demand models, it is necessary to analyse the empirical papers according to established statistical and econometric criteria. Since the primary purpose of each of these empirical papers has been to examine the relationships based on general economic-theoretic considerations between the variables underlying the determinants of tourism demand, it is important to analyse whether economic theory has had a significant impact on the analysis of tourism demand. It is also important to examine the empirical impact and

Table 1.8   Classification by method of estimation

Decades of publication	Only OLS	Unstated (OLS?)	OLS and GLS	Other	None	Total
1961–79	12	11	3	3	1	30
1980–89	16	8	11	14	1	50
1990–99	12	6	4	17	0	39
2000–03	2	0	0	3	0	5
Total	42	25	18	37	2	124

significance of the results, especially with regard to the econometric procedures used in the various studies.

In Table 1.8, the classification is by method of estimation. Five categories are listed, namely 'Only OLS', 'Unstated' (but presumably OLS), 'OLS and GLS' (generalised least squares, specifically Cochrane–Orcutt), 'Other' (which includes six entries for maximum likelihood (ML), five for {OLS, seemingly unrelated regression equations (SURE)}, three 2-stage least squares, ten {OLS, ML}, three SURE, one Unstated, one forward stepwise regression, and one for each of {OLS, GLS-AR(1), SURE}, GLS(pooling), {OLS, GLS-AR(1), ML}, {OLS, GLS, Ridge}, {ML, GLS-AR(1)}, {OLS, nonlinear least squares}, Probit ML, and {OLS, Tobit}), and None (with two entries). Of the 124 entries, 42 used only OLS, 25 presumably used OLS (where the method of estimation has not been stated explicitly), namely OLS(?), and another 38 ($= 18 + 20$, where 20 entries arise in the Other category) used OLS (or OLS(?)) in conjunction with GLS-AR(1) or GLS-AR(1?), SURE, ML, Ridge, nonlinear least squares, or Tobit. Thus, a total of 105 studies reported OLS estimates, with or without considering other methods of estimation. Although OLS and GLS were used in 18 studies, it is astonishing that 11 of the 18 did not state explicitly whether the Cochrane–Orcutt method had been used for an AR(1) process or, indeed, even report the (presumed) AR(1) parameter estimate and its standard error. Moreover, there was no discussion as to why an AR(1) process might have been used instead of a higher-order autoregressive process, or a moving average process of first order or higher order.

Diagnostic tests
Finally, the classification in Table 1.9 is by use of diagnostics to test one or more of the auxiliary assumptions of the models. The role of diagnostic tests has become well established in the econometric literature in recent years, and plays an important role in modern applied econometrics

Table 1.9   Classification by use of diagnostics

Decades of publication	Only DW	Other	None	Total
1961–79	16	0	14	30
1980–89	25	9	16	50
1990–99	11	16	12	39
2000–03	0	5	0	5
Total	52	30	42	124

(McAleer 1994). Most diagnostic tests are standard, and have been available in modern econometric software programs such as MICROFIT, PC-GIVE, SHAZAM and EViews since the 1980s. They include the Durbin and Watson (1950, 1951) DW statistic, the Durbin (1970), the Ljung–Box (1978) Q-statistic for serial correlation, Lagrange multiplier (LM) tests for serial correlation (LM(SC)) (Godfrey 1978), heteroscedasticity (LM(H)) (Breusch and Pagan 1979), normality (LM(N)) (Bera and Jarque 1981), and functional form (LM(F)), the White (1980) test for heteroscedasticity, the Ramsey (1969, 1974) regression specification error (RESET) test of functional form misspecification, the Engle (1982) test for autoregressive conditional heteroscedasticity (ARCH), the Chow (1960) test for structural change (Chow 1), the Box and Cox (1964) test for functional form, the Dickey and Fuller (1979, 1981) (DF) and augmented DF (ADF) tests for unit roots, and the Hylleberg et al. (1990) (HEGY) test for seasonal and non-seasonal unit roots.

Forty-two studies did not report any diagnostics whatsoever. In 52 studies, only the Durbin–Watson (DW) statistic for first-order serial correlation of the residuals was reported, with 65 (= 52 + 13, where 13 entries arise from the 'Other' category) studies reporting DW in total. Surprisingly, the DW statistic was reported in several cases, without explanation, even when quarterly or monthly data were used. Thus, 94 (= 52 + 42) of 124 studies reported minimal or no information regarding the adequacy of the underlying assumptions of the estimated models. Indeed, 23 of the 39 papers published in the 1990s used the DW statistic, or provided no diagnostics at all. Since diagnostic tests were not widely available in econometric software packages until the 1980s, it is understandable that empirical studies published before 1980 may have used only the DW statistic, or provided no diagnostic whatsoever. Given its vintage, the use of the DW statistic is not altogether surprising. However, the lack of any other diagnostic provided in papers published since the mid-1980s is of concern, especially in studies where few observations are used, and suggests that the inferences from the estimated models may be highly sensitive to the assumptions. Such sensitivity must be examined if the empirical results are to be interpreted with confidence.

Conclusion

Fluctuations in the demand for international tourism are influenced by many factors, but most studies focus on the economic variables in estimating a satisfactory explanation. The purpose of this chapter has been to analyse critically the types of data used, sample sizes where only annual data are used, model specification, and variables used in 124 published empirical studies of international tourism demand.

Two of the major deficiencies found in the published empirical studies include:

1. the use of small sample sizes, especially with annual data, which renders the regression estimates in such circumstances as imprecise; and
2. the concentration on estimating log-linear models, with virtually no discussion as to its merits relative to its linear counterpart, and a lack of discussion of the appropriate functional form used.

In view of the undoubted significance of empirical tourism demand studies for policy purposes, an econometric review of these studies has also been undertaken to examine the method of estimation, the type of diagnostic tests used to check the auxiliary assumptions and adequacy of the various models, and the implications of the lack of diagnostic testing for empirical analysis. As many as 105 of the 124 empirical studies reviewed used OLS estimation, either alone or in conjunction with other methods of estimation. Studies which use single equations to determine tourism demand elasticities may have omitted important information about the feedback between the explanatory variables and tourism demand.

The lack of reporting of diagnostic tests, especially in the more recently published papers, is an issue that can easily be redressed by using a range of widely available econometric software packages. Where a diagnostic has been reported, it has invariably been only the Durbin–Watson statistic. In the absence of testing the validity of the auxiliary assumptions of the reported models, the empirical conclusions reached regarding the factors which determine the demand for international tourism should be interpreted with some caution.

Past tourism studies have focused primarily on the economic variables affecting tourism demand. These factors are predominantly exogenous variables over which destinations or tourist-receiving countries have little control. Although there has been a proliferation of studies since the 1960s on the relationship between tourism demand and its determinants, specific areas still remain under-researched, particularly those related to marketing and non-economic factors.

Over time, tourism demand modelling practice has gone from using simple to state-of-the-art statistical and econometric techniques. The use of unit root tests and statistical analysis for non-stationary processes, through the use of cointegration methods, has revolutionised the understanding of tourism and macroeconomic time-series data. These developments permit both long- and short-run tourism demand models to be estimated and tested. However, there are many unanswered questions regarding the plethora of test procedures now available, particularly regarding their small sample properties. Future research to evaluate and extend existing procedures for modelling tourism and tourism-related macroeconomic time-series data through the use of Monte Carlo numerical experiments is imperative.

Acknowledgements

The author wishes to thank the editors for helpful comments and suggestions, and to acknowledge the financial support of the Australian Research Council. The author is also grateful to Elsevier, Professors Jafar Jafari and Stephen Wanhill, editors of *Annals of Tourism Research* and *Tourism Economics*, respectively, for permission to reproduce material from her papers.

Bibliography

Alperovich, G. and Y. Machnes (1994), 'The role of wealth in the demand of international air travel', *Journal of Transport Economics and Policy*, **28**, 163–73.

Anastasopoulos, P. (1989), 'The US travel account: the impact of fluctuations of the US dollar', *Hospitality Education and Research Journal*, **13**, 469–81.

Arbel, A. and S. Ravid (1985), 'On recreation demand: a time-series approach', *Applied Economics*, **17**, 979–90.

Artus, J.R. (1970), 'The effect of revaluation on the foreign travel balance of Germany', *International Monetary Fund Staff Papers*, **17**, 602–17.

Artus, J.R. (1972), 'An econometric analysis of international travel', *International Monetary Fund Staff Papers*, **19**, 579–613.

Ashworth, J. and P. Johnson (1990), 'Holiday tourism expenditure: some preliminary econometric results', *The Tourist Review*, **3**, 12–19.

Askari, H. (1971), 'Demand for package tours', *Journal of Transport Economics and Policy*, **5**, 40–51.

Askari, H. (1973), 'Demand for travel to Europe by American citizens', *Economia Internazionale*, **26**, 305–17.

Bakalis, S., A. Morris and K. Wilson (1994), 'Tourism trends to 2000 from the Antipodes to the Old Continent', in A.V. Seaton (ed.), *Tourism: The State of the Art*, Chichester: Wiley, pp. 415–27.

Bakkal, I. (1991), 'Characteristics of West German demand for international tourism in the northern Mediterranean region', *Applied Economics*, **23**, 295–304.

Bakkal, I. and A. Scaperlanda (1991), 'Characteristics of US demand for European tourism: a translog approach', *Weltwirtschaftliches Archiv*, **127**,119–37.

Barry, K. and J. O'Hagan (1972), 'An econometric study of British tourist expenditure in Ireland', *Economic and Social Review*, **5**, 143–61.

Baum, T. and R. Mudambi (1996), 'A country-of-origin analysis of tourist expenditure: the case of Turkey', *Tourism Economics*, **2**, 137–49.

Bechdolt, B. (1973), 'Cross-sectional travel demand functions: US visitors to Hawaii, 1961–70', *Quarterly Review of Economics and Business*, **13**, 37–47.

Bera, A.K. and C.M. Jarque (1981), 'An efficient large sample test for normality of observations and regression residuals', Working Paper in Economics and Econometrics, No. 040, Australian National University, Canberra.

Blackwell, J. (1970), 'Tourist traffic and the demand for accommodation: some projections', *Economic and Social Review*, **1**, 323–43.

Bond, M. (1979), 'The world trade model: Invisibles', *International Monetary Fund Staff Papers*, **26**, 257–333.

Bond, M. and J. Ladman (1972), 'International tourism and economic development: a special case for Latin America. Mississippi Valley', *Journal of Business and Economics*, **8**, 43–55.

Box, G.E.P. and D.R. Cox (1964), 'An analysis of transformations', *Journal of the Royal Statistical Society*, B 26, 211–43.

Brady, J. and R. Widdows (1988), 'The impact of world events on travel to Europe during the summer of 1986', *Journal of Travel Research*, **26**, 8–10.

Breusch, T.S. and A.R. Pagan (1979), 'A simple test for heteroscedasticity and random coefficient variation', *Econometrica*, **47**, 1287–94.

Bureau of Transport and Communications Economics (BTCE) (1988), 'Trends and prospects for Australian international air transport', Occasional Paper 88, Canberra.

Carey, K. (1991), 'Estimation of Caribbean tourism demand: issues in measurement and methodology', *Atlantic Economic Journal*, **19**, 32–40.

Carmody, G. (1988), 'Potential tourism demand in Australia: a review of the lessons of history', Submission to Industries Assistance Commission Inquiry into Travel and Tourism, Australian Tourism Industry Association.

Chadee, D. and Z. Mieczkowski (1987), 'An empirical analysis of the effects of the exchange rate on Canadian tourism', *Journal of Travel Research*, **26**, 13–17.

Chow, G.C. (1960), 'Tests of equality between sets of coefficients in two linear regressions', *Econometrica*, **28**, 591–605.

Cigliano, J.M. (1980), 'Price and income elasticities for airline travel: the North Atlantic market', *Business Economics*, **15**, 17–21.

Cline, R. (1975), 'Measuring travel volumes and itineraries and forecasting future travel growth to individual Pacific destinations', in S.P. Ladany (ed.), *Management Science Applications to Leisure-Time Operations*, New York: North-Holland, pp. 134–45.

Covington, B., E.M. Thunberg and C. Jauregui (1994), 'International demand of the United States as a travel destination', *Journal of Travel and Tourism Marketing*, **3**, 39–50.

Crampon, L.J. and K.T. Tan (1973), 'A model of tourism flow into the Pacific', *The Tourist Review*, **28**, 98–104.

Crouch, G.I. (1994), 'The study of international tourism demand: a review of findings', *Journal of Travel Research*, **33**, 12–23.

Crouch, G.I., L. Schultz and P. Valerio (1992), 'Marketing international tourism to Australia: a regression analysis', *Tourism Management*, **13**, 196–208.

Davies, B. and J. Mangan (1992), 'Family expenditure on hotels and holidays', *Annals of Tourism Research*, **19**, 691–9.

Di Matteo, L. and R. Di Matteo (1993), 'The determinants of expenditures by Canadian visitors to the United States', *Journal of Travel Research*, **31**, 34–42.

Diamond, J. (1977), 'Tourism's role in economic development: the case reexamined', *Economic Development and Cultural Change*, **25**, 539–53.

Dickey, D.A. and W.A. Fuller (1979), 'Distribution of the estimators for autoregressive time-series with a unit root', *Journal of the American Statistical Association*, **74**, 427–31.

Dickey, D.A. and W.A. Fuller (1981), 'Likelihood ratio statistics for autoregressive time-series with a unit root', *Econometrica*, **49**, 1057–72.

Divisekera, S. (1993), 'International demand for Australian travel and tourism', Proceedings of the National Conference on Tourism Research, Bureau of Tourism Research, University of Sydney.

Divisekera, S. (1994), 'A model of demand for international tourism: a multi-country demand system', Paper presented to the PhD Conference in Economics and Business, Australian National University, Canberra, 7–9 December.

Divisekera, S. (1995), 'An econometric model of international visitor flows to Australia', *Australian Economic Papers*, **34**, 291–308.

Durbin, J. (1970), 'Testing for serial correlation in least-squares regression when some of the regressors are lagged dependent variables', *Econometrica*, **38**, 410–21.

Durbin, J. and G.S. Watson (1950), 'Testing for serial correlation in least-squares regression I', *Biometrika*, **37**, 409–28.

Durbin, J. and G.S. Watson (1951), 'Testing for serial correlation in least-squares regression II', *Biometrika*, **38**, 159–78.

Edwards, A. (1976), 'International tourism development forecast to 1985', Special Report, 33, London: Economist Intelligence Unit Limited.

Edwards, A. (1979), 'International tourism development forecasts to 1990, Special Report, 62, London: Economist Intelligence Unit Limited.

Engle, R.F. (1982), 'Autoregressive conditional heteroscedasticity with estimates of the variance of United Kingdom inflation', *Econometrica*, **50**, 987–1007.

Ffrench, R. (1972), 'The effect of devaluation on the foreign travel balance of Jamaica', *Social and Economic Studies*, **20**, 443–59.

Franses, P.H. and M. McAleer (1998), 'Cointegration analysis of seasonal data', *Journal of Economic Surveys*, **12**, 651–78. Reprinted in M. McAleer and L. Oxley (eds) (1999), *Practical Issues in Cointegration Analysis*, Blackwell: Oxford, pp. 235–62.

Fujii, E., M. Khaled and J. Mak (1985), 'An almost ideal demand system for visitor expenditures', *Journal of Transport Economics and Policy*, **19**, 161–71.

Fujii, E., M. Khaled and J. Mak (1987), 'An empirical comparison of systems of demand equations for tourist expenditures in resort destinations', *Philippine Review of Economics and Business*, **24**, 79–102.

Fujii, E. and J. Mak (1981), 'Forecasting tourism demand; some methodological issues', *Annals of Regional Science*, **15**, 72–82.

Gerakis, A.S. (1965), 'Effects of exchange rate devaluations and revaluations on receipts from tourism', *International Monetary Fund Staff Papers*, **12**, 365–83.

Gibbons, J.D. and M. Fish (1985), 'Devaluation and US tourism expenditure in Mexico', *Annals of Tourism Research*, **12**, 547–62.

Godfrey, L.G. (1978), 'Testing against general autoregressive and moving average error models when the regressors include lagged dependent variables', *Econometrica*, **46**, 1293–302.

Gray, P. (1966), 'The demand for international travel by the United States and Canada', *International Economic Review*, **7**, 83–92.

Gray, P. (1967), 'Tourism as an export industry in South-East Asia: a long-run prognostication', *The Philippine Economic Journal*, **6**, 155–69.

Gu, Z. and T.L. Martin (1992), 'Terrorism, seasonality and international air tourism arrivals in Central Florida: an empirical analysis', *Journal of Travel and Tourism Marketing*, **1**, 3–17.

Gunadhi, H. and K.B. Chow (1986), 'Demand elasticities of tourism in Singapore', *Tourism Management*, **7**, 239–53.

Guthrie, H.R. (1961), 'Demand for tourists' goods and services in a world market', *Papers and Proceedings of the Regional Science Association*, **7**, 159–75.

Haitovsky, Y., L. Salomon and L.A. Silman (1987), 'The economic impact of charter flights on tourism to Israel', *Journal of Transport Economics and Policy*, **21**, 111–34.

Hollander, G. (1982), 'Determinants of demand for travel and from Australia', Working Paper, 26, Canberra: Bureau of Industry.

Holmes, R.A. and A.F.M. Shamsuddin (1997), 'Short- and long-term effects of world exposition 1986 on US demand for British Columbia tourism', *Tourism Economics*, **3**, 137–60.

Hultkrantz, L. (1995), 'On determinants of Swedish recreational domestic and outbound travel, 1989–93', *Tourism Economics*, **1**, 119–45.

Hylleberg, S., R.F. Engle, C.W.J. Granger and B.S. Yoo (1900), 'Seasonal integration and cointegration', *Journal of Econometrics*, **99**, 215–38.

Industries Assistance Commission (1989), *Travel and Tourism*, Report No. 423, Canberra: Australian Government Publishing Service.

International Monetary Fund, *Balance of Payments Statistics Yearbook*, Part 2 (various issues), Washington, DC: IMF.

Johnson, R.L. and D.B. Suits (1983), 'A statistical analysis of the demand for visits to US national parks: travel costs and seasonality', *Journal of Travel Research*, **22**, 21–4.

Jorgensen, F. and G. Solvoll (1996), 'Demand models for inclusive tour charter: the Norwegian case', *Tourism Management*, **17**, 17–24.

Jud, G.D. (1974), 'Tourism and economic growth in Mexico since 1950', *Inter American Economic Affairs*, **28**, 19–43.

Jud, G.D. and H. Joseph (1974), 'International demand for Latin American tourism', *Growth and Change*, **5**, 25–31.

Kanafani, A. (1980), 'Price elasticities of non-business air travel demand', *Transportation Engineering Journal*, **2**, 217–25.

Kim, S. and H. Song (1998), 'Analysis of inbound tourism demand in South Korea: a cointegration and error correction approach', *Tourism Analysis*, **3**, 25–41.

Klein, L.R. (1962), *An Introduction to Econometrics*, Englewood Cliffs, NJ: Prentice-Hall.

Kliman, M.L. (1981), 'A quantitative analysis of Canadian overseas tourism', *Transportation Research*, **15** (1), 487–97.

Kulendran, N. (1996), 'Modelling quarterly tourist flows to Australia using cointegration analysis', *Tourism Economics*, **2**, 203–22.

Kulendran, N. and M. King (1997), 'Forecasting international quarterly tourist flows using error-correction and time-series models', *International Journal of Forecasting*, **13**, 319–27.

Kwack, S.Y. (1972), 'Effects of income and prices on travel spending abroad, 1960III–1967IV', *International Economic Review*, **13**, 245–56.

Laber, G. (1969), 'Determinants of international travel between Canada and the United States', *Geographical Analysis*, **1**, 329–36.

Lee, C., T. Var and T.W. Blaine (1996), 'Determinants of inbound tourist expenditures', *Annals of Tourism Research*, **23**, 527–42.

Lim, C. (1997a), 'Review of international tourism demand models', *Annals of Tourism Research*, **24**, 835–49.

Lim, C. (1997b), 'An econometric classification and review of international tourism demand models', *Tourism Economics*, **3**, 69–81.

Lim, C. (1997c), 'The functional specification of international tourism demand models', *Mathematics and Computers in Simulation*, **43** (3–6), 535–43.

Lim, C. (1999), 'A meta-analytic review of international tourism demand', *Journal of Travel Research*, **37** (3), 273–84.

Lim, C. and M. McAleer (2001), 'Cointegration analysis of quarterly tourism demand by Hong Kong and Singapore for Australia', *Applied Economics*, **33**, 1599–619.

Lim, C. and M. McAleer (2002), 'A cointegration analysis of annual tourism demand by Malaysia for Australia', *Mathematics and Computers in Simulation*, **59**, 197–205.

Lim, C. and M. McAleer (2003), 'Modelling international travel demand from Singapore to Australia', *Anatolia*, **14**, 23–43.

Lin, T.B. and Y.W. Sung (1983), 'Hong Kong', in E.A. Pye and T.B. Lin (eds), *Tourism in Asia: The Economic Impact*, Singapore: Singapore University Press, pp. 50–62.

Little, J.S. (1980), 'International travel in the US balance of payments', *New England Economic Review*, May/June, 42–55.

Ljung, G.M. and G.E.P. Box (1978), 'On a measure of lack of fit in time series models', *Biometrika*, **65**, 297–303.

Loeb, P.D. (1982), 'International travel to the United States: an econometric evaluation', *Annals of Tourism Research*, **9**, 7–20.

Mak, J. and J. Moncur (1980), 'The demand for travel agents', *Journal of Transport Economics and Policy*, **14**, 221–31.

Mak, J., J. Moncur and D. Yonamine (1977), 'Determinants of visitor expenditures and visitor lengths of stay: a cross-section analysis of US visitors to Hawaii', *Journal of Travel Research*, **15**, 5–8.

Mak, J. and K. White (1992), 'Comparative tourism development in Asia and the Pacific', *Journal of Travel Research*, **31**, 14–23.

Martin, C.A. and S.F. Witt (1987), 'Tourism demand forecasting models: choice of appropriate variable to represent tourists' cost of living', *Tourism Management*, **8**, 233–46.

Martin, C.A. and S.F. Witt (1988), 'Substitute prices in models of tourism demand', *Annals of Tourism Research*, **15**, 255–68.

McAleer, M. (1994), 'Sherlock Holmes and the search for truth: a diagnostic tale', *Journal of Economic Surveys*, **8**, 317–70.

Morgan, J.N. (1986), 'The impact of travel costs on visits to US national parks: intermodal shifting among Grand Canyon visitors', *Journal of Travel Research*, **24**, 23–8.

Morris, A., K. Wilson and S. Bakalis (1995), 'Modelling tourism flows from Europe to Australia', *Tourism Economics*, **1**, 147–67.

Moshirian, F. (1993), 'Determinants of international trade flows in travel and passenger services', *Economic Record*, **69**, 239–52.

Mutti, J. and Y. Murai (1977), 'Airline travel on the North Atlantic', *Journal of Transport Economics and Policy*, **11**, 45–53.

O'Hagan, J.W. and M.J. Harrison (1984a), 'Market shares of US tourist expenditure in Europe: an econometric analysis', *Applied Economics*, **16**, 919–31.

O'Hagan, J.W. and M.J. Harrison (1984b), 'UK and US visitor expenditure in Ireland: some econometric findings', *Economic and Social Review*, **15**, 195–207.

Oliver, F.R. (1971), 'The effectiveness of the UK travel allowance', *Applied Economics*, **3**, 219–26.

Ong, C. (1995), 'Tourism demand models: a critique', *Mathematics and Computers in Simulation*, **39**, 367–72.

Papadopoulos, S.I. (1987), 'Strategic marketing techniques in international tourism', *International Marketing Review*, Summer, 71–84.

Papadopoulos, S.I. and S.F. Witt (1985), 'A marketing analysis of foreign tourism in Greece', in S. Shaw, L. Sparks and E. Kaynak (eds), *Proceedings of Second World Marketing Congress*, UK: University of Stirling, pp. 682–93.

Papatheodorou, A. (1999), 'The demand for international tourism in the Mediterranean region', *Applied Economics*, **31**, 619–30.

Poole, M. (1988), 'Forecasting methodology', BTR Occasional Paper, 3, Canberra: Bureau of Tourism Research.

Pyo, S.S., M. Uysal and R.W. McLellan (1991), 'A linear expenditure model for tourism demand', *Annals of Tourism Research*, **18**, 443–54.

Qiu, H. and J. Zhang (1995), 'Determinants of tourist arrivals and expenditures in Canada', *Journal of Travel Research*, Fall, 43–49.

Quayson, J. and T. Var (1982), 'A tourism demand function for the Okanagan, BC', *Tourism Management*, **3**, 108–15.

Ramsey, J.B. (1969), 'Tests for specification errors in classical linear least squares regression analysis', *Journal of the Royal Statistical Society B*, **31**, 350–71.

Ramsey, J.B. (1974), 'Classical model selection through specification error tests', in P. Zarembka (ed.), *Frontiers in Econometrics*, New York: Academic Press, pp. 13–47.

Rosensweig, J.A. (1986), 'Exchange rates and competition for tourists', *New England Economic Review*, July/August, 57–67.

Rugg, D. (1973), 'The choice of journey destination: a theoretical and empirical analysis', *Review of Economics and Statistics*, **20**, 64–71.

Schulmeister, S. (1979), *Tourism and the Business Cycle*, Vienna: Austrian Institute for Economic Research.

Seddighi, H.R. and D.F. Shearing (1997), 'The demand for tourism in North East England with special reference to Northumbria: an empirical analysis', *Tourism Management*, **18**, 499–511.

Sheldon, P.J. and J. Mak (1987), 'The demand for package tours: a mode choice model', *Journal of Travel Research*, **25**, 13–17.

Silberman, J. (1985), 'A demand function for length of stay: the evidence from Virginia Beach', *Journal of Travel Research*, **23**, 16–23.

Smeral, E. (1988), 'Tourism demand, economic theory and econometrics: an integrated approach', *Journal of Travel Research*, **26**, 38–43.

Smeral, E. and S.F. Witt (1996), 'Econometric forecasts of tourism demand to 2005', *Annals of Tourism Research*, **23**, 891–907.

Smeral, E., S.F. Witt and C.A. Witt (1992), 'Econometric forecasts: tourism trends to 2000', *Annals of Tourism Research*, **19**, 450–66.

Smith, A.B. and J.N. Tom (1978), 'Factors affecting demand for international travel to and from Australia', Occasional Paper 11, Canberra: Bureau of Transport Economics.

Song, H., P. Romilly and X. Liu (2000), 'An empirical study of outbound tourism demand in the UK', *Applied Economics*, **32**, 611–24.

Steinnes, D.N. (1988), 'A statistical analysis of the impact of oil price shocks on tourism', *Journal of Travel Research*, **26**, 39–42.

Stronge, W.B. and M. Redman (1982), 'US tourism in Mexico: an empirical analysis', *Annals of Tourism Research*, **9**, 21–35.

Summary, R. (1987), 'Estimation of tourism demand by multivariable regression analysis', *Tourism Management*, **8**, 317–22.

Sunday, A.A. (1978), 'Foreign travel and tourism prices and demand', *Annals of Tourism Research*, **5**, 268–73.

Sunday, A.A. and J.K. Johansson (1975), 'Advertising and international tourism', in S.P. Ladany (ed.), *Management Science Applications to Leisure-Time Operations*, New York: North-Holland, pp. 81–96.

Syriopoulos, T.C. (1989), 'Dynamic modelling of tourism demand in the Mediterranean', *Studies in Economics*, 89/12, Canterbury: University of Kent.

Syriopoulos, T.C. (1995), 'A dynamic model of demand for Mediterranean tourism', *International Review of Applied Economics*, **3**, 318–36.

Syriopoulos, T.C. and M.T. Sinclair (1993), 'An econometric study of tourism demand: the AIDS model of US and European tourism in Mediterranean countries', *Applied Economics*, **25**, 1541–52.

Taplin, J.H.E. (1980), 'A coherence approach to estimates of price elasticities in the vacation travel market', *Journal of Transport Economics and Policy*, **14**, 19–35.

Taplin, J.H.E. (1982), *Tourist travel to Tasmania: An Econometric Analysis*, University of Tasmania: Transport Economics Centre.

Tremblay, P. (1989), 'Pooling international tourism in Western Europe', *Annals of Tourism Research*, **16**, 477–91.

Truett, D.B. and L.J. Truett (1987), 'The response of tourism to international economic conditions: Greece, Mexico and Spain', *Journal of Developing Areas*, **21**, 177–89.

Truett, L.J. and D.B. Truett (1982), 'Public policy and the growth of the Mexican tourism industry, 1970–1979', *Journal of Travel Research*, **20**, 11–19.

Uysal, M. and J.L. Crompton (1984), 'Determinants of demand for international tourist flows to Turkey', *Tourism Management*, **5**, 288–97.

Van Dijk, J.C., J.S. Hagens and F.A.G. Windmeijer (1991), 'A simulation model of the Dutch tourist market: a technical report on "Toermodel"', SEO, Foundation for Economic Research, University of Amsterdam.

Var, T., G. Mohammad and O. Icoz (1990a), 'Factors affecting international tourism demand for Turkey', *Annals of Tourism Research*, **17**, 606–10.

Var, T., G. Mohammad and O. Icoz (1990b), 'A tourism demand model', *Annals of Tourism Research*, **17**, 622–6.

Vogt, M.G. and C. Wittayakorn (1998), 'Determinants of the demand for Thailand's exports of tourism', *Applied Economics*, **30**, 711–15.

Webber, A.G. (2001), 'Exchange rate volatility and cointegration in tourism demand', *Journal of Travel Research*, **39**, 398–405.
White, H. (1980), 'A heteroscedasticity-consistent covariance matrix estimator and a direct test for heteroscedasticity', *Econometrica*, **48**, 817–38.
White, K.J. (1985), 'An international travel demand model: US travel to Western Europe', *Annals of Tourism Research*, **12**, 529–45.
White, K.J. and M.B. Walker (1982), 'Trouble in the travel account', *Annals of Tourism Research*, **9**, 37–56.
Witt, S.F. (1980a), 'An abstract mode–abstract (destination) node model of foreign holiday demand', *Applied Economics*, **12**, 163–80.
Witt, S.F. (1980b), 'An econometric comparison of UK and German foreign holiday behaviour', *Managerial and Decision Economics*, **1**, 123–31.
Witt, S.F., M. Dartus and A.M. Sykes (1992), 'Modelling AIEST congress attendance', *The Tourist Review*, **47**, 27–9.
Witt, S.F. and C.A. Martin (1987), 'Econometric models for forecasting international tourism demand', *Journal of Travel Research*, **25**, 23–30.
World Tourism Organization (2002), *Tourism Highlights*, Madrid: World Tourism Organization.
Yoon, J. and E.L. Shafer (1996), 'Models of US travel demand patterns for the Bahamas', *Journal of Travel Research*, **34**, 50–56.

2 Microfoundations of tourist choice
Andreas Papatheodorou

Introduction

The knowledge of the formation mechanisms and determinant factors of tourist choice is of primary importance for all tourism stakeholders. From an inner psychological perspective, tourists need to know themselves better, become more informed about the process of decision making and choose destinations and tourist activities that will hopefully increase their utility and prosperity. From the supply side, the deciphering of tourism choice can help service providers and destination policy makers to design appropriate marketing and advertising campaigns for specific consumer target groups. It can also assist them to manage the quality of their product integrally and face periods of crisis in tourism successfully. Similarly, theoreticians should be knowledgeable of tourist choice factors to produce robust econometric models and forecasts that can facilitate resort planners (among other stakeholders) in their long-term projections and decisions: unless accurate, the planning exercise may fail to improve the resort to the detriment of the environment (natural and built), the local community and of course the end users of tourism.

It is not surprising, therefore, that tourism choice and its microfoundations have received substantial attention by researchers in social sciences from both a theoretical and an empirical perspective. As in most cases with tourism, researchers are predominantly interested in applying the principles of their discipline to explain tourist choices. The economists would mainly focus on rational behaviour and utility maximisation issues, the geographers would examine tourist flows in space, the psychologists would discuss motivation while other social scientists would highlight socio-cultural factors. Likewise, researchers in marketing and advertising would study how tourist choice can be affected in favour of a targeted product or destination. To understand, therefore, tourist choice in full it is important to integrate the above approaches and produce a creative, interdisciplinary amalgam. Such a task, however, is beyond the scope of this chapter, which essentially explains how economics has treated the issue. With this in mind, the next section discusses the foundations of tourist choice in the context of the mainstream classical microeconomic theory. This is the standard benchmark in consumer demand analysis upon which other approaches are presented and evaluated. In fact, despite some advantages, the classical theory fails to address essential issues including separability of preferences, discreteness in choice and product differentiation. As a valid alternative, therefore, the third section analyses the characteristics theory and its application in tourism economics. This is an interesting framework that deals successfully with many of the classical theory caveats. The fourth section focuses on information issues and the fifth considers developments from a dynamic perspective. The final section concludes and proposes areas for further research.

Classical microeconomics
In the textbook case, the consumers derive utility from the consumption of available goods; the aim is to maximise this utility subject to an income constraint. Formally:

$$\max U = f(\mathbf{x})$$
$$\text{s.t. } \mathbf{p} \cdot \mathbf{x} = Y; p_i, x_i, Y \geq 0; i = 1, \ldots, N \tag{2.1}$$

where U is utility as a function of quantities of goods x_i, $\mathbf{x}$ is the column vector of quantities of goods, $\mathbf{p}$ is the row vector of prices associated with these goods, Y is available expenditure and N is the total number of goods.

Separability in choice structure
This simple model, however, is very inadequate to explain tourist choice, largely because it is too generic to account for choice microfoundations. The first issue arises with respect to the number of goods involved in the utility function. Should tourism goods be put together with non-tourism goods, that is, does the consumer make a rational choice by considering all different goods (for example, refrigerators, cars, holidays, healthcare) at the same level? Or is it better to assume separability of the choice structure (Deaton and Muellbauer 1980b), where the consumers allocate the first part of their total budget to tourism (for example, 10 per cent) and subsequently make a choice among different tourist products (in terms of specific destinations and/or activities)?

Van Raaij (1986) argues that the potential tourist first takes a generic decision on whether to take a holiday or not. In this context, tourism expenditure is examined in relation to other household outlays, such as on consumer durable products. The decision relies heavily on the various constraints faced by the tourist. In the case of financial difficulties, for example, or lack of necessary durable goods, it seems rather unlikely that the tourist will opt for an international holiday. From a realistic perspective, it also makes good sense to assume separability, as the actual process of choice is quite complicated and time consuming: it is unlikely that a consumer is able to draw a simultaneous rational choice decision on hundreds or thousands of goods. In fact, it is acceptable to assume multiple levels of separability: for example, having decided that they want to spend Y amount of money on tourism goods, the representative consumer allocates Y_1 on tourism in the Mediterranean and Y_2 on tourism in the Caribbean – subsequently, he or she decides how to allocate Y_1 among Mediterranean destinations and Y_2 among Caribbean resorts. On the basis of separability, therefore, the column vector $\mathbf{x}$ in equation (2.1) would contain only the tourist goods under consideration at each level.

Discreteness in choice
Furthermore, the separability-adjusted model cannot explain another main feature of the choice structure, namely discreteness. In fact, the classical model assumes that the representative tourist consumes all goods under consideration simultaneously. This assumption might be acceptable at a micro level, as the tourist consumes goods and services from a range of tourist sectors, for example, transport, accommodation, catering. Nonetheless, this assumption is unrealistic both at the macro (that is, destination) and very micro (for example, within the restaurant sector) levels: as the representative tourist is not omnipresent, choice is essentially discrete. A similar problem arises from the fact that for some tourist products, individual consumption might be restricted to one (for example, air ticket) or very few units (for example, nights spent at a hotel). For these reasons, discrete choice modelling would be more realistic to use. The multinomial logit model is a good example:

$$P_i = e^{V_i} \bigg/ \sum_{k=1}^{N} e^{V_k} \qquad (2.2)$$

where P_i is the probability of choosing destination i out of the available N, e is exponentiation and V is the indirect utility associated with destination i. For more information, see Ben-Akiva and Lerman (1985) and Morley (1994).

The existence of a representative consumer
The classical model can bypass the discreteness caveat at an aggregate level. It may be argued that while the representative consumer is obviously not omnipresent, all tourist goods are consumed when the total number of tourists is taken into consideration. In other words, if three tourists go to Spain and one to Greece, out of a total four, then the representative tourist spends on average three-quarters of their money in Spain and one-quarter in Greece, other things equal. Although this assumption might be convenient enough especially for empirical research, it challenges the very existence of a representative consumer as such: to a major extent, people travel

to different places simply because they have different preferences. The standard classical utility model cannot account for consumer heterogeneity – discrete choice modelling can offer a better approach on this issue.

The essence of tourist choice
The question on the representative tourist opens the sack of Aeolus to address more fundamental issues about tourist choice. The classical model assumes that tourists derive utility from consuming goods *per se*. At a macro level, it is absurd to assume consumption of whole destinations; it makes better sense to talk about number of days spent in a particular destination. At a micro level, the notion of a good may be valid, for example, in the form of an air ticket or a restaurant meal. But do tourists actually derive utility by the consumption of goods as such? Is a meal consumed at home different from a meal at a restaurant in our hometown and dissimilar to a meal consumed under the palm trees of a beautiful tropical tourist island? The classical model cannot give a satisfactory answer to this question, not least because it cannot account for issues of horizontal or vertical differentiation. In the mid-1970s, however, product diversity received further attention. In this context, Dixit and Stiglitz (1977) assumed a utility function U that can accommodate differentiation, albeit of a restricted nature, within the classical framework. This usually takes the following form:

$$U = U\left[q_0, \left(\sum_{i=1}^{n} q_i^\rho \right)^{1/\rho} \right] \qquad (2.3)$$

where q_0 is the quantity of a unique good, q_i is the quantity of the differentiated product i and $\rho \leq 1$ is a parameter of substitutability. The sub-utility function for the differentiated goods is of the constant elasticity of substitution (CES) form. The main problem with this model is the absence of any notion of remoteness or neighbourhood relative to other products. In particular, this approach is poorly adapted to describe a confined space, since the CES utility function treats all differentiated products in a symmetric way. This seems to be an important drawback for the analysis of tourism choice: it is highly implausible, for example, that a German tourist would treat the British tourist product similarly to the Japanese or the Spanish ones. However, symmetry can still survive within a narrower defined group of products; for example, the German tourist may treat the Spanish tourist product similar to the Greek one. Traditional theory, however, does not provide a clear explanation of how products can be classified together. Most importantly, it cannot model the tourism experience as such, which is related not to goods *per se* but to characteristics associated with these goods. For example, the tourist does not derive

utility by spending a day in a hotel as such: what matters, are the characteristics of the hotel, for example, the size and quality of the room and the
available facilities.

Empirical research on tourist choice
Despite all these caveats, the classical microeconomics model has been
very popular among tourism researchers. In many cases, tourist choice is
understood as revealed demand for a destination and usually expressed in
numbers of tourist arrivals or nights spent in tourist accommodation. These
enter as dependent variables in single-equation models and are regressed on
the tourist's available income and a number of cost-related variables for the
particular destinations and its competitors such as local tourist prices,
transport costs and exchange rates (Witt and Martin 1987; Johnson and
Ashworth 1990; Sheldon 1990). Dummy variables may also appear to
account for exceptional items (Gunadhi and Boey 1986), while dynamic
considerations may take the form of lagged variables, time trends or
other more sophisticated modelling (Witt 1980; Martin and Witt 1988;
Syriopoulos 1995). None the less, the single-equation approach is only
indirectly related to the classical model. It is not a result of an optimisation
process and it fails to account for explicit complementarity or substitutability in destination choice. This is because in many cases, the inadequate number of observations and degrees of freedom requires that prices
of competing destinations are only collectively considered in a weighted
index. Moreover, the single-equation approach cannot account for the
impact of price changes in the destination under consideration on all other
competing destinations. For these reasons, the development of demand
systems has been a step forward. Their application in tourism has been
mostly related to the 'almost ideal demand system' (Deaton and Muellbauer
1980a): expenditure destination market shares are regressed on income, cost
and other variables (Papatheodorou 1999; De Mello et al. 2002).

The characteristics framework
The characteristics model developed by Lancaster (1966, 1971) and Gorman
(1980) can provide a valid alternative to the classical setting. It has been
applied in tourism by various researchers such as Rugg (1973), Morley
(1992) and Papatheodorou (2001). In its standard version, it takes the following form at the destination level:

$$\max U = g(\mathbf{z})$$

$$\text{s.t.} \quad \mathbf{z} = \mathbf{B} \cdot \mathbf{x}; \quad \mathbf{p} \cdot \mathbf{x} + \sum_{i=1}^{N} F_i \le Y; \quad \sum_{i=1}^{N} (x_i + t_i) \le T; \quad Y, T \ge 0, \quad (2.4)$$

where **z** is the column vector of quantities of characteristics j and **x** is the column vector of the number of days spent in each destination i (non-integer issues left aside). **B** is the consumption technology matrix whose elements show the quantity of each characteristic j produced by spending one day in each destination i: the technology is linear and additive so for each characteristic j we have:

$$z_j = \sum_{i=1}^{N} b_{ji} x_i .$$

p is the row vector of daily cost of living in the tourist destinations and F_i is the return fare to destination i. Y is total available expenditure, T is total available time and t_i is the return travelling time to destination i. The maximisation problem can be solved using standard linear programming techniques.

Separability in the characteristics model
Similar to the classical case, the characteristics model makes the convenient assumption of separability. Nonetheless, the present framework offers a natural justification as it focuses on attributes rather than products. In fact, tourist products can be easily distinguished from non-tourist ones as they have different characteristics: on the other hand, classical microeconomics cannot offer a satisfactory explanation for separability. In terms of subsequent levels of separability and decisions on the choice set of available destinations, the present model is again superior as it can directly address the reason for travelling. In fact, it is natural to assume that the actual consumer choice is largely determined by the tourist activities sought after – these effectively shape the choice set of both destinations and characteristics. Flexibility of decisions is of primary importance to consider at this point. Business-related tourism is usually associated with significant spatial and activity constraints. For example, if the tourist is required to travel on business to Athens in Greece, the destination choice set will only contain Athens, as there are no effective substitutes. In this case, the characteristics set would only matter at a micro destination level, for example, choice of a suitably located hotel. If the tourist travels to practise a sport, then the destination set would contain all places potentially suitable for this sport – likewise for the characteristics set. If the tourist travels on general leisure without any apparent preferences, then both sets can be very wide.

Territorial scale and discrete choice
Interestingly, the above discussion raises two issues. First, destination and characteristics sets should be set at an appropriate and equivalent level of spatial aggregation. If comparison is made among different city hotels then the characteristics set should comprise attributes such as location, type of

accommodation and entertainment facilities. On the other hand, in the case of tourist resorts appropriate characteristics include the overall level of facilities and tourist attractions. From an empirical point of view, however, the process of aggregation can be difficult. The construction of an aggregate index of facilities or tourist attractions might be subject to many assumptions (such as preference weightings) and even slight changes could endanger the robustness of the outcome. To complicate things further, decisions at different spatial levels are effectively interdependent: a destination might be favoured because it has an attractive seafront but the seafront will not be visited unless the destination is favoured. In other words, although tourist choice might be subject to separability, the tourist takes different territorial scales simultaneously into consideration. The second related issue is the discrete nature of tourist choice. As in the case of the classical model, it is absurd to assume omnipresence of the tourist at least at the destination level. Therefore, the framework described in equation (2.4) should be best combined with a discrete model such as the one highlighted in (2.2). Admittedly, the mathematics can be very complicated in this case and the interested reader is referred to Papatheodorou (2003b) for an analytical exposition.

Price and time constraints
As in the classical model, the characteristics framework acknowledges the existence of an expenditure constraint. In the present case, however, travelling costs are also taken into consideration. Moreover, the model gets closer to the reality of tourism by introducing an additional constraint, namely time. This consists of both the sojourn at the destination and the duration of the return trip. Although from a superficial perspective these two constraints are straightforward, a number of issues emerge at the level of microfoundations.

First, the derivation of an aggregate destination tourist price index might be very complicated. The consumer price index (CPI) might be unsuitable as it is usually calculated at a national level and refers to goods not consumed by tourists. Various tourist baskets can be used as a benchmark such as that proposed by Cosmos (1999). Nevertheless, Witt and Witt (1992) argue that the use of CPI does not generate dissimilar results in econometric analysis. In the case of international tourism, appropriate adjustments for foreign exchange rates should be made (Dwyer et al. 2002). On the other hand, at lower levels of spatial aggregation, individual prices of tourist goods may be used, that is, the rate of hotel accommodation or the price of a tourist meal. From a tourist choice perspective, prices clearly depend not only on quantities of goods but also on quality and variety. The characteristics framework can easily accommodate issues of horizontal and vertical differentiation by considering different consumption technologies. A well-endowed destination can generate higher quantities of attraction and facility characteristics on a daily basis: its expensiveness, however, may render it unaffordable for some tourists.

Nonetheless, prices are also affected by tourist choices on travel arrangements. In particular, when tourists make individual arrangements, they usually pay separately for each element of the composite tourist product (that is, transportation, accommodation, catering and so on). By creating essentially their own customised bundle, the tourists may derive greater satisfaction, but are also subject to a number of risks. First, if they do not have a good knowledge of the destination and the marketplace, they may be overcharged: frequent travelling and repeat visiting reduce this possibility in conjunction with a sound institutional framework. Second, tourists are exposed to the individual corporate risk and market power of each company with which they transact: contingency plans might prove very expensive in this case. On the other hand, a tourist may decide to buy a pre-arranged all-inclusive package offered at a set price by a tour operator. The occurring loss in customisation might not be significant when tourist preferences are not sophisticated. Moreover, tourists incur lower transaction costs and face only the corporate risk and market power related to the particular intermediary. Although they are charged for the provision of tour operating services, they may achieve a better price compared to individual arrangements. This is more likely when the tour operators exercise successfully their oligopsonistic power on tourist producers but behave competitively in the consumer market. In reality, most travellers opt for a mix of individual and group travel arrangements.

The second issue to consider is the interrelation of the expenditure and time constraints at different levels. First, most people need to work to generate sufficient funds for their tourist activities: working time, however, means less available time for travelling. This is the essence of the leisure paradox (Cooper et al. 1998): students, for example, have plenty of time but little money to travel, while upwardly mobile young workers the converse. On the other hand, expenditure and time become positively associated when substitutability of tourist transport modes is taken into consideration. Standard train services are usually much cheaper than high-speed trains *ceteris paribus*, but they involve much longer trip duration. Similar results hold in sea (for example, steamers *vis-à-vis* hydrofoils) and air transport (for example, turboprops *vis-à-vis* jets). Still, comparisons among different transport modes might be less clear. For example, it is cheaper to travel from Athens to the Greek islands by sea than by air; on the other hand, it is more expensive to cross the Atlantic now by ship than by plane. In any case, when a tourist has a loose expenditure constraint, he or she is likely to choose a faster transport mode as the marginal dis-utility of extra travel time increases in the generalised (monetary and time) cost function (Quandt 1970). This does not apply in the case where the transport mode is an end itself, as with the cruise ships. From a dynamic perspective, the two constraints are also positively correlated albeit due to a factor unrelated to consumer choice, that is, transport technology. In fact, over time, travelling becomes cheaper and faster allowing a relaxation of both constraints. There might be some limits, of course, in terms of how much the world can shrink: although Concorde has proved a major technological success, for example, it was commercially unsustainable and finally taken out of service. Moreover, technological advancements may lead to the reduction of travelling altogether through the development of teleconferencing and virtual reality (Cheong 1995).

In addition to expenditure and time constraints the tourist has to take other factors into consideration. Some can be captured indirectly by the two modelled constraints while others are beyond the scope of the present characteristics framework. First, tourist choice is affected by personal circumstances such as family structure. This may have a severe impact on both tourist preferences and discretionary expenditure available for leisure travelling. Oppermann (1995), for example, observes that in the age cluster 34–48 years, overseas travel is less frequent than in other age group: as many people have children in this stage of their life cycle, international travel becomes much more troublesome and expensive. Old people may also prefer not to travel far away from their residence, because of health problems.

Second, there are factors related to the human environment in a tourist destination. Safety and hygiene are of primary importance but tourist choice is also dependent on the similarity of the destination institutional framework in comparison to the origin. In other words, many tourists prefer places that are cognitively proximate to them to avoid exposure to unfamiliar situations: in fact, most tourists are risk-averse irrespective of whether or not they are 'psychocentrics' to use Plog's (1973) classification. Cultural and linguistic similarities between the origin and the destination can be important in this context. For international tourism, good external relations, low levels of travel bureaucracy, and the adoption of a single currency may affect choice to a major extent. The introduction of the euro, for example, is likely to boost tourism flows among euroland countries because of price transparency, lower transaction costs and elimination of foreign exchange instability. With this in mind, the time constraint of the characteristics framework can be generalised to account for cognitive distance and conceptual accessibility. This may be at odds with physical distance leading to a 'perversion of geography': although Tirana, Albania, for example is much closer to Athens, Greece, than London, most Athenians would feel more familiar in the British capital – moreover, it may be cheaper to visit London than Tirana anyway.

Empirical research on the characteristics model

The characteristics model can be empirically validated by using hedonic price analysis, where equilibrium prices are regressed on a number of characteristics (Lancaster 1971; Triplett 1975). In a pure hedonic framework, specific factors (for example, the producer of the product) become irrelevant in explaining price differentials – the vector of characteristics is all that matters. In reality, however, hybrid models combining attributes and other factors perform better (Dickie et al. 1997). In this context, the hedonic price approach is appropriate for the study of efficiency and competitiveness: positive (negative) product-specific coefficients reveal bad (good) value for money *ceteris paribus*. In tourism, prices of most goods and services are set directly by producers; they constitute equilibrium once the consumer accepts them by the act of purchase. Most hedonic price studies in tourism focus on holiday packages and assess *inter alia* the competitiveness of specific operators and destinations (Clewer et al. 1992; Taylor 1995; Papatheodorou 2002).

Tourist choice and information

The previous discussion on cognitive distance raised the importance of available information about a destination. Tourism falls in the category of experience goods and services (Tirole 1988): quality and other characteristics are revealed to the tourist only after the actual choice. The poetic wording and beautiful destination and hotel pictures in a tour operator's brochure may sometimes differ from the reality. Moreover, as tourism involves substantial monetary and time resources, experience comes at a high cost. Therefore, to avoid any disappointment *ex post*, the tourist should better take appropriate decisions *ex ante*. Following an earlier argument, the tourist may reject individual travel arrangements in favour of a fully organised package. In reality, however, information deficiencies are difficult to evade.

Signalling in tourist choice

For this reason, price may be used as a signal of quality. Intuitively, a high quality good is usually more expensive to produce than a low quality one; therefore, firms will supply the high quality only at a satisfactory price. Furthermore, if the mark-up on price is also high then the low quality good becomes less attractive since firms are keen to keep their high profit margin. The Folk Theorem of game theory suggests that repeat purchases by tourists may provide firms with a very strong incentive to sustain a reputation for quality for fear of losing future sales (Keane 1996). This is effectively related to the establishment of a brand name both at spatial and corporate levels. The island-state of Mauritius, for example, has a reputation for its quality tourism service – this is likely to affect consumer choice accordingly. Similarly, many international hotel chains offer a standardised product globally that is recognisable and understood by the tourist irrespective of the actual destination. This may of course lead to the 'McDonaldisation' of the tourism industry to the detriment of tourist choice. It is, therefore, important to find ways to minimise information risks without losing variety at either vertical or horizontal levels: product customisation through the use of flexible production methods may be the way forward (Poon 1990).

In any case, tourist choice nowadays is more informed than in the past. First, many people have gained substantial tourism experience over time through a learning-by-doing process: they have not only become knowledgeable of destinations and various tourist services, but they have also developed a cosmopolitan culture to address unknown and complex situations as they occur. Second, the cost of information acquisition has been reduced dramatically due to the internet revolution. Search engines may provide a multitude of websites on every subject within seconds. Ironically perhaps, tourist choice today becomes a matter of effective information overload management. As barriers to entry in the web are low for tourist producers and general information providers (for example, destination tourist authorities), reliability and trustworthiness of sources is of primary importance. In fact, the experiential character of tourism re-emerges and to avoid unnecessary search costs, the tourist may choose to rely only on websites of private and public organisations, which have gained their reputation in the real world.

Information and revealed tourist preferences
So far, we have analysed how tourists can shape their decisions and choice based on the available information. It is also important, however, to consider the converse question, for example, what is the information revealed by tourist choices as such? Though this issue may well be treated by disciplines other than economics, it is still important to comment on tourist activities and especially on Veblen effects. More specifically, the tourist activity vector together with vacation frequency and duration reveals tourist preferences. Activities may be active or passive, may take place in an individual or group setting and also may be classified in various other ways (van Raaij 1986). Time allocation studies can reveal similarities and differences in tourist activity and behavioural patterns. Empirical research on sightseeing

shows that time is allocated consistently according to site significance: despite its discretionary character, therefore, holiday time is used rationally by tourists (Pearce 1988).

As for Veblen effects in consumer choice, these are said to exist when individuals exhibit a willingness to pay a higher price for a functionally equivalent good, that is, the demand for a good increases simply because of its higher price. To maintain rationality, utility in this case should be defined over both consumption and status. In other words, and as suggested by Bagwell and Bernheim (1996: 366–7), 'to signal wealth effectively, the act of burning money must be observed readily by large numbers of people and it must be interpreted as evidence of substantial resource dissipation'. International tourism may be used as such a signal quite effectively, especially when the tourist destination is well known to be expensive: for example, in the past rich Europeans used to go skiing in Switzerland just to show off. But now that, Switzerland has become much more affordable for the average tourist due to the increase in disposable income, such tourism is directed more towards exotic places, such as some secluded Caribbean Islands. Indeed, recent time-series analysis has shown a negative trend for Swiss tourism (Witt and Witt 1992). In other words, although the level of services provided by Switzerland still remains high or might even be higher than in the past in both absolute and relative terms, the existence of Veblen effects opens the way for choice of new tourist destinations.

Tourist choice in a dynamic context
Most of the discussion so far has been set in a static context. To understand tourist choice fully, however, dynamic issues should also be considered. From a modelling perspective, intertemporal optimisation techniques, such as optimal control and dynamic programming may be used to derive dynamic paths of efficient tourism choice and consumption over time (Mananyi 1998). Nonetheless, this area is beyond the scope of this chapter, which now focuses on two issues, namely the formation of expectations and urbanisation.

Tourist choice and expectations
More specifically, tourist choice in a stochastic environment is essentially based on expectations about the attributes of a particular destination and its tourist providers. These expectations are subsequently compared to the perceived service performance. Similarly, tourist firms produce services based on their own expectations about tourist choice and performance. An optimal choice path emerges when expectations of tourists and producers match each other. In this game theory framework, however, mismatch may

also occur. When tourist expectations exceed perceived performance then the tourist becomes satisfied. This may be, however, to the detriment of profitability of producers if the latter offer a product of quality better than expected for its price. Conversely, unconfirmed expectations or an unfair balance of costs and benefits may create dissatisfaction: profit margins may rise, but this may be unsustainable in the longer term. People are often subjective in identifying satisfaction to internal and dissatisfaction to external factors (van Raaij 1986) such as infrastructure problems at the destination. Effective integrated quality management, therefore, should aim at minimising these potential gaps between different expectations and perception (European Commission 2000). If successful, this strategy will ensure the necessary tourist and producer satisfaction to sustain resort development over time. This presupposes of course that both expectations and *ex post* perception are formed rationally taking all the available information into consideration at a given point in time. Nonetheless, expectations may be adapting to changing conditions only slowly due to habit formation or other factors: in this case, destination authorities should make an extra effort by designing clever marketing and advertising campaigns. These should be based on the result of appropriate studies that reveal patterns of tourist preferences and measure service quality and customer satisfaction (Ekinci and Riley 2001).

Spatial impacts of tourist choice
Turning now to the issue of urbanisation, this is essentially related to the dynamic impact of tourist choice in space. In addition to ensuring repeat visiting, tourist satisfaction from a destination and its service providers may induce new tourists to opt for this area: positive word-of-mouth and favourable comments by travel guides may lead to a subsequent tourism boom. This will create the need for additional infrastructure in terms of transport networks, accommodation and other tourist services. If this materialises, then a process of tourism urbanisation may start with self-reinforcing characteristics. In particular, additional infrastructure endows a resort with more facilities and ancillary services: therefore, more tourists are induced to make this their primary choice. But, on the other hand, the very reason that ensures the financial viability of this expansion in infrastructure is persistent tourist choice. This urbanisation process is of course not perpetual but is subject to the carrying capacity of the physical environment and the emergent diseconomies of scale in the form of traffic congestion and inflation in land rents and tourist services. Consequently, the resort may subsequently wane in popularity. In this case, tourist choice will have set its own territorial footprint in the various stages of a tourist area life cycle (Butler 1980; Papatheodorou 2004).

Conclusions and the way forward

This chapter aimed at exploring the microfoundations of tourist choice. Alternative theoretical approaches were discussed (such as the classical microeconomics model and the characteristics framework) to highlight the nature of tourist choice and its determination – relevant empirical research was also presented. Information and dynamic implications complemented the analysis. Despite the theoretical contributions of the existing academic literature, there is much scope for further research in this area and for actual implementation. First, the spatial expression of tourist choice should be explored and modelled in detail perhaps with the assistance of geographical information systems. This will allow theoreticians and practitioners to understand interrelations among different territorial scales in tourism. National and regional policy makers can then design integrated and coherent policies that will not contradict the local authorities and their tourism planning – converse implications also apply. Second, the study of information and expectation issues in tourism should be further promoted to improve transparency in the institutional framework of consumer protection and to advance communication effectiveness among the various stakeholders. From an empirical perspective, the sophisticated techniques of the classical econometric modelling should be suitably adjusted to account for the characteristics framework and discrete choice analysis. This is essential to produce more realistic models and subsequently more meaningful econometric estimations and tourism forecasts. Finally, in our effort to study microfoundations in detail, we should not lose sight of the wider picture. It would make no sense to provide sophisticated explanations at a micro level that result in a fragmented and incompatible for aggregation structure. In other words, synthesis is of great importance: microfoundations should be amalgamated creatively to produce a holistic theory of choice in tourism.

In retrospect, it should be noted that tourist choice in this chapter is approached mainly from the demand side. Nevertheless, the structure of the supply side is quite important as it can potentially affect tourist choice to a major extent. More specifically, the tourism industries worldwide are characterised by a rise of market concentration and the creation of global conglomerates through horizontal and vertical integration practices: TUI, the largest tour operator in Europe, is a representative example. By taking advantage of scale and scope economies these companies fortify their position in the marketplace. They can exercise oligopolistic power against consumers, oligopsonistic pressure on other tourist producers and destinations and engage in restrictive anti-competitive practices. From this perspective, they can also influence tourist choice in terms of prices, available information and other dimensions. Studies on political economy (Britton

1991; Shaw and Williams 1994) and industrial geography of tourism (Ioannides and Debbage 1998; Papatheodorou 2003a) deal with such topics extensively as do other contributions in this book. This research area is, therefore, beyond the scope of this chapter. Nonetheless, supply-side issues should be thoroughly understood by tourism authorities and corporate strategists who wish to affect tourist choice – any policy implementation without such consideration can at best be only partially successful.

References

Bagwell, L.S. and B.D. Bernheim (1996), 'Veblen effects in a theory of conspicuous consumption', *American Economic Review*, **86**, 349–73.

Ben-Akiva, M. and S.R. Lerman (1985), *Discrete Choice Analysis: Theory and Application to Travel Demand*, Cambridge, MA: MIT Press.

Britton, S. (1991), 'Towards a critical geography of tourism', *Environment and Planning D. Society and Space*, **9**, 451–78.

Butler, R. (1980), 'The concept of a tourist area cycle of evolution: implications for management of resources', *Canadian Geographer*, **14**, 5–12.

Cheong, R. (1995), 'The virtual threat to travel and tourism', *Tourism Management*, **16** (6), 417–22.

Clewer, A., A. Pack and M.T. Sinclair (1992) 'Price competitiveness and inclusive tour holidays in European cities', in P. Johnson and B. Thomas (eds), *Choice and Demand in Tourism*, London: Mansell, pp. 123–43.

Cooper, C., J. Fletcher, D. Gilbert, R. Shepherd and S. Wanhill (1998), *Tourism Principles and Practice* (second edition), Harlow: Longman.

Cosmos (1999), *Summer Sun 2000*, Bromley: Cosmosair Plc.

De Mello, M., A. Pack and M.T. Sinclair (2002), 'A system of equations model of UK tourism demand in neighbouring countries', *Applied Economics*, **34** (4), 509–21.

Deaton, A. and J. Muellbauer (1980a), 'An almost ideal demand system', *American Economic Review*, **70**, 312–26.

Deaton, A. and J. Muellbauer (1980b), *Economics and Consumer Behaviour*, Cambridge: Cambridge University Press.

Dickie, M., C.D. Delorme Jr and J.M. Humphreys (1997), 'Hedonic prices, goods-specific effects and functional form: inferences from cross section–time series data', *Applied Economics*, **29** (2), 239–49.

Dixit, A.K. and J.E. Stiglitz (1977), 'Monopolistic competition and optimum product diversity', *American Economic Review*, **67**, 297–308.

Dwyer, L., P. Forsyth and P. Rao (2002), 'Destination price competitiveness: exchange rate changes vs inflation rates', *Journal of Travel Research*, **40**, 328–36.

Ekinci, Y. and M. Riley (2001), 'Validating quality dimensions', *Annals of Tourism Research*, **28** (1), 202–23.

European Commission (2000), *Towards Quality Coastal Tourism: Integrated Quality Management (IQM) of Coastal Tourist Destinations*, Brussels: European Commission.

Gorman, W.M. (1980), 'A possible procedure for analysing quality differentials in the egg market', *Review of Economic Studies*, **47**, 843–56.

Gunadhi, H, and C.K. Boey (1986), 'Demand elasticities of tourism in Singapore', *Tourism Management*, **7**, 239–53.

Ioannides, D. and K.G. Debbage (1998), 'Neo-Fordism and flexible specialisation in the travel industry: dissecting the polyglot', in D. Ioannides and K.G. Debbage (eds), *The Economic Geography of the Tourist Industry: A Supply-Side Analysis*, London: Routledge, pp. 99–122.

Johnson, P. and J. Ashworth (1990), 'Modelling tourism demand: a summary review', *Leisure Studies*, **9** (2), 145–60.

Keane, M.J. (1996), 'Sustaining quality in tourism destinations', *Applied Economics*, **28**, 1545–53.

Lancaster, K.J. (1966), 'A new approach to consumer theory', *Journal of Political Economy*, **74**, 132–57.
Lancaster, K.J. (1971), *Consumer Demand: A New Approach*, New York: Columbia University Press.
Mananyi, A. (1998), 'Optimal management of ecotourism', *Tourism Economics*, **4** (2), 147–69.
Martin, C.A. and S.F. Witt (1988), 'Substitute prices in models of tourism demand', *Annals of Tourism Research*, **15**, 255–68.
Morley, C.L. (1992), 'A microeconomic theory of international tourism demand', *Annals of Tourism Research*, **19**, 250–67.
Morley, C.L. (1994), 'Experimental destination choice analysis', *Annals of Tourism Research*, **21**, 780–91.
Oppermann, M. (1995), 'Travel life cycle', *Annals of Tourism Research*, **22**, 535–52.
Papatheodorou, A. (1999), 'The demand for international tourism in the Mediterranean region', *Applied Economics*, **31**, 619–30.
Papatheodorou, A. (2001), 'Why people travel to different places?', *Annals of Tourism Research*, **28** (1), 164–79.
Papatheodorou, A. (2002), 'Exploring competitiveness in Mediterranean resorts', *Tourism Economics*, **8** (2), 133–50.
Papatheodorou, A. (2003a), 'Corporate strategies of British tour operators in the Mediterranean region: an economic geography approach', *Tourism Geographies*, **5** (3), 280–304.
Papatheodorou, A. (2003b), 'Modelling tourism development – a synthetic approach', *Tourism Economics,* **9** (4), 407–30.
Papatheodorou, A. (2004), 'Exploring the evolution of tourist resorts', *Annals of Tourism Research*, **31** (1), 219–37.
Pearce, D.G. (1988), 'Tourist time budgets', *Annals of Tourism Research*, **15**, 106–21.
Plog, S.C. (1973), 'Why destination areas rise and fall in popularity', *Cornell Hotel, Restaurant and Administration Quarterly*, **14**, 13–16.
Poon, A. (1990), 'Flexible specialisation and small size – the case of Caribbean tourism', *World Development*, **18** (1), 109–23.
Quandt, R.E. (1970), 'Introduction to the analysis of travel demand', in R.E. Quandt (ed.), *The Demand for Travel: Theory and Measurement*, Lexington, MA: D.C. Heath, Lexington Books, pp. 1–15.
Rugg, D. (1973), 'The choice of journey destination: a theoretical and empirical analysis', *Review of Economics and Statistics*, **55**, 64–72.
Shaw, G. and A.M. Williams (1994), *Critical Issues in Tourism: A Geographical Perspective*, Oxford Blackwell.
Sheldon, P.J. (1990), 'A review of tourism expenditure research', in C.P. Cooper (ed.), *Progress in Tourism, Recreation and Hospitality Management*, London: Belhaven.
Syriopoulos, T. (1995), 'A dynamic model of demand for Mediterranean tourism', *International Review of Applied Economics*, **9**, 318–36.
Taylor, P. (1995), 'Measuring changes in the relative competitiveness of package tour destinations', *Tourism Economics*, **1**, 169–82.
Tirole, J. (1988), *The Theory of Industrial Organization*, Cambridge, MA: MIT Press.
Triplett, J.E. (1975) 'Consumer demand and characteristics of consumption goods', in N. Terleckyj (ed.), *Household Production and Consumption*, Washington, DC: National Bureau of Economic Research, pp. 305–23.
Van Raaij, W.F. (1986), 'Consumer research on tourism: mental and behavioural constructs', *Annals of Tourism Research*, **13**, 1–9.
Witt, S.F (1980), 'An abstract mode, abstract (destination) node model of foreign holiday demand', *Applied Economics*, **12**, 163–80.
Witt, S.F. and C.A. Martin (1987), 'Econometric models for forecasting international tourism demand', *Journal of Travel Research*, **25**, 23–30.
Witt, S.F. and C.A. Witt (1992), *Modelling and Forecasting Demand in Tourism*, New York: Academic Press.

3 Tourism demand forecasting
Haiyan Song and Lindsay Turner

Introduction

Tourism researchers and practitioners are interested in tourism demand forecasting for the following reasons. First, tourism demand is the foundation on which all tourism-related business decisions ultimately rest. Companies such as airlines, tour operators, hotels, cruise ship lines, and recreation facility providers are interested in the demand for their products by tourists. The success of many businesses depends largely or totally on the state of tourism demand, and ultimate management failure is quite often due to the failure to meet market demand. Because of the key role of demand as a determinant of business profitability, estimates of expected future demand constitute a very important element in all planning activities. It is clear that accurate forecasts of tourism demand are essential for efficient planning by tourism-related businesses, particularly given the perishable nature of the tourism product. Second, tourism investment, especially investment in destination infrastructures, such as airports, highways and rail links, requires long-term financial commitments and the sunk costs can be very high if the investment projects fail to fulfil their design capacities. Therefore, the prediction of long-term demand for tourism-related infrastructure often forms an important part of project appraisal. Third, government macroeconomic policies largely depend on the relative importance of individual sectors within a destination. Hence, accurate forecasts of demand in the tourism sector of the economy will help destination governments in formulating and implementing appropriate medium- to long-term tourism strategies.

Tourism forecasts may be generated by either quantitative or qualitative approaches. However, this chapter focuses on quantitative forecasting methods, especially econometric approaches. By econometric forecasting, we mean that the forecast variable is specifically related to a set of determining forces; future values of the forecast variable are obtained by using forecasts of the determining variables, in conjunction with the estimated quantitative relationship between the forecast variable and its determinants.

International tourism demand is generally measured in terms of the number of tourist visits from an origin country to a destination country, or in terms of tourist expenditure by visitors from the origin country in the destination country. The number of tourist nights spent by residents of the origin in the destination is an alternative tourism demand measure.

International tourism demand data are collected in various ways. Tourist visits are usually recorded by frontier counts (inbound), registration at accommodation establishments (inbound) or sample surveys (inbound and outbound). A problem with frontier counts is that in certain cases a substantial transit traffic element may be present. Accommodation establishment records exclude day-trippers and tourists staying with friends or relatives or in other forms of unregistered accommodation. Sample surveys may be applied at points of entry/exit to returning residents or departing non-residents, or household surveys may be carried out (outbound), but in both cases often the sample size is relatively small. International tourist expenditure data are usually collected by the bank reporting method or sample surveys. The former method is based on the registration by banks and agencies of the buying and selling of foreign currencies by travellers. There are many problems associated with this method of data collection such as identifying a transaction as a tourism transaction, the non-reporting of relevant transactions and the unreliability of its use for measuring receipts from specific origin countries (the geographic breakdown relates to the denomination of the currency and not the generating country). Sample surveys provide more reliable data on tourist expenditures, but as with visit data the sample size is often relatively small.

The determinants of tourism demand depend on the purpose of the visit. Approximately 70 per cent of international tourist trips take place for holiday purposes, 15 per cent for business purposes, 10 per cent in order to visit friends and relatives and 5 per cent for other purposes (where 'other' includes pilgrimages, and sports and health reasons). Therefore, the emphasis in empirical research on tourism demand modelling has been on holiday tourism, with only a few studies being concerned with business tourism. Consequently, we shall also concentrate on the demand for foreign holidays. Substantial agreement exists about the explanatory variables that are important in the case of international holiday tourism and they are discussed below.

Population
The level of foreign tourism from a given origin is expected to depend upon the origin population, an increase in population resulting in an increase in demand. Sometimes population features as a separate explanatory variable, but generally the effect of population is accommodated by modifying the dependent variable to become international tourism demand per capita.

Income
The appropriate income variable is personal disposable income or private consumption expenditure in the origin country (in constant price terms),

and is expected to have a positive influence on tourism demand. Income commonly enters the demand function in per capita form, corresponding to the specification of demand in per capita terms.

Own price

There are two price components – the cost of travel to the destination, and the cost of living for tourists in the destination (both in constant price terms) – and these are expected to have negative influences on demand. The cost of travel is often measured by the economy airfare. Usually the consumer price index (CPI) in a destination country is taken to be a proxy for the cost of tourism in that country on account of lack of more suitable data, and Martin and Witt (1987) have shown this to be a reasonable approximation. The CPI is then adjusted by the exchange rate between the origin and destination currencies. If data relating to the price of the tourist's basket of goods/services are available these would be more appropriate, but usually such data do not exist.

Exchange rates are also sometimes used separately to represent tourist living costs, possibly in addition to the exchange rate-adjusted CPI. The justification is that consumers are more aware of exchange rates than destination costs of living for tourists, and hence are driven to use the exchange rate as a proxy variable. However, the use of exchange rates alone can be misleading because even though the exchange rate in a destination may become more favourable, this could be counterbalanced by a relatively high inflation rate.

Substitute prices

The prices of substitutes may be important determinants of tourism demand, and are expected to have a positive influence. For example, an increase in holiday prices to Spain is likely to increase the demand for holidays to Portugal. The impact of competing destinations may be allowed for by specifying the tourist cost of living variable as destination cost relative to a weighted average value calculated for a set of alternative destinations; and by specifying the travel cost variable as travel cost from origin to destination relative to a weighted average value calculated for travel from the origin to competing destinations. The weights are generally based on previous market shares and are often allowed to vary over time.

Marketing

National tourist organisations engage in sales-promotion activities specifically to attempt to persuade potential tourists to visit the country, and these activities may take various forms including media advertising and public relations. Hence, promotional expenditure (in constant price terms) is expected to play a positive role in determining the level of international tourism demand. However, much tourism-related marketing activity is not specific to a particular destination (for example, general travel agent and tour operator advertising) and is likely to have little impact on the demand for tourism to that destination. The promotional activities of national tourist organisations are destination specific, and are more likely to influence tourist flows to the destination concerned.

Lagged dependent variable
A lagged dependent variable, that is an autoregressive term, can be justified on the grounds of habit persistence. Once people have been on holiday to a particular country and liked it, they tend to return to that destination. There is much less uncertainty associated with holidaying again in that country compared with travelling to a previously unvisited foreign country. Furthermore, knowledge about the destination spreads as people talk about their holidays and show photographs, thereby reducing uncertainty for potential visitors to that country. In fact, this 'word-of-mouth' recommendation may well play a more important role in destination selection than commercial advertising. A type of learning process is in operation and as people are in general risk averse, the number of people choosing a given alternative in any year depends (positively) on the numbers who chose it in previous years.

A second justification for the inclusion of a lagged dependent variable in tourism demand functions comes from the supply side. Supply constraints may take the form of shortages of hotel accommodation, passenger transportation capacity and trained staff, and these often cannot be increased rapidly. Time is also required to build up contacts among tour operators, hotels, airlines and travel agencies. Similarly, once the tourist industry in a country has become highly developed it is unlikely to dwindle rapidly. If a partial adjustment mechanism is postulated to allow for rigidities in supply, this results in the presence of a lagged dependent variable in the tourism demand function, with the parameter lying between zero and unity (Song and Witt 2000, pp. 7–8).

Qualitative effects
Dummy variables are often included in international tourism demand functions to allow for the impact of 'one-off' events. For example, the imposition by governments of foreign currency restrictions on their residents is likely to reduce the level of international tourism, as are threats of terrorism (for example, after September 11, 2001 in New York and October 12, 2002 in Bali), and threats of war (for example, the threat after the Iraqi invasion of Kuwait in 1990, followed by the Gulf wars of 1991 and 2003).

Similarly, various events are likely to stimulate international tourism, such as hosting the Olympic Games and other major attractions.

Overview of main contributions in tourism forecasting
Studies on tourism forecasting published before the 1990s are reviewed in Uysal and Crompton (1985), Johnson and Ashworth (1990), Crouch (1994a,b), Witt and Witt (1995), Lim (1997) and Frechtling (2001). Therefore, the main focus of this review is on studies published after 1990.

Single-equation econometric models with fixed parameters
It should be noted that the division of single-equation and system-of-equations models is based on the number of measurement equation(s) of tourism demand, rather than simply the number of equations in the model. Although the TVP (time varying parameter) model is a multiple-equation model, it is still regarded as a single-equation approach, as only one equation in the TVP model is used to measure the demand for a destination's tourism.

Model specification Tourism, especially long-haul tourism, is normally regarded as a luxury product, which often exhibits a nonlinear relationship between the demand for tourism and its determinants. Therefore, many published studies of tourism forecasting use the double log linear (LL) functional form to linearise the relationship for ease of estimation, although a few studies use simple linear and semi-log linear forms. Witt and Witt (1995) reviewed 40 studies published between 1966 and 1992 and found 31 of these 40 (78 per cent) articles used the LL functional form in their empirical analysis. Lim (1997) examined 100 articles published during the 1961–94 period and 73 (73 per cent) of these 100 publications employed the LL model. In a recent survey, Li (2004) found 39 out of 45 (87 per cent) published studies during the 1990–2003 period used the LL model in forecasting tourism demand. One of the advantages of using an LL functional form is that the estimated coefficients of the explanatory variables can be interpreted directly as the demand elasticities, which provide useful information for policy makers in tourism destinations.

Studies published between the 1960s and early 1990s mainly follow the traditional regression approach in that the models are specified in static form with very limited diagnostic statistics being reported. Static regression models suffer from a number of problems including structural instability, forecasting failure and spurious regression relationships (see further discussion on this below). In the mid-1990s, dynamic specifications such as the autoregressive distributed lag model (ADLM), and error correction model (ECM), began to appear in the tourism literature. Syriopoulos (1995),

Kulendran (1996), Kulendran and King (1997), Seddighi and Shearing (1997), Kim and Song (1998) and Vogt and Wittayakorn (1998) were the first authors to apply recent advances in econometrics, such as cointegration and error correction techniques, to tourism forecasting. The monograph by Song and Witt (2000) was the first book that systematically introduced a number of modern econometric methods to tourism demand analysis. Over the last few years there has been a surge in the application of modern econometric techniques to tourism demand modelling and forecasting, including Morley (2000), Song et al. (2000, 2003a,b,c), Kulendran and Witt (2001, 2003a,b), Lim and McAleer (2001, 2002), Webber (2001) and Dritsakis (2004).

Diagnostic checking of the forecasting models   Witt and Witt (1995) point out the problems in tourism forecasting prior to the 1990s, one of which refers to the ignorance of diagnostic checking. However, this has changed since the mid-1990s. In addition to conventional statistics such as the goodness of fit, and the Durbin–Waston (DW) statistic for autocorrelation, reported in earlier studies, many recent publications have paid attention to the diagnostic statistics of the demand models. These tests include the tests for integration orders (unit roots) of the data used in the demand models, heteroscedasticity, non-normality, inappropriate functional form, and structural instability. In particular, Kim and Song (1998), Song et al. (2000, 2003a,b,c), Kulendran and Witt (2001), Lim and McAleer (2001, 2002), Payne and Mervar (2002), Dritsakis (2004) and Song and Witt (2003) all reported a full battery of available diagnostic statistics. The evidence has shown that a model is likely to generate more accurate forecasts if it passes all the available diagnostic statistics.

Selection of variables in the demand analysis   Above, we discussed the potential variables for tourism demand analysis. Here, we examine the utilisation of these variables in empirical studies. The demand variable measured by total tourist arrivals is still the most frequently used measure of tourism demand, followed by tourist expenditure. Li (2004) pointed out in his literature survey that among the 45 selected studies published after 1990, 37 of them used tourist arrivals as the dependent variable while only six employed tourist expenditure as the dependent variable. Recent studies have also paid more attention to disaggregated tourism markets according to travel purpose (Turner et al. 1995; Morley 1998; Turner and Witt 2001a) or modes of transportation (Witt and Witt 1992). In terms of market segmentation, holiday and leisure travel has attracted the most research attention (Johnson and Ashworth 1990; Song et al. 2000, 2003b; Kulendran and Witt 2003b), followed by business travel (for example, Kulendran and Witt

2003a). Some interest is also placed on the demand for international conferences (for example, Witt et al. 1992, 1995) and the demand for ski tourism (Riddington 1999, 2002).

Lim (1997) argued that discretionary income, defined as the remaining income after spending on necessities in the country of origin, should be used as the appropriate measure of tourist income in the demand model. However, this is a subjective variable and the data cannot easily be obtained in practice. Therefore, alternative measures of income have to be used as a proxy for tourist discretionary income. Among these alternatives, real personal disposal income (PDI) is the best proxy to be included in a demand model related to holiday or visiting friends and relatives (VFR) travel (Syriopoulos 1995; Song et al. 2000; Kulendran and Witt 2001). National disposal income (NDI), gross domestic product (GDP), gross national product (GNP) and gross national income (GNI), all in constant prices, have also been used in many empirical studies. These variables are more suitable for the study of business travel or the combination of business and leisure travel when these two types of data are inseparable (Song and Witt 2000). Other possible proxies include real private consumption expenditure (Song et al. 2003b) and the industry production index (González and Moral 1995). Although most studies have found that income is the most important factor influencing the demand for international tourism, this finding has not always been conclusive. For example, the income variable was found to be insignificant in some of the error ECMs in Kulendran and King (1997), Kim and Song (1998) and Song et al. (2003b), and specifically, an insignificant income variable tends to be associated with models that relate to demand for international tourism by residents from Japan and Germany. One possible reason is that there are measurement errors in the data, and this is particularly true for the German income data as a result of unification.

In terms of income elasticity, Li (2004) looked at published studies on the demand for international tourism by UK residents between 1990 and 2003. Li found that 54 of the 80 estimated income elasticities are greater than one, 24 are between zero and one and only in two cases was the income elasticity less than zero, and these two cases were related to European destinations. These findings suggest that international tourism is generally regarded as a luxury product, while long-haul travel is more income elastic than short-haul travel. In terms of the magnitudes of long- and short-run income elasticities, Syriopoulos (1995), Kim and Song (1998), Song and Witt (2000) and Song et al. (2003b,c) show that the values of the long-run income elasticities tend to be higher than short-run counterparts, suggesting that it takes time for income changes to take effect on the demand for tourism due to information asymmetry and relatively inflexible budget allocations (Syriopoulos 1995).

Own price of tourism is another variable that has been found to have an important role to play in determining the demand for international tourism. In theory this variable should contain two components: costs of living in the destination and travel costs to the destination. However due to data unavailability, travel costs have been omitted in most studies with Witt and Witt (1991, 1992), Lim and McAleer (2001, 2002), Dritsakis (2004) and Turner and Witt (2003) being some of the exceptions. The cost of living in the destination is normally measured by the destination CPI. Another factor that may also contribute to the cost of living in the destination is the exchange rate between the origin country and destination country, as a higher exchange rate in favour of the origin country's currency could result in more tourists visiting the destination from the origin country. Witt and Witt (1992) and Qiu and Zhang (1995) used CPI in the destination and the exchange rates between the destination and origin separately to account for the costs of tourism, while the majority of published studies (especially the most recent ones) have commonly employed an exchange rate adjusted relative price index between the destination and origin as the own price variable (Turner and Witt 2003).

With respect to the own-price elasticity, Li (2004) found that 68 out of 78 estimates show negative values ranging from 0 to − 1, in line with the theoretical assumption. Smaller values of own price elasticity compared with income elasticity suggest that sensitivity of tourist responses to tourism price changes, is much lower than to income changes; indicating that international tourism tends to be price inelastic.

In addition to the relative prices between the destination and origin, substitute prices in alternative destinations have also been shown to be important determinants. There are two forms of substitute prices: one allows for the substitution between the destination and separately, a number of competing destinations (Kim and Song 1998; Song et al. 2000) and the other calculates the cost of tourism in the relevant destination relative to a weighted average cost of living in various competing destinations; and this index is also adjusted by relevant exchange rates. The weight is the relative market share (arrivals or expenditures) in each competing destination (Song and Witt 2003). The second form is used more often in empirical studies, as fewer variables are incorporated into the model; hence more degrees of freedom are available for the model estimation.

Marketing is also an important factor that influences tourism demand. The inclusion of this variable in the demand model with disaggregated data is expected to generate significant results. However, in aggregated studies the unavailability of marketing expenditure data across different origin countries has constrained its inclusion in the demand models. Only three studies incorporate this variable in their demand analyses (Witt and Martin 1987b; Crouch et al. 1992; Ledesma-Rodríguez et al. 2001).

In the studies by Kulendran and King (1997), Song et al. (2000, 2003a,b,c) and Lim and McAleer (2001, 2002) the lagged dependent variables have been found to be important factors that influence the demand for tourism, and their significance suggests that consumer persistency and word-of-mouth effects should be properly considered in demand forecasting models. The exclusion of this variable in the modelling process can result in biased forecasts.

In order to account for the impacts of one-off events and tourist taste changes on the demand for tourism, dummy and time trend variables have been used in some studies. As far as one-off events are concerned, the impacts of the two oil crises in the 1970s are examined in some empirical studies, followed by the Gulf War in the early 1990s and the global economic recession in the mid-1980s. Other regional events and origin/destination-specific effects have also been included in some studies. As for the trend variable, the deterministic linear trend has been used, especially in studies prior to the 1990s. Of the 100 papers reviewed in Lim (1997), 25 incorporated a trend variable in the model specification. However, a time trend tends to be highly correlated with the income variable and can cause a serious multicollinearity problem in the model estimation. This is why most recent studies have avoided including a deterministic trend in the model specification. Li (2004) discovered that of the 45 selected papers published after 1990, only six considered time trend in the model specification.

Forecasting Evaluation The forecasting performance assessment of single-equation econometric models is normally based on *ex post* forecasts. Different measures of forecasting performance are available. The predominant measure is the mean absolute percentage error (MAPE), which is used 127 times in 155 individual comparisons according to Li (2004). The next most popular measures are the root mean squared error (RMSE) and root mean squared percentage error (RMSPE), used 91 and 83 times, respectively, in the 155 comparisons. Other evaluation measures, such as mean absolute error (MAE) and Theil's U statistic (Turner et al. 1997a; Kim and Song 1998; Song et al. 2000), the acceptable output percentage (Z) and normalised correlation coefficient (r) (Law and Au 1999) have also been used. The tendency for the MAPE and RMSE (or RMSPE) to give the same rankings is small, as Li (2004) found in only 26 of 108 cases were MAPE and RMSE (or RMSPE) models in the same order. This discrepancy is due to the different assumptions imposed on the forms of the loss function.

Time-series models including the naïve no-change model and a variation of the Box–Jenkins ARIMA models have been used as benchmarks to assess the forecasting performance of econometric models in many of the published empirical studies. However, it has not been found that econometric models are superior to time-series models in terms of forecasting accuracy, and the conclusion normally depends on the type of econometric and time-series models included in the comparison. For example, when the static regression model is compared with time-series models (such as those in Witt and Witt 1991, 1992; Law and Au (1999); Law 2000), the econometric models have always been outperformed by time-series models. In particular, Witt and Witt (1991) show that the naïve model is superior to the causal econometric models where the econometric models are traditional static regressions. However, Li (2004) found that the particular time-series models used outperformed the econometric models in only 52 out of 133 cases. In particular, the naïve model generates the most accurate forecasts in only 34 of 131 studies (typically in Kulendran and Witt 2001). These results suggest that the use of advanced econometric techniques can improve the forecasting performance of econometric models, and also raises the question of the capacity of more modern time-series methods such as structural modelling (Turner and Witt 2001b) and neural networks (Kon and Turner 2005).

Single-equation econometric models with time varying components
The structural time series model (STSM) and the time varying parameter (TVP) model belongs to this category of single-equation models. The STSM incorporates stochastic and seasonal components into the classical econometric model. The stochastic and seasonal components in the STSM are specified in the state space form (SSF) and estimated by the Kalman filter algorithms (Kalman 1960). However, the coefficients of the explanatory variables are still treated as fixed parameters in the STSM. Applications of STSM in tourism demand studies include González and Moral (1995, 1996), Greenidge (2001), Kulendran and Witt (2001, 2003a) and Turner and Witt (2001b). These studies have shown that the STSM can successfully capture the time varying properties of the time series and reflect the seasonal characteristics of tourism demand. Although the trend, seasonal and cyclical components in the STSM are allowed to vary over time, the parameters of the explanatory variables are still fixed over time and this can be a drawback, as these parameters may also change over time due to changing tourist preferences. As an alternative to the STSM, the TVP model may be more appropriate if the coefficients of the explanatory variables in the econometric models change over time. Song and Witt (2000) and Song and Wong (2003) demonstrate that the demand elasticities related to long-haul travel tend to vary over the sample period as a result of tourist expectations and preferences changing. It has been shown that changes in

demand elasticities can be best simulated by TVP models (Song and Witt 2000; Song and Wong 2003). Song and Witt (2000) and Song et al. (2003b) also suggest that the TVP model can improve short-term (one to two periods ahead) forecasting performance.

Neural network models
As Law (2000) described, a neural network contains many simple processing units known as 'nodes' operating in parallel with no central control and the connections between these nodes have numeric weights that can be adjusted in the learning process. This learning process can be seen as a computational tool that mimics a human brain. Law and Au (1999) applied a feed-forward neural network to model the demand for Hong Kong tourism by Japan. In addition, Law (2000) extended the study by incorporating the back-propagation learning process to a nonlinear tourism demand relationship. Pattie and Snyder (1996) employed the same method to forecast over-night backcountry stays in US national parks. All three studies have shown a superior performance of neural network models in terms of forecasting accuracy. Burger et al. (2001) and Uysal and Roubi (1999) also used neural networks to forecast tourism demand with some success. In-depth discussion and application of different neural models and their relative forecasting accuracy compared with the basic structural model (BSM), naïve and Holt Winters methods is given in Kon and Turner (2004), where the BSM and neural models are found to be the most accurate. However, the application of neural network models and other univariate time-series methods including Box Jenkins ARIMA (Turner et al. 1995), BSM (Turner and Witt 2001b) and simpler methods such as Holt Winters (Grubb and Mason 2001) to tourism forecasting has been limited by their inability to provide policy implications, as the construction and estimation of the models are not based on solid economic theories. It is often an overlooked limitation of econometric models that they also assume that the determinant variables can be forecast ahead (most often using univariate time-series methods) before the econometric models can generate out of sample forecasts.

System demand models
Vector autoregressive models The main focus so far has been on single-equation tourism demand models in which an endogenous tourism demand variable is related to a number of exogenous variables. The single-equation approach depends heavily on the assumption that the explanatory variables are exogenous. If this assumption is violated, a researcher would have to model the economic relationships using a system (or simultaneous) equations method. The popularity of the simultaneous equation approach

dates back to the 1950s and 1960s within the context of structural macro-economic models that were used for policy simulation and forecasting. In estimating these structural models, restrictions were often imposed in order to obtain identified equations. Sims (1980) argued that many of the restrictions imposed on the parameters in the structural equations were 'incredible' relative to the data-generating process, and hence he suggested that it would be better to use models that do not depend on the imposition of incorrect prior information. Following this argument, Sims developed a vector autoregressive (VAR) model in which all the variables apart from the deterministic variables such as trend, intercept and dummy variables, are modelled purely as dynamic processes, that is, the VAR model treats all variables as endogenous.

More importantly, the VAR technique has been closely associated with some of the recent developments in multivariate cointegration analysis, such as the Johansen (1988) cointegration method. Although there has been increasing interest in using the VAR technique in macroeconomic modelling and forecasting, relatively little effort has been made in using this method to forecast tourism demand. Exceptions are Song et al. (2003b), Witt et al. (2003, 2004) and Wong et al. (2006) who used VAR models to forecast demand for tourism and tourism generated employment.

Almost ideal demand system (AIDS) model Eadington and Redman (1991) noted another deficiency of the single-equation approach, that is, such approaches are incapable of analysing the interdependence of budget allocations to different consumer goods/services. For example, tourism decision making normally involves a choice among a group of alternative destinations. A change of price in one destination may affect the tourists' decision on travelling to a number of alternative destinations, and also influence their expenditures in those destinations. Clearly, the single-equation methodology cannot adequately model the influence of a change in tourism price in a particular destination on the demand for travelling to all other destinations. An additional limitation of the single-equation approach is that it cannot be used to test either the symmetry or the adding-up hypotheses associated with demand theory.

The system of equations approach initiated by Stone (1954) overcomes these limitations. By including a group of equations (one for each consumer good) in the system and estimating them simultaneously, this approach permits the examination of how consumers choose bundles of goods in order to maximise their preference or utility with budget constraints. Although there are a number of system approaches available, the AIDS model, introduced by Deaton and Muellbauer (1980), has been the most commonly used method for analysing consumer behaviour.

Although the AIDS model has received considerable attention in food demand analysis, the application of this approach to tourism demand studies is still relatively rare. A thorough literature search has identified the following publications. O'Hagan and Harrison (1984) examined American tourists' expenditure in each of 16 individual destinations, while White (1982, 1985) divided the 16 destinations into seven regions and added a transportation equation into the demand system. Syriopoulos and Sinclair (1993) and Papatheodorou (1999) studied the demand for Mediterranean tourism by tourists from the US and various European countries. De Mello et al. (2002) introduced a three-equation system to examine the expenditure allocations of UK tourists in France, Portugal and Spain. Divisekera (2003) applied the AIDS models to Japanese, New Zealand, UK and US demands for tourism to Australia and chosen alternative destinations. Lyssiotou (2001) specified a nonlinear AIDS model to study UK demand for tourism to the US, Canada and 16 European countries and a lagged dependent variable was included in the AIDS specification to capture the habit persistence effect. However, a few neighbouring destinations were aggregated in this study, thus the substitution and complementary effects between these individual countries is not available.

All of the above studies focus on tourist expenditure allocation to different destinations, whereas Fujii et al. (1985) investigated tourist expenditure on different consumer goods in a particular destination. Apart from Lyssiotou (2001), the specification of the AIDS model is static and can only give estimates of long-run demand elasticity. Although Lyssiotou incorporated the lagged dependent variable into the model specification, neither the long-run equilibrium relationship nor the short-term adjustment mechanism is examined. In comparison with the studies above, Durbarry and Sinclair (2003) estimated an error correction AIDS in analysing the demand for tourism to Italy, Spain and the UK by French residents. This is the first attempt to use the error correction AIDS approach in tourism demand modelling and forecasting. However, the error correction AIDS models in their study omitted all the short-run explanatory variables due to their statistical insignificance. Thus, tourist short-run behaviour was not analysed in the study. Moreover, the forecasting performance of the dynamic AIDS model was not examined.

Li et al. (2004) examined the UK demand for tourism in Western Europe using both the long-run static and the short-run error correction AIDS models. Five destinations were considered in this study: France, Greece, Italy, Portugal and Spain. The tests for homogeneity and symmetry suggest that the dynamic version of the AIDS model satisfies demand theory well, and that the short-run adjustment should not be ignored when examining the demand for Western European tourism by UK residents. Various elasticities have been calculated and the results provide a basis for tourism policy making in these destinations.

Status of current tourism forecasting research: a critique

Most published studies on causal tourism demand models before the 1990s and some of the recent publications on the topic are classical regressions with ordinary least squares (OLS) as the main estimation procedure (Witt and Witt 1995). The functional form of most of these models is single equation in either linear or power form. Normally the simple-to-general modelling approach is followed. This approach starts by constructing a simple model that is consistent with demand theory, and the model is then estimated and tested for statistical significance. The estimated model is expected to have a high explanatory power (R^2), and the coefficients are expected to be both 'correctly' signed and statistically significant. In addition, the residuals from the estimated model are assumed to be a white noise process. However, if the estimated model is unsatisfactory, the model is then re-estimated by introducing new explanatory variables, and/or using a different functional form, and/or selecting a different estimation method.

This procedure is repeated until the final model is both statistically and theoretically acceptable. The specific-to-general modelling approach is often criticised for its excessive data mining, since researchers normally only publish their final models, with the intermediate modelling process omitted. Different researchers equipped with the same data set and statistical tools can end up with totally different models. In addition, the data used in estimating tourism demand models based on the simple-to-general approach are mainly time series, and most of these time series, such as tourist expenditure, tourist arrivals, income, tourist living costs and transport prices are trended (non-stationary). The estimated tourism demand models have tended to have high R^2 values due to these common trends in the data. Statistical tests based on such regression models with non-stationary variables are unreliable and can be misleading, and therefore any inferences drawn from these models are suspect. Moreover, tourism demand models with non-stationary variables tend to cause the estimated residuals to be autocorrelated, and this invalidates OLS. The problem of autocorrelation in tourism demand models has normally been dealt with by employing the Cochrane–Orcutt iterative estimation procedure. However, this diverts attention from searching for the correctly specified model (autocorrelation is normally indicative of model misspecification).

Some of the seminal works in the tourism forecasting literature follow the specific-to-general modelling approach and they include, Uysal and

Crompton (1985), Witt and Martin (1987a), Martin and Witt (1988), Crouch (1992), Witt and Witt (1992) and Sheldon (1993). Witt and Witt (1992) found that the econometric models estimated based on the specific-to-general approach, tend to be outperformed by simple time-series approaches including the naïve no-change model. The majority of the empirical studies using the specific-to-general approach to tourism forecasting did not perform rigorous diagnostic checking during the model selection process. Most of those studies only reported the DW autocorrelation and goodness of fit (R^2) statistics. As a result the functional form of the model, residual normality, homscedasticity and structural stability were largely ignored and this can lead to the model being mis-specified. In her review of tourism forecasting studies during the 1980s and early 1990s, Lim (1997) found that only 10 per cent of published articles reported diagnostic statistics other than the DW autocorrelation statistic. Many econometric software programs used by researchers during the same period, such as E-views, Microfit, RATS, PC-Give and STAPMS, contain standard diagnostic statistics, and the lack of diagnostic checking in tourism forecasting seems 'unusual' suggesting that the tourism forecasting literature has lagged well behind mainstream economic research.

Witt and Witt (1995) point out that the failure of the econometric models in accurately forecasting tourism demand may be caused by ignoring the standard diagnostic checking and failing to utilise modern econometric techniques, such as cointegration and error correction approaches, that have been developed since the mid-1980s (Engle and Granger 1987; Johansen 1988). Recent advances in econometrics, specifically the use of general-to-specific approach to modelling, overcome the problems associated with the traditional modelling procedure discussed above. The general-to-specific modelling methodology was first suggested by Hendry and von Ungern-Sternberg (1981), and later theorised by Engle and Granger (1987) and Hendry (1995). The general-to-specific approach to modelling is centred on the cointegration and error correction analysis and the aim of this approach is to identify both the long- and short-run dynamic relationships within a single framework. Tourism researchers have introduced this methodology to forecast tourism demand since the mid-1990s. The first published study on tourism forecasting using this methodology was Syriopoulos (1995) followed by Kulendran (1996), Kulendran and King (1997), Kim and Song (1998), Song et al. (2000), Song and Witt (2000), Kulendran and Witt (2001), Song and Witt (2003) and Song et al. (2003a).

In contrast to the specific-to-general modelling procedure, the general-to-specific approach starts with a general model that contains as many variables as possible, suggested by economic theory. According to this framework, if a dependent variable is determined by k explanatory variables, the data generating process (DGP) may be written as an autoregressive distributed lag model (ADLM) of the form:

$$y_t = \alpha + \sum_{j=1}^{k} \sum_{i=0}^{p} \beta_{ji} x_{jt-i} + \sum_{i=1}^{p} \phi_i y_{t-i} + \varepsilon_t, \qquad (3.1)$$

where p is the lag length, which is determined by the type of data used and is normally decided by AIC (Aikake Information Criterion) and SBC (Schwarz-Bayesian Criterion) statistics. In equation (3.1) ε_t is the error term which is assumed to be normally distributed with zero mean and constant variance, σ^2, that is, $\varepsilon_t \sim N(0, \sigma^2)$.

The general-to-specific modelling approach involves the following steps. First, a general demand model that has a large number of explanatory variables, including the lagged dependent and lagged explanatory variables, is constructed in the form of equation (3.1). Economic theory suggests the possible variables to be included, and the nature of the data suggests the lag length. Second, the t, F, and Wald (or LR or LM as appropriate) statistics are used to test various restrictions in order to achieve a simple but statistically significant specification. Third, the normal diagnostic tests, such as those for autocorrelation, heteroscedasticity, functional form and structural instability, are carried out to examine whether or not the final model is statistically acceptable. Fourth, the final model can be used for policy evaluation or forecasting.

The general-to-specific methodology allows both the long-run equilibrium (cointegration) and short-run dynamic (error correction) relationships to be analysed in the same framework. Therefore, the estimated models can provide useful information for both long- and short-term policy making. The step-by-step illustration on how to use this methodology was given in Song and Witt (2000, 2003), and its application to forecasting the demand for tourism in specific destinations were provided in Song et al. (2003a,b,c). Although the general-to-specific modelling approach has been widely used in other areas of applied economics, the application to tourism forecasting is still small in number and low in quality. The discussion in the following sections is aimed to give the reader an appreciation of this methodology.

State-of-the-art thinking on tourism forecasting

The cointegration and error correction approach to modelling has now become a standard research methodology in applied econometrics and forecasting. This methodology was associated with the seminal work of Engle and Granger (1987), for which both Engle and Granger won the Nobel Prize in economics in 2003 'for [developing the] methods of analyzing economic time series with common trends (cointegration)' (Source: www. Nobelprize. org/economics/laureates). Although this methodology has been available since 1987, the first studies on tourism demand modelling and forecasting using this methodology did not appear until the mid-1990s, and this gap is still widening given that the cointegration and error correction theory in the general economic literature has been developing quickly over the last few years. This growing gap, and some resistance from tourism researchers to adopt new methodologies, especially quantitative methodologies (and the increasing tendency for some tourism journals to be reluctant to publish quantitative work), calls for tourism researchers to absorb new research methodologies in general economic and business fields, in order to close the gap and make tourism research a more rigorous field of study.

Engle and Granger (1987) show that cointegrated variables can always be transformed into an ECM and vice versa. This bidirectional transformation is often called the 'Granger Representation Theorem' and implies that there is some adjustment process that prevents economic variables from drifting too far away from their long-run equilibrium time path. The cointegration and error correction models are very useful in situations where both long-run equilibrium and short-run disequilibrium behaviour are of interest. In tourism demand analysis, the long-run equilibrium behaviour of tourists is expected to be a major concern of policy makers and planners while the short-run dynamics are likely to provide useful information for short-term business forecasting and managerial decisions.

From ADLM to ECM

In the previous section we introduced the general-to-specific approach to modelling, which begins with a general ADLM as specified by equation (3.1). Our discussion here also begins with this general ADLM. With some algebraic manipulation, equation (3.1) can be re-parameterised into an ECM of the form :

$$\Delta y_t = (\text{current and lagged } \Delta x_{jt}s, \text{ lagged } \Delta y_t s)$$

$$- (1 - \phi_1)[y_{t-1} - \sum_{j=1}^{k} \xi x_{jt-1}] + \varepsilon_t. \tag{3.2}$$

We shall demonstrate this in the case of an ADLM(1, 1) model, but the derivation can be extended to a general ADLM(p, q) process. The ADLM(1, 1) model takes the form

$$y_t = \alpha + \beta_0 x_t + \beta_1 x_{t-1} + \phi_1 y_{t-1} + \varepsilon_t. \tag{3.3}$$

Subtracting y_{t-1} from both sides of equation (3.3) yields:

$$\Delta y_t = \alpha + \beta_0 x_t + \beta_1 x_{t-1} - (1 - \phi_1) y_{t-1} + \varepsilon_t$$

or:

$$\Delta y_t = \alpha + \beta_0 \Delta x_t + (\beta_0 + \beta_1) x_{t-1} - (1 - \phi_1) y_{t-1} + \varepsilon_t. \qquad (3.4)$$

Equation (3.4) can be further re-parameterised to give:

$$\Delta y_t = \beta_0 \Delta x_t - (1 - \phi_1)[y_{t-1} - k_0 - k_1 x_{t-1}] + \varepsilon_t. \qquad (3.5)$$

where: $k_0 = \alpha/(1 - \phi_1)$, $/k_1 = (\beta_0 + \beta_1)/(1 - \phi_1)$.

The parameter β_0 is called the impact parameter, $(1 - \phi_1)$ is the feedback effect, k_0 and k_1 are the long-run response coefficients, and the combination of the terms in the square brackets is called the error correction mechanism. Since the coefficient ϕ_1 is less than 1 and greater than 0, the coefficient of the error correction term, $-(1 - \phi_1)$, is greater than -1 and less than 0. This implies that the system will adjust itself towards equilibrium by removing $(1 - \phi_1)$ of a unit from the error made in the previous period. Although equations (3.3) and (3.5) are different in their functional forms, they actually represent the same data-generating process.

Equation (3.5) has the following advantages over equation (3.3):

1. Equation (3.5) reflects both the long- and short-run effects in a single model. The specification indicates that changes in y_t depend on changes in x_t and the disequilibrium error in the previous period.
2. Equation (3.5) overcomes the problem of spurious correlation by employing differenced variables. It can easily be shown that the term $[y_{t-1} - k_0 - k_1 x_{t-1}]$ is a stationary process if y_t and x_t are cointegrated. Therefore, it is unlikely that the residuals in (3.5) will be correlated. Many tourism forecasting models prior to the 1990s use level demand variables and therefore, suffer from spurious regression. The use of ECM in tourism forecasting will avoid the spurious regression problem.
3. The ECM fits in well with the general-to-specific methodology. Since the ECM is another way of writing the general ADLM, so that acceptance of the ADLM is equivalent to acceptance of the error correction model.
4. The estimation of equation (3.5) reduces the problem of data mining, since in the model reduction process one is permitted to eliminate the differenced variables according to statistical significance. However, the

elimination of lagged level variables is not permitted since they represent the cointegration relationship. For example, suppose that a cointegration relationship is found between the variables y_t, x_t and z_t. In the estimation of the ECM in which both differenced and lagged level forms of y, x and z are involved, the researcher is free to eliminate, Δy, Δx and/or Δz, but the lagged level variables, y, x and z should always appear in the final ECM.

5. Estimation of the general ADLM (3.3) which involves a large number of explanatory variables tends to suffer from the problem of multi-collinearity, that is, several of the explanatory variables are likely to be highly correlated which will result in abnormally large standard errors, and hence the calculated t-statistics cannot be used as a reliable criterion for hypothesis testing. However, the corresponding variables in the ECM are less likely to be highly correlated. In fact, Engle and Granger (1987) show that the explanatory variables in the ECM are almost orthogonal (that is, the correlation is almost zero). This is a desirable property, as the t-statistics provide a reliable guide for the elimination of differenced variables. Consequently, it is easier for a researcher to arrive at a sufficiently parsimonious final preferred model using the testing down procedure of the general-to-specific methodology.

From ECM to cointegration regression
Engle and Granger (1987) demonstrate that if a pair of economic variables are cointegrated, they can always be represented by an ECM and vice versa. This can be shown by the following transformation. The long-run steady state suggests that $y_t = y_{t-1}$ and $x_t = x_{t-1}$, that is, $\Delta y_t = \Delta x_t = 0$. Therefore, the ECM (3.5) becomes:

$$0 = -(1 - \phi_1)[y_t - k_0 - k_1 x_t], \text{ that is, } y_t = k_0 + k_1 x_t \qquad (3.6)$$

Equation (3.6) is the long-run cointegration regression with k_0 and k_1 being the long-run cointegration coefficients. Now $k_0 = \alpha/(1 - \phi_1)$ and $k_1 = (\beta_0 + \beta_1)/(1 - \phi_1)$, therefore the long-run cointegration coefficients (vector) can be obtained from the estimates of the general ADLM model (3.1).

The estimation of ECM and the test for cointegration are discussed fully in Song and Witt (2000). Advanced readers could also consult Hendry (1995).

Not only does the ADLM allow cointegration and error correction analysis, it also encompasses a number of econometric models that have been used in tourism demand modelling and forecasting and these include the static model, leading indicator model (Turner et al. 1997b), growth rate model, partial adjustment model, autoregressive model, and finite distributed lag model. The TVP and VAR models are also special cases of the ADLM specification if some restrictions on the coefficients of the ADLM are satisfied (for a detailed illustration about how to derive these specific models based on the general ADLM, see Song and Witt 2000, Chapter 3).

One of the criticisms of the general-to-specific approach is the complexity of the model selection process, as the general ADLM encompasses a large number of potential econometric models that can be used to model the demand for specific destinations. The testing procedure was discussed in Song and Witt (2000, 2003). But the following is a summary of criteria that can be used in the model selection process.

Thomas (1997) has summarised the various criteria for model selection within the framework of general-to-specific modelling. These criteria include consistency with economic theory, data coherency, parsimony, encompassing, parameter constancy and exogeneity. The first criterion for model selection is that the final model should be consistent with economic theory. This is very important because in general we cannot use a demand model for policy evaluation and forecasting if the model has negative income elasticity. Although such a model may be acceptable according to the diagnostic statistics, it should still be rejected because it invalidates a law of economics. The data coherency criterion ensures that economic data also have a role to play in the determination of the structure of the final model. It implies that the preferred model should have been subject to rigorous diagnostic checking for mis-specification. The parsimony criterion states that simple specifications are preferred to complex ones. In the case of modelling tourism demand, if two equations have similar powers in terms of explaining the variation in the dependent variable, but one has six explanatory variables while the other has only two, the latter should be chosen as the final model. This is because we gain very little by including more variables in the model, and moreover large numbers of explanatory variables tend to result in inadequate degrees of freedom and imprecise estimation. The encompassing principle (Mizon and Richard 1986) requires that the preferred model should be able to encompass all, or at least most, of the models developed by previous researchers in the same field. The encompassing criterion does not necessarily conflict with that of parsimony; the preferred model may be structurally simpler than other models, but still encompass them. The parameter constancy criterion is particularly important when we use econometric models to forecast. In order to generate accurate forecasts, the parameters of the model should be constant over time. The final criterion for selecting a model is that the explanatory variables should be exogenous, that is they should not be contemporaneously correlated with the error term in the regression.

In modelling tourism demand, the final preferred model should ideally satisfy all of the above criteria. However, this can sometimes be very difficult for various reasons, such as data limitations, errors in variables and insufficient knowledge of the demand system. Any of these may result in the above criteria not being satisfied. Even if we find a demand model that satisfies all the criteria, it should be borne in mind that the model can still only serve as an approximation to the complex behaviour of tourists, and it is possible that the decision making process of tourists will change due to changes in expectations, tastes and economic regimes. Therefore, we should always be prepared to revise our model to take account of such changes.

Issues for further research

A review of the literature on the recent published studies of tourism forecasting suggests that the following issues deserve more attention.

First, although some researchers have used modern econometric techniques, such as cointegration and ECM, in modelling and forecasting tourism demand, more effort needs to be made to continuously follow new developments in econometrics. For example, tourism forecasters are very much interested in the seasonal properties of the demand model when quarterly and monthly data are used. Although the seasonal cointegration and ECM can be employed to discover the seasonal patterns of tourism demand, the application of the seasonal cointegration and ECM is based on the time series possessing seasonal unit roots. However in practice, some tourism time series may not have unit roots, but still possess the properties of a non-stationary series. If this is the case, fractional cointegration and ECM (Robinson 1994; Gil-Alana and Robinson 1997, 2001) would be more appropriate. No research in this area has been carried out in the context of tourism forecasting.

Second, the emphasis of tourism forecasting research has been primarily on selecting forecasting methods that are likely to generate the lowest error magnitudes (Witt and Witt 1992, 1995). Here, forecasting accuracy is usually measured in unit-free terms, such as MAPE or RMSPE, when examining various time series. Empirical studies by Martin and Witt (1989) and Kulendran and Witt (2001) show that simple time-series models, and the no-change naïve model in particular, tend to outperform more sophisticated econometric models. Kim and Song (1998), Song et al. (2000) and Li (2004) on the other hand, found that econometric models are superior to univariate time series models. These conflicting findings are likely to be caused by the use of different data sets, the difference in the specifications of the econometric models, the nature of the time-series models used for comparison, and the different forecast horizons. This suggests that more research still needs to be done in evaluating forecasting performance in tourism between modern econometric techniques and traditional time-series models in order to reach some agreement in this area. It is unclear that more modern time-series methods (neural models and BSM) will not continue to outperform more modern econometric methods just as it remains unclear that more modern econometric methods (despite greater theoretical rigour) are actually capable of producing more accurate (statistically significantly better) forecasts over the older econometric methods in a post-sample forecast analysis. There seems to be a need to have a tourism forecasting competition between researchers using the same data set.

Third, for certain strategic business decisions it may be more important to forecast correctly the direction of change in either tourism demand (that is, whether tourism demand is likely to increase or decrease over a particular time period) or the rate of growth of tourism demand, rather than to minimise error magnitude. Failure to predict major downturns or upswings in tourism demand could have serious financial consequences. For example, downturns in tourism demand are often associated with economic and/or political and/or social instability, and therefore accurate forecasts of directional changes could signal to government and businesses in a destination that appropriate risk management strategies should be implemented. Very little attention has been paid to the issue of directional analysis in the tourism literature except Witt and Witt (1991) and Witt et al. (2003) who have examined forecasting performance in terms of directional change, and concluded that econometric models tend to generate more accurate forecasts than univariate time-series models, and Turner et al. (1997b) who suggest the use of leading indicators to forecast directional change. Further research is still needed to examine whether the empirical results obtained on relative forecasting performance in the studies above, in terms of directional change, still hold when more destination and origin country pairs, more modern time-series methods and different forecasting horizons are involved.

Fourth, more research is needed into examining the nature and breadth of economic determinants used. The assumption that currently accepted determinants are comprehensive, is challenged by Turner et al. (1998) and Turner and Witt (2001a). As tourism becomes a more universal social activity undertaken for a wider range of reasons by more diverse cultures, so the causal determinants of tourist flows may also change.

Fifth, according to Song and Witt (2002), forecasting performance of different econometric and time-series models varies across different destination–origin country pairs and over different forecasting horizons. Therefore, it is very difficult to obtain a single model that consistently outperforms all other models in all situations. In addition, researchers, policy makers and practitioners have different interests in the ways in which the forecasting models are used. For example, researchers are interested in achieving high accuracy at the expense of losing simplicity while practitioners are keener on achieving more accuracy with simple models. Moreover, policy makers are more interested in the policy impact assessment than forecasting itself. Therefore, policy makers prefer econometric models over time-series models while pure forecasters and many industry practitioners are concerned only with the accuracy of the forecasts rather than the type of the forecasting model used. Given all these different requirements, tourism forecasters have to estimate a number of econometric and time-series models. If this happens, combining forecasts generated from different models would be beneficial to all stakeholders. Chong and Hendry (1986) and Fair and Shiller (1990), among others, have shown that composite forecasts, if combined properly, are superior in terms of lack of bias and accuracy to the original forecasts generated by each of the individual models. However, forecast combination is not a straightforward process and can include non-quantitative methods such as expert opinion (Turner and Witt 2003); and there are different ways in which the forecasts can be combined, all of which calls for serious research to be undertaken in the area of tourism forecasting.

References

Burger, C.J.S.C., M. Dohnal, M. Kathrada and R. Law (2001), 'A practitioners' guide to time series methods for tourism demand forecasting – a case study of Durban, South Africa', *Tourism Management*, **22**, 403–9.

Chong, Y.Y. and D.F. Hendry (1986), 'Econometric evaluation of linear macroeconomic models', *Review of Economic Studies*, **53**, 671–90.

Crouch, G.I. (1992), 'Effects of income and price on international tourism', *Annals of Tourism Research*, **19**, 643–64.

Crouch, G. (1994a), 'The study of international tourism demand: a review of findings', *Journal of Travel Research*, **33**, 12–23.

Crouch, G. (1994b), 'The study of international tourism demand: a survey of practice', *Journal of Travel Research*, **33**, 41–54.

Crouch, G.I., L. Schultz and P. Valerio (1992), 'Marketing international tourism to Australia: a regression analysis', *Tourism Management*, **13**, 196–208.

De Mello, M., A. Pack and M.T. Sinclair (2002), 'A system of equations model of UK tourism demand in neighbouring countries, *Applied Economics*, **34**, 509–21.

Deaton, A.S. and J. Muellbauer (1980), 'An almost ideal demand system', *American Economic Review*, **70**, 312–26.

Divisekera, S. (2003), 'A model of demand for international tourism', *Annals of Tourism Research*, **30**, 31–49.

Dritsakis, N. (2004), 'Cointegration analysis of German and British tourism demand for Greece', *Tourism Management*, **25**, 111–19.

Durbarry, R. and T.M. Sinclair (2003), 'Market share analysis: the case of French tourism demand', *Annals of Tourism Research*, **30**, 927–41.

Eadington, W.R. and M. Redman (1991), 'Economics and tourism', *Annals of Tourism Research*, **18**, 41 56.

Engle, R.F. and C.W.J. Granger (1987), 'Cointegration and error correction: representation, estimation and testing', *Econometrica*, **55**, 251–76.

Fair, R.C. and R.J. Shiller (1990), 'Comparing information in forecasts from econometric models', *American Economic Review*, **80**, 375–89.

Frechtling, D.C. (2001), *Forecasting Tourism Demand: Methods and Strategies*, Oxford: Butterworth-Heinemann.

Fujii, E., M. Khaled and J. Mark (1985), 'An almost ideal demand system for visitor expenditures', *Journal of Transport Economics and Policy*, **19**, 161–71.

Gil-Alana, L.A. and P.M. Robinson (1997), 'Testing unit roots and other nonstationary hypotheses in macroeconomic time series', *Journal of Econometrics*, **80**, 241–68.

Gil-Alana, L.A. and P.M. Robinson (2001), 'Testing of seasonal fractional integration in the UK and Japanese consumption and income', *Journal of Applied Econometrics*, **16**, 95–114.

González, P. and P. Moral (1995), 'An analysis of the international tourism demand in Spain', *International Journal of Forecasting*, **11**, 233–51.

González, P. and P. Moral (1996), 'Analysis of tourism trends in Spain', *Annals of Tourism Research*, **23**, 739–54.

Greenidge, K. (2001), 'Forecasting tourism demand: an STM approach', *Annals of Tourism Research*, **28**, 98–112.

Grubb, H. and A. Mason (2001), 'Long lead-time forecasting of UK air passengers by Holt–Winters methods with damped trend', *International Journal of Forecasting*, **17**, 71–82.

Hendry, D.F. (1995). *Dynamic Econometrics*, Oxford: Oxford University Press.

Hendry, D.F. and T. von Ungern-Sternberg (1981), 'Liquidity and inflation effects on consumers expenditure', in A.S. Deaton (ed.), *Essays in the Theory and Measurement of Consumer Behaviour*, Cambridge: Cambridge University Press, 237–61.

Johansen, S. (1988), 'A statistical analysis of cointegration vectors', *Journal of Economic Dynamics and Control*, **12**, 231–54.

Johnson, P. and J. Ashworth (1990), 'Modelling tourism demand: a summary review', *Leisure Studies*, **9**, 145–60.

Kalman, R.E. (1960), 'A new approach to linear filtering and prediction problems. Transactions ASME', *Journal of Basic Engineering*, **82**, 35–45.

Kim, S. and H. Song (1998), 'Analysis of tourism demand in South Korea: a cointegration and error correction approach', *Tourism Analysis*, **3**, 25–41.

Kon, S.C. and L.W. Turner (2005), 'Neural network forecasting of tourism demand', *Tourism Economics*, **11**(3), 301–28.

Kulendran, N. (1996), 'Modelling quarterly tourism flows to Australia', *Tourism Economics*, **2**, 203–22.

Kulendran, N. and M. King (1997), 'Forecasting international quarterly tourism flows using error correction and time series models', *International Journal of Forecasting*, **13**, 319–27.

Kulendran, N. and S.F. Witt (2001), 'Cointegration versus least squares regression', *Annals of Tourism Research*, **28**, 291–311.

Kulendran, N. and S.F. Witt (2003a), 'Forecasting the demand for international business tourism', *Journal of Travel Research*, **41**, 265–71.

Kulendran, N. and S.F. Witt (2003b), 'Leading indication tourism forecasts', *Tourism Management*, **24**, 503–10.

Law, R. (2000), 'Back-propagation learning in improving the accuracy of neural network-based tourism demand forecasting', *Tourism Management*, **21**, 331–40.

Law, R. and N. Au (1999), 'A neural network model to forecast Japanese demand for travel to Hong Kong', *Tourism Management*, **20**, 89–97.

Ledesma-Rodríguez, F.J., M. Navarro-Ibánez and J.V. Pérez-Rodríguez (2001), 'Panel data and tourism: a case study of Tenerife', *Tourism Economics*, **7**, 75–88.

Li, G. (2004), 'Tourism forecasting – an almost ideal demand system approach', Unpublished PhD Thesis, University of Surrey, Guildford.

Li, G., H. Song and S.F. Witt (2004), 'Modelling tourism demand: a linear AIDS approach', *Journal of Travel Research*, **43**, 141–50.

Lim, C. (1997), 'Review of international tourism demand models, *Annals of Tourism Research*, **24**, 835–49.

Lim, C. and M. McAleer (2001), 'Cointegration analysis of quarterly tourism demand by Hong Kong and Singapore for Australia', *Applied Economics*, **33**, 1599–619.

Lim, C. and M. McAleer (2002), 'A cointegration analysis of tourism demand by Malaysia for Australia', *Mathematics and Computers in Simulation*, **59**, 197–205.

Lyssiotou, P. (2001), 'Dynamic analysis of British demand for tourism abroad', *Empirical Economics*, **15**, 421–36.

Martin, C.A. and S.F. Witt (1987), 'Tourism demand forecasting models: choice of appropriate variable to represent tourists' cost of living', *Tourism Management*, **8**, 233–46.

Martin, C.A. and S.F. Witt (1988), 'Substitute prices in models of tourism demand', *Annals of Tourism Research*, **15**, 255–68.

Martin, C.A. and S.F. Witt (1989), 'Forecasting tourism demand: a comparison of the accuracy of several quantitative methods', *International Journal of Forecasting*, **5**, 7–19.

Mizon, G.E. and J.F. Richard (1986), 'The encompassing principle and its application to testing non-nested hypotheses', *Econometrica*, **54**, 657–78.

Morley, C.L. (1998), 'A dynamic international demand model', *Annals of Tourism Research*, **25**, 70–84.

Morley, C. (2000), 'Demand modelling methodologies: integration and other issues', *Tourism Economics*, **6**, 5–19.

O'Hagan, J.W. and M.J. Harrison (1984), 'Market shares of US tourism expenditure in Europe: an econometric analysis', *Applied Economics*, **16**, 919–31.

Papatheodorou, A. (1999), 'The demand for international tourism in the Mediterranean region', *Applied Economics*, **31**, 619–30.

Pattie, D.C. and J. Snyder (1996), 'Using a neural network to forecast visitor behavior', *Annals of Tourism Research*, **23**, 151–64.

Payne, J.E. and A. Mervar (2002), 'A note on modelling tourism revenues in Croatia', *Tourism Economics*, **8**, 103–9.

Qiu, H. and J. Zhang (1995), 'Determinants of tourist arrivals and expenditures in Canada', *Journal of Travel Research*, **34**, 43–9.

Riddington, G. (1999), 'Forecasting ski demand: comparing learning curve and time varying parameter approaches', *Journal of Forecasting*, **18**, 205–14.

Riddington, G. (2002), 'Learning and ability to pay: developing a model to forecast ski tourism', in K.F.Wong and H. Song (eds), *Tourism Forecasting and Marketing*, New York: Haworth Hospitality Press, 111–26.

Robinson, P.M. (1994), 'Efficient tests of nonstationary hypotheses', *Journal of the American Statistical Association*, **89**, 1420–37.

Seddighi, H.R. and D.F. Shearing (1997), 'The demand for tourism in North East England with special reference to Northumbria: an empirical analysis', *Tourism Management*, **18**, 499–511.

Sheldon, P. (1993), 'Forecasting tourism: expenditures versus arrivals', *Journal of Travel Research*, **22**, 13–20.

Sims, C. (1980), 'Macroeconomics and reality', *Econometrica*, **48**, 1–48.

Song, H., P. Romilly and X. Liu (2000), 'An empirical study of outbound tourism demand in the UK', *Applied Economics*, **32**, 611–24.

Song, H. and S.F. Witt (2000), *Tourism Demand Modelling and Forecasting: Modern Econometric Approaches*, Oxford: Pergamon.

Song, H. and S.F. Witt (2003), 'Tourism forecasting: the general-to-specific approach', *Journal of Travel Research*, **42**, 65–74.

Song, H., S.F. Witt and T.C. Jensen (2003a), 'Tourism forecasting: accuracy of alternative econometric models', *International Journal of Forecasting*, **19**, 123–41.

Song, H., S.F. Witt and G. Li (2003b), 'Modelling and forecasting the demand for Thai tourism', *Tourism Economics*, **9**, 363–87.

Song, H. and K.F. Wong (2003), 'Tourism demand modelling: a time varying parameter approach', *Journal of Travel Research*, **42**, 57–64.

Song, H., K.F. Wong and K. Chon (2003c), 'Modelling and forecasting the demand for Hong Kong tourism', *International Journal of Hospitality Management*, **22**, 435–51.

Stone, J.R.N. (1954), 'Linear expenditure systems and demand analysis: an application to the pattern of British demand', *Economic Journal*, **64**, 511–27.

Syriopoulos, T. (1995), 'A dynamic model of demand for Mediterranean tourism', *International Review of Applied Economics*, **9**, 318–36.

Syriopoulos, T. and T. Sinclair (1993), 'An econometric study of tourism demand: the AIDS model of US and European tourism in Mediterrean countries', *Applied Economics*, **25**, 1541–52.

Thomas, R.L. (1997), *Modern Econometrics: An Introduction*, Harlow: Addison-Wesley.

Turner, L.W., N. Kulendran and H. Fernando (1997a), 'Univariate modelling using periodic and non-periodic analysis: inbound tourism to Japan, Australia and New Zealand compared', *Tourism Economics*, **3**, 39–56.

Turner, L.W., N. Kulendran and H. Fernando (1997b), 'The use of composite national indicators for tourism forecasting', *Tourism Economics*, **3**, 309–17.

Turner, L.W., N. Kulendran and V. Pergat (1995), 'Forecasting New Zealand tourism demand with disaggregated data', *Tourism Economics*, **1**, 51–69.

Turner L.W., Y. Reisinger and S.F. Witt (1998), 'Tourism demand analysis using structural equation modelling', *Tourism Economics*, **4**, 301–23.

Turner, L.W. and S.F. Witt (2001a), 'Factors influencing demand for international tourism: tourism demand analysis using structural equation modelling revisited', *Tourism Economics*, **7**, 21–38.

Turner L.W. and S.F. Witt (2001b), 'Forecasting tourism using univariate and multivariate structural time series models', *Tourism Economics*, **7**, 135–47.

Turner, L.W. and S.F. Witt (2003), *Pacific Asia Tourism Forecasts 2003–2005*, Bangkok: PATA.

Uysal, M. and J.L. Crompton (1985), 'An overview of approaches used to forecast tourism demand', *Journal of Travel Research*, **24**, 7–15.

Uysal, M. and M. Roubi (1999), 'Artificial neural networks versus multiple regression in tourism demand analysis', *Journal of Travel Research*, **38**, 111–18.

Vogt, M.G. and C. Wittayakorn (1998), 'Determinants of the demand for Thailand's exports of tourism', *Applied Economics*, **30**, 711–15.

Webber, A. (2001), 'Exchange rate volatility and cointegration in tourism demand', *Journal of Travel Research*, **39**, 398–405.

White, K.J. (1982), 'The demand for international travel: a system-wide analysis for US travel to Western Europe', Discussion Paper, 82-28, Department of Economics, University of British Columbia.

White, K.J. (1985), 'An international travel demand model: US travel to Western Europe', *Annals of Tourism Research*, **12**, 529–45.

Witt, S.F., M. Dartus and A.M. Sykes (1992), 'Modeling conference tourism, tourism partnerships and strategies – merging vision with new realities', in TTRA, *Proceedings of Travel and Tourism Research Association 23rd Annual Conference*, Wheat Ridge: TTRA, 116–24.

Witt, S.F. and C.A. Martin (1987a), 'Econometric models for forecasting international tourism demand', *Journal of Travel Research*, **15**, 23–30.

Witt, S.F. and C.A. Martin (1987b), 'International tourism demand models – inclusion of marketing variables', *Tourism Management*, **8**, 33–40.

Witt, S.F. and H. Song (2000), 'Forecasting future tourism flows', in S. Medlik and A. Lockwood (eds), *Tourism and Hospitality in the 21st Century*, Oxford: Butterworth-Heinemann, 106–18.

Witt, S.F., H. Song and P. Louvieris (2003), 'Statistical testing in forecasting model selection', *Journal of Travel Research*, **42**, 151–8.

Witt, S.F., H. Song and S. Wanhill (2004), 'Forecasting tourism generated employment', *Tourism Economics*, **10** (2), 167–76.

Witt, S.F., A. Sykes and M. Dartus (1995), 'Forecasting international conference attendance', *Tourism Management*, **16**, 559–70.

Witt, S.F. and C.A. Witt (1991), 'Tourism forecasting: error magnitude, direction of change error and trend change error', *Journal of Travel Research*, **30**, 26–33.

Witt, S.F. and C.A. Witt (1992), *Modelling and Forecasting Demand in Tourism*, London: Academic Press.

Witt, S.F. and C.A. Witt (1995), 'Forecasting tourism demand: a review of empirical research', *International Journal of Forecasting*, **11**, 447–75.

Wong, K.F., H. Song and K. Chon (2006), 'Tourism forecasting: a Bayesian VAR approach', *Tourism Management* (forthcoming).

PART TWO

TOURISM SUPPLY

4 Structure conduct performance and industrial organisation in tourism
Brian Davies and Paul Downward

Introduction

Tourism is invariably referred to as the world's largest industry.[1] Yet it is also a risky business venture subject to a highly volatile business environment. Such volatility has been examined in terms of the influence of tourism demand.[2] What has received little attention is the supply environment. Any analysis requires at least some discussion of the generality of competition involved. From a microeconomic perspective, the supply of tourism can be understood in terms of the models and concepts developed and refined in the structure conduct and performance paradigm (SCP) and, relatedly, the industrial organisation (IO) literatures. To provide a critical overview and assessment of the relevance of these concepts, and thus put forward a balanced insight into the main issues that the literature reveals is, in many respects, an ambition that cannot be adequately addressed in one chapter. On the one hand, the SCP and IO literature is immense. On the other, tourism is such a wide-ranging concept that it has yet to find one accepted definition, for example, in official statistics, so the definition of supply is accordingly fluid (Allin 2005).

Facing up to these constraints, this chapter draws upon the authors' previous research in the travel agency/tour operations business and hotels to provide what we feel are key issues that need further investigation and refinement, and which could have application to sectors other than those discussed. The next section begins the discussion by indicating the scale and economic importance of tourism, its definition, and how regulators implicitly draw upon SCP–IO concepts in terms of competition policy. The third section outlines the key concepts and links between the SCP and IO literature. There then follows a critical review of the existing tourism literature on travel and tourism and hotels. The fifth section presents results from our research which, we feel, helps to increase the robustness of previous analysis and leads to some conceptual and applied insights into future research in the following section. Finally, conclusions are drawn suggesting the need for more robust industry insights together with a comment on the state of research into tourism industry supply economics.

The importance of tourism
The World Tourism Organisation (2000) estimated that for the 1990–2000 period the average annual growth of tourism receipts ran at approximately 4 per cent. As an economic force, it accounted for 10–11 per cent of world gross domestic product (GDP) and, in terms of employment, in 1999 tourism and related activities employed an estimated 200 million world-wide. This represents 8 per cent of total global employment. Such economic activity places it alongside oil and motor vehicles in terms of economic activity.

With respect to the UK economy, the British Tourist Authority Marketing Intelligence Department (2003), using official statistics, estimated that tourism's share of GDP was 4.8 per cent in 1995 and 4.1 per cent in 2001. Tourism spending accounted for 7.8 per cent in 1995 and 6.4 per cent in 2001. In 2001, combined overseas and domestic tourism expenditure amounted to £37 000 million, and overseas visitor spending accounted for 19 per cent of total export of services and 3.5 per cent of total exports.

Yet, such figures may be a gross underestimate. Allin (2005) notes that the data upon which analysis is often based is in fact rather unsystematic. In the UK it draws upon sources within the Office for National Statistics and the national tourist boards. Rather by convention a group of industries have become known as the 'tourism-related industries' because it is believed that they account for a significant proportion of tourism spending. Their description and size in terms of jobs is indicated in Table 4.1.

In addition, tourism statistics associated with international transactions are available, as implied above, as part of the balance of payments, where

Table 4.1   Employment in tourism-related industries in Great Britain, September 2001

Industry	SIC category	Number of jobs
Hotels and other tourist accommodation	551/552	410 900
Restaurants, cafes etc.	553	556 200
Bars, public houses and nightclubs	554	528 000
Travel agencies and tour operators	633	140 900
Libraries, museums and other cultural activities	925	81 800
Sport and other recreational activities	926/927	414 600
All tourism-related industries of which:		2 132 400
Employee jobs		1 955 800
Self-employment jobs		176 600

Source: Allin (2005).

the 'travel account' records expenditure within the UK by visitors, and by UK visitors abroad. Finally, the development of Tourism Satellite Accounts (TSAs) by the World Travel & Tourism Council has enabled tourism's economic importance, in both demand and supply terms, to be reflected in macroeconomic statistics. A TSA provides a means of separating and examining both tourism supply and the tourism demand within the general framework of the System of National Accounts and within supply and use tables. It also facilitates a broad picture of the quantifiable effects of travel and tourism on economies. The emphasis here is upon identifying tourism as a demand-side activity because many businesses serve tourists but they also serve other customers.

Despite the tension between the importance of tourism and the measurement of its significance, industrial policy is nonetheless constructed and implemented. For example, in the UK the Competition Commission (CC), formerly the Monopolies and Mergers Commission, investigated the travel agency/tour operator business in 1986, 1989 and 1997. The persistent issue investigated was the degree of vertical integration between travel agents and tour operators, particularly for the larger companies conventionally regarded as market leaders, including Thomson, and the then in existence, Horizon. In the latter report, while in general it was felt that there was competition, only one company, Thomson, survived as one of the big companies between the two reports. Smaller suppliers felt increasing vertical integration was putting them under undue pressure and potentially squeezing them out of business. Over time this would reduce consumer welfare and be against the public interest. The CC eventually ruled that there were some anti-competitive practices, particularly the tying of insurance to discounted holidays, the forcing of travel agents to offer the same discounts between tour operators and generally, keeping the vertically integrated links unclear to consumers. The Holiday 2003 report, by Travelcare – the UK's largest independent travel agency – which has the backing of Trading Standards, also called for the Office of Fair Trading (OFT) to re-investigate big travel agents to force them to tell customers about their links to holiday firms.

Significantly, the CC drew upon its own primary and secondary research to inform its discussions. Moreover, the main theoretical ideas discussed were developed from the SCP and IO literatures. The next section of the chapter thus describes developments in SCP and IO studies and looks at the current literature on the industry. Surprisingly, little congruence between these studies and the CC findings are established. The main reasons for this are then discussed in a review of the authors' research before some suggestions for enhancing the academic research approach are provided.

The SCP–IO approaches

As Davies and Downward (2001) note, a useful way to think about the SCP–IO approaches is that they emerged out of a synthesis of two disparate research emphases in economic analysis that have developed since Alfred Marshall's *Principles of Economics*. While Marshall strove to unite optimising economic theory, expressed in the form of differential calculus, with the need to understand practical business life, subsequent developments drove a wedge between this synthesis. One strand of development emphasised the deductive theory expressed in the mathematics of optimisation. Ultimately this found its highpoint in 'general equilibrium' analysis. Thus a lineage can be traced from, for example, Stanley Jevons, Francis Edgeworth, past Marshall, through to John Bates Clark, Frank Knight and Piero Sraffa to Kenneth Arrow and Gerard Debreu's formal presentation of general equilibrium. The objective of such theorists was to formally analyse general principles said to govern economic behaviour.

The second strand of research effort comprised an essentially inductive approach exploring industries descriptively through case studies, prime examples of which are R.F. Hall and C.J. Hitch, P.W.S. Andrews, Gardiner Means and Adolf Berle. In these cases, detailed and qualitative case-study work was used to develop theses about pricing and business behaviour. While generalities were sought, therefore, they were grounded in primary empirical investigation.

Subsequently, the SCP paradigm sought to realign economic theory with the analysis of business actuality. The emphasis was to forge a link between the deduction of formal optimising theory and the more specific inductive agenda by econometrically assessing the predictions of such theory. The roots lie in the seminal works of Robinson (1933), Mason (1939), Bain (1956) and Chamberlin (1965). The SCP model postulates a linear–causal link between features of a market's structure, the subsequent conduct of firms and their 'performance' in terms of economic welfare. So, aspects of market structure such as the market share of firms, when combined with an assumption about firm behaviour, for example, profit maximisation, has implications for performance, that is economic welfare. The benchmark of maximum welfare, that is efficiency for society, is perfect competition in which prices reflect the opportunity cost of resources, that is, marginal costs. Thus, consumer welfare is at a maximum. In general, other market structures in which there is a degree of monopoly power implies that prices are above marginal costs because output is restricted. Consequently this erodes consumer welfare.[3] Market share of individual firms, and its industry-level counterpart as the degree of concentration, are seen as the determinants of market power. This is a symptom of the ability to prevent competitive entry into the market. The CC reports, referred to above, spend considerable time exploring these variables.

This linear conception of market analysis has actually been challenged, leading to the extension of the SCP approach into a broader IO literature. For example, the advent of oligopoly theory, following from the key work of von Neumann and Morgenstern (1944), Shubik (1959) and Demsetz (1974), reversed the direction of causality suggesting that market structures were essentially endogenously determined. Firm strategic behaviour affected market shares and thus industry concentration. Oligopoly theory, however, retains the view that prices above marginal costs lead to inefficiency, that is a loss of economic, consumer welfare.

More recently, large-scale production and even market dominance have been allied to efficiency. Transaction cost analysis, as has been popularised by Williamson (1975) as a seminal contribution, suggests that the internalisation of market transactions leads firms to high profits through efficient organisation rather than market power. Similarly, if technology and freedom of entry and exit of firms from markets determines market structure, then it has been proposed that this will lead to optimal conduct and performance, though under restrictive assumptions concerning the price response of incumbents when new firms enter. Baumol et al. (1982) thus present the 'contestable' markets hypothesis. Regardless of the small number and size of current incumbents in a market, their behaviour has to be 'as if' there exist perfectly competitive markets because of the threat of potential competition.

While there have been many other developments in the SCP–IO literatures, the basic qualitative thrust has been to examine the proposition that profitability is positively related to market characteristics proxying market power and/or efficiency. The absence of such a relationship conversely implies competition and/or contestability. It is indeed these issues that, for example, the CC referred to with the travel agent–tour operator business.

Tourism literature review
Literature on SCP and IO in relation to tourism supply is somewhat limited to an examination of UK hotels and the package tour industries. The hotel industry has been examined by Baum and Mudambi (1995), Davies and Downward (1996) and Davies (1998). The former is basically a study of supply in relation to demand. The authors suggest that the industry behaves oligopolistically and their findings support the Ricardian model of pricing being asymmetrically related to the state of demand. Prices are well behaved during periods of excess demand, but are unrepresentative of the state of demand in the face of excess supply.

Davies and Downward (1996) sought to test the general applicability of SCP to tourism via the medium of the UK hotel industry. It opened up a research agenda carried forward by Davies. This chapter aims to test the general applicability of IO generating 'stylised facts' and to build up case-study material on tourism supply. The results demonstrate that market share was more easily explained than profitability and appeared to be the key variable. The overall situation represented fights for market share reducing concentration. The possibility of return on sales and market power being related, indicating oligopoly, was noted.

Given this paucity of empirical work, our analysis concentrates on the UK package tour industry. An examination of the academic literature suggests that the key characteristics of its competitive structure are not well understood, and they certainly do not accord with the view of the CC.

In terms of the package tour operations, early work concentrated on oligopoly in supply. Studies of competition and strategies appear in the work of Sheldon (1986) on US tour operators, Fitch (1987) and Evans and Stabler (1995). Since then, the structure and nature of competition in the UK package tour industry has been subject to a debate in the literature in terms of competition and contestability. Baum and Mudambi (1994) favour an oligopolistic structure with price stability whereas Taylor (1996) suggests that the industry may be competitive, contestable or oligopolistic. Further, Taylor (1998) suggests, in line with Evans and Stabler (1995) that price wars and non-cooperative behaviour persists. The literature tends to be purely theoretical or draws upon a description of features of the market which is then compared to the assumptions of the theories.

More indirectly, the pricing of package tours has also been investigated in terms of the relationship between price and product characteristics. Sinclair et al. (1990), Clewer et al. (1994) and Pastor (1999) have pursued this through the use of a hedonic pricing framework. More recently, Aguilo et al. (2001, 2003) have undertaken an analysis of German package prices, and German and UK package prices, respectively, in relation to product characteristics including transport costs, time of the year, hotel quality and complementary offers. Use is made of analyses of variance and covariance. Their finding is that tour operators are significant in determining price. The implication they draw is that this is the result of monopolistic competition and increased concentration. This is in line with the work of van Dijk and van der Stelt-Steele (1993), Gratton and Richards (1997) and Gauf and Hughes (1998). Unfortunately, the form of competition is not directly investigated.

In general, some progress appears to be being made but, somewhat worryingly, over broadly the same periods of time and subject matter, many studies contradict one another. The UK studies are particularly interesting. Key aspects of them are presented in Table 4.2.

The table indicates two important features. The first is that, unlike the emphasis of SCP–IO literature generally, there is methodological slippage

Table 4.2   The SCP–IO literature on the package tour industry

Author	Period	Subject	Method	Conclusion
Fitch (1987)	1980–86	UK outbound tour operators	Descriptive examination of market shares and product segmentation	Market power of the large tour operators/ conglomerates
Baum and Mudambi (1994)	1986–91	UK package tour industry	Game-theoretic predictions of demand and price and stylised description of the industry	Oligopolistic market with asymmetric demand responses
Taylor (1996)		Reply to Baum and Mudambi		If firms react market structure is endogenous
Evans and Stabler (1995)	1970s–90s	Outbound package holidays	Descriptive	Excess capacity/ price wars pre-1991. Oligopoly and non-price competition since 1991
Gratton and Richards (1997)	1988–93	UK and German package tour markets	Descriptive	UK – contestable German – stable oligopoly

Source: Davies and Downward (2001).

away from testing predictions and focusing on the descriptive and anecdotal comparison of evidence and theory. The second feature is that the results and conclusions vary. This can be illustrated with respect to the UK studies. For example, over broadly the same periods of time and subject matter, Gratton and Richards and Evans and Stabler contradict one another. The same is true of Baum and Mudambi, Fitch, and Evans and Stabler. This naturally raises the question, 'How can this be?'. The next two sections of this chapter begin to answer this question with a look at what we would argue are more apposite research findings as well as issues for further research.

Econometric findings

Recognising the limitations of the existing literature, Davies and Downward (1998, 2001) attempted to use econometric methods to address the *predictions* of the UK package tour industry in a manner more consistent with the methodological roots of the SCP–IO literature as discussed in the second section.

In these chapters, annual micro data based on 63 sets of company accounts, for firms having a turnover larger than £2 million p.a. over the 1989–93 period,[4] were employed. This was necessary because, as discussed above, Allin (2005) notes that official data exist only at a more aggregate level. The basic aim was to assess the qualitative proposition, discussed above, that profitability is positively related to market characteristics proxying market power and/or efficiency and that the absence of this would imply competition and/or contestability.

To this end, pre-tax profit–sales ratios and market shares were calculated from the raw data. Because the sample comprises a panel data set, dummy variables were also used to capture firm-specific effects. This was important to measure any firm-specific differences between observations as well as to help to minimise specification errors in the absence of data on product differentiation which also implies barriers to entry. In basic terms, they can be interpreted as variables measuring shifts in the intercept of the general equation attributable to individual firms. Because it had a time dimension, the panel data also allowed the calculation of the Herfindahl index of concentration for the industry as a measure of the degree of market power of the industry. The aggregate UK unemployment rate was used as a control for macroeconomic effects in the economy in the analyses. The industry so defined is directed at outbound tourism. The following basic model was analysed in Davies and Downward (1998):

$$ROS_{it} = \sum_{i=1}^{i=63} b_i D_i + b_{64} Conc_{it} + b_{65} MS_{it} + b_{66} Unem_{it} + u_{it},$$

where:

Ros	=	return on sales;
D	=	firm-specific dummy variables;
$Conc$	=	Herfindahl index of concentration;
MS	=	market share;
$Unem$	=	unemployment;
u	=	random disturbance;
i	=	1, . . ., 63; number of firms;
t	=	1, . . ., 5; time periods.

While the above specification could be argued to capture the main influences implied in the SCP IO literature, matters are more subtle than this. The SCP–IO hypotheses raise two important issues for the econometric analysis of the industry using this equation. First, market shares and profitability can be viewed as endogenous variables. This follows directly from oligopoly theory and the strategic behaviour of firms. In this case, market share may well be an objective addressed through pricing behaviour and thus profits. Market share may be actively sought at the expense of profits. Profits could be sacrificed for market share and, likewise, profits and market share could be contemporaneously determined. Partially to address this issue, Davies and Downward (2001) extended the research by running regressions in reverse, as detailed below:

$$MS_{it} = \sum_{i=1}^{i=63} b_i D_i + b_{64} Conc_{it} + b_{65} Ros_{it} + b_{66} Unem_{it} + u_{it}$$

This enabled the comparison of results in a manner akin to testing for causality in time-series econometrics (see Granger 1969).[5] Such an approach allows the economic interpretation of results to be more transparent.

This said, and from a more statistical point of view, both Davies and Downward (1998, 2001) made use of instrumental variable methods to address endogeneity statistically. This involved following a two-stage least squares procedure that required replacing the specified 'independent' variable of a particular equation, that is suspected to be endogenous, by a proxy that is not endogenous. In these cases predictions of the current variables, based on lagged values of the variable, were used to replace the actual values of the independent variable.[6]

A final innovation of the research was to recognise, what is effectively implied in the CC reports, and indeed by Evans and Stabler (1995) that the industry is segmented into a group of large companies and a long tail of much smaller companies. In keeping with the desire to investigate the hypothesis that best represents the data, the regressions were run for the whole sample and then for segregated samples comprising the top seven companies and the remainder of the industry, that is, small companies.[7]

The tour operations industry
For the industry as a whole, both the ordinary least squares (OLS) and instrumental variable (IV) regressions indicated that only the macroeconomic measures significantly affected the profitability of the industry countercyclically. Two plausible explanations are that most package tours are booked in advance so any reduction in demand will not be apparent until

the next time period – usually next year. On the other hand, profits may rise in a period of falling demand because the capacity constraints in terms of airline seats and accommodation are relieved and this is reflected in more favourable contractual arrangements with suppliers. With reference to the firm-specific variables, the OLS regressions indicated that a group of companies outperformed the largest firm, Thomson. Yet these findings were not supported in the IV estimates.

Interestingly, in the case of the market share regressions, the R^2 were much higher, a finding borne out in the subsequent analyses as well. However, the results indicated no feedback from return on sales to market share, or a significant effect of concentration. This implies that contestability between sectors of the industry is not present. The strength of competition depends not only on the number of actual firms in the market, but also on how easy new competitors can enter and take away market share from existing firms by influencing costs and/or prices. Therefore, it cannot be argued that the existence of potential competition and the threat of entry by new competitors is influencing market shares and firm behaviour in the tour operator/ travel agency industry. Finally, the macroeconomic effect is not statistically significant, while the firm-specific variables confirmed the relative scale of Thomson.

In summary, little support for the market power and efficiency hypotheses existed, though the nature of competition remained an open question.

Statistical tests did reveal that pooling the data was justifiable. For the reasons given above, however, the sample was segmented in order to further the investigation. It was assumed that there exists a higher strategic grouping of seven firms, namely, Thomas Cook Ltd., Airtours PLC, Lunn Poly Ltd., Going Places Leisure Travel Ltd., A.T. Mays, Owners Abroad and Thomson Tour Operators Ltd.

The Top 7
In both the OLS and IV regressions the only market power variable indicated as significant in terms of profitability is concentration, with a negative sign. This suggests, as an industry-level indicator, that expansion of the individual firms within the industry is an unprofitable exercise. In neither case does the macroeconomic proxy have an effect. In the market share regressions there was no evidence of any feedback from return on sales to market share. In total, these results would tend to suggest that this is a stable industry. Little evidence of actual firm competition exists as the firm-specific dummies also show that profitability can persistently differ. The members appear to have relatively settled market shares with little incentive to welcome new members and a cost in seeking to increase market share.

This may be an indication that this is not a competitive industry but more akin to a stable oligopoly

Small companies

What of the rest of the industry? One initial area of concern is that a priori one would expect that most of the remaining firms may not share the similarities in the products that the members of the higher strategic group do and hence do not have the common interests of that class. Indeed, it is often suggested that firms outside the top group are more specialist and concentrate more on niche markets. Yet the statistical analysis indicated that pooling the data was acceptable. This said, the instruments for the IV regressions were rejected, implying that the results may exhibit simultaneity bias.

Despite this concern, the results of the OLS regression with profitability as the dependent variable, revealed a positive relationship with concentration. This suggests that the market situation is different from those previously examined. The inference is that firms could gain from increases in industry density, that is, a shake-out of firms would improve the profit position of surviving firms. Surviving firms can earn and increase profit if competitors are eliminated. Unlike the Top 7, there seems to be potential gains from market power/efficiency. Firm-specific effects reinforced this view, indicating that nearly every firm underperformed compared to Kuoni, the largest company in this group. In contrast, with market share as the dependent variable, only firm-specific effects appear to be present, confirming Kuoni's relative size.

Collectively, the regressions suggested the need to segment the industry, that overall market power/efficiency cannot be detected, particularly in the larger firms, with the results suggestive of oligopoly. Differential profit margins also seem to rule out contestability. Contestability would compete away this position as a result of entry. In contrast, market power/efficiency seems to have a role to play in the small-firm sector of the industry. Elimination of the competition can produce higher profits when viewed at the industry level. It follows that erosion of their relatively distinct markets by the larger players can also affect profitability. In general, the market share equations had better explanatory power than the return on sales equations, which implies that explaining market share is more straightforward than return on sales. The ubiquitous significance of firm-specific factors suggests that market share is heavily influenced by the individual actions firms take. This suggests that the larger companies have the potential to pick off their smaller rivals, if not one another. Such a possibility is implied in the CC reports. It follows that more robust SCP–IO insights are possible when explored appropriately.

Future research

Despite the above discussion, there are some interesting conceptual and methodological issues that need addressing if the SCP–IO analysis of tourism is to advance. One can begin to appreciate these issues by, once again, thinking about the conflicting findings implied in the literature review.

In many respects, the general lack of econometric endeavour can be seen to repeat a fallacy of 'misplaced concreteness' identified by Machlup (1946), in the first 'tests' of the models now commonplace in the SCP–IO literature.[8] These tests became part of what was known as the 'marginalist controversy', which, among other issues, involved a methodological discussion over the use of descriptive case-study evidence to test the assumptions of optimising models of pricing and competition. As discussed in the third section, moves were made to generate a more inductive approach to economic theory and this prompted many early case-study investigations into pricing and competition. Work by Hall and Hitch, and Andrews, noted earlier, implied that firms did not literally identify and equate marginal revenues and costs to (attempt to) maximise short-run profits as per the SCP–IO literature. They set prices on the basis of a mark-up on average full costs evaluated at a normal level of output. The objective was to stabilise prices to create long-run profits in an uncertain environment by generating goodwill from customers. Consequently, they postulated that prices tended to change more in relation to cost changes than demand changes.

Subsequent investigations, such as Hague (1971), generalised these insights to a consideration of the budgeting process, arguing that this was indicative of 'satisficing' behaviour as opposed to optimising behaviour. This was also evident because firms pursued a multiplicity of goals that often needed to be traded off.[9]

Responses to these arguments were put forward by Machlup (1946) and subsequently Friedman (1953). They reminded researchers that the appropriate test of the relevance of the marginalist theories was the predictions of aggregate firm behaviour at the level of markets and not the processes followed by specific firms in setting prices, that is, examining the implications of the assumptions. The IO literature, as a manifestation of optimising economic behaviour, is, thus, essentially predictive in content and emphasises an instrumentalist orientation (Mair and Miller 1992). Indeed, it seems remarkable that one might expect that 'behaviour' logically postulated to construct predictions of aggregate outcomes in markets will be grounded in firm-specific investigations. In part, of course, this motivated the research discussed in the previous section. As Downward (1994, 1999) argues, however, one need not dismiss the descriptive case-study research in relaxing one's methodological precepts. While the evidence is not the appropriate basis of a test of optimising models, nonetheless as causal narratives the insights need not be ignored. Indeed, Post Keynesian, Behavioural and Institutional economics traditions emphasise such theories in precisely this way.

There are other reasons for this, too. It is increasingly accepted philosophically that quantitative and econometric methods will have difficulty decomposing complex social and economic phenomena. As Downward and Mearman (2002) argue, regression analysis entails an ontological commitment to constant conjunctions of events – subject to a stochastic error.[10]

The above comments might seem somewhat contradictory in the light of the previous discussion of the historical descriptive investigation into the IO theories. There is no contradiction, however. The concern with this method voiced above focused upon the attempt to assess mathematical constructs such as optimising decisions with reference to actual decision-making processes. A more appropriate use of such methods would be to explore and reveal the processes that are actually at work and then link these to the statistically defended predictions of either optimising models or other models. In this respect the combination of methods would address real contexts and causes as well as their general implications.

Of course, what is being argued is the need to triangulate broadly quantitative and qualitative methods.[11] This is not a particularly new argument. For example, as far as economics is concerned, Keynes (1973) put forward a similar approach to inference.[12] In social science, 'grounded theory', for example, associated with Glaser and Strauss (1967), suggests how quantitative and qualitative research can combine in producing theory. Essentially, grounded theory implies that the researcher approaches phenomena of interest with as little a priori contamination as possible to allow core theoretical concepts to emerge. One should then seek to generalise on emerging theories by appeal to a diversity of groups or categories. Such 'theoretical' sampling is conceptually different from 'statistical' sampling wherein pre-existing theoretical concepts and sample designs are involved. More generally, Davies (2003: 14) summarises the literature in the context of tourism noting that tourism research has some history of triangulating quantitative and qualitative investigations. Using Miller and Crabtree's (1994) design possibilities, illustrations are drawn as follows. Archer (1980) suggests both quantitative and intuitive techniques should be used concurrently in forecasting tourism demand. Uysal and Crompton (1985) also suggested concurrent use of qualitative and quantitative tourism demand forecasts to improve accuracy. Stabler (1996) and Stabler and Goodall (1996) use nested approaches within the context of environmental economics. Opperman (1995) uses multiple methods to investigate travel patterns and Seaton (1997) evaluates an eight-day 'Arts fest' using both visitor survey data and unobtrusive observation measures.

However, the triangulation that is being offered here has a more specific interpretation and reflects the ontological discussion above. The argument is that statistical and econometric work can produce empirical descriptions of events, but their causes need to be investigated qualitatively. It is possible to provide different answers to different questions about the same theory, with the same ontological presuppositions (Downward and Mearman 2002). It is argued that such an approach is necessary to refine our understanding of competition. Of particular significance is help in explaining the dynamics of profitability and market share among tourism providers more precisely as well as the role of pricing and marketing as part of the firm-specific influences on behaviour. More qualitative evidence – for example, deriving from descriptive case-study research – will help to draw out the causal process underpinning pricing and competition. With the notable exception of the CC's use of such primary research in to the package tour industry, tourism remains relatively virgin territory empirically.

To illustrate the potential of this approach, it is worth noting some recent results presented in Davies and Downward (2003), who investigated the pricing and marketing organisation and behaviour in 20 UK small-scale package tour companies defined as having a turnover of up to £3 million using interviews and questionnaires. The following main themes emerged from the research, though it is important not to overstate the conclusions drawn from such a small-scale study. In general the results were highly resonant with many early case studies of pricing and competition in manufacturing that pre-dated the SCP–IO paradigm and its methodological emphasis upon prediction. The main themes that come from the work are that prices are set to achieve long-run objectives, typically profit and growth. In order to meet these objectives, prices are set by executives following mark-up procedures based on costs set by tour operators or as a result of short-term contracts with tourism suppliers. This facilitates the promotion of goodwill and meets long-run competition among known rivals. Contingent events may cause unexpected and, indeed, frequent changes in prices. To help to meet these challenges, firms respond by typically changing their non-price marketing activities. The response to changes in prices or marketing efforts from competitors echoed these patterns. Even though these are small companies, they seemed to appreciate who their key rivals were. As well as the obvious rivalry with the larger firms, this suggests a degree of oligopolistic interdependence between the relatively small-scale suppliers as well, either directly or indirectly, in having to meet mutual competition from the larger firms.

This is an interesting finding in that it suggests that oligopoly as a concept is a more general behavioural phenomenon, and is not, in essence, tied to the scale of production *per se* as typically emphasised in the SCP–IO analysis. This accords with an institutionalist approach to economics. Behaviour can only be analysed within the institutional context. This said, it should be noted that early case-study research in economics emphasised oligopolistic interaction. This led Hall and Hitch (1939) to propose the kinked demand curve. Moreover, Andrews (1949) stressed the concern with potential competition, that is, 'contestability' in its modern guise. If this is the case, then the relatively inflexible adjustments of prices and marketing variables is explicable.

In many respects we were somewhat surprised by these results and anticipated less resonance with the previous case-study literature on pricing in manufacturing because, in principle, one was dealing with a different industry involving the provision of services. It is argued that tourism may not be an easily identified specific industry, unlike manufacturing. It has significant differences in both production and consumption consisting of a complex bundle of physical, social and experiential characteristics.[13] Moreover, one might expect more of an 'auction' approach to price setting from a demand-side perspective given that, typically, holidays may be treated more as one-off purchases by consumers as opposed to repeat deals. Yet, on reflection there is probably little difference here with small-scale manufacturers, say, producing bespoke components,[14] and may bring into doubt viewing tourism as differing from conventional industries in this respect. Firm and industry boundaries may not be as clearly defined among tourism suppliers. Nor may they be based on technological substitutability with high degrees of cross-elasticity of supply among homogeneous products. However, in terms of behavioural reaction to the market context, tourism suppliers may be seen as manufacturers.

Interestingly, these results offer a way of accounting for the variations in econometric results noted earlier. Because of the 'structural' emphasis of the IO literature, oligopoly has typically been confined to discussion of the larger firms in markets. By definition, here structural features such as relatively large market shares can figure in econometric work. Of course, for many smaller firms their rivalrous 'segment' is less well defined and difficult to identify in secondary data. However, the behaviour is the same, because it reflects a similar decision-making scenario, but scaled down. The only difference may well be the unknowable feedback from the overall scale of industry demand which sets a capacity for the industry. In this respect for this sector, though behaviour is the same, it is possible for market demand to squeeze out suppliers to raise profits for the remainder in the aggregate. Concentration of the industry rather than specific firms' market share was significant.

Importantly, however, embracing an approach in which the historical causal processes are emphasised seems to suggest that policies may also need to be more fine-tuned. While the CC and the Travelcare (2003) reports clearly seem to have captured aspects of the relationships in terms of the vertical integration of the industry, other potential scenarios are possible. An example, based on the typical public policy ramifications of the SCP–IO literature, can be given to support such an argument. On the basis of the econometric evidence one might argue that the smaller firms have collective opportunities for exploiting consumers if the industry becomes more concentrated and, to the extent that the degree of competition is limited to the smaller firms, this suggests that there may well be opportunities for localised exploitation. Such a possibility has recently been discussed by Waterson (2003) in discussing the problems of search behaviour by consumers as being one aspect of consumer welfare, the other being the traditional focus on the existing choices possible as defined by the extent of current supply. In this hypothetical scenario, supported implicitly by the econometric analysis discussed above, there would be segmentation between the large and small firms, this could be associated with niche markets, but also simply because of the search costs and habits which prevents consumers looking for the 'best deal' as implied in optimising explanations of behaviour.

Conclusion

This chapter has discussed the SCP–IO analysis of tourism by taking the package tour industry as a case study. It argues that from a microeconomic perspective, the supply of tourism can be, and is, understood in terms of the models and concepts developed and refined in the structure conduct and performance paradigm (SCP) and, relatedly, the industrial organisation (IO) literatures. This is demonstrated by, for example, public policy concerns. In critically reviewing the academic literature, however, the chapter indicates that there are serious econometric and methodological shortcomings. By drawing upon our own research it is argued that a more appropriate econometric strategy, combined with insights from more descriptive analysis can be united to produce results that help to provide more robust industry insights. To this extent, it is shown that the authors' own work produces results that seem to accord more readily with those of the CC. Importantly, however, it is also argued that academic primary research can also help to qualify the more formal quantitative analysis required of the SCP–IO literatures. In this respect public policy can be better informed in a manner consistent with the aspirations of the competition authorities.

What is also significant is that economic investigations into tourism supply and especially the nature of interfirm relationships remains underdeveloped territory. As illustrated above, existing academic investigation concentrates mainly on the UK, although some exists for other country studies, as per the literature review. However, in terms of SCP and IO the works forming the basis of this chapter are almost the sum total of investigations. Yet, the approaches championed here are clearly applicable in other contexts. Davies and Downward (1996) and Davies (1998) show that this is the case with the UK hotel industry. Davies (2003) makes the first tentative steps towards generating an integrating framework encompassing an alternative logic of inference, the changing nature of the business environment and linking and bridging mechanisms. All are necessary as an integrating framework is a necessity but also requires an interrelationship between the measures.

This requires refinement of existing approaches together with a broader research methodology. As suggested there, such frameworks will improve our understanding of not just SCP and IO but of the tourism industry. A 'truer analysis' of business behaviour, hotels, tour operators, travel agents and the tourism business will result.

Notes

1. Almost all standard textbooks on tourism start by pointing this out. See, for example, Theobald (1998, part 1). Similarly, organisations such as the World Travel & Tourism Council estimate that tourism is the world's largest industry (WTTC 1996).
2. For a comprehensive survey of methods and articles, see Sinclair and Stabler (1997, chapters 2 and 3).
3. Assuming no externalities and so on. In this discussion we implicitly ignore the concept of producer surplus.
4. The data derive from the 'Financial Analysis Made Easy' package based on company records lodged at Companies' House, London.
5. See Davies and Downward (1996) for an application of this approach elsewhere.
6. This approach is consistent with the two broad strategies that econometricians have, in general, adopted in IO work elsewhere. One strategy has been to embrace a non-structural role for econometrics. Schmalensee (1989) emphasises the role of econometrics in identifying 'stylised facts' leading to robust correlations between simultaneous variables. The other strategy has been to re-embrace structural identification. Bresnahan (1989) suggests that the identification of structural parameters is possible by employing micro data to explore an industry's characteristics more specifically. A synthesis of these approaches was thus employed to look for robust correlations as per Schmalensee's hypothesis and to explore the data for inference about various industry characteristics, as per Bresnahan.
7. Davies (1998) conducted similar work on hotels.
8. The 'misplaced concreteness' here concerns the theory of the firm. The theory of the firm is incorrectly titled and ought to be the theory of the market. The theory is concerned with what happens in the aggregate in the market. Any assessment should be about the market and not firms.
9. Satisficing as a concept had been originally presented by the behavioural economist Simon (1952) to indicate that in contexts of uncertainty, and bounded rationality, when agents lack the computational power required to optimise, decision makers focused upon achieving adequate values of objectives.
10. Thus regressions break down variation in data into two categories. One category is argued to be relatively invariant. The other is random variation. In the former case it is clear that the underlying structure of the subject matter needs to persist to obtain robust descriptions. In the latter case, using inferences made statistically, it is assumed that the

world (at least partially) comprises unconnected individual drawings from a probability distribution. Of course, this is why statistical methods are employed. The problem with this characterisation is that in a non-experimental realm, and particularly one in which innovational human agency is involved, it is problematic to assume that structures do not change and evolve. Such is the case in tourism, which, due to the volatility in tourism demand created by such as the seeking of novelty, changes in fashion the need to offer new experiences and destinations and the nature of competition and cost structures, operates as a living organism creating and responding constantly to dynamic changes in both external and internal influences.

On the other hand, even if one believes that there are relatively enduring features of the world, the approach maintains that there is a fundamental randomness that contaminates all phenomena. To an extent there is an ontological paradox in juxtaposing structures and randomness. This is, of course, a problem if one uses nothing but statistical analysis as a basis of offering inferences. An alternative would be to argue that, in fact, the world is a structured open system in which all phenomena are causally linked. Complexity rather than randomness thus creates problems of predicting and decomposing phenomena. In this sense statistical analysis can be embraced in a partially instrumentalist fashion as a form of proxy for complexity. This might be useful for offering predictions as part of an understanding of the underlying structures. Yet, one can still recognise that complexity will affect the ability to predict. The corollary, of course, is that understanding real causes is needed to help to instigate and thus be integrated into the quantitative and econometric analysis. It is here that qualitative analysis is required. This argument draws upon a critical-realist philosophical position as discussed in Downward and Mearman (2002).

11.   One of the earliest references to triangulation is in Campbell and Fiske (1959) in psychology. The notion is essentially taken from mapping in which measurements taken from two or more points provide a more accurate source of navigation.

12.   To avoid the problem of induction, relevant evidence was obtained through a process of 'negative analogy'. Keynes argued that one should examine a particular phenomenon in different contexts. If a phenomenon appears to be a common element between various contexts then it is this commonality that indicates the relevance of a particular phenomenon, which adds weight to a particular account of that phenomenon. These arguments were part of a broader philosophical discussion of probabilities which were, in general, not simply 'objective numerical' features of the world, but a qualitative, possibly numerical, expression of rational belief.

13.   See Davies (2003).

14.   It should be emphasised at this point that while the case-study work into manufacturing referred to above does not specifically address small-scale firms, in general the literature finds little difference in behaviour. Studies such as Haynes (1962) and Hankinson (1985) are specific examples of such research. Indeed, Lee (1998) provides a large summary of the work done from which the interested reader can identify research into smaller firms.

References

Aguilo, P.M., J. Alegre and A. Riera (2001), 'Determinants of the price of German tourist packages on the island of Mallorca', *Tourism Economics*, **7** (1), 59–74.

Aguilo, E., J. Alegre and M. Sard (2003), 'Examining the market structure of the German and UK tour operating industries through an analysis of package holiday process', *Tourism Economics*, **9** (3), 255–78.

Allin, P. (2005), 'Understanding national statistics', in P.M. Downward and L. Lumsdon (eds), *Essential Data Skills for Leisure and Tourism Management: A Guide to Using Official Statistics*, Office for National Statistics.

Andrews, P.W.S. (1949), *Manufacturing Business*, London: Macmillan.

Archer, B. (1980), 'Forecasting demand – quantitative and intuitive techniques', *International Journal of Tourism Management*, **1** (1), 5–12.

Bain, E. (1956), *Barriers to New Competition*, Cambridge, MA: Harvard University Press.

Baum, T. and R. Mudambi (1994), 'A Ricardian analysis of the fully inclusive tour industry', *Services Industries Journal*, **14** (1), 85–93.

Baum, T. and R. Mudambi (1995), 'An empirical analysis of oligopolistic hotel pricing', *Annals of Tourism Research*, **22** (3), 501–16.

Baumol, W.J., J.C. Panzar and D.R. Willig (1982), *Contestable Markets and the Theory of Industrial Structure*, New York: Harcourt Brace.

Bresnahan, T.F. (1989), 'Duopoly models with consistent conjectures', *American Economic Review*, **71**, 934–45.

British Tourist Authority Marketing Intelligence Department (2003), *Tourism Trend update*, http://www.tourismtrade.org.uk/MarketIntelligenceResearch.

Campbell, D.T. and D.W. Fiske (1959), Convergent and Discriminant Validity by the Multi-trait Multi-method Matrix, *Psychological Bulletin*, **56**, 81–105.

Chamberlin, E. (1965), *The Theory of Monopolistic Competition*, Cambridge MA: Harvard University Press.

Clewer, A., A. Pack and M.T. Sinclair (1994), 'Price competitiveness and inclusive tour holidays in European cities', in P. Johnson and B. Thomas (eds), *Choice and Demand in Tourism*, London: Mansell, 123–8.

Competition Commission (1997), *Foreign Package Holidays: A report on the supply in the UK of tour operators' services and travel agents' services in relation to foreign package holidays*, London: HMSO, Cm 3813.

Davies, B. (1998), 'Industrial organisation: the UK hotel industry', *Annals of Tourism Research*, **25** (4), 294–311.

Davies, B. (2003), 'The role of quantitative and qualitative research in industrial studies of tourism', *International Journal of Tourism Research*, **5**, 1–15.

Davies, B. and P. Downward (1996), 'The structure, conduct, performance paradigm as applied to the UK hotel industry', *Tourism Economics*, **2** (2), 151–8.

Davies, B. and P. Downward (1998), 'Competition and contestability in the UK package tour industry: some empirical observations', *Tourism Economics,* **4** (3), 241–51.

Davies, B. and P. Downward (2001), 'Industrial organisation and competition in the UK tour operator/travel agency business, 1989–93: an econometric investigation', *Journal of Travel Research*, **39** (4), 411–25.

Davies, B. and P. Downward (2003), 'Exploring competition in the package tour industry: insights from small scale travel agents and tour operators', Staffordshire University, Division of Economics Working Paper 2.

Demsetz, H. (1974), 'Two systems of beliefs about monopoly', in H.J. Goldshmidt, H.M. Mann and J.F. Weston (eds), *Industrial Concentration*, Cambridge, MA: The New Learning MIT Press, 164–84.

Downward, P.M. (1994), 'A reappraisal of case-study evidence on business pricing: a comparison of neoclassical and post Keynesian perspectives', *British Review of Economic Issues*, **16** (39), 23–43.

Downward, P.M. (1999), *Pricing Theory in Post Keynesian Economics*, Cheltenham, UK and Northampton, MA, USA: Edward Elgar.

Downward P.M. and L. Lumsdon (eds) (2005), *Essential Data Skills for Leisure and Tourism Management: A Guide to Using Official Statistics*, Office for National Statistics.

Downward, P.M. and A. Mearman (2002), 'Critical realism and econometrics: constructive dialogue with Post Keynesian economics', *Metroeconomica*, **53** (4), 391–415.

Evans, N. and M. Stabler (1995), 'A future for the package tour operator in the 21st century?', *Tourism Economics*, **1** (3), 245–63.

Fitch, A. (1987), 'Tour operators in the UK: survey of the industry, its markets and product diversification', *Travel and Tourism Analyst*, March, 29–43.

Friedman, M. (1953), 'The methodology of positive economics', in *Essays in Positive Economics*, Chicago: Chicago University Press.

Gauf, D. and H. Hughes (1998), 'Diversification and German tour operators: the case of TUI and coach tourism', *Tourism Economics*, **4** (4), 325–37.

Glaser, B.G. and A.L. Strauss (1967), *The Discovery of Grounded Theory: Strategies for Qualitative Research*, Chicago: Aldine.

Granger, C.W.J. (1969), 'Investigating causal relations by econometric models and cross spectral methods', *Econometrica*, **37** (3), 424–38.

Gratton, C. and G. Richards (1997), 'Structural change in the European package tour industry: UK/German comparisons', *Tourism Economics*, **3** (3), 213–26.

Hague, D.C. (1971), *Pricing in Business*, London: George Allen & Unwin.

Hall, R.F. and C.J. Hitch (1939), 'Price theory and business behaviour', *Oxford Economic Papers*, **2**, 13–33.

Hankinson, A. (1985), *A Study of Pricing Behaviour of Dorset–Hampshire Small Engineering Firms*, Dorset Institute of Higher Education, unpublished.

Haynes, W.W. (1962), *Pricing Decisions in Small Business*, Lexington, KY: University of Kentucky Press.

Keynes, J.M. (1973), *Treaties on Probability, Volume VIII: The Collected Writings of John Maynard Keynes*, London: Macmillan.

Lee, F.S. (1998), *The Foundations of Post Keynesian Price Theory*, Cambridge: Cambridge University Press.

Machlup, F. (1946), 'Marginal analysis and empirical research', *American Economic Review*, **36**, 112–47.

Mair, D. and A. Miller (eds) (1992), *A Modern Guide to Economic Thought*, Aldershot, UK and Brookfield, US: Edward Elgar.

Mason, E.S. (1939), 'Price and production policies of large scale enterprises', *American Economic Review*, **29**, 61–74.

Miller, W.L. and B.F. Crabtree (1994), 'Clinical research', in N.K. Denzin and Y. Lincoln (eds), *Handbook of Qualitative Research*, Thousand Oaks, CA: Sage, 607–31.

Monopolies and Mergers Commission (1986), *Foreign Package Holidays*, London: HMSO.

Monopolies and Mergers Commission (1989), *Thomson Travel Group and Horizon Travel Ltd*, London: HMSO.

Opperman, M. (1995), 'Multitemporal perspective of changing travel patterns', *Journal of Travel and Tourism Marketing*, **4** (3), 101–9.

Pastor, V.J. (1999), 'Un analisis de los prices hoteleros empleando funciones hedonicas', *Estudios Turisticos*, **139**, 65–87.

Robinson, J. (1933), *The Economics of Imperfect Competition*, London: Macmillan.

Schmalensee, R. (1989), 'Inter industry studies of structure and performance', in R Schmalensee and R.D. Willig (eds), *Handbook of Industrial Organisation*, Amsterdam: North-Holland, 951–1008.

Seaton, A.V. (1997), 'Unobtrusive observational measures as a quality extension of visitor surveys at festivals and events: mass observation revisited', *Journal of Travel Research*, **35** (4), 25–30.

Sheldon, P.J. (1986), 'The tour operator industry an analysis', *Annals of Tourism*, **13**, 349–65.

Shubik, M. (1959), *Strategy and Market Structure*, London: Wiley.

Simon, H.A. (1952), 'A behavioural model of rational choice', *Quarterly Journal of Economics*, **69**, 99–118.

Sinclair, M.T., A. Clewer and A. Pack (1990), 'Hedonic prices and the marketing of package holidays: the case of tourism resorts in Malaga', in G.J. Ashworth and B. Goodall (eds), *Marketing Tourism Places*, London: Routledge, 85–103.

Sinclair, M.T. and M. Stabler (1997), *The Economics of Tourism*, London: Routledge.

Stabler, M. (1996), 'The emerging new world of leisure quality: does it matter and can it be measured?', in M. Collins (ed.), *The Third International Conference of the Leisure Studies Association*, **49**, Brighton: LSA, 32–54.

Stabler, M. and B. Goodall (1996), 'Environmental auditing in planning for sustainable island tourism', in L. Briguglio, R. Butler, D. Harrison and W.L. Filho (eds), *Sustainable Tourism in Islands and Small States: Issues and Policies*, London: Pinter, 170–96.

Taylor, P. (1996), 'Oligopoly or contestable markets in the UK package tour industry?', *The Service Industries Journal*, **16** (3), 379–88.

Taylor, P. (1998), 'Mixed strategy pricing in the UK package tour industry', *International Journal of the Economics of Business*, **5** (1), 29–46.

Theobald, W. (1998), *Global Tourism*, Oxford: Butterworth-Heineman.

Travelcare (2003), 'Holiday 2003 Report', Manchester.
Uysal, M. and J.L. Crompton (1985), 'An overview of approaches used to forecast tourism demand', *Journal of Travel Research*, **23**, 7–14.
van Dijk, J.C. and D.D. van der Stelt-Steele (1993), 'Price formation in industry tourism branches', *Annals of Tourism Research*, **20**, 716–28.
von Neumann, J. and O. Morgenstern (1944), *Theory of Games and Economic Behaviour*, Princeton, NJ: Princeton University Press.
Waterson, M. (2003), 'The role of consumers in competition and competition policy', *International Journal of Industrial Organisation*, **21**, 129–50.
Williamson, O.E. (1975), *Markets and Hierarchies: Analysis and Antitrust Implications: A Study in the Economics of Internal Organisation*, New York: Free Press.
World Tourism Organisation (WTO) (2000), 'A strategic project for the World Tourism Organisation', report by the General Secretary: The Tourism Satellite Account (TSA) CE 63-64/4 Add. 1, www.world tourism.org/statistics/tsa_project/TSA_STRATEGIC_PROJECT.pdf.
World Travel and Tourism Council (1996), *Progress and Priorities*, Brussels: WTTC.

5 Industrial economics and pricing issues within tourism enterprises and markets

Adrian O. Bull

Importance of the issue

The conventional view in economics that a product is a scarce good or service, and represents an output resulting from a production process, provides a starting definition for much of tourism. However, such a definition does not provide an adequate description of what constitutes a product from a consumer needs perspective, or an adequate specification of the boundaries of a commodity class. In perfect competition, perfect homogeneity among a number of products automatically defines a commodity class, a market and an industry. In other cases, the boundaries of a commodity class may be defined in theory by reference to the degree of substitutability between objects, but the less substitutable products are, the fuzzier the commodity class boundaries become. Tourism involves a huge range of products, only some of which are substitutable, and therefore the 'market' for tourism is in fact fragmented into markets for many products (Leiper 1995: 18–19).

Nonetheless, there may be some substitutability between different classes of tourism product; for example, a tourist may trade off expenditure for a poorer class of travel for better accommodation, or vice versa. The degree of substitutability and the cohesiveness of the purchasing group, determine the nature of the market structure within which tourism enterprises operate.

Additionally, the tourism experience (product) involves a range of characteristics that may cause problems for a classical analysis of industrial economics and markets within tourism. Pine and Gilmore (1999) note the characteristics of intangibility, heterogeneity, a shared experience, simultaneous production and consumption, perishability, high fixed or sunk costs and cyclical demand. To those we may add that there are often fixed capacity constraints and multiple market segments with different elasticities of demand.

Suppliers of tourism products face a range of market conditions where it is possible to question and challenge the assumptions of neoclassical economic analysis on market structure and supplier behaviour, particularly with reference to pricing. A more useful analysis requires further insight into these market conditions.

Overview of main themes
The main themes that concern analysts within this field are:

- definitions of tourism markets;
- structures of these markets;
- competitive and pricing strategy; and
- market performance and conduct.

Tourism market definitions
In many ways, tourism markets are unusual: the boundary of a market may or may not relate to where consumers actually purchase products, market jurisdiction and policy may reside within a completely different country or region from that where consumer protection may be needed, and often product definitions themselves are exceptionally fuzzy.

Tourism market structures
Given the degree of personal experience encapsulated within a tourist trip (that is, the consumer actually contributes to production), it is almost impossible to envisage a market of perfect competition for tourism products. Is the importance of a market structure then dependent on contestability, concentration or other factors? In many local areas, countries and international situations, there may be a few large suppliers – and there may be barriers to entry into the 'club' of large suppliers – but there may also be a number of smaller enterprises surviving alongside, perhaps in the hotel sector, travel or transport, or tourist attractions. Does this constitute oligopoly or merely imperfect competition?

Competitive and pricing strategy
Classical economic theory predicts a range of supplier strategies relating to output, price and other responses to competitors. It is important to review the extent to which theory is actually useful within the special case of tourism through a discussion of both the empirical literature and an analysis of the reasons why theory may fail to predict accurately within the tourism sector.

Market performance and conduct
Industrial organisation within tourism, its relationship with structure, performance, conduct models and its implications for policy are a main theme within this area of study. However, they are not dealt with here since they form the subject of another chapter within this handbook.

Critical evaluation of existing literature
The discussion and evaluation of literature in the topic area is divided here
into sections relating to the same themes noted above. Where necessary, the
discussion incorporates elements of theoretical material that relate strongly
to the industrial economics of tourism sectors.

Definitions of tourism markets
Until recently little attention has been paid to the definitions of tourism
markets. There is an inherent problem in tourism that a single definition
under theoretical substitutability paradigms (see, for example, Brooks
1995) cannot apply across the board. Tourism products including accommodation and tourist attractions are an example of place-sensitive products (Bull 1998) with spatial fixity, where not only must the purchaser travel
to the point of supply, but also the location is an integral characteristic of
the product supplied. With differentiated products, the notion of what constitutes an individual and specific market may be problematical. Any two
or more products are usually considered to be of the same generic commodity class if there is a reasonably high level of substitutability between
them, which may be measured by a positive cross-price elasticity of
demand. However, there is no clear definition of the degree of substitutability (or of a specific value of cross-price elasticity) necessary to determine the cut-off point for products to be classified as being within the same
market. This lack of definition results in considerable legal argument in
antitrust law cases (Watson 1977).

The boundaries of a market may be 'defined' qualitatively by recognition
among producers, and among consumers, that the products traded are per-
forming essentially the same function, or possess some basic homogeneous
characteristics. This implies, for tourists, that there is some determination
of indifference between products based on these characteristics. In the long
run this may lead to an identifiable price nexus among products, although
in the short run the differentiating characteristics between products and the
way they are marketed may produce price and demand variations which
suggest that products are not really in the same market at all (Dilley 1992).
Within any one market, the level of homogeneous characteristics should be
such as to create substitutability on both the supply and the demand sides
(Carlton and Perloff 1990: 739). In supply terms this implies that both the
production function and the cohesiveness of the marketplace constrain the
pricing of products.

A market may be bounded within a geographic area (Watson 1977). As
location theory shows in terms of supply, production costs and methods may
differ greatly from one area to another. Alternatively, transport costs may be
so high as to constrain supply areas (Isard 1956). In terms of demand,

transaction costs and poorer consumer information about more spatially remote alternatives act as constraints limiting demand to a specific geographical area. In addition, governments may impose trading regulations that bound markets. This is the case, for example, in China where outbound tourism is constrained to government-approved operators and destinations.

In the case of tourism services, the property of non-storability often means that markets in different locations are essentially separated (Holmstrom 1985), and that access to those services determines the boundaries of each market. Ultimate markets for tourism attractions or destinations are geographically bounded in both supply and demand in terms of basic locational characteristics, which are both an input to and a component of the product.

'The market' in one sense is therefore the destination area or areas within which purchasers regard tourism activities as substitutable. (This was the view taken, for example, by the Australian Competition and Consumer Commission (ACCC) in Australia regarding joint operations by Qantas/BA and Air Alliance [Australian Trade Practices Report (ATPR) [CCH] 50-184 (1995) and ATPR [CCH] 50-265 (1998)].) In selecting tourism destination products, consumers are clearly not indifferent between products in totally different geographical areas. The extent of a geographical tourist area or destination within which there is a high level of substitutability between products is limited by consumers' perceptions, image and access (Smith 1989: 178–86). This determination of what constitutes a tourism market area is a particular case of the general notion that markets involving a set of contact points between buyers and sellers are often primarily geographically bounded (Watson 1977). Smith (1989: 163) notes that any distinct tourism market area is one which is perceived as internally homogeneous in terms of tourism image. Places outside this area are perceived differently and so constitute different tourism markets.

Goodall (1991) and Stabler (1991) find that consumers of tourism services make a choice of product from within specific sets of choices. Goodall shows, through the behavioural theory of opportunity sets, that consumers would consider only services of the same type, within the same area, and offering the same general characteristics, as being members of a single decision set (or marketplace) from which to make a purchase. Sets are held to be place specific. Stabler suggests that both consumers and producers operate within limited opportunity sets, which form a hierarchy, although they do not necessarily involve sequential choice. For a consumer, the type of holiday required may be at the highest level of the hierarchy, followed by type of destination, what is attainable, and then a specific set of choices of accommodation and other tourism products within that smaller attainable set. Different consumer groups have different attainable sets, by destination and by type of product. This behavioural work reinforces the concept of a destination area as a boundary to each tourism market.

Within a destination city or region, the number of tourism suppliers is likely to be related to the range and importance of key tourist attractions for recreational tourism, and the destination's commercial importance for business tourism. Clearly, a small destination offering some unique property such as a production plant that business people from elsewhere come to visit may possess only one or two hotels. A large destination city or homogeneous destination region may have a large range of attractions, accommodation, local tours and support services. Unless a destination consists of an entire, very small, country, however, the literature cited suggests that direct competition is not nationwide (Slattery 1994).

However, the market for travel and transport products differs in that it relates to an area within which substitutability is possible for a group of potential consumers at the point where they live (the tourist-generating market). Researchers agree that for tourism products there are: (i) a generating market area, (ii) an intermediate or travel zone and (iii) a destination area, which are geographically separate and cognate (see, for example, Leiper 1995). Products such as travel, travel arrangements, inclusive tours and travel insurance are related geographically to areas (i) or (ii) and are clearly sold in a specific area of type (i). However, destination *tourism* products, including accommodation and attractions, normally involve suppliers in area (iii) and may be on sale to several areas of type (i). The global perspective on the competitive consequences is partly summarised by Souty (2003).

Additionally, markets in tourism have historically been considered imperfect, owing to asymmetric market information that leaves consumers (tourists) generally less well informed about products and prices than suppliers, especially within destinations. A feature of tourism is that consumers must travel to the location of the product in order to consume. It is therefore likely, particularly if the consumer has to travel for some distance to reach the product, that the nature and quality of the product cannot be determined by consumers by inspection prior to purchase, and such products are therefore experience (or in some cases, credence) products rather than search products (Gilbert 1991). That is to say, experience products (such as tourism products) cannot be demonstrated to consumers, and their nature is known to consumers only through any prior experience or by description. The physical remoteness of many consumers from the product up to the point of purchase may result in imperfect market information on the demand side, whereas suppliers (particularly in oligopoly) are likely to have much better information about their competitors and their products. Market information is likely to be asymmetric.

One of the most significant implications of asymmetric market information is held to be market failure caused by the adverse selection of low-quality (known) products in preference to those of (unknown) high quality (Akerlof 1970). Akerlof also finds that since buyers may have a greater expectation that experience products may be of low rather than high quality, there is downward pressure on market prices and quality.

Under these conditions, should the suppliers of differentiated products wish to establish positive price differentials to represent the presence of particular characteristics, they need to convey market signals (Spence 1974) to consumers. Signalling involves an objective identification of quality and/or other characteristics, and the communication of that information to consumers. Tourism suppliers are able to use their reputation as a market signal only to repeat consumers; for operators of chains the signal of standardisation can only apply to those product characteristics which are replicable at every location, and clearly cannot apply to every outlet. Some of the most important signals in this type of market are objectively compiled guides offering ratings and full product descriptions. Gitelson and Crompton (1983) and Goodall (1991), for example, note the importance of government information, ratings organisations and objective guide books in providing consumer information about destination products to prospective tourists.

Objective ratings systems not only provide market signalling, but also help to delimit the boundaries of markets themselves by specifying the quality and other characteristics by which products may or may not be held to be substitutes.

Structures of tourism markets
Since tourism products are largely real-time services directed at people, it follows that the ability to on-sell and create secondary markets is limited. Furthermore, since most products are experience rather than search products, it follows that factors conducive to perfect competition are missing, and most suppliers are likely to use product differentiation and personalisation as a strategic tool.

It is possible that a supplier of a tourism product may be a monopoly, that is, the sole producer of a product with no close substitutes. For example, a unique tourist attraction such as the Eiffel Tower in Paris has no direct substitutes. However, most tourism products consist of a set of characteristics, some of which are unique (such as location), and some of which may not be unique. These products will only be monopoly products if the unique characteristic is the major, and perhaps sole, determinant of consumer choice (Lancaster 1971), and if the market can only support a single producer. If the unique characteristic is not the only determinant of choice, then some substitutability between products is possible, and the appropriate model of market structure is some form of imperfect competition. This includes monopolistic competition and oligopoly.

If there is a positive, but not infinite, cross-price elasticity of demand between products in a marketplace, then the structure of that market is one of monopolistic competition or oligopoly. A monopolistically competitive market has many firms, and no restriction on entry. Despite similarity in the basic characteristics or performance of products, each firm sells a version of the product that is differentiated from others. Differentiation may be vertical, horizontal, or both. The formal properties of a monopolistically competitive market are discussed by Chamberlin (1933):

- each firm faces a downward-sloping demand curve;
- each firm makes no long-run profit, since any profits earned in the short run make the industry attractive to new entrants, causing a loss of market share and a downward shift in the demand curve of each incumbent; and
- a price change for product i has only a limited effect on the demand for product j.

In tourism particularly, where market information relies on experience or communication, one property of monopolistic competition which continues to receive attention is the role of advertising in reinforcing, or even in creating, product differentiation. Schmalensee (1986), for example, notes that advertising may on the one hand provide information or market signalling about products, fostering competition and encouraging vertical differentiation through the revelation of quality in the advertising. On the other hand, advertising is perceived as creating artificial differentiation through persuasive means, reducing competition and forming a barrier to entry.

Full monopolistic competition implies contestability (Baumol et al. 1982) where it is possible for any number of firms to operate sustainably. Free entry to and exit from the market will allow the possibility of a large number of firms being present. Sinclair and Stabler (1997: 61) find that sunk costs are insignificant in tourism, yet for tourist attractions, hotels and airports, specific location involves a sunk cost which is incurred at the investment stage in developing production at that location. This may constitute an entry deterrent to other firms. Since one firm 'controls' the locational input, it may be seen as a contrived barrier to entry. Specific location is also an input which may produce a non-replicable product characteristic, or at best may only be replicable at considerable cost. (For example, a resort offering downhill skiing may have prime snow and good slopes, which are replicable elsewhere by grading and artificial snow-making machines, but its specific mountain view is not replicable.) Therefore, it is likely that there will be few (geographical) locations that will be good substitutes for each other in any market. Markets thus become subdivided in the same way that any markets for highly-differentiated products do, and where consumers, seeking to maximise individual utility, have different preferred sets of product characteristics. Eaton and Lipsey (1989: 750) describe this effect: 'the location of existing goods and products balkanizes the market into a number of over-lapping submarkets. As a result competition is localized – each good only has a few neighbouring goods with which it competes directly, regardless of the number of goods serving the entire market'. This situation has been termed 'natural oligopoly' (ibid.), and is seen very commonly within tourism destinations.

The structure of imperfect competition is very common among travel and tourism markets, especially where there are many small enterprises (Bull 1995). A key differentiator is the style and level of service. Service as an attribute – and product input – can be cheaply and easily varied so that the marginal revenue obtained from extra service (or a different style) will exceed the marginal cost of providing it. One important consequence of this concern with service, however, is that there may only be limited needs for expansion and amalgamations of businesses, since expansion in service is less likely to provide economies of scale than expansion in technical pro-duction of goods. Many travel and tourism businesses in monopolistic competition therefore remain small.

Barriers to entry exist in a range of tourism sectors. In addition to the spatial fixity of place-sensitive products, there are licensing regimes such as those for travel agencies, heavy investment costs in some sectors such as ocean cruising or convention centres, and the prospect of predatory pricing by existing suppliers. Together with the limited boundaries of many tourism markets, these create the conditions for local, or sometimes national, oligo-polies. Oligopolies within tourism have been shown generally to operate with high levels of product differentiation (Bull 1995) owing to the ease of changing service product attributes, both real and perceived.

There are a number of models of oligopoly that allow for product differentiation with regard to more than one attribute. These include, for example, that of the 'chain market' of Chamberlin (1933), which restricts the cross-price effects on demand for the (differentiated) product of firm i to the price changes of a limited number of other firms. A common feature of concern among these models of multiple-differentiated oligopoly is whether firms generally operate under a Cournot- or Bertrand-type system. This question has significance for both the long- and short-run operation of markets for tourism products.

The conjectural variation model of oligopoly originally proposed by Cournot (1838) is a single-period model in which prices are assumed to be unvarying, and each firm then sets a profit-maximising output for itself while assuming that other firms do not change their output levels. Market equilibrium occurs when, holding the strategies of all other firms constant, no firm can obtain a higher profit by selecting a different output. Such an equilibrium is termed a 'Nash equilibrium', after Nash (1951). Cournot's original model refers to static analysis with homogeneous products, but the principle of selecting output levels as decision variables can be, and has often been, applied to other situations. This is notwithstanding the fact that the contradictions of conjectural variations models mean that game-theoretic approaches are now almost universal instead; Cournot is still important for modelling the existence of equilibrium and the choice of a decision variable.

The critique of Cournot made by Bertrand (1883) argues that there needs to be a more explicit mechanism to determine oligopolists' prices. Bertrand's own model suggests that firms set prices, rather than output quantities, as a strategic variable. It assumes that products are homogeneous and each firm sets a price, while other firms continue to charge whatever prices they have already set. The model shows that a Nash equilibrium in prices is attained when price equals marginal cost, since (as in perfect competition) no firm can make any profit by reducing price below marginal cost, and will lose its market share to its rivals if it seeks to raise its price. Output, revenue and profit become a discontinuous function of price. This situation, which is rarely found empirically, is less of a problem for the Bertrand model if products are differentiated, since an equilibrium may exist with differing prices, above marginal cost, to reflect product heterogeneity (Shapiro 1989).

Many tourism producers are also faced with a capacity constraint. Airlines and other transport providers operate with the physical constraints of loading capacity, as do hotels and other accommodation providers with occupancy limits. A recreational amenity may possess a technical or authorised carrying capacity, which represents an output constraint. Under this condition, any one firm selling at marginal cost may not be able to satisfy all market demand, and hence other firms may be able to find buyers at higher prices than the first firm. Edgeworth (1897) and (1925) shows that capacity constraints on a Bertrand model can prevent a simple stable equilibrium from being achieved, although a long-run equilibrium is possible in a large market (Allen and Hellwig 1986).

With differentiated products and capacity constraints, it can be shown that Cournot and Bertrand–Edgeworth models produce similar solutions (Shapiro 1989), and that the choice of model to represent differentiated oligopoly depends on how easily firms in an individual industry can vary either output or price in practice. Shapiro suggests that the choice of model would reflect the technology of production and exchange within an industry (Shapiro 1989: 351). With this in mind, at the development and entry stage of an industry sector supplying tourism products, decision making is likely to be Cournot-type, representing competition to set output levels and install sunk productive capacity. Once capacity exists, prices become the strategic variable, denoting Bertrand–Edgeworth-type decision making. This two-stage approach is typical of sunk-cost models (Schmalensee 1992). The concentration on price as a strategic variable is enhanced since tourism products are mostly services which are non-storable and perishable, so that producers must adjust prices to influence demand or be left with useless output (Carlton and Perloff 1990: 274). An example of this type of decision making in practice is shown by Chung (2000) in a longitudinal study of luxury hotels in Korea. Chung shows that the sector does not attain a Nash equilibrium, but individual suppliers follow a monopolistic pricing strategy.

Competition issues, and competitive and pricing strategy
Within either an imperfectly competitive or an oligopolistic market, tourism suppliers are likely to place a major dependence on product differentiation and price as strategic variables. This is especially true for those suppliers whose capacities are constrained and who are therefore limited in their selection of levels of output. As a result, the generic strategy framework based on Porter (1980) is commonly used as an analytical tool in the tourism field. Evans et al. (2003) note its acceptance and provide a number of examples within tourism (p. 213) despite criticisms of the framework by Poon (1993) and others. The framework broadly suggests that on the market side there are three generic strategies (excluding hybrids):

● low cost and price leadership;
● product differentiation, including quality differentiation; and
● focusing on a specific niche market.

The first of these strategies requires a supplier to identify costs accurately, to assess and utilise any available production advantages, and to have some knowledge of competitors' likely response strategies and their impact. Within the low-cost airlines sector, some suppliers have attempted to gain very low cost and low price leadership, such as Southwest Airlines and Ryanair (Calder 2002; Gillen and Morrison 2003). Attempts are made to reduce costs at all points, and if necessary to unbundle products, such as separating out a charge for carrying baggage in an aircraft hold, in order to reduce the perceived main price of the core product. This corresponds with Bertrand–Edgeworth type decision making within an oligopolistic market.

The second strategy is relatively easy to achieve within tourism with its experience-product nature and emphasis on services. Product differentiation creates a degree of monopolisation, reduces price elasticity of demand and creates repeat business, especially when allied with branding, through customer loyalty. The main requirement for a supplier is only to be able to identify the marginal cost of any differentiating product attribute, and to ensure that the marginal revenue obtained from its inclusion exceeds this cost. Throughout all tourism sectors, product differentiation is used extensively and provides a major platform for the construction of marketing programmes.

In the case of capacity-constrained tourism services, differentiation within a supplier's product, as well as from others' products, can provide the basis for price discrimination, where one or more of the sub-products created is a partial monopoly. It is now readily accepted that lead booking times for travel and accommodation are an attribute upon which differentiation can be based, and price elasticity of demand can vary widely for different sub-products thus created. Yield management systems can then operationalise pricing and are used extensively across many areas of tourism; see, for example, Relihan (1989) on hotels, Carroll and Grimes (1995) on car rentals, Doganis (2001) on air travel and Perdue (2002) on ski resorts.

Focusing on a niche market implies an inward attention that aligns a supplier's competences with the needs of a known and specific market segment. It is particularly appropriate for smaller enterprises that may well exist for some other business objective than formal profit maximisation (Bull 1995: 57–8) such as entrepreneurs with a 'hobby' interest in an area of special interest tourism. While they may effectively be operating within a structure of imperfect competition, they may have little interest in the activities of other suppliers and no real understanding of profit maximisation strategy.

Empirical examples can be found of all of these strategies. Wu (2004) finds that travel businesses in Taiwan, operating in an imperfectly competitive market, tend to use one of three main strategies: focus on their own customer needs (ignoring competition), product differentiation, or low cost and low price, effectively covering all of the potential Porter strategies. In an attempt to model the industrial organisation of the hotel industry in the UK, Davies (1999) likewise finds a diversity of strategies that not only suggest that the market is neither oligopolistic nor contestable but also cast doubt on the axioms of neoclassical market structure theory. However, once again an important factor is that many firms appear not to be classic profit maximisers but use market share as their key strategic variable. This is echoed by Skalpe (2003) in a study of the Norwegian hospitality industry, where expected strategies to relate business risk and return are rare, owing to the common objective of personal non-profit incentives and 'concealing performance': 'hotels and restaurants provide excellent opportunities for integrating personal lifestyle and household expenses into the business' (Skalpe 2003: 632).

In the American ski resort sector, Perdue (2002) finds that under oligopolistic market conditions, suppliers operate with a price leadership/follower strategy, following the lead of one of the major resorts that is likely to have set its quantity (capacity) for the season and then applies yield management systems to manage demand. Baum and Mudambi (1995) find that with inflexible supply and volatile demand in the Bermuda resort hotel market, suppliers both differentiate heavily and use 'withholding' strategies to reduce supply in off-peak periods, thus avoiding drastic price cutting that might result from a Ricardian approach to competition that would bid marginal prices of unused stock (hotel rooms) down to zero.

Strategies of integration, whether by means of full takeover or strategic alliances such as in the global airline sector, have increased the market power of (especially horizontally) integrated suppliers, and raised barriers to entry. Whether they have reduced competition, as might theoretically be expected, or increased it by opening up new tourism markets and enhancing the economics of density (Wang et al. 2004) seems to vary from sector to sector.

As different sectors of tourism become more concentrated and perhaps shift from a structure of imperfect competition to one of oligopoly, so an awareness of competitors' strategies kicks in (Milman 2001) and price reactive strategies often follow. However, owing to the particular characteristics of tourism outlined in the introduction, products are naturally heterogeneous and it is often simple to develop a strong strategy of product differentiation, especially through service and perceived quality standards.

State-of-art thinking on the topic

A number of issues are coming to the fore in current research.

First, the development of the internet is having a profound impact not only on the marketing of tourism products but also on the markets themselves. The internet is providing an open information source that is changing the asymmetric nature of market knowledge, and providing more consumer information to redress the historic problem of tourism being only an experience product. Research is moving from analysing the effectiveness of the internet as a marketing tool to more sophisticated applications such as its ability to create potential monopsonist or buying power tourist groups through on-line communities (Kim et al. 2004), or for product and price information to become more readily available for analysis by competitors.

The internet also helps to permit customisation as the offspring of product differentiation. Suppliers with an investment in database marketing, or with the ability to unbundle and create bespoke travel and tourism products, are able to re-position themselves into a different market structure where the neoclassical rules of oligopoly or imperfect competition may not apply so readily.

Second, many suppliers in tourism face a situation of competition to sell a core product, but then provide additional products under monopolistic conditions to tourists that buy the core product from them. For example, low-cost airlines may face a highly competitive market in selling air trips, but once the passengers are on board the airline can act as a monopoly supplier of food and beverages, duty-free goods and so on. Similar 'supplemental spending' situations apply in leisure clubs (Alcock and Bull 1993), hotels (Adams 2000), cruises and theme parks (Milman 2001) and resorts (Perdue 2002). Under these conditions, suppliers may select a non profit-optimal strategy for their core product, but one that maximises sales volume in order to maximise the captive market to which they can sell monopoly products at high profit. Current research in this area is utilising the economics of competitive clubs as a theoretical framework of analysis.

Third, the issue of defining market boundaries more exactly is receiving increased attention. This is largely due to an emphasis on the actioning of competition policy in a number of countries including the EU, the USA, Australia and New Zealand. Market definition is becoming an object of demand- rather than supply-side study in many cases (European Commission 1999, 2002), since consumers can be more accurately surveyed to determine potential substitutability where products are complex as in tourism, rather than relying on official industrial classifications that in many cases do not serve tourism at all well. As a result, competition policy analysts are finding many new situations to be liable for investigation that might not previously have been considered (Souty 2003).

Fourth, researchers are finding new uses for methodologies such as hedonic pricing. This technique has been used to demonstrate how tour operators, supposedly under oligopolistic conditions, operate with market-share objectives for market power in the Balearic Islands (Aguilo et al. 2003). It has also been used to show how inefficient pricing by resort hotels in under- or overvaluing their attributes compared with those of competitors can quickly lose demand in a local market (Bull 1998).

Issues for further research
There are a number of issues concerning industrial organisation at the local or destination level, and that at the inter-destinational level. For example, there is currently no good analytical framework to deal with the paradox

between the need for tourism businesses, especially small ones, to undertake cooperative promotion and other marketing to gain external economies of scale, and competition between these selfsame suppliers. This problem is noted, for example, by Weber and Ladkin (2003), in the convention sector. The 'economics of alliances' between partners whose activities are rarely competitive with each other is an insufficient tool for dealing with competitive cases.

Researchers have attempted to analyse the supply side of economic activity using standard economic and econometric tools derived from market structure and industrial structure analysis. However, the complexity of market definition and product definition means that it is perfectly possible to adjust slightly the specification of a 'product' or 'supplier' from a parametric perspective and yield completely different results from an analysis. For example, Davies and Downward (2001a, 2001b) note the contradictory findings from analyses of the UK tour operating sector by Baum and Mudambi (1994), Evans and Stabler (1995), Taylor (1996) and themselves. Clearly, the specification of 'competing suppliers' in sectors with such fuzzy boundaries as many of those in tourism is a continuing problem for analysis, and particularly for competition regulation authorities. Some authorities such as the EU are turning to consumer studies to identify and specify market boundaries, and there is clearly a need for research using, for example, Tourism Consumption Systems methods (Woodside and Dubelaar 2002) to help to develop demand-side specifications.

It is clearly important to establish to what extent suppliers are operating with objectives other than profit maximisation. A number of the articles referred to in the literature above produce contradictory results since empirically many firms are not operating with the expected profit-maximising strategy. What impact do market-share maximisation or personal 'concealing performance' objectives have on market structure and performance, given that they could well be common objectives for many suppliers within travel and tourism?

References

Adams, B. (2000), 'Maxing out', *Hotel and Motel Management*, **215** (14), pp. 38–40.
Aguilo, E., J. Alegre and M. Sard (2003), 'Examining the market structure of the German and UK tour operating industries through an analysis of package holiday prices', *Tourism Economics*, **9** (3), pp. 255–78.
Akerlof, G.A. (1970), 'The market for lemons: quality uncertainty and the market mechanism', *Quarterly Journal of Economics*, **84** (August), pp. 488–500.
Alcock, K.M. and A.O. Bull (1993), 'Patron preferences for features offered by licensed clubs', *International Journal of Contemporary Hospitality Management*, **5** (1), pp. 28–32.
Allen, B. and M. Hellwig (1986), 'Bertrand-Edgeworth oligopoly in large markets', *Review of Economic Studies*, **53**, 175–204.
ATPR [CCH] (1995), *Qantas Airways Ltd and British Airways Plc*, Australia Trade Practices Reports, Canberra: Federal Court of Australia.

ATPR [CCH] (1998), *Re Ansett Australia Ltd*, Australian Trade Practices Reports, Canberra: Federal Court of Australia.

Baum, T. and R. Mudambi (1994), 'A Ricardian analysis of the fully-inclusive tour industry', *Service Industries Journal*, **14** (1), pp. 85–93.

Baum, T. and R. Mudambi (1995), 'An empirical analysis of oligopolistic hotel pricing', *Annals of Tourism Research*, **22** (3), pp. 501–16.

Baumol, W., J. Panzar and R. Willig (1982), *Contestable Markets and the Theory of Industry Structure*, New York: Harcourt Brace Jovanovich.

Bertrand, J. (1883), 'Book review of *Théorie Mathématique de la Richesse Sociale and of Recherches sur les Principes Mathématiques de la Théorie des Richesses*', *Journal des Savants*, **67**, pp. 499–508.

Brooks, G.R. (1995), 'Defining market boundaries', *Strategic Management Journal*, **16** (6), pp. 535–49.

Bull, A.O. (1995), *The Economics of Travel and Tourism*, 2nd edn, Melbourne: Longman.

Bull, A.O. (1998), *The Effects of Location and Other Attributes on the Price of Products which are Place-Sensitive in Demand*, Griffith University, Brisbane: ADT.

Calder, S. (2002), *No Frills: The Truth Behind the Low-cost Revolution in the Skies*, London: Virgin Books.

Carlton, D.W. and J.M. Perloff (1990), *Modern Industrial Organization*, New York: HarperCollins.

Carroll, M.M. and R. Grimes (1995), 'Evolutionary change in product management: experiences in the car rental industry', *Interfaces*, **25** (5), pp. 84–104.

Chamberlin, E.H. (1933), *The Theory of Monopolistic Competition*, Cambridge, MA: Harvard University Press.

Chung. K.Y. (2000), 'Hotel room rate pricing strategy for market share in oligopolistic competition', *Tourism Management*, **21** (2), 135–45.

Cournot, A.A. (1838), *Recherches sur les Principes Mathematiques de la Richesse Sociale* (Bacon, N.T., Trans.), (English, 1897 edn), New York: Macmillan.

Davies, B. (1999), 'Industrial organisation: the UK hotel sector', *Annals of Tourism Research*, **26** (2), pp. 294–311.

Davies, B. and P. Downward (2001a), 'Industrial organisation and competition in the UK tour operator/travel agency business, 1989–1993: an econometric investigation', *Journal of Travel Research*, **39** (May), pp. 411–25.

Davies, B. and P. Downward (2001b), 'Industrial organisation of the package tour industry: implications for researchers', *Tourism Economics*, **7** (2), pp. 149–61.

Dilley, R. (1992), *Contesting Markets*, Edinburgh: Edinburgh University Press.

Doganis, R. (2001), *The Airline Business in the 21st Century*, London: Routledge.

Eaton, B.C. and R.G. Lipsey (1989), 'Product differentiation', in R. Schmalensee and R.D. Willig (eds), *Handbook of Industrial Organisation*, Amsterdam: Elsevier Scientific, pp. 723–68.

Edgeworth, F. (1897), 'La teoria pura del monopolio', *Giornali degli Economisti*, **40**, pp. 13–31.

Edgeworth, F. (1925), 'The pure theory of monopoly', in F. Edgeworth (ed.), *Papers Relating to Political Economy*, 1, London: Royal Economic Society, pp. 111–42.

European Commission (1999), *EU Case No. IV/M.1524 Airtours/First Choice*, Brussels: EU Commission.

European Commission (2002), *EU Case T-342/99 Judgment on Airtours*, Brussels: EU Commission.

Evans, N., D. Campbell and G. Stonehouse (2003), *Strategic Management for Travel and Tourism*, Oxford: Butterworth-Heinemann.

Evans, N. and M. Stabler (1995), 'A future for the package tour operator in the 21st century?', *Tourism Economics*, **1** (3), pp. 245–63.

Gilbert, D.C. (1991), 'An examination of the consumer behaviour process related to tourism', in C. Cooper (ed.), *Progress in Tourism, Recreation and Hospitality Management*, London: Belhaven Press, pp. 78–105.

Gillen, D. and W. Morrison (2003), 'Bundling, integration and the delivered price of air travel: are low-cost carriers full-service competitors?', *Journal of Air Transport Management*, **9** (1), pp. 15–23.

Gitelson, R.J. and J.L. Crompton (1983), 'The planning horizons and sources of information used by pleasure vacationers', *Journal of Travel Research*, **23** (3), pp. 2–7.

Goodall, B. (1991), 'Understanding holiday choice', in C. Cooper (ed.), *Progress in Tourism, Recreation and Hospitality Management*, London: Belhaven Press, pp. 58–77.

Holmstrom, B. (1985), 'The provision of services in a market economy', in R.P. Inman (ed.), *Managing the Service Economy: Prospects and Problems*, Cambridge, UK: Cambridge University Press, pp. 183–213.

Isard, W. (1956), *Location and Space-Economy*, New York: John Wiley & Sons.

Kim, W.G., C. Lee and S.J. Hiemstra (2004), 'Effects of an online virtual community on customer loyalty and travel product purchases', *Tourism Management*, **25** (3), pp. 343–56.

Lancaster, K.J. (1971), *Consumer Demand: A New Approach*, New York: Columbia University Press.

Leiper, N. (1995), *Tourism Management*, Melbourne: RMIT Press.

Milman, A. (2001), 'The future of the theme park and attraction industry: a management perspective', *Journal of Travel Research*, **40** (November), pp. 139–47.

Nash, J.F. (1951), 'Non-cooperative games', *Annals of Mathematics*, **54**, pp. 286–95.

Perdue, R. (2002), 'Perishability, yield management and cross-product elasticity: a case study of deep discount season passes in the Colorado ski industry', *Journal of Travel Research*, **41** (August), pp. 15–22.

Pine, J. and J.H. Gilmore (1999), *The Experience Economy*, Boston, MA: Harvard Business School Press.

Poon, A. (1993), *Tourism, Technology and Competitive Strategies*, Wallingford, UK: CAB International.

Porter, M.E. (1980), *Competitive Strategy: Techniques for Analysing Industries and Competitors*, New York: Free Press.

Relihan, W.J. (1989), 'The yield management approach to hotel room pricing', *Cornell Hotel and Restaurant Administration Quarterly*, **30** (2), pp. 40–45.

Schmalensee, R. (1986), 'Advertising and market structure', in J. Stiglitz and F. Mathewson (eds), *New Developments in the Analysis of Market Structure*, Cambridge, MA: MIT Press.

Schmalensee, R. (1992), 'Sunk cost models and market structure: a review article', *Journal of Industrial Economics*, **40** (2), pp. 125–34.

Shapiro, C. (1989), 'Theories of oligopoly behavior', in R. Schmalensee and R.D. Willig (eds), *Handbook of Industrial Organisation*, Amsterdam: Elsevier Scientific, pp. 329–414.

Sinclair, M.T. and M. Stabler 1997), *The Economics of Tourism*, London: Routledge.

Skalpe, O. (2003), 'Hotels and restaurants – are the risks rewarded?', *Tourism Management*, **24** (6), pp. 623–34.

Slattery, P. (1994), 'The structural theory of business demand: a reply to Hughes', *International Journal of Hospitality Management*, **13** (2), pp. 173–76.

Smith, S.L.J. (1989), *Tourism Analysis*, Harlow, UK: Longman.

Souty, F. (2003), 'Passport to progress: competition challenges for world tourism and global anti-competitive practices in the tourism industry', World Tourism Organisation Discussion Paper, Madrid, WTO, www.world-tourism.org/quality/E/trade/passport_to_progress.pdf.

Spence, M. (1974), *Market Signaling*, Cambridge, MA: Harvard University Press.

Stabler, M.J. (1991), 'Modelling the tourism industry: a new approach', in M.T. Sinclair and M.J. Stabler (eds), *The Tourism Industry: An International Analysis*, Wallingford, UK: CAB International, pp. 15–43.

Taylor, P. (1996), 'Oligopoly or contestable markets in the UK package tour industry?', *Service Industries Journal*, **16** (3), pp. 379–88.

Wang, Z.H., M. Evans and L. Turner (2004), 'Effects of strategic airline alliances on air transport market competition: an empirical analysis', *Tourism Economics*, **10** (1), pp. 23–43.

Watson, D.S. (1977), *Price Theory and its Uses*, 4th edn, Boston, MA: Houghton Mifflin.

Weber, K. and A. Ladkin (2003), 'The convention industry in Australia and the United Kingdom: key issues and competitive forces', *Journal of Travel Research*, **42** (November), pp. 125–32.

Woodside, A. and C. Dubelaar (2002), 'A general theory of tourism consumption systems: a conceptual framework and an empirical exploration', *Journal of Travel Research*, **41** (November), pp. 120–32.

Wu, J.-J. (2004), 'Influence of market orientation and strategy on travel industry performance: an empirical study of e-commerce in Taiwan', *Tourism Management*, **25** (3), pp. 357–66.

6 Travel and tourism intermediaries
Nevenka Čavlek

Introduction
The aim of this chapter is to discuss the main issues in travel and tourism intermediation. Focus is set on the following:

- the role played in the market today by travel agencies and tour operators, as the main travel and tourism intermediaries;
- the business environment of travel agencies and tour operators on the largest tourism generating markets;
- the economics of travel agencies;
- the principles of tour operating and the main commercial risks;
- the economics of tour operation; and
- yield management in the tour operating business.

There is no doubt that people would travel even if intermediaries in travel and tourism did not exist. However, since everything in life is easier with good organisation, by providing professional help in this kind of travel arrangement travel and tourism intermediaries have justified their existence. From a historical point of view, intermediation in the sphere of travelling reached a higher stage with the start of travelling for the purpose of tourism, as a higher phase in the development of travel. The need for intermediaries is conditioned by the specificity of the tourism demand and tourism supply. Intermediaries in travel and tourism link those who offer services (service providers) with those who make use of these services (travellers and tourists). The main representatives of travel and tourism intermediaries are travel agents and tour operators, although they are not the only channels of distribution of travel and tourism services on the market. Sometimes different organisations in the sphere of tourism can also act as intermediaries, like travel clubs and associations, tourist offices and similar organisations.

One of the most noticeable differences between tour operators and travel agencies is that tour operators operate as wholesalers, and travel agencies as retailers. Therefore, travel agencies do not face the risk of unsold capacities, because they do not purchase in advance the services from suppliers, but sell their services only when they have a buyer for them. However, a travel agency can also sporadically appear as an organiser of a particular tour.

In tourism literature, the terms 'tour operator' (widely used in Europe) and 'wholesaler' (mostly used in the United States) are usually used as synonyms, although they do not always denote the same idea. A wholesaler can be any bulk buyer and seller of a single travel and tourism service (for example, acting as a broker in the sector of air transport, or hotel accommodation). Other companies that occasionally organise and sell package tours are also called tour operators or wholesalers (although their main source of income comes from a different field of activity), as well as companies who do not package their own programme, but 'contract the work out to a wholesaler and pass on the bookings as they come in' (Cooper et al. 1998, p. 257), as is the case with affinity groups. For a tour operator, however, the purchase of different services in bulk, the packaging of these services into a single product and the sale of these products usually indirectly to the customers is its primary activity. Therefore, a tour operator might be defined as an economic entity which, by uniting the services of different suppliers, creates and organises inclusive tours in its own name and on its own account, for yet unknown buyers, and by doing so continuously realises its main source of income. In this sense it could be said that every tour operator is a wholesaler, but not every wholesaler is a tour operator.

The prevailing organisational function of a tour operator has created the illusion that it has lost its function as an intermediary, since this is the most significant and most noticeable function of the travel agency. For this reason, some theoreticians, as pointed out by Freyer (1998) and Holloway (1998), tend to deny the role of tour operators as an intermediary on the tourism market. However, in the view of this author, this role is clearly visible, not only from the tour operators' position in relation to customers, but equally so from their relation to the providers of the services which they buy in bulk, unite into a 'package' and then sell individually to their customers. Regardless of the fact that today many tour operators in the world own airline companies, hotels, rent-a-car organisations, ship companies and so on, their role as intermediaries has not disappeared, because these services are still not offered by the tour operator itself, but directly by the providers mentioned above. In other words, the nature of the work of the hotel chains or airline companies does not lose its economic characteristics in any way. Although it might be said that such activities are altered in terms of economic conditions or characteristics, they are not transformed into something different (in this case, into tour operating activities).

Travel and tourism intermediaries act in the market as coordinators and representatives of the interests of the suppliers and of the users of travel and tourism-related services. Tourism consumers find their interest in using the services of intermediaries since the latter help them organise their travel and many other single services they will use in tourist resorts. By buying an integrated product like a package holiday, customers not only save the time they would need to contact personally each service provider, supposing they know who to contact and for which service, but they also save money. For tour operators' products, this means that the price must be even lower than the price which a travel agency would offer its clients if it arranged such a holiday itself. The price must be different, since the tour operator, unlike the travel agency, appears to the suppliers as a wholesaler and in a certain way guarantees to its partners a better use of capacities. Furthermore, since tour operators offer the market a wide choice of tourism destinations and accommodation facilities, they attract clients by freeing them of the worries of organising the journey and holiday themselves. On the other side, the organiser of a tour is also responsible for protecting the interests of its clients in a manner which guarantees certain service quality standards from all the suppliers whose services are an integral part of the package. Equally, there is a duty to ensure the clients' safety during the journey and during the holiday itself.

The role that these intermediaries play today on the market is not disappearing with the individualisation of tourism travel, or with the new possibilities that modern information technology offers to consumers of travel and tourism services. The reason for this is that travel and tourism intermediaries are adapting quickly to the changing business environment. In fact, those who are considering modern technology as a partner and not as a threat have the best chances of surviving in the increasingly competitive market. The business practice of travel intermediaries shows that new information technology has been revolutionising the role of travel agencies and redefining their function, just as it has been supporting tour operators' efficiency and promotions (Buhalis 2003).

Economics of travel agencies

Retail travel agencies in the majority of cases are small businesses. However, it should be pointed out that the distribution network worldwide differs from country to country. It can range from very small enterprises, often family owned, to large multinational companies. According to the research of the world's largest association of travel professionals, ASTA (American Society of Travel Agents) (2002), agencies on the US market work with an average of four to five full-time employees. In 2002, 51.2 per cent of ASTA agencies reported an annual sales volume of less than $2 million. Although the trend of consolidation processes among distribution channels in the USA is not so prominent as it is on the European market, changing business conditions on the market are also pushing these travel agencies towards a trend of increasing their size. Therefore, the number of small agencies has been decreasing, while the number of medium and large agencies has been increasing since 1998. The main reason lies in the fact that agencies in a franchise or in cooperation are better able to secure an over-ride commission with carriers. In this way, travel agencies can secure up to 5 per cent additional commission. In this low net-profit business this is of enormous significance, since such commissions can increase a travel agent's profit by up to 50 per cent (Lundberg et al. 1995).

The situation in the European market is different. For the European market, consolidation seems to be the best answer for market survival. The main generating markets are characterised by an ongoing process of con-centration in the travel distribution trade. The German market, as the largest generating market in the world, proves that the turnover of inde-pendent travel agencies is decreasing while at the same time the turnover of chains, franchise systems and cooperatives is increasing. If the turnover of all travel agencies is analysed, the relation of sales outlets to turnover changed significantly in the period from 1997 to 2000. In 1997, 52 per cent of the travel agency market was covered by independent agency outlets, achieving 22 per cent of total turnover (DRV 1999). In 2000, the number of independent agency outlets decreased, representing only 36 per cent of the travel agency market, while their share in the total agency turnover dropped to just 13 per cent (FVW International 2001; DRV 2001). In 2002, independent travel agency outlets represented just 5 per cent of the total German travel agency market (DRV 2003).

There is a difference in the structure of sales items between Europe and the USA. The main sales items among European travel agencies are package tours which account for more than 50 per cent of total agency sales, followed by air tickets which account for over one-third of an agency's sales. However, the sales items ratio in Europe is quite different from that on the US market (Table 6.1). Small travel agencies in Europe usually do not sell airline tickets because they would need to obtain an IATA (International Air Transport Association) licence which would entail additional costs. In the USA there are ARC-accredited (Airlines Reporting Corporation) and non-ARC sellers of travel services. ARC retailers are also usually members of IATA and are allowed to sell both international and domestic airline tickets. Air sales generally represent over 50 per cent of total agency sales in the USA.

While in Europe it is not yet common practice for travel agents to charge fees for a variety of services, in the USA close to 95 per cent of ASTA agen-cies charge fees for some or all of their services (ASTA 2002). This is the result of the implementation of 'zero base commissions', and therefore most agencies charge a standard amount when issuing an airline ticket. In Europe the main source of a travel agency's income in the revenue statement

Table 6.1   Sales item structure of European and US agencies

Turnover/travel agency sales

	Percentage of total sales	
	Europe	USA
Tour packages	53–55	27–30
Air tickets	33–34	34–52
Other transport tickets	5–6	3–4
Others (insurance, car rental, cruise, hotel, money exchange, etc.)	6–8	16–35
Total sales	100	100

Source: Trade information compiled by author.

is still commission earned from principals (service providers) whose services they sell.

Based on trade information from the main European tourism-generating markets, Table 6.2 presents a simplified illustration of the retailing agency operating account, standardised to one million currency units (EUR) of total sales/turnover. These data clearly show that the revenue of a travel agency represents only 10 per cent of the agency's total turnover/sales. Since the operating costs of a travel agency amount to some 85–95 per cent of the agency's revenue, the pre-tax earnings can account for only 5 per cent of its achieved revenue. In other words, pre-tax earnings represent only 0.5–1.5 per cent of the total turnover/agency sales.

The percentage of commission that principals approve to retailers on the price of sold products or services varies depending on the service being sold and on the commission policy of the principal. The highest commissions can be earned in selling travel insurance (between 30 and 40 per cent), package holidays (10 per cent on average) and airline tickets (between 7 and 10 per cent). Some principals, like tour operators, usually determine the level of commission with the volume of sales, and therefore commissions can range from 7–14 per cent. Usually agencies in a franchise or as a cooperative can secure bonus commissions negotiated with large leisure travel concerns, which means that additional commissions are paid for exceeded targets. Since these commissions are usually paid at the end of the season, agencies have to take this into account in cash flow estimations (see Figure 6.1). However, the increased share of clients making direct bookings with suppliers through the internet, the increased discounting of package holidays, 'no fee' low-cost airlines, and commission cuts by scheduled airlines have all contributed to the reduced profitability of travel agencies. Therefore, some

Table 6.2   An illustration of retailing agency operating accounts in Europe

Turnover/travel agency sales

Sales items	Structure of sales items	
	Average range (%)	Example (€)
Tour packages	53–55	540 000
Air tickets	33–34	330 000
Other transport tickets	5–6	60 000
Others (insurance, car rental, cruise, hotel, money exchange, etc.)	6–8	70 000
Total sales	100	1 000 000

Revenue structure

Items of income	Average share (%)	Example (€)
Commission	95	95 000
Other income	5	5000
Total revenue	100	100 000

Operating costs

	Average share of total revenue (%)	Example (€)
Personnel costs (salaries, pensions, training, etc.)	48–51	51 000
Establishment costs (rent, energy, insurance, cleaning, maintenance, etc.)	14–17	17 000
Communication + CRS costs	9–12	12 000
Advertising costs	2.5–3	3000
Administration costs (printing, stationery, bank charges, fees, etc.)	6–8	8000
Depreciation	2	2000
Total	85–95	93 000

Pre-tax earnings

	Average share of total revenue (%)	Example (€)
Pre-tax earnings	5–15	7000

Source: Trade information gathered from different European markets.

agencies in Europe have been forced to start charging service fees, too. A survey conducted by ABTA (Association of British Travel Agents) reports that those agencies which started charging fees between 2000 and 2002 almost doubled profitability in the same period (ABTA 2002). Besides commission, travel agencies also generate income from interest on clients' deposit money, from margins earned on the sale of travel goods, and similar means.

The main costs in the retailing business are associated with personnel costs which usually account for over 50 per cent of total costs. They also include payments to owners and directors. An analysis of travel agencies operating accounts on the German market leads to the conclusion that many cost items, with the exception of personnel costs, decrease with the increase in size of a travel agency (Kreilkamp et al. 1996). However, although the share of personnel costs in total revenue remains constant with the increase in size of travel agencies, the productivity of employees changes. Travel agencies with higher revenue achieve a better ratio of cost coverage contribution per employee, and with it also better productivity, than small agencies. Usually, small travel agencies tend to secure their profitability by strictly controlling costs. Therefore they try to keep staff salaries low, postpone staff training for 'better times', and/or cut advertising costs. However, practice has shown that this cannot be a successful long-term strategy. The already-mentioned survey among ABTA's agents has proved that agency staff with proper incentives achieved profits 57 per cent better than the average, and those agencies that were spending over £500 per employee on training achieved improved profitability that was 30 per cent above the survey average.

As Mundt (1998) points out, the share of profit in the total agency sales is not the strongest indicator of the economic success or failure of a travel agency. The reason for this is that the majority of the agency's turnover lies on the agency's account only as interim payments. Although clients pay for services directly to the travel agency, after the service is consumed the travel agency makes payments for the provided service to the service providers. This means that most of the achieved turnover (see Table 6.2) has to be transferred either to various service providers on whose account the travel agency sold these single services, or to the tour operator whose package holidays were sold. Therefore a much better indicator of a travel agency's economic performance would be the share of profit in its total revenue. For a travel agency, it is not always best to maximise turnover at any cost, since high turnovers do not always guarantee high profits.

Since the financial playing field of travel agencies is limited, they often face the problem of liquidity. Cash-flow gaps create a financial situation which can easily bring a travel agency to a critical stage, particularly in times when bookings fail and when payment to service providers falls due. Since

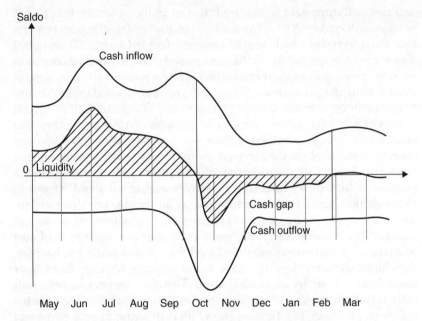

Source: Trade information from a German franchise travel agency.

Figure 6.1   Liquidity in retailing travel agency.

the whole tourism business is very much characterised by seasonality, travel
agencies are also confronted with the consequences of this problem, which
means that their money inflow and outflow is the reflection of seasonality
and can have very high fluctuations. Figure 6.1 illustrates the liquidity
problem of a typical franchise travel agency on the German market.

   In times when travel agencies' revenue is stagnating and at the same time
when operating costs are increasing, cost management becomes a priority
for success. The question necessarily arises: how can travel agencies overcome the problem of cash gaps? One of the possible solutions is to try to
obtain short-term bank loans. Usually this will be possible if the agency has
a good structure of capital, that is, if in the total agency capital, own capital
prevails. One has to bear in mind that paid interest ultimately reduces the
agency's already low profit. However, in travel agency management the
principle 'liquidity before profitability' always applies. In times of crisis,
travel agencies in a franchise or as a cooperative can also attempt to negotiate the advance payment of commission with principals. Since commissions are in the best case paid after the departures of clients, such advance
payments could solve the risk of poor liquidity.

Tour operator economics

Principles of tour operating and the main commercial risks.
As already mentioned, tour operators appeared on the tourism market as
entrepreneurs in the sphere of organising leisure travel. Although it might
seem easy to 'manufacture' travel products by combining transport, accommodation and other tourist services and facilities, and distribute it as a
single product at an inclusive price directly or indirectly to customers, the
whole business is very complex, highly demand driven and very risky. The
main risks in the tour operating business are connected with projections of
tourism demand, capacity planning and pricing. The better the demand
forecasting, the more likelihood there is of achieving better capacity planning and pricing. However, this is easier said than done. Forecasting
tourism demand is always connected with many risks, since there are a large
number of factors that can lead to sudden changes. Since tour operators
have to finalise the prices of packaged tours at the latest some six to eight
months before their first tour operation begins, the risks are very high. Some
risks, such as fluctuations in the currency of the destination country (where
the contracted prices of accommodation, local transfers and so on, are fixed
in the local currency), or volatility in the currency in which payment is made
for aircraft (which is usually in US dollars), can be pre-empted by buying
the needed currency in advance. Unfortunately, this business activity is
highly dependent on economic movements on the generating and receiving
markets, on all kinds of safety and security risk, and since this is a very low
net-profit business it makes managers in this field feel as though they are
'dancing on thin ice' almost every day (Čavlek 2002b, p. 413).

Based on forecasted tourism demand, a tour operator plans total capacity and decides on the number of destinations and volume of its programme. All the contracts with suppliers of single services must be signed
well in advance, usually between 12 and 18 months before the start of
the holidays. This means that in planning their capacities for different
destinations, tour operators have to anticipate many factors that might
influence demand for a destination before negotiations for capacities begins.
The business philosophy of tour operators is based on the principle of
economies of scale and enlarged scope of operations, thus allowing them to
offer products at very competitive prices. By buying services in bulk, the
tour operator runs the risk of not selling them. However, it is through this
principle of contracting a large number of facilities that a lower price per
unit from the suppliers is obtained. The lower the price of a package holiday
which the tour operator can achieve in comparison with individually organised travel allows the tour operator greater opportunities in finding clients
on the market to whom it will be able to sell the programme and, at the same

time, lower the risk of contracting large capacities. The level of risk greatly depends on the contracts signed, since the terms and conditions between tour operators and service providers specify commitments. In the case of hotel contracts, there are two possible types of contracts: an allotment and a firm contract or a guarantee. A contract of allotment allows a tour operator to return an unsold allocation of rooms to the hotelier within agreed release dates at no charge or penalty. The contract is usually signed for one season. In the case of a firm contract or guarantee, hotel rooms may not be returned, and tour operators have to pay for the whole contracted capacity no matter whether they are sold or not. Such firm contracts are frequently signed for a longer period (three to five years). In this case, tour operators can secure the best possible prices, but at the highest risk.

When a tour operator contracts aircraft seats, it usually does so with a charter airline. In this case, it is the tour operator that takes the commercial risk of the operation. In addition, some tour operators deal with scheduled airlines, which is usually the case with small tour operators and with specialist long-haul operators. However, the commercial risk of the operation still applies, since tour operators purchase a certain number of seats in bulk on a scheduled flight based on a net group airfare per person. In this situation, too, it is the tour operator and not the airline that takes the responsibility for selling the seats.

There are various types of contracts such as a 'time charter' when a tour operator contracts an aircraft for the whole season, or charters a block of seats (a 'part charter') which can also be purchased on a scheduled flight. Large tour operators usually have their own charter airlines and thus can better control the costs and the operation as a whole. The most developed form of charter operation is the 'back-to-back charter' where a tour operator runs a series of flights on a systematic and continuous basis throughout a season, known as a chain of charter flights, to a certain destination to achieve better utilisation of the aircraft. The tour operator uses the same aircraft which flies a group of holidaymakers to the destination to bring back the group that has just finished their holiday.

Pricing an inclusive tour
Only after all the components of a package holiday have been defined can the tour operator determine its selling price, which mostly depends on the type of transport in a particular package and on the type of accommodation, because these are the direct costs which make up somewhere between 65 and 75 per cent of the selling price of a package holiday. Other costs that have to be included in the price are transfer costs from airports, harbours or railway stations to the hotel and vice versa, the costs of the representatives in the resort, and the costs of the tour operator (including brochures,

travel agent's commission, administrative costs and staff salaries). Since the commercial risks for a tour operator are highest in the organisation of air-package tours, the pricing of this type of package will be more closely considered.

In principle, tour operators connect a contracted bed to a contracted flight seat, that is, one contracted bed is related to one contracted flight seat, and the total availability is featured as a package. Tour operators calculate the price of a package on the basis of prices contracted with the suppliers. Table 6.3 illustrates the main steps in the calculation of the price of an air package tour.

Since the tour operator guarantees payments for *n* flights, in this case 24 rotations, it has to bear in mind that it cannot sell seats on all the flights, but has to add in a so-called 'empty leg'. In the case of back-to-back charters, the first inbound flight and the last outbound flight of the series are empty. This is because at the beginning of the season, once the aircraft carries the first group of passengers to their destination, there are no

Table 6.3   Price structure of a seven-night inclusive tour

Item	Currency unit	Average cost structure (%)
Cost per seat including airport tax	160	
Flight costs	514 560	
(Based on 24 departures = 160 × 134 × 24)		
Cost per seat including 'empty leg'	167	
(Flight costs ÷ 23 commercial flights ÷ total seats)		
Cost per seat at 90 per cent occupancy	185	35
Hotel costs per person, based on 7 nights, half board in a 3 star hotel	210	40
Cost of the ground service (handling fee)	18	3
Costs of resort representative	8	2
Total cost per person	421	
Costs of the tour operator (approx. 25% to cover agency commission, marketing costs, personnel, administrative costs)	105	20
Selling price	526	100

Note: *Destination MUC–DBV–MUC (Munich–Dubrovnik–Munich); type of chartered aircraft: Airbus 319–134 seats.

Source: Trade Information compiled by author.

passengers at the destination to carry home. Likewise, for the last flight of the season there are no passengers to take to the destination; the aircraft arrives at the destination empty to carry home the passengers who have finished their holiday. In the above case the cost per seat has to be calculated on 23 commercial flights. However, if the average duration of stay in the destination is 14 days, and not seven days, this means that the tour operator will have to make a calculation on only 22 commercial flights, since the last two departures to the destination cannot be offered for sale. This is because on the last two departures the tour operator carries back clients who have completed their holiday and, since this is the end of the season, there are no further clients to carry to the destination. These costs are linear throughout the season, which is not the case with the hotel costs, since they depend on the time in the season (see more in Hofmann 2000).

The pricing model shown is the basis for determining the actual selling price of an inclusive tour. 'Cost-based pricing' which is strictly based on the real costs of the single services included is usually applied by smaller tour operators and specialist tour operators, provided that they do not operate on a particularly competitive market and that they have a highly competitive product. Market-based pricing (Youell 1994) is usually applied by mass market tour operators that dominate a particular market and this calculation takes into account the price which the market is ready to accept. This is an exceptionally delicate and complex method since the price depends on an estimation of the price which will be set by the competition. However, in the pricing policy, not only should the economic aspect of the price be considered, but also the psychological effect the price has on the consumer. Not every reduction in the price of a package holiday necessarily means increased demand for this product. Similarly, not every increase in price necessarily has to result in a decrease in demand. Therefore, the flexibility of demand is not always in proportion to the price of a tourism product.

Vertically and horizontally integrated tour operators, which include the majority of large tour operators on the European market, have more room to balance inclusive tour prices than is the case with small tour operators, since large tour operators can correct and control prices, in the areas of transport, accommodation, and/or in the distribution chain. Naturally, their profit margin decreases, but they can compensate this with a planned increase in turnover. For example, on the German market the largest leisure travel concerns, TUI, Thomas Cook and Rewe have their own chains of travel agencies and franchise systems, while many other agencies that want to sell their package holidays have joined alliances or strategic partnerships. In this way the largest German tour operators 'have trimmed the distribution under their control' (FVW 2002b). This is of extreme importance for vertically integrated leisure travel concerns, because in this way they can better and easily ensure both their turnover and the better capacity utilisation of their charter airline seats and hotel beds. TUI, which has the largest distribution system under its own control, aims to secure some 35 per cent of its turnover by using its own distribution network.

The data presented in Table 6.4 clearly show that the business of a tour operator has a very low profit margin and is therefore very risky. In good years most tour operators achieve a profit of 1–2 per cent net, whereas a profit of 4–5 per cent net is considered to be an exceptional achievement, and can usually be attributed to specialist tour operators that can charge premium prices for their specialised products.

The many failures and bankruptcies of tour operators irrespective of size prove that this is one of the riskiest industries. It is therefore understandable that tour operators try to use every single possibility to boost their revenue. Another source of income that tour operators usually have is interest on money held in account. Similar to the case of the travel agency's business, tour operators also record high turnovers since clients pay deposits for holidays many months in advance and final payments are due six to eight weeks before the holidays start. Payments to service providers are usually

Table 6.4   Income statement of a large vertically integrated tour operator (in %)

I	Sales	100
	Tour operators	78.2
	Flights	8
	Travel agencies	13.2
	Accommodation	0.4
	Other	0.2
II	Expenses for leisure travel services	69
	Cost of materials (operating supplies for aircraft, goods purchased and similar)	4
	Hotel services	36
	Flight and technical service costs	20
	Fees	5
	Transfer and other transportation costs	1
	Other costs of purchased services	4
Gross profit		31
	Personnel expenses	10
	Other operating expenses, depreciation and amortisation	20
	EBITA (earnings before interest, taxes and amortisation)	1
	EBTA (earnings before taxes and amortisation)	0.8

Source: Trade information compiled by author.

made after the clients have had their holidays. This leaves tour operators a good opportunity to earn extra on these deposits, which can amount to one per cent of net income when interest rates in the banks are favourable. However, the cash flow risk in this business is similar to that already described in the case of the liquidity problem in the travel agency business.

Another source of income derives from commission for services sold to clients through resort representatives in tourism destinations, such as car hire, excursions, and similar services. Rent-a-car companies and travel agencies grant commission not only to representatives to stimulate better sales, but to tour operators, too. Commission that tour operators can earn from the sales of such services can in the best case cover the cost of the resort representatives. Large tour operators can also speculate and earn on the currency exchange by buying needed currency when exchange rates are most favourable and holding the money until payments for services fall due.

Yield management in the tour operating business
Although very fragile, the tour operating business has become a multi-billion dollar industry. The continuous growth of international tourism, and with it the concentration of demand on the one side, and supply on the other, has forced companies involved in tourism to create corporations with very complex organisational and management structures. Tour operating companies have been doing the same. For mass-market tour operators on the European market to survive in a very competitive environment, it has become essential to merge with, or to take over, companies that deliver different components of the whole product, not only to be able to have quality control over the services provided, but also to share in the profit of as large a number of different components of the whole product that they supply on the market as possible (Čavlek 2000, p. 325). On the European market there are four giant vertically integrated leisure travel concerns: the TUI Group, with the mother company Preussag (renamed as TUI AG), Thomas Cook whose owners are 'Lufthansa' and the department store and mail order group 'Karstadt/Quelle', My Travel Group (the only British company, which breaks the domination of German companies in the business) and Rewe Touristik, in the hands of a large German utility chain. All have a similar structure: they consist of several tour operating companies on domestic markets and abroad, their own charter airlines, accommodation facilities in tourism resorts, chains of retail travel agencies and they provide very complex customer care. In this way they have created tourism concerns that work right across the travel value chain, providing tour operations, distribution, flights, accommodation, insurance, entertainment and so on, from a single source (Čavlek 2002a, p. 42). Together these four concerns have close to 60 million clients. The time when tour operators could

sell all they produced has long passed. Now they are operating in a highly competitive market. From year to year customers are becoming more quality conscious, are increasingly sensitive to prices, and tend to book holidays later and later, thus causing tour operators to think hard about cash flow management, flight consolidations and so on. Although vertically integrated travel concerns have more room to balance their revenue than small ones, the integration of different product components not only means the possibility of earning profits from different sides, but also carries the risk of accumulating business failures in more than one area. 'The more integrated the travel and tourism concern are, the more complex and riskier are their business operations' (Čavlek 2002b, p. 416). Therefore yield management, especially for integrated leisure travel concerns, has become a priority, since such concerns have a very high share of fixed costs in their operation. However, as Hilz (2000, p. 455) states, the implementation of yield management is not profitable for every company.

Yield management can in short be defined as the optimisation of revenue through the differentiation of prices. Tour operators cannot expect that all their products will be sold at brochure prices. If, hypothetically, 60–70 per cent of the tour operator's products can be sold at brochure prices, there are still 30–40 per cent of packages that may stay unsold if the tour operator does not alter the brochure prices. However, it has to be stressed here that some of these 60–70 per cent of already sold package holidays might have been sold at higher prices. Changes in demand have to be detected in the early stages, and reaction has to be fast! The task of yield management is to come up with the best solutions (in the case of a fall in demand, to decide on booking incentives). The complexity of the task lies in the fact that demand varies for different destinations, different hotel categories and different flight departures. On top of this the question arises of how many packages can be sold, for example, at a price reduction of only 5 per cent if demand is low, when to start with a reduction of 10 per cent or even more and so on. Yield management in the tour operating business is therefore extremely complex since tour operators deal with an integrated product that has to be purchased within a very limited time range, and has a precise date of consumption without the possibility of being stored. Yield management models are relatively new models in the business practice of airlines and hotels. However, the problem for tour operators is that none of the existing software can be applied in the tour operating business. Unlike an airline or hotel company that has to optimise capacity utilisation in just one field of activity, tour operators have to optimise capacity utilisation combining the yield management of different flights, hotels and destinations. This becomes more complex when optimisation has to take into account own hotels versus hotel capacities under contracts of allotment, own aircraft and so on.

How can yield management help tour operators to achieve higher revenues? In short, yield management enables tour operators to optimise the utilisation of capacities and at the same time enables the sale of products at the highest possible prices at a particular moment. This means that tour operators have to differentiate the prices of their product in such a way that they achieve an optimal balance between demand and the selling price. This is of extreme importance for all tour operators who have fixed contracts with service providers (hoteliers and airlines), or who partially or completely own these companies. Since tourism demand is very seasonal, which means that throughout a season tour operators would need different sizes of aircraft and continually flexible hotel contracts, which would not only be uneconomic, but taking into consideration everything that has been said so far, also unrealistic. Total fixed costs, in simple terms, are based on lower capacity utilisation than the average expected throughout a season. Therefore, once the break-even point is achieved, and the fixed costs are covered, any new customer makes an extra contribution to the company's profit. However, again it has to be pointed out that yield management has a role in optimising utilisation not only when demand is low, but also when demand is high.

Prices quoted in brochures could in the future be seen more as orientation prices, since the role of yield management is to 'govern' and to modify prices depending on actual demand. As already discussed earlier, tour operators determine the brochure prices many months in advance, and therefore there is quite a large time gap between the stipulated offer and actual demand. The aim of yield management is therefore to carefully monitor and alter prices in order to achieve the best possible results. It can be foreseen that this alteration of prices depending on the behaviour of seasonal demand will increasingly lead in the future to so-called 'fluid pricing' (Hilz 2000, p. 473).

Conclusion
Considering the role and importance that travel and tourism intermediaries have gained over the past on the tourism market, it would be difficult to imagine that they would allow their business to disappear. However, it has also become obvious that the business environment within which travel and tourism intermediaries operate has undergone radical changes. Therefore travel and tourism intermediaries need to undertake necessary changes too. Some predictions have been made that travel intermediaries do not have a future, because the need for intermediaries will disappear with better-educated and more-travel-experienced customers, as well as with the new possibilities that modern information technology offers. The possibilities offered by new information and communication technologies might be seen

as a threat to traditional travel and tourism intermediaries. However, all those who accept modern technology as a partner may be in a better position to secure their future on the market. This means that travel and tourism intermediaries need to undertake some changes in their core businesses. For example, travel agencies can reposition their business from being information and booking offices to becoming professional travel advisers.

The rise of low-cost ('no-frills') airlines, and the possibility of direct bookings of flights and accommodation through the internet is a challenge to tour operators. Existing internet portals can already combine accommodation services from hotel data systems and flights from airline computer reservation systems to create a package at daily prices. How are tour operators responding to this challenge? Many of them have developed their own websites, and some are also already able to perform 'dynamic packaging' at daily prices. On the other hand, vertically integrated tour operators have started their own low-cost flight operations, and are offering city-breaks using low-cost carriers. As long as tour operators can add value to their products, save time and money for their clients, and ensure their protection, they can secure their competitiveness in the long term. However, as in any other business, some companies disappear from the market and new companies appear. Since the business environment in which these companies operate is becoming increasingly competitive, and since the risks of their operation are very high, travel and tourism intermediaries are constantly seeking better organisational forms. There will consequently be an increasing need in the future to put more emphasis on the economics of their business.

The trend of consolidation that has taken place among travel and tourism intermediaries in the European market is slowly moving to the American market. At the same time there are visible signs of disintegration among European leisure travel concerns. The new organisational structures require new management models, but above all require well-educated staff who will be able to lead the development of the industry. In general it can be concluded that the modern business of travel and tourism intermediaries is increasingly characterised by integration and cooperation as well as by the use of modern technology.

What is to be expected in the future? Most likely the market will be more polarised between vertically integrated concerns and 'small players'. Small companies will be able to survive the competition of vertically integrated concerns only if they are able to offer products of high quality standards for clients with specific requirements, and in the long term foster high quality management and innovative activity. This is particularly important since large companies, which may have at their disposal high-technology and which possess the capital for optimal development, cannot respond as quickly to changes as small companies. Large vertically integrated concerns will try to develop yield management techniques applicable to this very complex and risky business. Finally, one business function in particular that will gain in importance, no matter what the size of the company, will be risk management.

References

ABTA (2002), 'The 2002 travel agent's benchmarking survey', www.abtamembers.org, accessed 22 December 2003.
ASTA Research (2002), www.astanet.com, accessed 22 December 2003.
Buhalis, D. (2003), *eTourism*, Harlow: FT Prentice-Hall.
Čavlek, N. (2000), 'The role of tour operators in the travel distribution system', in W.C. Garter and D.W. Lime (eds), *Trends in Outdoor Recreation, Leisure and Tourism*, Wallingford: CAB International, 325–34.
Čavlek, N. (2002a), 'Business in tourism: SMEs versus MNCs', *Zagreb International Review of Economics and Business*, **5** (2), 39–48.
Čavlek, N. (2002b), 'The influence of vertically integrated travel concerns on education and training in tourism', in B. Vukonić and N. Čavlek (eds), *Rethinking of Education and Training for Tourism*, Zagreb: Graduate School of Economics and Business, 411–18.
Cooper, C., J. Fletcher, D. Gilbert and S. Wanhill (1998), *Tourism: Principles and Practice*, Harlow: Longman.
DRV (1999), *Facts and Figures: The German Travel Market*, Association of German Travel Agents and Tour Operators (DRV).
DRV (2001), *Facts and Figures: The German Travel Market*, Association of German Travel Agents and Tour Operators (DRV).
DRV (2003), *Facts and Figures: The German Travel Market*, Association of German Travel Agents and Tour Operators (DRV).
Freyer, W. (1998), *Tourismus: Einfuerung in die Fremdenverkehrsoekonomie* (Tourism:) Introduction to Tourism Economics, Munich, Vienna: Oldenburg Verlag.
FVW International (2001), *Reisebüro 2000: Ketten und Kooperationen*, Beilage zur FVW International, Beilage zur FVW International, 13.
FVW International (2002a), *Reisebüro 2001: Ketten und Kooperationen*, Beilage zur FVW International, Beilage zur FVW International, 13.
FVW International (2002b), *Europäische Veranstalter 2001*, 14.
Hilz, A. (2000), 'Yield management fuer Reiseveranstalter', in J.W. Mundt (ed.), *Reiseveranstaltung*, Munich, Vienna: Oldenburg Verlag, 452–74.
Hofmann, W. (2000), 'Die Flugpauschalreise', in Mundt (ed.), 116–54.
Holloway, J.C. (1998), *The Business of Tourism*, Harlow: Addison Wesley Longman.
Kreilkamp, E., U. Regele and D.J. Schmücker (1996), *Betriebsvergleich der deutschen Reisebüros 1994. Schwerpunktthema: Personal*, Hamburg: Verlag Dieter Niedecken.
Lundberg, D.E., M. Krishnamoorthy and M.H. Stavenga (1995), *Tourism Economics*, New York, Chichester, Brisbane, Toronto, Singapore: John Wiley & Sons.
Mundt, J.W. (1998), *Einfürung in den Tourismus*, Munich, Vienna: Oldenburg Verlag.
Mundt, J.W. (ed.) (2000), *Reiseveranstaltung*, Munich, Vienna: Oldenburg Verlag.
Youell, R. (1994), *Leisure and Tourism*, London: Pitman.

7 Pricing principles for natural and cultural attractions in tourism
John Loomis and Kreg Lindberg

Importance of pricing in tourism and cultural resource management

Many unique natural and cultural heritage attractions are owned by public or non-governmental organizations (rather than businesses). The very decision to retain these attractions in public ownership suggests that profit-maximizing pricing such as a private firm would pursue may not meet the objectives of public ownership. Public pricing goals often involve recovery of at least some of the management costs, while keeping sites affordable to allow for public exposure to the natural or cultural heritage. Thus a wider range of factors may affect the pricing decision in public agencies and non-profit organizations than in the private sector. This chapter will first describe economic approaches to pricing, then alternative approaches that are driven by economic (for example, decreasing production costs) or non-economic (for example, revenue requirements, social equity) considerations. Even when non-economic goals affect the pricing decision, economic principles can guide the decision. For example, if pricing is used to reduce negative ecological or congestion impacts, it is necessary to know the price responsiveness of demand to calculate the magnitude of a price increase needed to reduce visitation levels to a target amount. Also there are economic and recreation management consequences of pricing policies sensitive to social equity concerns (for example, low prices may result in overuse or excess demand, necessitating supplemental non-pricing rationing). We draw upon the relevant portions of the general public sector pricing literature (Layard and Walters 1978, among others) and tailor these general principles to the specifics of outdoor recreation and cultural sites.

The basic thesis of this chapter is that pricing plays many more roles in recreation and tourism management than might be imagined (Rosenthal et al. 1984). While the role of pricing to generate revenues for tourist-related businesses or park agencies is obvious, a less obvious role includes pricing for management of visitor use. For example, charging a higher price during periods of peak demand can reduce congestion and give some visitors an incentive to shift their visitation to less heavily used time periods. This results in more uniform levels of visitor use, and frequently reduces the need to expand facilities to meet peak demand. In addition, differential pricing to shift use from popular to less popular areas can be quite effective in more evenly distributing visitor use over a park system. The principles of using pricing as a visitor management tool will be highlighted in this chapter. While much of the literature and many of the examples relate to parks, the principles are equally applicable to cultural sites. Research on pricing of cultural sites and museums has a long history (Huszar and Seckler 1974; Steiner 1997; Yeoman and Leask 1999).

Appropriate pricing can also improve equity or fairness in financing tourist facilities (Loomis and Walsh 1997). For example, why should the general taxpayer finance provision and maintenance of facilities used only by tourists? Should not the tourists directly pay for use of the facilities? The notion of user pays is one principle for equitable financing of recreational facilities. Along these lines, users that impose greater costs should pay higher fees than users that impose lower costs.

Even the role of pricing in raising revenue is often misunderstood by managers. When faced with a decline in revenue or funding, an agency may be tempted to respond by raising prices. But, as we shall show, raising prices does not always lead to an increase in total revenue. The outcome depends on several factors to be discussed.

If the issues of scarcity and choice are the basic problems of economics, demand and supply functions are the basic empirical tools. Demand functions are used to estimate the relationship between the entry prices to a recreation site and the number of visits that consumers demand. Supply curves will be used to provide information on agency costs of providing alternative quantities of recreation resources and facilities, and hence the quantity of visitor capacity provided.

Principles of pricing

The appropriate price to charge for use of recreation facilities will depend on the manager's objective and the time perspective of the analysis. Prior to undertaking construction of a new facility, all costs are variable, and this is typically called a long-run decision. If the objective of the manager is to recover all the construction or capital costs as well as the operating costs, then the price will be set to reflect all these costs. However, even in the long-run case, budgetary appropriations from the legislature may be used to cover the construction or capital costs, and the manager might only need to set fees to cover the operating cost of the facility. Pricing decisions about existing facilities are often considered examples of short-run pricing. Here, the historic costs of building the facility have already been incurred and are considered sunk. The usual goal of short-run pricing is to generate the maximum benefits to society from the use of the existing facility. As such, fees may be set to recover just the variable or day-to-day management costs.

This distinction will be mentioned as we discuss below the alternative pricing strategies that agencies might adopt.

Marginal cost
In order to maximize economic efficiency so as to attain the largest total benefits in excess of costs, economists generally recommend that user fees be set equal to the added costs or variable costs of producing additional recreation opportunities. The additional cost of providing another visit is called the 'marginal cost of another visit'. This means that price would be set where marginal cost equals (that is, intersects) the demand (or marginal benefit) curve. If prices are set equal to the marginal cost, the greatest net benefits (that is, benefit minus cost) are achieved. In the long-run, when all costs are variable, charging the long-run marginal cost price results in the efficient scale of tourism operations, as long as either the tourist operation does not result in any negative spillovers (that is, externalities) or those externalities are included in the marginal cost curve (that is, it is a marginal social cost curve, rather than a marginal private cost curve).

However, in the short run with existing facilities in place, marginal cost pricing may not always result in break-even revenue or a profit. In the short run with an existing facility, setting price at marginal cost may not cover average total costs. This is because in the short run, marginal cost pricing, by definition, is not designed to specifically recover the fixed costs of the facility (see exceptions below). Marginal costs reflect just the incremental or variable costs of serving other visitors. By definition, there are no additional fixed costs of serving additional visitors, since fixed costs are costs that have to be paid whatever the visitor use level (for example, salary of the park superintendent).

To further understand the relationship between the principle of marginal cost pricing and the accountant's tendency toward average cost pricing, it is helpful to review the effect of alternative levels of demand on marginal and average total costs of production. There are three possible situations. An existing park and tourist operations exhibit either:

1. Constant cost production. In this case, because marginal cost of serving another visitor equals the average costs, then marginal cost pricing would result in pay-as-you-go operations.
2. Decreasing cost of production: falling per unit costs of serving additional visitors. In this case, the marginal cost prices are less than average total costs. Therefore marginal cost pricing will not cover fixed costs, resulting in a need for subsidies to cover fixed costs.
3. Increasing cost of production: increasing per unit costs of serving additional visitors which rise with increased numbers of visitors. In this

case marginal cost prices are greater than average total costs, resulting in surplus revenues to expand operations or profits in the short run.

Even in the short run with an existing facility, a constant cost facility may not always remain a constant cost facility. That is, the cost conditions may not be invariant to the use level. At first a large new park may exhibit falling per unit costs, but once its capacity is reached, the park may enter the increasing costs per visitor range. Thus, it is important to understand the dynamic relationship between marginal cost prices and demand. Initially when park and other recreation sites are developed, there may be excess capacity of facilities, justifying a low marginal cost pricing policy in the short run, which does not recover average total costs including investment costs. However, as visitor use increases, marginal cost prices would rise until a point is reached where the revenue from user fees covers average total costs including investment costs. User fees would be equivalent to the competitive equilibrium price in the long run. When demand in excess of capacity develops, marginal cost prices should rise still further to ration use to the available capacity in the short run, and provide an indicator of sufficient willingness to pay to justify an expansion of facilities in the long run. This illustrates the two roles of efficient pricing: in the short run, to encourage the best use of existing facilities; and in the long run, to find the optimum level of investment in capacity.

This dynamic process of moving from a short run of constant or falling costs to rising short-run costs spills over into a long-run decision of whether to expand the facility in the face of rising demand. Specifically, there can be economies of scale (falling long-run per unit costs) from expansion or diseconomies of scale (rising long-run per unit costs) of expanding facilities. If sufficient land exists, doubling the number of campsites in a campground might reduce the per unit costs of providing a campsite. For example, there is often little incremental cost of doubling the size of a water or sewage treatment plant, so that the cost per campsite served falls. However, if the topography makes land scarce, it might require very expensive engineering, construction and land stabilization methods to double the number of campsites. In this case, the additional sites provided will cost more per unit, raising the per unit costs of expanding the supply of campsites.

Minimum-cost production

Efficient pricing results when there is competition between many firms. Effective price competition among private suppliers would drive user fees to minimum-cost levels. However, without the discipline of competitive markets, it may be difficult for managers of government agencies to find the efficient solution. As a result, the efficient operation of recreation programs by public agencies is likely to depend on the ability of managers to adopt the correct least-cost price policy. Further, some tourist destinations are unique or almost unique and/or they purposely limit the number of visitors in order to protect the resource. Note that here there are two interacting objectives – maximum economic benefits and conservation. The Galapagos Islands of Ecuador and mountain gorilla tourism in Africa are examples of this phenomenon. This allows destinations to exercise market power in pricing (Microsoft is an equivalent example outside tourism). This leads to an economically inefficient level of visitation, but can be used to increase tourism-related fee revenue. Perhaps because host-country governments often receive this revenue, governments do not appear inclined to charge prices that would reflect a competitive market equilibrium.

Price not only influences quantity demanded – it also affects the quantity that will be supplied. This has always been true for private companies supplying outdoor recreation goods and services. It is increasingly the case for government agencies supplying outdoor recreation opportunities. If the price of lift tickets is so low that it does not cover the average total cost (AC) of operating most ski areas, little or no downhill skiing will be provided in the long run. If the price is raised somewhat, we may expect suppliers to provide more skiing opportunities. And at even higher prices, they may be willing to provide still more.

Pricing when there are long-run economies of scale in production
In many capital-intensive tourist operations, the average total costs fall as the number of visitors or scale of the operation increases. This is termed 'economies of scale'. A concern when there are economies of scale is that one firm can more cost-effectively service the entire tourist market, relative to several small firms. But one large firm that can drive out small competitors, will not voluntarily keep its prices at the minimum cost. Monopolists can use their market power to raise price above the lower costs that economies of scale bestow (again, think Microsoft). With monopoly pricing, consumers do not realize the cost savings from economies of scale. They are captured as excessive profits by the monopolist. Another important difference from the competitive solution is that at the efficient quantity ($P = MC$), marginal costs are less than average total costs. Marginal costs are always below average total costs when average costs are declining. Thus, there is a trade-off between economic efficiency and revenue self-sufficiency when there are economies of scale. This is the traditional problem with natural monopoly.

Since the principle of marginal cost pricing was first developed, its advocates generally have held that it is the proper solution to the problem of achieving economic efficiency under conditions of decreasing costs, such as occur in public recreation. They would set user fees at marginal cost.

Because the intersection of the demand curve and the marginal cost curve would occur at a price (P) where marginal cost is below the average cost of production (AC), the result would be a net loss from operating recreation programs (P – AC). The deficit would be subsidized from taxes or from a fixed seasonal fee. This latter approach is called 'two-part pricing', where one must pay an annual charge to consume at all (for example, purchase an annual membership), that then gives one the right to pay the price set equal to marginal cost (Layard and Walters 1978: 177). The annual membership essentially is priced to cover the difference between P – AC, at the efficient level of output (that is, P = MC).

Under conditions of decreasing costs of production, the most important advantage of marginal cost pricing is that it would result in larger output and lower average total cost per visit than would average cost pricing, which recovers all operating and capital costs. The inefficiencies resulting from average cost pricing under conditions of decreasing costs of production are that output would be overpriced and underprovided.

Pricing when there are diseconomies of scale
Several developments in the preceding decades contributed to the realization that more and more public recreation sites and tourist destinations experience increasing costs, especially on weekends and holidays. Suitable sites for many kinds of recreation were increasingly scarce, and land costs were rising rapidly. Managers have also become more aware of the environmental damages of excess demand for some types of recreation. As a result, emphasis has shifted toward the case of increasing costs.

MC pricing in the face of rising costs meets both roles of efficient pricing: in the short run, to encourage the efficient use levels of existing facilities; and in the long run, to find the optimum level of investment in capacity. Under conditions of increasing costs, the chief advantage of marginal cost pricing is that it serves these two basic purposes: first, to discourage excess demand, that is, avoid more recreation use than the optimum carrying capacity of existing facilities in the short run; and second, to generate surplus revenue for capital investment to expand recreation programs in the long run.

In order to make appropriate economic decisions with respect to prices, they should be related to appropriate measures of cost. In the usual recreation supply situation, there are: (i) capital costs to acquire land and to develop access roads and facilities; (ii) environmental resource protection costs; (iii) agency operation, maintenance and replacement costs; (iv) administrative overhead costs; (v) congestion costs of users; (vi) other associated costs; and (vii) opportunity costs of forgone resource development. The shape of the marginal cost curve depends on these inputs, which vary as the level of output is increased.

Peak load pricing as a special case of marginal cost pricing

The application of marginal cost pricing by managers of parks, tourist destinations and museums should result in variable user fees at different times of the day, week, or season of the year. Economists use the term 'peak load pricing' when they refer to the practice of charging different prices for the same services demanded at different points in time (Loomis and Walsh 1997; Yeoman and Leask 1999). It makes sense to charge higher prices during peak periods of demand and lower prices during off-peak periods. Since the demand for most recreation opportunities is higher at some times than others, capacity has to be large enough to accommodate demand during the peak periods. However, this results in substantial excess capacity during off-peak periods. The costs of this capacity can be covered by adoption of a marginal cost pricing policy that charges peak users more than off-peak users. In addition, higher prices are needed during peak periods to ration what would be excess demand to the available supply. Downhill ski areas, airlines, hotels and movie theaters are examples of situations where charging higher prices for peak holiday periods is quite common to ration use to available capacity.

Peak load pricing can be illustrated by referring to Figure 7.1. Assume that the demand curve, $D_{PeakTime}$, represents the weighted average demand curve for all peak days and $D_{Off-Peak}$ all off-peak days. During the off-peak period, low user fees are set at $P_{Off-Peak}$ where supply is equal to the marginal benefit of off-peak users. During the peak period, high user fees are set where marginal cost is equal to the marginal benefit of peak users. As a result, off-peak users pay only the lower operating costs to provide the recreation opportunities they consume. However, peak users pay both the operating costs and the costs of increased capacity to provide the additional recreation opportunities they demand at peak times.

For example, a peak price of $6 and an off-peak price of $2 would cover average total costs of $4 when one-half of the annual use of a site occurs on peak days and one-half on off-peak days (all monetary figures in this chapter are in US$, but the principles apply regardless of currency). Figure 7.1 illustrates the situation where the quantity demanded on peak days is double that on off-peak days. But there are roughly twice as many off-peak days in the midweek as peak days on weekends and holidays, so that approximately one-half of the annual recreation use occurs on peak days and one-half on off-peak days. Of course, if annual peak and off-peak use differs, then they must be weighted accordingly.

The difference between the $6 peak and $2 off-peak period prices represents two types of costs: (i) increased operating costs incurred to provide services to large numbers of visitors when operating at high levels of output; and (ii) a capacity charge, representing the annualized value of

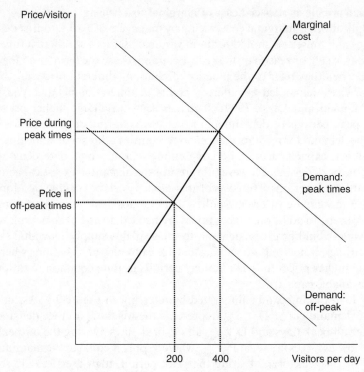

Figure 7.1   Peak load pricing

capital expansion at the site to accommodate peak periods, divided by the number of users in the peak period. This means that a capacity charge is added to the operating cost in the peak period so that demand and supply will be in equilibrium.

In the long run, the value of the capacity charge takes on added significance. As the demand for recreation use increases over time, the capacity charge also increases, to maintain the equilibrium between quantity demanded and capacity of the park. If the number of visitors in the peak period is known, then multiplying peak usage by the capacity charge per user represents the total revenue remaining after payment of the cost of operation. If this remaining revenue is greater than the annual capital costs of new construction, then expansion of park capacity is justified and should be done. This means that additions to capacity should be made until the daily capacity charge, multiplied by the number of users in the peak period, equals the annual capital costs associated with expansion. Hence, the value of the capacity charge required to clear the market during the peak period indicates whether expansion of park facilities is justified from an economic viewpoint.

Peak load pricing has two additional advantages. First, the approach provides casual users with an economic incentive to visit the facilities during off-peak periods when entrance fees are lower. This would tend to reduce the seasonal variation in the number of daily users and to partially equalize costs over time. Second, when peak period users pay an additional cost to reflect the scarcity of recreation opportunities during peak periods, this guarantees that those users who place the highest value on recreation use of the site at that time are the ones that actually are admitted. This is important because as a result, only those persons whose benefits equal or exceed the added costs of providing the recreation resources will use them. In this way, marginal cost pricing will result in the production of recreation opportunities that maximize total net benefit.

Peak load pricing also may reduce equity problems associated with pricing since low-income users (for example, college students, retired persons) can go during off-peak periods when charges are less. Thus, the imposition of peak load pricing may lead to desirable distribution results. However, if low-income workers can only visit on peak weekends and holidays due to fixed work schedules, then peak load pricing could worsen equity. Thus equity may require a dual system whereby half the sites are allocated using peak load pricing and the other half at low fees using a lottery.

Implementation of peak period pricing would require information that should not be difficult to obtain. The number of users during peak and off-peak days should be readily available from fee receipts. More difficult to obtain is information regarding the number of potential users turned away from the site on peak days. This would be needed to accurately estimate the quantity of use demanded at the given user fees. Peak load pricing would be contrary to many existing pricing practices where unrestricted annual passes can be used, even on peak days. A solution used by the ski industry is that annual passes are not honored at peak periods.

An example of using differential pricing for management and revenue
As is evident, pricing can be used as a management tool as well as to raise revenue. An example of this is the field experiment conducted by Bamford et al. (1988) at 14 Vermont State Park campgrounds. At the time of the study, the current pricing system charged the same fee for high amenity campsites such as those adjacent to lakes and streams, and less desirable sites located elsewhere in the campground (for example, by the main road). The natural result is competition and overuse of the desirable sites and underutilization of the other sites.

To evaluate the effect of a fee differential to spread use more evenly among sites, a price differential ranging from $1 to $5 was instituted at selected Vermont State Park campgrounds. The prices for the different types of campsites were displayed at the entrance station map so that campers knew the prices for various locations of sites when they were making their campsite selection. Visitor use before and after the fee was monitored, and a sample of campers was sent a survey to record their socioeconomic characteristics.

Regression and correlation analysis showed that the fee differential resulted in a strong and statistically significant shift in visitor use away from prime campsites as the fee differential increased between prime and non-prime campsites. Over half the variation in the demand for prime campsites can be explained solely by the fee differential.

The authors also noted a small, but consistent effect of visitor income on campsite choice with the fee differential. However, while the presence of any differential fee caused fewer low-income households to choose prime sites, the size of the differential fee did not further reduce the percentage of low-income households choosing prime sites. Nonetheless, it appears that fee differentials could be used as a potent tool for managing spatial patterns of visitor use.

It is worth noting that this differential pricing is quite effective at relatively low price differentials when the recreation sites of interest are not unique and there are many similar substitute sites (that is, the demand is relatively price sensitive). When a site is fairly unique, with few substitutes such that the demand is very price unresponsive, it may take a very large price differential to shift use to other sites. A large price differential may run into equity concerns, however.

Pricing, elasticity of demand, total revenue and price discrimination

If a manager of a tourist facility or park is faced with declining revenue, there may be a tendency to assume that raising the price or entrance fee will automatically increase total revenue. After all, if price goes up, and total revenue is price times quantity, total revenue should rise. But this is only true if the demand for the tourist destination or service is relatively price insensitive or what economists call 'price inelastic'. This determination draws upon the concept of elasticity of demand.

Elasticity of demand is defined as the percentage change in quantity consumed that is caused by a percentage change in a determinant of demand. Price elasticity of demand, for example, is a convenient way of comparing how price changes affect the quantity consumed. It is the ratio of two percentages – the change in quantity consumed that results from a change in price. When the percentage change in price results in a larger percentage change in quantity demanded, the demand is said to be 'price elastic'. By price elastic we mean that the quantity demand is quite sensitive or very responsive to price changes. Conversely, when the percentage change in price results in a smaller percentage change in quantity demanded is said to be price inelastic, that is, the quantity demanded is not very sensitive to changes in the price.

If the recreation activity or destination is price elastic and the price is increased, the total revenue will fall. For example, if the price elasticity of demand is −2 for castle tours and the price is raised by 10 percent, this will reduce the quantity demanded by 20 percent. The 20 percent reduction in the quantity demanded will more than offset the 10 percent increase in price, the result being a decrease in total revenues. Now, consider a unique tourist destination where demand is price inelastic. In this case, if the price or entrance fee is increased, the total revenue will increase. To see why, suppose that the price elasticity of demand for recreation activity is −0.5 and the entrance fee or lift ticket is increased by 10 percent. Because the price elasticity of demand is −0.5, the 10 percent price increase results in only a 5 percent decrease in the number of trips demanded. Since the total amount spent equals the quantity demanded times the price, the 5 percent decrease in the quantity demanded will be more than offset by the 10 percent increase in price. The result of the price increase will be an increase in total revenue. So the manager needs to know whether the current and proposed prices are in the inelastic portion of the demand curve before raising price in an attempt to increase revenue (a linear demand curve will have elastic and inelastic portions, while a nonlinear demand curve may have constant elasticity). If they are not in the inelastic portion of the demand curve (for example, prices are quite high already or there are many substitute sites), then total revenue could decrease with the price increase. This will only disappoint the manager and anger the visitors.

A pricing strategy that takes advantage of the fact that different users often have different price elasticities is called 'third degree price discrimination'. This is the maximization of total profits by setting prices of a product or service in two or more different submarkets so that marginal revenue equals marginal cost in each. To practice third degree price discrimination, sellers must have sufficient market power to set their own prices, serve two or more submarkets with different elasticities of demand, and be able to prevent transfers among types of customers in different submarkets. This can be demonstrated by an example. Suppose a national park is setting entrance fees for a park that caters to two separate submarkets of visitors – local residents and foreign tourists. These two groups can be easily identified and segregated at moderate cost. In many situations, foreign tourists are readily identifiable (and an identity card may be required to

Table 7.1   Estimated foreign visitation and revenue at various price levels in Costa Rica

Price ($)	Foreign visits (monthly)			Revenue from foreign visits ($000, annual)		
	Poás	Irazú	Manuel Antonio	Poás	Irazú	Manuel Antonio
1	6917	3881	7359	83	47	88
5	6487	2910	5602	389	175	336
10	6302	2492	4845	756	299	581
15	6194	2248	4402	1115	405	792
20	6117	2074	4088	1468	498	981

prove local residence), so preventing transfer of entrance tickets would be easy to detect. Third degree price discrimination increases total revenue by increasing the price to the price inelastic group (for example, the foreign tourists) and keeping prices low to the price elastic group (for example, the local residents). We use these examples, because the price elasticity of demand is related to percentage of the total purchase price reflected in the entrance fee. Thus for foreign tourists, whether the entrance fee is $5 or $10 may not matter when they have spent $2000 to fly there, $100 a night on a hotel and $40 a day on a rental car. A $5 or $10 entrance fee would be a small part of the overall trip cost. On the other hand, for local residents, whose only expense may be the cost of local transport, the difference between $5 and $10 entrance fee might be a 25 percent or greater difference in trip cost, and they would likely be quite sensitive to this. This type of price discrimination is practiced in Costa Rica and many African countries, which charge foreigners higher fees than they charge residents, and also in Beijing's Forbidden City (Lindberg and Aylward 1999). Developing the necessary information on the relative price elasticities of foreign tourists versus local residents is not too difficult and has been illustrated at Lake Nakuru, Kenya by Navrud and Mungatana (1994).

Table 7.1 illustrates the relative price inelastic response within a $1 to $20 range of entrance fees from three parks in Costa Rica. As can be seen, higher and higher fees reduce foreign visitation, but the decrease in visitation is less than the increase in fee, resulting in increasing revenue. No doubt if the fee was raised to $50 or $100, fee revenue would at that point fall.

Interaction of pricing and other public goals of tourism management
Pricing to recover recreation management costs and efficiently allocate limited capacity among visitors, sometimes conflicts with other public

goals or public perceptions about the management of natural or cultural sites. A common concern in some countries, is that people have viewed national parks and cultural sites as part of their national heritage. They feel that the areas should be provided by the government to all citizens, with funding ultimately being based on taxes or other government revenue sources. They feel that it is simply not appropriate to charge citizens to access publicly owned land.

Of course, equity concerns based on limited ability to pay have been a longstanding concern against pricing (Harris and Driver 1987). That is, fees may have a disproportionate effect on low-income citizens or other groups within society (for example, ethnic minorities and/or local residents, who often are also low income) whom we wish to have access to the recreational or cultural site. Some common sense or flexibility in setting prices can partially offset some of these concerns. If the recreational/cultural site is located near an urban city and frequently used by inner city residents, then it may very well be unfair to charge a very high price. Rather, establishing a discounted pricing system for local residents (who pay taxes to support these facilities) may be appropriate. At more distant sites, where significant automobile or other travel costs must be incurred to reach the site, distance screens out poor users. That is, the high costs for nearly all visitors to reach remote recreational/cultural sites often reduces the proportion of visitors that are low income or poor as they simply do not have the financial means to visit the site. For these sites, charging a fee to recover management costs from the users may be more equitable than requiring the general taxpayers to pay the management costs. In addition, such equity concerns are less relevant in the case of international visitation, particularly when the visitors tend to be much wealthier than residents of the destination country. Framed in economic terms, it may be difficult to justify retaining low or nonexistent fees in order to maximize the net benefits of foreign visitors. Many countries, including Costa Rica, have implemented multi-tiered fee systems in order to limit equity impacts for nationals while generating revenue from foreigners.

With a little flexibility and creativity, it is also often possible to devise fee systems to facilitate visitation by groups that might be disadvantaged, such as: (i) lower fees for students or the elderly, or through (ii) annual passes, off-peak fee reductions, or 'open' days with no fees, which implicitly favor local residents. However, several other countries have retained uniform fee systems, in some cases due to explicit or perceived legislative prohibitions on differential fees.

Future research
The measurement of marginal cost, particularly if there are negative externalities associated with tourism, requires more research. The relevant

costs should include more than the internal operation and maintenance costs of the tourist companies or public agencies administering recreation programs. For many recreation facilities, one of the greatest influences on long-run marginal cost is often external costs such as congestion, user conflicts and opportunity costs. Congestion results when too many users impose external costs on each other by physically interfering with each other or each other's quality of experience (for example, solitude). Conflict costs arise when one group of users, typically motorized, impose noise and air pollution costs on other users, typically non-motorized users. Recent examples include the skier–snowmobiler and jet skis–angler conflicts. Congestion and conflict are related concepts, but conflict illustrates that it is not simply a matter of the number of people that imposes costs.

Opportunity costs may result from using natural resources for recreation at the expense of another purpose. An example would be the opportunity cost of draining wetlands to build golf courses or hotel expansion. Wetlands provide many non-market functions such as storage of flood waters, groundwater recharge, nutrient removal, nursery for juvenile fish and so on. Most of these functions are not priced in a market, so the developer of the golf course would not pay for the lost social benefits provided by the wetland. Further, the large quantities of water used by the golf course may dry up streams or springs. The heavy use of fertilizers on the golf course may increase eutrophication of remaining water resources. These costs need to be included in the marginal costs paid by visitors to such developed tourist facilities in order that such facilities should not be overproduced, relative to natural resources.

Of course, to implement several of the types of pricing principles discussed in this chapter requires knowledge of visitor demand and price elasticity. This requires systematic research on a wide variety of tourist opportunities so that we can understand the likely range of elasticities for typical tourist sites, facilities as well as different types of users and their region of origin (for example, local residents versus foreign tourists). The research is worthwhile when the results can be applied broadly to management of an entire park system or at high volume sites, where fine tuning entrance fees could increase visitor benefits and agency revenues by hundreds of thousands of dollars. In this case, the value of the information generated by the research is well worth the cost of the studies.

References

Bamford, T., R. Manning, L. Forcier and E. Koenemann (1988), 'Differential campsite pricing: an experiment', *Journal of Leisure Research*, **20** (4), 324–42.
Harris, C.C. and B.L. Driver (1987), 'Recreation user fees: pros and cons', *Journal of Forestry*, May, 25–9.

Huszar, P. and D. Seckler (1974), 'Effects of pricing a "free" good: a study of admission at the California academy of sciences', *Land Economics*, **50** (4), 364–73.

Layard, P. and A. Walters (1978), *Microeconomic Theory*, New York: McGraw-Hill.

Lindberg, K. and B. Aylward (1999), 'Price responsiveness in the developing country nature tourism context: review and Costa Rican case study', *Journal of Leisure Research*, **31** (3), 281–99.

Loomis, J. and R. Walsh (1997), *Recreation Economic Decisions: Comparing Benefits and Costs*, 2nd edn, State College, PA: Venture Press.

Navrud, S. and E.D. Mungatana (1994), 'Environmental valuation in developing countries: the recreational value of wildlife viewing', *Ecological Economics*, **11**, 135–51.

Rosenthal, D., G. Peterson and J. Loomis (1984), 'Pricing for efficiency and revenue in public recreation areas', *Journal of Leisure Research*, **16** (3), 195–208.

Steiner, F. (1997), 'Optimal pricing of museum admission', *Journal of Cultural Economics*, **21**, 307–33.

Yeoman, I. and A. Leask (1999), 'Yield management', in A. Leask and I. Yeoman (eds), *Heritage Visitor Attractions: An Operations Management Perspective*, London: Cassell, 176–89.

PART THREE

TOURISM TRANSPORT

8 The evolution of alliances in the airline industry

Frédéric Dimanche and Dominique Jolly

Introduction

Business alliances represent a growing trend, particularly in the tourism sector. This chapter explores the nature of these business alliances, the effect of pulling resources together, and the types of benefits expected by the respective partners. After reviewing the existing literature on strategic alliances, the purpose of the chapter is then to use a new typology of alliances that we illustrate in the context of tourism and more specifically airlines. Two types of inter-firm alliances are identified: endogamy and exogamy. Endogamy occurs when partners share related profiles, whereas exogamy appears when allies exhibit unrelated profiles. The usefulness of this typology is that it enables the researcher to use resource-based approaches (Wernerfelt 1984; Grant 1991; Hamel 1991) so as to suggest a dichotomy between alliances generating opposite results and representing very different stakes and risks. For practitioners, this typology allows the distinction between two classes that call for significantly different managerial approaches. More specifically, we propose the use of this original alliance typology to cast a new light on the evolution of strategic alliances in the airline sector.

Importance of alliances

Quantitative evolution

For the past few years, observers of the tourism sector would certainly identify agreements between firms as one of the most significant business trends (Archambault 2000). Indeed, the professional press worldwide is replete with examples of mergers, acquisitions, takeovers, alliances, partnerships and other inter-firm agreements in all sectors of the industry. This trend has particularly been true of the airline industry (Wang and Evans 2002). The US airline deregulation, followed by similar European policies, has led to major changes worldwide with consolidation, hub systems, low airfares in competitive situations and high airfares where competition is lacking (Goeldner et al. 2000). The current situation demonstrates the continuing trend for airline alliances and concentration. Indeed, alliances such as code-sharing agreements have become very popular in the airline industry, as most airlines form partnerships with competitors to remain effective (Vander Kraats 2000).

Qualitative evolution

Not only have business alliances become more numerous, but the nature of these relationships has also evolved qualitatively. The objective of this chapter is to demonstrate that alliances have changed from being *endogamic* to becoming *exogamic*. Old alliances such as global distribution systems (GDSs), for example, focused on a single function (of the value chain) within a set of companies with related profiles that may originate from the same geographical area. New partnerships tend to mix companies originating from different geographical areas and covering a larger number of functions.

A global picture of alliances

Inter-firm alliances

Definitions of inter-firm alliances in the business literature constitute a large spectrum from definitions focused on equity joint venture to much broader approaches. Equity joint ventures were studied (for example, Killing 1982, 1988; Harrigan 1986, 1988; Geringer and Hébert 1991). They are usually defined as a legal and separate entity that was created and held by at least two distinct partners by transferring a part of their own resources in order to pursue a joint goal. Looser definitional approaches consider an alliance to be any transaction where partners share some interests, and have intimate, harmonious and emphatic relationships. This includes long-term agreements, taking some financial interests, subcontracting, licensing and so on.

There is a general agreement that inter-firm alliances can be explained by the reduction of transaction costs (Hennart 1988), as well as cost sharing, risk sharing (Kogut 1988), symbiotic effects, increase of market power, resource transfer (Hamel 1991; Mowery et al. 1996; Kumar and Nti 1998; Si and Bruton 1999), or knowledge creation (Inkpen 1996).

Inter-firm alliances in tourism

As Evans et al. (2003, p. 249) note, 'the (tourism) literature is far from clear as to what constitutes a "strategic alliance" and many definitions have emerged such as those of French (1997), Bennett (1997) and Glaister and Buckley (1996).' Vellas and Bécherel (1999, p. 17) loosely defined alliances as 'a co-operative relationship between businesses. They can be informal, such as a pooling of information, or contractual'. Alliances were defined more specifically by Evans et al. (p. 250) as 'a particular "horizontal" form of inter-organizational relationship in which two or more organizations collaborate, without the formation of a separate independent organization, in order to achieve one or more common strategic objectives'. In hospitality contexts, Go and Pine (1995, p. 341) indicate that strategic alliances 'have become an increasingly important means of conducting business in the hotel industry . . . to create value and to innovate'. The topic of globalisation and strategic airlines alliances was presented by Oum et al. (2000). The authors suggest that complementary alliances (exogamic) improved customer welfare while parallel alliances (endogamic) reduced flight frequency, and therefore choice and customer satisfaction.

Airline alliances and distribution systems
For twenty years, alliances in the airline industry were formed for distribution purposes. The example of global distribution systems such as Abacus, Galileo, Sabre, World Span and Amadeus illustrate this very traditional case. Each of these entities was searching for quantitative complementarities such as: reaching a critical mass; reaching the optimum scale; gaining scope economies; increasing joint economies of scale; spreading risks among members. The GDS business offers therefore several examples of endogamic partnerships (see Figure 8.1).

Most of these GDSs were originally developed with a focus on the reservation system of several airline companies. They operate as an interface between providers, such as airline companies, hotels or car rental companies, and end-users, such as travel agencies (which still represent the largest share), corporate services, on-line travel sites or multinational agencies. There are four main GDSs around the world: (i) Sabre, originally launched by American Airlines, is still the first in the North American

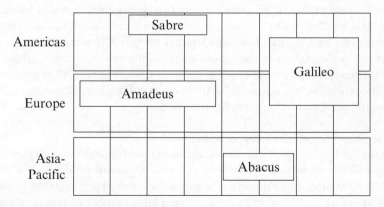

Figure 8.1   Old endogamic partnership

market; (ii) Galileo was founded by 11 major North American (3) and European (8) airlines (that is, Aer Lingus, Air Canada, Alitalia, Austrian Airlines, British Airways, KLM Royal Dutch Airlines, Olympic Airlines, Swissair, TAP Air Portugal, United Airlines and US Airways); (iii) Worldspan, founded in 1990 was originally owned by affiliates of Delta Air Lines, Northwest Airline, and Trans World Airlines. It is currently owned by affiliates of Delta Air Lines (40 per cent), Northwest Airlines (34 per cent) and American Airlines (26 per cent); and (iv) Amadeus, the youngest of the 'big four', is a European equity joint venture originally founded in 1987 by Air France, Iberia, Lufthansa and SAS, now held by three main shareholders, Air France (23 per cent), Lufthansa (5.1 per cent), and Iberia (18 per cent) – the rest being public.

At the end of the 1980s, 18 companies out of the first twenty in the world had some equity stake in a GDS. During the 1990s, most airline carriers tended to disengage from GDSs – even if they continued to work with them. The shareholding of these companies has changed significantly over the last ten years: Galileo was sold to Cendant – a conglomerate of hotel brands (for example, Days Inn, Ramada or Travelodge) with little original connection to the airline sector. The early founders are no longer equity owners. Sabre, originally founded by American Airlines, is now 100 per cent publicly owned. SAS, which was part of the original founders of Amadeus, left the joint venture. The recent disengagement of Lufthansa in Amadeus (February 2004), despite the fact that Amadeus is a profitable company in a difficult environment, stresses the fact that companies now consider these investments as less strategic and consequently appear to increasingly lose interest in endogamic alliances.

In addition to GDSs, internet travel agencies such as Orbitz represent another example of endogamic partnerships. Orbitz is an internet-based travel agency (such as Expedia.com or Travelocity.com) that was founded in 2001 by five major airline carriers – American, Continental, Delta, Northwest and United. Besides, Orbitz is open to Charter Associates. Its activity is focused on on-line travel reservations and ticketing. Compared to carrier-specific websites (such as the one of Southwest), Orbitz generates higher volumes; this allows collective savings on booking costs and consequently reduced booking fees for travellers.

The emergence of a new cooperation model
Since the beginning of the 1990s, the world air transportation sector has increasingly been slipping towards a fringed oligopoly: on the one hand, a reduced number of coalitions of world scope, centred around a few powerful founding members, and on the other, a large number of less significant companies which remain independent. These 'mega-networks' have deve-

loped around geographical poles and have generally been launched with the creation of a new all-encompassing brand that is superimposed over traditional flags. This quest for geographical complementarities, as well as for a larger range of covered functions, has changed the nature of alliances in the airline industry from being endogamic to exogamic. Three main clubs can be identified:

1. *Star Alliance:* The first large commercial confederation launched with great publicity in 1997 by United Airlines and Lufthansa, to which joined Thai Airways International, Singapore Airlines, Air Canada, Varig, All Nippon Airways, Air New Zealand, bmi British midland, Mexicana Airlines, SAS – Scandinavian Airlines, Austrian Airlines, Lauda Air, Tyrolean, LOT, Spanair and Asiana. The main measures, as defined by its management board, are product development (common facilities in airports or single agencies in cities); group purchase of parts, fuel and aircraft; business strategy (reciprocity of frequent flyer programmes, harmonisation of timetables, integrated reservation systems, sharing of information systems); and marketing communications (integration of staff and brand identity) (Archambault 2000).
2. *Oneworld:* A network launched in 1999 by American Airlines and British Airways to which joined Cathay Pacific, Qantas, Iberia, Aer Lingus, Finnair and LanChile. American Airlines and British Airways have had difficulties with their relationship because of their (too) strong competitive position in trans-Atlantic routes. However, Oneworld members have developed common actions such as developing an integrated timetable, common baggage handling processes, or frequent flyer reciprocity (Archambault 2000);
3. *SkyTeam:* A partnership between Air France and Delta Air Lines signed in 1999 for ten years led to the creation of SkyTeam in 2000, with Aeromexico and Korean joining in, then CSA Czech Airlines, and Alitalia in 2001. More recently, Air France took over the Dutch airline KLM, which will lead eventually to the participation of KLM in SkyTeam. Also, Aeroflot is a candidate as a member of SkyTeam to help reinforce the alliance in the emerging eastern European market.

Other alliances have been created with less success; some died (the Swissair-led European alliance Qualiflyer or the 'Atlantic Excellence' trans-Atlantic airline alliance between Swissair, Delta Air Lines, Sabena and Austrian Airlines) and some never really got off the ground (Wings). It is to be noted that one of the reasons for the failure of Qualiflyer was its restricted geographic focus (Europe). Successful alliances include partners from several continents (see Figure 8.2).

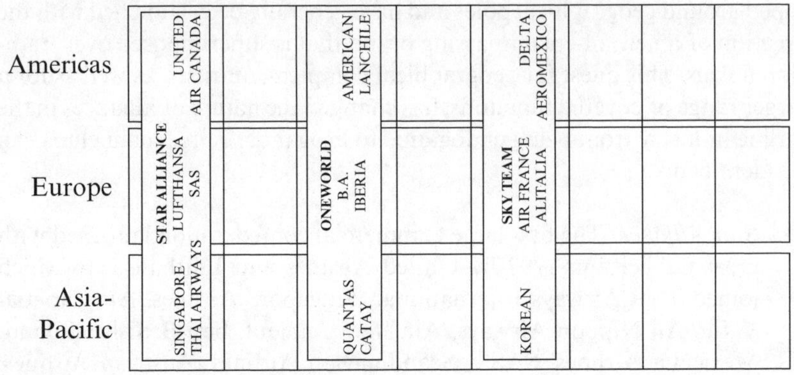

	STAR ALLIANCE	ONEWORLD	SKY TEAM		
Americas	UNITED AIR CANADA	AMERICAN LANCHILE	DELTA AEROMEXICO		
Europe	LUFTHANSA SAS	B.A. IBERIA	AIR FRANCE ALITALIA		
Asia- Pacific	SINGAPORE THAI AIRWAYS	QUANTAS CATAY	KOREAN		

Figure 8.2   New exogamic partnership

These alliances make it possible to offer customers a widened range of destinations and a reinforcement of the flight frequencies; an easier routing through various hubs; a reciprocity for reward programmes and even a common consumer loyalty programme; and an access to the services of all the member companies (for example, executive lounges).

At levels often less obvious or visible to the customer, these agreements also allow economies on the code share flights; the common use of information networks; sharing of invaluable statistics such as consumer flows; and a rationalisation of the network (for example, Alitalia suppressed up to 30 routes out of Milan Malpensa, after entering SkyTeam and using Air France and its Paris hub as a substitute).

These networks, which constantly redefine the air landscape, are not yet stabilised. These alliances evolve/move, are built and are demolished; there is sometimes, for some airlines, a superposition of old and new alliances. Thus, Air France chose to forsake its ally Continental Airlines to privilege its agreement with Delta Air Lines. In addition, some countries have yet to enter these networks (for example, the People's Republic of China). Much remains to be played. Global airlines alliances are steadily becoming major forces in the international marketplace, but they remain fragile because their survival depends upon the strength of a few major airlines. What would remain of SkyTeam if Air France or Delta faced major difficulties and disappeared? The United Airlines difficulties in 2003 created problems for Star Alliance. Even worse, Qualiflyer did not survive the bankruptcy of Swissair. Some alliances are still limiting their actions while waiting for final government decisions on competitive agreements. The major stake of these groupings is to find new members, other European, Asian or Latin-American companies, in order to create a network that would truly be worldwide.

Existing conceptual frameworks

On the definition of alliances

There appear to be numerous examples of confusion in the literature regarding the definition of alliances. Indeed, Wang and Evans (2002, p. 73) stressed the 'lack of precise definitions to specify different types of airline alliances in the literature'. Existing definitions suffer from at least three limitations. First, the concept is wrought in semantic uncertainty, which generates a loose agreement among academics regarding the definition of organisational forms of cooperation. In effect, contrary to what Crotts et al. (2000, p. 1) suggest, we do not think that mere buyer–seller relationships are enough to constitute alliances. Second, few studies conceptualising alliances have been conducted in the tourism sector. Third, typologies do not emphasise enough relatedness between allies' resource profiles.

We suggest that four conditions must be met in order to have a true inter-firm alliance (Jolly 2001). First, each of the partners must accept a loss of their autonomy in order to pursue a common goal in a well-specified area – whether this concerns an entire business or a specific function (for example, code sharing or joint purchase of catering services) or a well-defined project (for example, joint development of training programmes or technical procedures or developing together a new technology or service). Second, each partner has to pool a fraction of its own resources into the joint venture in the interests of cooperation (for example, ground crew of an airline providing ground services for passengers of another airline at one place, while the opposite occurs at another place). Third, the joint action should produce results that would not occur in the context of an independent action (for example, Delta Air Lines gains access to Asia and Europe through its alliance with Korean Air and Air France, respectively). And finally, apart from the alliance, each partner is supposed to keep autonomous a significant part of its global business – otherwise this will result in an imbalance that might reduce the freedom of the ally. This latter point exists de facto with the enforcing of international regulations that prohibit access to internal routes. For example, an American airline cannot run point-to-point routes in Europe.

Inter-firm agreements such as the formation of an equity joint venture, an industry consortium, or more simply a non-equity contract for technology development or swaps such as code-share agreements, are examples of organisational arrangements that respond positively to these four conditions. Taking a financial interest (A buying x per cent of B), or a complete takeover (where A becomes the parent company of B at 100 per cent), do not fall into the category of inter-firm alliances; the two scenarios imply a hierarchical relationship that cannot be considered a same-level relationship. Likewise, unilateral licensing agreements where A pays to get access to the knowledge of B for a certain amount of money, cannot be considered as the pursuit of a common goal. A similar argument can be made against subcontracting; joint action and pooled resources are usually very limited and subcontracting means that the subcontractor heavily depends upon the desiderata of the contractor while survival is more questionable for the subcontractor than for the contractor. Finally, in the case of franchising, there is no joint decision as most of the time the franchiser decides on what has to be done and forces the franchisee to implement its decisions.

Interfirm alliances in travel

We shall restrict our argument to inter-firm alliances and keep aside discussions, for example, of partnerships in destination planning and development, or of cooperative marketing actions between countries (Hill and Shaw 1995). The International Air Travel Association (IATA 2001) defines an alliance as at least three airlines engaging in a commercial relationship or Joint venture, where (i) a joint and commonly identifiable product is marketed under a single commercial brand; (ii) this brand is promoted to the public through the airlines participating in the alliance and its agents and (iii) the brand is used to identify the alliance services at airports and other service delivery points. This narrow definition is focused only on marketing activities. We need to broaden the scope of alliances.

Type of joint activities

The literature has typically put the emphasis on territorial/geographic dimensions (For example, Vander Kraats 2000) while demonstrating a more limited interest on the nature of the activities (For example, Glisson and Cunningham 1996). Figure 8.3 illustrates the various activities that can be undertaken in the context of an alliance.

Resources pooled

Resources pooled by partners in the context of an alliance can either be of the same nature (For example, development engineers who may come from different countries but who share similar technical backgrounds, skills and experiences) or of different types (for example, a company may give access to another airline to routes in a geographic market to which it has sole rights of access).

Nature of advantages of airline alliances

Benefits of airline alliances are well identified and covered in the literature (for example, Brueckner and Whalen 2000; Flores and Renato 1998). Alliances in the airline industry have been proven to contribute positively to performance when environments are rapidly changing and variable

Joint procurement	Joint operations	Joint back office	Co-marketing agreements	Co-services
• Joint procurement of fuel • Joint purchase of catering services • Joint aquisition of planes • Joint procurement of replacement parts	• Joint maintenance and repair • Common facilities in airports • Baggage handling	• Joint reservation systems • Harmonisation of time-tables. coordination of flight schedules	• Code sharing of international flights • Joint frequent flyers programmes	• Joint ticketing • Lending of flight attendants

Figure 8.3   Airline alliance activities

(Domke-Damonte 2000). The main motive for entering into an alliance agreement is typically to gain some sort of market share. For example, airlines want to expand networks overseas, gain entry to some markets, or eliminate a competitor to increase market share. This first set of motives comes from the qualitative complementarities of networks and is well documented in the literature. For example, Dev and Klein (1996) suggested the use of a market-based approach for the travel and tourism industry in selecting a marketing partner. They proposed that firms should have a complete understanding of their customers' buying behaviour before making partner selection decisions. In the same qualitative vein, alliances provide a better service to customers such as enhancement of the offer, smoother transitions on connecting flights, or coordination of flight schedules and connections.

However, less has been said on cost savings gained from scale and scope economies that result from quantitative complementarities. For example, alliances allow cost reductions when there is joint purchase of fuel or maintenance, joint acquisition of aircrafts, or even joint marketing activities. Motives for alliances are evolving and now appear to rely increasingly on qualitative rather than quantitative complementarities.

Mutual dependency

Alliances do create mutual dependencies between partners. Again, alliances should not be confused with a merger or even worse, with an acquisition. Flores and Renato (1998) have suggested that regulation is one reason for not going into mergers and acquisitions and alliances are one way to bypass those regulations. For some authors such as Crotts et al. (2000) the term 'alliance' seems no more than a buzzword. In the title of their book, the agreements discussed by the authors are most of the time traditional arm's-length contracts where there is no mutual dependency.

A new perspective: endogamic versus exogamic alliances

Some researchers suggested that inter-firm alliances in the airline industry have evolved qualitatively but failed to identify this move from endogamic to exogamic partnerships (Wang and Evans 2002). We distinguish between two types of inter-firm alliances: endogamy and exogamy (Jolly 2002). Endogamy occurs when partners share related profiles. In contrast, exogamy appears when allies exhibit unrelated profiles. We shall show that the benefits resulting from endogamies is essentially to gain quantitative complementarities such as economies of scale. It is suggested that endogamy serves for accumulating similar resources, whereas the benefits that can be achieved in an exogamic relationship are qualitative complementarities resulting from the combination of differentiated competences, such as the combination of different sets of knowledge or different geographical markets.

This section begins with an explanation of the concept of relatedness. Then, it elaborates on the dichotomy between endogamic and exogamic partnerships. Finally, this new perspective is applied to the airline industry to demonstrate the evolution of alliances.

Measuring relatedness between two profiles

An issue central to understanding alliances is that of a company's 'resource profile'. Indeed, we believe that the profile of the respective allies determine not only the resources that are brought into the alliance, but also the nature of the alliance. It is therefore essential to conceptualise 'profile' and understand how companies can measure the proximity or relatedness between their respective profiles. Ansoff (1965) was one of the early authors to propose an evaluation grid to assess a firm's capability profile. He noted four resource categories: buildings and equipment, personnel competences, capabilities related to the company structure, and managerial capabilities. These categories are examined through four functions: executive and financial management, research and development, marketing and commercialisation, and operations. A similar objective is pursued by Porter (1985) with his value chain model where a homogeneous strategic unit can be decomposed in operations that create value: main operations (logistics, production, sales and marketing, services) and support operations (supply systems, technological development, human resource management, infrastructure).

A resource profile is therefore the representation of an organisation, according to a model describing its assets and capabilities. The relatedness between two companies' profiles is examined not just through products, services and markets, but also through managerial processes, quality management, customer relationship management, purchasing strategies and so on. The following resources are typically identified: technological, financial, physical, human, organisational and brand (the image and reputation of the firm) (Grant 1991). Companies can then measure with competence analysis grids of the relations that may exist between other firms and themselves to determine how their needs as an ally can best be served.

Related versus unrelated resource profiles
In the interpersonal sphere, endogamy is the union of two partners coming from the same social milieu whereas exogamy is the wedding of two people originating from different backgrounds. In the business world, the concept of milieu can easily be understood as the industry in which a company operates. It refers, by extension, to the products and/or services it delivers. What can be an alliance between companies coming from the same milieu? Joint research and development (R&D) between companies of the same industry is an example of endogamy. Another example is a common central reservation system for two airlines from the same geographic area. Endogamies occur when two companies come from the same industry, deliver the same product and/or service, and exhibit like profiles. There is a good chance that the partners' profiles share some similarities – for at least three reasons. First, they operate within the same environment, with the same customers, distributors and suppliers. Second, they have to face the same rules of the game and therefore share the same key success factors. Third, if they share the same background, they might have very similar value chains, they might have comparable technology portfolios, they may employ similar types of manufacturing facilities, or they very often use similar distribution channels.

On the contrary, an exogamy occurs when a company teams up with a partner which does not share the same profile. Usually, this means that the two companies do not come from the same industry. For example, this would be the case of an airline company setting up an alliance with car rental companies to offer joint services to their customers. The two partners do not have the same competitors, suppliers or even sometimes the same distributors. They have completely different value chains, they master different technologies, they manage different operating facilities, and they have a different expertise at the commercialisation stage. Should we conclude that exogamies are only inter-industry partnerships? No! In some circumstances, companies belonging to the same business might have developed different resource profiles: this means that they have different expertise, or do not use the same operation processes, or exploit different distribution channels. This is, for example, the case of alliances between a well-established large airline carrier and a small regional, dedicated, airline company – the latter usually retaining a relevant local network but lacking a continental or worldwide network.

How far does the dichotomy of endogamy and exogamy differ from the traditional split between horizontal and vertical alliances? First, all vertical alliances are exogamic because the profiles of backward and forward firms are necessarily different. But not all horizontal alliances are endogamic. When companies operate in the same business sector and if they share similar profiles, their alliance will be endogamic. However, not all companies in a given business sector share similar profiles. Two companies in the same industry might then enter into an exogamic partnership. In a nutshell, the distinction between endogamy and exogamy does not come from the membership to one industry or another, but rather from the comparative profiles of the partners. Related profiles induce endogamic partnerships and unrelated profiles offer opportunities for exogamic partnerships.

Quantitative versus qualitative complementarities
As soon as two organisations share related profiles, have related assets, capacities, abilities, competencies and expertise, it can easily be assumed that there is a high probability that they will pool similar resources in their cooperation. For example, two national tourism organisations may pool their resources to market together their common region. In that case, they will bring together marketers with similar backgrounds. In a completely different field, if two airlines intend to merge their maintenance operations, which are hypothesised to be identical, they will add similar negotiation powers towards the service provider. When resources of the same nature are brought into the cooperation, the only aim that can be pursued by allies is the accumulation of identical resources. This set of relationships can be summarised as follows: similar environment and value chains → similar resources brought by the allies → accumulation of identical resources in the alliance.

In contrast, when two companies differ significantly in terms of profile, the resources that will be pooled, if they decide to form an alliance, will be highly differentiated. For example, the resources brought by the French National Railways Company (SNCF) and Expedia.com in their alliance are completely different. Expedia brought an expertise in the distribution of non-transportation services, while the SNCF focuses on its core business of railway transportation. The alliance allows the two partners to bundle a complete set of services. Each partner is bringing resources that cannot be brought by its counterpart; this means that resources pooled in the cooperation cannot be substituted. In such circumstances, the allies are not looking for the accumulation of similar resources, but for the combination of specific resources. These relationships can be expressed as follows: unrelated environment and value chains → different resources brought by the allies → combination of differentiated resources in the alliance.

To conclude, partners of an endogamy can only pursue quantitative complementarities whereas exogamy can only deliver qualitative complementarities. Looking for quantitative complementarities in exogamy is unrealistic. The resources pooled are too different to produce scale effects. In the same vein, looking for qualitative complementarities in an endogamy would be a curious quest as the resources brought by the allies are supposed to be fully substitutable. The following section illustrates this conceptual framework on endogamies and exogamies in the context of airline alliances.

From endogamic to exogamic alliances in the airline industry

Traditional endogamic partnerships
We suggest that inter-firm alliances such as Amadeus are endogamic partnerships while the new mega alliances such as SkyTeam or Oneworld are exogamic partnerships. Why are traditional alliances endogamic partnerships?

1. The joint action is focused on one single function, for example, reservation.
2. Resources pooled are of the same nature. In alliances such as Amadeus, partners have pooled managers with similar experiences, human resources with related expertises, technologies of the same nature and so on.
3. Complementarities gained are quantitative. When companies merge their reservation function, they are able to gain economies of scale and other size effects.
4. Independence of each partner stays intact.

New exogamic partnerships
Why are mega alliances exogamic partnerships?

1. The joint action is much broader than with old endogamic partnerships. These new partnerships are made to integrate networks of partners beyond simple code-sharing.
2. Resources pooled in the alliance are of a different nature. First, the airlines bring in their respective route networks. In addition, partners may share consumer information such as reservation or ticketing behaviour,

loyalty programmes, and executive lounges and benefits in respective hubs.
3. Complementarities gained are qualitative. The first rationalisation of this sharing of networks and commercial means lies in complementarities of a geographical nature: some of them cover the Americas, some cover Europe, and another airline would cover Asia. Companies try to strengthen and expand their international presence in ways that would not be possible without an alliance. Each company compensates each other's weaknesses in a given territory by the local strength of its partner. Second, allies offer to their customers a substantial increase in the number of flights available from their market, and increase the spectrum of possible destinations.
4. Finally, partners keep autonomous a significant part of their global business outside of the alliance. Mere code-share partnerships allow each partner to maintain a strong autonomy and to retain the opportunity to make independent strategic choices. For example, each partner remains autonomous in their respective local markets, in their pricing policies, and in their purchase decisions of new aircrafts.

The inter-firm agreements in the industry have suffered dramatic changes; the future will show additional changes. In the previous framework, one is not really aware of these alliances. They were mostly centred on back-office activities. GDSs were, for example, only known by specialists. Now, the cooperation is increasingly publicised and promoted. Any of the above-discussed alliances proudly displays the names of their members, and travellers increasingly know about these global brands and their members. In conclusion, these alliances have moved from the back to the front office.

Endogamic and exogamic alliances do not raise identical issues, and they are not managed the same way. In exogamic relationships, partners are different and must learn about and adapt to each other. The qualitative differences that exist between organisations can be threats to the success of the alliance and must therefore be managed. In addition, the two types of alliance do not produce the same results. Endogamic relationships standardise processes to obtain benefits of scale in at least one stage of the value chain. Exogamic relationships, in opposition, develop qualitative benefits that result from a synergy of differentiated resources.

Issues for further discussion and research (conceptual and applied)
The following briefly highlights three areas of future research that may be particularly relevant conceptually and practically useful. Those areas are the impacts of mega alliances on competitive environments, their impact on consumer behaviour and their effects on management.

Impacts of mega alliances on competitive environments

The mega alliances are changing the environment in which they operate, most notably with respect to competitive issues. Despite potential benefits for travellers (as mentioned earlier), exogamic mega alliances raise possible anti-competitive effects. With the joint effect of the disappearance of national airlines (for example, Swissair and Sabena in Europe) on the one hand, and the alliances on the other, one can wonder what will be the effects of such a decrease of the competitive environment (in addition to alliances, the consolidation trend also takes the form of mergers or acquisitions such as the Air France takeover of KLM Dutch Airlines). Indeed, it is paradoxical that private giants emerge as a result of the deregulation of the industry whose original aim was to fight public monopolies. The diminishing number of competitors may not be a problem, as long as there remain opportunities for new entries into the market. For example, the rapid growth of low-cost airlines, particularly in Europe, attests to the openness of the market, even if the size of these companies cannot rival that of major carriers. However, the case can be made that low-cost airlines, which operate exclusively point to point, are not directly competing with the international airlines that comprise the mega alliances. The fact that major US airlines such as Delta and United are developing their own low-fare airlines (Song and Ted, respectively) appears to support this point. Another simple question that remains to be fully answered is whether belonging to an alliance contributes to greater passenger volumes and to greater market share. Travel Business Analyst, for example, has reported that airlines in the four major world airline alliances may not have gained market share when compared with traffic of airlines that are not members (see www.travelbusinessanalyst.com/market_reports/).

Impacts of mega alliances on consumer behaviour

As the alliances grow and develop their marketing strategies, the recognition of their brands may slowly replace the recognition of the original airline brand. Two key strategic questions are: will it be advantageous for the airlines to replace their traditional brand marketing by alliance brand marketing, and will the establishment of standards across the alliance and the resulting homogenisation be more important than the quest for differentiation of the alliance members? It remains to be seen whether super brands will dilute and outpace existing carriers' brands. To date, much confusion still exists as to who belongs to what alliance. Indeed, we still know very little about customers' knowledge and perceptions of alliances, their services and benefits. It can be hypothesised that frequent travellers are more knowledgeable about the alliance and its members than non-frequent travellers.

Currently, customers dislike the lack of visibility that may exist when purchasing tickets. For example, they may book a ticket on one airline and have to fly with another carrier of the alliance, and despite the ease of travelling and the similar benefits on their frequent flyer programmes, they may be dissatisfied by this situation. Indeed, for the moment, alliance members often differ with respect to product features and service quality issues (from in-flight services such as catering standards, entertainment in multiple languages, crew able to communicate in the national languages of all member airlines, to marketing services such as booking facilities) despite the fact that they are under the same brand. Alliances are still far away from the idealistic 'seamless travel experience' they may promote as airlines develop heterogeneous marketing practices.

Another related issue is the choice of alliance communication strategies towards their 'global' customers. Are airlines going to communicate the same message featuring the same attributes to all targeted customers spanning several continents, or will it be more effective to have customised messages to geographic segments? Airlines have so far built their reputation with a long history of communication strategies to fit their respective markets.

Managing alliances
Airline alliances, despite the important economic stakes for their members, have not yet developed specific management models. The governance model seems to be based on consensus among members, rather than shared hierarchical decision power. Further, alliances are not legal entities that can sign contracts with service providers. An alliance might use its consolidation power to negotiate a service, but contractual relationships are with each individual member; this could bring controversial situations where one 'powerful' member might try to get even better conditions in a private bilateral negotiation with the service provider. Although membership rules might impose changes in some business practices, alliance members keep a big part of their independence, and in particular there is neither (i) distribution of financial benefits: revenues stay with the airline member transporting the passenger, which might promote biased behaviour on shared routes, (that is, 'stealing' passengers from other members) nor (ii) pool of resources: members might not feel compromised with others, which might prevent concessions 'for the benefit of the alliance' to the detriment of the acquired capabilities of one member.

An additional issue of interest may be that of cultural differences and their impact on trust (reference trust). Cultural influences contribute to management styles, may lead to conflict situations, and may affect trust relationships. Does the change from endogamic to exogamic partnerships have an impact on those issues?

It was the objective of this chapter to cast a new light on strategic business alliances, particularly in the context of airlines. Organisations are increasingly seeking exogamic alliances in broad networks including more than just two or three partners. As the size of the networks increases, so do the strategic and managerial issues that were discussed above. Whatever the research issue, we suggest that an understanding of the evolution of alliances from endogamic to exogamic should shed increasing light on the nature and the consequences of those alliances. Alliances represent opportunities and advantages for the organisations that build them. These benefits can only be fully sought and obtained with a thorough understanding of the evolution of alliances.

Acknowledgement

The authors wish to thank José Luis Rodriguez (Amadeus) and Georges Rochas (Air France) for their contributions to this chapter.

References

Ansoff, H. (1965), *Corporate Strategy*, New York: McGraw-Hill.

Archambault, M. (ed.) (2000), *Tourism and the Trend Towards Consolidation*, Montréal: Chair in Tourism, Université du Québec à Montréal.

Bennett, M. (1997), 'Strategic alliances in the world airline industry', *Progress in Tourism and Hospitality Research*, **3**, 213–23.

Brueckner, J. and T. Whalen (2000), 'The price effects of international airlines alliances', *Journal of Law and Economics*, **43** (2), 503–46.

Crotts, J., D. Buhalis and R. March (eds) (2000), *Global Alliances in Tourism and Hospitality Management*, New York: Haworth Hospitality Press.

Dev, C. and P. Klein (1996), 'A market-based approach for partner selection in marketing alliances', *Journal of Travel Research*, **35** (1), 11–17.

Domke-Damonte, D. (2000), 'The effect of cross-industry cooperation on performance in the airline industry', in Crotts et al. (eds), pp. 141–60

Evans, N., D. Campbell and G. Stonehouse (2003), *Strategic Management of Travel and Tourism*, Oxford: Butterworth-Heinemann.

Flores, R. and G. Renato (1998), 'Competition and trade in services: the airlines' global alliances', *World Economy*, **21** (8), 1095–108.

French, T. (1997), 'Global trends in airline alliances', *Tourism Analyst*, **4**, 81–101.

Geringer, J.M. and L. Hébert (1991), 'Measuring performance of international joint ventures', *Journal of International Business Studies*, **22** (2), 249–63.

Glaister, K.W. and P.J. Buckley (1996), 'Strategic moves for international alliance formation', *Journal of Management Studies*, **33**, 301–32.

Glisson, L.M. and W. Cunningham (1996), 'Airline industry strategic alliances: marketing and policy implications', *International Journal of Physical Distribution and Logistics Management*, **26** (3), 26–34.

Go, F. and R. Pine (1995), *Globalization Strategy in the Hotel Industry*, New York: Routledge.

Goeldner, C., B. Ritchie and R. McIntosh (2000), *Tourism: Principles, Practices, and Philosophies*, 8th edn, New York: Wiley.

Grant, R.M. (1991), 'The resource-based theory of competitive advantage: implications for strategy formulation', *California Management Review*, **33** (3), 114–35.

Hamel, G. (1991), 'Competition for competence and inter-partner learning within international strategic alliances', *Strategic Management Journal*, **12** (4), 83–103.

Harrigan, K.R. (1986), *Managing for Joint Ventures Success*, Lexington, MA: Lexington Books.

Harrigan, K.R. (1988), 'Joint ventures and competitive strategy', *Strategic Management Journal*, **9** (2), 141–58.

Hennart, J.-F. (1988), 'A transaction costs theory of equity joint ventures', *Strategic Management Journal*, **9** (4), 361–74.

Hill, T. and R. Shaw (1995), 'Co-marketing tourism internationally: bases for strategic alliances', *Journal of Travel Research*, **34** (1), 25–32.

IATA (2001), *Recommended Practice 1008*, 21st edn, International Air Transport Association.

Inkpen, A.C. (1996), 'Creating knowledge through collaboration', *California Management Review*, **39** (1), 123–140.

Jolly, D. (2001), *Alliances Inter-entreprises: Entre Concurrence et Coopération* (Inter-enterprise alliances: balancing competition with cooperation), Paris: Vuibert.

Jolly, D. (2002), 'Alliance strategy: linking motives with benefits', *European Business Forum*, **9** (Spring), 47–50.

Killing, J.P. (1982), 'How to make a global joint venture work', *Harvard Business Review*, **60** (3), 120–27.

Killing, J.P. (1988), 'Understanding alliances: the role of task and organizational complexity', in F.J. Contractor and P. Lorance (eds), *Cooperative Strategies in International Business*, Lexington, MA: Lexington Books, pp. 55–67.

Kogut, B. (1988), 'Joint ventures: theoretical and empirical perspectives', *Strategic Management Journal*, **9** (4), 319–32.

Kumar, R. and K.O. Nti (1998), 'Differential learning and interaction in alliance dynamics: a process and outcome discrepancy model', *Organization Science*, **9** (3), 356–67.

Mowery, D.C., J.E. Oxley and B.S. Silverman (1996), 'Strategic alliances and interfirm knowledge transfer', *Strategic Management Journal*, **17** (Winter Special Issue), 77–91.

Oum, T., J.H. Park and A. Zhang (2000), *Globalization and Strategic Alliances: The Case of the Airline Industry*, New York: Elsevier.

Porter, M. (1985), *Competitive Advantage*, New York: Free Press.

Si, S.X. and G.D. Bruton (1999), 'Knowledge transfer in international joint ventures in transitional economies: the China experience', *Academy of Management Executive*, **13** (1), 83–90.

Vander Kraats, S.A. (2000), 'Gaining a competitive edge through airline alliances', *Competitiveness Review*, **10** (2), 56–64.

Vellas, F. and L. Bécherel (1999), *The International Marketing of Travel and Tourism: A Strategic approach*, London: Macmillan.

Wang, Z. and M. Evans (2002), 'Strategic classification and examination of the development of current airline alliance activities', *Journal of Air Transportation*, **7** (3), 73–101.

Wernerfelt, B. (1984), 'A resource-based view of the firm', *Strategic Management Journal*, **5** (2), 171–80.

9 Airline alliances and tourism
Clive L. Morley

Importance of airline alliances

Alliances among international airlines, involving high levels of cooperation and coordination of services and operations, have become a prominent feature of the airline industry in recent times. The trend started with alliances between European and North American airlines, extending to Asian airlines and subsequently to include African and Latin American airlines. Figure 9.1 shows the growth trend in the number of alliances and the number of airlines involved in alliances. These trends are continuing: for example, Air China is considering joining one of the major alliances (Xinhua News Agency 2003) and US Airways is joining Star Alliance.

Most of the alliances take the form of code sharing of services by two airlines, in which one airline agrees to buy a block of seats on a flight service of another airline and then sells these seats under its own brand (the flight typically appears with both airlines' codes). But some involve greater degrees of cooperation such as recognition of each other's frequent flyer schemes, sharing of lounges and terminals, joint marketing and integration of booking systems. Alliances can include a degree of equity ownership (for example, British Airways part ownership of Qantas, both members of the Oneworld alliance), but usually do not. Indeed, equity positions do not necessarily translate into common alliance membership (for example, Singapore Airlines has a 49 per cent stake in Virgin Atlantic, but while Singapore Airlines is a member of Star Alliance, Virgin Atlantic remains independent). Notably, five major alliances emerged in the late 1990s which included many of the world's largest airlines. The membership of these has fluctuated to some degree; indicative of the unsettled state of such alliances is the fact that by 2003 the 'Qualiflyer' alliance had dissolved and the future of the 'Wings' alliance is very uncertain (Baker 2003; Baker and Field 2003). The alliances have also varied in their degree of coordination and integration.

Current memberships of the three major alliances and their market shares are shown in Table 9.1. The former 'Qualiflyer' alliance – of Swissair, Sabena, Turkish, Air Liberte AOM, TAP Portugal, LOT Polish, Crossair, Volare, Air Europe, Balair, LTU, Air Littoral and Portugalia – was dissolved as a result of the failures of its drivers Swissair and Sabena (it had about 5 per cent revenue and 3 per cent passenger shares in 1999: O'Toole

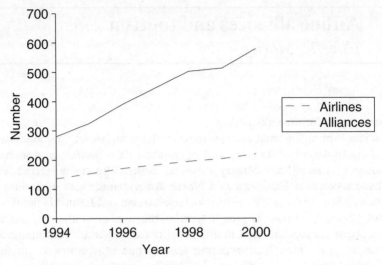

Source: Oum and Zhang (2001).

Figure 9.1   Growth in airline alliances

Table 9.1   Major alliances

Alliance	Key members	Worldwide share (%)	
		Revenue	Passengers carried
Star Alliance	United, Lufthansa, Singapore, All Nippon, Air Canada, Thai, Varig, SAS, Air New Zealand, Mexicana, Austrian, British Midland, Asiana, LOT Polish, Spanair	21	19
Oneworld	American Airways, British Airways, Qantas, Cathay Pacific, Iberia, LanChile, Finnair, Aer Lingus	14	13
SkyTeam	Air France, Delta, Aeromexico, Korean, Alitalia, CSA Czech	11	13
3 alliances totals		46	45

Source: Baker and Field (2003), figures generally for 2002.

and Walker 2000). The shaky 'Wings' alliance, between Northwest and KLM, has another 4 per cent share of both passengers and revenue (calculated from data in Baker and Field 2003), but in October 2003 Air France (a key driver of the SkyTeam alliance) announced a takeover of KLM. It can be seen that these alliances between them have a large share of international airline traffic and revenue. They are thus an important feature of the international airline industry, and hence of the tourism industry. Some of these alliances have built a profile of their own, alongside their member airlines, so that names of alliances such as Star and Oneworld are well known to many air travellers.

In addition to the major alliances there are many hundreds of smaller and one-to-one arrangements and alliances. It should be noted that, despite their wide spread and large market shares, alliances are neither a necessity for airlines to profit in their business, nor a strategy pursued by all. Some large and important airlines remain outside these major alliances, such as Emirates Airlines and Japan Airlines, and airlines such as Southwest Airlines, EasyJet and Ryanair have successfully remained independent of the major alliances with strategies of low cost and concentration on high traffic routes.

Civil aviation is the main mode of international travel, and for many tourist destinations (such as in the Caribbean and Mediterranean) over 90 per cent of arrivals are by air (Papatheodorou 2002, p. 381). Thus airline policy and regulation, including issues such as airline alliances, are very important for the tourism industry. For example, alliances give their member airlines the potential to collaborate to some extent, depending on the regulatory environment (for example, granting of anti-trust immunity) on trips involving more than one stage and airline. The impact on services and the fares paid by tourists could be marked.

Alliances can affect both the demand and supply sides of tourism (see the discussion in the following sections). Airlines are generally believed to benefit from lower costs, improved market access, coordination of services with partners improving productivity and reducing competition, and higher barriers to entry. Travellers (including tourists) are expected to benefit from the better service aspects and reduced fares consequent to reduced costs for the airlines. The balance of outcomes for tourists of improved efficiency of airlines versus a lessening of competitive forces needs to be determined empirically. Tourism demand could conceivably be greatly affected by the changes in the airline industry and airline operations that result from airline alliances.

Overview of main issues
The strong growth of alliances of international airlines raises two key issues for further consideration. The first is: are alliances likely to persist as an

important feature of the airline industry? The second issue is consequential: if airline alliances persist, what are the likely impacts on tourism?

The first question is relatively straightforward to address. Alliances are very likely to continue to be an important aspect of the strategy of many international airlines in the foreseeable future. This is because alliances have a number of important benefits for airlines in a changing and more competitive, globalising industry. These benefits, which have been discussed by many analysts, including the Organisation for Economic Cooperation and Development (OECD 2000), Oum et al. (2000, chapter 2) and Morrish and Hamilton (2002) are outlined in the following paragraphs.

Airlines enter into alliances in pursuit of both economic benefits, such as productivity gains, and a stronger competitive position from improved customer service (Oum et al. 2000, chapter 2). For some airlines there may be a desire to follow the strategy of others to minimise any strategic advantages competitors may gain or not leave themselves disadvantaged (Howarth and Kirsebom 1999, p. 4; Morrish and Hamilton 2002).

Airline alliances can affect productivity through potential cost reductions from shared use of lounges and terminal facilities, sharing risk through block space sales on flights to partners and code sharing, pooling purchasing and efficiencies in the use of staff (for example, sharing check-in and flight staff). Cost savings through joint purchasing and sharing parts can be achieved after adoption of common specifications (for example, in engineering, maintenance and even aircraft). This is a current focus for many airlines (Baker 2003). While there have been some such gains realised to date, alignment of specifications and purchasing have often proved difficult in practice, leaving room for further cost savings to be achieved in the future. Joint marketing and promotion provide opportunities for economies of scale and scope. However, sharing of facilities can raise anti-competitive concerns (Chen and Ross 2000).

Allied airlines feed passengers into their partners' routes, as alliances entail the link-up of airlines' networks. In effect, an allied airline can offer prospective passengers service to more destinations at greater frequency. Coordination of schedules to minimise passengers' waiting time between connecting flights and facilitate the ease of making connections (via closeness of gates, through booking of luggage and reducing check-in requirements) can add to the appeal of this expanded service. This is likely to make the allied airline more attractive to travellers and increase the airline's load factors.

Alliances also provide a means of gaining market access and growth where they might otherwise be restricted by government regulation. Partial deregulation, starting in the USA and spreading to other parts of the world, increasing integration of markets in Europe and the wide adoption of hub and spoke operations, put strong pressure on airlines to remain competitive via globalising strategies (Morrish and Hamilton 2002). In an industry constrained, by low and variable profits, in its funding for capital investment (for the new aircraft and facilities such strategies could entail), alliances provide a means to, in effect, grow and offer a global service.

Airline alliances have arisen due to the unique historical, strategic and regulatory circumstances of the industry and also the forces of globalisation affecting many industries (Alamdari and Morrell 1997; Seristö 1999, Fan et al. 2001; Pels 2001; Oum et al. 2000; Morley 2003a). As these factors impelling airlines to enter into alliances are not transitory, alliances are likely to continue to be an important feature of the international airline industry into the foreseeable future.

That future can be expected to be difficult in some respects for airlines. Most international airlines have been greatly affected recently by a series of external shocks – especially the terrorist attack on the twin towers in New York, the SARS crisis and Iraq war in 2003 – and the strategic challenge of new 'no frills' airlines, including Southwest Airlines in the USA and EasyJet and Ryanair in Europe. There is no reason to expect the future to be any less challenging and volatile. Alliances are one way of responding to future uncertainty, in an effort to reduce risk by sharing it with partners and by gaining some of the advantages of size in such an environment.

In strategy terms, international airline alliances are predominantly horizontal alliances (among peers and rivals in the same industry) rather than vertical alliances with suppliers or customers (up or down the value chain). In the airline industry case it has been found important to distinguish between two forms of horizontal alliance. This is the distinction between complementary and parallel alliances. In essence, complementary alliances involve two (or more) airlines with non-overlapping routes linked through a common destination that coordinate schedules and so on in an attempt to realise operational economies of scope and scale, while a parallel alliance is one between airlines formerly competing on a route who agree to cooperate on the route, thereby potentially reducing competition.

Other industries have also experienced moves to set up strategic alliances (Pekar and Allio 1994). A lesson from that experience is that such alliances often fail or change significantly (Brouthers et al. 1995).

The difficulties of alliances include potential negative impacts on brand and customer relationships from partners' actions (or lack thereof), loss of ability to take up opportunities due to being tied into the alliance and the need for trust in partners across national cultural differences. These difficulties are illustrated by the particular case of the question of whether or not to merge frequent flyer programmes. In the long term there are strong economic benefits to be garnered by airlines in an alliance from merging their frequent flyer programmes (Gudmundsson et al. 2002). These benefits come from greater purchasing power over their suppliers, cost savings from combining call centres and other back office operations and stronger, more coherent marketing. The resulting larger frequent flyer programme is likely to be more attractive to travellers. However, mergers entail compromises, which many airline managers feel are excessive, and there are concerns to do with how long lasting an alliance may turn out to be (ibid.).

The airline alliances are certainly not yet stable, there is recent history of airlines leaving or even changing alliances (for example, the break-up of the KLM–Alitalia alliance in 2000: Morrish and Hamilton 2002 list other examples) and of airlines going out of business (for example, Swissair, Ansett) with consequences for the alliances they were involved in. Despite this change and uncertainty in the membership of specific alliances, the factors outlined above are likely to continue to pressure airlines to continue growth and deeper consolidation of alliances (Fan et al. 2001).

The question of the impacts of airline alliances on tourism thus does follow – it requires more consideration. The issue of the impacts of alliances, on the airlines and on customers, has been a main focus of the literature on airline alliances. So this question is considered in the following section.

Critical review of the literature
Previous research has generally considered the issue in terms of the effects of airline alliances on both the airlines and their customers. These effects are linked, for example productivity gains (if realised) offer the potential for fare reductions. Productivity gains, however, may be appropriated as extra profits by the airlines and not lead to fare reductions, if alliances significantly reduce competition. Tourists are a special category of airline customers and have received less attention specifically. Hence this review will concentrate first on the general issues, and then seek to apply the results to tourism.

Productivity is expected to be boosted by alliances, as combined operations enable economies of scale and scope to be realised, and access to resources and learning from partners is facilitated (Oum et al. 2004). Profitability will therefore be enhanced by such productivity gains (improved efficiency) and a stronger competitive position deriving from market power. Oum et al. (2000) estimated productivity gains of up to 4.8 per cent from alliances involving the linking of networks previously not overlapping, but no real gains from lesser degrees of cooperation. Oum and Zhang (2001) found that alliances which involved the airlines combining their networks to open up access to new markets did improve partner airlines' profitability (+ 1.4 per cent) and productivity (+ 5 per cent) and lead to reduced fares (– 5.5 per cent), on average (although minor alliances confined to specific routes had no significant effects). A similar study reported by Oum et al. (2004) found similar results: alliances lead to improvements in productivity and profits for airlines. An alliance increased productivity (by $+1.9$ per cent) with higher levels of cooperation in the alliances increasing productivity further (an extra 4.4 per cent for stronger alliances). Profitability was seen to be less affected by the number of alliances (not significantly) but the higher cooperation alliances did lead to increased profits ($+3.7$ per cent).

Goh and Yong (2003), using a different econometric model, found statistically significant, but very small, cost savings for airlines from alliances. Their alliances variable was a count of the number of code-sharing partners an airline had, with no measure of the extent of the alliance beyond code sharing (and neglecting the distinction between parallel and complementary alliances – see below). The results are consistent with those from Oum et al. (2000) and Oum and Zhang (2001) that minor alliances yield only small, if any, productivity gains and that it is the more integrated and deeper alliances (going beyond the numerically much more common code-sharing arrangements) that result in cost reductions for the airlines involved. This consistency has now been seen across a number of econometric methods, model functional forms and data sets, indicating a degree of robustness in the finding.

These results from economic and regression model-based studies are supported by the results of a survey of airline executives conducted by Howarth and Kirsebom (1999) who identified cost savings of a similar magnitude, also increasing with the degree of cooperation and integration of the alliance.

There is thus evidence from econometric studies and an influential consulting report that airlines do generally benefit from entering into alliances. Airline executives, in receipt of such results, are likely to continue to pursue and maintain alliances, lending more weight to the arguments of the previous section that alliances will continue as a feature of the airline industry.

In reviewing the literature on fare effects of alliances, it is necessary to draw on the distinction between parallel and complementary alliances that is useful and important in both economic theory and empirical results.

In theory, complementary alliances should lead to lower fares, while parallel alliances lead to higher fares (Park 1997). An argument for complementary alliances reducing overall fares can be illustrated with the simple example of traffic between airports A and B which goes via airport C, rather than direct. The route A to C is served by one airline and C to B by another airline. In the absence of cooperation, each airline can have an incentive to increase fares on its route, to increase revenue and profit, even at the expense of some drop in passenger numbers. But the drop in passenger numbers affects the other airline, even if it does not change its fare, reducing its revenue and profit. If the two airlines cooperate in setting fares over the whole trip A to B they can do so to maximise their total profit in this market. The potential reduction in profit of the partner airline due to an airline's potential fare increase becomes a factor in consideration, leading to a tendency to rather lower fares (Brueckner 2001). Add to this theory the passenger benefits of schedule and terminal coordination and cost reductions from sharing operations, and there is a case for complementary alliances reducing fares, a case empirically confirmed (see below).

On the other hand, parallel alliances involve cooperation between airlines on the same route, thereby reducing competitive pressures on the route. This naturally raises concerns of quasi-monopoly power accruing to the alliance and potential for large, ongoing producer surpluses at the expense of customers. Although a parallel alliance between airlines with relatively small market shares may enable them to become a stronger competitor to a market leader on a route (Oum and Park 1997).

In many cases there is not only one route between an origin and destination, especially well separated ones. There is thus some competitive and price restraint pressure on a parallel alliance from alternate routes, even if they are less direct and may take a little longer in transit.

Park (1997) found that airfares did increase in the case of a parallel alliance (of Delta, Swissair and Sabena) but decreased after a complementary alliance (of Northwest and KLM). As most alliances in practice involve a mixture of complementary and parallel alliances it is necessary to turn to detailed empirical evidence to settle the issue of the effect of alliances on fares.

Oum et al. (2000) invoke an oligopolistic framework and the distinction between complementary and parallel alliances to develop a sophisticated economic theory of airline alliances. In their model complementary alliances are expected to result in lower fares due to improved efficiency for the partner airlines and no lessening of competition, increases in traffic for the partners and higher consumer welfare. A parallel alliance lowers the pressure of competition, and higher fares and lower consumer welfare result. These expectations are confirmed by empirical testing of their model.

A further theoretical economic model is developed by Park et al. (2001). The distinction between complementary and parallel alliances is again key to the predictions of the effects of alliances in this model, which shows that traffic carried by the alliance partners (and traffic in total) is expected to increase with a complementary alliance, but decrease with a parallel alliance. The argument is basically that complementary alliances lead to increased demand for the alliance partners' services, and increased profits, at the expense of competitor airlines. The increase in traffic carried increases the alliance partners' load factors, decreasing their average costs and allowing them to reduce fares (further expanding the market). Parallel alliances, by reducing competition, allow the partners to increase their total profit by increasing fares and reducing their total traffic carried. The model's predictions are confirmed by analysis of data on trans-Atlantic alliances in the early 1990s.

Brueckner (2003a) consolidates and furthers a stream of research (Brueckner and Whalen 2000; Brueckner 2001, 2003b) analysing the effects of alliances on fares. He found that alliances lead to large fare decreases, of more than 25 per cent (4 per cent from alliance membership, 7 per cent from code sharing and 16 per cent from anti-trust immunity). These figures are higher, although in the same direction, than the results of Oum et al. (2000) who found fare decreases of about 5 per cent, on average, from alliances.

The evidence is thus fairly strong and consistent that alliances benefit the airlines involved, and stronger alliances more than minor ones. Also, to some extent, the benefits to the airlines tend to be passed on to travellers in lower fares.

The state of the art
The empirical evidence, in summary, is that to date airlines have not used alliances to give themselves monopoly profits. They have benefited 'in terms of load factors and from a general rise in productivity levels, but these have been offset by increased flight frequencies and, more particularly, lower air fares' (Morrish and Hamilton 2002, p. 407). The state of the art on the issue of tourism impacts is less certain. As outlined in the previous section, most studies have focused on the impacts of alliances on the airlines and the airline industry, or considered general social and consumer welfare benefits. The fare decreases observed are generalised and average. Analysis of the impacts on tourists and tourism is just starting to emerge (Gilbert and Wong 2003; Morley 2003b).

The impact of attributes of airline alliances on tourists' choices is complicated by the (not unexpected) finding that nationalities differ markedly in their expectations of service dimensions (Gilbert and Wong 2003). For example, North Americans and West Europeans have higher expectations of airlines' frequent flyer programmes than do Chinese or Japanese. Leisure tourists tend to be price conscious and have lower expectations of alliance features such as convenient schedules and flight frequencies, frequent flyer programmes and waiting lounges than business travellers (ibid.). However, even for business travellers there is evidence that the attributes of airline alliances are not very important in choice of airline (Goh and Uncles 2003). They are likely to be even less so in tourists' choice of destination and their decision to travel or not – vital decisions for the tourism industry.

The study by Goh and Uncles (2003), of a sample of business travellers, found that many (average 40 per cent) were unsure of or incorrect in their awareness of specific benefits. Tourists (as they tend to be less frequent travellers, and as some of the alliance attributes are less relevant or important to them) would be expected to be even less aware of such benefits. The use of informed travel agents by both business and tourist travellers can mitigate against this point. Further, there is little indication that airlines can effectively differentiate themselves through alliance membership (ibid.; the business travellers tended to be either unsure of any differences or not to believe in them). Alliances are unlikely to have much impact on choice of airline. The tourism effects of alliances are thus to be sought in those factors which affect the size of market demand, namely any impacts through changes in fares, increased marketing of a particular destination or improved viability of certain services (which were not among the aspects considered by Goh and Uncles).

Morley (2003b) considers the case of tourism into Australia. He estimates that the effect of airline alliances is an increase of 2.5 per cent in tourist numbers. This estimate is a broad-brush calculation, using an overall fare elasticity of demand for tourists of –1 from previous studies and a decrease in fares of about 10 per cent due to alliances (Productivity Commission 1997). It incorporates the idea that most (75 per cent according to an Australian Competition and Consumer Commission study: ACCC 2000) economy class passengers are on discounted fares which were not changed by alliances (Productivity Commission 1997). Australia was identified as a case where the airfares were a larger than usual component of tourists' spending, and thus the effect of alliance was likely to be stronger than in other destinations. The fare decrease used is noticeably larger than estimates cited above in other regions and worldwide. In situations with smaller fare elasticities for tourists, which on the evidence of much of the tourism demand literature would also be the case for many tourist flows, the effects would be even smaller.

As Morley (2003b) notes, the figure of an increase of 2.5 per cent in tourists is likely to have elements of both over- and underestimation of the effects. It overestimates because it ignores the impact of alliances on other fares, such as those to competing destinations, as the elasticities drawn on are own fares rather than relative fare elasticities. Alliances on competitive routes may have reduced fares on these routes, making other destinations comparatively more attractive. The impact of this would be less than the direct impact calculated above, due to the generally smaller elasticities of other destinations and the generally smaller fare decreases observed (averaging 5 per cent according to Oum et al. 2000). The underestimation of effect comes from concentrating only on the fare effect and neglecting the (much harder to quantify) impacts of customer service improvements and increased marketing. However, the studies cited earlier in this section lend weight to the argument that the service improvement effects, at least, are likely to be quite small for tourism.

In 2003 Qantas proposed to buy a 22.5 per cent stake in Air New Zealand. The resulting proposed alliance would have been stronger than most alliances, involving an equity stake, operational integration and significantly reduced competition (especially on trans-Tasman routes). The impacts would thus be expected to be more marked than usual.

The New Zealand Commerce Commission (2003) considered the alliance but determined to decline to give its authorisation (necessary for the alliance to proceed). The tourism impacts of the proposed alliance were an important aspect of the determination. Both the airlines, in their submission to the Commission, and the Commission itself, attempted to quantify aspects of the alliance impacts, and these results are drawn on in the following discussion. Tourist numbers are converted to percentages of tourist flows in the following to facilitate comparison with percentages cited throughout this article. Tourists are equated with 'holidaymakers' to be consistent with the Commerce Commission usage (2003: paragraph 1275) and the tourist flow totals are sourced from Statistics New Zealand (2003). Australia is the largest source of foreign tourists entering New Zealand (23 per cent of the total), and so is considered separately in the analysis.

The proposed alliance was a parallel one, which would lead to market dominance by the alliance partners and likely fare increases. The airlines' submission estimated that the fare increases would lead to a decrease of 13.7 per cent in tourists to New Zealand from Australia and a decrease of 6.6 per cent in tourists from the rest of the world. The Commerce Commission's modelling estimated that larger fare increases would result than the airlines' modelling, leading the Commission to estimate decreases of 56.8 per cent in tourists to New Zealand from Australia and of 4.2 per cent in tourists from the rest of the world (it is not explained why the Commission's analysis results in a smaller impact on tourists from the rest of the world).

The impact of the alliance via increased marketing was also considered. Increases in tourist numbers were expected from Qantas having more incentive to sell New Zealand as a destination and as a result of more effective joint promotion of New Zealand by the airlines. The airlines' submission was that these marketing benefits would lead to an increase of tourists from Australia of 5.8 per cent, and 5.9 per cent from the rest of the world. The Commerce Commission's estimates were zero impact on Australian origin tourists, and an increase of 4.7 per cent from the rest of the world.

The ACCC (2003) also refused to approve the alliance. It argued that the trans-Tasman route is Australia's largest passenger market and the proposed alliance would control more than 90 per cent of that market, making it effectively a single airline market. Anti-competitive effects were also found in the Australia–North America market. 'The ACCC and tourism bodies agreed that the proposed alliance is unlikely to result in increased tourism or benefits to the economy from tourism' (ibid.). This last point is consistent with the ACCC's previous determination that it 'remained unconvinced that there were substantial tourism benefits arising' from the Joint Service Agreement between Qantas and British Airways (ACCC 2000, p. 82). Clearly the ACCC assesses that the marketing benefits of even such strong alliances will be small on tourism into Australia. The overridingly important factor is the effect on competition, and hence fares, of alliances.

It is reasonable to conclude that the marketing impacts of alliances may be important in smaller markets such as New Zealand (and regional markets, it is argued in Morley 2003c). But they are likely to be not very important in larger markets such as Australia, and even less so (by extrapolation of the argument) in major and very well known world tourism markets such as Spain.

Issues for further research
There is both room and need for much more research into the effects of airline alliances on tourism. The discussion of the literature and the state of current knowledge indicate some clear areas for further research. In the main this can most profitably expand on the basis already in place in previous work, rather than needing to set off in radical new directions.

Most of the studies carried out to date, and many of the best ones, have been broad and general in their conclusions, giving average and overall results. For example, the estimates of profit, productivity and fare impacts of alliances cited above (from Oum et al. 2000, Oum and Zhang 2001 and Oum et al. 2004), while based in sophisticated theoretical economic models, are derived from data at a high level of aggregation (such as productivity indices rather than specific measures) and, as regression coefficients, are, in a sense, averages over time and airlines. For policy and planning purposes they give an indication rather than a fully applicable magnitude for use in any particular case. It is obvious in tourism economics that many effects are particular to origins, destinations and market segments, particularly in the values of relevant parameters of models, such as demand elasticities and the relative importance of different market segments. Therefore there is a need for more focused data and estimates.

Morrison (1996) analysed the impacts of airline mergers in the USA on airfares. Using time series extending well before and after the mergers, he was able to consider consequences, in the companies and markets, that may not be immediate but come to fruition over a longer time scale. This is a valuable corrective to the immediacy of impacts assumption in much of the modelling on this topic. For example, Morrison identified that mergers could be tending to occur involving routes with fares much higher than on routes with otherwise similar characteristics. That is, a merger (and, by extension, alliances) may be influenced by the high fares predating it. The fare reductions seen post-merger are thus placed in an important context.

It is worth considering this finding when investigating the effects of alliances. Most modelling of alliance impacts assumes that the air fares before the alliances are sustainable and appropriate, so that any reduction is an efficiency gain from the alliance. Morrison's (1996) analysis shows that the situation can be more complex, and there could be an element of correcting unsustainably high prevailing fares. Many studies of airline alliances' effects have proceeded on the basis of an event study form of model. This has meant the formulation of a model and the incorporation into it of a dummy variable representing the presence of an alliance. But Morrison found that the effects of airline mergers would be distorted in such modelling, as alliances may not be independent of existing features of a route (say) such as the previous fare levels, and as effects can take some time to become fully apparent. An implication is that the straightforward use of dummy variables in econometric models to indicate the presence of an alliance, and other simple alliance indicators, can be misleading in the results they give.

Another important feature of the issue of airline alliances is their rapidly changing forms, members and natures. It is thus possible that studies from even as recent as five years ago (using data from years prior to that) are losing relevance.

The analysis to date has some key weaknesses that provide opportunities for further work. Important among these are the derivation of the elasticities used in most models, which assume that elasticities are constant in respect of other important variables such as incomes (that is, are constant over important market segments) and over time. Both of which assumptions are likely to be invalid and have been seen to be so when tested (for example, Morley 1994, 1998). It is thus necessary for accuracy that elasticities be continually re-estimated on up-to-date data. This is a matter of importance for tourism demand analysis in general, and of importance for such areas as assessing the effects of airline alliances where such elasticities are relied upon. The lack of sound estimates of cross-price elasticities is another aspect of this issue.

More particular to the studies of airline alliances is the use, in many studies to date, of posted, representative or average fares. Tourism flows, and much of the actual travel decisions of air travellers more widely, are often driven by discount, special or group fares. Alliances may not have a great impact on such fares, which are already very competitive and set by demand, rather than determined by cost considerations. The fares used in studies may not be a real representation of fares actually considered by tourists, and thus the impacts can be distorted. The impacts of alliances on marketing, and the flow on effects on tourism, are asserted but not well tested or estimated.

Models that include some of the features of alliances (such as lower fares, reduced stopovers, through ticketing and so on) as explanatory variables would be a step in advance of current models. Data for such variables might be obtained from specifically designed and conducted surveys. This would enable the estimation of the impacts on tourism numbers of the component aspects of alliances.

References

Alamdari, F. and P. Morrell (1997), 'Airline alliances: a catalyst for regulatory change in key markets?', *Journal of Air Transport Management*, **3**, 1–2.

Australian Competition and Consumer Commission (ACCC) (2000), *Joint Services Agreement between Qantas Airways Limited and British Airways Plc Determination*, ACCC Authorisation No. A30202, 10 May.

Australian Competition and Consumer Commission (ACCC) (2003), 'Qantas/Air New Zealand alliance, "Very anti-competitive and not in public interest" ', ACCC news release, MR065/03, www.accc.gov.au, 15 December.

Baker, C. (2003), 'Global shifts', *Airline Business*, Reed Business Information, **19** (1), 52–4.

Baker, C. and D. Field (2003), 'Where are they now?', *Airline Business*, Reed Business Information, **19** (7), 42–4.

Brouthers, K., L. Brouthers and T. Wilkinson (1995), 'Strategic alliances: choose your alliances', *Long Range Planning*, **28**, 18–25.

Brueckner, J.K. (2001), 'The economics of international code sharing: an analysis of airline alliances', *International Journal of Industrial Organization*, **19**, 1475–98.

Brueckner, J.K. (2003a), 'The benefits of code sharing and antitrust immunity for international passengers, with an application to the Star alliance', *Journal of Air Transport Management*, **9**, 83–9.

Brueckner, J.K. (2003b), 'International airfares in the age of alliances: the effects of code sharing and antitrust immunity', *Review of Economics and Statistics*, **85**, 105–19.

Brueckner, J.K. and W.T. Whalen (2000), 'The price effects of international airline alliances', *Journal of Law and Economics*, **43**, 503–45.

Chen, Z. and T.W. Ross (2000), 'Strategic alliances, shared facilities and entry deterrence', *RAND Journal of Economics*, **31** (2), 326.

Commerce Commission (New Zealand) (2003), *Final Determination: Air New Zealand Limited and Qantas Airways Limited*, New Zealand, www.comcom.govt.nz, 15 December.

Fan, T., L. Vigeant-Langlois, C. Geissler, B. Bosler and J. Wilmking (2001), 'Evolution of global airline strategic alliance and consolidation in the 21st century', *Journal of Air Transport Management*, **7**, 349–60.

Gilbert, D. and R.K.C. Wong (2003), 'Passenger expectations and airline services: a Hong Kong based study', *Tourism Management*, **24**, 519–32.

Goh, K. and M. Uncles (2003), 'The benefits of airline global alliances: an empirical assessment of the perceptions of business travellers', *Transportation Research Part A: Policy and Practice*, **37**, 479–97.

Goh, M. and J. Yong (2003), 'Impacts of code-share alliances on airline cost structure: a trun-

cated third order translog estimation', www1.econ.unimelb.edu.au/iaesrwww/seminar/
Air_v1.pdf, Seminar presented at the Institute of Applied Economic and Social Research,
University of Melbourne, 2 October.

Gudmundsson, S.V., E.R. de Boer and C. Lechner (2002), 'Integrating frequent flyer programs
in multilateral airline alliances', *Journal of Air Transport Management*, **8**, 409–17.

Howarth, G. and T. Kirsebom (1999), *The Future of Airline Alliances: Current Thinking,
Strategic Directions and Implications*, Sutton, UK: Gemini Consulting and Reed Business
Information.

Morley, C.L. (1994), 'Discrete choice analysis of the impact of tourism prices', *Journal of
Travel Research*, **33**, 8–14.

Morley, C.L. (1998), 'A dynamic international demand model', *Annals of Tourism Research*,
25, 70–84.

Morley, C.L. (2003a), 'Globalisation, airline alliances and tourism: a strategic perspective',
Asia-Pacific Journal of Tourism Research, **8**, 15–25.

Morley, C.L. (2003b), 'Impacts of international airline alliances on tourism', *Tourism
Economics*, **9**, 31–51.

Morley, C.L. (2003c), 'Tourism impacts of airline alliances on Australia and regional destinations', in S. Divisekra and L. Turner (eds), *Conference Papers, Managing Tourism in the
Global Economy*, CD publication, Melbourne: Victoria University.

Morrish, S.C. and R.T. Hamilton (2002), 'Airline alliances – who benefits?', *Journal of Air
Transport Management*, **8**, 401–7.

Morrison, S.A. (1996), 'Airline mergers: a longer view', *Journal of Transport Economics and
Policy*, **30**, 237–50.

O'Toole, K. and K. Walker (2000), '2000 Alliance Survey', *Airline Business*, Reed Business
Information, July, 45–93.

Organisation for Economic Cooperation and Development (2000), *Airline Mergers and
Alliances*, DAFFE/CLP (2000) 1, Paris: OECD.

Oum, T.H. and J.-H. Park (1997), 'Airline alliances: current status, policy issues and future
directions', *Journal of Air Transport Management*, **3**, 133–44.

Oum, T.H., J.-H. Park, K. Kim and C. Yu (2004), 'The effect of horizontal alliances on firm
productivity and profitability: evidence from the global airline industry', *Journal of Business
Research*, **57** (3), 844–53.

Oum, T.H., J.-H. Park and A. Zhang (2000), *Globalization and Strategic Alliances: The Case
of the Airline Industry*, Oxford: Pergamon.

Oum, T.H. and A. Zhang (2001), 'Key aspects of global strategic alliances and the impacts on
the future of Canadian airline industry', *Journal of Air Transport Management*, **7**, 287–301.

Papatheodorou, A. (2002), 'Civil aviation regimes and leisure tourism in Europe', *Journal of
Air Transport Management*, **8**, 381–8.

Park, J.-H. (1997), 'The effects of airline alliances on markets and economic welfare',
Transportation Research E: Logistics and Transportation Review, **33**, 181–95.

Park, J.-H., A. Zhang and Y. Zhang (2001), 'Analytical models of international alliances in
the airline industry', *Transportation Research Part B: Methodological*, **35**, 865–86.

Pekar, P. and R. Allio (1994), 'Making alliances work – guidelines for success', *Long Range
Planning*, **27**, 54–65.

Pels, E. (2001), 'A note on airline alliances', *Journal of Air Transport Management*, **7**, 3–7.

Productivity Commission (1997), *The Economic Impact of International Airline Alliances*,
Information Paper, Productivity Commission, Canberra, May.

Seristö, H. (1999), 'Regulation as a driver for international airline alliances', Paper presented
at the 3rd Air Transport Research Group Conference, Hong Kong, June.

Statistics New Zealand (2003), *Tourism and Migration 2002, Overseas Visitor Arrival
Characteristics by Country of Residence, Table 2.07*, www.stats.govt.nz, 2 January 2004.

Xinhua News Agency (2003), 'Air China investigating joining the Star Alliance', 22 July.

10 Aviation and tourism
Peter Forsyth

Introduction

Aviation and tourism are natural complements – for many tourist trips, aviation is the preferred means of travel and for some trips, it is the only means. For many journeys, the services of the air transport and the tourism industries must be consumed jointly. As a consequence, there are many ways in which the two industries impact on one another. Changes in the industry structure of one, such as those which came about due to liberalisation of air transport, have resulted in the stimulation of growth in the other, such as long-haul tourism. Technical progress in aviation has resulted in lower fares which have stimulated tourism growth. Government policies imposed on one industry, such as taxation of tourism, have impacted on the other.

In spite of this, the two have rarely been analysed together. The World Tourism Organization has studied the links between the two (WTO 1994), and has convened seminars on the subject (WTO 2000). Some government policy advisory bureaux, such as the Australian Industries Assistance Commission, have examined the policy implications of the links (IAC 1989). The implications of aviation policies for tourism in Europe have been analysed by Papatheodoru (2002). The links between them and the implications for trade in services have also been considered (Findlay and Forsyth 1988), as have their links in the context of microeconomic reform in Australia (Dwyer and Forsyth 1992). There have been some textbook-level studies which have highlighted the interdependence between the two (see Page 1999). Overall, however, while there is now a substantial literature on both tourism economics and the economics of aviation, there have been relatively few contributions which explore the connections.

In this summary of the issues, a brief background, which highlights the links, is presented. The underlying policy conflicts between the two industries are then outlined. What is positive for the aviation sector is often negative for tourism. Thus the restrictive regulation of earlier years ensured the profitability and stability of the aviation sector, but it discouraged tourism. The moves towards liberalisation, which have been taking place gradually but steadily over the past four decades, are then examined. These have taken place in various stages, and the ways in which they have promoted tourism are considered. Changes in aviation technology have had a major impact on tourism, most obviously through lower costs and fares stimulating tourism. However, they have also had important impacts on patterns of tourism flows; for example, the changing strength of the economies of market density which are present in aviation have had implications for primary and secondary destinations, and increasing aircraft ranges have had implications for stopover destinations. The ways in which the limitations of air transport infrastructure have acted as a constraint on tourism growth are considered next. Apart from regulation, the next most important aspect of government policy towards the two industries is taxation – governments have taxed both industries, and the implications of tax policies are considered. While the two industries are complements on the consumption side, there are not many examples of links on the production side. There are some examples of integration between airlines and tourism firms, such as tour companies' ownership of charter airlines, and airlines' ownership of travel agents – these links are examined. Finally, this chapter concludes by drawing some generalisations, and by pointing to areas for further research.

Background
One of the more striking aspects of air travel has been the trend in costs and prices over the past few decades. Air travel has become safer and more reliable, and it has become a lot cheaper. As Table 10.1 shows, there has been a consistent downward trend in air transport fares – this trend looks set to continue. It has been a result of changes in airline technology and

Table 10.1   Real revenue yields, 1967–1999

Year	Real average revenue per passenger kilometre (cUS 1999)
1967	17.8
1970	15.9
1975	16.1
1980	15.1
1985	11.3
1990	11.7
1995	10.3
1999	8.3

Note: Average revenues per kilometre deflated by US CPI.

Source: International Civil Aviation Organization, *Civil Aviation Statistics of the World*, various years.

liberalisation, two issues which will be explored later. Fifty years ago, air travel was expensive, and used only by business or well-off travellers. Now it is as cheap as most surface modes, with the exception of the car for family trips. With its speed and convenience, it is now the preferred mode for most international tourism trips except for short distances.

The result has been an ongoing boom in air travel. In Table 10.2, trends in air travel are shown for the world in total, and for some key regions. While there has been some slackening off in growth in North America and Europe, the growth rate still remains high, relative, for example, to GDP, and in some regions, notably the Asia Pacific, the growth rate is very high. Air travel demand is expected to continue to grow strongly for the next decade or so. Much of the growth has been in leisure travel, though business travel continues to grow steadily.

Air travel is now an important means of travel for tourism, especially for international tourism. Several countries which have good surface links still have a majority of their inbound tourists arriving by surface modes, though a growing proportion use air (for example, France, Italy and Hong Kong). For other countries, especially those which have limited surface links (such as the UK) or which are islands (such as New Zealand) air transport is the dominant means of transport for inbound and outbound tourism (see Table 10.3). For some of these countries, air travel is virtually a necessity for international tourism – without affordable air travel, tourism to these countries would be minimal. It is no longer necessary for countries to be well located close to their tourism markets, with good surface links to them, for their tourism industries to prosper.

Aviation and tourism – the policy conflicts

Aviation and tourism are two complementary industries. For air-based trips, the tourist needs to make use of the services of both industries to enjoy access to the product. This being so, it is in the interest of each of the industries that the prices, and perhaps profits, of the other be low. Lower air fares bring more tourists as customers of the tourism industry, and lower ground costs induce more tourists to use the services of the airlines. This means that there is an underlying conflict of interest between the two industries, which policy makers must recognise and address. Over time, in most countries, policy makers have changed the balance, and tilted it towards the tourism industry.

The main field on which policy has been exercised has been the airline industry. The airline industry of most countries is well defined (there are only a few airlines to be dealt with) and relatively easy to regulate or tax. By contrast, the tourism industry is quite diffuse, with very many firms in most segments, many small businesses and many firms, such as restaurants,

Table 10.2 Air transport passengers by region, 1976–1999

Year	Europe '000	% of total	North America '000	% of total	Asia Pacific	% of total	Total world (ICAO states) '000
1976	278 805	36.5	240 756	31.5	69 883	9.2	762 979
1980	234 250	31.3	316 639	42.3	103 024	13.8	747 877
1985	268 348	29.9	388 943	43.4	132 310	14.8	896 439
1990	340 938	30.5	472 085	42.3	183 365	16.4	1 117 008
1995	305 020	23.4	551 218	42.3	311 876	23.9	1 303 658
1999	398 289	25.6	656 478	42.1	339 023	21.8	1 558 629

Source: International Civil Aviation Organization, Civil Aviation Statistics of the World, various years.

227

Table 10.3   Share of air transport in total tourism arrivals, 1999

Country	Share of air transport (%)
Canada	37.87
USA	62.32
Australia	99.28*
New Zealand	99.07*
Japan	96.23
Hong Kong	53.51*
Singapore	73.90*
Thailand	83.96
France	14.52 (1997 data)
Italy	15.97*
Spain	69.64
Turkey	62.60*
United Kingdom	68.06*

Note: Arrivals by air as % of total visitors. Where indicated by *, arrivals by air as % of overnight visitors.

Source: World Tourism Organization, *Compendium of Tourism Statistics, 2002,* Madrid: WTO.

which lie partly inside, and partly outside, the tourism industry. Most firms in the industry (with some exceptions, such as domestic aviation) are difficult to regulate. Historically, airlines have been regulated closely until recently (Oum and Yu 2000; Doganis 2001), and tourism industry firms have not been subject to much economic regulation – for example, accommodation is usually subject to environmental and safety regulation, though not economic regulation. A further factor is that until recently, most international airlines were government owned, which made it easier for governments to control them.

Most of the economic regulation which was in place for the aviation industry was positive for that industry, but negative for the tourism industry. International regulation normally limited the number of airlines which could fly between the two countries at either end of a route – typically, only two were allowed, one from each country (sometimes it was possible for airlines of countries intermediate between the two to serve them on a '6th Freedom' basis). The number of seats which the airlines were permitted to offer for sale was also tightly controlled, and set at a level which would push prices up above costs. Regulation usually set minimum fares (Doganis 2001). The result was that airlines were insulated from competition, and supply was restricted, leading to increased profits. These profits went to the government if the airline was government owned – regulation could be seen as a tax on air travel and tourism. Often the profits would be dissipated through higher costs; employees of the airlines shared in the profits through gaining higher than market wages.

Regulation thus led to higher air fares, and thus it discouraged tourism, both inbound and outbound. From the home tourism industry's perspective, higher airfares were undesirable because they lessened the demand for its product. However, there was a partly offsetting advantage – higher air fares also discouraged outbound tourism, and to the extent that outbound tourists switched their spending to the domestic industry, the home tourism industry would gain. On balance, most tourism industries see low air fares as in their interest, and consider the gains in inbound tourism to outweigh the losses from outbound tourism, though it could go the other way. The third main group affected by regulation are the home country consumers who travel internationally – this group has an unambiguous interest in less regulation and low air fares.

Aviation regulatory policy represents a balance between the conflicting interests of the airlines, the home country travellers, and the tourism industry. In the early post-war years, this balance was very much tipped towards the interests of the airlines. Airlines were mainly few in number, government owned and had good access to policy makers – they were readily able to put their case. They prospered under tight regulation. Over time, consumer interests became stronger, and they sought lower fares for holidays abroad. Tourism industries became more articulate, and countries began to see themselves as tourism destinations, and they saw tourism as bringing economic benefits. Tourism interests were more explicitly recognised, and several countries included tourism representatives in their aviation negotiating teams. There was also criticism of high airfares leading to higher costs, not higher profits. As a result, the balance began to change.

Those countries which saw the potential for tourism development, but which were highly dependent on air travel to bring the tourists, revised their approach to airline regulation. Spain realised the potential for visitors from Northern Europe, who would be unlikely to travel on surface modes. Singapore, and other island destinations, saw potential for stopover tourism. Australia and New Zealand realised that they would only become major tourism destinations if the long-haul air fares to them became affordable. Other countries did not see themselves as tourism destinations, or did not see air travel as essential in bringing tourists, and were content to maintain restrictive aviation regulation – a good example is Japan (Yamauchi 1997). The dominant trend over the past four decades has been one of increasing liberalisation, and this has been a critical factor in the expansion of international tourism.

Over the past decade or so, there has been a growing recognition of tourism benefits when aviation policies are assessed. Aviation policies in several countries have been subjected to a much more explicit cost–benefit framework, in which costs and benefits are evaluated and compared, than was the case before. Proposals for liberalisation or strategic alliances have been analysed using this framework (Department of Transport and Communications 1988; BTCE 1991; Gillen et al. 1996; Productivity Commission 1999; Gillen et al. 2001). In several of these (Department of Transport and Communications 1988; Gillen et al. 1996; Productivity Commission 1999; Gillen et al. 2001), the relevance of tourism benefits is explicitly recognised, though benefits were not quantified. Recently, however, there have been attempts to measure tourism economic benefits in the context of aviation policy analysis. Qantas and Air New Zealand have been seeking to form a strategic alliance, and in their submissions to the respective competition authorities, they attempted to measure tourism benefits, along with other benefits and costs (Air New Zealand and Qantas Airways Limited 2002). Both competition authorities addressed the issue in their reports on the proposed alliance (Australian Competition and Consumer Commission 2003; New Zealand Commerce Commission 2003). While tourism benefits from aviation changes are not likely to be as large as the benefits and costs to travellers and airlines, they can be significant. What is notable is that measures of tourism benefits are now being used in aviation policy making.

By noting this critical conflict of interest between the aviation and tourism industries, it is not intended to suggest that there are no common interests. Both industries benefit from tourism promotion – hotels gain if airlines promote a destination, and airlines gain more demand if the tourism industry promotes itself. Both have an interest in lower taxes – airlines lose if hotels are taxed and there are fewer airline passengers. This said, however, many of the developments in aviation and tourism policy over recent decades can be seen in terms of this conflict. The overall trend has been strongly towards liberalisation, and there have been various stages of liberalisation which have had major impacts on tourism – these are considered in the following section.

While regulation and its liberalisation constitute the most important means by which aviation policy affects tourism, they are not the only way. Airline mergers and strategic alliances can also impact on tourism in several ways. Anti-competitive mergers and alliances can raise fares and discourage tourism. On the other hand, those mergers which result in improved networks and more convenient travel will encourage tourism. As noted above, competition authorities are now paying more attention to tourism implications of airline mergers and alliances (on alliances, see the chapters by Morley and by Dimanche and Jolly in this volume).

Airline liberalisation and tourism growth

The development of tourism over the last half century is closely intertwined with air transport liberalisation. Tourism, and especially international tourism, has grown rapidly because air travel has continued to get much cheaper. There are two main reasons for this: airline liberalisation and technological progress. The latter is considered in the next section. Liberalisation has meant that airline markets are more competitive, resulting in airlines being forced to keep their fares low, and to keep costs down. Liberalisation has also meant that a wider range of airlines is able to serve a given market – for instance, UK tourists can fly to France on an Irish airline. They are no longer limited, as they were, to only UK or French airlines.

In the 1950s and 1960s, air transport was very tightly regulated, both in international and domestic markets. On most markets between city pairs, only one or two airlines were permitted. The number of seats they were permitted to offer was tightly restricted, and thus they had little incentive to compete for traffic. Furthermore, they were not usually permitted to compete on price, since fares were regulated. Air travel was expensive, and used by business and the well off. Since the 1960s, air transport has been extensively liberalised (though some markets remain quite tightly regulated), and has become much cheaper. This has enabled mass international tourism.

It is possible to distinguish distinct phases of liberalisation. First, there was the development of the charter market, especially in Europe. Next, there was domestic deregulation, notably in the US. This was followed soon after by the liberalisation of international markets. Finally, there has been the boom in low-cost carriers (LCCs). These are considered in turn.

The charter market

The first major move away from regulation came with the development of the charter market. This got under way in a big way in the 1960s in Europe, especially with travel from the UK and Germany to the sun destinations of Southern Europe. Fares on scheduled airlines in Europe were high, too high for mass tourism. Charter airlines offered a way around this (Papatheodoru 2002). They were operated on a low-cost basis, and seats were sold in conjunction with a tour package. The limited flexibility enabled the airlines to achieve very high load factors, and thus low costs per passenger. Charter airlines were often owned by tour companies or the major scheduled airlines. The market was very competitive, and fares were much lower than those on scheduled airlines. Charter airlines were less tightly regulated than the scheduled airlines – for example, they were often, though not always, permitted to offer as many flights as they wished. However, they were regulated as to where they could fly to, and they could only offer air travel as part of a tour package (Doganis 2001).

The significance of charters is that they offered a way around the regulatory dilemma by segmenting the market. Most countries were unwilling to open up air transport markets to more competition and put their (state-owned) airlines at risk. Charters offered a way of serving tourism demands while not impacting too strongly on the scheduled airlines. Because of the restrictions put on charters, and the destinations they travelled to, direct competition between charters and scheduled airlines was limited. Charter airlines did pose a policy problem for countries with tourism potential, such as Spain. Should these countries insist on their airlines gaining an equal share of traffic to and from them, as was usual with air transport arrangements, or should they let airlines of the origin countries dominate the market? Spain did not have many charter airlines, but it allowed access to the charter airlines of Northern Europe, which soon dominated traffic into Spain. While Spain thus only had a minor share of air traffic, its tourism industries boomed.

Charter airlines enabled the growth of holiday tourism in Europe. They enabled tourists to travel internationally to holiday and cultural destinations of about one or two hours flying time away from their origin, for holidays of about one or two weeks' duration. People switched from domestic holidays, made by surface transport, to international holidays around Europe.

Charter airlines have long been mainly a European phenomenon. Charter operations have existed in the US, on trans-Atlantic routes, and even some long-haul charters, such as from the UK to Australia, have existed. However the reliance on charters has not been nearly as great in other markets as in the European market. This is primarily because of the ways other markets have been regulated.

Domestic deregulation
Prior to the late 1970s, most countries with significant domestic air transport markets, such as the US, Canada, Australia and Brazil, regulated their markets very tightly. As a result, air travel was oriented to business, with high fares and high convenience. The breakthrough came with domestic deregulation in the US, which took place over the late 1970s and early 1980s (Bailey et al. 1985). Other countries followed the US example later.

Deregulation in the US led to a much more competitive airline industry which was interested in serving low-fare markets. Initially, there was rush of new entrants, mainly operating on a low-cost basis, and offering simple, low fares. Then the established airlines fought back, with low-fare offerings of their own – ultimately most of the new entrants were forced out, and the older airlines re-established their dominance. This too was made possible by effective market segmentation. The airlines worked out ways to offer low fares to price-sensitive leisure travellers while keeping the high-yield business travellers (Frank 1983; Levine 1987). These included minimum stay restrictions on return tickets, and requirements that travellers stay at their destination over Saturday night – a restriction which would not appeal to business travellers. The result was that low fares did become readily available, and the range of fares became quite wide. A similar pattern emerged in the other deregulated domestic markets, such as those of Canada (Oum et al. 1991) and Australia (Forsyth 1991).

Airline deregulation led to major changes in the pattern of tourism within the countries which deregulated. Holidaymakers switched from surface transport to air transport, and made longer journeys. It also meant that these countries became more competitive as destinations for foreign tourists. For example, it became moderately cheap to fly to the US and fly to a number of destinations within the US during a short holiday – this made the US more attractive as a holiday destination for European and Japanese travellers.

Liberalisation on long-haul markets
The liberalisation of long-haul international markets came about at around the same time as domestic deregulation (though some countries, such as Australia, opened up their international markets before their domestic markets). Having deregulated its domestic market, the US sought to conclude liberal 'open skies' agreements with its international partners (Kasper 1988). Typically, these agreements allowed for several airlines, not just one from each country, to serve on a route, and they avoided fare and capacity restrictions. They opened up routes to new entry and competition (Doganis 2001). Other countries allowed airlines from third countries to serve routes between them and origin/destination countries. For example, Australia and the UK ceased to reserve the route between them for Australian and UK airlines, and they permitted airlines from countries between them, such as Thailand and Singapore, to serve the route (Findlay 1985). These intermediate countries could serve the Australia–UK market by combining their traffic rights to Australia and the UK, however they could still be restricted in terms of the capacity which they were permitted to schedule on each of the sectors they flew. This substantially added to competition, and because some of these countries' airlines had very low costs, this put considerable pressure on fares.

Liberalisation on international, long-haul markets has been gradual, and incomplete. Some markets, such as the North Atlantic are very competitive, while others, such as the trans-Pacific, are much less so. Air transport markets within Asia present a mixed picture, with some very open markets and other very restricted markets (Bowen 1997; Oum and Yu 2000). Japan and Hong Kong have been very slow to open up their markets. South America has also been slow to liberalise.

The consequence of this has been the development of a mass long-haul tourism market over the last two decades. This has been especially import-ant for countries which are relatively remote, such as Australia, New Zealand and South Africa. Prior to liberalisation, international tourism to these countries was modest, limited to business travel and niche markets for visiting friends and relatives (VFR) and well-off tourists. Nowadays, these countries are very much competitors for mass holiday tourism. Interestingly, areas which have been slow to liberalise, such as South America, have not developed as their tourism potential would suggest.

The low-cost-carrier phenomenon
Low-cost carriers are the new boom segment in air transport and they are having a major impact on tourism. LCCs are not new – Southwest, in the US, has been operating since the early 1970s. In the early days of US deregula-tion, many LCCs entered, and soon failed (Gudmundsson 1998). Since the mid-1990s, LCCs have been enjoying a resurgence in markets across the world. They are currently more profitable than the established carriers (which seem to be having more problems in adapting to competition from LCCs than they did in the US in the 1980s). It is possible that current LCCs have learned the lessons from the 1980s and many can be expected to survive for some time (Calder 2002; Lawton 2002; Williams 2002).

As their name suggests, LCCs seek to keep costs at a minimum. They operate simple point-to-point networks, and try to avoid costly connecting traffic. They obtain high utilisation from aircraft and crews, and often pay their staff lower salaries than the established airlines. Many, though not all, are 'no frills' airlines, and do not provide much in terms of flight service, lounges, or frequent flyer programmes. Several sell food and beverages on the flight. So far, they have been successful in keeping costs down, especially as compared with the costs of the established airlines.

The products which they are offering are new. Instead of cheap inclusive tour packages, or low return fares subject to restrictive conditions, they offer one-way low fares with minimum restrictions, though also with limited refundability. Sometimes they contract out tour packages but sell them on their websites. They often travel to secondary airports. Sometimes these airports are alternative gateways to major destinations (as Lübeck is for Hamburg, Senai in Malaysia is for Singapore, and Charleroi is for Brussels), sometimes these are smaller destinations in their own right (for example, Carcassonne in South West France) and sometimes they are both (Treviso in Italy which is near Venice but is also the gateway to the Veneto region). The LCCs are flying to these destinations partly because airports are cheaper to use, partly because airports are less congested and quick turnarounds are possible, and partly because they are not entering direct, head-to-head competition with strong established airlines.

LCCs are making an impact in markets across the world. In the US, Southwest continues to grow, and new LCCs such as JetBlue have entered. In Canada and Australia, LCCs such as Westjet (Lawton 2002) and Virgin Blue provide the main competition for the dominant national airline (Forsyth 2003). LCCs are gaining a foothold in Asia, especially in domestic markets such as those of Malaysia, where AirAsia has been successful, and Indonesia. Their further expansion will depend on their gaining access to international routes. However, it is in Europe where the growth of LCCs has been most spectacular. The intra-European aviation market became extensively liberalised only in the mid-1990s, and since then, the LCCs have been the main form of new competition. Several of the airlines, such as Ryanair, easyJet and Air Berlin are now quite large airlines, with very large orders for more aircraft (Lawton 2002).

Competition from the LCCs is creating problems for the major airlines, many of which are loss making, and which find it difficult to match the fares of the LCCs. Furthermore, the new breed of LCCs appears to be more financially secure than their predecessors. Some incumbent airlines, such as Lufthansa, have sought to compete aggressively against them (and encountered problems from competition authorities). Several major airlines have set up their own LCCs, such as British Airways' Go and KLM's Buzz, only to sell them off later on (Cassani and Kemp 2003). There seems to be a new wave of set-ups by major airlines, with United's Ted in the US, Singapore Airlines' Tiger and Qantas' Jetstar in Australia.

The LCCs are important because they are having significant impacts on tourism. Most of them are oriented to leisure travellers, though some, like easyJet, also seek out the price-sensitive business traveller. The most obvious impact is on the overall size of the market – lower fares mean more travel (though some of this is at the expense of surface modes). Furthermore, the products they are offering are changing tourism markets. The ready availability of low, and in some cases very low, fares makes trips of short duration possible. Thus a Londoner can easily afford a weekend in Dublin visiting the pubs, and it is now practical for a Berliner to have a holiday house in the South of France. Neither of these markets would have been well served by the expensive scheduled airlines or the restrictive charter airlines. On top of this, the low fares are encouraging a growth in the overall market for traditional destinations.

A further impact which the LCCs are having is on the development of secondary destinations. Holiday travellers are discovering the attractions of places which are less well known, and sometimes less crowded. These destinations in turn have realised the importance of LCCs in bringing tourists, and they have been offering financial inducements to the LCCs to operate services (within Europe their ability to do this may be constrained by recent limits on subsidies imposed by the European Commission, see European Commission 2004). LCCs are thus both growing, and changing, tourism markets.

It is likely that these impacts on tourism will be permanent, and that further impacts will come about. LCCs have brought about a major change in airline markets. Their expansion plans are bold, and new entrants continue to arrive. It is quite possible that there will be a shakeout, and that many will not survive. Nevertheless, it currently does not seem as though the major airlines will be able to force them out of the market as they nearly did in the 1980s. Quite possibly, airline markets will be characterised by traditional airlines, with a smaller market share, operating alongside LCCs, in a larger overall market.

Aviation technology and patterns of tourism
It is to be expected, given that air transport is a key determinant of tourism flows, that the technology of aviation will have an important impact on tourism. Technology determines costs, and thus it determines which destinations are price competitive and which are not.

One aspect of aviation technology which is very obvious is that it has been improving steadily over the last century. For example, fuel use is becoming more efficient, leading to cost savings, and extending the range of aircraft. The unit costs of travelling by air are falling, and they can be expected to continue to do so for the next couple of decades at least. Lower unit costs lead to lower fares, and lower fares lead to increased tourism. Even without the changes in industry structure and competition dealt with in the last section, the gradual but consistent fall in costs would have produced rapid growth in tourism by air. Some of these changes have required changes in other dimensions to become fully effective. Achieving lower costs through larger aircraft is only possible if they can be filled. Developments in information technology and yield management, along with deregulation of fare setting, have contributed to making it possible to fill the large aircraft, and achieve low per unit costs.

One particularly pertinent feature of aviation technology is that it gives rise to economies of density (Tretheway and Oum 1992). Airlines are generally considered to not be subject to substantial economies of scale – small as well as large airlines can operate at low cost per passenger. However, economies of density are important in the airline industry. These economies pertain to routes – costs per passenger fall as the traffic density on the route increases. One of the main reasons for this lies in aircraft technology – it is possible to operate large aircraft such as the Boeing 747 at lower cost per seat kilometre than it is to operate smaller aircraft such as the Boeing 737. Further, there are also economies in passenger handling at airports.

The upshot is that fares on routes with low traffic volumes will be higher than fares on routes with high traffic volumes of the same length. Since smaller origins and destinations tend to be only able to support low traffic volumes, they will inevitably have high fares. Hence, smaller, secondary destinations will be less price competitive than large destinations, even when they obtain direct air services (and often smaller destinations can only be accessed indirectly through larger gateways).

The impact of economies of density changes over time, as aviation technology changes. When the Boeing 747 was introduced in the 1970s, it increased economies of density, since the per seat kilometre costs which it offered were much lower than on smaller aircraft then in service. This gave a boost to the dense markets able to support services with 747s. It meant that all but the largest cities in most countries would have to have indirect long-haul services through the main gateways. Over time, the cost advantages of the Boeing 747 were eroded, with aircraft such as the Boeing 767, the Boeing 777 and the Airbus A340 entering long-haul markets. With these smaller aircraft offering relatively low per seat kilometre costs, airlines began to offer direct services to the secondary cities, such as London to Tampa or Baltimore, rather than just London to New York. These newer aircraft have made secondary destinations easier and quicker to get to than they had been before and thus encouraged tourism to them. This process might be reversed when the Airbus A380, which is much larger than the Boeing 747, and which is forecast to have significantly lower costs per seat kilometre, comes into service. Secondary cities may again be bypassed.

Economies of density not only exist in long-haul traffic – they also exist at the short-haul end. Costs per seat kilometre are lower using Boeing 737 and Airbus A320 aircraft than they are using smaller regional jet and turboprop aircraft. This means that fares on dense city pairs are lower than on less busy routes. This provides a challenge for the development of regional tourism. The larger cities and resort areas are always easier and cheaper for tourists to access than the smaller ones. Many promising smaller resort areas lament that they are unable to attract direct air services, and when they do obtain these services, they tend to be relatively expensive. The introduction of regional jets has made some difference, and it is possible that the next generation of regional jets will tilt the balance further, and lessen the impact of economies of density, making secondary destinations easier to access and more price competitive.

Another aspect of change in aviation technology, which is having an impact on patterns of tourism, is the development of longer-haul aircraft.

Over time, the range of aircraft is increasing. This means that they are needing to make fewer stops for refuelling, and can make long, direct flights. Thus destinations which used to prosper as stopover destinations are now being bypassed. In the early days of jets, flights from the US to the South Pacific had to stop in Hawaii and Fiji. With the development of longer-range aircraft, first Fiji, then Hawaii were bypassed. The range of aircraft is continuing to increase – with the introduction of the Airbus A340–500, it is no longer necessary for flights to stop en route from South East Asia to Los Angeles, and flights from Australia to the Middle East need not stop at Singapore. The era of stopover tourism may be ending.

Aviation technology encompasses more than just airliner hardware. Over time, aviation has become more and more information technology dependent – airlines are IT industries with wings. IT plays a critical role in airline booking and yield management – significantly though, the role has been changing.

By the 1970s, computer reservation systems (CRSs) had become established as the critical tool in handling airline bookings and in the management of capacity – allocation of passengers to flights, provision of information about loadings, and in setting prices. They also provided the airline's links to travel agents. Initially, each airline had its own simple CRS, but as their complexity grew, CRSs became more expensive to develop and expand. By the early 1980s, smaller airlines were attaching themselves to the CRSs of larger airlines, and there was a growing belief that CRSs were something of a natural monopoly (Bailey et al. 1985). Ownership of a major CRS would give an airline a strong competitive advantage in the marketplace. For example, when listing flights on the travel agents screen, the airline could ensure that its own flights were listed first, even if more convenient or cheaper flights were available from its rivals. It was considered that CRSs might result in concentration of the airline industry – while economies of scale, *per se*, were not important, if an airline had a major CRS, it could dominate the market. In the US, airlines with major CRSs such as United and American strengthened their position in the late 1980s. Governments began regulating the use of the CRSs, in an attempt to ensure that the owners did not gain an anti-competitive advantage from their CRSs. The period was one of consolidation in the liberalised markets, and it seemed possible that competition in the industry would falter.

However, technology does not always change in the same direction, and the development of the internet meant that ownership of a CRS became of much less significance. Airlines set up internet booking systems and passengers bypassed travel agents and the CRSs which they used. The internet meant that CRSs lost their potency as barriers to entry.

This was shown most clearly with the new LCCs. In earlier phases of competition from LCCs, the new airlines found it difficult to access potential passengers and sell their product. They often needed to work through travel agents, which charged a commission that was a high proportion of the fare, and they also needed to be listed on the major CRSs, which were owned by the incumbent airlines. Several airlines failed because they were not able to distribute their product in a cost-effective way. With the internet, they were able to bypass the travel agents and the CRSs. In addition, the handling cost per passenger of internet bookings is only a small fraction of the cost using other methods.

Not surprisingly, the LCCs have been pioneers in the use of the internet for bookings (Doganis 2001). Some airlines, such as easyJet, have long had a majority of their seats sold on the internet (86.5 per cent by 2001: Lawton 2002, p. 116). Of all tourism industries, airlines have perhaps made the most effective use of the internet. The new technology has made it much easier for the new entrant LCCs to survive and grow, and it has resulted in an industry which is significantly more competitive.

Air transport infrastructure as a constraint on tourism growth
The presence of air transport services enables tourism in a region to develop. When these services are constrained, tourism growth is hampered. Airline services are quite flexible, and are not likely to be a constraint except when they are regulated. Air transport infrastructure, especially airports, but also including air traffic control, is much more likely to be a brake on tourism growth.

Airport capacity is a constraint on tourism development in the major cities of Europe, North America and Japan (Graham 2003). Airport developments have a long lead time, and they tend to be controversial. This is primarily because of their environmental impacts, on noise and air quality. Thus, in many cities, further expansion of airport capacity is strongly resisted, and as a result, capacity has fallen well short of demand. The excess demand is handled in two ways – congestion and slot restrictions.

In the US, when there is excess demand for an airport, congestion, in the form of delays to flights, is allowed to build up. Congestion acts as a rationing device, and fewer flights are scheduled into the congested airport. Traffic is discouraged, and there is less tourism from, and to, the city (Brueckner 2002).

In Europe and elsewhere, the favoured approach to handling excess demand is through slot controls (Boyfield 2003). Airport capacity is declared in terms of a number of slots, and slots are usually allocated to the airlines which have been using the airport before it became congested. To use the airport, an airline must have a slot for the time it wishes to land or take off. For some airports, slots are scarce and difficult to obtain – this is so for the London and Tokyo airports. A slot pair (to land and take off daily) at London Heathrow airport recently sold for 10 million pounds sterling. While slot control systems lessen congestion, they reduce the number of flights into the city and make them more expensive, thus discouraging tourism. At various stages in the past, airport capacity limitations have been a major restriction of the growth of tourism into and out of Japan (Dempsey and O'Connor 1997). Airport capacity constraints are likely to become more of a brake on tourism growth in these countries over the future, notwithstanding the increasing use by LCCs of secondary airports. The region with least problems of airport capacity appears to be Asia, outside Japan. While air transport has been growing very rapidly in recent years, there have been significant increases in capacity in cities such as Hong Kong, Kuala Lumpur and Shanghai.

At the other end of the scale, lack of airport capacity can prove a barrier to tourism development in smaller cities, the regions and in remote locations. Some developing countries may have tourism potential, but their airport facilities may be inadequate, and they may not have the resources to upgrade them. Smaller cities and regions may possess airports, but they can have operational restrictions (because of runway length or strength) which prevent the use of cost-effective aircraft. As a result, tourism is hampered because air fares are higher than they might be, and frequencies are low. Usually in these circumstances the barriers to expanding capacity are not as strong as they are with the environmentally constrained major cities of North America and Europe.

While inadequate capacity can be a brake on tourism, excessive capacity can also have the same effect. Excessive investment often takes place in airports. Airports are often government owned, or regulated, and they can usually pass on higher costs through higher charges. These are initially paid by airlines, but ultimately paid by the passengers. A city or country may see an airport as a prestige project, and build a large and lavishly appointed facility. However, tourists do not come to a city or region just because there is a large airport there – rather they will be discouraged by the higher air fares they have to pay so that the airport can be funded. Tourism is best served when airport investments are of a size and quality matched to the demand.

When investment to expand capacity at international airports takes place, a high proportion of the benefits accrue to airlines and passengers. Airlines and passengers both gain from reduced congestion, from additional flights and from operational economies enabled by better airport facilities. Many of the airlines and passengers who gain from airport investment will be foreign – this will be especially true in the case of airports in developing countries which serve mainly incoming tourists, not the local population, few of whom are sufficiently well off to fly. From the perspective of the country doing the investing, most of the costs will fall on residents, but most of the benefits will be enjoyed directly at least, by foreigners.

This poses a problem for evaluation. If these investments in airport capacity are to be justified from the perspective of the home country, this must be done in terms of the tourism and other economic benefits which flow from the extra capacity. Additional tourism will bring economic benefits to a country or region, through tax payments, terms of trade effects, additional profits, possible positive impacts on employments and general stimulation of economic activity. Measurement of the benefits from additional tourism from outside the country or region is not a well-developed science, and many of the claimed benefits of airport expansion can be argued to be exaggerations (Niemeier 2001). Nevertheless there can be real economic benefits, especially when the stimulation of the economy takes place where there are unemployed resources.

Taxing tourism and aviation
While regulation is one of the main arms of policy, especially in respect of aviation, taxation is the other. Tourism and aviation can be subject to general taxation, and both can be subject to industry-specific taxes, such as bed taxes and passenger levies. To an extent, both will be taxed, though there are constraints on the government's ability to impose taxes in the ways it wants. Taxes are desired by governments in that they raise revenue, however the downside is that they discourage activities, such as tourism, which they may be seeking to encourage. To this extent, governments will need to treat aviation and tourism together to ensure that they impose the right mix of taxes given their objectives.

Some countries see tourism as a tax base, and seek to use their market power in tourism to transfer the burden of taxes to foreigners rather than to domestic residents. Countries do have some market power in tourism, because they are not perfect substitutes for one another. They can increase the prices of their tourism products to some extent without reducing demand to zero (Tisdell 1983; Fujii et al. 1985). This market power enables them to regulate their airlines – if there were no market power, any regulation which had the effect of raising fares would lead to air travel being eliminated or reduced substantially (Findlay and Forsyth 1988). Once a country has decided to exercise its market power, the question arises of how much to tax aviation and how much to tax tourism.

By taxing aviation, for example with a passenger levy, all tourists, both inbound and outbound, will be taxed. This tax has the effect of discouraging both inbound and outbound tourism – it has both positive and negative effects on the home tourism industry. A tax on tourism, for example a bed tax, however discourages inbound tourism and encourages outbound tourism – it has only negative impacts on the home tourism industry. These patterns of effects come about because it is usually only feasible to discriminate imperfectly among inbound, outbound and domestic tourists when taxes are levied. The negative effects on the tourism industry may lead the government to prefer taxes on aviation rather than tourism products directly.

In many countries it may not be practical to tax tourism directly. In developing countries, much of tourism may be supplied by the informal sector, for example, household businesses, which may be very difficult to include in the tax system. Taxes at the aviation level, collected from only a few firms or directly from passengers, may be much simpler to collect. Thus countries with less extensive tax systems may prefer aviation taxes.

Other countries, however, may prefer not to tax tourism. Rather they may see tourism as a source of economic benefits, and seek to encourage it, if need be, by keeping the price of a visit low. However, most developed countries these days have general systems of indirect taxes, such as value added tax (VAT) or goods and services tax (GST), which tax tourism goods and services along with other goods and services. The rate at which these taxes are levied is sometimes quite high, above 15 per cent. This poses a problem for taxing of exports, including tourism exports. Most VAT/GST systems allow for taxes paid on the inputs into exports to be refunded, making exports tax free. The problem is that this is difficult with tourism, since the tourists buy goods and services directly when they are in the country. It is possible to refund this tax for large items, though it would be difficult to refund it for all purchase made by tourists. Thus tourism exports are taxed more heavily than other exports.

To this end, countries may wish to encourage tourism, rather than discourage it by imposing taxes on it. Such countries would not impose additional taxes either at the aviation level, or at the tourism level, through specific tourism taxes. They may also take compensatory measures, such as government funding of tourism promotion. Some countries, and more particularly regions, also seek to encourage tourism through subsidising aviation, or more likely, aviation infrastructure. Thus several regions in Europe have sought to increase tourism by subsidising airport use of low-cost airlines.

Few countries make a systematic assessment of the extent to which they want to encourage or tax tourism and aviation, and it is quite possible that tourism promotion and tax policies work at cross-purposes. Some countries seem keen to encourage tourism, yet they are also imposing more taxes on tourism and aviation, especially the latter. In recent years there is evidence of a growth in taxes levied on aviation – air travel is easy to tax, and its growth makes it an attractive source of revenue. To an extent, current taxes may be more transparent than the implicit taxes raised on aviation through regulation, which have been declining, though tourism industry groups have expressed concern about the trend towards them (WTTC various years).

While levies on airports and their passengers have been growing, not all of these are true taxes. In some cases these represent a charge for services. For example, security levies have been increasing, and these pay for the additional security now implemented at airports. There is some debate about who should pay for these services. While passengers and airlines gain from safer skies, much of the benefit of tighter security is enjoyed by the community at large – thus it is suggested that these should be provided by the government, not at the expense of passengers. Environmental charges at airports are also growing in terms of coverage and levels – these cover the noise and emissions externalities created by air transport at airports. To some extent these are used to compensate persons adversely affected (through sound insulation grants for houses around airports), though not all revenues collected are spent in this way. These levies may be present to correct an externality, though they do add to the already high taxation of air travel, and do have the effect of discouraging tourism.

Aviation and tourism: supply-side integration
Aviation and tourism services are clearly linked on the demand side. To consume tourism, the tourist must purchase a range of related products, such as accommodation, meals, local travel and long-distance travel, such as air travel. These are sometimes sold jointly as a package. The question then arises of how integrated the supply of these products might be.

By and large, with some important exceptions, the links between aviation and tourism on the supply side are not particularly significant. Airlines and other tourism operators tend to be owned and operated independently of one another. This suggests that there are few strong economies to be gained from integration, and that there are managerial advantages in specialisation in one part of the industry (see the chapter by Čavlek in this volume).

Perhaps the most important exception to the general rule occurs with inclusive tour companies. Tour companies, especially in Europe, such as the Thompson Group in the UK, often operate their own airlines. With the development of inclusive tours, relying on charter airlines, tour companies set up their own airlines. To provide package tours competitively, the various parts of the chain need to be integrated closely – for example, available supplies of accommodation and air capacity need to be matched closely to the demand, so that high utilisation can be achieved. Tour companies found that they could do this when they owned and operated their own airlines, and the load factors of the tour company airlines are very high. It will be interesting to see whether these links persist, as market conditions change. The development of the LCCs has meant that the advantages of inclusive tours and charter airlines have been eroded, as travellers are willing to pay a little extra for the additional flexibility that the LCCs provide. Some tour companies have set up LCCs of their own. This may be a defensive move, as they see their market share as slipping. It has yet to be seen whether there are any economies to be reaped from integration of tours and LCCs, and whether this is a likely pattern for the future.

Another exception of some significance is airline ownership of travel agents. This may reflect economies of integration on the production side – travel agents are intensive users of the CRSs which the airlines develop and own. Airlines may also have considered that ownership of a travel agent would give them marketing advantages, as the agent would be a direct link with their customers. However, another major reason for ownership of travel agents was probably to create an entry barrier. If all or most of the travel agents are owned by the incumbent airlines, it is difficult for new entrant airlines to sell their product. Airline ownership of agents is often mentioned as a barrier to entry into the airline industry. This barrier has been considerably weakened by the development of internet booking, which bypasses the travel agent. The new entrant LCCs have been particularly effective users of the internet, and the older airlines are well behind them in their internet use. In the light of this, it may well be that the major airlines no longer see ownership of travel agencies as being as strong a competitive weapon as it was, and they may divest themselves of these businesses.

Beyond these examples, there are few significant cases of cross-ownership between tourism and aviation businesses. For a time, the major international airlines owned or operated hotels (for example, Pan Am with Intercontinental and Air France with Meridien), however, they were quick to divest themselves of these when they encountered cash crises in the 1980s and 1990s. Some of the new LCCs have invested in car hire and similar firms, but this is probably the result of opportunistic investments rather than to reap economies of integration at the production level (they also have been investing in mobile phone companies and credit cards). Within the tourism industry, specialisation probably pays – it probably is better to concentrate on providing airline services, hotel services or local bus tours well than to develop unwieldy conglomerates which do not excel in any of the products they sell.

Concluding remarks
Changes in aviation have had profound implications for tourism. The availability of low fares has made air travel affordable for leisure tourism, and

has greatly stimulated international tourism. Aviation shapes tourism – changes in aviation prices, technology and constraints have determined where tourists go to, have made destinations and bypassed them.

Many of these changes at the aviation level, especially those to do with regulation, have been the result of deliberate policy decisions. As noted, there is a conflict of interest between aviation and tourism, and over the past half century, the balance of interests between the two industries has been shifting in the direction of tourism. There has been a secular trend towards liberalisation. This trend has reflected the recognition that overall gains are made by having a liberal environment, even if some interests are adversely affected. It reflects a greater understanding of the economic and other benefits tourism can bring to a country, and it reflects a more articulate tourism industry in many countries. While there has been some cost in terms of airline profits and staff remuneration, countries see gain in encouraging tourism through more efficient and lower-cost airlines.

This said, not all issues are settled. One aspect of the link which will repay further research concerns the impacts of aviation changes on tourism, and the measurement of the economic benefits from consequent changes in tourism. As noted, this is something which is now being factored into aviation policy making, though explicit measurement of benefits is still in its infancy.

Related to this is the need for a better understanding of the determinants of tourism demand. Tourism demand modelling is becoming more sophisticated (see the chapter by Lim in this volume), and some models explicitly include aviation (for example, air fare) and ground component (for example, ground component prices) variables as determinants of tourism demand. Both types of variables are significant, and they influence demand in different, though related, ways. They will influence not only total visitor flows, but also duration of trips, and expenditure in total, and per night. More detailed evidence on how aviation changes, such as falls in fares, impact on these variables will enable more accurate measures of the impact of aviation changes on tourism economic benefits.

A final aspect of the aviation–tourism connection which has been examined briefly here concerns aviation and tourism taxes. The impacts that taxes on one level can have on the other can easily be understood. However, policy makers rarely put all the pieces of the jigsaw together. Does a country wish to encourage tourism, and maximise economic benefits of tourism, by keeping taxes, on both aviation and ground tourism, low? Or does it wish to make use of its market power, and use foreign tourists as a source of revenue? Whichever of these options it chooses, it will need to determine at which level – aviation or ground tourism – such taxes are best levied. Furthermore, if there is already general taxation of tourism and aviation services, it will need to determine how best to counteract these if it wishes to keep taxes low. Aviation and tourism taxation need to be considered jointly – though often they are not.

Acknowledgements
I am grateful to John King for comments on an earlier draft and to Anthony Bell for research assistance. Any errors are mine.

References

Air New Zealand and Qantas Airways Limited (2002), *Submission to the Australian Competition and Consumer Commission in Support of the Application for Authorisation*, December.
Australian Competition and Consumer Commission (2003), *Applications for Authorisation A 30220, A30221, A30222, A90862, and A90863, Acquisition by Qantas Airways Limited of Ordinary Shares in Air New Zealand Limited and cooperative arrangements between Qantas, Air New Zealand and Air Pacific Limited, Final Determination*, Canberra, September.
Bailey, B., D. Graham and D. Kaplan (1985), *Deregulating the Airlines*, Cambridge, MA: MIT Press.
Bowen, J. (1997), 'The Asia Pacific airline industry: prospects for multilateral liberalisation', in C. Findlay, Chia Lin Sien and K. Singh (eds), *Asia Pacific Air Transport Challenges and Policy Reforms*, Singapore: Institute of Southeast Asian Studies, pp. 123–53.
Boyfield, K. (ed.) (2003), *A Market in Airport Slots*, London: Institute of Economic Affairs.
Brueckner, J. (2002), 'Airport congestion when carriers have market power', *American Economic Review*, **92** (5), 1357–75.
Bureau of Transport and Communications Economics (BTCE) and Jarden Morgan NZ/CS First Boston New Zealand Limited (1991), *Costs and Benefits of a Single Australasian Aviation Market*, Canberra: Australian Government Publishing Service.
Calder, S. (2002), *No Frills: The Truth behind the Low Cost Revolution in the Skies*, London: Virgin Books.
Cassani, B. and K. Kemp (2003), *Go: An Airline Adventure*, London: Time Warner Books.
Commerce Commission (New Zealand) (2003), *Application for Authorisation of Certain Restrictive Business Practices between Air New Zealand Limited and Qantas Airways Limited, Final Determination*, Wellington, October.
Dempsey, P. and K. O'Connor (1997), 'Air traffic congestion and infrastructure development in the Pacific Asia region', in C. Findlay, Chia Lin Sien and K. Singh (eds), *Asia Pacific Air Transport Challenges and Policy Reforms*, Singapore: Institute of Southeast Asian Studies, pp. 23–47.
Department of Transport and Communications (Australia) (1988), *Negotiating International Aviation Rights*, Canberra, June.
Doganis, R. (1991), *Flying Off Course*, 2nd edn, London: Harper Collins Academic.
Doganis, R. (2001), *The Airline Business in the 21st Century*, London: Routledge.
Dwyer, L. and P. Forsyth (1992), 'Microeconomic reform in aviation and tourism', in P. Forsyth (ed.), *Microeconomic Reform in Australia*, St Leonards: Allen & Unwin, pp. 151–70.
European Commission (2004), *Decision on Subsidies to Charleroi Airport*, February, Media release, IP/04/157.
Findlay, C. (1985), *The Flying Kangaroo: An Endangered Species? An Economic Perspective of Australian International Civil Aviation Policy*, Sydney: Allen & Unwin.
Findlay, C. and P. Forsyth (1988), 'Trade in air transport and tourism services', in L. Castle and C. Findlay (eds), *Pacific Trade in Services*, Sydney: Allen & Unwin, pp. 99–122.
Forsyth, P. (1991), 'The regulation and deregulation of Australia's domestic airline industry', in K. Button (ed.), *Airline Deregulation: International Experiences*, London: David Fulton, pp. 48–84.

Forsyth, P. (2003), 'Low cost carriers in Australia: experiences and impacts', *Journal of Air Transport Management*, **9**, 277–84.

Frank, R. (1983), 'When are price differentials discriminatory?', *Journal of Policy Analysis and Management*, **2** (2), 238–55.

Fujii, E., M. Khaled and J. Mak (1985), 'The exportability of hotel occupancy and other tourist taxes', *National Tax Journal*, **38**, 169–77.

Gillen, D., R. Harris and T.H. Oum (1996), *Assessing the Benefits and Costs of International Air Transport Liberalization: Report to Air Policy Group*, Ottawa, Canada.

Gillen, D., H. Hinsch, B. Mandel and H. Wolf (2001), *The Impact of Liberalizing International Aviation Bilaterals: The Case of the North German Region*, Aldershot: Ashgate.

Graham (2003), *Managing Airports: An International Perspective*, 2nd ed., Oxford: Butterworth-Heinemann.

Gudmundsson, S. (1998), *Flying Too Close to the Sun: The Success and Failure of the New-entrant Airlines*, Aldershot: Ashgate.

Industries Assistance Commission (Australia) (IAC) (1989), *Travel and Tourism, Report No 423*, Canberra: Australian Government Publishing Service, September.

Kasper, D. (1988), *Deregulation and Globalization: Liberalizing International Trade in Air Services*, Ballinger: American Enterprise Institute.

Lawton, T. (2002), *Cleared for Take-Off: Structure and Strategy in the Low Fare Airline Business*, Aldershot: Ashgate.

Levine, M. (1987), 'Airline competition in deregulated markets: theory, firm strategy and public policy', *Yale Journal on Regulation*, **4** (2), 393–494.

Niemeier, H. M. (2001), 'On the use and abuse of impact analysis for airports: a critical view from the perspective of regional policy', in W. Pfähler (ed.), *Regional Input–Output Analysis: Conceptual Issues, Airport Case Studies and Extensions*, HWWA Studies 66, Nomos Verlagsgesellschaft, pp. 201–22.

Oum, T., W. Stanbury and M. Tretheway (1991), 'Airline deregulation in Canada', in K. Button (ed.), *Airline Deregulation: International Experiences*, London: David Fulton, pp. 124–87.

Oum, T.H. and C. Yu (2000), *Shaping Air Transport in Asia Pacific*, Aldershot: Ashgate.

Page, S. (1999), *Transport and Tourism*, Harlow: Longman.

Papatheodoru, A. (2002), 'Civil aviation regimes and leisure tourism in Europe', *Journal of Air Transport Management*, **8** (November), 381–8.

Productivity Commission (1999), *International Air Services, Report No. 2*, Canberra: AusInfo.

Tisdell, C. (1983), 'Public finance and the appropriation of the gains from international tourism', *Singapore Economic Review*, **28**, 3–20.

Tretheway, M. and T.H. Oum (1992), *Airline Economics: Foundations for Strategy and Policy*, Vancouver: Centre for Transportation Studies, University of British Columbia.

Williams, G. (2002), *Airline Competition: Deregulation's Mixed Legacy*, Aldershot: Ashgate.

World Tourism Organization (1994), *Tourism and Aviation Policies, Balancing the Benefits*, Madrid: WTO.

World Tourism Organization (2000), *Tourism and Air Transport: Seminar Proceedings*, Madrid: WTO.

World Travel and Tourism Council (WTTC) (various years), *Travel and Tourism Tax Barometer*, East Lansing, MI: WTTC Tax Policy Center.

Yamauchi, H. (1997), 'Air transport policy in Japan: limited competition under regulation', in C. Findlay, Chia Lin Sien and K. Singh (eds), *Asia Pacific Air Transport Challenges and Policy Reforms*, Singapore: Institute of Southeast Asian Studies, pp. 106–22.

PART FOUR

TOURISM TAXATION
AND INFRASTRUCTURE

11 Taxation of travel and tourism
James Mak

Introduction

During the second half of the twentieth century, travel and tourism grew spectacularly, becoming one of the world's major economic and social forces. According to the World Tourism Organization (WTO), in 2002, 714 million tourists left their own country to visit other countries, compared to only 25 million in 1950.[1] Since the 1970s, the number of tourists travelling abroad has grown 1.4 times as fast as the world's economy.[2] While comprehensive statistics on domestic tourism are not available, it is believed that domestic tourism may be ten times as large as international tourism.[3] The World Travel & Tourism Council (WTTC), a tourism advocacy group whose membership comprises some of the world' largest travel businesses, estimates that tourism accounts for more than 10 per cent of the world's gross domestic product, 8 per cent of worldwide employment, and 12 per cent of global exports.[4]

The growing importance of tourism has not escaped the attention of policy makers. Travel destinations see tourism development as an attractive economic benefit, generating income, employment, foreign exchange and tax revenues. But tourism development is not a free good. Like residents, tourists and their suppliers demand public services which have to be paid for through taxes and user charges. The production of tourism goods and services requires resources which may have to be diverted from other economic uses. Frank Mitchell notes:

> If all resources [employed in tourism] are priced at their opportunity cost, at a minimum, the net value of tourism will consist of (1) indirect taxes paid on goods purchased by tourists, plus (2) receipts to government for services provided, minus (3) the cost to government of providing the services used by tourists and promoting tourism.[5]

Thus, the net benefit from tourism development depends critically on how a destination designs its public finance/revenue system to tax travel and tourism. Richard Bird argues that many tourist countries, especially among the developing nations, 'seem to under tax their tourist exports'.[6]

Since the 1980s, taxes levied on travel and tourism have proliferated around the world. The growth of tourism has provided destinations an excellent opportunity to broaden their tax base and export taxes to tourists. Tax exporting occurs when 'the burden of a tax is shifted to someone outside the jurisdiction'.[7] Tax exporting is not unique to tourism. Mary Gade and Lee Adkins, for example, found that US states structure their local tax/revenue systems to tax exports more heavily in order to lower taxes on their own residents and to shift the cost of public services that benefit residents to non-residents.[8] Some explain that politically it is easier to tax tourists rather than residents because tourists are not constituents. Evidence, however, indicates that where tourism is an important contributor to the local economic base, tourism suppliers constitute powerful political interest groups which are quite capable at defeating or delaying efforts to impose new or increase existing tourist taxes.[9]

Nonetheless, by the early 1990s the travel industry became quite alarmed by the proliferation of taxes levied on tourism. So much so that in October 1993 the WTTC established the World Travel and Tourism Tax Policy Centre at Michigan State University 'to track and monitor the status of taxes imposed on travellers and travel and tourism companies around the world . . . Its aim is to provide timely information and analysis of tax policy issues and considerations to government policy makers, industry leaders, and the general public'.[10] In its first report the WTTC notes: 'It has been clear . . . that Travel and Tourism is vulnerable to non-productive taxation. This vulnerability is based on the lack of quality information and knowledge of taxation and the industry as a whole'.[11] The WTTC further notes: 'The industry and the travelling public are increasingly called upon to contribute more to the global tax base. The fundamental question that must be addressed by both the industry and policy makers is: What are the impacts of a growing tax burden on the world's largest industry?'.[12]

This chapter examines the economics of taxing travel and tourism. It tries to answer the following questions: What is a tourist tax? What are the economic reasons for taxing travel and tourism? Who ultimately bears the burden when tourists and tourism suppliers are taxed? Is it economically 'efficient' and 'fair' to single out travel and tourism for special taxation? The chapter ends with a brief discussion of user charges, indications for further research, and some concluding observations.

What is a tourist tax?
When tourists travel, they encounter a large array of taxes. They may have to pay an entry tax when they visit another country, or an exit tax when they leave. During their stay, they may encounter more taxes levied on their purchases ranging from hotel room rentals, restaurant meals, gifts and souvenirs, car rentals, admission to visitor attractions and so on. These taxes are not 'discriminatory' in that residents of these destinations must also pay them when they make the same purchases. But for some items, most of the purchases at the local businesses are made by tourists (for example, hotel

room and car rentals), while other purchases (generally) are largely made by residents (for example, gasoline and restaurant meals). Likewise, 'tourist businesses' such as hotels, travel agencies and car rental companies must pay local business and property taxes that are also levied on 'non-tourist businesses'.[13] Taxes which fall largely on tourists or 'tourist businesses' are often referred to as 'tourist or tourism taxes'. Under such a restrictive definition, few taxes imposed on tourists and tourism businesses would qualify as 'tourist taxes'. Not surprisingly, selective excise/sales taxes on lodging and car rentals are among the most commonly employed tourist taxes when it comes to targeting travellers for taxation.

Travellers in most countries pay a value-added tax (VAT), when they make purchases. In the European Union and some South American countries, VAT ranges from 15–25 per cent. In theory VAT can be designed as an income tax. In practice, it is a consumption-based, national sales tax. Liam Ebrill et al. note that 123 out of 180 countries in the world employ VAT; the US and Australia, among industrialized countries, are the notable exceptions.[14] Unlike state and local sales taxes employed in the US which are levied at the retail level, VAT taxes the value added – that is, the increase in the value of the commodity – at every stage of distribution from the producer to the middlemen, and finally, to the consumer. Typically, the 'value added' is never actually calculated because sellers simply subtract the VAT they pay on their purchases from the VAT they receive from their own sales; the difference is the seller's VAT tax liability. While VAT eliminates the undesirable effects of tax pyramiding, it also induces a one-time spike in the prices of commodities.[15] Some countries permit a refund on the VAT paid by tourists on merchandise they take home from their visits, confirming the view that VAT is a consumption tax and is levied where the good is consumed, not where it is produced or sold.[16]

Why destinations tax tourism?
Destinations tax tourism for at least four reasons: (i) to expand and diversify their tax base; (ii) to export taxes to non-resident tourists; (iii) to tax away excess profits or economic rents from tourism to benefit residents; and (iv) to correct for market failure.

Diversify tax base
As demand for travel and tourism is income elastic, tourism – and its potential tax base – is expected to grow faster than the world's income. By taxing travel and tourism, destinations are able to build in greater revenue elasticity into their own fiscal systems. Not surprisingly, tourism has become – and will likely continue to be – an increasingly important source of public revenues to travel destinations.

Tax exporting

Successful tax exporting requires two conditions to be satisfied: (i) the tax must be passed on to the consumer; and (ii) the consumer must be someone who does not live in the jurisdiction.[17] In their study of tax exporting in Hawaii, Walter Miklius et al. found that almost all of Hawaii's taxes are exportable to tourists in varying degrees. Hawaii's hotel occupancy tax is almost entirely exported to tourists; by contrast only 22 per cent of Hawaii's broad-based general excise tax, 16 per cent of the taxes levied on corporations, banks and other financial institutions, 9 per cent of the real property tax, and none of the state's personal income tax falls on tourists.[18]

The US Advisory Commission on Intergovernmental Relations (ACIR) notes that tax exporting in tourism can improve economic efficiency:[19]

> non-residents, or visitors, may be major beneficiaries from certain services provided by a local or state government. In such cases, the interests of an efficient allocation of resources to those public services can be furthered by the use of taxes that – by virtue of their exportability – makes it possible to collect an appropriate share of the costs of those services from the non-resident beneficiaries.

No one disagrees that it is appropriate to tax tourists to pay for the cost of public services they enjoy. But what about a fiscal system that generates more revenues from tourists than the cost of providing public services to them?[20] Destination residents regard the excess revenue – that is, the 'profit' from tourism – as a benefit to the community. The problem with this beggar-thy-neighbour policy is that it misrepresents the true cost to residents of public services financed by such revenues. Indeed, if voters think the services are cheaper than what they actually cost, too much of the community's resources would be allocated to meet the demand for public services.[21]

The industry, by contrast, emphasizes that high taxes that increase the cost of travel can discourage people from travelling and thus hurt the industry and the local economy. High taxes in one destination may also induce travellers to switch to other destinations.[22] Low taxes, on the other hand, encourage people to travel. Stephen Wanhill argues that the reduction in VAT in Ireland 'might have been the single most important driver of the recovery in tourism during the late 1980s'.[23]

New York City is often cited as an example where exorbitant hotel room taxes became counterproductive.[24] In 1990, the New York State Legislature enacted a 5 per cent room tax on hotel rooms priced at $100 or more per night. As a result the combined state and city room taxes increased to 19.25 per cent plus $2 per night on rooms priced at $100 or more. By comparison, the average effective hotel room tax rate among the top 50 US cities in the mid-1990s was about 12 per cent.[25] It was widely accepted that as a result of the new tax, tourist travel declined in New York City, prompting the Legislature to rescind the tax in 1994.[26] The WTTC notes that New York State lost $962 million in taxes on visitor spending to collect $463.2 million from a 5 per cent room tax.[27] As in New York City, the WTTC alleges that many cities throughout the world have adopted short-sighted tax policies that have deterred travel, slowed tax revenue collections and stifled job creation.

More recently, in the Balearic islands, a 10 per cent decrease in visitor numbers in eight months has been blamed on the imposition of a daily 'eco-'tax on tourists beginning in May 2002.[28]

Travel destinations vary tremendously in the effort they put into taxing tourism. Since 1994 the WTTC Tax Policy Center has been tracking the amount of taxes paid as a percentage of the total bill (that is, the average tax rate or the tax effort) for four nights of lodging, five days' car rental, 12 meals, and one set of international arrival and departure airport charges at 52 leading tourist destinations. In 2002, the destination with the highest tax effort was Copenhagen at 24.25 per cent and the average tax effort among the 52 destinations was around 14 per cent (Mumbai and São Paulo) while Asian destinations like Tokyo (6.27), Taipei (5.54) and Hong Kong (2.18) were at the tail end.[29] Whether such differences in average tax rates have a significant influence on travel demand still has to be rigorously studied. To date, evidence on the negative impact of taxes on travel demand remains largely anecdotal.

Taxing economic rents/excess profits

Because every tourist destination has distinctive attributes determined by its location, natural amenities or man-made attractions, tourism generates economic rents. Tourism's economic rents are returns that are in excess of the marginal social cost of providing services to tourism.[30] Tourism suppliers obviously will try to capture these rents by charging higher prices where and when they can. On the other hand, destination lawmakers may wish to extract as much of the rents as possible to increase tourism's benefit to residents. Taxation is one way to extract the economic rents from tourism.

In theory, taxes on economic rents are an excellent source of public revenue in that there are no negative allocative impacts on the economy. Because rents are returns in excess of what profit-maximizing suppliers are willing to accept, taxing away the excess profits will not influence the suppliers' pricing and output decisions. If the rents are left to private suppliers, they could be dissipated by the entry of new competitors in the absence of restrictions on entry.[31]

Taxing rents from tourism invariably leads to the question of which 'tax handles' to use? Tourism is an 'elusive' tax base.[32] Tourism is not a typical product in that it is not a single commodity; nor is it only sold by specialized suppliers or even a single industry. The tourism product is a collection of heterogeneous goods and services provided by diverse suppliers and industries which sell their products to both tourists and residents, and to tourist and non-tourist businesses. Designing a tax system to single out tourists and tourist businesses for taxation is not a trivial challenge. It is difficult to calibrate tax rates which only tax rents. Thus tax rates can be set either too high or too low; in the former case, they can be distortionary. In developing countries it is also difficult to resort to income/profits taxes to tax tourism. The burden of the general excise/sales tax falls more heavily on residents than on tourists. This leaves special taxes.

Generally, there are two types of special taxes on tourism used to appropriate gains from tourism: (a) entry and exit/departure taxes and (b) hotel occupancy taxes.[33] Clem Tisdell also suggests entertainment and restaurant taxes.[34] However, Fujii et al. have shown that even in a tourism dependent state like Hawaii restaurant and entertainment taxes fall largely on residents.[35] Likewise, amusement taxes in most US major cities also fall disproportionately on locals than on tourists.[36]

Correcting for market failure
Tourism gives rise to many environmental problems, and taxes levied to correct for the negative environmental externalities stemming from tourism have become more prevalent. For example, in 2002 Venice began imposing a 'coach tax' of up to €250 per motor coach depending on where the coach is parked in the city; the city of Florence had imposed a smaller (€100) coach tax earlier. A round trip airline ticket between Sydney and London includes an A$3.58 noise tax. Norway imposes a carbon dioxide tax on domestic flights. The European Commission has recommended a European-wide 'green tax' on all air tickets to discourage greenhouse gas emissions.[37]

There are two other areas of tourism where taxation has made a significant contribution to correct market failure: destination tourism promotion and convention centre financing.

Governments of just about every country and destination fund destination tourism promotion. The dominant role that government plays in tourism promotion is still not well understood by policy makers and the public. Destination tourism promotion has all the properties of a public good.[38] It is both non-rival and non-excludable. Once money is spent to promote a destination, all destination businesses benefit whether or not they helped to fund it. Even if every business owner agrees that more money should be spent on promotion, each has an incentive to be a free-rider. Indeed, if many choose to free ride, not enough money will be available to be spent on promotion. Not surprisingly, tourist bureaux chronically complain about the shortage of funds. Free-riding results in the misallocation of economic resources because by underfunding promotion, the destination is unable to achieve its potential.

Agricultural producers are able to band together to assess themselves to pay to promote their products, typically with the aid of enabling legislation, but not tourism. The diversity of tourism makes it difficult for suppliers to come to agreement on an acceptable assessment formula to raise funds to pay for generic promotion. The State of California provides an excellent example of tourism's inability to fund collective promotion using the agricultural self-assessment model. In 1995 the California Legislature passed legislation, the California Tourism Marketing Act, directing the industry to come up with a formula to assess tourism businesses in the state to finance tourism promotion. The state promised to contribute $7.5 million each year towards the promotion budget and expected the industry to raise at least $25 million per year from its own assessments, but in 2003, the industry collected only $6.8 million.[39] In 1993 when voters in the State of Colorado refused to renew funding for its tourism board, the industry sought voluntary contributions to pay for tourism promotion but could not raise as much money as previously.

The efficient solution to free-riding is for the government to tax the tourist industry to pay for destination promotion. The most frequently employed tax to fund tourism promotion is a dedicated or earmarked hotel room tax. Despite the industry's general opposition to tourism taxes, it has often strongly supported legislation to levy lodging taxes to fund tourism promotion. Many destinations still use general revenue funds rather than special taxes on tourism to pay for promotion. Funding tourism promotion using money from the general treasury amounts to giving a subsidy to the tourist industry.[40]

Convention centre financing is another example of market failure that is often corrected through appropriate taxation. As stand-alone facilities, convention centres typically operate in the 'red'. Convention centres are not built with the idea that rental fees and other revenues will enable the facilities to break even. The case for building convention centres is based on the additional economic activity, income, employment and tax revenues that conventions will generate in the community. Since private for-profit developers cannot capture those benefits, they would not be interested in building and operating a convention centre unless there were direct subsidies to cover annual operating losses and debt service. Not surprisingly, convention centres are largely built by local governments and funded through special taxes levied on tourism. In the US, convention centres are typically financed by using hotel room tax revenues supplemented by excise/sales taxes.

The incidence of tourist taxes

The most numerous studies available on the incidence of tourist taxes are on the hotel room occupancy/bed tax. The economics of the hotel room tax is well known.[41] Assuming that the market for lodging is competitive, it can be shown under comparative statics that the introduction of a room tax creates a wedge between the tax-inclusive price hotel guests pay for the rooms and the net after-tax price the hotelier receives; the difference between the two 'prices' is the revenue going to the government.[42] Under the usual assumptions about the demand and supply for lodging, the room tax also raises the rental price of the hotel rooms, meaning that at least a portion of the room tax is passed on to the hotel guests. Who pays most of the room tax? It depends on the market conditions for hotel room rentals. The ratio of the price increase to hotel guests and the reduction in the net price received by hoteliers is (approximately) equal to the ratio of the supply and demand elasticities for lodging. The greater (smaller) the elasticity of supply relative to the elasticity of demand, the larger (smaller) the portion of the room tax passed on to the guests as a higher price.

There is also an efficiency loss – or excess burden – due to the tax because the higher tax-inclusive room rate means that less lodging will be demanded. Thus, both tourists and hoteliers are worse off as a result of the tax.

Empirical studies of the incidence of hotel occupancy/bed taxes have taken several approaches.[43] Some have used time-series data; others have used cross-section data. Most of them estimate only the demand elasticities for lodging; supply elasticities are rarely estimated.[44] Extant studies suggest that demand for lodging is generally price inelastic while the supply of lodging is price elastic, implying that hotel room taxes are largely passed on to hotel guests as higher prices.[45] These studies examine the effects of a room tax *ex ante*, that is, before the tax is actually levied. By contrast, Carl Bonham et al. employed interrupted time-series analysis to evaluate, *ex post*, the impact of a newly imposed 5 per cent hotel room tax in Hawaii.[46] They found that the new tax had no statistically significant negative impact on hotel room rental revenues, implying that the room tax was fully passed on to hotel guests.[47] However, they conclude:

> [The findings] may not be entirely surprising since a five per cent increase in lodging expenditures represents less than 1.5 per cent of the total cost of a typical vacation in Hawaii inclusive of round-trip airfare. That may not be true of travel to other destinations. Therefore it is important to perform similar analyses for other travel destinations.[48]

By contrast, a survey of 1000 UK tourism and leisure operators conducted by the consulting firm Touche Ross for the British Tourist Authority found that when VAT was increased in 1991/92 from 15 per cent to 17.5 per cent, 19 per cent of the respondents indicated that they passed the entire tax increase on to their customers, over half absorbed the tax increase, and the rest passed on some of the increase.[49] Of course, what they said they did and what actually happened based on rigorous economic analysis may be quite different.

Efficiency and equity of tourist taxes

Goods and services purchased mostly by tourists are often taxed at higher rates. For example, in the US, it is not uncommon to see both the local general sales tax and a hotel room tax levied on tourist lodgings. The piggy-backing of the hotel room tax on top of the general excise/sales tax can make the effective tax rate on lodging several times that of rates applied to most other goods and services.[50]

The travel industry has argued that levying higher tax rates on tourist goods violates the neutrality principle of taxation and reduces economic efficiency. Therefore, all goods should be taxed at a uniform rate. Higher tax rates imposed on goods largely purchased by tourists are also judged to be unfair. According to the WTTC, 'In the even handed capturing of tax revenue, it is unreasonable to assess special fees or levies on specific goods or services'. In its view, unequal taxation violates its Fair Revenue Generation Principle of Intelligent Taxation.[51] However, a strong case can be made for the opposite views.

The neutrality principle states that taxes should not inadvertently influence people's purchase decisions. If a higher tax rate on Good A unintentionally induces consumers to switch to substitute Good B because the tax-inclusive price of Good A is increased by more than the price of Good B, then the tax system favours Good B over Good A. An excess burden is created by the substitution because consumers actually prefer Good A over Good B, but are instead induced to switch to Good B by the higher tax rate imposed on Good A. By contrast, a uniform rate, to the extent that it does not change the relative prices of the two goods, would have a neutral effect on consumer choices. This suggests that the excess burden can be eliminated by taxing all goods at the same rate.[52]

But, as a practical matter, it does not follow that a uniform tax system is necessarily preferable to a variable tax rate system. In the real world, it is not feasible to tax all goods; some, such as leisure goods and goods bought and sold in the underground economy, are difficult to tax. Indeed, under the best-designed tax system, some goods will be taxed while others will escape taxation. In other words, there will always be some excess burden even under the best-designed tax system. The practical question for policy makers is to decide what rates minimize – rather than eliminate – the excess burden. Tax rates that minimize the excess burden are 'optimal' tax rates.[53]

Leaving aside the relative costs of compliance and administrating differ-ent tax regimes, uniform tax rates are usually not optimal.[54] The inverse elasticity rule states that 'the optimal tax rate on each good is proportional to the inverse of its own price elasticity'.[55] In other words, higher tax rates should be levied on goods that have lower price elasticities of demand.[56] It is optimal to tax goods at the same rate only if they all have the same price elasticity of demand, a situation which is never encountered. The intuition underlying this rule is quite simple: if excess burdens are created because consumers substitute lower- for higher-priced goods, then one ought to tax more heavily goods for which consumer demand is not very price sensitive because that would induce relatively little substitution among goods. On the other hand, goods for which demand is very price sensitive should be lightly taxed. Because the demand for tourist goods (for example, lodging) is generally determined to be price inelastic, it is not inappropriate on effi-ciency grounds to tax them at higher rates than on other goods that have higher price elasticities of demand. In practice, it is not easy to fine tune tax rates based on optimal tax principles.

Is it 'unfair' to tax more heavily goods that are largely purchased by tourists? That depends on which definition of 'fairness' we accept. In the matter of what is fair in taxation, two concepts of equity have been widely discussed – the benefit principle of taxation versus the ability-to-pay prin-ciple. The benefit principle states that taxpayers should be required to pay taxes in accordance with the government expenditure benefits received. The ability-to-pay principle espouses the notion that taxpayers should pay taxes in accordance with their ability to pay. Between the two, the latter appears to be the dominant principle in taxation today, and this is validated by the widely adopted graduated income tax system.[57] Tourism is a luxury good, and to the extent that tourists tend to have higher incomes and thus greater ability to pay than locals, it is not unfair to tax them more heavily. Since it is not possible for travel destinations to tax tourists' incomes directly, an alternative is to levy higher tax rates on goods that are largely purchased by tourists. In sum, taxing tourist goods more heavily does not necessarily reduce economic efficiency or equity.

User charges in tourism

User charges are prices charged by governments to users to pay for specific public services or for the privilege of engaging in certain activities. Airport facilities and security charges, port charges, and admissions to public beaches, pools, parks and preserves are examples of user charges in tourism. Unlike taxes which are paid under coercion, user charges, like prices in private markets, are 'voluntary' payments in that only those who choose to use those services are required to pay. User charges are most appropriately used to finance public services when most or all of the benefits go to identifiable users, and those who do not pay can be denied use at a reasonable cost. Sometimes, user charges – such as entrance fees – are employed to ration the use of scarce resources. When used in this way, user charges are most effective when the demand for the use of the resource is price elastic. Thus, admission charges to must-see tourist attractions are not very effective in rationing attendance at these unique attractions because the demand for visits is invariably very price inelastic. Peter Forsyth et al. show that, under several circumstances such as where there are problems of uncertainty, difficulty in monitoring tourist behaviour, high transactions costs, and where it is difficult to control movement of visitors, price (and quantitative) restrictions lose their effectiveness.[58]

Generally, there are sound reasons why entrance fees at popular public parks and natural preserves should be imposed. First, entrance fees can help to limit the number of visits to congested attractions. Second, the revenues generated could be used to maintain the attractions. Third, they are also an excellent way to extract the economic rent from the scarce resource for the benefit of the public. Despite the obvious advantages, during the early 1990s, only half of the world's protected areas charged admission fees. And where they were levied, the fees were typically quite modest. In many places they were well below what visitors were willing to pay.[59] Moreover, fees collected were often siphoned off to the general funds rather than for the maintenance of the visitor attractions. Not surprisingly, funds for maintenance and conservation are chronically in short supply everywhere.

An argument against the use of entrance fees is that they are widely regarded as regressive. But that is not necessarily true. To the extent that fees fall largely on high-income visitors, admission fees can actually be progressive rather than regressive.[60] Another argument against the use of entrance fees is that they are unpopular among local residents, and hence lawmakers are reluctant to impose them.[61] Richard Bird argues that local residents should be exempt from paying the entrance fees on the grounds either that 'residents contribute sufficiently through their regular taxes or that they are entitled to enjoy their own country without further payment'.[62] Harry Clarke and Yew-Kwang Ng show that even if residents are required to pay the entrance fees, they would still be better off as long as the revenues collected from the fees are used to provide services that benefit them.[63]

Further research
It is transparent from the above that a lot remains to be learned about the impacts of taxation on travel and tourism. The agenda for future research is wide open. Clearly, more research needs to be done on the direct impacts of travel and tourist taxes on the demand for travel. As well, we need to

know more about the incidence and exportability (*ex post*) of tourist taxes. We also need to know more about how to tax and collect revenues from multinational tourism businesses given that their activities take place in different countries and tax jurisdictions. A topic which has not received much attention is the effect of tax incentives on tourism investment. To date, studies of tourism's tax impacts have relied on static partial equilibrium analysis. In the future the greatest value added would undoubtedly come from examining the impacts of tourism taxation from a general equilibrium perspective using computable general equilibrium modelling techniques.

Concluding observations

Taxing tourism is one way for tourist destinations to reap the economic gains from tourism development. Tourism can be overtaxed although evidence of this remains anecdotal and sketchy. Within the tourist industry, it is widely believed that the industry and tourists are being unfairly singled out for taxation to the detriment of both tourism and destination residents. This chapter explains that there are sound economic reasons for taxing tourism beyond simply collecting revenues to provide public services to tourists and their suppliers. A well-designed system of tourist taxation can benefit the residents of destinations in a number of ways; it can broaden and increase the revenue elasticity of the destination's tax base, extract economic rents, and protect the environment (which also benefits tourism). It can also benefit tourism by making more money available for tourism promotion and for the construction and operation of convention centres. Finally, this chapter has argued that levying higher taxes on goods and services that are largely purchased by tourists does not necessarily reduce economic efficiency or equity.

Notes

1. See www.world-tourism.org/market_research/facts/menu.html.
2. Mak (2004), p. ix.
3. Ibid., p. 24.
4. See www.wttc.org/tsal.htm.
5. Mitchell (1970), p. 4. Indirect taxes – also referred to as 'commodity taxes' – are taxes levied on goods and services while direct taxes – such as personal and corporate income taxes – are levied on 'persons'.
6. Bird (1992), p. 1147.
7. Bruce (1998), p. 635. However, Bill Fox (University of Tennessee-Knoxville) prefers a stricter definition which states that tax exporting occurs only if taxes paid by non-residents exceed the cost of public services provided to them.
8. Gade and Adkins (1990).
9. Mak (2004), Chapter 12.
10. See www.traveltax.msu.edu/. Funding for the Centre was terminated recently and the WTTC Tax Barometer, an annual series of tax rankings of 52 of the most popular tourist cities in the world, has not been updated since 2002. See Mak (2004) Chapter 12 for more detail and analysis of the WTTC Tax Barometer.

11. Ibid. 'Economics of travel and tourism taxes', *Issues in Tax Policy*. By 'non-productive taxation', the WTTC apparently means taxation that slows tax revenue generation and economic growth.
12. Ibid.
13. A conventional definition of a 'tourist business' or 'tourist industry' is one that derives a significant portion of its business from tourism. The US Department of Commerce defines 'significant' in that the business or industry's 'revenues and profits would be substantially affected if tourism ceased to exist'. Okubo and Planting (1998).
14. Ebril et al. (2001); see also Tait (1999), pp. 422–6.
15. Tait (1999), p. 423. Tax pyramiding refers to a tax levied on top of an earlier tax; this could occur, for example, in the case of a gross receipts tax. VAT can also contribute to intergovernmental fiscal mismatches due to differences in the distribution of tourists within a country. See Mak (2004), pp. 160–61.
16. Refunds on business expenses may include a variety of services, including lodging.
17. Fujii et al. (1985).
18. Miklius et al. (1989), Table 4, p. 10.
19. US ACIR (1989), p. 192.
20. See, for example, Mathematica, Inc. (1970).
21. See US ACIR (1989), p. 192 and Forsyth and Dwyer (2002).
22. Rugg (1973) and Mak and Moncur (1980).
23. Wanhill (1995), p. 217.
24. Likewise, Dwyer and Forsyth argue that a bed tax in Sydney to help pay for the 2000 Sydney Olympics is 'not good public policy' because it disproportionately burdens one industry and will also have negative macroeconomic consequences. Dwyer and Forsyth (4 June 1999).
25. State of Hawaii Tax Review Commission (1996), Appendix B-5 and B-6.
26. Mak (2004), p. 155.
27. WTTC, *Economics of Travel and Tourism Taxes* at www.traveltax.msu.edu.
28. See www.traveltax.msu.edu.
29. WTTC Tax Barometer at www.traveltax.msu.edu, reproduced in Mak (2004), Table 12–1.
30. Bird (1992), p. 1147.
31. Ibid. and Mak (2004), Chapter 11.
32. Bird (1992), p. 1148.
33. Tisdell (1983) and Bird (1992).
34. Tisdell (1983).
35. Fujii et al. (1985).
36. Blair et al. (1987).
37. Mak (2004), pp. 143–4.
38. Mak and Miklius (1990), Dwyer and Forsyth (1993), Bonham and Mak (1996) and Mak (2004), pp. 155–60.
39. See www.twcrossroads.com, Article ID=39126.
40. Mak and Miklius (1990) and Bonham and Mak (1996).
41. See Mak and Nishimura (1979) and Mak (1988).
42. See Mak (1988).
43. See, for example Mak and Nishimura (1979), Arbel and Ravid (1983), Fujii et al. (1985), Sakai (1985) and Hiemstra and Ismail (1992).
44. Estimates of supply elasticities for lodging can be found in Arbel and Ravid (1983) and Fujii et al. (1985).
45. Presumably the supply elasticity estimates are for the 'intermediate' or the 'long run'; in the 'immediate' run supply is likely to be 'inelastic'.
46. Bonham et al. (1992).
47. Ibid. See also Bonham and Gangnes (1996).
48. Bonham et al. (1992), p. 439.
49. Wanhill (1995), p. 216.

50. See, for example, Mak (1988).
51. 'Principles of intelligent taxation', *Issues in Tax Policy* at http://traveltax.msu.edu/intro/issues/part4.htm.
52. Bruce (1998), p. 450.
53. Ibid., p. 459.
54. Gentry (1999), p. 262.
55. Bruce (1998), pp. 459–60.
56. There could be 'distributional' (that is, equity) reasons why this might not apply to some goods (for example, food). See Bruce (1998), pp. 463–5.
57. Ibid., p. 461.
58. Forsyth et al. (1995).
59. International Monetary Fund et al. (2002), pp. 25–6, and Mastny (2002), p. 114.
60. Knapman and Stoeckle (1995), pp. 5–15.
61. Mak (2004), pp. 178–9.
62. Bird (1992), p. 1152.
63. Clarke and Ng (1993).

References

Arbel, A. and A. Ravid (1983), 'An industry energy price impact model: the case of the hotel industry', *Applied Economics*, **15**, pp. 705–14.

Bird, Richard, (1992), 'Taxing tourism in developing countries', *World Development*, **20** (8), pp. 1145–58.

Blair, Andrew R., Frank Giarratani and Michael H. Spiro (1987), 'Incidence of the amusement tax', *National Tax Journal*, **XL** (1), March, pp. 61–9.

Bonham, Carl, Edwin Fujii, Eric Im and James Mak (1992), 'The impact of the hotel room tax: an interrupted time series approach', *National Tax Journal*, **XLV** (4), December, pp. 433–42.

Bonham, Carl and Byron Gangnes (1996), 'Intervention analysis with cointegrated time series: the case of the Hawaii hotel room tax', *Applied Economics*, **28** (10), October, pp. 1281–93.

Bonham, Carl and James Mak (1996), 'Private versus public financing of state destination promotion', *Journal of Travel Research*, **XXX** (2), Fall, pp. 3–10.

Bruce, Neil (1998), *Public Finance and the American Economy*, Reading, MA: Addison-Wesley.

Clarke, Harry R. and Yew-Kwang Ng (1993), 'Tourism, economic welfare and efficient pricing', *Annals of Tourism Research*, **20** (4), pp. 613–32.

Dwyer, Larry and Peter Forsyth (1993), 'Government support for inbound tourism promotion: some neglected issues', *Australian Economic Papers*, **32** (61), December, pp. 355–74.

Dwyer, Larry and Peter Forsyth (1999), 'Should accommodation providers pay for the Olympics? A critique of the Sydney bed tax', *Tourism and Hospitality Research: Surrey Quarterly Review*, **1** (3), pp. 253–64.

Ebrill, Liam, Michael Keen, Jean-Paul Bodin and Victoria Summers (2001), *The Modern VAT*, Washington, DC: International Monetary Fund.

Forsyth, Peter and Larry Dwyer (2002), 'Market power and the taxation of domestic and international tourism', *Tourism Economics*, **8** (4), pp. 377–99.

Forsyth, Peter, Larry Dwyer and Harry Clarke (1995), 'Problems in use of economic instruments to reduce adverse environmental impacts of tourism', *Tourism Economics*, **1** (3), pp. 265–82.

Fujii, Edwin, Mohammed Khaled and James Mak (1985), 'The exportability of hotel occupancy and other tourist taxes', *National Tax Journal*, **38** (2), June, pp. 169–78.

Gade, Mary N. and Lee C. Adkins (1990), 'Tax exporting and state revenue structures', *National Tax Journal*, **43**, March, pp. 39–52.

Gentry, William (1999), 'Optimal taxation', in Joseph Cordes, Robert D. Ebel and Jane G. Gravelle (eds), *The Encyclopaedia of Taxation and Tax Policy*, Washington, DC: Urban Institute Press, pp. 261–4.

Hiemstra, S. and J. Ismail (1992), 'Analysis of room taxes levied on the lodging industry', *Journal of Travel Research*, Summer, pp. 42–9.

International Monetary Fund, United Nations Environment Programme and the World Bank (2002), *Financing for Sustainable Development*, Washington, DC: World Bank.

Knapman, Bruce and Natalie Stoeckle (1995), 'Recreational user fees: an Australian empirical investigation', *Tourism Economics*, **1** (1), March, pp. 5–16.

Mak, James (1988), 'Taxing hotel room rentals in the US', *Journal of Travel Research*, **27** (1), Summer, pp. 10–15.

Mak, James (2004), *Tourism and the Economy, Understanding the Economics of Tourism*, Honolulu: University of Hawaii Press.

Mak, James and Walter Miklius (1990), 'State government financing of tourism promotion in the US', in *Proceedings of the National Tax Association and Tax Institute of America Meeting*, pp. 58–63.

Mak, James and James E.T. Moncur (1980), 'The choice of journey destinations and lengths of stay: a micro analysis', *Review of Regional Studies*, **10** (2), pp. 38–47.

Mak, James and Edward Nishimura (1979), 'The economics of a hotel room tax', *Journal of Travel Research*, **17** (4), pp. 2–6.

Mastny, Lisa (2002), 'Redirecting international tourism', in *State of the World, 2002*, A Worldwatch Institute Report on Progress Toward a Sustainable Society, New York: W.W. Norton, pp. 101–26 and 225–34.

Mathematica, Inc. (1970), *The Visitor Industry and Hawaii's Economy, A Cost–Benefit Analysis*, Princeton, NJ.

Miklius, Walter, James E.T. Moncur and Ping Sun Leung (1989), 'Distribution of state and local tax burden by income class', in Hawaii Tax Review Commission, *Working Papers and Consultant Studies*, 2, Honolulu: State of Hawaii Department of Taxation, pp. 7–19.

Mitchell, Frank (1970), 'The value of tourism in East Africa', *East Africa Economic Review*, **2** (1), pp. 1–21.

Okubo, Sumiye and Mark A. Planting (1998), 'US travel and tourism satellite accounts for 1992', *Survey of Current Business*, July, www.bea.doc.gov/bea/bea/an/0798ied/maintext.htm.

Rugg, Donald (1973), 'The choice of journey destination: a theoretical and empirical analysis', *Review of Economics and Statistics*, **55**, pp. 64–72.

Sakai, Marcia (1985), 'A micro-analysis of demand for travel goods: an application to the business traveller', PhD dissertation in economics, Honolulu: University of Hawaii-Manoa.

State of Hawaii Tax Review Commission (1996), *Report of the 1995–1997 Tax Review Commission*, 16th December.

Tait, Alan (1999), 'Value-added tax', in Joseph Cordes, Robert D. Ebel and Jane G. Gravelle (eds), *The Encyclopaedia of Taxation and Tax Policy*, Washington, DC: Urban Institute Press, pp. 422–6.

Tisdell, Clem A. (1983), 'Public finance and the appropriation of gains from international tourists: some theory with ASEAN and Australian illustrations', *Singapore Economic Review*, **28**, pp. 3–20.

US Advisory Commission on Intergovernmental Relations (ACIR) (1989), 'Intergovernmental fiscal relations in Hawaii', in Hawaii Tax Review Commission, *Working Papers and Consultant Studies*, 2, Honolulu: State of Hawaii Department of Taxation, pp. 139–314.

Wanhill, Stephen (1995), 'VAT rates and the UK tourism and leisure industry', *Tourism Economics*, **1** (3), pp. 211–24.

12 Public sector investment in tourism infrastructure

Marcia Sakai

Introduction

Tourism infrastructure is foundational for tourism development, second in importance only to a destination's attraction resource base, because infrastructure is vital to the commerce of tourism. Infrastructure increases the efficiency of privately producing and distributing tourism services, and in certain cases, such as tourism enclaves or remote destinations, makes possible the supply of tourism services. Tourists travel to destinations in other countries or to other regions within their own country, thus making passenger transportation infrastructure a key element. Whether travel is by land, air or sea, the supporting airport and harbor transportation nodes, as well as railway, road, bridge and tunnel networks, are required. Tourists also add to the effective population of a destination, requiring the same basic services that are ordinarily consumed by residents. The demand for infrastructure services of water supply and waste disposal, communication and electricity is thereby increased.

Infrastructure has also been defined to include public safety, mail and freight services, medical systems, financial systems, education systems, national defense and other services that support both resident and tourism demand, such as retail and shopping (Ritchie and Crouch 2005). In the current discussion, infrastructure is defined as capital-intensive, long-lived physical assets that provide benefits to the general public or to promote economic development (US Department of Transportation 1993; Gramlich 1994, p. 1177).

The provision of tourism infrastructure is of particular importance in the long-term environment of tourism growth. Expanded facilities are needed to accommodate anticipated growth and to maintain a relatively uninterrupted service level. At the same time, environmental changes in the technology that supports the various infrastructure networks, geo-political changes that affect oil resources heavily used in modern transportation, and socio-political changes that affect government ability to finance tourism infrastructure are anticipated to affect the look of tourism infrastructure finance for the future. Despite the pause in global tourism capital investment that followed 11 September 2001, the WTTC (2004) estimates that total capital investment in tourism is expected to reach US$1402 billion by the year 2014, at real annual growth rates of 4.23 percent.

Why does the public sector invest in infrastructure?

Infrastructure may be provided by the public sector or the private sector and the outcome is often determined by domestic economic, social and political policies. From an economic perspective, public investment is rationalized when private markets fail to produce an efficient amount. In principle, if private markets are operating efficiently, the behavior of buyers and sellers in markets accurately reflects the marginal social benefit and cost of different amounts of infrastructure, so that marginal social benefit is equal to marginal social cost at the amount provided. But, this may not happen if infrastructure is a public good, if it represents a natural monopoly, or if its use results in externalities (Fisher 1996, pp. 39–44). It is not expected that private firms would provide public goods in efficient amounts. Public goods are nonrival in consumption, so that one person's use does not reduce any other person's ability to similarly use the good, as with parks and bridges up to some congestion point. They may also be nonexcludable, so that it is impossible or difficult to exclude consumers from use, as with many road networks. Because the marginal cost of an additional user is zero, market-based marginal cost pricing would result in a zero price that would not allow private providers to collect revenues to cover fixed costs. Because consumers cannot be excluded from benefits, they have little incentive to reveal how much they are willing to pay. Instead, they have an incentive to free ride and benefit from the payments of others. Not only would private firms have difficulty in assessing a charge, but all users would understate their marginal valuation of the public good. The same is true for merit goods, which have positive externalities and high costs of exclusion.

Efficient results may not occur when production exhibits increasing returns to scale, that is, when average costs of production are declining over a large range. Industries with this characteristic are described as natural monopolies and are typically associated with large fixed costs relative to operating cost. Average cost is always above marginal cost, and marginal cost pricing would not allow the producer to recover fixed costs, unless a private producer was able to exercise its monopoly powers. In the classic monopoly situation, however, the producer would reap monopoly profits but still underproduce. Infrastructure examples of increasing returns to scale abound. They include electric, water and sewer utilities, airports (up to a point), roads and other transportation networks, and parks. In the case of electric utilities and airports, it is common to see significant private sector provision; in the case of roads, water and sewer utilities and parks, it is more common to see public provision.

Optimal public infrastructure investment and finance

In practice, publicly provided goods are rarely pure public or merit goods, but may provide sufficient public benefits to be supported by general taxation. The solution to the optimal provision and use of these infrastructure goods lies largely in determining the relative shares of public and private benefits. Public benefits accrue because of the economic benefits derived from the use of infrastructure by others and because of the option value of the infrastructure. For example, benefits from a transportation network flow to individuals for reasons other than their direct use. Such networks enable the tourism economy to function smoothly. Government may then use its taxing power to finance infrastructure investment with general taxes in proportion to the public benefit.

If private benefits are large and if direct users are easily identified and charged for their use of infrastructure, government may assess user charges or benefit taxes to finance that portion of the infrastructure investment associated with private benefits (Fisher 1996, pp. 179–90). These user charges function as a pricing mechanism and provide a signal to users of the opportunity costs of the resources used. This would be appropriate not only for infrastructure investment, but also for recovering costs of operation and efficient pricing in the presence of congestion externalities. User charges may be earmarked or deposited into special funds that support specific infrastructure spending, such as highway or aviation funds. Although earmarking of general tax revenues create budget inflexibility and inefficiency in allocation (Forsyth and Dwyer 2002, p. 385), this is less so with user charges, particularly when the amount of user charge reflects marginal costs and benefits. Overall, user charges or benefit taxes are attractive as an efficient and equitable method of paying for the private benefits derived from infrastructure.

Under conditions of natural monopoly, infrastructure may be publicly or privately provided, the latter usually with some form of government regulation. When user charges are feasible, fixed cost may be covered through a flat access charge, such as entry to national and regional parks, and variable charges, such as daily camping charges. Similarly, users pay a flat fee for access to water and waste disposal service, along with a per unit usage charge. Alternatively, a form of two-part pricing may be applied, with the highest charges assessed against the first units of use and lower charges for subsequent units.

Given the common finding that infrastructure exhibits increasing returns to scale and that tourism infrastructure users are easy to identify, it is no surprise that roads, water systems and waste systems, and parks are managed as quasi-public enterprises, funded by special taxes earmarked to the enterprise fund; and that new roles for a larger private share of infrastructure investment are emerging as important methods of financing airports, seaports, stadia and sporting venues, and convention centers.

Public infrastructure investment for economic development

Public investment in tourism infrastructure may occur for redistributive economic development or competitive positioning reasons. In the case of developing countries, capital markets are also undeveloped, and governments assume a larger role in the provision of infrastructure. International organizations have been major suppliers of capital for these projects, including the World Bank, the Asian Development Bank, the Inter-American Development and the Arab Development Bank, on occasion even taking a direct investment role.

Public infrastructure investment, and other forms of government intervention in providing infrastructure, is supported by new theories of economic growth. These suggest that economic growth arises not only from physical equipment capital, but also from public infrastructure and human capital. In this expanded definition of capital, airport and roadway infrastructure would clearly support tourism driven economic growth, shifting the country's comparative advantage toward a targeted tourism sector and moving the economy to a higher growth path by producing a product with a higher income elasticity of demand (Sinclair and Stabler 1997, pp. 149–50).

Government participation in providing tourism infrastructure is likely to be high if tourism has a significant role in the economy or its development and thus is not limited to developing countries. In North America and increasingly in Europe, rejuvenation of urban core areas is being accompanied by public infrastructure investment. Destination cities are discovering the economic potential of developing the city as a recreational center, linking existing cultural attractions and building new ones to create tourist cities of play. Among the growing examples of infrastructure for this vision of the city are convention centers, stadia or other sporting venues, festival malls, and to a lesser extent casino gambling (Perry 2003, p. 19). Olympics and other mega events fall into this category too, but are distinguished by the magnitude of the investment scale needed to stage large, multiple sporting events. As noted by Baade (1997, p. 1501), 'you are seeing a linkage between airport, highway, convention center, stadia financing. They are being integrated into a single economic package that's designed to draw people into that entity – a destination city'.

Roads and highways
Intra-urban roadways, inter-urban highway networks and other forms of ground transportation, are among the most visible and most commonly provided infrastructure by the public sector. In the US, public spending on transportation is dominated by spending on roads and highways, and about half of those expenditures represent capital investment (US Department of Transportation 2003). Transportation in personal vehicles also dominates among the modes of ground passenger travel in France, Germany, the UK, and to a lesser extent in Japan. Road infrastructure is characterized by economies of scale. That government provides for roadways is due to the public benefit associated with a smoothly operating transportation system to support commerce and national defense, even though private benefits may be large. Aside from general transportation services that tourism requires, tourism-specific roadways include those that service major recreational areas or that serve as scenic byways or heritage corridors.

Large private benefits and ease of user identification explain why user charges and taxes represent the vast majority of the revenue stream used to finance road infrastructure. Because of the largely technological difficulty in assessing direct user charges, the major revenue sources (i) approximate use, such as motor fuel taxes, highway toll charges and parking fees, (ii) charge for access, such as motor vehicle license fees, motor vehicle operator license fees, or (iii) charge for excess wear, such as truck and trailer taxes and special use charges for trucks. The motor fuel tax, assessed at a money rate per gallon or liter of fuel purchased, is a good proxy for a highway user charge, because amounts collected vary by the amount and type of road use and can be collected at a relatively low administrative cost. But, it is an imperfect proxy because it overlooks the effects of fuel efficiency, the substantial use of motor fuels in off-highway settings, and the differences in highway use by location and time. Revenues derived from motor fuel tax collections are typically held in a trust fund for disbursement to cover both operating and capital expenditures. To the extent that the motor fuel tax pre-finances capital expenditures, current users subsidize future users, an efficiency issue that also arises with air passenger taxes. This is the US approach. In most other countries, taxes on motor fuel vastly exceed any costs of road provision.

The need for roadway and other network infrastructure, such as water systems, may occasionally be identified with specific tourism developments, such as destination resorts. But, in the US, taxpayers are rejecting the principle of cost sharing for new infrastructure development, forcing local governments to look for other ways of finance. Impact fees are one such alternative reflecting the thinking that new growth should pay for itself.

An impact fee is a compulsory exaction typically levied on developers for the purpose of funding investment in off-site facilities, such as roads, sewage treatment plants and parks that are expected to provide benefits for the users of the new development.

Impact fees are levied as a condition for permit approval and must pass a legal test of 'rational nexus'. The rational nexus criterion states that there must be proportionality between the need for the new capital facilities generated by the development and there must be a reasonable connection between the funds collected and the benefits accruing to the development (Simmonds 1993, p. 4). Funds collected in this fashion may not be applied to any other general public use. Thus, impact fees, which pay for the capital cost of development infrastructure, are essentially user charges for the purpose of capital investment. Impact fees have also had limited use for economic diversification, as in the case of the Haseko resort development in Hawaii. While this application did not meet the rational nexus test, the issue was resolved by a formal agreement between the developer and the government over the terms of the assessment (Mak 1993, p. 254).

Airports

Airports, seaports and railroad hubs are key drivers of regional economic growth. Large, efficient, well-located airports offer economies of scale and convenience for the transportation hubs upon which much of today's passenger traffic depends. It is no surprise that cities around the world are aggressively seeking to expand their airport capacity to boost regional economic growth in an environment of growing globalization (Gold 2000).

National and local governments have historically owned airports and funded their development through public sector funds and debt financing, supported by a combination of general and special taxes and user fees, or through investments by major development banks. The airport was viewed as a public utility with public utility obligations. This was manifested virtually throughout the world by national government ownership of major international airports and regional government ownership of regional airports. It was typical to find government transport departments operating major airports, although semi-autonomous airport authority and concession arrangements existed. In the US, municipalities or states were and still are largely responsible for airport development.

The global pattern of public ownership, management and financing is changing, however, as the need for new aviation infrastructure, estimated to be $250 billion in the 2000–2010 decade (Hooper 2002, p. 289), is taxing government ability to pay for it. Since the 1990s, airport ownership and management has shifted to the private sector, through corporatizations, concession arrangements, project finance privatization and management contracts. Airport privatization is seen as a way of injecting additional finance into the airport system (Graham 2003, p. 12), first in the UK in Europe, then Australia, South Africa, South America, New Zealand, and more recently in Asia. For example, BAA plc is a London-based public corporation owning and operating London's Heathrow, Gatwick and Stansted airports, Scotland's Glasgow, Edinburgh and Aberdeen airports, Southampton airport, and World Duty Free retailing.

The need to be competitive in private capital markets is driving greater focus on the enhancing revenues and minimizing costs associated with targeted service levels, increasing airport productivity, and developing more comparable accounting methods of airport performance. Airports are taking on a greater commercial, customer-based orientation to enhance revenues, as indicated by the growing share of non-aeronautical revenues from concessions, rents, direct sales, parking facilities and other charges. This is particularly the case in European airports where non-aeronautical revenues exceeded 50 percent of total revenues in 2001.

Growth in the aeronautical revenue stream, derived from landing fees, passenger fees, aircraft parking fees, baggage handling fees, and other fees such as air traffic control, security and lighting, is more constrained by tariff regulation, long-term lease agreements with airlines, or legislation. Airports are natural monopolies. A 1999 International Civil Aviation Organization study reports that the average cost of a work load unit (WLU, equivalent to one passenger or 100 kg of freight) declines from \$15 for airports handling less than 300 000 WLUs, to \$9.40 for airports with WLUs between 300 000 and 2.5 million, and \$8.00 for airports with WLUs between 2.5 million and 25 million WLUs (Graham 2003, p. 59). Where privatization of airports has occurred, concern over the monopoly's ability to charge monopoly prices has resulted in tariff regulation by bodies such as the UK's Civil Aviation Authority and Competition Commission.

In the US, public sector airports have good access to capital markets, through tax exempt bond issues supported by revenues from legally binding long-term (between 20 and 50 years) lease and use agreements between the airports and the airlines. This reduces the pressure to privatize. These agreements typically detail the user charges – the fees and rental rates which an airline has to pay, the method by which these are to be calculated and the conditions for the use of both airfield and terminal facilities. The agreements reduce the risk for private investors and reduce the cost of capital for US airports. In addition, US airports have access to sources of capital that are generally funded by user taxes or charges. They include capital grants from the Airport and Airway Trust Fund funded by a passenger tax, funds generated by the \$4.50 passenger facility charge, state aviation fuel tax and general funds and property taxes, as well as revenues generated from concessions and non-aeronautical sources. The tax-exempt bonds, airport improvement grants, passenger facility charges, state and local contributions, and other sources represent, 60, 20, 16, 4 and 2 percent of airport funding, respectively (Busey 2002).

Disincentives for the corporatized form of privatization in the US exist because of federal regulations that prohibit the use of airport-generated funds for non-airport uses. Private airport owners are thus not able to reap the benefits of growing non-aeronautical revenues as their European counterparts have. The Hawaii state government, for example, was denied the use of revenues from an off-airport site of Duty-Free Shoppers for non-airport uses. Privatization in the US more often takes the form of project finance and management contract. Nevertheless, US public finance practices governing the relationship between airports and airlines is providing a global financial model for privatized airport companies to reduce risk for the debt they issue.

Convention centers
Major cities seeking to regenerate their economic base in a post-industrial manufacturing era view convention centers as drivers of economic development and destination competitiveness, and a source of civic pride. Since the 1960s, over 400 convention centers with exhibition space entered the US marketplace, more than 70 percent of them since 1970. These facilities stand ready to meet the demand of the large meetings and conventions market, fueled by the demand of over 20 000 associations and seven million business organizations, estimated to represent 2 percent of US gross domestic product in 1998. Although the pace of convention center development slowed during the 1990s, municipal leaders view them to be the most important tourist facility for attracting outside visitors (Judd et al. 2003, pp. 53–4).

Convention centers confer private benefits on users who are typically visitors, but revenues from direct user charges are usually not sufficient to break even. Instead, the benefits conferred by convention centers are largely public, deriving from economic development and the extra economic activity when conventioneers are in town. Because these benefits are generally external to the development or use of the convention center, a private convention center developer and operator cannot capture these benefits. Thus, hotel occupancy taxes, food and car rental taxes, sales taxes and property taxes, are the major sources of revenue for convention center debt service. They approximate benefit taxation to the extent that they fall on convention center users and the businesses that benefit from convention center activity. But they are not without imperfections, as they also fall on residents and non-convention tourists and business activity.

Nevertheless, revenue from visitors is key to convention center financing strategies. Local residents do not view convention centers as public infrastructure, as they would a bridge or road or water system, so that in the US 'in one city after another, convention center general obligation bond referendums were voted down and it was not until public authorities placed the capital spending for tourism infrastructure "off-budget" that the lion's share of convention centers began to be built' (Perry 2003, p. 41).

Stadia and arenas
Stadia are public assembly facilities providing amenities for spectator viewing of sporting events and may include arenas where non-sporting uses are a significant part of the use mix (Stevens 2001, p. 59). Because of the growing linkages established between tourism and spectator sporting events, the stadium is now becoming part of the tourism infrastructure and appeal of a city. Newly constructed stadia are promoted as supporting economic development, regenerating urban areas, and enhancing civic pride and city marketing image.

The stadium story is evolving differently in North America and in Europe. Stadium construction and renovation has by far the largest presence in the US, with 33 percent of the new stadium count and 52 percent of the refurbishment count, according to a 2001 survey of stadium construction plans (ibid., p. 66). The UK is second largest with some 21 and 15 percent, respectively.

Stadia and arena construction in North America is growing apace, as existing facilities are rendered commercially obsolete by the demand for deluxe, fully loaded arenas with higher revenue-generating capabilities and by the cartel powers of major league sports. Heavily funded by local governments during the 1970s and early 1980s, new stadia development is marked by increasing private sector investment as a share of facility costs. Reasons for this shift include generous lease agreements that increase the franchise owners' ability to pay (a form of subsidy), the generic trend toward greater privatization, and public contentiousness with the merits of subsidizing major league facilities. The direct contribution from public sources for these facilities dropped from a high of 93 percent in the 1970s and 1980s to 51 percent during the period from 1995 on into the early 2000s. The public share of arena funding alone declined from 100 to 39 percent (Crompton et al. 2003, p. 165).

In the UK developments were always privately funded, although a public investment case is being made for facilities that serve a 'national' sporting need. Such notions were instrumental in leveraging public funds to support the development of stadia, such as the £130 million Cardiff Millennium Stadium funded by a £40 million National Lottery grant (Jones 2002, p. 823).

Who should pay for the financing of stadia? Users are easily identified and assessed, and they should pay according to the level of benefits received. Stadia beneficiaries in North America include the middle- and upper-income portions of the population who are willing to pay for the luxurious, private accommodation found in the newer facilities, fans that live both inside and outside the taxing jurisdiction where the stadium is located, future users and citizens who benefit from enhanced factor incomes. Retail businesses in proximity to the stadium also benefit, through the capitalization of economic benefits into property values (Zimmerman 1997, p. 1491). At the same time, stadia provide a level of public benefit (Noll and Zimbalist 1997, p. 58), arising from the satisfaction of living in a 'big league town', the promotional value of the image-making stadium, and the extra economic activity generated, as in the convention center case. While these benefits may be small on average, they are potentially large in the aggregate and accrue to the general public.

Given the mix of private and public benefits associated with stadia, Zimmerman (1997, p. 1491) suggests a mix of public–private funding:

1. the largest share should derived from direct user charges, such as ticket taxes or other stadium-related revenues, because the incidence of theses taxes and fees fall upon stadium attendees and fans and on owners and players, the groups who receive the most private benefit from the stadium;
2. a broad-based tax that touches all citizens, such as a property tax, to pay for the public consumption benefits of the stadium;
3. tax bases selected that cover the entire geographic attendance area;
4. taxes on factor income gains associated with real estate or business entertainment, such as a special taxing district to access the appreciation in property values or an additional tax on luxury box tickets; and
5. long-term debt financing, so that future users pay their share of infrastructure costs.

Determining the public–private mix in financing stadia construction is unlikely to be easily resolved. Despite the reduced dependence on public sector investment, the absolute level of public investment in the US is virtually identical to the level that existed when public funding dominated stadia financing. In real 2003 dollars, public stadia financing has remained constant at approximately $200 million per facility since 1970 (Crompton, et al. 2003, p. 170). The principles of public finance are best observed if the share of public subsidy is proportional to the share of public benefit, and if the focus of the debate is less on whether the investment will be profitable, although this is no small consideration for communities who are still repaying the debt on stadia from which teams have departed, but more on whether larger benefits could be derived from alternative opportunities.

Olympic cities

Olympic Games fall into the class of hallmark or mega events, defined as 'major one-time or recurring events of limited duration, developed primarily to enhance the awareness, appeal and profitability of a tourist destination in the short and/or long term. Such events rely for their success on uniqueness, status, or timely significance to create interest and attract attention' (Ritchie 1984, p. 2). They are characterized by infrastructure investments large enough to stage competitions for thousands of athletes and accommodate millions of spectators. The 1996 Atlanta Olympics, for example, drew more than 10 000 athletes from 197 countries and over two million visitors (French and Disher 1997, p. 380). They have been promoted for the same reasons as convention centers and stadia, as a means of economic stimulus, as urban redevelopment, and as a visible marketing opportunity. In addition, Olympic infrastructure is unique in having a legacy benefit flowing from future use of the sporting facilities built for the event.

Mounting these events requires huge investments in infrastructure. It is estimated that the 1996 Atlanta Olympics cost $1.58 billion in direct facility construction and public infrastructure upgrades, the 2000 Sydney Olympics cost A$3.23 billion in infrastructure, and the 2002 Salt Lake City Olympics cost $1.3 billion (Andranovich et al. 2001, p. 125; Hall 1996, p. 373; Chappelet 2002, p. 19). The price tag for the 35 venues to accommodate the 28 sporting events in the 2004 Athens Olympics, estimated to be $5 billion at the outset, might double before it is over (Quinn 2004).

Who should pay for Olympic infrastructure? Outside of the US, this is typically financed by the municipal government in the city winning the bid process, often with the assistance of the national government. This would imply large public legacy and economic benefits. But when the public sector finances Olympic infrastructure, it bears all of the risk associated with staging the one-time Olympic games, and it is claimed that private returns far exceed those to the public (Hall 1996, p. 374). The growing scale of required investment and the lack of financial success for some events, such as the 1976 Montreal Games (Levine 2003, p. 248), makes the role of private investment increasingly important.

Nowhere is this more evident than in the US, where Olympic cities typically depend on private consortia to raise funds for the sporting venues through ticket sales, corporate sponsorships and television broadcasting rights. A study of three US Olympic events, Los Angeles (1984), Atlanta (1996) and Salt Lake City (2002), reports that all were privately organized with authority to develop the necessary venues, organize fund raising, and operate the sporting, housing and ancillary game venues, even when public funds were involved (Andranvich et al. 2001). Voters in Los Angeles approved an Olympic ticket tax and an increase in the hotel occupancy tax to pay for the city's contribution to the games. Voters in Utah approved a referendum campaign to divert $59 million of sales tax revenues to a fund for the construction of Olympic facilities. In Atlanta, a 'no new taxes' pledge limited the city's contribution to the Olympic effort. All three Olympic cities ended with a financial surplus, legacy funds and public use facilities. All three were able to accelerate and change the timing of investment in transportation, telecommunication, or waste disposal infrastructure through federal, state or local funding. But urban regeneration was not achieved (ibid., p. 126). Although only Atlanta specifically planned for redevelopment of targeted areas of the city, the Olympic games did not directly result in major business relocation. Expecting these events to substantially eliminate urban problems may be too ambitious.

In Sydney, funds were diverted to Olympic related infrastructure spending (for example in rail), away from spending elsewhere.

To the extent that private funds paid for Olympic infrastructure development, these results appear to be efficient. But the accelerated infusion of public investment suggests the need for detailed studies that estimate the net benefits of Olympic Games, including the opportunity cost of resources allocated to infrastructure development, to determine whether the amounts of public investment are efficient.

Conclusion and further research
Public investment in infrastructure that serves the needs of tourism is common, because it serves both tourists and residents. The dominating public finance issue, however, is whether public investment is commensurate with marginal public benefits and costs. This may be characterized alternatively as determining whether the incremental addition of infrastructure yields only private benefits. This issue is highlighted by greater efforts to increase the level of private investment and funding through user charges and by the trend to privatization or public–private partnerships.

Public policy decisions would be better informed by research that establishes the marginal benefit and marginal cost of public infrastructure investment, as well as the distribution of these benefits and costs. This analysis is needed for deciding how to finance the investment itself, as well as how to finance operations. Opportunity costs need to be assessed, including the costs of externalities. And the long-lived nature of the infrastructure asset requires an analysis that takes into account benefits and costs over time. Besides the traditional static partial equilibrium or input/output analyses, dynamic general equilibrium analysis has significant promise to better assess infrastructure projects and their public finance.

Bibliography

Andranovich, Greg, Matthew J. Burbank and Charles H. Heying (2001), 'Olympic cities: lessons learned from mega-event politics', *Journal of Urban Affairs*, **23** (2), 113–31.

Baade, Robert A. (1997), 'Professional sports and economic impact: the view of the judiciary', *State Tax Notes*, **13**, 1495–505.

Busey, Brian (2002), 'US airport finance overview', presented at USAID Conference on Airport Planning, Cairo, Egypt, 6 March.

Chappelet, Jean-Loup (2002), 'From Lake Placid to Salt Lake City: the challenging growth of the Olympic Winter Games since 1980', *European Journal of Sport Science*, **2** (3), 1–21.

Crompton, John, Dennis R. Howard and Turgut Var (2003), 'Financing major league facilities: status, evolution and conflicting forces', *Journal of Sport Management*, **17**, 156–84.

Fisher, Ronald C. (1996), *State and Local Public Finance*, 2nd edition, Chicago: Irwin.

Forsyth, Peter and Larry Dwyer (2002), 'Market power and the taxation of domestic and international tourism', *Tourism Economics*, **8** (4), 377–99.

French, Steven P. and Mike E. Disher (1997), 'Atlanta and the Olympics', *Journal of the American Planning Association*, **63** (3), 379–92.

Gold, Barry P. (2000), 'Privatization and financing of airport development and expansion projects', *Journal of Project Finance*, **6** (1), 47–60.

Graham, Ann (2003), *Managing Airports, An International Perspective*, 2nd edition, Amsterdam: Elsevier Butterworth Heinemann.

Gramlich, Edward M. (1994), 'Infrastructure investment: a review essay', *Journal of Economic Literature*, **32**, 1176–96.

Hall, Colin M. (1996), 'Hallmark events and urban reimaging strategies: coercion, community, and the Sydney 2000 Olympics', in Lynn C. Harrison and Winston Husbands (eds), *Practicing Responsible Tourism*, New York: John Wiley & Sons.

Hooper, Paul (2002), 'Privatization of airports in Asia', *Journal of Air Transport Management*, **8** (5), 289–300.

Jones, Calvin (2002), 'The stadium and economic development: Cardiff and the Millennium Stadium', *European Planning Studies*, **10** (7), 819–29.

Judd, Dennis R., William Winter, William R. Barnes and Emily Stern (2003), 'Tourism and entertainment as local development: a national survey', in Dennis R. Judd (ed.), *The Infrastructure of Play*, Armonk, NY: M.E. Sharpe.

Levine, Mark (2003), 'Tourism infrastructure and urban redevelopment in Montreal', in Dennis R. Judd (ed.), *The Infrastructure of Play*, Armonk, NY: M.E. Sharpe.

Mak, James (1993), 'Exacting resort developers to create non-tourism jobs', *Annals of Tourism Research*, **20**, 250–61.

Noll, Roger G. and Andrew Zimbalist (eds) (1997), 'The economic impact of sports teams and facilities', in *Sports, Jobs and Taxes: The Economic Impact of Sports Teams and Stadiums*, Washington, DC: Brookings Institution Press, pp. 55–91.

Perry, David C. (2003), 'Urban tourism and the privatizing discourses of public infrastructure', in Dennis R. Judd (ed.), *The Infrastructure of Play*, Armonk, NY: M.E. Sharpe.

Quinn, Patrick (2004), 'Cost for Athens games far surpasses estimates', *The Honolulu Advertiser*, Associated Press, 13 June, p. c12.

Ritchie, J.R. Brent (1984), 'Assessing the impact of Hallmark Events', *Journal of Travel Research*, **23** (1), 2–11.

Ritchie, J.R. Brent and Geoffrey Crouch (2005), *The Competitive Destination: A sustainable tourism perspective*, Cambridge, MA: CABI Publishing.

Simmonds, Keith C. (1993), 'Impact fees: a method of paying for growth in Florida', *International Journal of Public Sector Management*, **6** (3), 3–16.

Sinclair, M. Thea and Mike Stabler (1997), *The Economics of Tourism*, London: Routledge.

Stevens, Terry (2001), 'Stadia and tourism-related facilities', *Travel and Tourism Analyst*, **2**, 59–73.
US Department of Transportation (1993), *Financing the Future: Report of the Commission to Promote Investment in America's Infrastructure*, Washington, DC.
US Department of Transportation (2003), *Transportation Statistics Annual Report 2003*, Washington, DC.
World Travel and Tourism Council (WTTC) (2004), *2004 Travel & Tourism Economic Research*, London: WTTC.
Zimbalist, Andrew (2003), *May the Best Team Win*, Washington, DC: Brookings Institution Press.
Zimmerman, Dennis (1997), 'Who benefits from and who pays for stadiums?', *State Tax Notes*, **13**, 1489–94.

PART FIVE

EVALUATION FOR POLICY MAKING

13 Tourism Satellite Accounts
Ray Spurr

Introduction

Measuring the contribution of tourism to the national economy has presented a long-running problem for policy makers, industry lobbyists and researchers. Proponents of tourism argue that the absence of credible economic measures of tourism has led to governments underestimating the benefits that tourism brings to their economies, particularly in comparison with other industries such as manufacturing where the outputs are easier to observe and quantify and which, for historical reasons, are more clearly reflected in government statistical collections.

The difficulty in measuring the economic contribution of tourism arises from problems of both methodology and from the lack of comprehensive data. The economic impacts of tourism are complicated by the highly fragmented and dispersed nature of the suppliers of tourism goods and services, spread as they are across the economy generally. Conventional industries, as they have been defined in the System of National Accounts (SNA) as adopted by governments internationally, are characterized by the existence of a clearly identifiable product and set of producers. They can usually be measured by the direct economic effects incurred in the production of that product or products. To compare tourism with such existing industries, however, requires the construction of a 'composite' or 'artificial' tourism industry. This 'composite industry' has to be identified, at least initially, from the demand side by examining what it is that tourists purchase, rather than by going direct to the 'supply-side' producers of a clearly defined product. These statistical measurement problems have been exacerbated by the historical absence of a classification within the SNA framework to allow for the clear identification and economic measurement of a tourism industry. While the various components of tourism supply are all included within the SNA, they cannot be readily aggregated to provide figures for tourism as a whole because the classifications under which they appear combine both tourism and non-tourism production (Cockerell and Spurr 2002).

Irrespective of whether governments have in fact underestimated the benefits of tourism, it is certainly true that tourism has not been well served in statistical and information terms. This has reduced the quality and reliability of research and analysis on the industry. And it is probably fair to assume that it will have also had its effects on the quality of policy decision making and planning by governments, and probably by tourism industry operators as well.

The strong growth in service industries over the past thirty years, and in international trade in tourism services in particular, has led to a growing acknowledgement of the need to better understand these industries and the role which they play in our economies. This has highlighted the statistical measurement challenges that these industries often present. In this environment and with tourism a key component in the growth in international trade in services, increasing attention has been directed in recent years to the question of improving the statistical measurement of tourism in economic terms. The concept of a Tourism Satellite Account (TSA) took root at the beginning of the 1990s with the broad structure and form for a TSA emerging through international consultations following the 1991 Ottawa Conference on Tourism Statistics. This culminated in OECD, WTO and EUROSTAT endorsement of an agreed comprehensive model, the 'Tourism Satellite Account: recommended methodological framework' following an international conference hosted by the World Tourism Organization in Nice, France in May 1999 (WTO 1999).

Since that time an increasing number of countries have established, or begun to develop, national TSAs based on this agreed international framework. This chapter explains what a TSA is, why it is necessary, the benefits it provides and possible future developments and uses for TSAs.

The System of National Accounts and the concept of a 'satellite account'
The national accounts of a country provide the primary statistical framework for the measurement and consequent analysis of economic activity within that country. They are established in broad accordance with an internationally agreed set of conventions laid out in the United Nations endorsed 'System of National Accounts'.

The SNA provides concepts, definitions, classifications, accounting rules, accounts and tables to present a comprehensive, integrated framework for the estimation of production, consumption, capital investment, income, stocks and flows of financial wealth, and other related economic variables in an economy. This framework makes it possible to match and analyse demand for a specific variety of goods or services with the supply of these goods and services within an economy.

The current version of the SNA, SNA93, specifically includes provision for the development of 'satellite accounts' which may be used to expand the analytical capacity of the existing system (UN 1993). The possible use of satellite account structures is being increasingly turned to where the traditional SNA structure fails to meet emerging statistical needs. Examples of emerging areas of interest for their use include the monitoring of community health, the state of the environment, and leisure and sporting activities. Satellite accounts are designed to sit alongside the main structure of the national accounts but to follow a consistent conceptual approach with it.

The term 'satellite account' is used to describe the fact that these accounts sit outside, or rather alongside, the mainstream SNA tables. They do this because much of the data they contain already exists within the SNA under existing classifications. To simply add new tables which duplicate some of this data would thus involve double counting. For example, tourist expenditures on air travel or on meals consumed in restaurants will appear within the existing SNA classifications for Air Transportation and for Take Away Meals and Restaurants. If tables measuring the value of 'tourism' were to be simply added into the SNA, tourist expenditures on these items would be counted twice in the calculation of overall national expenditure.

Why is a 'tourism' satellite account necessary?
The SNA identifies economic outputs by reference to a list of observable products, independent of the use to which those products are put. It measures the value of production of identifiable goods and services and is essentially a measure of supply side activity. The difficulty which arises in relation to tourism is that tourism is not restricted to a set of predefined goods and services but is rather defined by who these products are delivered to. That is, by whether or not the purchaser or tourist meets the definition of being a 'visitor'.

Thus many of the things which tourists buy are not normally perceived to be tourism-related products – for example clothes, groceries, telecommunications, books or newspapers. But to measure the economic impact, or value, of tourism activity in our economy, purchases of these items by tourists need to be included as well as the purchase of items which are more frequently associated with tourism such as hotel accommodation, restaurant meals, postcards and transport expenses. Further complicating the issue is that many of these items may be purchased not only by visitors, but also by local residents as well in the course of their everyday activities. Clearly since these purchases are not made in the context of tourism activity they should not be included in the measurement of tourism.

So while all of the components of tourism-related production are in fact already in the traditional SNA tables they cannot be simply aggregated and identified as 'tourism'. This is because these component activities appear under separate classifications of their own which will often include items which are not tourism-related as well as those which are. Before the advent of the TSA it was therefore not possible to clearly identify either the components of tourism production, or the aggregate level of tourism production, in a reliable and officially sanctioned manner.

The Tourism Satellite Account

A TSA thus comprises a set of concepts, definitions, classifications and accounting rules designed to enable a country to properly understand and evaluate tourism within its overall economy. It provides a framework of monetary flows which can be traced from the tourism consumer to the producing unit or supplier within the economy. In doing so it defines and identifies the various tourism 'industries' or groups of suppliers which produce or import the goods and services purchased by visitors (Massieu 2000).

The TSA is designed to provide a measure of tourism-related economic activity: demand, supply, taxes, wages, trade and capital formation, although few if any of the countries which have developed TSAs have yet been able to fully incorporate all of these elements. The TSA brings together components of economic demand and supply activity from across the economy which relate to tourism demand. These are identified and quantified so as to present a balanced picture of supply and demand for these goods and services within that economy and to enable them to be studied, both individually and in aggregated form.

As a measure of value added, rather than of total expenditure, the TSA tells us what tourism's contribution is to national production. Thus, for example, the purchase by a visitor of goods such as bottles of spirits or perfume which have been imported will generate less value added than the purchase of accommodation or restaurant services which have drawn heavily on local inputs of labour and materials.

History of development

By the 1980s it was apparent that services had become a driving engine of growth in the economies of many, and particularly the most developed, countries as well as a major factor in global trade. With this came a growing recognition of the importance of tourism as a key component in the services economy constituting as it did over 30 per cent of international trade in services in the OECD area. Meanwhile for many of the poorer countries tourism was emerging as a rapid source of growth in foreign exchange earnings, employment and contributor to regional development (Dupeyras 2002).

This increasing focus on the economic importance of tourism was accompanied by growing frustration among many in the tourism industry, and among government officials concerned with tourism issues, at the poor state of tourism statistics and their lack of credibility in the eyes of government economic policy makers. There were those in government who were beginning to believe that tourism had the capacity to create employment and income faster and more effectively than other industries and were interested in the way in which tourism could be used as a development tool to tackle issues of regional development, employment generation and foreign exchange earnings. However, there was a belief that the industry's claims to be taken more seriously in government policy making were failing because its increasing importance was not being adequately recognized (Lapierre 1994; and Meis Dupeyras 2002).

Prior to the development of the TSA methodology, however, statistics on tourism in most countries tended to be restricted to data of an essentially marketing kind such as the number of travellers, their socioeconomic characteristics, nationality or country of residence, length and purpose of stay, type of accommodation, occupancy rates and places visited. Sometimes estimates of average expenditure were added to this based on a variety of survey methodologies. But little information was available to policy officials on macroeconomic aspects of tourism activity, its impact on economic growth, employment, government income, foreign currency receipts and fixed capital formation. And industry or official claims regarding the growing importance of the tourism within many economies were often treated quizzically if not with positive scepticism.

During the 1960s, France developed satellite accounts as a way of designating accounting practices which were not correctly identified in the SNA but that could be considered as satellite subsystems of it. These were initially used for analysing the housing sector although the French did develop preliminary plans for quantifying tourism's economic impacts (Laimer and Smeral 2001). In the international arena, work began in the WTO in 1982 to develop a 'uniform and comprehensive means of measurement and comparison' for tourism with other sectors of the economy following the recommendations of the then existing SNA (United Nations 1993). During the 1980s the OECD was also working on the development of a 'Manual on tourism economic accounts' which proposed means for treatment of a number of the more complex issues in tourism measurement (OECD 1991).

At a conference on Tourism Statistics, held in Ottawa in 1991, Statistics Canada presented a proposal 'to establish a credible and comparable means for assessing tourism economic activities in relation to other industries in a domestic economy, and to develop a framework for relating other relevant data regarding tourism activities in an organized and consistent manner'. The recommendations of the Ottawa Conference were endorsed by the United Nations Statistical Commission in 1993 at which point the WTO appointed a consultant to develop a conceptual framework for a TSA (WTO 1994). An Intergovernmental Ad Hoc Group was formed to review and comment on the methodological framework being developed. Important participants in this process included Canada, the World Travel & Tourism Council (WTTC) on behalf of the private sector, the OECD and the Statistical Office of the European Community (EUROSTAT).

The proposed methodological framework was presented to the 1999 'Enzo Paci World Conference on the Measurement of Economic Impact of Tourism', held in Nice in the south of France. A WTO–OECD–EUROSTAT Inter-Secretariat Working-Group was then charged with bringing the proposed methodological framework to finality. The final proposal known as TSA: RMF (OECD, the Statistical Office of the European Communities 2000 (2)), was adopted by the United Nations Statistical Commission in 2000 (OECD et al. 2000)

For the private sector the WTTC, using the WEFA Group as its consultants, had begun developing what it characterized as 'simulated' Tourism Satellite Accounts from shortly after the WTTC's establishment in 1990. Through the 1990s it produced estimates for the global economic significance of tourism, for major international regions, and a number of more in-depth studies on individual countries. The WTTC continued to lobby for the adoption of TSAs and played an active role in the work of the Intergovernmental Ad Hoc Group and at the Enzo Paci Conference. It continues to produce simulated TSAs at the global, regional, national and in some cases subnational levels, now drawing on the agreed methodological framework. Since 2000, the WTTC has used Oxford Economic Forecasting as its consultants in this work (WTTC/WEFA 1996a,b; WTTC 2005).

Concepts and definitions
A critical element of the TSA is the adoption of a common set of concepts and definitions for measuring the economic dimensions of tourism. This provides a basis for calculation of key impacts and relationships of tourism which is consistent with national accounting standards and therefore allows comparability of results with other industry sectors and across time. Some of these concepts and definitions are fundamental to understanding what it is that the TSA measures.

Thus tourism is defined for purposes of the TSA as the activities of persons travelling to and staying in places outside their usual environment for not more than one consecutive year for leisure, business and other purposes.

The TSA includes but distinguishes between international and domestic visitors, and between visitors who stay for one or more nights in the place visited and same-day visitors who visit for less than one night.

Visitor activities include consumption activity in anticipation of trips, for example, the purchase of luggage or travel insurance, and some trip-related expenditure incurred after returning such as developing photographs which were taken during the trip.

In order to identify a 'tourism industry' which can be compared to other industries in the economy, or to the tourism industry of another economy, the TSA adopts the concept of 'tourism characteristic industries'. These are 'industries' or sectors of the economy which are typical of tourism and either would cease to exist in their present form or would be significantly affected if tourism were to cease. In the Australian TSA this is defined as requiring that at least 25 per cent of the industry's output is consumed by visitors. It thus includes travel agency and tour operator services, taxi transport, air and water transport, motor vehicle hire, accommodation, and cafés, restaurants and food outlets.

The TSA also distinguishes tourism-connected industries, which are industries other than tourism characteristic industries for which a tourism-related product is directly identifiable and where the products are consumed by visitors in volumes which are significant for the visitor and/or for the producer. These can include a wide range of industries such as clubs, pubs, taverns and bars; rail transport; road transport (other than where included as characteristic, above); food manufacturing; automotive fuel retailing; retail trade; casinos and other gambling services; libraries; museums and arts; entertainment services; and education.

Vacation homes and other secondary residences are included through the use of imputed rentals to ensure consistency with the treatment of owner-occupied dwellings in the SNA generally.

It is important to understand that the TSA considers only direct tourist demand. It requires that there be a direct physical and economic relationship between the visitor and supplier and does not consider the indirect effects of tourist demand triggered by the delivery linkages in the economy. To take account of these indirect impacts, which are important for understanding the full contribution and impact of tourism on an economy, requires the use of extensions to the basic TSA structure such as those referred to under 'applications for macroeconomic modelling and forecasting' later in this chapter (WTO 1994, 1999).

Expenditure on the purchase of dual-use durable consumer goods which may be used from time to time in relation to tourism activities, such as motor vehicles or cameras, is not included in the definition of tourism expenditures adopted under the TSA unless they are purchased during the trip or immediately before it and for the purpose of the trip. This became a point of significant contention during the negotiations leading up to agreement on the methodological framework for the TSA. The WTTC argued for inclusion of a portion of the value of multi-purpose consumer goods which are used by visitors for tourism as well as other purposes. This position was eventually rejected on the grounds that it would be inconsistent with the treatment of other industries under the SNA, and would therefore compromise inter-industry comparison.

Other areas of contention during the negotiation of the Recommended Methodological Framework for the TSA included the handling of tourism-related investment including investment in infrastructure utilized by tourism such as roads and airports, tourism collective consumption items including government-provided immigration and marketing services, business-related travel, and the export of goods for tourism use in other countries. In the event, tables for capital formation and tourism collective consumption were included within the Recommended Framework although they are not included in the tourism supply and consumption tables and therefore do not contribute to the calculation of tourism GDP, gross value added or employment. And exports of tourism goods are not included, although this could lead to problems of consistency with national TSA numbers in the production of regional and subregional TSAs.

How a TSA works

The overall SNA framework relies on basic accounting principles under which the supply of goods and services within the economy in monetary terms is matched to the demand for those goods and services. The centrepiece of the system is an input–output (I–O) model of the national economy. The I–O model defines the supply of goods and services as a series of spreadsheets. Each industry in the economy is listed down the rows and each commodity across the columns with each cell providing a value of the commodity produced by each industry per annum. Further spreadsheets provide the value of each commodity consumed by each industry and final demand by consumers, governments, non-residents and investment by the private and public sectors (Smith and Wilton 1997).

A TSA represents an extension or subset of these spreadsheets. Tourism products such as accommodation and restaurant meals are consumed by both visitors and non-visitors, while non-tourism commodities such as newspapers or laundry services are also consumed by visitors. To deal with this the percentage of production of each tourism commodity which is consumed by visitors is calculated to generate a tourism ratio. Other commodities consumed by visitors are treated similarly (Laimer and Smeral 2001; Smith and Wilton 1997).

These tourism shares can then be applied to calculate the differences between the value of output attributable to visitor consumption and to intermediate consumption and the value added generated by visitor consumption can be computed (Massieu 2000).

The overall TSA report is made up of a series of tables which can be related to the tables of SNA93. These convey the core data regarding the main aggregates of Tourism Consumption; Tourism Supply; Tourism Value Added; Tourism GDP; Tourism Employment; and Tourism Gross Fixed Capital Formation. The ten core tables which comprise the agreed TSA structure are set out in Table 13.1.

Table 13.1   Tourism Satellite Account: the constituent tables

Table	Coverage	Notes
1	Inbound tourism expenditure	Exports of tourism services
2	Domestic tourism expenditure	Part of domestic total consumption
3	Outbound tourism expenditure	Imports of tourism services. Often not included as not integrated to the key TSA tables and data are frequently not available
4	Domestic 'tourism final consumption'	Synthesized from Tables 1 & 2
5	Production of tourism commodities	Total production of tourism goods and services including but not limited to tourism characteristic industries
6	Domestic supply and consumption by product	Reconciliation of Tables 4 & 5. The key table of the TSA
7	Employment & labour use	Structure not yet agreed
8	Tourism fixed capital formation (investment)	Structure not yet agreed
9	Tourism collective consumption	Services provided simultaneously to all members of the community or all members of a particular section of the community such as public administration or security. This table has not been widely implemented to date
10	Non-monetary indicators	e.g., tourism volumes/nights; types of tourist etc. structure can reflect most useful indicators

Sources: OECD, EUROSTAT, UN and WTO (2000); Jones et al. (2004).

Benefits of a TSA

A TSA provides a range of important benefits. In particular:

- It brings together basic data on the key economic variables relating to tourism and presents it in a consistent and authoritative way. This includes information on tourism's contribution to and share of GDP, its gross value added, the employment it generates, the taxes it pays and tourism's contribution to exports. In doing so a TSA provides answers to questions such as: how important is tourism demand for commodities produced by a country; how much direct and indirect value added is generated for the economy from satisfying tourism demand; how much in taxes does government recover from tourism; and how much employment depends on tourism?

- Because it is derived from the overall SNA structure, the TSA enables tourism to be compared with other industries in the economy using consistent and accepted national accounting principles. This helps to raise awareness of tourism and its contribution to the national economy and helps to legitimize or give credibility to the tourism industry in the minds of politicians and the general public. In doing so it can help to solicit and justify funding for tourism development and marketing. In the case of Canada, for example, publication of the first TSA in 1994 coincided in time with a decision by the Canadian government to restructure the institutional arrangements for government involvement in tourism and to provide a dramatic increase in government funding (which was subsequently backed by matching private sector funds). This objective has often underpinned industry support for development of TSAs and it is has often been identified as the primary benefit which has flowed from the introduction of a TSA.

- It identifies the tourism-related industries within the economy, their production functions and the interrelationship of tourism industries with the rest of the economy. Thus it answers questions such as: what are the main commodities purchased by visitors; what industries benefit from tourism demand; and how are those benefits distributed between industries across the economy?

- It brings the composite components of the industry together identifying and defining a core 'tourism industry', that is, the sectors of the economy which produce 'tourism characteristic goods'. From this the TSA can provide the information from which to profile the development of the key tourism-related sectors in the economy and their links to tourism demand.

- It provides a base for developing national tourism indicators such as the quarterly performance measures published by Statistics Canada (Statistics Canada 1994b)
- It provides policy makers with insights into tourism and its socio-economic functions and impacts on their economies which should help improve the effectiveness of tourism policies and actions and measures to evaluate these policies in the context of broader policy agendas.
- It provides a basic starting point, definitions and data sources for use in the development of analytical extensions such as tourism employment/labour force modules, state or regional TSAs, and for the application of further analytical tools such as economic impact and forecasting models.
- It provides a measure of the size of tourism capital investment and the means to analyse the link between capital investment and tourism supply and demand.

Seven of the eight APEC member economies which reported having developed a TSA in a survey conducted for the Asia Pacific Economic Cooperation (APEC) Tourism Working Group in 2001 rated its major benefit as being the TSA's use as an indicator of tourism industry performance together with its value as a comprehensive framework for identifying the economic impact of tourism. Enhancing awareness and recognition of tourism's economic importance was identified as a close second, while other uses and benefits identified in the survey included that the TSA helped to strengthen the industry's identity, that it enhanced knowledge, provided a core definition of the industry and that it served as a medium for public information (Cockerell and Spurr 2002).

In the longer term, the existence of a TSA undoubtedly provides a core resource for improved understanding of the role played by tourism within an economy and thus a major contribution to improved research, policy making and decision making generally on tourism.

Progress to date in implementing TSAs
Starting with Canada in 1994 there has been a steady expansion in the number of countries embarking on the development of a TSA. Early adopters included Australia, Norway, New Zealand, Singapore, Sweden, Switzerland and the United States.

A review of 20 of the 21 APEC member economies in 2001 found that eight had already developed a TSA at some level and a further five were in the process of doing so. Of the remaining seven APEC member economies, three were hoping to develop a TSA in the near future (Cockerell and Spurr 2002).

A EUROSTAT survey of EU member countries in 2001 found that of 15 EU members only one, Sweden, had implemented a TSA. Austria, Spain and France were in the process of implementation and Finland, Italy and the UK had undertaken pilot or feasibility studies (Laimer and Smeral 2001). Subsequent progress has included joint public sector/private research agency pilot projects in Austria and the UK (Laimer and Smeral 2001; Jones et al. 2004).

Practical implementation difficulties

Of the countries that have embarked on the development of a TSA, Canada, as the country with the longest experience and largest investment in TSA development, comes closest to fully implementing the Recommended Methodological Framework. As yet, however, no country completes all of the tables in the recommended TSA framework. Most countries complain of data deficiencies and few have yet begun to develop tables on outbound tourism, employment, capital formation and collective consumption.

Difficulties emerge at every step in the development process. Many countries, especially those with less sophisticated statistical systems, lack the comprehensive I–O tables for their economies which are required and most lack sufficiently detailed visitor expenditure data. The 2001 survey of APEC member economies identified difficulties in accessing the technical expertise and resources which were required (Cockerell and Spurr 2002; Massieu 2002).

Estimates of the cost and development time involved varied enormously from a few thousand US dollars and less than a year to US$620 000 and three years in the case of Australia. For Canada it took in excess of six years and an extensive commitment of resources in its pioneering development role. The APEC survey found an average cost of US$250 000 and staff resource requirements of between 30 and 120 person months. Clearly these estimates are heavily influenced by data quality and completeness and whether new data collections were implemented as part of the process.

The development of a national TSA generally requires a considerable commitment by governments at an inter-agency level, with a particular need to include the national statistical agency. It requires the allocation of financial, technical and staff resources, and the existence of basic statistical structures including some form of national I–O tables. The quality of expenditure data, including in relation to domestic travel, the treatment of expenditure on package tours which have been paid for in the foreign source country, and the imputation of holiday home rents are just examples of issues which will frequently present particular difficulties.

Given these problems in implementation, one of the principal objectives of the TSA – comparability with other industries and between nations – remains problematic. Individual circumstances also differ significantly, even between countries at relatively similar levels of development, with international tourism accounting for less than 25 per cent of tourism expenditure in some countries (for example, the US, Australia and New Zealand) and for more than 50 per cent in others (for example, Austria and Switzerland). Table 13.2, which is drawn from a more extensive table in 'Satellite accounts first steps – United Kingdom,' provides some examples of headline TSA results from seven OECD countries (Jones et al. 2004).

Further directions and extensions for TSAs
Discussion and research is continuing on further extensions and applications of the basic TSA structure. The following are areas of particular interest and potential.

The employment module
An important policy interest for governments is to gain a better understanding of tourism employment and the role of tourism in creating, preserving and diversifying jobs in the economy, the number and structure of those jobs and the levels of remuneration. Tourism employment is more difficult to measure than employment in most other sectors because of both the fragmented nature of the industry, which has given rise to the need for a TSA in the first place, and also its particular characteristics of high seasonality, predominantly small enterprise employers, shift work, casual and part-time employment and extensive involvement of family labour. Improving information in this area would contribute to better targeting of education and training and a reduction in skill and occupation supply and demand mismatches as well as to the identification of more efficient labour practices.

The OECD have developed an 'Employment Module' to complement or extend the basic TSA structure by extending the range of information on the characteristics of the tourism labour force beyond that which is found in the existing TSA design. To do this it adopts a supply-side perspective including only employment in a set of selected characteristic tourism industries and provides information on numbers employed, socio-demographic characteristics of the labour force, labour conditions, mobility labour structures, productivity, labour costs, job qualifications and skills recruitment strategies and education and training provisions (Dupeyras 2002). Like the TSA itself, full development of the module provides significant challenges to governments. However, countries such as Australia and Canada have set out to incorporate elements of the module into their TSA systems.

Table 13.2 TSA headline results: international comparisons

	Canada (1998 $CAN)	New Zealand (1999 $NZ)	USA (1997 $US)	Austria (1999 ATS)	Norway (2000 NOK)	Australia (1998 $AUS)	Switzerland (1998 CHF)
Total tourism expenditure (m)	45 886	12 078	291 500	302 161	76 417	58 200	30 610
of which:							
International tourism consumption (%)	33.7	23.3	24.0	53.5	30.3	22.0	47.4
Domestic household consumption (%)	66.3	72.5	43.0	37.0**	46.3	67.0	34.2**
Domestic business consumption (%)		4.2	29.0	9.5	23.4	11.0	5.8
Government & other (%)	n/a	0.1	5.0	n/a	n/a		12.5
Direct value added (% of total industry contribution to gross value added)	2.3	4.6	2.2*	7.2	3.8	4.5	
Total employment, 000s (direct)	533	87 FTE	1452*	n/a	133	513	165 FTE
% cf workforce	3.7	5.6	3.5*	n/a	6.8	6.0	5.2

Notes:
*US accounts report for only 'tourism industries' – these figures are therefore likely to be slight under-estimates.
** Includes adjustment for expenditure while at second home.

Source: This table is drawn from a more extensive table in Jones et al. (2004). The data were sourced from: www.bea.gov.uk; www.statistick.at; www.statcan.ca; www.stats.gov.nz; www.abs.gov.au; www.statistik.admin.ch; www.ssb.no.

Capital formation

The way in which capital formation should be handled in the TSA was a subject of some controversy during much of the negotiations on the Recommended Methodological Framework. Although the direct cost of capital acquisition is not included in calculating tourism consumption and tourism value added in the TSA, the services provided by capital are assumed to be included because the price of products such as air transport implicitly includes a component to cover the cost of capital, gaining more information about capital investment to support tourism remains an area of substantial analytical interest for tourism policy making. Questions of handling have ranged across how capital which is not solely used by tourists should be treated (for example, the restaurant which serves both local residents and tourists), whether tourists need to come into physical contact with the capital asset in order for it to be included, for example, if the aircraft that the visitor travels on is included then what about the airline's head office building and its investment in computer reservations systems, how unimproved land should be treated, and how to handle public infrastructure ranging from a convention centre or a concert hall to roads and airports or the infrastructure of the national tourism organization or of government visa offices. A WTO Committee on Statistics working group was established in 2000 to compile statistical sources and resolve conceptual and measurement difficulties associated with analysis of gross fixed capital formation of public authorities and gross capital formation associated with tourism consumption. An initial report was presented by the group in January 2001 (Holtz-Eakin 2001; Miller 2002).

Subnational or regional TSAs

Regional and provincial administrations expend significant resources in developing and marketing tourism attractions, promoting events and supporting tourism-based operations. Good policy decision making on these issues requires that they have accurate and reliable methods for measuring the size and performance of tourism in their economies. Extending the existing TSA structure down to the subnational level has become a priority for many state and provincial governments. In Australia the Queensland state treasury has developed a TSA for that state (OESR 2001). Elsewhere in Australia, the Sustainable Tourism Cooperative Research Centre (STCRC) has developed a TSA for the state of New South Wales and state-level TSA results have been modelled for Victoria and Western Australia by Access Economics, a private consultancy company. Internationally, TSAs have been developed or model generated for Wales (Wales Tourist Board 2001) while the WTTC have produced simulated TSAs for the US states of South Carolina and Hawaii (WTTC 2005). The resource costs involved and data problems, including the shortage of adequately disaggregated I–O tables, remain a barrier to the rapid implementation of subnational level TSAs.

Applications for macroeconomic modelling and forecasting
A TSA represents a 'snapshot' or description of the significance of direct tourism demand within an economy at a point in time and in a strictly defined context. It considers only direct tourist demand, excluding indirect and induced effects of tourism demand, and adopts a narrow definition which requires a direct physical and economic relationship between the visitor and producer to have occurred in the context of a trip. Some commentators have questioned these limitations and some TSAs add an extra layer of indirect impacts through the addition of further tables (Laimer and Smeral 2001). Certainly TSAs cannot provide a measure of the net impacts on the economy of a change in tourism expenditures, although they do provide critical information for developing such estimates. Enormous scope remains for the use of TSAs as an input to macroeconomic modelling and forecasting. The data and common definitions they provide are an invaluable aid to constructing economic impact models for analysis of tourism and the effects of policy changes impacting on tourism. Canada has developed an impact model which draws on its TSA data while other examples include the work done under the Australian STCRC Computable General Equilibrium modelling project to examine the impacts of different tourism source markets and of special events on the Australian and New South Wales economies (Dwyer et al. 2000, 2003a,b and c), and tourism economic modelling carried out by the Queensland State Treasury (OESR 2001).

Indicators of tourism economic performance
For a combination of reasons, including the short time frame in which TSAs have been in existence, their use for benchmarking tourism industry structures and performance remains in its infancy. Measurement complexities and data limitations mean that for most countries the reference year to which a TSA refers will usually be several years prior to the TSA's publication. High resource costs will generally mean that updates will be spread several years apart. Nevertheless, the use of TSAs as a benchmarking tool to assist in policy making and private sector management holds considerable promise. Canada, with its lengthier TSA history, has provided quarterly tourism data benchmarked against its TSA since 1996 (Statistics Canada 1994b, 1999). The United States also produces a limited range of tourism indicators benchmarked to its travel and Tourism Satellite Account. The Australian Bureau of Statistics commenced issuing an initial set of quarterly tourism gross value added indicators benchmarked against Australia's TSA in late 2004. It seems likely that the number of countries

using TSAs as a tool for benchmarking the performance of their tourism industries, and the range of indicators presented, will grow substantially over time.

Conclusions

The development of an agreed methodology and consistent definitions for measuring tourism within an economy has been a significant step forward in the maturing of tourism as an acknowledged and significant sector within national economies. The spread of TSAs can be expected to continue to countries which have not already developed them and with that will come increasing recognition of tourism and understanding of the way it interacts with other areas of the economy. All this is still in its infancy with no country having yet implemented the TSA structure in its entirety. The extensions and potential applications of TSAs are also still in the early stages of development. For researchers national, and in the future sub-national, TSAs present a valuable research resource which they have barely begun to tap.

References

Australian Bureau of Statistics (2000), *Australian National Accounts Tourism Satellite Account* 1997–9' (Cat. No.5249.0), ABS: Canberra, www.abs.gov.au.

Australian Bureau of Statistics (2003), *Australian National Accounts Tourism Satellite Account 2001–2002* (Cat. No.5249.0), ABS: Canberra, www.abs.gov.au.

Cockerell, N. and R. Spurr (2002), 'Overview', in *Best Practice in Tourism Satellite Account Development in APEC Member Economies*, Asia-Pacific Economic Cooperation (APEC) Secretariat Publication #202-TR-01-1: Singapore, June, pp. 9–17.

Dupeyras, A. (2002), 'OECD including the employment dimension in APEC', in N. Cockerell and R. Spurr (eds), *Best Practice in Tourism Satellite Account Development in APEC Member Economies*, Asia-Pacific Economic Cooperation (APEC) Secretariat Publication #202-TR-01-1: Singapore, pp. 35–40.

Dwyer, L., P. Forsyth, J. Madden and R. Spurr (2000), 'Economic impacts of inbound tourism under different assumptions about the macro economy', *Current Issues in Tourism*, 3 (4), 325–63.

Dwyer, L., P. Forsyth and R. Spurr (2003a), 'Inter-industry effects of tourism growth: some implications for destination managers', *Tourism Economics*, 9 (2), 117–32.

Dwyer L., P. Forsyth and R. Spurr (2003b), 'Evaluating tourism's economic effects: new and old approaches', *Tourism Management*, 26 (2), 307–13.

Dwyer, L., P. Forsyth, R. Spurr and T. Ho (2003c), 'Estimating the regional and national economic impacts of tourism growth and special events', *ASEAN Journal of Hospitality and Tourism Management*, 2 (2), July, 118–30.

Holtz-Eakin, D. (2001), 'Capital in a tourism satellite account', *Tourism Economics*, 7 (3), 215–32.

Jones, C., M. Munday, J. Bryan, A. Roberts, I. McNicoll and D. McLellan (2004), 'Tourism satellite accounts first steps – United Kingdom', Welsh Economy Research Unit: Cardiff Business School, www.culture.gov.uk/global/research/statistics_outputs/uk_tsa_fsp.htm, accessed 2 December 2005.

Laimer, P. and E. Smeral (2001), 'A tourism satellite account for Austria: the economics, methodology and results', Statistics Austria and WIFO (Austrian Institute of Economic Research), Article number 20-5940-99, Vienna.

Massieu, A. (2000), 'Developing the tourism satellite account: WTO perspective', in N. Cockerell and R. Spurr (eds), *Best Practice in Tourism Satellite Account Development in APEC Member Economies,* Asia-Pacific Economic Cooperation (APEC) Secretariat Publication #202-TR-01-1, Singapore, pp. 19–34.

Meis, S. and J. Lapierre (1994), 'Measuring tourism's economic importance – a Canadian case study', *Travel and Tourism Analyst,* **2**, 79–89.

Miller, R. (2002), 'A private sector perspective in APEC', in N. Cockerell and R. Spurr (eds), *Best Practice in Tourism Satellite Account Development in APEC Member Economies,* Asia-Pacific Economic Cooperation (APEC) Secretariat Publication #202-TR-01-1, Singapore, pp. 41–52.

OECD (Organization for Economic Cooperation and Development) (1991), 'Manual on tourism economic accounts', Tourism Committee OECD, Document OCDE/GD (91)82, Paris.

OECD, EUROSTAT, UN and WTO (2000), 'Tourism satellite account: recommended methodological framework', Brussels/Luxemburg, Madrid, New York, Paris.

OESR (2001), 'The contribution of international and domestic visitor expenditure to the Queensland economy: 1998–99', Queensland Government Treasury Office of Economic and Statistical Research, www.oesr.qld.gov.au/queensland_by_theme/industry/services/index.shtml, accessed 2 December 2005.

Smith, S.L.J. and D. Wilton (1997), 'TSAs and the WTTC/WEFA methodology: different satellites or different planets?', *Tourism Economics,* **3** (3), 249–63.

Statistics Canada (1994a), 'The tourism satellite account', *National Income and Expenditure Accounts,* 2nd Quarter 1994, Catalogue No.13-001, Statistics Canada, Ottawa.

Statistics Canada (1994b), 'National tourism indicators. Historical estimates 1987–1996', *System of National Accounts,* Catalogue No. 13-220-XPB, Ottawa.

Statistics Canada (1999), 'National tourism indicators, quarterly estimates', *System of National Accounts,* Catalogue No. 13-009-XPB, Ottawa.

United Nations (1993), *System of National Accounts,* New York: United Nations statistics Division.

United Nations (UN) (1993), 'System of National Accounts', New York.

Wales Tourist Board (2001), 'A tourism impact and planning model for Wales: Final report', Cardiff.

WTO (World Tourism Organization) (1994), 'Recommendations on tourism statistics', World Tourism Organization Series M, 83, United Nations: New York.

WTO (1999), 'Tourism satellite account: the conceptual framework', Enzo Paci World Conference on the Measurement of the Economic Impact of Tourism, Nice, France, May.

WTTC (2005), 'Travel and tourism forging ahead: the 2004 travel and tourism economic research', World Travel and Tourism Council, London, http://wttc.org/2004tsa/frameset2a.htm, accessed 2 December 2005.

WTTC, WEFA (1996a), 'Principles for travel and tourism national satellite accounting', World Travel and Tourism Council, London.

WTTC, WEFA (1996b), 'Simulated satellite accounting research, documentation', World Travel and Tourism Council, London.

14 CGE tourism analysis and policy modelling
Adam Blake, Jonathan Gillham
and M. Thea Sinclair

Introduction

Computable general equilibrium (CGE) models are eminently suited to tourism analysis and policy, given their multi-sectoral basis and ability to examine a wide range of actual and counter-factual scenarios. In contrast to partial equilibrium approaches, CGE models can take account of the interrelationships among tourism, other sectors in the domestic economy and foreign producers and consumers. The modelling can be tailored to alternative conditions, such as flexible or fixed prices, alternative exchange rate regimes, differences in the degree of mobility of factors of production and different types of competition. CGE tourism models are particularly helpful to policy makers, who can use them to provide guidance about a wide variety of 'What if?' questions, concerning the range of domestic or international shocks or policy scenarios that can arise.

Given CGE models' versatility and long-standing acceptance and use within the field of international trade and development (Deverajan et al. 1982; de Melo 1988; Shoven and Whalley 1992; François et al. 1996), it is surprising that their application to tourism has been relatively recent and limited in geographical scope. Much of the pioneering work on CGE tourism modelling was undertaken in Australia, with additional research being largely concentrated in the UK and North America, following earlier studies that paved the way for CGE modelling by using the input–output (I–O) approach. Further use of CGE models has been facilitated by the development of Tourism Satellite Accounts (TSAs), which have provided substantial increases in the quantity and quality of the data that can be used in the models. Encouraged by the World Tourism Organisation and the World Travel & Tourism Council, many countries throughout the world now have a TSA that explicitly quantifies the contribution of tourism and travel to different sectors of the economy. TSAs provide an ideal basis for CGE models that can examine the analytical and policy-related questions that the more descriptive TSAs are not designed to answer. It is within the context of further and more geographically widespread TSA development that the use of CGE tourism models throughout the world is taking off.

This chapter will document the main contributions that CGE modelling has made to tourism analysis, initially outlining the theory that underlies the models and subsequently providing an overview of the empirical studies that have been undertaken in the tourism field. The contributions to CGE tourism modelling to date will then be evaluated, in terms of both their theoretical and empirical contributions. The final section will discuss the most recent thinking on the topic and will suggest some directions for further research.

Contributions to CGE analysis

The theoretical framework
Partial equilibrium analysis permits the examination of one sector or market in the economy, in isolation from the remainder. This may be appropriate for some types of analysis but within the context of tourism, it is clear that interrelationships between different economic sectors are fundamental. For example, Nicholson (1995) has pointed out that pricing outcomes in one market usually have effects in others, that these interactions cause feedbacks throughout the economy and may even affect the price–quantity equilibrium in the original market. De Melo and Tarr (1992) argue that such inter-industry linkages are best captured in a general as opposed to a partial equilibrium framework.

The literature on CGE analysis stemmed from developments of the Walrasian general equilibrium (GE) framework, formalised and refined at an early stage by Arrow and Debreu (1954), Debreu (1959) and Arrow and Hahn (1971), who showed that the viability and efficiency of the market system are amenable to analysis. The Arrow–Debreu framework identifies a number of consumers who possess an endowment of factors and commodities. Consumers have individual preferences and are assumed to maximise utility over each commodity. Commodity market demands depend on prices and are continuous, non-negative, homogeneous of degree zero and subject to the condition that at any set of prices, the total value of consumer expenditure equals consumer income. Producers are assumed to maximise profits so that in the case of constant returns to scale, no production activity can do better than break even at equilibrium prices, so long as there are no barriers to entry or exit. Many features can be built into this framework, to tailor it to the different conditions that characterise alternative real-world circumstances. In this way, the framework provides a widely encompassing means of evaluating the effects of policy changes and exogenous shocks on resource allocation and can also permit assessment of the distributional effects of such changes.

CGE models are based on the GE framework and consist of a set of equations, characterising the production, consumption, trade and government activities of the economy, which are solved simultaneously. There are four types of equation (Blake et al. 2001): equilibrium conditions for each market ensure that supply is equal to demand for each good, service, factor of production and foreign currency; income–expenditure identities ensure that the economic model is a closed system; behavioural relationships give economic agents' reactions to changes in prices and incomes, determining consumers' demand for each good and service; production functions determine how much is produced for any given level of factor utilisation. The number of equations and degree of detail to which the economic activities are examined, such as the number of production sectors, factor types and consumer demands, depend upon the availability of data for the economy in question. For example, in the case of the US economy, available data relate to 494 production sectors and 37 types of consumer demand. In contrast, a country such as Malta has data for 27 production sectors and a single type of consumer demand. Thus, the degree of detail of the modelling can be much higher for some countries than for others.

Imperfect competition and the use of dynamics

CGE models can be set up under conditions of perfect or imperfect competition. The former may be suitable for generating the long-run outcomes that occur after prices and factors have adjusted to their equilibrium positions, assuming that there are no significant barriers to competition in the economy in question. However, it has been argued that a perfectly competitive market structure may not be suitable for modelling service provision that is characterised by heterogeneous products with high mark-ups and barriers to entry. In this case, a CGE model incorporating an imperfectly competitive market structure can be developed. An early example of the latter is Harris (1984), who considered the case of small open economies with scale economies and imperfect competition. Subsequent studies incorporated industrial organisation features into multi-country CGE models that were used to examine the effects of regional integration, such as EU membership (Gasiorek et al. 1992; Harrison et al. 1996, 1997). To date, virtually no CGE tourism modelling has been undertaken using an imperfectly competitive framework, partly owing to the increasing complexity of the analysis and calibration required by this approach.

Although there appears to be an intuitive case for incorporating dynamics into CGE models, the majority of models to date are static. In reality, static models may be appropriate for much of the analysis that is undertaken, where inter-temporal allocation is not the major concern, for example, involving inter-country and/or inter-sectoral effects. Palstev (2000) noted that dynamic CGE models can provide reasonably accurate predictions if there are no major structural changes in the economy and if the future growth of fundamental parameters, such as the rate of economic growth, population change and depreciation, is fairly straightforward to forecast. In cases characterised by greater levels of uncertainty, both the forecasts and the predictions provided by the models tend to be less accurate. However, dynamic CGE models can be operationalised using a range of forecasts, depending upon alternative assumptions about the future, thereby assisting businesses or governments to plan for the range of possible outcomes that may occur.

Early applied dynamic general equilibrium models tended to have only one sector (Auerbach et al. 1983; Perroni 1995; Kotlikoff 1998) and emphasised such issues as the impact of tax changes on long-run growth, investment, savings and capital formation (Bhattari 1999). More disaggregated dynamic CGE models have begun to appear, those that are most widely used tending to incorporate different underlying equations. This is illustrated by Ianchoivchina and McDougall's (2000) explanation of the dynamic GTAP (global trade analysis project) approach and Dixon and Rimmer's (2002) explanation of the Monash model, which is a development of the ORANI model (Dixon et al. 1982; Dixon and Parmenter 1996). The overlapping generations (OLG) approach to CGE modelling, as part of the DREAM model, is documented by Madsen and Sorensen (2002), who also attempt to model the non-steady state.

The range of applications of the models to policy issues has been wide, owing to the fact that the models are constructed by project teams whose members have a range of expertise. The models have provided specialist forecasts for such issues as different aspects of the domestic macro economy, world commodity markets, alternative trade policies and a range of tax and tariff issues. International tourism has sometimes been examined using the models; for example, using the Monash model (Adams and Parmenter, 1991, 1992, 1993, 1995). However, with a number of exceptions cited below, relatively little attention has been paid to tourism analysis or tourism policy modelling.

Applications of CGE models to tourism

From input–output to CGE
Initial applications of multi-sectoral modelling to tourism used the specific form of I–O modelling, based on the assumptions of fixed prices and fixed coefficients. I–O modelling played an important role in stimulating general acceptance of multi-sectoral analysis of tourism (for example, Johnson and Moore 1993; Archer and Fletcher 1996). However, a number of the underlying assumptions are not be applicable in many contexts (as noted by

Briassoulis 1991 and Dwyer and Forsyth 1994, among others), so that I–O models can give rise to excessively high estimates of tourism economic impacts. For example, Zhou et al. (1997) examined the impact of a decline in tourism demand in Hawaii, comparing the results obtained from CGE analysis with those obtained from I–O modelling. They found that the results obtained from their I–O model of Hawaii exceeded those obtained from their CGE model. The reason for this is that I–O analysis is nested within the wider CGE framework by imposing fixed prices and fixed coefficients on the CGE model. The imposition of these constraints means that the economic impact estimates that are obtained from I–O models are higher than those that arise from CGE models, as I–O models fail to take account of the crowding-out effects that occur as prices rise. Although the assumptions of fixed prices and fixed coefficients may be valid within some empirical contexts, in cases where the assumptions do not hold, I–O models provide overestimates of economic impacts. The implication is that policy makers should use the more widely encompassing framework of CGE modelling, within which the I–O model is but one of a set of alternative models.

Thus, in recent years, there has been a 'paradigm shift' in favour of CGE models of tourism (Dwyer et al. 2003a, 2004), which supplanted the modified models that were developed to overcome some of the deficiencies of the basic I–O model (Andrew 1997; Wagner 1997; Jensen and Wanhill 2002). The CGE modelling framework is sufficiently flexible to allow for the incorporation of different sets of assumptions concerning consumption and production relationships, in accordance with the empirical circumstances or scenarios under consideration. The development of CGE models designed specifically for tourism has been geared mainly towards examining the economic impact of changes in tourism demand on the macro economy and the different economic sectors within it. Subsequent studies have examined alternative tourism-related policy options that the government can follow.

Research on tourism and the Australian economy
Adams and Parmenter's pathbreaking work (1991, 1992, 1993, 1995) acted as an important catalyst to research on tourism using the CGE modelling framework. They examined the economic impact of changes in tourism demand in a CGE model of Australia, using a 19-sector model with a simplified dynamic structure in which the growth path is determined exogenously. The impact of tourism expansion was predicted for key macroeconomic variables, sectoral and regional growth rates. Their findings illustrate the results that CGE tourism models can provide. For example, in the case of Australia, they found that the appreciation of the exchange rate leads to import substitution and the contraction of the traditional export

sectors of mining and agriculture which, coupled with the high import content of the tourism sector, causes the balance of trade to worsen. Thus, they provided empirical evidence to support Copeland's (1991) argument that some sectors benefit and some lose as the result of tourism expansion.

Some sectors experience direct stimulation (air transport, restaurants, hotels), others experience indirect stimulation due to the rising prices of intermediate inputs supplied to the tourism sectors (food, clothing) and others (traditional exports) contract as the result of adverse exchange rate effects. At the regional level, Queensland, the state with the greatest tourism orientation, experiences an overall negative effect due to the crowding-out of traditional exports, which are highly concentrated in the state. Victoria, with little reliance on traditional exports and where one of the country's principal airports is located, experiences the largest expansion.

Subsequent studies have also examined the economic impact of changes in tourism. Dwyer et al. (2000) considered tourism within the context of the macro economy, allowing for different assumptions about factor supplies, exchange rates, government fiscal policy and the public sector borrowing requirement (PSBR). For example, the assumptions about labour supplies included the alternatives of no skills shortages in tourism or related industries, labour shortages and real wage increases in all or some sectors, fixed money wages and fixed real wages. Assumptions about government policy involved fixed or endogenous government borrowing. The results show how alternative conditions in the macro economy give rise to differences in GDP, real household consumption expenditure, employment, tax revenue and the balance of trade, indicating the way in which CGE modelling can quantify the degree of the different responses.

Dwyer et al. (2003b) have also shown the ways in which tourism analysis using the CGE framework can provide results and implications for policy, some of which may not, at first sight, be evident. They examine tourism demand at the intra-state, inter-state and national levels, by tourists from New South Wales (NSW), Australia and the rest of the world. Their multi-regional CGE tourism model provides both short- and long-run solutions, relating to capital constraints, fixed real wages and a fixed PSBR in the short run but flexibility over the long run. Their results highlight the importance of domestic tourism demand for NSW and international tourism demand for Australia. The policy implication that NSW, along with other states, should promote domestic tourism may give rise to unanticipated costs, in that the gains that one state receives from rising demand may occur at the cost of a loss of demand by others. Hence, there is a case for inter-state policy collaboration. However, the form of collaboration must be based on careful prior analysis if such costs are to be precluded. For example, CGE modelling (Adams and Parmenter 1995, 1999; Dwyer et al. 2003a) has shown that a state (such as Queensland) that fails to increase its market share of a rise in international tourist arrivals may experience a fall in its income and employment. The direction of the change depends upon the composition of tourism expenditure across states, the industrial composition of the gross state products and the related multiplier effects. Thus, there may be a trade-off between the political exigency of ensuring that no state loses as the result of an increase in demand and the total gain to the economy as a whole.

Tourism impacts in the UK, USA and Indonesia
Other studies that have developed CGE models of tourism in different economies have also provided results that are relevant to policy making. Blake et al. (2003a) examined the case of government policy towards foot and mouth disease in the UK. The context for the modelling was the UK government's policy of slaughtering animals that were deemed to have or be at high risk of having the disease and banning access to large areas of the countryside. The foot and mouth outbreak and policy response led to large decreases in domestic and international tourism. The development and application of the CGE tourism model of the UK economy showed that the effects of the tourism decreases were to reduce GDP by £2 billion, compared with a £1.6 billion fall in GDP resulting from the loss of agricultural production. The total cost of the policy was even greater, as it also included the cost of slaughter and carcass disposal, as well as compensation payments. The implication was that a policy geared towards supporting tourism would have been far less costly than the government's policy of supporting agricultural exports by means of slaughtering animals and prohibiting access to many rural areas.

A further study that examined the implications of policies recommended by the government and members of the tourism industry concerned the US government's response to the events of September 11 (Blake and Sinclair 2003). The study involved building a 98-sector model of the US economy, involving 23 types of labour and four types of tourism demand. Examination of the US government's crisis response of subsidising airlines showed that the fall in GDP was under $10 billion compared with a fall of $30 billion that would have occurred without the response. The measures also succeeded in saving around 250 000 jobs that would otherwise have been lost, the air transport sector being the main sector to benefit. The model indicated that the tourism industry's recommended alternative responses of tax credits for travel (that is, tourism consumption) and for the workforce employed in the industry (that is, tourism production) would have been less effective in reducing the losses in income and employment

CGE-related research has also considered the impact of tourism in developing countries. Using a CGE model of the Indonesian economy, Sugiyarto et al. (2003) examined the economic impact of tourism demand and trade liberalisation on income, employment, the government budget and the balance of payments. Trade liberalisation has been a particularly contentious topic for developing countries, many of which perceive it as imposed on them by external international organisations such as the World Bank or the International Monetary Fund. Indonesia is an interesting case study as it has experienced both trade liberalisation and tourism growth during the past decades. Two main macroeconomic policy scenarios were examined, each being considered with and without tourism growth. The first involved a reduction of tariffs on imported commodities and the second involved both tariff reductions and decreases in indirect taxes on domestic commodities. The results showed that the effects of foreign tourism demand are to increase the positive effects of the tariff and tax reductions, particularly with respect to increases in the levels of GDP and employment. At the same time, the adverse effects of the reductions are lower, notably in terms of a reduced balance of payments deficit.

CGE tourism models and taxation
CGE modelling can also provide important insights into policies relating to different types and levels of taxation. Alavalapati and Adamowicz (2000) examined the interactions between tourism, natural resources and the environment in British Columbia, paying specific attention to the effects of an environmental tax on each sector of the economy. They considered two scenarios: one in which environmental damage occurs because of natural resource extraction activities, notably the pulp industry, and the other in which the environment deteriorates because of both natural resource extraction and tourism. The simulated results indicated that the imposition of an environmental tax on the resource sector is beneficial if the environmental damage results only from the extraction activities but that it has adverse effects if the damage results from both resource extraction and tourism. The policy implications are analogous to those provided by the model of the US economy in that they indicate that the policy measure should be targeted directly on the sector that is most directly affected.

Blake (2000) studied the impact of different types of taxation using a CGE model that he developed for the Spanish economy. He showed that foreign tourism activities in Spain are highly taxed relative to other sectors. In the case of domestic tourism, the tax system levies lower rates of taxation on tourism and subsidises domestic transport. Blake examined the issue of near-marginal tax incidence in the Spanish case and found that marginal increases in taxes on foreign tourism are likely to result in higher domestic welfare. This is because the effect of the increases is to reduce the pre-existing distortions in the domestic economy that result from low levels of domestic taxation. The elimination of indirect taxation would benefit foreign tourists but would decrease the quantity of domestic tourism, indicating that the existing tax structure, in its entirety, has the net effect of taxing foreign tourists but subsidising domestic tourists. The removal of value-added tax from accommodation would have adverse effects on the economy. However, an increase in the tax on accommodation would be beneficial over the long run, partly because it would counteract the effects of the subsidies on domestic transport. Blake also pointed out that both the short-run transition costs and any externalities associated with tax changes should also be taken into account in the process of policy formulation.

Indirect commodity tax reform has been examined by Gooroochurn and Milner (2003), in the context of the tourism-dependent economy of Mauritius. They use the concept of marginal excess burden to examine marginal tax reforms in tourism-related and non-tourism sectors. Marginal excess burden (MEB) is a measure of the incremental welfare cost of raising additional revenue from a tax that is already distortionary, while other taxes remain constant. It is, thus, concerned with the welfare effects of marginal tax reform, rather than of lump-sum tax changes that are designed to minimise welfare loss. Gooroochurn and Milner use a CGE model of Mauritius to explore the effects of changes in production taxes and of sales taxes on different sectors of the economy, in alternative contexts of exogenous and endogenous tourist arrivals. The MEB was found to be higher for almost all economic sectors in the case when tourist arrivals are exogenous. However, the MEB was higher for restaurants and hotels when tourist arrivals are endogenous, as the increase in welfare associated with a rise in domestic consumption outweighed the fall in welfare associated with a smaller increase in government revenue. Consideration of the distributional effects of an increase in sales tax on the tourism sector indicated that an increase in the tax rate has smaller adverse effects on poorer than on richer households. The overall results indicate that the structure of indirect taxation in Mauritius is not optimal and that tourism-related sectors appear to be undertaxed, although any tax increases should be considered in conjunction with estimates of the incidence of the tax on tourists and their price elasticity of demand.

The effects of EU membership and associated changes in fiscal policy on the islands of Cyprus and Malta is examined by Blake et al. (2003b), using CGE models that they developed for each of the island states. The results from this study showed that EU membership will be beneficial for both countries and in the long run will lead to modest increases in tourism demand in these destinations. Malta, however, by virtue of having stronger commodity trading links with the EU will have larger benefits from membership, which in the short term may lead to reductions in tourism demand as increased demand for Maltese non-tourism exports attracts resources away from tourism-related sectors and increases costs for these sectors. In the long run Malta is still expected to have an increase in tourism demand as the necessary resource transfers can occur with lower price effects, and therefore fewer tourists will be deterred by rising prices, while reductions in transactions costs for tourists will lead to tourism increases.

Evaluation of CGE tourism analysis
CGE analysis provides a comprehensive framework for examining tourism, particularly given tourism's multi-product composition. However, it is important to evaluate the criticisms that have been levelled at the approach, from both a theoretical and an applied policy perspective. Perhaps the most fundamental point concerns the general equilibrium nature of CGE analysis, involving the assumption of market clearing. It has been argued that although there are forces pushing economies towards equilibrium, there are also forces that prevent such equilibrium outcomes from being achieved. This criticism is one that is levelled at a large part of economic analysis and modelling. However, all models provide a simplified representation of reality and if they provide an effective means of understanding and/or predicting economic interrelationships and outcomes, they are useful. In this context, it is clear that the versatility of CGE analysis allows the models to be tailored to fit different real-world circumstances. Thus, for example, constraints can be imposed on the model to allow for rigidities in factor prices or mobility, exchange rates or government borrowing. Similarly, alternative functional forms can be used to take account of different types of market structure and competition and it is likely that more CGE models involving imperfect competition will be developed in the future.

Other criticisms that have been made of CGE analysis are that it tends to rely on static models, based on I–O tables that are dated. However, an increasing number of dynamic CGE models are now being developed, in line with improvements in software and increasing computational power. Such models may provide a richer set of information than that available from static models, depending on the assumptions that are made about the changes that are occurring in the economy. In cases where economies are not changing rapidly, static models, based on I–O tables that, though dated, provide accurate representations of the ongoing structural interrelationships between different sectors in the economy, may provide useful information and policy guidance. Such models may provide a cost- and time-effective means of policy modelling for economies for which limited data and resources are available, such as developing countries. It has also been argued that the results obtained from CGE models may be particularly sensitive to some of the parameter values that are included in them. If such parameter values are inaccurate, the results obtained from the models are also likely to be inaccurate, as well as misleading for policy purposes. However, sensitivity analysis can be conducted by including alternative parameter values in the model, to determine the bounds within which the model results lie, for changes in the parameter values that are deemed to be realistic.

CGE models provide useful guidance for policy formulation, as they can quantify the effects of actual policies, such as changes in taxation, subsidies or government borrowing, as well as predicting the effects of a range of alternative policies or exogenous shocks. As Dwyer et al. (2004) point out, issues that can be examined by using the models include the impact of changes in domestic and/or international tourism, special events, taxes on tourism or other economic sectors, alternative types of aviation regulation, and tourism crises such as September 11 or the SARS outbreak. The economic impacts can be quantified for changes in the macro economy, in terms of efficiency, GDP, employment, the PSBR, balance of payments and economic welfare. Results can be provided at the international, national, regional and/or local levels, depending upon data availability, and some models have also provided outcomes for different groups of households or workers within the population.

The state of the art in CGE tourism analysis: implications for further research

Future research on CGE tourism analysis is likely to focus on three main areas. The first involves further research on dynamic CGE analysis. This is currently at the frontier of developments in tourism modelling, in terms of both theoretical and empirical contributions. For example, Gómez Gómez et al. (2003) formulate a dynamic GE model that examines the conditions that are required for a tourism tax to contribute a double dividend of environmental improvement and an increase in consumption. They highlight the role of the terms of trade in giving rise to a double dividend in an economy specialising in tourism. Gillham (2005) develops a dynamic model with imperfect competition that can take account of increasing returns to scale in different sectors of the Spanish economy. He uses the model to evaluate the impact of foreign direct investment on tourism and other economic sectors in Spain. He also uses a CGE model developed specifically for the Canary Islands to examine the interrelationships between tourism and trade and taxation policies in the islands (Gillham et al. 2003).

The second area concerns the incorporation of more microeconomic information into CGE models of tourism. This is an innovative area of research on CGE modelling (Hertel et al. 2001; Bourguignon et al. 2002). The incorporation of detailed information at the level of individual households' consumption and firms' production behaviour and their interactions with the macroeconomic representations of economic behaviour characterised by CGE models would improve the quality, accuracy and insights available from the analysis. It would also provide interesting results about the distributional implications of tourism shocks or tourism-related policies. This type of information is a prerequisite for effective strategies to enable tourism development to contribute effectively to poverty alleviation. Such developments in CGE tourism modelling should not be considered in isolation but should complement developments in econometric modelling. The latter can provide more accurate estimates of the parameter values that are included in CGE models, relating to more disaggregated levels of analysis, providing improved means of policy formulation.

Thus, the future of CGE tourism analysis depends upon both improvements in modelling and on the provision of a superior quantity and quality of data. In the context of tourism modelling, such improvements should encompass the provision of a more disaggregated range of data for different types of tourism production and consumption, such as business tourism, short breaks, educational tourism and adventure tourism. Improved data at the regional and local levels would also assist more effective policy formulation, along with better coordination between policy making at the local, regional, national and international levels.

The third area concerns policy analysis. CGE modelling can show the ways in which tourism impacts and policies are integral to wider macroeconomic events and policy making, demonstrating the ways in which shocks or policies that affect one sector of the economy impact upon others. The modelling can shed specific light on a wide range of issues, including foreign direct investment in tourism, tourism productivity and competitiveness, fiscal policies for tourism, policies within wider international groupings such as the European Union, policies for transportation, the environment and related externalities. The future for CGE modelling of tourism is bright, particularly given the context of ongoing development of Tourism Satellite Accounts for countries across the world. Clearly, TSAs provide the means of describing and quantifying tourism's contribution to different economies. However, they must be complemented by tourism modelling if they are to provide businesspeople and governments with effective guidance for dealing with the range of events and policy decisions that have to be made on an ongoing basis. CGE tourism modelling provides a versatile and effective means of examining the wide range of scenarios that can occur.

References

Adams, P.D. and B.R. Parmenter (1991), 'The medium term significance of international tourism for the Australian economy', Report prepared for the Bureau of Tourism Research, part I, Canberra.

Adams, P.D. and B.R. Parmenter (1992), 'The medium term significance of international tourism for the Australian economy', Report prepared for the Bureau of Tourism Research, part II, Canberra.

Adams, P.D. and B.R. Parmenter (1993), 'The medium term significance of international tourism for state economies', Report prepared for the Bureau of Tourism Research, Canberra.

Adams, P.D. and B.R. Parmenter (1995), 'An applied general equilibrium analysis of the economic effects of tourism in a quite small, quite open economy', *Applied Economics*, **27** (10), 985–94.

Adams, P.D. and B.R. Parmenter (1999), 'General equilibrium models', *Valuing Tourism. Methods and Techniques*, Canberra: Bureau of Tourism Research.

Alavalapati, J.R.R. and W.L. Adamowicz (2000), 'Tourism impact modelling for resource extraction regions', *Annals of Tourism Research*, **27** (1), 188–202.

Andrew, B.P. (1997), 'Tourism and the economic development of Cornwall', *Annals of Tourism Research*, **24** (3), 721–35.

Archer, B.H. and J. Fletcher (1996), 'The economic impact of tourism in the Seychelles', *Annals of Tourism Research*, **23** (1), 32–47.

Arrow, K.J. and G. Debreu (1954), 'Existence of an equilibrium for a competitive economy', *Econometrica*, **22**, 265–90.

Arrow, K.J. and F.H. Hahn (1971), *General Competitive Analysis*, San Francisco: Holden-Day.

Auerbach, A.J., L.J. Kotlikoff and J. Skinner (1983), 'The efficiency gains from dynamic tax reform', *International Economic Review*, **24**, 81–100.

Bhattari, K. (1999), 'A forward-looking multisectral general equilibrium tax model of the UK economy', Hull Economic Research Papers No. 269, School of Economic Studies, University of Hull.

Blake, A.T. (2000), 'The economic effects of tourism in Spain', Christel DeHaan Tourism and Travel Research Institute Discussion Paper, www.nottingham.ac.uk/ttri/series.html, 2000/2.

Blake, A.T., R. Durbarry, M.T. Sinclair and G. Sugiyarto (2001), 'Modelling tourism and travel using tourism satellite accounts and tourism policy and forecasting models', Christel DeHaan Tourism and Travel Research Institute Discussion Paper, www.nottingham.ac.uk/ttri/series.html, 2001/4.

Blake, A.T. and M.T. Sinclair (2003), 'Tourism crisis management: US response to September 11', *Annals of Tourism Research*, **30** (4), 813–32.

Blake, A.T., M.T. Sinclair and G. Sugiyarto (2003a), 'Quantifying the impact of foot and mouth disease on tourism and the UK economy', *Tourism Economics*, **9** (4), 449–65.

Blake, A.T., M.T. Sinclair and G. Sugiyarto (2003b), 'Tourism and the effects of EU accession on Malta and Cyprus', Paper Presented at the Conference on Tourism Modelling and Competitiveness, Paphos, Cyprus, October.

Bourguignon, F., A. Robilliard and S. Robinson (2002), 'Representative versus real households in the macroeconomic modelling of inequality', Paper presented at the Development Economics Study Group Annual Conference, University of Nottingham, April, www.shef.ac.uk/uni/projects/desg/cinfo/cpapers/robinson.pdf.

Briassoulis, H. (1991), 'Methodological issues: tourism input–output analysis', *Annals of Tourism Research*, **18**, 435–49.

Copeland, B.R. (1991), 'Tourism, welfare and de-industrialisation in a small open economy', *Economica*, **58** (4), 515–29.

de Melo, J. (1988), 'Computable general equilibrium models for trade policy analysis in developing countries: a survey', *Journal of Policy Modelling*, **10** (4), 469–503.

de Melo, J. and D. Tarr (1992), *General Equilibrium Analysis of US Foreign Trade Policy*, London: Oxford University Press.

Debreu, G. (1959), *Theory of Value*, New York: Wiley.

Devarajan, S., J.D. Lewis and S. Robinson (1982), *General Equilibrium Models for Development Policy*, New York: Cambridge University Press.

Dixon, P.B. and B.R. Parmenter (1996), 'Computable general equilibrium modelling for policy analysis and forecasting', in H. Aman, D. Kendrick and J. Rust (eds), *Handbook of Computational Economics*, 1, Amsterdam: Elsevier Science, pp. 4–85.

Dixon, P.B., B.R. Parmenter, J. Sutton and D.P. Vincent (1982), *ORANI: A Multisectoral Model of the Australian Economy*, Amsterdam: North-Holland.

Dixon, P.B. and M. Rimmer (2002), 'Forecasting and policy analysis with a dynamic CGE model of Australia', Preliminary working paper, Monash University: Centre of Policy Studies, OP-90.

Dwyer, L. and P. Forsyth (1994), 'Foreign tourism investment: motivation and impact', *Annals of Tourism Research*, **20** (4), 751–68.

Dwyer, L., P. Forsyth, J. Madden and R. Spurr (2000), 'Economic impacts of inbound tourism under different assumptions regarding the macroeconomy', *Current Issues in Tourism*, **3** (4), 325–63.

Dwyer, L., P. Forsyth and R. Spurr (2003a), 'Inter-industry effects of tourism growth: implications for destination managers', *Tourism Economics*, **9** (2), 117–32.

Dwyer, L, P. Forsyth, R. Spurr and T. Ho (2003b), 'Tourism's contribution to a state economy: a multi-regional general equilibrium analysis', *Tourism Economics*, **9** (4), 431–48.

Dwyer, L., P. Forsyth and R. Spurr (2004), 'Evaluating tourism's economic effects: new and old approaches', *Tourism Management*, **25** (3), 207–317.

François, J.F., B. McDonald and H. Nordström (1996), 'A user's guide to Uruguay Round assessments', CEPR Discussion Paper, 1410, Centre for Economic Policy Research, London.

Gasiorek, M., A. Smith and T. Venables (1992), 'Trade and welfare; a general equilibrium model', in L.A. Winters (ed.), *Trade Flows and Trade Policy After 1992*, Cambridge: Cambridge University Press, 35–61.

Gillham, J. (2006), 'The economic interrelationships of tourism: a computable general equilibrium analysis', PhD thesis, University of Nottingham.

Gillham, J., A. Blake, R. Hernández Martín, G. Reed and M.T. Sinclair (2003), 'Modelling the impact of tourism on a small island economy', Paper Presented at the Conference on Tourism Modelling and Competitiveness, Paphos, Cyprus, October.

Gómez Gómez, C.M., J. Lozano Ibáñez and J. Rey-Maquieira Palmer (2003), 'Tourism taxation in a dynamic model of an economy specialised in tourism', Paper Presented at the Conference on Tourism Modelling and Competitiveness, Paphos, Cyprus, October.

Gooroochurn, N. and C. Milner (2003), 'Assessing indirect tax reform in a tourism-dependent developing country', Paper Presented at the Conference on Tourism Modelling and Competitiveness, Paphos, Cyprus, October.

Harris, J.R. (1984), 'Applied general equilibrium analysis of small open economies with scale economies and imperfect competition', *American Economic Review*, **74**, 1016–32.

Harrison, G., T. Rutherford and D. Tarr (1996), 'Increased competition and completion of the market in the European community', *Journal of Economic Integration*, **11** (3), 332–65.

Harrison, G., T. Rutherford and D. Tarr (1997), 'Economic implications for Turkey of a customs union with the European Union', *European Economic Review*, **41**, 861–70.

Hertel, T.W., P.V. Preckel, J.A.L. Cranfield and M. Ivanic (2001), 'Poverty impacts of multilateral trade liberalization', unpublished research paper available from the Center for Global Trade Analysis, Purdue University, West Lafayette, IN, USA.

Ianchoivchina, E. and R. McDougall (2000), 'Theoretical structure of dynamic GTAP', GTAP Technical Paper, 17, Purdue University, West Lafayette, IN, USA: Department of Economics.

Jensen, T.C. and S. Wanhill (2002), 'Tourism's taxing times: value added tax in Europe and Denmark', *Tourism Management*, **23**, 67–79.

Johnson, R. and E. Moore (1993), 'Tourism impact estimation', *Annals of Tourism Research*, **20**, 279–83.

Kotlikoff, L.J. (1998), 'Intergenerational transfers and savings', Journal of Economic Perspectives, **2**, 41–58.

Madsen, A.D. and M.L. Sorensen (2002), 'Effects of trade and market integration in a small open economy – dynamic CGE approach, Danish rational economic agents model (DREAM)', Working Papers Series, Denmark: Danish Ministry of Finance.

Nicholson, W. (1995), *Microeconomic Theory: Basic Principles and Extensions*, London: Thomson Learning.

Palstev, S. (2000), *Moving from Static to Dynamic General Equilibrium Economic Models*, Department of Economics, University of Colorado, Boulder, CO, http://debreu.colorado.edu/papers/move.pdf.

Perroni, C. (1995), 'Assessing the dynamic efficiency gains of tax reform when human capital is endogenous', *International Economic Review*, **36**, 907–25.

Shoven, J. and J. Whalley (1992), *Applying General Equilibrium*, Cambridge: Cambridge Surveys of Economic Literature.

Sugiyarto, G., A. Blake and M.T. Sinclair (2003), 'Tourism and globalization: economic impact in Indonesia', *Annals of Tourism Research*, **30** (3), 683–701.

Wagner, J.E. (1997), 'Estimating the economic impacts of tourism', *Annals of Tourism Research*, **24** (3), 592–608.

Zhou, D., J.F. Yanagida, U. Chakravorty and P. Leung (1997), 'Estimating economic impacts of tourism', *Annals of Tourism Research*, **24** (1), 76–89.

15 Economic evaluation of special events
Larry Dwyer, Peter Forsyth and Ray Spurr

Introduction

Special events are now highly sought after in many countries, regions and cities, internationally. Special events may be defined as, 'major one-time or recurring events of limited duration, developed primarily to enhance awareness, appeal and profitability of a tourism destination' (Ritchie 1984: 2). Events are generally seen as increasing economic activity and creating new jobs resulting from the net increase in demand for goods and services they generate. Governments are often prepared to offer generous funding incentives to attract events, and to allocate large expenditure to upgrading the facilities needed for the events. Several states in Australia, for example, have now set up events corporations, to win events, to facilitate their operations and sometimes to subsidise them. In some cases, they are prepared to enter expensive bidding wars to secure footloose events. Thus, Victoria bid the Formula 1 Grand Prix away from South Australia, and also bid the Motor Cycle Grand Prix away from New South Wales, which had previously bid it away from Victoria. What can be an economic gain for one state can be an economic loss for another, and Australia as a whole need not gain because the event is held within its borders. Clearly, this competitive federalism, whereby states spend real resources in shifting events from one state to another, with little or no gain to the nation, can be very wasteful. Probably the main reason for this growing enthusiasm for events is their perceived economic benefits. It is recognised that there may be other perceived benefits from events, such as 'putting a city on the map', facilitating business networking and civic pride. These aspects are very difficult to test or evaluate. Granted this, however, much of the public justification of events funding centres around the perceived positive economic impacts of events.

The theme of this chapter is that the economic impacts and net benefits of events, if rigorously assessed, are very much lower than those invariably claimed. The techniques of analysis widely used have inherent biases, which lead to overstatement of impacts on output and jobs. As a result there is likely to be misallocation of events funding, and excessive overall spending in promoting events. We begin by summarising the current state of event evaluation and promotion, and then examine what is wrong with it. Next, highlighting a recent study undertaken by the authors, we outline how the economic impacts and benefits of events can be estimated much more accurately using computable general equilibrium (CGE) modelling. We then argue that arguments advanced by proponents of the continued use of I–O models in event impact analysis are based on misunderstandings of the preferred CGE model. Finally, we identify what is needed to improve evaluation, and discuss the institutional framework under which this might come about.

Event impact assessment

The theoretical basis of economic impact assessment of special events is to be found in the pioneering work of Burns et al. 1986 in their study of the Adelaide Grand Prix. Since then, contributions have been made by several authors (including Getz 1987; Crompton and McKay 1994; Crompton 1995; Dwyer and Forsyth 1997; Delpy and Li 1998; Mules 1999; Dwyer et al. 2000c). The key input to economic impact assessment is the amount of expenditure by visitors, accompanying persons, organisers, delegates, sponsors and others, for example, media. Only that proportion of expenditure which represents an injection of 'new money' into an area is relevant to the calculation of the economic impacts. This proportion of expenditure is referred to as 'inscope' expenditure (Burns et al. 1986). Since this inscope expenditure has secondary (indirect plus induced) effects on the economy, multipliers are used to determine the contribution to value added and to employment. It has also been recognised that the holding of an event may also generate what are called 'intangible' costs and benefits Dwyer et al. 2000c). By their nature, these costs and benefits are not quantifiable as precisely or objectively as are the economic impacts. For the most part, discussion has focused on the estimation of the economic impacts of events.

Economic impact studies invariably claim that events will produce big increases in output (measured in terms of gross state product (GSP) or GDP) and jobs – often these are referred to (incorrectly) as 'economic benefits'. The economic impact on Victoria of events other than the Commonwealth Games is claimed to be an increase in GSP of A\$277.3 million in a year (Victorian Auditor-General 2001). The gain to Victorian GSP as a result of the Commonwealth Games is projected to be A\$373 million (ibid.). A study of the Formula 1 Grand Prix estimated that the gain to GSP would be A\$130.7 million, and the gain in tax receipts would be A\$9.8 million. The Motor Cycle Grand Prix in 1997 was estimated to have added A\$54 million to GSP and A\$3.7 million to tax receipts (ibid.).

Events strategies: what is wrong?
There are three serious weaknesses in the ways government agencies evaluate and promote special events:

1. Because biased evaluation techniques are used, which generate high multipliers, the economic impacts of events have been grossly overstated, leading to support for events which do not deliver promised changes in output and jobs. More accurate information on the economic impacts of events, on host and non-host states, will provide valuable information on the extent to which events strategies are a zero-sum game, or produce net benefits for the nation.
2. There is a failure to distinguish between the impacts on output and jobs, and the net benefits which this increased economic activity brings.
3. Because the benefits to one region are often at the expense of other regions, events will be supported which do not produce net benefits for the national economy.

The outcome of these weaknesses in strategy is that events do not deliver the benefits which are expected, and government support for events is often wasted on events which are uneconomic. Overall, there is highly likely to be excessive funding of events; the funds allocated could be better used elsewhere.

Derivation of the multipliers

Input–output models
Something which is remarkable about event assessment internationally is that, except for some isolated sceptics (Matheson 2002; Matheson and Baade 2003) claims of enormous economic impacts or benefits from events have been so uncritically accepted. The multipliers used to estimate impacts on output, income and employment are invariably based on I–O models (Bushnell and Hyle 1985; Turko and Kelsey 1992; Dawson et al. 1993; Wang 1997; Donnelly et al. 1998; Crompton 1999). I–O models are based on the following assumptions (Briassoulis 1991; Fletcher 1994):

- All inputs and resources are supplied freely and no resource constraints exist. In real-world economies, however, resource constraints generally are present and must be taken into account when estimating impacts of the increased visitor expenditure on economic activity.
- There are constant proportions between inputs and output, between labour and output, and between value added and output.

These assumptions are unrealistic if relative prices change and cause businesses to change the composition of their inputs, or if resources must be drawn away from other parts of the economy.

● All price effects and financial effects are treated as being neutral.

In reality there are likely to be capacity constraints in the economy which cause prices and costs to rise in an expansion of economic activity. If the prices of inputs and wages increase due to an increase in demand, the net impact of output and jobs from the increase in demand is much less than the initial injection of spending. These price rises will limit the extent of the expansion; and may even lead to contractions in economic activity in some sectors.

● The behaviour of the government budget sector is treated as being neutral.

In reality tax revenue will increase in an economic expansion, enabling the government to increase spending, reduce other taxes, or some combination of the two.

Multipliers based upon I–O models have been widely used in estimating the economic impacts of stadium investments and attracting major league teams to cities in the US. Their use has been attacked on both theoretical and empirical grounds. They are claimed to exaggerate the impacts on economic activity (Noll and Zimbalist 1997; Siegfried and Zimbalist 2000). A number of *ex post* studies have now been carried out, but they have been unable to detect any significant impacts on economic activity resulting from the stadiums or the attraction of major league teams (Siegfried and Zimbalist 2002).

A recent article entitled 'A guide for undertaking economic impact studies: the Springfest festival' by Crompton et al. (2001) is noteworthy for its use of the IMPLAN I–O modelling system. While these authors discuss the validity of different multiplier measures, warning the reader against the uncritical acceptance of several types of economic impact estimates, the appropriateness of the (I–O) model itself remains unanalysed. This is unfortunate given that the article purports 'to offer a generalizable model for undertaking economic impact studies that tourism professionals can use to implement similar studies in their own communities' (2001: 79). In the same journal issue, in an article that purports to develop 'a standardized method for assessing economic impacts associated with tourist events', it is stated that 'Input–Output analysis may be applied to assess secondary, indirect or induced impacts of the initial tourist expenditure'

(Tyrrell and Johnson 2001: 94). Elsewhere, they state that without accurate visitor expenditure estimates, 'even the most detailed, theoretically appropriate [sic] input–output model will provide misleading results' (ibid.). While aware of some of the limitations of the I–O method, these authors explicitly assume that the technique has an important ('theoretically appropriate'?) role to play in event assessment.

The results of 30 economic impact studies undertaken in the US have been summarised by Crompton (1999). Crompton's commentary is interesting because he devotes a good deal of discussion to the need for accurate and objective presentation of the economic impact results to make the case for government and organisational support and 'guidance for priority in promotional effort' (p. 58). And yet, accepting the arguments presented in this paper, the IMPLAN I–O model underlying Crompton's results render his estimates of limited real use to these decision makers.

Because of the very restrictive assumptions upon which it is based, I–O modelling is rejected in most other areas of economic evaluation. Events evaluation by tourism researchers and consultants is one of the few areas left in which I–O/multiplier models are still used for evaluation and policy advice purposes. In industrialised countries such as Australia, the US and the UK, I–O techniques are recognised as being based on an incomplete model of the economy, and thus inappropriate for economic impact assessment (Dixon and Parmenter 1996; Partridge and Rickman 1998; Harrison et al. 2000; Fossati and Wiegard 2001). If the government were to fund a new road, there would be a requirement that it be evaluated using cost–benefit analysis (CBA). If there is a need to evaluate the impact on GDP or jobs of some change, such as in motor vehicle protection, greenhouse gas emissions limits or in tax structures, CGE models would be used. I–O analysis would not be used. Sometimes, both CGE models and CBA are used side by side, as they were in the study of the Melbourne City Link road project (Allen Consulting 1996). In Australian economic policy discussion, for example, these techniques have almost completely supplanted I–O analysis, except in areas such as industry assistance (where project boosterism is still rife).

I–O models estimate the positive economic impacts on spending brought about by changes such as special events; however they do not measure the equally real negative economic impacts. An event brings additional demand to the economy – as this demand is met, additional output and jobs are created. However, the process does not end with the positive effects. I–O analysis essentially assumes that all resources and inputs are provided freely, and that no resource constraints exist. In real-life economies, when more resources are required in one area of the economy, they are drawn away, at least in part, from productive activities elsewhere in the economy. Prices of inputs and wages get bid up, and other activity is discouraged. The net impact on output and jobs from a boom in demand, such as would be created by a special event, is much less than the initial injection of spending.

CGE models
The deficiencies in I–O analysis have given rise to the development of CGE models, which are supplanting it as a means of estimating the impact on output and jobs of a change in spending. CGE models represent world best practice in assessing economy-wide economic impacts of changes in tourism expenditure. CGE analysis is being employed to explore the economic impacts of policy initiatives and frameworks and broader changes as diverse as hazardous waste management, trade liberalisation, tariff protection, environment–economy interactions, structural adjustment, agricultural stabilisation programmes, technological change, labour market deregulation, financial market deregulation, taxation changes, macroeconomic reform, economic transition, international capital linkages, public infrastructure and industry sector studies (Dixon and Parmenter 1996; Harrison et al. 2000; Yao and Liu 2000). Proponents of CGE modelling point out that economy-wide, interactive, effects must be taken into account in determining the impacts of increased tourism expenditure on a destination. Resource supplies are constrained, and greater resource requirements in one part of the economy will lead to lower use, and output, in other parts of the economy. Prices for goods and services which are used as inputs will be bid up, discouraging production elsewhere in the economy. When there is an increase in spending in the economy from visitors from abroad, the exchange rate will be bid up, discouraging exports and economic activity in other parts of the economy. Many of the impacts which I–O analysis ignores will be in the opposite direction from that of the initial spending boost – thus it will lead to an overestimate of the final impact on overall activity. Depending on the key relationships in the economy, the extent of this overestimation could be very large (Dwyer et al. 2004b). These mechanisms can only properly be taken into account using CGE rather than I–O modelling (Dwyer et al. 2000a, 2004a).

CGE models are being used increasingly in assessing the economic impacts of tourism (Zhou et al. 1997; Adams and Parmenter 1999; Blake 2000; Blake et al. 2000, 2003; Sugiyarto et al. 2002; Dwyer et al. 2003b, 2004b). They are also beginning to be used in evaluating the impacts of events – see Industry Commission (1996, Appendix 7) and NSW Treasury and Centre for Regional Economic Analysis (1997). Nonetheless, tourism researchers seem to be relatively unaware of this extensive and evolving CGE modelling literature with its potential to inform impact analysis and policy making in their own field. Meanwhile, adjusting I–O models to render them more realistic (Manete 1999; West and Gamage 2001) does not address the key limitation, namely that by assuming perfectly elastic supply of inputs, they take into account only the positive, but not the negative, impacts.

The use of a CGE model in event assessment can be illustrated using results generated by the CGE modelling project supported by the CRC for Sustainable Tourism. The model used was a development of the Monash MMRF multi-regional model, specially adapted to enable detailed modelling of tourism issues. It consists of three models: NSW, Rest of Australia and Australia wide. It has been used to analyse the economic impacts of events in NSW (Dwyer et al. 2005).

I–O versus CGE results: a comparison
In 1996, the Industry Commission in Australia undertook an evaluation of the Formula 1 Grand Prix using CGE technique, which are more rigorous than those used by consultants commissioned by the state government (Industry Commission 1996). It found that the impacts on economic activity were much lower than those claimed, and it also highlighted the negative impacts on states other than the host state (see also Banks 2002). The methodology used in the state-based studies of the Formula 1 Grand Prix has been severely criticised (Economists at Large & Associates 2000).

A CGE model was recently employed to estimate the economic impacts of the Sydney Olympics (Arthur Andersen/CREA 1999). The model enabled estimates to be made of the economic impact of the event on New South Wales and Australia for each of the pre-event, event year and post-event phases. Results indicated that in the post-event phase (to 2006), New South Wales would suffer reductions in real GSP, real consumption and employment, while nationally, there would be a reduction in real consumption and employment.

In 2003 the Department of Industry Tourism and Resources commissioned an economic evaluation of the Rugby World Cup using a CGE model. This model will enable estimation of any adverse impacts of the Rugby World Cup on some states.

A recent study compared the results of using CGE and I–O modelling to estimate the economic impacts of a special event. The expenditure data were based on that for the Qantas Australian Grand Prix 2000. The I–O model used was that contained within the CGE model developed by the CRC economic modelling group (Dwyer et al. 2003c). The project team estimated the economic impacts of the event on the NSW and Australian economies, and on the economy of the rest of Australia using both a CGE and an I–O model. The comparison revealed substantial differences between the techniques with respect to estimates of the economic impacts.

The assumptions of the I–O and CGE models used to assess the event are displayed in Table 15.1. The expenditure data fed into the I–O and CGE models included the total injected amount of expenditure associated with visitation and administration of the event from interstate and overseas sources (A$51.25 million). Expenditure injected from interstate sources was A$29.5 million, while expenditure injected from overseas was A$22.7 million. The same as for visitor expenditure, injected organiser expenditure was allocated to the main industry sectors.

Differences in real output, GSP and employment
Table 15.2 contains estimated impacts of the event that injects A$51.25 million into the NSW economy. The impacts are distinguished according to the model used (I–O, CGE) and the impact on the host state (NSW), the rest of Australia (RoA) and the nation as a whole (Aus). I–O modelling projects a much greater impact on real output on both New South Wales and Australia (A$112.0 million and A$120.1 million), as compared to CGE modelling (A$56.70 million and A$24.46 million).

The differences in the projected impacts of the event on real output are substantial. The percentage by which the I–O model overestimates the impact on real output, compared to CGE, is 80 per cent for New South Wales and 491 per cent for Australia. The output multiplier for New South Wales is 2.185 using the I–O model but only 1.106 using the CGE model. For Australia as a whole, the I–O model yields an output multiplier of 2.343 whereas the CGE model yields a substantially smaller output multiplier of 0.487.

A further difference relates to the magnitude of the impacts on the state and the nation as a whole. I–O modelling projects that the effects of the event on real output are A$8.1 million greater for Australia than New South Wales, a difference of just under 7 per cent. The CGE model, however, projects that the impact on Australia ($24.46 million) is much less than the impact on the state (A$56.70 million). In percentage terms the impact on real output in Australia is only 43 per cent of the impact on the state.

Another difference between the two sets of results relates to the effect on real output in the rest of Australia. The I–O model projects an increased real output, GSP and employment in RoA as interstate firms supply industrial or consumer goods and services to meet the additional demand associated with the event in New South Wales. The CGE model, in contrast, projects decreased real output, GSP and employment in RoA. This is due to the fact that the expenditure by interstate visitors to the event must be financed by reduced expenditure within other states.

Table 15.1   Assumptions underpinning the models

Assumptions of I–O model	Assumptions of CGE model
All final demand components are exogenous. The assumption is that final demand components (private consumption, exports, private investment etc.) are not explained within the model but are given exogenously; that is, outside the model	All main final demand components are endogenous. The model provides theories to explain the behaviour of these final demand components following an expenditure shock to the system. While final demand components such as real public investment and government consumption are determined exogenously, the nominal values of these components are changed under the simulations as prices vary
Capital, labour and land are endogenous. This assumption implies that there is an elastic supply of these factors which enables output to be increased with no constraints	Capital and land are given exogenously – essentially a short-run approach is adopted. It would be feasible to allow all factors to vary, as they would in the long run. However a short-term event is unlikely to result in significant changes in the capital stock. Thus we assume: fixed public investment and fixed capital
There are no price-induced substitution effects. This implies that there are no price changes affecting the behaviour of consumers, suppliers, investors etc. Real wages are fixed and no changes occur in the real exchange rate	Price-induced substitution effects occur. Real wages are flexible; regional nominal and income real wages are allowed to move differently among the states. Flexible private investment, where private investment is a function of the rate of return on investment
Government expenditure remains constant, and is given exogenously (unless a change in government expenditure is the assumed shock to the system)	Government budget deficits are fixed. Government expenditures are variable. Since changes in economic activity affects government receipts, and ultimately affect spending, which in turn affects economic activity, these must be taken into account. Tax rates are fixed. We assume that additional taxation revenue leads to equal new public expenditures
State employment is flexible (perfectly elastic). This implies that sufficient additional labour is available to produce the goods and services required by the event	State employment can be regarded as fixed (zero elasticity) or flexible (perfectly elastic). For the purpose of the comparison, simulations were undertaken using both assumptions and the results were averaged. Neither of these two extremes is considered ikely, though it is common to report them to illustrate the sensitivity of the results to the assumptions. In order to simplify presentation, we have taken a mid-point between the extremes – this should give a best estimate which is realistic
Fixed nominal exchange rate and world price of imports	Fixed nominal exchange rate and world price of imports

Table 15.2   I–O and CGE output, GSP and employment multipliers
for NSW and RoA, for a large event held in NSW
(shock = A$51.25m)

Macro variables	NSW (I–O)	RoA (I–O)	Aus (I–O)	NSW CGE	RoA CGE	Aus CGE
Change in real output ($m)	112.00	8.1	120.1	56.70	−32.24	24.46
Change in real GSP/GDP ($m)	38.90	4.4	43.3	19.41	−10.61	8.80
Change in employment (number of jobs)	521	71	592	318	−189	129
Output multiplier	2.2	0.16	2.3	1.2	−0.3	0.9
GSP/GDP (or value-added multipliers)	0.8	0.09	0.8	0.4	−0.2	0.3
Employment multiplier (per $m)	10.2	1.4	11.6	6.2	−3.7	2.5

The absolute differences in value added yielded by the two methods are smaller but the percentage differences are even greater than the percentage differences in real output. On the I–O model, the projected change in GSP/GDP due to the event is A$38.9 million for New South Wales and A$43.3 million for Australia, a difference of +11 per cent. In contrast, the CGE model projects a change in GSP/GDP of A$19.41 million for the state and A$8.80 million for Australia, a difference of −55 per cent. The value-added multiplier using I–O modelling is 0.759 and 0.844 for New South Wales and Australia, respectively, as compared to value-added multipliers of 0.432 and 0.267 using CGE analysis. Interestingly, while substantially higher than the CGE value added multipliers, the value-added I–O multipliers are themselves less than those I–O multipliers employed in many event impact assessment studies in Australia and internationally (Dwyer et al. 2000c). This suggests that the I–O multipliers used are not themselves exaggerated so as to bias the comparison.

The two models give different employment projections also. The projected increase in employment using an I–O model is 521 (full-time equivalent) jobs in NSW and 592 jobs throughout Australia. Using a CGE model the projected employment effects are 318 jobs and 129 jobs, respectively. The CGE employment projections are 61 and 22 per cent of the I–O employment projections. Once again the I–O model projects increased employment in RoA whereas the CGE model projects relatively large job losses in RoA. The I–O employment multiplier is 10.169 for New South Wales and 11.548 for Australia, while the CGE employment multipliers are 6.2 and 2.5, respectively. Similarly as for the value-added multiplier, the employment multiplier generated within the I–O model is conservative compared to other studies using I–O models (Dwyer et al. 2000c). That said, the estimation of employment changes using I–O models is fraught with problems (Dwyer et al. 2000c) and use of I–O-generated employment multipliers is eschewed by even the strongest advocates of I–O (Mules 1999).

Industry differences
I–O modelling projects a positive change in output and employment in all industries in New South Wales except oil, natural gas and brown coal where no change is projected. In contrast, the CGE model projects reduced output and employment in several industries in New South Wales. Table 15.3 indicates the impact of the event-related expenditure on employment in various industries in New South Wales and RoA. Only the ten industries most positively impacted upon are shown.

Both models project that hotels, culture and recreation, air transport, repairs, retail trade, and road transport are included in the top ten industries experiencing the greatest positive impacts on employment. The I–O model indicates that food and drink, agriculture and wholesale trade experience relatively large positive increases in employment, while, as we shall see below, the CGE model projects a decline in employment in each of these sectors. In contrast, the CGE model projects relatively large increased employment in construction, health and administration/other while the I–O model projects increases of only 0.0056, 0.0028 and 0.0034 per cent, respectively, for these industries (not shown in Table 15.3).

Table 15.3   Projected greatest positive impact on industry employment in New South Wales resulting from event-related expenditure (percentage change)

I–O model	CGE model
Hotels (0.1404)	Hotels (0.1598)
Air transport (0.0588)	Culture/recreation (0.0723)
Culture/recreation (0.0556)	Repairs (0.0355)
Repairs (0.0357)	Air transport (0.0348)
Food and drink (0.0290)	Construction (0.0227)
Road transport (0.0278)	Retail trade (0.0201)
Retail trade (0.0193)	Health (0.0195)
Agriculture (0.0163)	Road transport (0.0191)
Wholesale trade (0.0136)	Administration/other (0.0179)
Finance/business services (0.0128)	Welfare (0.0148)

A major difference between the two modelling techniques is that CGE modelling projects that the event-related expenditure has negative impacts on the level of employment of some industries, both in NSW and RoA. Table 15.4 lists the industries experiencing the largest reductions in employment in the host state. Interestingly, the CGE model projects reduced employment in the host state for some industries that might be regarded as closely associated with tourism – motor vehicles, water transport and transport services (and also rail transport, communications and insurance not shown in the table).

In some cases, the reduced employment in the industry within the state is offset to some extent by expanded employment in RoA (for example, water transport, motor vehicles, other manufacturing, metal products, chemicals, TCF, wood, paper, black coal and agriculture). In the case of some industries, however, the decline in employment in NSW is reinforced by a decline also in RoA (mineral ore, aluminium, magnesium and transport services). Other industries which experience reduced employment in both the state and RoA include petroleum refining, non-metal products, urban gas distribution, rail transport, transport services and communication. Wholesale trade, which I–O modelling indicates experiences a relatively large increase in employment in the state (see Table 15.3), is shown to experience a decline in employment in both New South Wales and the RoA when the CGE model is used.

Projected estimates of the economic impacts of events based on I–O models are incapable of identifying industries that may contract as a result

Table 15.4 CGE model: projected greatest negative impact on industry employment resulting from event-related expenditure (percentage change)

Industry	NSW	RoA
Water transport	−0.0883	0.0036
Motor vehicles	−0.0528	0.0064
Other manufacturing	−0.0511	0.0025
Metal products	−0.0458	0.0033
Chemicals	−0.0423	0.0030
Mineral ore	−0.0393	−0.0008
Aluminium, magnesium	−0.0377	−0.0013
TCF, wood, paper	−0.0328	0.0040
Transport services	−0.0303	−0.0055
Black coal	−0.0269	0.0006
Agriculture	−0.0181	0.0037

of the event. Two recent examples are the pre-Olympics estimates for the 1996 Games in Atlanta (Humphreys and Plummer 1995), and the projected impacts of the proposed World Cup in South Africa in 2010 (South Africa Football Association 2000). In neither case were interactive industry effects accounted for in the analysis, leading to greatly exaggerated economic impacts (Matheson 2002).

Although the comparison of I–O and CGE presented here is based on one particular event, the results are indicative of the types of differences that would exist for other events. That said, it would be useful to develop other examples. In particular, it would be helpful to see what the differences look like for different kinds of events (large versus small, sport versus arts and so on) in different settings (urban versus rural), using real data. This is an area for future research.

Event assessment in practice

What guidance on the model to use can be given to those individuals or organisations who wish to assess an event? Although even the strongest advocates of I–O would generally agree that the CGE approach is conceptually superior, several types of (interrelated) claims are often made for continuing to use I–O models to estimate the multiplier effects of events:

1. The choice of model depends on the size of the event.
2. The choice of model depends on the location of the event.
3. The choice of model does not matter since adjustments can be made to I–O results to make them more realistic.
4. CGE models are required to make too many assumptions making them too complex to use.
5. CGE models are costly, and often unavailable.

On the basis of such arguments, I–O analysis continues to receive support in some quarters as the preferred technique of event assessment. We need to consider carefully the nature of each claim and the qualifications that must be made to each.

Size of event

Does the choice of model depend on the size of the event? It is sometimes claimed that CGE is appropriate for calculating the impacts of large events, but that it is not suitable to calculate the impacts of small events and that I–O can be used in this context (Mules 1999).

Proponents of CGE analysis in event assessment respond that it is not the size of the event which determines the appropriate model for analysing the impacts. For a small event the negative impacts on economic activity elsewhere will be small, though they may still be significant relative to the positive effects of the event on activity, and thus it is necessary to take them into account. Small events have much the same types of impact as large events, and they work through the economy in exactly the same way. In the case of a large event, such as the Olympics or the Rugby World Cup, the negative impacts on other parts of the regional and national economies are obvious – accommodation prices are bid up, as is the price of skilled labour. For a small event these effects still exist, though they are not so obvious, For example, they impact on factor and other input prices in the same way, only their magnitude is smaller. Strictly, any size event will have interactive effects that must be accounted for. Small changes can be analysed using CGE analysis just as readily and correctly as large changes. Thus, in principle, CGE analysis should be used for events, however small they might be.

The source of an increase in expenditure brought about by an event can affect how large its economic impact will be. An increase in spending as a result of interstate visitors to an event will not have any impact on the country's exchange rate. However, an increase in spending as a result of additional visitors from abroad will have an impact on the real exchange rate, pushing it up. This will have a negative impact on other export and import competing industries, both within and outside the state (Dwyer et al. 2003a). Thus the net impact on economic activity within the state, in the rest of the economy, and the national economy as a whole, will be different according to the source of the additional spending. I–O analysis relies only on the total of injected expenditure, regardless of its source, and thus is incapable of estimating the differential effects due to exchange rate movements. CGE models, which explicitly allow for the exchange market, will capture these effects. Underlying the simulations in Table 15.1 is a projected 0.0047 percentage change in the real value of the Australian dollar as a result of the special event.

Location of the event
Does the choice of model depend on the location of the event? It has been claimed that CGE analysis is inappropriate to evaluate small, local events, and that I–O analysis is sufficient for this purpose (Mules 1999). To explore this claim we need to distinguish between an event held in a regional or remote area and one held in an urban area.

Regional and remote events   Some claim that there is a case for using I–O models to estimate local impacts of events in areas that are separate from the main centre of the economy (for example, rural towns and cities). CGE models are rarely available at this level of detail, but, more to the point, the assumptions which I–O analysis makes – that all inputs are in elastic supply to the area – may be approximately met (Mules 1999; Burgan and Mules 2000).

It is acknowledged that an event in a rural city will draw many of its required resources (labour, services, goods) from outside the area – resource constraints do not limit the expansion of economic activity by very much. The event will draw on resources from the rest of the region and nation – economic activity, and jobs, will rise, temporarily, in the local area. While general equilibrium effects will still exist, the assumptions of free supply of inputs, made by I–O analysis, may be approximated.

At least two qualifications must be made to this view, however.

First, even in this context, the assumptions of I–O analysis may not be met – some key inputs cannot be expanded readily if at all. In a restricted local area, such as a rural town, the displacement effects are likely to be greater than in the main centre of economic activity. Consider accommodation: an event will increase accommodation demand, and the local accommodation supply may be tightly constrained. With the increased demand associated with the event, prices are increased, and other potential visitors may go elsewhere. I–O analysis will not pick up these effects and will overestimate the size of the economic impact unless the resource constraints are allowed for by making downward adjustments to the estimated impacts.

Second, while economic activity, including household income, within the area will increase, some of this will have only a peripheral impact on the local economy. During the event, labour and services from outside the region will be hired in – this will count as increased economic activity within the area, though it will not have any real impact on it, since the incomes earned will be mainly spent outside it.

Urban event   The concept of a 'local event' has a clear meaning if an event is taking place in a rural city, some distance from the capital city or main centre of economic activity. Here there is a distinct local economy. However, when the area under consideration is a suburb of the main city, or close to the main city, there is really no 'local' economy. Suburbs of large cities do not have their own local economies, separate from the urban, and indeed, state economy. Thus, if only the local effects were of interest, it may suffice to use the simpler I–O approach (taking note of the above considerations). However, for an event in a large city, or in a supra-metropolitan region like the Gold Coast or Riviera, there are likely to be feedback effects on a significant scale within the local economy which require CGE analysis.

Some advocates of I–O do not appear to realise that the analysis is not appropriate to estimate the local effects of an event which takes place within a major centre of economic activity, such as a large city. If the event is held in a major centre of activity, the resource constraints will be critical as the resources needed in the area hosting the event will be drawn from other parts of the city. Here, the local effects are more or less meaningless. This is because the existing resource constraints and feedback effects will lead to negative impacts on activity in other parts of the regional economy.

Multi-state events   Since I–O models focus on a single area and the expenditure injected into it, they cannot handle multi-state events. Some large events, such as the Olympic Games and the Rugby World Cup, are held across several states or regions in economies (and now, across more than one country as is the case for World Cup Soccer). This gives rise to a pattern of flows of visitors both into, and out of, the states hosting the event. It is a simple matter for a multi-regional CGE model to take account of these flows and estimate the net impact of the event on state and national economies.

Adjusting the results of I–O
It has been claimed that differences between the estimates of the two techniques are fairly small for most events, and, in any case, adjustments can be made to the I–O results in recognition of any such differences. Some have suggested a percentage downwards revision to input I–O multipliers for this purpose. This raises the question of whether there are systematic differences between the two models in estimating the economic impacts of events in general or for different events by size or type. If there are, then I–O models can be used and the estimates adjusted accordingly.

The problem with any such 'rule-of-thumb' adjustment is that it ignores the information lost to the analyst and clients by using I–O instead of CGE modelling. This information includes those industries negatively impacted upon as a result of event-related expenditure, both in the host region and elsewhere in Australia, as well as the extent of gains and losses of GSP, real output and employment in other regions of Australia. The particular industries affected and the extent of expansions or contractions depends on the industrial structure of the host economy. Such information may well be critical to event assessment and, depending on the types of effects projected, may well determine the willingness of governments to support the funding for some events (as well as sponsorship from interstate depending on the projected industry effects elsewhere).

A further problem with any such proposed rule of thumb is that we would not expect that there would be any systematic differences between the two techniques, except that the impacts would be much lower using CGE. However, exactly how much lower depends on the nature of the shock, the expenditure patterns, government fiscal policy stance, flexibility of real wages, industry structure and so on (Dwyer et al. 2000a). In short, we should not hold out hope that there might be some particular scaling factors which could be relied on, and the comparison estimates in Tables 15.1–3 appear to support this.

The results of I–O analyses tend to be rather predictable; the final change in activity is some multiple of the initial change in expenditure. By contrast, those of a CGE analysis are far less so; quite often, unexpected results turn up. This suggests that the model is capturing the complexities and interrelationships in the economy that are missed in more simple approaches. In a real economy, the ultimate consequences of some change on variables such as economic activity cannot be easily predicted. In this respect, the CGE approach is a valuable research device, which goes beyond simplistic rules of thumb.

Of course, sometimes, I–O and CGE analyses may estimate changes in activity of a similar order of magnitude. This could happen if the CGE model being used embodied assumptions about resource supplies (easy access to unemployed resources) which approximate those on which I–O analysis relies. In short, if essentially implausible assumptions are fed into a CGE analysis, it can give similar outputs to an I–O analysis. When more plausible assumptions, which recognise resource limitations, government fiscal policy, and the ways labour markets work, CGE and I–O approaches will typically give very different results, with the measured change in economic activity being significantly lower under the former. It does matter which approach is more complete and more correct as a representation of the economy.

The assumptions of CGE
It is sometimes claimed that use of CGE analysis in event impact assessment requires making too many assumptions. This claim must be heavily qualified.

CGE models are indeed more comprehensive, and incorporate more markets and processes; hence more assumptions must be made. These involve how markets work, how taxes are levied, how production is structured, and how consumers behave. The assumptions will be based on available empirical work, which in turn will embody assumptions, and they will be chosen to give the best practical representation of the economy. To make any model tractable, simplifying assumptions must be made. I–O analysis makes fewer assumptions than does CGE analysis, but the assumptions it does make about production processes are highly stylised, and open to the same types of criticism (Briassoulis 1991). However the real objection to I–O analysis is that it avoids making assumptions about how the rest of the economy works by ignoring it. It is preferable to have a complete representation of the economy, even if this involves making some further assumptions.

The proponent of CGE modelling would also claim at this point that a major strength of CGE analysis is that its assumptions can be varied and the sensitivity to them tested. Unlike the assumptions of the typical I–O model, the implications of which are rarely conveyed to stakeholders, the assumptions of CGE analysis can be identified and discussed for their realism. The fact that CGE simulations can be undertaken using different assumptions, the realism of which can be discussed and debated, provides a transparency to the assessment process that rarely exists in I–O modelling.

Indeed, these considerations highlight one of the practical advantages of using CGE models for policy analysis. As with all kinds of models, results are sensitive to the assumptions made. The I–O approach locks one into extreme assumptions about input availability (free availability with no constraints) and feedback effects from other markets (they do not exist). The CGE model provides us with a mechanism for investigating the sensitivity of the results to changes in assumptions about the parameters. For example, the labour markets can be modelled differently; at one extreme, unemployed labour can be freely available, and at the other extreme, additional demand for labour leads not to more employment, but only higher wages. Assumptions in between these extremes can also be used (Dwyer and Forsyth 1998). CGE models also typically allow for alternative assumptions about government tax and spending policies, exchange rate mechanisms, and consumer behaviour. This can provide very useful information to policy makers in predicting the economic impacts of particular types of events in different macroecoconomic contexts (Dwyer et al. 2000a).

Cost and availability
We reject the exaggerated view that '[i]nput–output analysis is simple, quick, reliable and accepted technique' (Hunn and Mangan 1999: 22) as false on all counts. Sometimes, these advocates of I–O further overstate their case by claiming that '[d]ata for the model is readily available' (p. 16). This is certainly not true for many economic impact assessment exercises. Also, the availability CGE model is sometimes criticised as too time consuming and expensive to build (Hunn and Mangan 1999; Mules 1999). While cost considerations would be one important element in a decision as to how to model the event impact, one might point out here that CGE modelling techniques and software systems are now routinely available, and the data should be assessed in terms of their importance for the question to be investigated, other than just in terms of the ease of data mobilisation (McDougall 1995).

It is sometimes maintained that the overall cost of undertaking CGE analyses is prohibitive, and simpler techniques such as I–O are more cost effective (Mules 1999: 37). This claim is not necessarily true. Assuming that both a CGE and an I–O model are available, the cost of analysing a change with them would be much the same; most of the cost is in preparing the inputs and in interpreting the outputs, not in developing or running the model.

It does cost more to develop a CGE model from the beginning, but in many cases, it is unnecessary to do this. In Australia, for example, several CGE models, national and regional, have been developed, with more under construction. Research Centres (Centre of Policy Studies, Centre for Regional Economic Analysis) have developed models that can be readily used, and most of the main economic consulting firms have their own models or access to a model. Some state treasuries in Australia are spending considerable sums in developing their own CGE models, but this is in order to have substantial in-house expertise with which to examine a very wide range of issues (tax, industry policy, major projects), and not just for tourism.

It is recognised, of course, that estimating the economic impacts of a single event may not justify the expense of constructing a new CGE model if no suitable model already exists. In the discussion above we considered the use of I–O modelling in a small regional economy or substate region where relative prices can safely be assumed to be set outside such economies which are typically very open to commodity and factor flows and face no external account constraint. In these circumstances, the range of mechanisms encompassed by a CGE model, over and above those included in an I–O model, may not be of much practical importance. In such cases I–O analysis can be employed to estimate economic impacts as long as its assumptions and deficiencies are acknowledged. It must be recognised, of course, that the positive impacts cannot be extrapolated to the wider national or even state level. The practical advantage of using I–O modelling in certain contexts is, however, a separate issue from its conceptual status.

Should the cost of the analysis determine which model is used in event impact assessment? Clearly, the cost of the assessment exercise should be commensurate with the benefits from obtaining information about it. Neither CGE nor I–O analyses are costless. A local I–O analysis, which adequately captures the unique features of the locality, may well be more expensive than a run of an existing CGE model. These practical issues require further exploration, requiring an answer to the question of when does theoretical rigour give way to practical consideration?

Additional issues

On the basis of this discussion we see that each of the claims advanced by advocates of I–O analysis, while having superficial plausibility, must be at least heavily qualified.

Two other issues are relevant to the question of whether CGE modelling should replace I–O modelling in the economic impact assessment of events. One issue concerns the use of modelling to help in the estimation of the net benefits generated by a special event. CGE models can generate estimates of real benefits as an output of the modelling. The other issue concerns the role of government and its jurisdiction of interest in event assessment. In the discussion thus far, the role of government has been neglected. A government deciding whether or not to provide financial or other form of support to an event may wish to have background information that is not obtainable unless a CGE model is employed to forecast the impacts.

Measuring benefits, not impacts
The changes in economic activity (such as in GDP) which are estimated to flow as a result of an event are often described as the 'economic benefits' of the event (for example, Ingerson and Westerbeek 1999; Ryan and Lockyer 2001). Similarly, we find statements such as 'Benefits in terms of increased GSP' (Johnson 1999: 107). This may just be loose talk, but it certainly makes events look more attractive than they really are. When a study estimates that 'benefits' of A\$100 million will flow as a result of an event which will come about if a A\$10 million subsidy is given to it, it looks like a very attractive deal. In fact, it may be a very poor deal, because 'benefits' may not mean what they seem.

Economic impacts, such as the change in GDP resulting from an event, are not the same thing as the economic benefits which arise. The impact on GDP is a gross measure of the change in value of output as a result of an event. This addition to output normally requires additional inputs, of land, labour and capital, to enable it to be produced. These inputs have a cost, and this cost must be deducted from the change in value of gross output if a measure of the net economic gain is to be made (Dwyer and Forsyth 1993). When allowance is made for this, a change in gross output, of say A\$100 million, might give rise to a net economic benefit of something much less, such as A\$5–10 million. Thus, a subsidy of A\$10 million to secure an event which adds A\$100 million to GDP might not be worthwhile. It needs further analysis. The conclusion of Ryan and Lockyer (2001) that, since the Masters Games in Hamilton contributed A\$250 000 to the local economy this appears to be 'sufficient reason' to continue with future promotion of the Games, confuses 'impacts' with 'benefits'.

Neither I–O models nor CGE models produce, as part of their normal outputs, measures of net economic benefit. They typically report changes in the gross value of output, as measured by GDP or GSP – they do not subtract out the additional cost of factors needed to produce this additional output. CGE models, however, can be constructed to do this. Some

Table 15.5　Net benefits to different areas from event (A$m)

Macroeconomic variable	NSW	RoA	Aus
Change in GSP/GDP	19.41	−10.61	8.80
Less cost of additional labour	−15.03	+7.84	−7.19
Plus additional payroll taxes received	0.36	−0.24	0.11
Change in net real benefit	4.73	−3.01	1.73

Notes:　In this (short-run) simulation, there were no changes to the use of land or capital. Figures do not add due to rounding.

Source:　Own calculations, as reported in Dwyer et al. (2003b).

are constructed with an explicit measure of economic welfare, which forms an integral part of the model (Dixon et al. 2002). Alternatively, a standard model can be adapted to produce, as part of its output, an estimate of net benefits – the cost of additional inputs is subtracted from the value of the additional output. Referring to the event comparison above, the net benefit to NSW from hosting the Grand Prix type event, which brought an additional A$51.25 million in spending into the state, is estimated to be A$4.73 million. This is much less than the addition to GSP of A$19.41 million. The net benefit to Australia from this event is estimated to have been A$1.73 million, which is an order of magnitude less than the change in GDP of A$8.80 million.

The estimate of the change in net real benefit in Table 15.5 is somewhat narrow of course since it does not account for the various social and environmental costs and benefits that are associated with different events. Other than their impact on economic activity, most events create other benefits and costs. To judge whether an event is worthwhile in overall economic terms, it is essential to conduct a CBA. Nevertheless, the estimate of net real benefit will be an important input into any wider CBA.

Relevance of the jurisdiction

An issue neglected thus far concerns the interests of the different levels of governments involved in the event assessment process. To make informed decisions about events policy, governments need to know the answers to the following questions: how much will the event add to economic activity and jobs after accounting for inter-industry effects? Is the event likely to produce net economic benefits, and if so, how much is it worth subsidising? To what extent do the benefits of the event come at a cost to other jurisdictions?

Thus, a local council might undertake an economic impact study to determine whether to support a festival in the town or to finance road construction. If the perspective of the local government is taken, it is only the local effects of the event that are relevant. However, where a state or federal government is contemplating financial support for an event, it will be interested in not just the impact in the local area, but also the impacts on the state and/or nation. The impact on economic activity in the state as a whole cannot be determined from a local I–O analysis. An event may increase economic activity substantially within a local area but its net impact on the economic activity within the state will normally be much less, and conceivably negative. The impact on national output will be even less than this, and it is more likely to be negative. This is evident from the discussion above in terms of the interstate effects of events. Local impact studies will not provide public sector decision makers with enough guidance as to whether they should support local events financially or otherwise, since they will also need to know the overall state-wide impacts. This fact seems to have escaped Hunn and Mangan who make the indefensible claim that CGE models 'produce a range of results which are not relevant for local government authority, state or Territory, for example balance of payments, exchange rates and the prices and quantity supplied of factors such as labour' (Hunn and Mangan 1999: 20). Likewise, national governments will be interested in the impacts of events or projects on activity in the nation, not just the impact in particular states or regions.

Another issue is relevant. In standard event assessment, expenditures of residents in the host destination are ignored on the grounds that this represents expenditure 'transferred' within the one destination rather than expenditure 'injected' from outside (Getz 1987; Crompton and McKay 1994; Delpy and Li 1998). An advantage of the CGE approach is that it can estimate the impacts of intrastate (intraregional) expenditure shifts on GSP and employment, which, in other simulations, have been found to be substantial (Dwyer et al. 2004b). Any event can have an impact on the overall level of economic activity and jobs through changing the patterns of spending within the state. I–O modellers ignore this effect, by concentrating only upon 'injected expenditure' as having economic impacts. The impacts from 'transferred expenditure' may not be very large, and they may be positive or negative. However, the impact on certain variables, such as state government revenue, could be moderately large since different commodities are taxed differently. CGE models are able to estimate these effects. They are also able to capture the effect on economic activity from state residents spending less on tourism outside the state as a result of the event taking place. In the comparisons appearing in Table 15.1, unfortunately, no data were available on spending by intrastate visitors to the event so the impacts from 'transferred' expenditure could not be simulated.

For these reasons, the perspectives on an event from the local, state and national levels will be quite different. An event may be highly attractive to a rural city, though only of marginal or negative benefit to a state. Notwithstanding this, a state government may be prepared to subsidise the event, even though it is basically shifting, rather than creating, economic activity and jobs. This could be so if a region is depressed, and the state government wishes to give it some stimulus. For this to be worthwhile, the event must be assessed in comparison with other forms of stimulus – there may be ways in which the same funds could generate a greater impact on local economic activity, or a similar impact without as large a negative impact on other parts of the state. If so, it would be more effective to subsidise these alternatives rather than the event. And such decisions should be taken in full awareness of who the winners and losers within the state will be, both in regional and industry terms. The losers might well be other depressed regions, or industries, within the state. An I–O analysis will provide no information on this. Where an event receives financial support from the state government, assessment of the statewide effects is critical.

Two further jurisdictional issues are relevant – taxation revenue and subsidies.

Taxation revenue   A higher-level government outside of the local area may be interested in the implications of an event on state and national tax revenues. Changes in the patterns of expenditure brought about by the event give rise to increases and decreases in tax revenues, because different aspects of economic activity are taxed differently. Furthermore, changes in tax revenues lead to changes in government spending and tax rates, which in turn, influence economic activity. These effects are captured in CGE models. Since I–O models do not estimate the negative as well as the positive impacts on expenditure and activity, they cannot be used to estimate the net effects on net tax revenue.

Subsidies   Events are often subsidised by governments. These subsidies need to be financed from government revenue or reductions in other government spending. These changes have implications for economic activity and jobs in the state and beyond. Subsidies cannot be modelled using I–O models, however they can be in CGE models, and their implications for economic activity can be estimated. This can be done by making assumptions about the financing of the government subsidies. They could be financed from increased taxes, or decreased spending on other goods and services. In each of these cases, financing the subsidies will have a negative impact on economic activity.

Summary
The discussion above is summarised in Table 15.6.

Notwithstanding the above discussion it must be acknowledged that the application of CGE analysis to events is in its embryonic stage. To date, the most significant study has been the estimated impacts of the Sydney Olympics on GSP and employment in New South Wales (New South Wales Treasury 1997) and the Rugby World Cup (Department of Industry 2003). Much more detailed work needs to be undertaken using CGE analysis on a range of events of different types and sizes and under different assumptions about factor constraints, real wages flexibility and government fiscal policy stance.

Modelling the economy's structure
There are many issues which need to be resolved in building a model of regional and national economies to estimate the effects of shocks such as special events. We concentrate on three here. The first concerns the degree of integration of the regional economies within the national economy. This is of major importance when using CGE models to examine the economic impact of events, because particular attention is normally paid to the regional impacts of events. The second issue concerns the labour market. This is an issue which is important for all modelling work, because the ways the labour market is modelled has a large impact on the results. The third issue, recognising that events produce displacement effects on economies, concerns how such effects are modelled.

Integrating regional and national economies
Suppose that we have a CGE model for each of several regional/state economies and that these are to be integrated to form a model of the national economy. It is unlikely that there would be separate models for local areas, though, in principle these could be developed if needed.

The critical issue is the extent to which the states are integrated. Do they simply consist of geographical parts of a single national economy, or do they operate, to some extent, as distinct economies? If a state operates as a moderately separate economy, the economic impact of an event taking place within its borders will be smaller than if the state is simply part of a seamlessly integrated national economy. This is because resource constraints will be more binding in the separate economies case than in the integrated economy. An event will increase economic activity within the state, but resource limitations (for example, limited availability of labour) will limit the extent to which economic activity can increase. In a more integrated economy, labour will flow to the state that is experiencing increased demand for resources as a consequence of an event. At heart, there is an

Table 15.6   Summary: I–O versus CGE

Issue	I–O versus CGE
Event size	CGE relevant equally to large and small events
Event Location	I–O is best suited to analysis of events in remote locations, but resource constraints should be taken into account I–O incapable of modelling multi-state events I–O inappropriate for modelling events in urban areas where feedback effects exist
Adjusting results of I–O	No systematic differences between the techniques to enable use of 'rules of thumb' Information on negative industry effects lost unless CGE is used
Assumptions of CGE	CGE models can make more assumptions about how markets work, how taxes are levied, how production is structured and how consumers behave, but this is a plus, not a minus Assumptions of I–O ignore real-world behaviour Assumptions of CGE can be varied and their realism discussed CGE can explore sensitivity of results under different policy scenarios
Cost and availability	CGE models cost more to develop from scratch Operating costs similar for each type of model CGE modelling techniques and software becoming more available Theoretical rigour versus practical considerations If I–O model is available and used, its limitations must be recognised and estimates adjusted
Measuring the real benefits	I–O modelling does not produce measures of real benefit A standard CGE model can be adapted to produce, as part of its output, an estimate of net benefits – the cost of additional inputs is subtracted from the value of the additional output
Relevance of jurisdiction	State and federal government interest beyond local impacts requires a CGE analysis Estimating changes in taxation revenues requires CGE analysis Implications of subsidies to support events can only be modelled using CGE analysis

issue of how freely resources, goods and services can flow from one state to another in response to an increase in demand.

Consider labour – is there a local state (regional) labour market, or is there a wider national market? If the latter is the case, an event will increase demand for labour, and labour will flow from other regions to meet this demand. Interregional differences in wages and in unemployment rates will be unsustainable. If there is unemployment in a region, an event will not reduce unemployment by much because labour will flow from other regions to take up the jobs. By contrast, with state-wide labour markets, an increase in labour demand that comes about because of an event will lead to some combination of reduction in unemployment within the state and increase in wage rates in the state. In the longer run, the integration of regional labour markets will be greater than in the short to medium run, because it takes time for workers to shift residence (Dwyer and Forsyth 1998). The degree of integration, particularly in the short run, will depend on how far separated the states are, and on cultural factors such as the willingness of workers to move out of their home state to seek employment. The long-term persistence of regional unemployment in many industrial countries of Europe suggests that labour markets there are far from perfectly integrated. Clearly, it is an empirical matter as to how well integrated the state or regional labour markets are in a particular country.

Different states/regions will have separate stocks of capital and land in the short run, and separate stocks of land in the long run. An increase in the demand for, say, accommodation in one state in the short run, as a result of an event taking place, can only be met from the accommodation stock within that state – for many special event locations it is not feasible to supply accommodation from other states regardless of how much excess capacity there is. In the long run, capital investment is flexible, and investment can increase the supply of fixed capital where this is needed.

Further, there is the question of the extent to which goods and services flow between states in the short and long runs. If demand increases, will it be met by increased production by industries within the state, or flows of imports from interstate and abroad? This depends on the nature of the goods (whether heavy or perishable) and how readily traded they are. Some services can be readily supplied from outside the state borders (for example, call centre services) while others cannot (plumbers).

If we are interested in the extent to which a change in demand, resulting from an event, stimulates economic activity within a state as well as the national economy, the extent of integration of the state economies will affect the answer. If resource markets (for example, labour) are highly integrated, the event will lead to a greater impact on economic activity than if they are not. On the other hand, the level of economic activity in the state is of less policy significance than when markets are less integrated – for example, when there is chronic unemployment, it will be difficult for the state to lower it through promoting economic activity.

The reverse is true of goods and services markets. If these are highly integrated, a demand increase stimulated by an event will be less likely to stimulate local economic activity, because the goods and services will tend to be imported from interstate and abroad.

Obviously, the ideal is to have a suite of state and national models which accurately reflect the degree of integration of state and national economies. To the extent that actual economies have well-integrated resource markets and less-integrated goods markets than is captured in the model, the measured impact of an event will be an underestimation of the actual impact – and vice versa. This needs to be borne in mind in interpreting the results of a model which incorporates state and national economies.

Labour markets
The ways in which labour markets are modelled will normally have a large influence on the results of CGE simulations There are different views that can be taken of the labour market. If there is unemployment in the economy, and when demand increases the real wage stays constant, unemployment will be reduced, and economic activity will increase significantly. On the other hand, if the response to an increase in demand for labour is a wage increase (which can take place even though there is considerable unemployment), the impact on unemployment will be much less, as will the impact on overall economic activity (Dwyer and Forsyth 1998). How labour markets actually work is a controversial area in economics. A CGE model can incorporate different views of how the labour market works and illustrate the sensitivity of results to the different assumptions (Dwyer et al. 2000a). For example, the assumptions of fixed real wages/flexible unemployment and fixed unemployment/flexible wages can be simulated to give the range of possible outcomes. The most realistic assumption probably lies somewhere between these two extremes.

Modelling displacement effects
The nature of events is that they produce displacement effects on economies. They result in temporary, but intense, increases in the demand for a range of products and facilities, often in only one locality of the economy. As a result of an event, for a few days accommodation in the vicinity becomes high priced and difficult to obtain, restaurants become crowded and roads congested. Potential visitors respond by going elsewhere, or by visiting at a different time. Local residents may leave the area for the duration of the event. The result of this process is that the increase

in demand, which comes about because of the event, is smaller than that due to the event itself and associated tourism flows, due to these displacement effects. In estimating the economic impacts of an event, it is necessary to take these displacement effects into account (Dwyer et al. 2000a).

By their very nature, CGE models incorporate displacement effects. Increases in demand push up against supply constraints, pushing up prices and inducing shifts in expenditure patterns. These lessen the ultimate impact on output. By contrast, I–O models make no allowance for displacement effects. In I–O modelling of events, displacement effects are generally taken into account through simply adjusting the amount of injected expenditure to allow for expenditure 'switched' in time or geographically (Delpy and Li 1998). Such a procedure does not capture any consumption effects resulting from price changes.

While a normal CGE model will automatically take displacement effects into account, one can ask how well it will do so. It may be that specific adjustments to CGE models are desirable to improve accuracy in the context of modelling specific shocks such as events.

The typical shock analysed using a CGE model is one which affects the whole economy for the whole time period (for example, a year). However, events are peculiar shocks to economies in that their effects are very intense though also very localised. They lead to sharp increases in demand for a short period, and this demand increase is focused usually on facilities within a specific area. Demand for labour and other services, for accommodation in the vicinity of the event, and for restaurants and local transport, may increase several-fold for a short period, perhaps of only a few days. This intense and highly specific shock may have different and larger impacts on the economy from those of a more sustained and widespread shock of similar overall magnitude.

The latter type of change, typical of longer-term tourism growth in a destination, will result in marginal or small changes in any affected sector of the economy. Consider accommodation – it will result in a small increase in overall demand and thus lead to a small price rise, which will displace some demand. An increase in demand due to an event will often lead to a large temporary increase in demand. Most likely, it will result in demand greatly exceeding capacity and prices being bid up sharply. Because the temporary demand increase is pushing up against capacity, the price increase, averaged over the whole period, will be higher than the price increase of the small sustained demand increase. The impact in terms of changes in demand patterns will be correspondingly greater.

The relevance of disaggregation is illustrated in Figure 15.1. Suppose the supply of some service, such as accommodation, is shown by the curve S_1, up to the quantity A, the maximum capacity at a point of time. There is

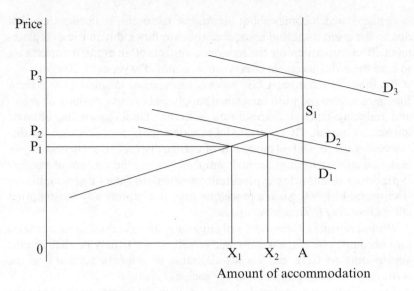

Figure 15.1   Relevance of disaggregation

a demand/supply equilibrium at a price of P_1 and quantity X_1. Suppose that the event doubles demand for about five weeks, or adds 10 per cent to demand over the whole year. A 10 per cent increase in demand is represented by D_2 and a doubling of demand by D_3. With a doubling of demand the increase in price is more than ten times the price increase with a 10 per cent increase in demand, but the increase in output, constrained to A, is less than ten times. Short demand shocks are likely to have a smaller impact on output than comparably sized shocks of longer duration.

Perhaps the best means of handling this type of problem is to undertake a preliminary study of the event and estimate the price and output changes. The net changes in demand, after allowing for these displacement effects, can then be fed into the CGE model. This is a relatively demanding approach in terms of information and analytical effort. It would be worthwhile to undertake detailed case studies of medium to large events in different regions.

A less demanding approach is to adapt the CGE model to capture these effects more accurately than normally. Allowing for the short duration of events is a relatively simple matter. While the normal time period of analysis of CGE models is one year, they can be run for shorter periods, such as one week. The impact of an event lasting one week in a year can be estimated by running the model for a week with the event, and for 51 weeks without the event (that is, the base case), and aggregating the results. If the model is basically linear, this will yield similar results to those of a simple simulation not distinguishing time periods, and spreading the impact of the event over the year. On the other hand, if non-linearities are present – for example with supply constraints – the results could differ markedly.

Another adaptation to better model localised events is to introduce supply constraints. I–O modellers do this, but do not allow for price changes in the model (Wanhill 1988). For the event period, it would be possible to run the model with the output of key services, such as accommodation, constrained to the supply in the base case (or some other level if preferred). This would result in prices for services in short supply being bid up, and demand being rationed away. As a result, the overall change in output would be smaller because of these displacement effects. In an economy-wide model, it would be necessary to constrain the output of the relevant services across the whole economy (for the region or state) but, in reality, an event would create a larger proportionate effect spread across a smaller area. In economy-wide models it is not feasible to attain this level of disaggregation, but modelling changes in this way would give a reasonable approximation to the displacement effects. Of the various services which might be constrained during the event period, accommodation is likely to be the most binding. In principle, other services such as restaurant services, local transport and recreational services could be constrained in this way if considered appropriate.

It should also be recognised that sometimes events are scheduled to take place at times when infrastructure has excess capacity. For example, an event may take place when there would otherwise be a lull in the accommodation industry. This can be allowed for in a CGE model. Excess capacity in the short run can be built into the model for the relevant sector, and the fixed capacity constraint can be imposed at a level of output greater than the current use. The displacement effect will only take place if the event leads to an increase in demand which cannot be handled using the excess capacity.

Cost–benefit analysis of events   The role of CBA is to express, as far as is possible, all the benefits and compare them to all the costs. The overall balance can then be determined. Some of these benefits and costs can be measured directly; this would be so of benefits to patrons, and the environmental costs of staging the event (such as noise and traffic congestion). The event may leave a legacy of facilities, such as improved roads or better sports arenas, which will be of value in the future. The value of these need not show up in increased measured economic activity. Some events require that public facilities, such as parks, be alienated – this has a cost that should be counted.

Some key types of benefit and cost which are likely to be present in the event context are:

- Benefits to patrons and sponsors. Typically, the aggregate willingness to pay to attend or sponsor the event will exceed the amount that patrons and sponsors actually pay because of the degree of uniqueness of the event (some patrons would be willing to pay much more than they will have to for the Rugby World Cup Final). In addition, many events such as football grand finals are priced intentionally below the market-clearing level. Events provide benefits to those who attend them. Once upon a time, events were actually put on for this reason. Motor sports lovers enjoyed seeing the Indy 500, football fans enjoyed the game, and music lovers were pleased to go to the concert. With many events, what patrons are willing to pay to attend the event exceeds what they are required to pay to attend – there is a net gain to the patrons from the event being available. In short, the monetary value of the benefits exceeds the revenues that the organisers are able to collect from the patrons, even with quite sophisticated pricing structures. This will be especially so when prices are held down intentionally to enable a wide cross-section of the community to attend, not just the well-off. When tickets are in short supply and are rationed, this indicates that the benefits to patrons exceed the revenues collected from them by some margin. It is a comment on the way event evaluation has developed internationally that what is likely to be the main source of benefits of an event is so often ignored, while dubious calculations of impacts on economic activity are presented as measures of 'economic benefits'.
- The costs of staging the event. Resources have value in alternate uses.
- Costs and benefits from environmental externalities, such as noise and congestion.
- The additional deadweight cost of raising taxation if government subsidies are to be provided for the event. If subsidies are to be provided, their full cost should be factored in. If a government spends A$1, it normally costs it significantly more than A$1 to raise the funds – this is because it must rely on distortionary taxes to raise the revenue (Freebairn 1995; Campbell and Bond 1997). This is especially true for the Australian state governments, which often claim, with some justification, that it is expensive for them to raise revenue because they must rely on narrow and inefficient tax bases. Thus, if the additional cost of raising an additional A$1 in tax is A$1.25, then an event would be economically worth subsidising by A$10 million only if it produces net benefits of at least A$12.5 million, because

there is an additional A\$2.5 million cost associated with raising taxes. This aspect of subsidies is rarely if ever considered, though it was recognised by the ACT Auditor-General (ACT Auditor-General 2002) in its discussion of events subsidisation.

- Benefits from the stimulation of economic activity in the region hosting the event, resulting from additional spending by visitors from outside the region, and any benefits or costs resulting from the switching of expenditure by residents in the region. Some local residents may experience increased household income from the event, but increased incomes may well come largely as a result of additional work done, and work effort has a cost.
- The discounted net benefits from additional economic activity created by additional tourism to the region stimulated by the event.
- In addition to these effects, which can be evaluated in the CBA, there will also be intangible effects, which may be positive or negative. In accordance with standard practice in CBA, these should be identified and measured as far as is possible, and included in the cost–benefit calculation.

The first three of these can be valued directly without need for general equilibrium analysis. Where there is good reason to believe that prices paid or received do not represent true opportunity costs (for example, where the event is provided with valuable land free of charge), shadow prices should be used. 'Shadow pricing' refers to changes made to nominal prices to reflect real costs. In addition, some shadow prices might be evaluated using a CGE approach (Dwyer et al. 2003a).

The fourth and fifth types of benefit cannot be valued using normal partial equilibrium methods. They represent benefits from adding to, or switching, economic activity, and their value depends on the pattern of taxes and distortions in the economy. Nevertheless they cannot be ignored as they might account for a significant proportion of the overall benefits from the event. They can be measured using CGE analysis.

The sixth type of benefits, relating to the so-called 'intangible' effects of an event may not be able to be quantified in an objective manner but should be specifically acknowledged and considered in the overall CBA assessment.

With information about the net economic benefits from the event, the government or agency is in a position to make an informed decision about the event. If the net benefits are positive, it can give its approval to the event, if that is required. If benefits exceed costs, it can judge how much subsidy would be justifiable, if the event will only go ahead with a subsidy or with tax concessions.

The political economy of events strategies   It is not difficult to see why the economic impacts of events are so oversold around the world. Many groups in the economy have their interests linked to the promotion of events. Not all groups do – taxpayers have an interest in their taxes being spent effectively. However, taxpayers are not likely to be articulate when highly specific types of expenditure such as government subsidies to events are on the agenda. The forces pushing for rigorous assessment of events do not appear to be strong, though this need not remain so always. Within governments, the treasury and the auditor-general's office are uneasy about the uncritical acceptance of the economic benefits of events (ACT Auditor-General 2002).

The promoters of events naturally will highlight their positives. Sporting bodies, artistic organisations, the media and private sector promoters will be keen to ensure that the event occurs, and that it gathers maximum financial support from the government. Hence they will willingly use studies which highlight the large economic impacts of their event. For their part, consulting firms eager to please clients will employ models that generate large event 'output multipliers'. Tourism bodies, such as peak industry councils and government agencies, may be more ambivalent. While events may not be the ideal way of promoting tourism, if governments are prepared to fund them generously, they will not object. Most events will have a positive impact on tourism overall in the host area, and on the performance of tourism businesses. Thus tourism bodies may welcome government support for events, though they might prefer more direct and effective support for tourism.

The institutional environment is hardly conducive to the sober assessment of events, and if anything, changes in recent years have exacerbated the problem. Many governments have set up events corporations – these bodies focus either solely, or largely, on events. Their task is to 'win' events for the state, and some have been given large budgets with which to do this. They measure their success in terms of events attracted, and the size of these events. Naturally they wish to see their own budgets in a healthy state, and so they have a strong incentive to advertise the large economic impacts of events, both to the community at large, and within the government. The narrow focus of events corporations, and the system of incentives they operate under, appears to create an institutional structure which gives them little encouragement to improve event evaluation techniques.

Towards a rational events strategy

A rational events strategy involves funding events at a level which is appropriate given the benefits they create, and which reflects the benefits which could be obtained by using the funds elsewhere. It also involves allocating the funds available to the events which create the greatest net benefits.

Achieving this requires at least two things to happen. First, there needs to be rigorous economic evaluation of events, implying a move away from the current practice of exaggerating economic impacts. Second, there needs to be an institutional framework under which there is the incentive for this to happen.

Improving evaluation

Good economic evaluation of events is a precondition for good decision making. At present, it is not possible to make adequate judgements of the economic impacts and benefits of many events because the standard of economic analysis has been so poor. Even when the attempt has been made to summarise the economic impacts of an event to provide a basis for informed decision making (Crompton 1999), the analysis has relied on I–O modelling as the basis for comparison, as does the 'Template for the economic impact of a special event' (ibid. Appendix 4). The best-practice approach to measuring the impact on economic activity, and in particular, on output (GSP or GDP) and employment is to use a CGE approach.

Estimation of the economic impacts is only part of the evaluation story. If funds are to be provided to assist an event, it is necessary that the cost of these funds be compared to the benefits from the event. The event should be subjected to a cost–benefit calculation. We have demonstrated that it is straightforward to adjust the output of CGE analyses to produce measures of net benefit (Dwyer et al. 2005). In the cost–benefit calculation, these should be added to the other benefits of the event, such as those enjoyed by patrons over and above the prices they pay for entry. Other benefits, and costs such as environmental and disruption costs, should also be added in to form a complete picture. With this information, it is possible for the decision maker to make a judgement of whether the economic benefits of the event are greater than the costs, and to also judge whether the event would represent the best use of the funds when funds are limited and alternative calls on funds exist.

The minimum requirement is that the jurisdiction considering attracting the event should undertake these calculations to determine whether the event is in its own interest. However, as noted earlier, the economic impacts and benefits on other jurisdictions, and on the nation as a whole, will differ from the impacts on the host jurisdiction. Typically, some of the benefits of an event in one area will be at the expense of costs in other areas, and the gain to the state or nation as a whole will be less than the gain to the host area. A rational approach to event strategy will require that benefits and costs to all affected jurisdictions be evaluated, particularly those jurisdictions falling under the authority of the level of government being called upon to provide financial subsidies for the event.

Reforming institutions
In some cases, institutions responsible for event strategies have too great an incentive to oversell events, and to be seen as 'winning' events, and too little an incentive to evaluate events rigorously, and to only fund those events that can pass rigorous tests of economic benefit. An institutional structure which sets up events corporations which have events promotion and subsidising as their sole or main objective can create poor incentives for rigorous event evaluation. The key requirement is that events evaluation and funding be allocated to an agency which can compare the relative merits of events subsidies with other uses of public funds.

One of the major benefits of events (indeed the only one which many evaluations acknowledge) comes through their impact on economic activity, which stems from their role in attracting tourists. One option therefore, is to allocate events strategies to a tourism corporation: this would ensure that events will be compared to other initiatives that promote tourism, and their comparative performance would be assessed. In short, there will be some benchmarks measuring the effectiveness of, and benefits created by, events spending when other spending options are competing with it. The available evidence does not suggest that events subsidies are an effective means of promoting tourism. The A\$10 million spent on the Formula 1 Grand Prix in Melbourne brings little more than A\$50 million into the Victorian economy. By way of contrast, estimates of tourism promotion elasticities imply that an extra A\$10 million spent on international tourism promotion by Australia would bring an additional A\$80–100 million (Tourism Council of Australia 1997) or, possibly, A\$300 million (Crouch et al. 1992) in tourism expenditure into Australia.

The downside of this option is that tourism corporations will be less interested in the other benefits and costs of events – events are broader than just tourism promotion. None the less, additional promotion, or reductions in some of the quite distortionary taxes which are imposed on the industry, may well be a much more effective and efficient use of the funds that are currently used in attracting events.

This is not the only option. An alternative adopted by some states in Australia is to assign event strategies and funding to a general coordinating agency (in Australian states, this could be the Premier's department). Such an agency would have an overview of a wide range of spending priorities, and it would need to assess the claims of one against the other. Such an agency is likely to be aware of evaluation approaches being used across the spectrum of government spending areas, and to have an interest in ensuring both consistency and rigour.

Designing an institutional framework which resolves problems such as those that arise in federal political structures such as Australia or Canada is not an easy task. It is a problem which is recognised as having ramifications well beyond event strategies. Coordinated action by states, facilitated and encouraged by the federal government, has helped the implementation of competition policy in Australia and similar approaches might be tried with investment incentives and events attraction. Whichever institutional approach is taken, what is certain is that it will have to rely on rigorous evaluation of the economic costs and benefits of events in the host states, and to be fully effective in the non-host states and Australia as a whole as well. An improved approach of event evaluation is a precondition for a better institutional framework to succeed.

Concluding remarks

There is a serious need for improved economic evaluation of events. Fortunately, the techniques are readily available. Where the need is for an estimate of the impacts of a policy or investment on the GDP or jobs, computable general equilibrium analysis is the appropriate tool. Where there is a need to compare the benefits of a policy or investment with the costs of funding it, cost–benefit analysis is the appropriate tool; such a CBA will need to draw upon the results of a CGE analysis if benefits from increasing or switching overall economic activity are to be included. These methods of evaluation give very different – and much lower – estimates of impacts and benefits from those methods conventionally used in events evaluation. With ready availability of models and expertise, their cost of use is comparable to that of the conventional methods.

A heavy reliance on techniques of analysis which not so much evaluate the economic impacts of events as cast them in a highly favourable light has been inconsistent with the rigorous assessment of events. There is a strong presumption that overall, there is excessive funding being devoted to subsidising events, and that the funds being used are probably being misallocated.

Improving event evaluation is a straightforward matter. More accurate and rigorous techniques of analysis are readily available, and they are used widely in other areas of the economy. However, institutional frameworks are hardly conducive to good evaluation of events. The key decision makers have an incentive to promote, not scrutinise events projects. To improve matters, it is essential that events and the economic benefits they create be assessed and compared to the benefits that would flow from alternative public spending options.

Acknowledgements

The authors wish to acknowledge the support given to this research by the Sustainable Tourism Cooperative Research Centre Tourism, Australia. Special acknowledgement is due to the modelling work of Thiep van Ho.

References

ACT Auditor-General (2002), 'Performance Audit Report V8 Car Races in Canberra – Costs and Benefits', Canberra, July.

Adams, B. and B. Parmenter (1999), 'General equilibrium models', in *Valuing Tourism: Methods and Techniques*, Canberra: Bureau of Tourism Research, pp. 3–12.

Allen Consulting Group, J. Cox and Centre of Policy Studies (1996), 'The economic impact of the Melbourne CityLink transurban project', Consulting Report to the Melbourne City Link Authority, April.

Arthur Andersen and Centre for Regional Economic Analysis (CREA) (1999), *Economic Impact Study of the Sydney 2000 Olympic Games*, Centre for Regional Economic Analysis, University of Tasmania, January.

Banks, G. (2002), 'Inter-state bidding wars: calling a truce', Speech to the Committee for Economic Development of Australia, Brisbane, November, www.pc.gov.au.

Blake, A. (2000), 'The economic effects of tourism in Spain', Tourism and Travel Research Institute Discussion Paper, 2001/2, Nottingham.

Blake, A., R. Durbarry, T. Sinclair and G. Sugiyarto (2000), 'Modelling tourism and travel using tourism satellite accounts and tourism policy and forecasting models', Tourism and Travel Research Institute Discussion Paper, 2001/4, Nottingham.

Blake, A., T. Sinclair and G. Sugiyarto (2003), 'Quantifying the impact of foot and mouth disease on tourism and the UK economy', *Tourism Economics*, 9 (4), pp. 449–65.

Briassoulis, H. (1991), 'Methodological issues: tourism input–output analysis', *Annals of Tourism Research*, 18, pp. 435–49.

Burgan, B. and T. Mules (2000), 'Event analysis – understanding the divide between cost benefit and economic impact assessment', in J. Allen, R. Harris, L. Jago and A. Veal (eds), *Events Beyond 2000: Setting the Agenda*, Sydney: Australian Centre for Event Management, University of Technology, pp. 256–64.

Burns J.P.A., J.H. Hatch and T.J. Mules (1986), *The Adelaide Grand Prix: the Impact of a Special Event*, Adelaide: Centre for South Australian Economic Studies.

Bushnell, R.C. and M. Hyle (1985), 'Computerized models for assessing the economic impact of recreation and tourism', in D.V. Propst (ed.), *Assessing the Economic Impact of Recreation and Tourism*, Asheville, NC: Southeastern Forest Experiment Station, pp. 135–46.

Campbell, H. and K. Bond (1997), 'The cost of public funds in Australia', *Economic Record*, 73 (220), pp. 22–34.

Crompton, J.L. (1995), 'Economic impact of sports facilities and events: eleven sources of misapplication', *Journal of Sport Management*, 9, pp. 14–35.

Crompton, J. (1999), 'Measuring the economic impact of visitors to sports tournaments and special events', National Recreation and Park Association, Division of Professional Services, Missouri.

Crompton, J., S. Lee and T. Shuster (2001), 'A guide for undertaking economic impact studies: the Springfest festival', *Journal of Travel Research*, 40 (1), pp. 79–87.

Crompton, J.L. and S.L. McKay (1994), 'Measuring the economic impact of festivals and events: some myths, misapplications and ethical dilemmas', *Festival Management and Event Tourism*, 2 (1), pp. 33–43.

Crouch, G., L. Schulze and P. Valerio (1992), 'Marketing international tourism to Australia – a regression analysis', *Tourism Management*, 13 (2), pp. 196–208.

Dawson, S.A., D.J. Blahna and J.E. Keith (1993), 'Expected and actual regional economic impacts of Great Basin National Park', *Journal of Park and Recreation Administration*, 11 (4), pp. 45–59.

Delpy, L. and M. Li (1998), 'The art and science of conducting economic impact studies', *Journal of Vacation Marketing*, 4 (3), pp. 230–54.

Department of Industry, Tourism Resources (2003), *Economic Evaluation of Rugby World Cup*, Canberra.

Dixon, P. and B. Parmenter (1996), 'Computable general equilibrium modelling for policy analysis and forecasting', in H. Aman, D. Kendrick and J. Rust (eds), *Handbook of Computational Economics*, 1, Amsterdam: Elsevier Science B.V., pp. 4–85.

Dixon, P., M. Picton and M. Rimmer (2002), 'Efficiency effects of inter-government transfers in Australia', *Australian Economic Review*, **35** (3), pp. 304–15.

Donnelly, M.P., J.J. Vaske, D.S. DeRuiter and J.B. Loomis (1998), 'Economic impacts of state park: effect of park visitation, park facilities, and county economic diversification', *Journal of Park and Recreation Administration*, **16** (4), pp. 57–72.

Dwyer, L. and P. Forsyth (1993), 'Assessing the benefits and costs of inbound tourism', *Annals of Tourism Research*, **20** (4), pp. 751–68.

Dwyer, L. and P. Forsyth (1997), 'Impacts and benefits of MICE tourism: a framework for analysis', *Tourism Economics*, **3** (1), pp. 21–38.

Dwyer, L. and P. Forsyth (1998), 'Estimating the employment impacts of tourism to a nation', *Tourism Recreation Research*, **23** (2), pp. 1–12.

Dwyer, L., P. Forsyth, J. Madden and R. Spurr (2000a), 'Economic impacts of inbound tourism under different assumptions about the macroeconomy', *Current Issues in Tourism*, **3** (4), pp. 325–63.

Dwyer, L.,P. Forsyth and R. Spurr (2003a), 'Inter-industry effects of tourism growth: some implications for destination managers', *Tourism Economics*, **9** (2), pp. 117–32.

Dwyer L., P. Forsyth and R. Spurr (2004a), 'Evaluating tourism's economic effects: new and old approaches', *Tourism Management*, **25**, pp. 307–17.

Dwyer, L., P. Forsyth, R. Spurr and T. Ho (2003b), 'The contribution of tourism to a state and national economy: a multi-regional general equilibrium analysis', *Tourism Economics*, **9** (4), pp. 431–48.

Dwyer, L., P. Forsyth, R. Spurr and T. Ho (2003c), 'Estimating the regional and national economic impacts of tourism growth and special events', *ASEAN Journal of Hospitality and Tourism Management*, **2** (2).

Dwyer, L., P. Forsyth, R. Spurr and T. Ho (2004b), 'General equilibrium modelling in tourism', CRC for Sustainable Tourism, Australia, **25**, 307–17.

Dwyer, L., P. Forsyth, R. Spurr and T. Ho (2005), 'Economic impacts and benefits of tourism in Australia: a general equilibrium approach', *STCRC Sustainable Tourism Management Series*, February.

Dwyer, L., R. Mellor, N. Mistilis and T. Mules (2000b), 'Forecasting the economic impacts of events and conventions', *Event Management*, **6** (1), pp. 192–204.

Dwyer, L., R. Mellor, N. Mistilis and T. Mules (2000c), 'A framework for assessing "tangible" and "intangible" impacts of events and conventions', *Event Management*, **6** (3), pp. 175–91.

Economist at Large & Associates (2000), 'Grand Prixtensions: the economics of the magic pudding', Melbourne: Economist at Large & Associates.

Fossati, A. and W. Wiegard (eds) (2001), *Policy Evaluation with Computable General Equilibrium Models*, London and New York: Routledge.

Fletcher, J. (1994), 'Input–output analysis', in S. Witt and L. Moutinho (eds), *Tourism Marketing and Management Handbook*, second edition, London: Prentice Hall International, pp. 480–84.

Freebairn, J. (1995), 'Reconsidering the marginal welfare cost of taxation', *Economic Record*, September, pp. 21–30.

Getz, D. (1987), 'Events tourism: evaluating the impacts', in J.R.B. Ritchie and C.R. Goeldner (eds), *Travel, Tourism and Hospitality Research: a Handbook for Managers and Researchers*, New York: John Wiley & Sons, pp. 27–38.

Harrison G., S. Jensen, L. Pedersen and T. Rutherford (2000), 'Using dynamic general equilibrium models for policy analysis', in G. Harrison, S. Jensen, L. Pedersen and T. Rutherford (eds), *Contributions to Economic Analysis*, 248, Amsterdam: North-Holland; Oxford and New York: Elsevier.

Humphreys, J. M. and M.K. Plummer (1995), 'The economic impact on the State of Georgia of hosting the 1996 summer Olympic games', mime, Athens, GA: Selig Centre for Economic Growth, University of Georgia.

Hunn, C. and J. Mangan (1999), 'Estimating the economic impact of tourism at the local, regional and state or territory level, including consideration of the multiplier effect', in *Valuing Tourism: Methods and Techniques*, Bureau of Tourism Research Occasional Paper No. 28, Canberra, pp. 34–39.

Johnson, R. (1999), 'Input–Output models with and without the multiplier effects', in *Valuing Tourism: Methods and Techniques*, Occasional Paper No. 28, Canberra: Bureau of Tourism Research.

Industry Commission (1996), *State Territory and Local Government Assistance to Industry Report 55*, October, Canberra AGPS.

Ingerson, L. and H. Westerbeek (1999), 'Determining key success criteria for attracting hallmark sporting events', *Pacific Tourism Review*, **3** (3, 4), pp. 239–53.

Manete, M. (1999), 'Regional and inter-regional economic impacts of tourism consumption: methodology and the case of Italy', *Tourism Economics*, **5** (4), pp. 425–36.

Matheson, V. (2002), 'Upon further review: an examination of sporting event economic impact studies', *The Sport Journal*, **5** (1), pp. 2–11.

Matheson, V. and R. Baade (2003), 'Bidding for the Olympics: fools gold?', in C. Barros, M. Ibrahim and S. Szymanski (eds), *Transatlantic Sport*, Cheltenham, UK and Northampton, MA, USA: Edward Elgar, pp. 67–78.

McDougall, R. (1995), 'Computable general equilibrium modelling: introduction and overview', *Asia-Pacific Economic Review*, **1** (1), pp. 88–91.

Mules, T. (1999), 'Estimating the economic impact of an event on a local government area, region, state or territory', in *Valuing Tourism: Methods and Techniques*, Bureau of Tourism Research Occasional Paper No. 28, Canberra, pp. 40–46.

Noll, R. and A. Zimbalist (1997), 'The economic impact of sports teams and facilities', in R. Noll and A. Zimbalist (eds), *Sports, Jobs and Taxes; The Economic Impact of Sports Teams and Stadiums*, Washington, DC: Brookings Institution, pp. 55–91.

NSW Treasury and Centre for Regional Economic Analysis (1997), 'The economic impact of the Sydney Olympic games, final report', NSW Treasury and University of Tasmania, November.

Partridge, M.D. and D.S. Rickman (1998), 'Regional computable general equilibrium modelling: a survey and critical appraisal', *International Regional Science Review*, **21** (3), pp. 205–48.

Ritchie, J.R. Brent (1984), 'Assessing the impact of hallmark events: conceptual and research issues', *Journal of Travel Research*, **23** (1), pp. 2–11.

Ryan, C. and T. Lockyer (2001), 'An economic impact case study: the South Pacific masters games', *Tourism Economics*, **7** (3), pp. 267–75.

Siegfried, J. and A. Zimbalist (2000), 'The economics of sports teams and their communities', *Journal of Economic Perspectives*, **14** (3), pp. 95–114.

Siegfried, J. and A. Zimbalist (2002), 'A note on the local economic impacts of sports expenditures', *Journal of Sports Economics*, **3** (4), pp. 361–6.

South Africa Football Association (2000), World Cup Bid Details, www.safa.ord.za/html/bid_det.htm, accessed 9 January 2002.

Sugiyarto, G., A. Blake and T. Sinclair (2002), 'Economic impact of tourism and globalisation in Indonesia', Discussion Paper 2002/2, Tourism and Travel Research Institute, www.nottingham.ac.uk/ttri/series.htm.

Tourism Council of Australia (1997), 'Is there a case for generic tourism marketing?', *Access Economics*, Canberra.

Turko, D.M. and C.W. Kelsey (1992), *Conducting Economic Impact Studies of Recreation and Parks Special Events*, Washington, DC: National Recreation and Park Association.

Tyrrell, T. and R. Johnson (2001), 'A framework for assessing direct economic impacts of tourist events: distinguishing origins, destinations and causes of expenditures', *Journal of Travel Research*, **40** (1), pp. 94–100.

Victorian Auditor-General (2001), *Report of the Auditor-General on the Finances of the State of Victoria, 2000–2001*, Melbourne.

Wang, P.C. (1997), 'Economic impact assessment of recreation services and the use of multipliers: a comparative examination', *Journal of Park and Recreation Administration*, **15** (2), pp. 32–43.

Wanhill, S. (1988), 'Tourism multipliers under capacity constraints', *Service Industries Journal*, **8**, pp. 136–42.

West, G. and A. Gamage (2001), 'Macro effects of tourism in Victoria: a nonlinear input–output approach', *Journal of Travel Research*, **40** (1), pp. 101–9.
Yao, S. and A. Liu (2000), 'Policy analysis in a general equilibrium framework', *Journal of Policy Modelling*, **22** (5), pp. 589–610.
Zhou, D., J. Yanagida, V. Chakravorty and P. Leung (1997), 'Estimating economic impacts from tourism', *Annals of Tourism Research*, **24** (1), pp. 76–89.

PART SIX

APPLICATIONS

16 Valuation of tourism's natural resources
Clem Tisdell

Introduction and importance

Much tourism depends on the environment(s) at the destination(s) of tourists. Such environments may be natural, cultural, or partly man-made and partly natural. In fact, few tourist destinations involve completely natural environments. For example, the environments of most national parks are to some extent human modified, for instance by access roads, walking tracks, built facilities such as toilets, picnic tables and camping areas (often near entry points) and so on.

Because access to many environmental goods, such as beaches, national parks and other open-air recreational facilities are either not priced or only partially priced, there is a danger of their not being valued (when they are economically valuable) or of their being undervalued from an economic point of view. Consequently, this can distort economic resource allocation. Land areas which would be best left in a relatively natural state for tourism and other purposes may, for example, be developed for uses such as agriculture or housing. From an economics perspective, rational decisions about resource use or allocation require appropriate economic valuations to be made about their alternative uses.

Pigou (1938), in developing the subject of welfare economics, suggested that economic valuation might be best based, from an operational viewpoint, on monetary values. Money enables economic values to be expressed in a single unit of measurement and facilitates the comparison of economic values. It is the basis of social cost–benefit analysis. According to this approach, the aim of economic valuation of a natural resource or an area of land is to determine its social economic value for all of its alternative uses in monetary terms. The use with the highest net monetary value (determined by social cost–benefit analysis) constitutes the best economic use of the natural resource. This may involve its preservation in a relatively natural state, with tourism being one of its uses.

Much economic discussion about this matter has centred on the theory of economic valuation and on techniques that might be applied to assign monetary values to alternative uses or environmental states for natural resources. After discussing generally some background theory on economic valuation, including the theory of total economic valuation, this chapter reviews various techniques, such as the travel cost method and contingent valuation method in relation to tourism's natural resources, and then considers the relevance of a more recent development, choice modelling, to this subject, and refinements of the contingent valuation method. This is followed by a critical assessment of the current state of the subject, suggestions for future research and concluding observations.

An overview of the main theories and techniques involved in valuing tourism's natural resources

Measures of consumers' surplus have typically been the basis for assigning monetary economic values to possible alternative states for environmental resources. Willingness to pay by stakeholders for a particular state of a natural resource has been most frequently used as the indicator of the economic value of the resource in that particular state. This involves the independent estimation of the willingness to pay of each individual stakeholder for this particular environmental state and the addition of all these amounts to determine an aggregate economic valuation. Thus, in accordance with standard microeconomic theory, it assumes that the valuations by individuals are independent. Such independence does not necessarily occur in practice (compare Leibenstein 1950). Second, this type of valuation is used as a basis for social cost–benefit analysis which relies on the Kaldor–Hicks principle; namely, the assumption that if aggregate net value determined in this way rises, social welfare increases because gainers could in principle compensate losers for any losses involved. However, if compensation is not paid, issues involving income distribution become relevant.

An alternative approach is to consider the aggregate monetary sum that individuals would have to be paid to compensate them for the loss of an environmental asset. Empirically it has been found that the willingness to accept compensation for the loss of an environmental resource usually exceeds the willingness to pay for its retention (Knetsch 1990; Perman et al. 2003, pp. 429–30). The difference is often considerable. That raises the awkward question of which of the two approaches is to be preferred. The first alternative allocates property rights or entitlements in favour of those who want to retain the environmental or natural resource. The second alternative assigns property rights or entitlements in favour of those who may want to exploit the natural resources. The choice of the technique, therefore, involves a question of distributional justice. According to 'new welfare economics', the choice cannot be resolved without a value judgement.

Despite this problem, there can be a large number of cases in which both approaches (willingness to pay and willingness to accept compensation) lead to the same conclusion about optimal resource use. This strengthens any economic policy prescription based on this type of social cost–benefit analysis, even though it does not render such analysis flawless.

Few, if any natural resources, are valued just for tourism. Natural resources used for tourism are typically mixed goods and possess economic values for multiple purposes. Consequently, there are few natural resources that are just tourism's resources and normally this ought to be taken into account when valuing natural resources used for tourism. Bearing this in mind, we turn now to an overview of the main theories and techniques of valuation of tourism's natural resources, then consider some current developments of these valuation techniques, including those involving choice modelling. This will be followed by a critical assessment of the state of the subject and suggestions for future research and development.

Main theories of valuation of tourism's natural resources

The theory of the demand for and optimal use of natural resources is complex because such resources are normally used for multiple purposes and on occasion, more intensive use for one purpose, for example tourism, can be in conflict with other uses, such as nature conservation. In addition, there can be conflicts between uses of such resources for different types of tourism and recreation, for example body versus board surfing. Not all the complexities of multiple use can be examined here but the theory of total economic valuation provides a useful introduction to this subject.

According to the theory of total economic valuation, the economic value of a natural resource may be assessed by taking into account its total economic value consisting of its use value plus its non-use value. Developers of the concept include Albani and Romano (1998) and a useful outline of it can be found in Pearce et al. (1994). Subject to some qualifications, most of the value of a natural site for tourism derives from its on-site use. The economic value of a site for tourism constitutes a use value. Furthermore, in principle, exclusion from the site is possible. However, the commodity involved is not a pure private good because it involves shared or common facilities. Nature-based tourism is, therefore, appropriately classified as a quasi-public good or in the absence of an entry fee to the site, it is common property. However, few tourism sites can be classified as open access because usually some rules or regulations apply to their use. They are thus usually *res communis*.

Use values may derive from consumptive or non-consumptive use of natural resources. Passive forms of tourism are often non-consumptive of natural resources at a location, up to a point. But as discussed later, even in the case of passive tourism, incidental consumption of natural resource assets can occur with growing use of a site by tourists. On the other hand, some forms of tourism and recreation are basically consumptive of natural resources, for example, recreational hunting and fishing. Nevertheless, depending upon institutional constraints, all these forms of tourism can be sustainable.

Many natural tourist sites have non-use values. Non-use values of a site or natural resource are usually of an intangible nature and to a large extent, have the characteristics of pure public goods; they involve non-rivalry in their consumption and non-excludability from their benefits. Such values can include the existence value of nature (for example, wildlife species) associated with a site, its bequest value and arguably options for its future use. For some natural resources, non-use values constitute most of their value. For example, Bandara and Tisdell (2003) found from a study of the contingent value of the Asian elephant in Sri Lanka that its non-use value accounts for more than half of its total economic value.

An environmental resource has pure existence value if individuals are willing to pay to support its continuing existence independently of any thought of using it, for example, viewing it or visiting it. Individuals are willing to pay, for instance, to conserve some wildlife species independently of their using these, for example, whales or Australian tree kangaroos (Tisdell and Wilson 2004a). Bequest value refers to the willingness of individuals to preserve environmental assets for the benefit of future generations. Option values may exist either for use values or for non-use values and conservation of natural resources can add to economic value by leaving future use values and non-use values partly open. For example, it may be impossible to know precisely the preferences of future generations for different wildlife species. By erring in favour of conservation of varied species, expected benefits to future generations are increased by leaving options open.

It should be emphasised that total economic value only refers to economic values and usually these are based on the willingness of individuals to pay for attributes of (environmental) goods. Money is the measuring rod of value in this valuation and usually the Kaldor–Hicks criterion (potential Paretian improvement criterion) is adopted. Many normative assumptions are involved and the valuations that emerge are liable to be sensitive to the distribution of income. Some of these limitations are discussed in Tisdell and Wen (1997).

Total economic valuations can play a useful role in determining the economically optimal allocation of resources. Resources should be allocated to maximise net total economic value if the Kaldor–Hicks criterion of maximising social economic gain is adopted. The benefit of using net total economic benefit is that it takes into account both market values and non-market values. For example, suppose there is an area of land that may either be cleared for farming or left in a natural state, and used for tourism. Its use for farming is assumed to result in a net annual profit of $1 million per year. If used for tourism and entry is free, visitors may obtain a net economic surplus from the areas of $2 million annually. In addition, the area may conserve rare wildlife and even those who do not visit it may be prepared to pay for its preservation. For example, non-use values may amount to $1 million per year from its preservation. Clearly, net total economic value of this area is maximised by conserving the area for tourism rather than allowing it to be used for farming, which in this case is assumed to be inconsistent with tourism and to provide no non-use values.

Because tourism is our main focus here, our analysis of optimal resource use can be developed further by dividing the total economic value obtained from a natural site into its economic value for use for tourism or outdoor recreation and its value in a natural state for other purposes. Its value for non-tourist purposes will include its non-use values (values assigned to its public goods attributes) plus other external values such as for example, its value in sustaining clean water flows in the catchment area to which it belongs. As in most expositions of total economic value, its components are assumed to be additive.

Let us, therefore, envisage the following relationship:

$$TEV = TTV + NTV \qquad (16.1)$$

where TEV represents total economic value of a natural site, TTV its total on-site value from tourism and outdoor recreation and NTV is its total non-tourism value in a natural state. While the additivity assumption is a limitation of this approach, it seems to be a minor problem compared to ignoring completely the totality of the economic valuation problem.

Other things equal, the total tourist value of a natural site and its total non-tourist value may depend on its number of tourist visits, X_1, per unit of time. Typically, the NTV of a site may be constant up to a threshold, X_1, of tourist visits per unit of time and then decline as X increases further, for example, because visitors in large numbers damage the natural site. However, TTV may continue to rise when X exceeds X_1 even though it may eventually decline because of the crowding effect (Wanhill 1980; McConnell 1985) or because of visitor-induced deterioration in the natural assets that attract tourists.

In these circumstances, the economically optimal number of tourist visits (using the Kaldor–Hicks criterion) required to maximise TEV is less than that needed to maximise TTV but greater than that which maximises NTV. The optimal solution is a compromise one.

This can be illustrated by Figure 16.1. There curve 0BCEF represents the marginal TTV of the site and 0ACD represents its marginal NTV. Hence, the maximum TEV from the site is obtained by having X_2 visits per unit of time. At this point, the marginal value obtained by tourists from visits just equals the loss in marginal NTV as a result of increased tourist visits. Note

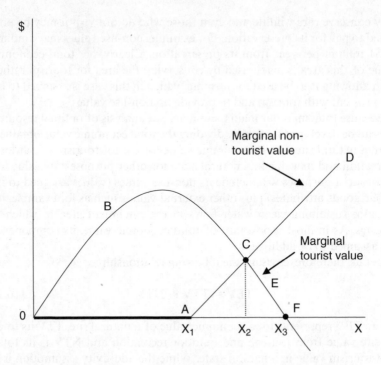

*Figure 16.1   Optimisation of total number of tourist visits so as to
            maximise the total economic value of a natural site*

that X_2 has a value intermediate between X_1, the value maximising NTV,
and X_3, the value maximising TTV.

While the case illustrated by the figure may be typical, other possibilities
can occur (compare Wen and Tisdell 2001, Sec 7.5). For example, the marginal tourism value might become zero before the threshold, X_1, is reached.
In this case, there is no conflict between maximising TTV and NTV.

If a natural site is quite popular with tourists, then the number of visits
is likely to be of a magnitude that reduces its non-tourism values, such as
those derived from the conservation of nature. Does this mean that the use
of a natural site by tourists will commonly reduce the value of the site in
conserving nature? This may be so. However, this raises the broader question of whether nature conservation necessarily suffers as a result of the
utilisation of natural sites by tourists. The answer is no.

Even if tourism at a particular natural site is to some extent at the
expense of nature conservation, in aggregate nature conservation may
benefit from the use of natural sites for tourism (compare Tisdell and
Broadus 1989). Tourist use of such sites adds to political pressure for the

provision and conservation of natural sites by stakeholders with an interest in nature-based tourism, including tourists themselves. For example, the self-interest of railroad companies in the United States played an important role in the nineteenth century in the creation of national parks, such as Yellowstone, in the west of the USA. Railroad companies supported the creation of such parks in anticipation of carrying extra passengers to them for vacations. In addition, the contacts and experience of tourists with nature may strengthen their political and economic support for its conservation. Overall, it seems likely that if all protected areas were locked away and were not available for tourism, a much smaller land area would be allocated for nature conservation than now is the case, with even more serious consequences for nature conservation than currently. In such a case, reduced political pressure can be expected for the creation of protected areas for nature.

While the economic value of natural resources for tourism can provide a strong case for their conservation, this case can often be bolstered if account is also taken of off-site non-tourism values of a natural site that would not be preserved in the absence of tourism. For example, ecosystem services enjoyed off site, such as clean water, might be maintained if tourism is allowed on the natural site and the existence value of biodiversity on the site might be retained also. Hence, those who want the site conserved for tourism purposes rather than developed would find it worthwhile not only to stress the tourism value of the natural site but also its other economic values as well. Conversely those who want the site preserved primarily for its ecological or off-site values would do well not to ignore its value for tourism purposes. In real political situations, all these sets of economic values can make a difference in influencing political decisions about whether a natural area is conserved.

Techniques for valuing tourism's natural resources
The longest-established techniques for valuing tourism's natural assets are (i) travel cost methods; (ii) contingent valuation methods; and (iii) hedonic pricing approaches. More recently choice modelling techniques have been increasingly used for this purpose. The first three techniques will be considered here and choice modelling will be covered in the next section.

Travel cost and hedonic pricing methods are usually classified as revealed preference methods. Contingent valuation and choice modelling approaches are normally viewed as stated preference methods. While it is often believed that the revealed preference methods are more objective in their derived valuations than stated preference approaches, because the latter depend on subjective responses by respondents, it is wrong (as discussed later) to believe that the former are necessarily scientifically more accurate than the latter and free from subjective influences. In any case, the different techniques often measure the value of different things, so they are rarely perfect substitutes. For example, the travel cost method usually values visits to a site whereas the contingent valuation method may measure the whole economic value that visitors place on the conservation of the site. In fact, what the contingent valuation method measures depends on the type of questions asked visitors; on what they are actually asked to value.

The travel cost method
The travel cost method for valuing outdoor recreational assets was originally suggested by Harold Hotelling (1947). It was developed by Clawson (1959), Knetsch (1963) and was followed up in Clawson and Knetsch (1966). Basically it involves using the travel costs incurred by travellers to a natural area plus any entry fee paid as a proxy for their effective price for visiting the area. Those travelling greater distances to visit the natural area will usually incur greater travel cost. Therefore, the effective price or cost of a visit is higher than for those who live closer to the natural area. Other things equal, a lower relative frequency of visits would be expected from residents living more distant from the natural attraction than those closer by, given that the demand for visits is a normal economic good.

Usually, the areas that provide the source of visitors to the outdoor attraction are divided into zones to simplify the application of this technique. The researcher has to make a judgement about how many zones to use and how to determine their boundaries (Stymes 1990). The coarseness of zoning will be influenced to some extent by the geographical availability of data; for example, the 'fineness' of the availability of population data for different areas.

The operational core of the zoned travel cost method is the trip generation function (see, for example, Perman et al. 2003, Ch. 12). This specifies the relative frequency of visits to the attraction from the different zones in relation to the travel cost involved in visiting the site. It is the basis for estimating the demand curve for visits to the natural site and subsequently for measuring the economic surplus derived by visitors or tourists from their visits to the site (Tisdell 2005, Ch. 7). The Marshallian measure of consumers' surplus is used to derive the economic value that visitors obtain from their visit to the natural site. If entry to the site is free, this surplus is equivalent to the area under the demand curve for visits. It is the difference between the maximum amount that visitors pay to enter the natural site and the maximum amount they would be prepared to pay for entry. It is an economic value not explicitly taken into account by the economic system, but ought to be taken into account when assessing alternative uses for natural areas.

For example, suppose that the most profitable alternative use of the natural area is for beef production. Assume steady-state situations for comparative purposes. Beef production yields an annual net income of $2 million per year, and because this production from this site is negligible in relation to the total market, it has no impact on beef prices. Consequently, consumers' surplus from beef is not altered by use of the natural area for beef. The use of the natural area for tourism is estimated (for instance, using the travel cost method) to generate a visitors' surplus of $5 million annually, but involves associated costs of $0.5 million per year, giving a net economic benefit of $4.5 million annually. From a social economic perspective, retention of the natural area and its use for tourism is the more attractive economic option of the two.

Nevertheless, it is important to realise that the travel cost method has several limitations. One of the most important of these is how to measure the cost of travel and in particular what allowance to include in total cost for the time involved in travel. Should this be some fraction of possible income forgone? This is in fact often used. But it is in some cases the travel itself that is enjoyable and income is not always forgone when undertaking recreational travel. In most cases, it is alternative leisure possibilities that are forgone. In fact, Randall (1994) argues that often the allowances made for such travel costs reflect convention rather than reality. Randall argues that recreational decision making depends on the subjective, and unobservable price of travel, whereas the travel cost method uses the observer's assumed cost of travel. Common et al. (1999) demonstrate by undertaking a travel cost study of visits to Tidbinbilla Nature Reserve that the problem raised by Randall is both of empirical and theoretical significance. Randall correctly emphasises that revealed preference methods of measuring the value of recreational or tourist resources are not necessarily more objective than stated preference methods.

Problems for this method also arise when there are substitute sites, or if visitors visit several sites on the one trip, or if individuals have limited knowledge of the site to be visited, or if the site covers a large area (Tisdell and Wilson 2002). The second-mentioned problem has been noted widely in the relevant literature. Multi-purpose journeys are in fact, quite common, especially in the case of international travel by tourists. When visits to a particular site involve a journey with visits to multiple sites or other attractions, the value of the particular site is liable to be overestimated by the travel cost method unless appropriate adjustments are made. Navrud and Mungatana's (1994) estimation of the economic value of Lake Nakaru National Park in Kenya using the travel cost method appears to suffer from this problem (Tisdell and Wilson 2004b). The third problem can arise for first-time visitors to a natural area. If their information is distorted, they may spend more to travel to the natural area than they feel is justified *ex post*. Hence, their actual travel expenditure overstates their true demand to visit. An experiential good is involved. Fourth, some natural tourist areas are very large, such as the Great Barrier Reef World Heritage area. It can, therefore, be misleading to model these as a single point, as is the theoretical assumption in the travel cost approach. Within such a large area, multiple tourist sites have to be considered.

The significance of these problems will vary with the particular case under consideration. In many circumstances, despite errors, approximations still result in appropriate policy choices. Perfect theoretical models are not always required or optimal for refined decision making about natural resource use.

As pointed out in the previous section, the economic value of a natural area just for tourism or recreation rarely measures its total economic value. Therefore, the economic value of retaining a natural area rather than developing it, as in the above example for beef production, may be much greater than the economic value of the natural area for tourism. Contingent valuation methods can be used to help account for a broader range of economic values provided by the natural area.

The contingent valuation method
The contingent valuation of a natural area (by stakeholders with interests in it) usually measures its economic value *contingent* on its preservation. Contingent valuation is valuation contingent upon some event or circumstance, and often (but not always) it involves willingness to pay to retain the status quo of a natural resource. If it is a natural area, the complete contingent valuation of it would include its total tourist value plus its total non-tourist value. In such a case, it is not the stated preference analogue of the travel cost approach. If the natural area has non-use values, the contingent valuation method (CVM) should ascribe a higher economic value to the natural area than the travel cost method.

But there is a stated preference analogue to the travel cost method. It involves eliciting from visitors the maximum fee that they would be prepared to pay to visit the natural area, everything else held constant, and deducting the actual fee charged to determine their consumers' surplus. Such an estimate would exclude the existence and bequest value of the area as well as other non-tourist values. It is a stated preference method for estimating visitors' surplus.

Nevertheless the CVM can be used, in principle, to elicit from visitors to a natural area the total economic value that they place on the tourism asset. This economic valuation will include not only their economic surplus from visits but also existence, bequest and other values of the site in the opinion of visitors. However, the total valuation placed on the natural resources by visitors may fall far short of its aggregate economic value because those who do not visit the natural area may also value the area highly for its existence, bequest and option values, for example (as previously defined).

Navrud and Mungatana (1994) apart from using the travel cost method estimate the economic value of Nakaru National Park, Kenya, for tourism by adopting what they describe as the contingent valuation method. However, basically they use a stated preference approach to estimate the aggregate economic surplus of visitors to the park and do not estimate the CVM of this park as an asset. That would involve total economic evaluation. Using their method, they find that the annual visitors' surplus from visits to the park is about US$7.5 million.

Tisdell and Wilson (2001) used a dichotomous choice model to determine the willingness of visitors to Mon Repos Conservation Park (near Bundaberg in Queensland) to contribute financially to the conservation of sea turtles. This provides an indication of the contingent economic valuation of sea turtles by visitors. Analysis revealed that this measure of contingent valuation of marine turtles tends to rise with the respondent's level of education, level of income, the respondent's sighting of marine turtles, whether they donated to sea turtle conservation at Mon Repos, and whether they reported a positive learning experience at Mon Repos. Tisdell and Wilson (2001) found that the ecotourism experience of visitors to Mon Repos turtle rookery on average increased their economic valuation of the existence of sea turtles.

Consider now some of the details of the contingent valuation technique of eliciting from visitors their maximum willingness to pay for a recreational asset.

The CVM was originally developed by Davis (1963, 1964), who used a bidding game approach, a method that is still widely used, to determine willingness to pay. It involves asking the respondent whether he or she is prepared to pay a designated amount to retain a particular resource. This amount is called the starting point. If the respondent says 'yes' then the same question is asked with a higher amount. If the respondent says 'no', a lower amount is tried, asking the same question. This procedure is repeated until the highest amount is found that the respondent is willing to pay. This represents the individual's contingent valuation of the resource.

An alternative simpler approach is to employ an open-ended question to elicit the maximum amount that respondents are willing to pay to retain an asset. For example, visitors to a natural site may be told that there is a proposal to withdraw a natural site from outdoor recreational use and develop it for housing. They may then be asked what is the maximum amount they would be prepared to pay to retain the current situation, everything else unaltered.

A third approach involves the use of a payment card. This card lists a series of alternative payments that could be made by the respondent who after considering the question posed and the payment card is asked to circle (or otherwise mark) the maximum amount he or she would be willing to pay. The card may be 'anchored', for example, by indicating amounts on average that individuals provide to finance various other goods supplied collectively. This, however, can introduce 'anchor bias'. Bidding games are believed to be subject to some extent to a starting-point bias. This means that the estimated value may be influenced by the level of the payment initially presented to respondents. The open-ended question approach on the other hand is often believed not to stimulate respondents to think carefully about their alternative levels of payment. Typically, it places a lower value on tourism assets than the bidding game approach (Bishop and Heberlein 1990, p. 85) and most likely a lower value than the payment card approach. However, the open-ended question approach is simple and can be a cost-effective basis for many social decisions about alternative method resource use. It can be (in a world of bounded rationally) a suitable basis for optimally imperfect decision making (Baumol and Quandt 1964; Tisdell 1996).

A more recent method for determining contingent valuation is the dichotomous-choice technique (Bishop and Heberlein 1990). One variant of this method involves presenting each respondent with a single bid that the respondent may either accept or reject. The bids offered to the sample of those surveyed are drawn randomly from a range of potentially relevant values. The relative frequencies of respondents are then used to estimate the mean willingness to pay of respondents in the sample and this is extrapolated to the relevant population to estimate the contingent value of the resource to be valued. This method (also called referendum CVM) is designed to overcome the problem of starting-point bias, and simulates the type of choice that is made in markets about whether or not to purchase a private good.

Starting-point bias is sometimes found to be present when the bidding game approach is used. This means that the respondents can be influenced by the magnitude of the starting value tested in the bidding game. According to Bishop and Heberlein (1990, p. 87) disagreement continues about the most desirable CVM and new methods continue to be developed. Furthermore, they point out that in many cases the various methods give similar results and that 'the choice of questioning technique is still largely a matter of individual judgment'.

Naturally CVM has a number of additional limitations to those already mentioned. For example, strategic bias may occur. In such a case, respondents do not give their real values but vary those in an attempt to influence policy outcomes. Hypothetical bias may also arise. In such cases, individuals find it hard to imagine accurately the alternatives they are asked to value so their answers may not reflect their values in a real situation. Instrument bias can also occur. Answers may be influenced by the way in which respondents are hypothetically asked to pay for their choices. Furthermore, one should be aware that most CVM studies are based on a partial approach.[1] While this approach has a range of valid applications, errors can be made in generalising from partial studies to aggregate circumstances. Suppose, for example, that several natural sites are substitutes. The evaluation of each independently may result in the conclusion that each has low economic value for recreation and other purposes. However, it cannot be concluded that all have low economic value because withdrawal of the availability of some will increase the economic value of the remainder if they are substitutes (compare Samples and Hollyer 1990). As usual, caution and judgement are required when drawing policy conclusions from the application of economic techniques.

Hedonic pricing techniques
Usually CVMs are not used to value the attributes of the natural resources attracting tourists. Hedonic pricing techniques can potentially be used for this purpose. These are revealed preference type of techniques. From observed behaviour, inferences are drawn about attributes or characteristics of goods that give pleasure to those that consume them. The marginal utility of those attributes may for instance be estimated using such studies.

The hedonic method relies on the existence of complementarity between the demand for private goods and environmental attributes associated with them. For example, housing land values may be higher for blocks giving an ocean view or a view of a national park, than comparable blocks without such a view (compare Pearson et al. 2002). By making various assumptions, it is often possible to estimate the economic value placed on the environmental amenity. A comparable case in relation to tourism may be differences in hotel or accommodation tariffs for facilities located so as to provide tourists with superior environmental attributes compared to those with less salubrious environs.

However, as discussed below, hedonic travel cost models have been developed in an attempt to take into account the influences of varied attributes or characteristics of sites or natural resources on the valuation of these by tourists. Brown and Mendelsohn (1984) provide an early contribution along these lines.

Some current developments of relevant valuation techniques
Techniques used to value tourism's natural resources continue to develop, and change in the degree of their popularity. Furthermore, hybrids of different methods have also evolved (see, for example, Cameron 1992).[2]

It is widely accepted that standard environmental valuation techniques have not given enough attention to valuing the attributes of sites. This is so for standard travel cost analysis and for most applications of contingent valuation. As Pendleton (1999, p. 168) observes,

> A single value for the recreation benefits of a given site is rarely of interest for management purposes unless the manager is considering the loss of an entire site. Instead managers usually are concerned about the economic impacts of changes in the quality of a site or the quality of all sites. Effective management requires valuation techniques that can determine the economic impact of quality changes in recreation sites.

The hedonic travel cost method and random utility models were developed in an attempt to address this issue (Pendleton 1999). As explained by Brown and Mendelsohn (1984, p. 427), the process involved in the application of the hedonic travel cost method is as follows: 'The prices of recreational attributes are estimated by regressing travel costs on bundles of characteristics associated with each of several potential destination sites. The demand for site characteristics . . . is then revealed by comparing the site selection of users facing different attribute prices'.

Brown and Mendelsohn helped to develop the hedonic travel cost method and applied the technique to determine the demand for recreational inland fishing, taking into account the characteristics of scenery, lack of congestion, and fish density. In principle, the method is a revealed preference one. But only some attributes of a site may be objectively measurable. For example, in this case, although fish density can be approximated objectively, scenic value is more subjective.

This method has been subject to considerable criticism, as for example referenced in Font (2000). Font in fact uses a two-stage travel model to assess the economic value of natural areas in Mallorca for travel there. Using that method, he finds such resources to be of considerable economic value in attracting international tourists to Mallorca.

The hedonic travel cost method faces all of the limitations of the ordinary travel cost method plus others even though its objective of taking into account the varied attributes of tourist resources is admirable. It requires the researcher to decide what attributes are important and some of those may not be objectively measurable. Also the sites visited may not have sufficient diversity of attributes or may not have enough visitors to measure empirically the value of the full possible range of attributes, or to do so significantly.

In such cases, choice modelling can be superior. Choice modelling approaches are becoming increasingly popular for environmental valuation. Like contingent valuation, choice modelling is a stated preference method. It differs from contingent valuation methods because it considers the choices that individuals make when offered hypothetically or 'experimentally' environmental goods with different attributes or characteristics. In the case of CVM, usually only two alternative states of the environmental good are compared, and these usually are its availability compared to its non-availability.

Choice modelling (involving choice experiments) has a similar theoretical basis to the characteristics approach to demand theory developed by Lancaster (1996a, b). It is also related to dichotomous-choice contingent valuation based on the random utility model (Luce 1959; McFadden 1974) or also to referendum CVM (described earlier in this chapter as dichotomous-choice CVM).

Hanley et al. (2001) provide a useful overview of choice modelling, and Boxall et al. (1996) present a readable introduction to the choice experiment approach to choice modelling and compare it with a referendum contingent valuation approach. Boxall et al. illustrate their article with a case study involving the demand for recreational moose hunting and Hanley et al. illustrate their review with examples involving the demand for rock climbing in Scotland.[3]

Both referendum and dichotomous-choice CVM present respondents with the possibility of making one choice from a set of alternatives. Typically, however, choice modelling presents respondents with many more scenarios about which they must choose than does CVM. For example, the moose hunting case study of Boxall et al. (1996) involved 32 scenarios requiring 32 choices. However, they varied the scenarios presented to respondents so that each respondent only had to consider 16 scenarios and make 16 choices.

The stages involved in choice modelling are clearly set out in Hanley et al. (2001, p. 437), who also point out that there are four main types of choice modelling: (i) choice experiments developed initially by Louviere and Hensher (1982) and Louviere and Woodworth (1983); (ii) contingent ranking; (iii) contingent rating; and (iv) paired comparisons. The choice experiment approach, applied, for example, by Boxall et al. (1996), requires respondents to choose between two or more alternatives in each of a range of scenarios. One of the alternatives included is maintaining the status quo. Contingent ranking involves respondents ranking the alternative scenarios presented, contingent rating requires the respondents to assign a value on a Likert scale, usually of 1–10, to each of the alternative scenarios presented; and paired comparisons requires a similar assignment but alternative scenarios are only presented to respondents in pairs.

The approach involving choice experiments is usually favoured by economists because of its grounding in economic welfare theory. The other methods are more problematic in terms of their economic basis. However, it is possible that their application could on occasion be justified if they provide economical rules of thumb for decision making (Baumol and Quandt 1964; Tisdell 1996).

In their case studies, both Boxall et al. (1996) and Hanley et al. (2001) use travel costs as the proxy for the price of taking advantage of alternative scenarios involving different attributes. However, as pointed out by Randall (1994), actual travel costs are difficult to measure because many of the cost elements involved are subjective. In such cases, economic inferences drawn from choice experiments can be subject to some of the limitations of travel cost methods.

General limitations and future research needs
Most attempts by economists to measure the value of outdoor natural assets used by tourists or visitors concentrate on their value for recreation. In doing so, their focus is on a particular aspect of use value. For some resources, this may be their complete or prime source of economic value. But for other resources used for tourism and recreation, their source of economic value is mixed and only partially accounted for by their tourism or recreational value. The passive or non-use value of many natural areas is considerable and measurement solely of their tourism and recreational value is liable to understate significantly the economic value of conserving such areas. On the other hand, some sites (such as recreational parks surrounding some man-made reservoirs) may have little or no passive use value.

Travel cost methods do not measure non-use values, and applied choice models to date have not done so either. In that respect, Boxall et al. (1996, p. 252) speculate that

> The real test of the choice experiment method, however, may lie in its ability to address non-use economic values such as preservation and existence. While these issues are presently under examination, the authors believe that this SP [stated preference] should become more widely used in the valuation of environmental amenities.

It is possible for applications of CVM to measure total economic value. But that depends on the questions asked and the population surveyed.

The various evaluation techniques suggested all involve application costs and the accuracy of most varies with sample sizes. More attention needs to be given to assessing the net operational benefits of using the different available techniques, desirable sample size in relation to cost and so on. This would be a useful step towards optimally imperfect decision making in this area.[4] There is also a related but somewhat different issue involving the extrapolation of results from one site to others and the extrapolation of historical or existing estimates of economic value to the future. There is also the possibility that developments in economic valuation by economists have been restricted by the existing theory of economic welfare. This focus is too narrow for many policy applications. Hanley et al. (2001, p. 453) observe 'There is increasing interest among policy makers to be able to somehow combine environmental CBA with multi-criteria analysis and with participatory approaches, such as citizen juries (Kenyon and Hanley, 2000). Whether and how this can be done is an important area for future research'.

While there is a need to examine this approach, it changes the focus to the exploration of methods of social conflict resolution. It involves an interdisciplinary search for 'socially optimal methods' of conflict resolution subject to political and institutional constraints. The definitions of social optimality in such cases could therefore, be different from those used traditionally in welfare economics. It may, however, be appropriate to consider such approaches as complements rather than substitutes for existing economic approaches to optimal resource use.

It is extremely desirable to consider the attributes of different natural resources used by tourists or recreationists in assessing the value of those resources and the possible economic impacts of a variation in these attributes. Choice experiments provide useful insights in this regard. But they are subject to the limitation that the utility function in relation to the characteristics taken into account is usually assumed to be linear; no multiplicative effects on utility of the attributes is allowed. While linear relationships can be used to approximate nonlinear ones as a rule over a range, linearity remains a restriction. The appropriateness of this assumption will however, depend operationally on whether it promotes optimally imperfect decision making in this subject area.

Concluding comments

Considerable progress has been made since the early 1960s in developing and applying techniques for the economic valuation of environmental/natural resources. However, as far as tourism and recreation are concerned, these developments have concentrated on estimating the use value of natural sites or resources for this purpose. While this emphasis has its relevance, this chapter emphasises the risk of neglecting non-use economic values. Taking these values into account can often strengthen the economic case for conserving a natural area used by tourists and recreationists.

Choice modelling is a positive development despite several limitations. Nevertheless, it needs to be supplemented by other approaches that pay more attention to issues involved in social conflict resolution.

Finally, this chapter emphasised that in many policy applications, variations in results obtained by applying different (but related) techniques for natural resource valuation do not alter the selected policy choice. In such cases, the least cost technique is economically advantageous. More attention should be given to identifying circumstances in which this is so.

Acknowledgements
Preparation of this chapter has been assisted by 'spin-off' benefits from a large Australian Research Council Discovery Grant. Their financial support has been of considerable help and is appreciated. I wish to thank Christopher Fleming for comments on the first draft of this chapter. The usual caveat applies.

Notes
1. A short list of additional limitations of CVM can be found in Bennett and Blamey (2001, pp. 4–5).
2. Some of these hybrids are reviewed in Bateman et al. (2002, Ch. 11).
3. For further overviews of choice modelling, see Bennett and Adamowicz (2001) and Bateman et al. (2002, Chs 6 & 7). Bateman et al. provide an excellent coverage of most stated preference methods of economic valuation.
4. There are encouraging signs of increasing attention to the decision-making costs and benefits of alternative economic valuation techniques. See for example, Bateman et al. (2002, pp. 69–70, 79–80, 139). For instance, Bateman et al. point out (p. 139) that the use of single-bounded dichotomous-choice or referendum methods tends to be expensive relative to the information generated and is also quite sensitive to the indirect assumptions used.

References
Albani, M. and D. Romano (1998), 'Total economic value and evaluation techniques', in R.C. Bishop and D. Romano (eds), *Environmental Resource Valuation: Applications of the Contingent Valuation Method in Italy*, Boston, MA: Kluwer Academic, pp. 47–71.

Bandara, R. and C. Tisdell (2003), 'Use and non-use values of wild Asian elephants: a total economic valuation approach', Economics, Ecology and the Environment, Working Paper No. 80, Brisbane: School of Economics, University of Queensland, 4072.

Bateman, I.J., R.T. Carson, B. Day, M. Hanemann, N. Hanley, T. Hett, M. Jones-Lee, G. Loomes, J. Mourato, E. Özdemiroğlu, D.W. Pearce, R. Sugden and T. Swanson (2002), *Economic Valuation with Stated Preference Techniques: A Manual*, Cheltenham, UK and Northampton, MA, USA: Edward Elgar.

Baumol, W.J. and R.E. Quandt (1964), 'Rules of thumb and optimally imperfect decisions', *American Economic Review*, **54**, 23–46.

Bennett, J. and V. Adamowicz (2001), 'Some fundamentals of environmental choice modelling', in Bennett and Blamey (eds), pp. 37–69.

Bennett, J. and R. Blamey (eds) (2001), *The Choice Modelling Approach to Environmental Valuation*, Cheltenham, UK and Northampton, MA, USA: Edward Elgar.

Bishop, R.C. and T.A. Heberlein (1990), 'The contingent valuation method', in R.L. Johnson and G.V. Johnson (eds), *Economic Valuation of Natural Resources: Issues, Theory and Applications*, Boulder, CO: Westview, pp. 81–104.

Boxall, P.C., W.L. Adamowicz, J. Swait, M. Williams and J. Louviere (1996), 'A comparison of stated preference methods for environmental valuation', *Ecological Economics*, **18**, pp. 243–53.

Brown, G. and R. Mendelsohn (1984), 'The hedonic travel cost method', *Review of Economics and Statistics*, **66**, pp. 427–33.

Cameron, T.A. (1992), 'Combining contingent valuation and travel cost data for the valuation of non-market goods', *Land Economics*, **68**, pp. 302–17.

Clawson, M. (1959), 'Methods of measuring the demand for the value of outdoor recreation', Resources for the Future, Reprint No. 10.

Clawson, M. and J.L. Knetsch (1966), *Economics of Outdoor Recreation*, Baltimore, MD: Johns Hopkins University Press for Resources for the Future.

Common, M., T. Bull and N. Stoeckel (1999), 'The travel cost method: an empirical, investigation of Randall's difficulty', *Australasian Journal of Agricultural and Resource Economics*, **43**, pp. 457–77.

Davis, R.K. (1963), 'Recreational planning as an economics problem', *Natural Resources Journal*, **3**, pp. 238–49.

Davis, R.K. (1964), 'The value of big game hunting in a private forest', *Transactions of the Twenty-Ninth North American Wildlife and Natural Resource Conference*, **29**, pp. 393–403.

Font, A.R. (2000), 'Mass tourism and the demand for protected natural areas: a travel cost approach', *Journal of Environmental Economics and Management*, **39**, pp. 97–116.

Hanley, N., S. Mourato and R.E. Wright (2001), 'Choice modelling approaches – a superior alternative for environmental valuation?', *Journal of Economic Surveys*, **15**, pp. 435–62.

Hotelling, H. (1947), 'Economic study of monetary evaluation of recreation in national parks', Letter quoted in R.E. Prewitt (ed.), *United States Department of the Interior*, Washington, DC, 1949.

Kenyon, W. and N. Hanley (2000), 'Economic and participatory approaches to environmental evaluation', Discussion Papers in Economics, 2000–15, University of Glasgow.

Knetsch, J.L. (1963), 'Outdoor recreation demands and benefits', *Land Economics*, **39**, pp. 387–96.

Knetsch, J. (1990), 'Environmental policy implications of disparities between willingness to pay and compensation demanded', *Journal of Environmental Economics and Management*, **18**, pp. 227–37.

Lancaster, K. (1966a), 'Change and innovation in the technology of consumption', *American Economic Review*, Supplement, May, pp. 14–23.

Lancaster, K. (1966b), 'A new approach to consumer theory', *Journal of Political Economy*, **76**, pp. 122–57.

Leibenstein, H. (1950), 'Bandwagon, snob and Veblen effects in the theory of consumers' demand', *Quarterly Journal of Economics*, **64**, pp. 183–207.

Louviere, J. and Hensher, D. (1982), 'On the design and analysis of simulated choice or allocation experiments in travel choice modelling', *Transportation Research Record*, **890**, pp. 11–17.

Louviere, J. and G. Woodworth (1983), 'Design and analysis of simulated consumer choice or allocation experiments: an approach based on aggregate data', *Journal of Marketing*, **20**, pp. 350–67.

Luce, R.D. (1959), *Individual Choice Behavior: A Theoretical Analysis*, New York: Wiley.

McConnell, K.E. (1985), 'The economics of outdoor recreation', in A.H. Kneese and J.L. Sweeney (eds), *Handbook of Natural Resources and Energy Economics*, 2, Amsterdam: Elsevier Science Publishers.

McFadden, D. (1974), 'Conditional logit analysis of qualitative choice behavior', in P. Zaremka (ed), *Frontiers in Econometrics*, New York: Academic Press, pp. 105–39.

Navrud, S. and E.D. Mungatana (1994), 'Environmental valuation in developing countries: the recreational value of wildlife viewing', *Ecological Economics*, **11**, pp. 135–51.

Pearce, D.R., K. Turner and I. Bateman (1994), *Environmental Economics*, Hemel Hempstead, UK: Harvester Wheatsheaf.

Pearson, L.J., C.A. Tisdell and A.J. Lisle (2002), 'The impact of Noosa National Park on surrounding property values: an application of the hedonic price method', *Economic Analysis and Policy*, **32** (2), pp. 158–71.

Pendleton, L. (1999), 'Reconsidering the hedonic vs. RUM debate in the valuation of recreational environmental amenities', *Resource and Energy Economics*, **21**, pp. 167–89.

Perman, R., Y. Ma, J. McGilvray and M. Common (2003), *Natural Resource and Environmental Economics*, Harlow, UK: Pearson Education.

Pigou, A.C. (1938), *Economics of Welfare*, 4th edn, London: Macmillan.

Randall, A. (1994), 'A difficulty with the travel cost method', *Land Economics*, **70**, pp. 88–96.

Samples, K.C. and J.R. Hollyer (1990), 'Contingent valuation of wildlife resources in the presence of substitutes and complements', in R.L. Johnson and G.V. Johnson (eds), *Economic Valuation of Natural Resources: Issues Theory and Applications*, Boulder, CO: Westview, pp. 177–92.

Stymes, D.J. (1990), 'A note on population distributions and the travel cost method', in R.L. Johnson and G.V. Johnson (eds), *Economic Valuation of Natural Resources: Issues, Theory and Applications*, Boulder, CO: Westview, pp. 139–49.

Tisdell, C.A. (1996), *Bounded Rationality and Economic Evolution*, Cheltenham, UK and Brookfield, USA: Edward Elgar.

Tisdell, C.A. (2005), *Economics of Environmental Conservation*, 2nd edn, Cheltenham, UK and Northampton, MA: Edward Elgar.

Tisdell, C. and J. Broadus (1989), 'Policy issues related to the establishment and management of marine reserves', *Coastal Management*, **17**, pp. 37–53.

Tisdell, C. and J. Wen (1997), 'Total economic evaluation of protected areas', *Annals of Tourism Research*, **24**, pp. 992–1994.

Tisdell, C.A. and C. Wilson (2004b), 'Economics of wildlife tourism', in K. Higginbottom (ed.), *Wildlife Tourism: Impacts, Management and Planning*, Altona, Australia: Common Ground Publishing, pp. 145–63.

Tisdell, C.A. and C. Wilson (2004a), 'The public's knowledge of and support for conservation of Australia's tree-kangaroos and other animals', *Biodiversity and Conservation*, **13**, pp. 2339–59.

Tisdell, C.A. and C. Wilson (2002), 'World heritage listing of natural sites: tourism stimulus and its economic value', *Economic Analysis and Policy*, **32** (2), pp. 27–49.

Tisdell, C. and C. Wilson (2001), 'Wildlife-based tourism and increased support for nature conservation financially and otherwise: evidence from sea turtle ecotourism at Mon Repos', *Tourism Economics*, **7**, pp. 233–49.

Wanhill, S.R.C. (1980), 'Charging for congestion of tourist attractions', *International Journal of Tourism Management*, **1**, pp. 168–74.

Wen, J.J. and C.A. Tisdell (2001), *Tourism and China's Development*, Singapore: World Scientific.

17 Implications of human capital analysis in tourism

Javier Rey-Maquieira, Maria Tugores and Vicente Ramos

Importance of the issue

Even though Adam Smith in *The Wealth of Nations* had already pointed out the importance of human capital as an explanatory factor of growth, there is no doubt that in the last forty years the economic theory has improved outstandingly its understanding of the role of human capital in economic development. From the first studies of Shultz (1960, 1961), an important part of the economic growth literature has focused on the effects of human capital on productivity.

Starting with Solow (1957), an important part of the research dealing with growth accounting has tried to explain the determinants of growth apart from raw labour and capital accumulation. In some of the main papers on the issue (Griliches 1970, 1977; Kendrick 1976, 1994), human capital has been identified as one of the explanatory elements of the Solow residual 'black box'. From a theoretical perspective, the proposal of Lucas (1988) has turned into a benchmark in the modelisation of human capital accumulation as the driving force of economic development. In fact, many of the new theories of growth are based on the existence of externalities in education (Topel 1998).

From the microeconomic perspective, Gary Becker is considered to be the father of the contemporary human capital economic literature. The goal of these studies is the analysis of individual, family and social investment decisions in human capital and their policy implications. The topics under consideration are, among others, the relationship between individual demand for education and the supply of educated labour, the variance in earnings that can be explained through differences in the components of human capital endowments as education, on-the-job training, experience, migration or health, and the connection between them and labour productivity.

During the last decades, an important increase in the average level of human capital has taken place in all developed economies. This has put the analysis of human capital issues at the forefront of labour studies. As

Freeman (1986, p. 357) points out, 'The human capital revolution of the 1960s and 1970s turned the previously peripheral topic of demand for education into a major area of research for labour economists'. There is no doubt that in the modern world in which flexibility and competitiveness are essential, investment in human capital could be a good tool to deal with these challenges (Groot and Maaseen van den Brinks 2000).

In the case of tourism, whose direct and indirect impact is estimated by the World Travel & Tourism Council to account for about 234 million jobs worldwide in 2006, the role of human capital is essential at least for two reasons.

First, a general subject has to do with the relation between human capital, productivity and growth in the different sectors of the economy. As Solow (2000) pointed out, one of the main unsolved problems in the economics of growth literature is the link between sectoral composition and development. The common thought in the literature is that manufacturing is the key sector for economic development and, consequently, the increasing trend of income and employment share of the service sector could be deleterious to growth given its believed flat productivity path. However, some authors (Baumol 1985; Fuchs 1985; Kendrick 1985; Griliches 1992; Dollar and Wolff 1993; McLachlan et al. 2002) reject this idea. Still, it is difficult to measure the implications of specialisation in tourism for different reasons, such as problems in the measurement of productivity (Kendrick 1985; Griliches 1992; Debbage and Daniels 1998) the delimitation of the sector (Roehl 1998; Smith 1998) or the unresolved role in tourism of productivity-enhancing activities as innovation or human capital investment. There is no doubt that the statement that relates low levels of productivity and low salaries to the tourism industry must be examined in depth[1] (Keep and Mayhew 1999).

The second reason has to do with the role of human capital within the sector. Logically, the problem of delimitation of the tourism sector makes it difficult to analyse training and education needs as well as individuals' demand for education. Most of the relevant issues related to the role of human capital have already been studied in depth in the manufacturing or service sectors as a whole (Freeman 1986). Some of these general topics that can be further applied to the tourism industry are: the substitution possibilities between educated labour and other inputs, the demand for education, the relationship between qualifications and productivity, the role of training, the policy implications, or the relationship between migrations and qualifications, among others. Moreover, the importance of personal services in the tourism sector, where the customer is directly in contact with the worker (Baumol 1985), makes it necessary to study some other specific topics such as the relationship between quality of the product and employees' education. Maxwell et al. (2001) and Fleetwood (2002b) state that only a properly educated workforce could be able to sustain the high level of friendly, efficient and professional service, which is a major ingredient in ensuring satisfied customers and continued growth. However, labour conditions in the sector are very poor, with low salaries, high rates of turnover, high seasonality, anti-social working hours, a lack of a career path design, and comprising a significant proportion of informal tasks, that make the acquisition of skills and, therefore, the improvement of the final service, difficult (ILO 2001; Maxwell et al. 2001).

Summarising, some of the relevant questions about human capital in the tourism sector coincide with general issues of the economic analysis: what is the contribution of educated labour to productivity? What are the strategic sectors of an economy? What is the role of sectoral policies? However, other questions stem from specific tourism characteristics: is tourism a sector with a low level of productivity? How can productivity be measured in this sector? What are the education and training needs of the sector? What is the role of general and specific training? What is the relationship between education, training and the quality of the product supplied? What is the role of human capital in the innovation decisions of the tourism industry? Could it be the driving force of the sector? What is the relationship between investment in human capital and earnings?

The structure of the rest of the chapter will be as follows. The next section shows how human capital issues have been studied in the tourism literature so far. The third section critically evaluates these main contributions. Then some general considerations are presented on the state of the art in human capital research, specifying the topics that could be further developed in the tourism field. The final section concludes with a summary of the main ideas and issues of the chapter, with special attention to future research.

Overview of the main contributions
In the economic literature, there is a consensus that education and training are important for any firm to ensure its success in a changing and intensely competitive environment. It is also argued that this importance is particularly high in the tourism and hospitality industry, where the quality of service continues to be the most important characteristic differentiating a company or a destination from its competitors.

In this section, we examine the fundamental issues that have been developed in the last decades in the field of human capital resources related to the tourism industry. Most of the main ideas that have been treated are presented but, of course, not all papers are referenced. Table 17.1 summarises the main topics that can be found in the literature.

Table 17.1   Human capital topics in the tourism literature

Topic	References
Curriculum planning and evaluation	Formica (1996); Airey and Johnson (1999); Chung (2000); Churchward and Riley (2002); Collins (2002)
Career paths and skills	Finegold et al. (2000); Ladkin (2002)
Training needs	Sheldon and Gee (1987); McColl-Kennedy and White (1997); Formica and McCleary (2000); Aktas et al. (2001); Beeton and Graetz (2001); Agut and Grau (2002)
Training incidence	Kelliher and Johnson (1997); ILO (2001); Ramos et al. (2004)
Evaluation of education and training activities	Hocutt and Stone (1998); Pizam (1999); Jameson (2000); Davies et al. (2001)
Government involvement	Pollock and Ritchie (1990); Esichaikul and Baum (1998); Light and Dumbraveanu (1999); Pizam (1999)

Curriculum planning and evaluation
The discussion about the contents of specific tourism studies is one of the most elaborated areas in the literature. Some of the questions that researchers tried to answer were: (i) What are these courses currently offering? (ii) What are the graduate students' perceptions regarding the effectiveness of the tourism education? (iii) What recommendations can be made to improve the system?

Airey and Johnson (1999) try to answer the first question for the case of the UK. The study's data come from the prospectuses of the nearly 100 graduate and postgraduate courses in the UK that include tourism in their title. The main finding is that most courses include common areas of knowledge whose aims are substantially vocational and business orientated.

Chung (2000), Churchward and Riley (2002) and Collins (2002), centre on the evaluation of the tourism education from the stakeholders' perspective, specifically by questionnaire responses of the professionals in the sector and the current and graduate tourism students in different countries. All of them agree that there is a need for improving the mix of academic and practical experience and point out, among others, marketing, finance and second languages as subjects where there is room for enhancement. It is worth mentioning the methodology used by Chung. He tested his hypothesis by using statistical techniques such as factor analysis, canonical correlation analysis, multiple regression analysis and discriminant analysis.

Related to this topic, Formica (1996) points to the internationalisation of hospitality curricula in the last decade because of the necessity to cover the demand for future professionals in one of the most global sectors, the tourism industry.

Career paths and skills

A second topic that has been studied in the literature is the relationship between education and training on the one hand and the career paths of workers on the other. Two of the studies that tackle this topic in the tourism sector are Finegold et al. (2000) and Ladkin (2002). Focusing on the hotel business, both conclude that specific studies are becoming increasingly important in career development.

Finegold et al. analyse the link between national skill-creation systems and individual career paths through a comparative study of the US, the UK and Germany. Ladkin refers to the Australian hotel managers' case. The authors highlight the importance not only of general education but also of on-the-job training for promotion.

Training needs

A significant proportion of the papers on human capital in tourism have dealt with the study of training needs of the tourism sector. Some of the findings of this branch of the literature are summarised in Table 17.2. The results show that different subsectors in the tourism industry and different locations have different training requirements. However, there is a consensus on the need to improve the employees' qualification in languages, customer service and new technologies.

Agut and Grau (2002) highlight the differences between technical competence needs and training requests. McColl-Kennedy and White (1997) have made a significant contribution by measuring customer perceptions of the service quality. Specifically, the results show a significant difference between customer and employee perceptions, with customer perceptions of service quality being significantly lower than those of the employee. The main conclusion of the authors is that it would be advisable to restructure training activities, taking into account customer preferences. Only then will training design be appropriate. Sheldon and Gee (1987) compare the different opinions of both employees and employers with respect to training needs.

Training incidence

A logical step after detecting training needs is to quantify the incidence of training among workers and firms. It is difficult to establish exactly the

Table 17.2   Classification of the main results in the training needs research

Author	Sector and location	Qualifications most needed
Agut and Grau (2002)	Hotels and restaurants in Spain	Information technology Languages
Aktas et al. (2001)	Hotels in Turkey	Foreign languages General education
Beeton and Graetz (2001)	General tourism sector in Australia	Sales and service (marketing) Business
Formica and McCleary (2000)	Hotels in Italy	Human resources Marketing
McColl-Kennedy and White (1997)	Hotels in Australia	Customer service
Pizam (1999)	General tourism sector in Latin America	Customer service Foreign language Computers
Saibang and Schwindt (1998)	Hotels in Thailand	Customer service A second language
Sheldon and Gee (1987)	General tourism sector in Hawaii	Human relations and courtesy Communications

percentage of firms and workers involved in training processes because of the different definitions used in different works. For example, while Kelliher and Johnson (1997) report that on-the-job training was carried out in all hotels in the UK, Ramos et al. (2004) found a much lower incidence, especially in low category hotels, in the Balearic Islands (Spain). This sharp difference could be due to the different definition of training.

Ramos et al. (2003) use a discrete choice model in order to identify which characteristics of both employer and employee determine the provision of training. The main finding is that, between high- and low-quality hotels, there are large differences in on-the-job training but there are no differences in formal education.

Evaluation of education and training activities
The evaluation of education and training involves the attempt to measure their effects on productivity and service quality. Over a decade ago, research

undertaken in the UK, published as *Training in Britain: A Study of Funding, Activity and Attitudes* (HMSO 1989), revealed that 85 per cent of UK employers made no attempt to assess the benefits gained from undertaking training because of the difficulties in quantifying the effects and the lack of interest of employers regarding monitoring. However, nowadays the business climate suggests that such an attitude is no longer tenable and the evaluation of education and training activities is the goal of many tourism studies.

With respect to the evaluation of education, Pizam (1999) shows that most Latin American countries lack the qualified and motivated tourism human resources to effectively compete with other tourism areas. In many countries, the education provided in public schools is perceived to be inadequate for the needs of the tourism business. The number of external tourism training institutions is insufficient to meet the needs of an expanding industry. Moreover, the number of in-house training programmes is insufficient and their quality is deemed to be mediocre.

In the case of training activities, Davies et al. (2001) conclude that in Western Australia there is a link between the provision of training and an improvement in quality, commitment and productivity, and that training activities can also work towards reducing labour turnover. Moreover, Jameson (2000) examines the training practices of small tourism and hospitality firms in four regions of England. He stresses the low incidence of training activities in small tourism and hospitality firms. However, in these cases most of the participants evaluate them positively. In both papers, the study focuses on employer responses through questionnaires.

In all of these papers there is an indirect evaluation of training activities through employers or institutions related to the sector. In no cases have employees been interviewed or a measurement undertaken of the possible consequences (reduction of turnover, increase in productivity, among others). Therefore, there is a lack of a more accurate analysis in that sense.

From a methodological point of view, Hocutt and Stone (1998) use two surveys where more than 300 undergraduate students were asked for their impressions on employee and customer responses to the provision of training in a restaurant context. It was shown that empowerment via training led to higher employee and customer satisfaction.

When evaluating the effectiveness of training programmes, the literature clearly indicates that training is an important component of successful tourism and hospitality organisations but that it must be approached with caution: training objectives must be clearly articulated and action plans must be developed.

Government involvement
Finally, the hospitality and tourism literature analyses the role that government and other public institutions may play in the process of increasing the human capital stock in the tourism industry.

Most papers agree that the government and other public institutions, such as national tourism organisations, have a key role to play in the provision of training and in the improvement of tourism-orientated education. This is especially important for countries where a developed and education-conscious private sector is absent. Esichaikul and Baum (1998) and Pizam (1999) find that this is the case for Thailand and South America, respectively. From a different point of view, Light and Dumbraveanu (1999) examine the role of institutions on tourism restructuring in post-communist Romania. Related to this topic, Pollock and Ritchie (1990) describe the efforts of two provincial governments in Canada to formulate an integrated strategy for the planning and development of a tourism education and training system in order to ensure a greater degree of interdependence among different levels of the total education system.

Critical evaluation of existing literature
Although the literature reviewed above makes interesting contributions to the understanding of the role of human capital in tourism, it suffers from several shortcomings that limit its scope and open possibilities of new research on the topic.

First, most of the human capital studies reviewed in the previous section have limited their analysis to specific segments of the tourism sector, mainly hotels and restaurants, and have focused on the analysis of the tourism education system or the training needs in a specific region or country. Exceptions are Finegold et al. (2000), who compare the training incidence (that is, the amount of training provided, the number of cases where workers receive training and the percentage of workers that have been trained) in the US, the UK and Germany, and Beeton and Graetz (2001), who differentiate between the different segments of the tourism sector. More effort should be made to make geographical comparisons and to compare the characteristics of the different segments of the tourism sector.

Second, an important problem that arises in the existing literature is the imprecision in the definition and measurement of human capital. On the one hand, when the role of formal education is evaluated, no attempt is made to differentiate among different levels of education (such as university study, tourism management degrees, or vocational schools, among others). On the other hand, educational and training needs may differ with the job hierarchy and the department in which the employee is actually working. However, most of the studies do not disaggregate among jobs, and the few who do have only differentiated the role of education for managers.

Third, a similar problem arises when we analyse the incidence and consequences of on-the-job training. In many cases, the definition of training is based on the fulfilment of formal or informal courses, the place where the training has been provided, the instructors, or the institution that pays for the courses. This situation creates a wide range of classifications, making it difficult to compare training activities through different papers. An important effort in that sense is Langer (2003), who introduces the 'training activity degree', a new method for the quantitative measurement of training activities, by presenting an empirical application to the Austrian and German accommodation sector.

Fourth, from a methodological point of view, the existing tourism literature is mainly empirical and based on descriptive analysis. Most of the studies have been conducted through questionnaires addressed to managers or experts in the sector, and sometimes to customers, which reflect opinions or quantify some particular actions. However, scant attention is paid to the direct measurement of human capital investment effects on salaries, productivity or turnover, based on worker responses. Moreover, there are serious shortcomings in the use of modern econometric techniques and the availability of large representative samples.

Finally, another important gap in the literature is the lack of theoretical support to the empirics. There is little attempt to examine the relationship between human capital theoretical models and empirical applications to the tourism sector. This is due to the fact that most of the topics have been analysed from a management, marketing or sociological perspective. In fact, it seems that the need to analyse the relationship between human capital and the tourism sector, which contributes significantly to the gross national product of many developed and developing countries, has been neglected by the experts in economic theory and political economy.

State-of-the-art thinking on the topic

The deficiencies of the economic analysis on human capital in the field of tourism go beyond some temporal shortcomings. First, we examine the origins of the shortcomings from a general point of view. Second, we present some topics that have been covered by the labour economics literature but have not been fully explored in the tourism sector analysis.

Introduction and some general problems

One of the reasons for the lack of economic analysis in tourism, which has been pointed out by Sinclair and Stabler (1997) and Tisdell (2000) among others, stems from the low priority given to services in economic studies historically.

Some of the shortcomings in the economic analysis of services have their roots in classical economics. The distinction between goods and services made by Adam Smith was linked to the difference between productive and unproductive work. This was due to the fact that, for many classical economists, the term 'productive' was associated with an increase in the stock of material wealth and therefore, given that services could not be accumulated, they were regarded as unproductive. As Preissl (2000, p. 125) states 'The immaterial nature of services has long been one of the factors which formed the perception of them as low-tech, low-productivity industries with little impact on a country's economic performance'.

Another possible cause of the marginal emphasis put on tourism arises from the fact that the economic importance of the services sector is a relatively recent phenomenon. As Fuchs (1985, p. 319) stresses,

> The gaps in data result primarily from the heavy hand that history plays in the shaping and funding of the government's statistical programs. Because we were originally an agricultural nation, it is relativity easy to find out how many plums were grown in South Carolina last year, or to obtain other detailed information about minor crops. Because we have been industrialized for a century, the manufacturing sector is also covered thoroughly. The service sector, however, which accounts for more employment and more gross national product than agriculture and industry combined, receives much less attention.

Although it seems to be a growing interest in the analysis of the services sector and especially in the evolution of its productivity, tourism has not been a preferential subsector in this analysis (Inman 1985; Griliches 1992; Wolff 1999). This explains the lack of data and national accounting classifications that could contribute to the economic analysis of tourism (Baum 1993). Moreover, as Smith (1998) points out, the heterogeneous and unconventional nature of tourism conflates with the focus on manufactures in the information systems to produce a lack of useful data.

The special nature of tourism in conjunction with the historically low interest in services in the economic analysis has led to an array of conceptual and measurement complications in the study of the determinants and evolution of productivity in tourism in which human capital plays a primary role. Here again some lessons can be learned from the incipient literature on the services sector:

- The analysis of the evolution of productivity in the tourism sector is influenced by the traditional view that services have a low productivity performance relative to manufactures. However, as Inman (1985),

Miles and Tomlinson (2000) and McLachlan et al. (2002) put forward for the case of services, this view can be misleading because of the lack of homogeneity of services. This heterogeneity, which is one of the main obstacles for an economic analysis of tourism (Smith 1998), may render any statement about productivity, innovation or human capital needs in the tourism sector imprecise. Several new classifications of output have been proposed that could be useful to analyse the tourism case. First, Hill (1999) proposes a new taxonomy for the classification of output in tangibles, intangibles and services. The distinction between intangibles and services is based on the idea that services, contrary to intangibles, do not exist independently from the producers or consumers and that the services typically consist of some kind of improvement to an existing entity. The fact that part of the tourism product can be considered as an intangible could simplify the study of the sector. Second, Baumol (1985) in his analysis of the current productivity performance in services, distinguishes among stagnant personal services, progressive impersonal services and asymptotically stagnant impersonal services. Baumol's analysis regarding a possible change in the evolution of productivity in services due to innovation, technological progress or substitution effects could be of interest for the special case of tourism. That is, his statement that there are no services segments where innovations have no role to play can be applied to the tourism sector and therefore challenges the conventional wisdom that the specialisation in tourism necessarily leads to low productivity and skills.

- The general measurement problems in tourism are even greater when we address the productivity issue. Again the problems are similar to those of the service sector: difficulties in the measurement of output, problems in the measurement of the quality of services, lack of good databases, problems in the measurement of relative prices and so on (Kendrick 1985; Griliches 1992; McLachlan et al. 2002). The problems in the measurement of productivity have key implications for the analysis of the role of human capital in tourism. Specifically, how can the effects of education, training and experience on productivity be evaluated without a valid measurement of the latter? How can the relationship among skills, productivity and wages be analysed or international comparisons be made? A substantial improvement of productivity measures in tourism is needed for a complete and rigorous analysis of the impact of human capital on the tourism industry.
- Another problem in the analysis of the role of human capital in tourism is the lack of literature on innovation in the tourism sector (Jacob et al. 2003). This is relevant since human capital is

a complementary factor to innovations and is necessary for both the adoption of existing innovations and the production of new innovations (Orfila et al. 2005). Again, this shortcoming traces back to the literature on the services sector, where few efforts have been made to study the relationship between innovations and services (Miles and Tomlinson 2000). Beyond the practical problem of innovations measurement in services through the conventional indicators used in manufactures (number of patents and research and development expenditure), this field of research is encumbered with the historical perception that the services activities are unproductive and, therefore, there is no room for productivity improvements through innovations.

- The last general problem that we wish to consider is the role that the labour conditions of the sector may play regarding the possibilities and efficacy of training efforts. On the one hand, an initial issue presented in many reports related to human capital considerations in the field of tourism is that the workforce generally has lower qualifications and that the sector is faced with skill shortages and recruitment difficulties (Keep and Mayhew 1999; ECC 2001; HtF 2002). Moreover, there is also evidence that the most-qualified workers are the first to leave the sector (Fleetwood 2002b). On the other hand, a well-argued topic in the literature is that, given the personal service nature of tourism activity, the endowment of human capital is particularly relevant. How can these two contradictory facts be reconciled? It is possible that, despite the importance of human capital in tourism, the poor labour conditions in this sector exert a negative effect on the workforce's incentives to invest in human capital (Baum and Nickson 1998; ILO 2001). Hence, even if there is a consensus on the benefits to be achieved from increasing the sector's human capital endowment, those efforts may be unsuccessful if they are not within the bounds of a broad change in the sector.

The labour economics approach to human capital: the case of tourism
As we have already mentioned, there is a consensus about the key role of the human input and its education and training endowment in the performance and competitiveness of the tourist sector. However, there has been little effort to adapt the research in labour economics to the specificity of the sector. In this section, we present some of the main issues on the human capital research that we consider should be further developed in the tourism literature. We differentiate four topics: the determinants of the investment in human capital, the returns to schooling, labour demand and training evaluation.

Determinants of investment in human capital The literature has extensively analysed the determinants of workers and firms' decisions on investment in human capital. We highlight three main areas of research.

First, the analysis of general versus specific human capital investment has been one of the main issues to be considered since the initial theoretical considerations on human capital investment (Becker 1964). In fact, the private incentives to general human capital investment and specific human capital investment have key implications in the design of institutional policies. It would be worthwhile to expand the theoretical analysis that may directly affect tourism activities. Whereas the conventional human capital literature states that firms will not finance generic human capital but may have incentives to co-finance specific human capital, nowadays there are theoretical approaches based on imperfectly competitive labour markets that justify firms financing generic human capital investments (Booth and Bryan 2002). Seasonality and turnover issues must also be considered in order to understand the tourism case.

Second, research on training determinants has been shown to improve when information from both individuals and firms is included (Lillard and Tan 1992). The literature has also shown that the effect of many of the determinants is not homogeneous among different kinds of workers or training systems. Therefore, it would be relevant to carry out this research for the different activities in the tourism sector.

Third, regarding the expected effect of labour condition on individual education decisions, the vast literature on the issue (Freeman 1976; Hansen 1980) concludes that there is a high supply elasticity and that expected wages is a variable that explains, at least to some extent, the variation in degrees and enrolment decisions (Freeman 1986). As we have already mentioned, this finding may have a role to play in the tourism sector given its unfavourable labour conditions. Related to the individual decisions' effect on the qualifications supply, the impact of the growing migration incidence in many developed countries should be studied. The effect of the human capital endowments of the immigrant population on the relative qualifications supply may be non-negligible for many tourism destinations.

Returns to schooling Since the contributions made by Becker, the classical theory approach considers education decisions as an investment in human capital. The establishment of large databases in the 1970s allowed researchers to test empirically the returns to such investments. Since then, many studies have expanded the Mincer (1974) wage regression specification in order to estimate the impact of the components of human capital on earnings. The general conclusion that one can draw from this literature is that the returns to schooling are positive but moderate (Freeman

1986). One remarkable fact is that most of this research is applied to the economy as a whole, or even at the very best, to manufacturing, but much less effort has been devoted to the analysis of tourism. The endogeneity of the human capital variables is one of the main methodological problems that the literature has dealt with (Card 1998). The conventional treatment of endogeneity is to use instrumental variables. It would be worth analysing whether there are particularities in the choice of instruments for the tourism case.

There is a need to improve our knowledge about the impact of the different components of human capital in tourism workforce earnings. Again, given the heterogeneity of the sector it would be necessary to perform a disaggregated analysis in order to obtain appropriate results for policy design. Moreover, the analysis of returns to schooling in tourism should be extended to international comparisons just as Trostel et al. (2002) do for the general case.

Another research issue on returns to schooling that would be particularly appropriate to develop, given the tourism employment particularities, is the difference between job education requirements and the actual endowment of the individual, that is the job-matching problem. One of the main issues in this field is related to workers' overeducation, which may be quite common among the casual tourism workforce and also has a different intensity in the various branches that comprise the tourism sector. When overeducation is detected, the research should identify the inefficiencies of such a mismatch. Additionally, there is scope to investigate the substitution possibilities of overeducation and other components of the human capital endowment as experience and on-the-job training by means of multinomial logit specification (Sloane et al. 1996). In order to extend this research to the field of tourism, proper measures of overeducation are needed. The proposed measurement methods are based on job analysis, worker self-assessment or realised matches.

Labour demand issues   A third topic of potential interest in the study of human capital in tourism is to apply the progress made by the labour economics literature in labour demand research. We want to stress specifically two areas of research, the sectoral change effect and the analysis of the complementarity or substitutability relations among productive inputs.

Given the high degree of heterogeneity that defines the tourism sector, it is reasonable to assume that changes in the relative weight of each activity, or in the productive structure of the activity (for example, innovations implementation or a movement towards increasing the service quality), will lead to relevant changes in the demand for education. The sectoral change effect on the demand for education can be approximated by means of fixed-coefficients input–output techniques, or better, through use of computable general equilibrium models. The models for applying this methodology to the case of tourism require data with sufficiently disaggregated information of tourism activities and with information on the educational endowment of the labour input. There are also additional conditions needed, beyond the conventional input–output techniques, to obtain reliable results. Specifically, there must be differences in the educational endowment of the activities under analysis, there must be differences in the employment growth between the activities, and there must be low input substitution possibilities in order to keep the fixed-coefficients specification. The conclusion from the general economic research is that a substantial amount of the change in education demand is due to sectoral composition shifts (Freeman 1977, 1980).

Another branch of the labour demand analysis is devoted to the analysis of the substitution possibilities between inputs in the production process. In the case we are dealing with, the topics of interest are the complementarity or substitutability relations between workers with different educational endowments, or between them and the capital input. Hamermesh (1993) makes a comprehensive examination of both methodological possibilities and results in the literature. The general conclusion is that investment in education reduces the price substitutability between capital and labour, and also reduces labour demand elasticity. This is a research field that could be very informative in its tourism application in order to estimate projections of the educational requirements of the workforce under alternative possibilities of sectoral composition and the effect on earnings of changes in the relative supply of qualifications.

Training evaluation The evaluation of training activities is one of the issues in human capital literature to which more efforts are being devoted (Van der Klink and Streumer 2002). As we have already pointed out above, it is reasonable to presume that there are some topics that can be further developed. Studies should include the evaluation of both public active labour market policies and firms' training programmes. In the general labour literature, there is more research in the case of public policy evaluation. This can be due to a lack of data and a greater ease in receiving funds for studies in the public sector (Heckman et al. 1993)

There are aspects of tourism activities, such as high turnover or the relevance of the informal sector, which may involve difficulties in evaluating the active labour market polices. These issues increase the inherent problems that arise from the impossibility of comparing the effects of applying or not applying the programme to the same individual. One of the issues which researchers should address is the appropriate definition of the control group and whether experimental or non-experimental techniques are used (Heckman et al. 1999).

Evaluation of firms' training programmes must include an in-depth analysis of the performance variables to be considered. Among the ones most frequently suggested are: wage growth, firms' performance evaluation, turnover and absenteeism (Krueger and Rouse 1998). The heterogeneity of the different training programmes must also be considered in order to identify differences in the efficiency of alternative proposals. Finally, the conventional problem of these evaluations, that is the programme participant's selection, can be tackled using longitudinal data in order to control for individual effects.

The results of both public and private training evaluation research can shed light on the question of whether the low levels of training are due to a lack of information by the stakeholder about the effectiveness of training, or else to his/her knowledge that training is not profitable. Of course, the answer implies opposite policy proposals.

Issues for further research (conceptual and applied)
In the course of this chapter, we have identified some shortcomings in the research on human capital in the field of tourism. In this last section, we shall summarise some issues for further research.

From a general perspective, there is a need to improve the definition of what we consider as the tourism sector. This will be helpful in order to clarify the main concepts and obtain better data. Both issues are essential for future research on tourism as a whole and for the analysis of human capital in the sector.

There is also a need to improve the use of economic analysis in tourism research. The incipient research in the services sector as a whole challenges the conventional wisdom that only manufactures and agriculture create wealth and, therefore, it can offer guidance for the economic study of the tourism sector. In the specific context of human capital research, we have pointed out the need for improving the definition and measurement of the relevant variables. Moreover, there is a lack in the use of modern econometric techniques and the availability of large representative samples. Another important gap in the literature is the lack of theoretical support to the empirics.

Finally, two matters have been pointed out that are especially relevant for future research. One of them is the lack of literature on innovation in the tourism sector. This is relevant since human capital is a complementary factor to innovations and is necessary for the adoption of existing innovations or the production of new innovations. Regarding the second one, there must be serious reflection on whether human capital policies require an improvement in the conditions of the workforce in order to break the vicious circle of low qualifications and poor labour conditions.

Note

1. An ILO (2001) report shows that the wage level in the tourism sector is lower than the national average in the case of Switzerland, Canada, Great Britain and the US. With respect to productivity, Fleetwood (2002a) and McLachlan et al. (2002) present evidence on the labour productivity differences in tourism activities, with some above, and others below, the economy's average.

References

Agut, S. and R. Grau (2002), 'Managerial competency needs and training requests: the case of the Spanish tourist industry', *Human Resource Development Quarterly*, **13** (1), pp. 31–51.

Airey, D. and S. Johnson (1999), 'The contents of tourism degree courses in the UK', *Tourism Management*, **20**, pp. 229–35.

Aktas, A., A. Aksu, R. Ehtiyar and A. Cengiz (2001), 'Audit of manpower research in the hospitality sector: an example from the Antalya region of Turkey', *Managerial Auditing Journal*, **16** (9), pp. 530–34.

Baum, T. (1993), 'Collecting and using information about human resources in tourism – the direct survey method', in Tom Baum (ed.), *Human Resource Issues in International Tourism*, Oxford: Butterworth-Heinemann, pp. 60–76.

Baum, T. and D. Nickson (1998), 'Teaching human resources management in hospitality and tourism: a critique', *International Journal of Contemporary Hospitality Management*, **10** (2), pp. 75–9.

Baumol, W.J. (1985), 'Productivity policy and the services sector', in Robert Inman (ed.), *Managing the Services Economy. Prospects and Problems*, Cambridge: Cambridge University Press, pp. 301–17.

Becker, G. (1964), *Human Capital*, New York: Columbia University Press.

Beeton, S. and B. Graetz (2001), 'Small business – small minded? Training attitudes and needs of the tourism and hospitality industry', *International Journal of Tourism Research*, **3**, pp. 105–13.

Booth, A. and M. Bryan (2002), 'Who pays for general training? New evidence for British men and women', *IZA Discussion Paper* (Institute for the study of Labor, Bonn), 486, April.

Card, D. (1998), 'The causal effect of education on earnings', in O. Ashenfelter and D. Card (eds), *Handbook of Labour Economics*, **3A**, Amsterdam: North-Holland; Oxford and New York: Elsevier, pp. 1801–63.

Chung, K.Y. (2000), 'Hotel management curriculum reform based on required competencies of hotel employees and career success in the hotel industry', *Tourism Management*, **21**, pp. 473–87.

Churchward, J. and M. Riley (2002), 'Tourism occupations and education: an exploration study', *International Journal of Tourism Research*, **4**, pp. 77–86.

Collins, A.B. (2002), 'Are we teaching what we should? Dilemmas and problems in tourism and hotel management education', *Tourism Analysis*, **7**, pp. 151–63.

Davies, D., R. Taylor and L. Savery (2001), 'The role of appraisal, remuneration and training in improving staff relations in the Western Australian accommodation industry: a comparative study', *Journal of European Industrial Training*, **25** (7), pp. 366–73.

Debbage, K. and P. Daniels (1998), 'The tourist industry and economic geography: missed opportunities', in D. Ioannides and K. Debbage (eds), *The Economic Geography of the Tourist Industry*, London: Routledge, pp. 17–30.

Dollar, D. and E. Wolff (1993), *Competitiveness, Convergence, and International Specialization*, Cambridge, MA: MIT Press.

ECC (European Community Commission) (2001), 'Improving training in order to upgrade skills in the tourism industry', Final report of Working Group B, Tourism and Employment, June.

Esichaikul, R. and T. Baum (1998), 'The case for government involvement in human resource development: a study of the Thai hotel industry', *Tourism Management*, **19** (4), pp. 359–70.

Finegold, D., K. Wagner and G. Mason (2000), 'National skill-creation systems and career paths for service workers: hotels in the United States, Germany and the United Kingdom', *International Journal of Human Resources Management*, **11** (3), pp. 497–516.

Fleetwood, S. (2002a), 'Research report no. 2: Tourism productivity and profitability', Tourism Division, Department of Industry, Tourism and Resources, Australian Government.

Fleetwood, S. (2002b), 'Research report no. 4: Tourism workforce and training', Tourism Division, Department of Industry, Tourism and Resources, Australian Government.

Formica, S. (1996), 'European hospitality and tourism education: differences with the American model and future trends', *International Journal of Hospitality Management*, **15** (4), pp. 317–23.

Formica, S. and K. McCleary (2000), 'Professional-development needs in Italy', *Cornell Hotel and Restaurant Administration Quarterly*, **41** (2), pp. 72–8.

Freeman, R.B. (1976), 'A cobweb model of the supply and starting salary of new engineers', *Industrial Labour Relations*, **33**, January, pp. 236–48.

Freeman, R.B. (1977), ' Manpower requirements and substitution analysis of labour skills: a synthesis', *Research in Labour Economics*, **1**, pp. 151–83.

Freeman, R.B. (1980), 'An empirical analysis of the fixed coefficient manpower requirements model, 1960–1970', *Journal of Human Resources*, **15** (2), pp. 176–99.

Freeman, R.B. (1986), 'Demand for education', in O. Ashenfelter and R. Layard (eds), *Handbook of Labour Economics*, I, Amsterdam: North-Holland, pp. 357–86.

Fuchs, V.R. (1985), 'An agenda for research on the service sector', in Robert Inman (ed.), *Managing the Services Economy. Prospects and Problems*, Cambridge: Cambridge University Press, pp. 319–25.

Griliches, Z. (1970), 'Notes on the role of education in production functions and growth accounting', in L. Hansen (ed.), *Education, Income and Human Capital*, New York: Columbia University Press, pp. 71–127.

Griliches, Z. (1977), 'Estimating the returns to schooling: some economic problems', *Econometrica*, **45** (1), January, pp. 1–22.

Griliches, Z. (ed.) (1992), *Output Measurement in the Services Sector*, National Bureau of Economic Research, Chicago: University of Chicago Press.

Groot, W. and H. Maaseen van den Brinks (2000), 'Education, training and employability', *Applied Economics*, **32**, pp. 573–81.

Hamermesh, D. (1993), *Labour Demand*, Princeton, NJ: Princeton University Press.

Hansen, W. (1980), 'Forecasting the market for new PhD economists', *American Economic Review*, **70** (1), pp. 49–63.

Heckman, J.J., R.J. Lalonde and J.A. Smith (1999), 'The economics and econometrics of active labour market programs', in O. Ashenfelter and R. Layard (eds), *Handbook of Labour Economics*, **3**, Amsterdam: North-Holland Elsevier, pp. 1865–97.

Heckman, J., R. Roselius and J. Smith (1993), 'US Education and training policy. A re-evaluation of the underlying assumptions behind the new consensus', Chicago Working Papers, CSP94-1, Centre for Social Evaluation.

Hill, P. (1999), 'Tangibles, intangibles and services: a new taxonomy for the classification of output', *Canadian Journal of Economics*, April, **32** (2), pp. 426–46.

HMSO (1989), *Training in Britain: A Study of Funding, Activity and Attitudes*, London: HMSO.

Hocutt, M.A. and T.H. Stone (1998), 'The impact of employee empowerment on the quality of a service recovery effort', *Journal of Quality Management*, **3** (1), pp. 117–32.

Hospitality and Training Foundation (HtF) (2002), 'A review of staff training and development in the hospitality industry', Hospitality and Training Foundation Report 2002, HtF, London.

Inman, R. (1985), 'Introduction and overview', in Robert Inman (ed.), *Managing the Services Economy. Prospects and Problems*, Cambridge: Cambridge University Press, pp. 1–24.

International Labour Organisation (ILO) (2001), 'Human resources development, employment and globalisation in the hotel, catering and tourism sector', Report for discussion, TMHCT/2001, Genova: International Labour Organisation.

Jacob, M., J. Tintoré, E. Aguiló, A. Bravo and J. Mulet (2003), 'Innovation in the tourism sector: results from a pilot study in the Balearic Islands', *Tourism Economics*, **9** (3), pp. 279–95.

Jameson, S.M. (2000), 'Recruitment and training in small firms', *Journal of European Industrial Training*, **24** (1), pp. 43–9.

Keep, E. and K. Mayhew (1999), 'Skills task force. Research Paper 6. The leisure sector', ESRC Centre on Skills, Knowledge and Organisational Performance, Oxford and Warwick Universities.

Kelliher, C. and K. Johnson (1997), 'Personnel management in hotels – an update: a move to human resource management?', *Progress in Tourism and Hospitality Research*, **3**, pp. 321–31.

Kendrick, J. (1976), 'The formation and stocks of total capital', National Bureau of Economic Research, New York, distributed by Columbia University Press.

Kendrick, J. (1985), 'Measurement of output and productivity in the service sector', in Robert Inman (ed.), *Managing the Services Economy. Prospects and Problems*, Cambridge: Cambridge University Press, pp. 111–23.

Kendrick, J. (1994), 'Total capital and economic growth', *Atlantic Economic Journal*, **22**, pp. 1–18.

Krueger, A. and C. Rouse (1998), 'The effect of workplace education on earnings, turnover and performance', *Journal of Labour Economics*, **16** (1), pp. 61–94.

Ladkin, A. (2002), 'Career analysis: a case study of hotel general managers in Australia', *Tourism Management*, **23**, pp. 379–88.

Langer, G. (2003), 'A comparison of training activities in the Australian and German accommodation trade using the training activity degree', *International Journal of Tourism Research*, **5**, pp. 29–44.

Light, D. and D. Dumbraveanu (1999), 'Romanian tourism in the post-communist period', *Annals of Tourism Research*, **26** (4), pp. 898–927.

Lillard, L. and H. Tan (1992), 'Private sector training: who gets it and what are its effects?', in Ashenfelter, O. and R. Lalonde (eds), *The Economics of Training*, II, The International Library of Critical Writings, Aldershot, UK and Brookfield, USA: Edward Elgar.

Lucas, R. (1988), 'On the mechanism of economic development', *Journal of Monetary Economics*, **22**, pp. 3–42.

Maxwell, G.A., M. MacRae, M. Adam and A. MacVicar (2001), 'Great expectations: investors in people in Scottish tourism', *Total Quality Management*, **12** (6), pp. 735–44.

McColl-Kennedy, J. and T. White (1997), 'Service provider training programs at odds with customer requirements in five-star hotels', *Journal of Services Marketing*, **11** (4), pp. 249–64.

McLachlan, R., C. Clark and I. Monday (2002), 'Australia's service sector: a study in diversity', *Productivity Commission Staff Research Paper*, Canberra: AusInfo.

Miles, I. and M. Tomlinson (2000), 'Intangible assets and service sectors: the challenges of services industries', in Buigues, P., Jacquemin, A. and J.-F. Marchipont (eds), *Competitiveness and the Value of Intangible Assets*, Aldershot, UK and Brookfield, USA: Edward Elgar.

Mincer, J. (1974), *Schooling, Experience and Earnings*, New York: Columbia University Press.

Orfila, F., R. Crespí and E. Marinez-Ros (2005), 'Innovation activity in the hotel industry: Evidence from Balearic Islands', *Tourism Management*, **26** (2), pp. 851–65.

Pizam, A. (1999), 'The state of travel and tourism human resources in Latin America', *Tourism Management*, **20**, pp. 575–86.

Pollock, A. and B. Ritchie (1990), 'Integrated strategy for tourism education/training', *Annals of Tourism Research*, **17**, pp. 568–85.

Preissl, B. (2000), 'Service innovation: what makes it different? Empirical evidence from Germany', in J. Stanley Metcalfe and I. Miles (eds), *Innovation System in the Service Economy: Measurements and Case Study Analysis*, Boston, MA: Kluwer, pp. 125–48.

Ramos, V., J. Rey-Maquieira and M. Tugores (2004), 'The role of training for changing an economy specialized in tourism', *International Journal of Manpower*, **25** (1), 55–72.

Roehl, W. (1998), 'The tourism production system: the logic of industrial classification', in D. Ioannides and K. Debbage (eds), *The Economic Geography of the Tourist Industry*, New York: Routledge, pp. 53–76.

Saibang, P. and R.C. Schwindt (1998), 'The need for employee training in hotels in Thailand', *International Journal of Training and Development*, **2** (3), pp. 205–14.

Sheldon, P. and C. Gee (1987), 'Training needs assessment in the travel industry', *Annals of Tourism Research*, **14**, pp. 173–82.

Shultz, T. (1960), 'Capital formation by education', *Journal of Political Economy*, **68** (6), pp. 545–57.

Shultz, T. (1961), 'Investment in Human Capital', *American Economic Review*, **51**, March, pp. 1–17.

Sinclair, M.T. and M. Stabler (1997), *The Economics of Tourism*, London: Routledge.

Sloane, P.J., H. Battu and P.T. Seaman (1996), 'Overeducation and the formal education/experience and training trade-off', *Applied Economic Letters*, **3**, pp. 511–15.

Smith, E.L.J. (1998), 'Tourism as an industry: debates and concepts', in D. Ioannides and K. Debbage (eds), *The Economic Geography of the Tourist Industry*, New York: Routledge, pp. 31–52.

Solow, R. (1957), 'Technical change and the aggregate production function', *Review of Economics and Statistics*, **39** (August), pp. 312–20.

Solow, R. (2000), *Growth Theory*, Oxford: Oxford University Press.

Tisdell, C. (2000), 'Introduction: basic economics of tourism', in Tisdell (ed.), *The Economics Of Tourism*', The International Library of Critical Writings in Economics, Elgar Reference Collection, Cheltenham, UK and and Northampton, MA, USA, pp. xv–xxix.

Topel, R. (1998), 'Labor markets and economic growth', in O. Ashenfelter and D. Card (eds), *Handbook of Labour Economics*, 3C, Amsterdam: North-Holland; New York and Oxford: Elsevier, pp. 2943–84.

Trostel, P., I. Walker and P. Woolley (2002), 'Estimates of the return to schooling for twenty-eight countries', *Labour Economics*, **9**, pp. 1–16.

Van der Klink, M.R and J.N. Streumer (2002), 'Effectiveness of on-the-job training', *Journal of European Industrial Training*, **26** (2), pp. 196–9.

Wolff, E. (1999), 'The productivity paradox: evidence from indirect indicators of service sector productivity growth', *Canadian Journal of Economics*, **32** (2), pp. 281–308.

18 Tourism information technology
Pauline J. Sheldon

Importance of the issue

Knowledge, information and information technology (IT) are important economic resources that must be added to the traditional economic resources of land, labor and capital. This is particularly true for the field of tourism due to its reliance on, and production of, information, and the intangible and perishable nature of the tourism product. Added to this is the fact that tourism is both a service industry and an experience industry, requiring unique applications of IT. Since many models of technological development are in manufacturing industries, tourism requires special consideration of its use of IT. Information and IT are needed to manage the experience and to process the information that contributes to the creation of quality tourism in both the private and public sectors.

Information technology represents a strong force for change in tourism development as it creates new products, new communication networks, new business models, new industry structures and new types of firms. The entire travel distribution system is being transformed due to the electronic channels and consumer access to these on-line channels. Impacts are also prevalent in the area of human resources, the automation of jobs, and the production function of travel firms. Information is a critical resource for all travel firms and destinations in their search for improved competitiveness and maximum socio-economic benefit in the global marketplace.

As information technology becomes more advanced, it is being infused with more intelligence and is used for strategic decision making and innovation. Expert systems, knowledge management systems, intelligent agents, neural networks, artificial intelligence, and even virtual reality are finding productive applications in tourism. Mobile technologies are increasingly important for travelers en route and at unfamiliar destinations. Connection to databases on travel product information and location-specific destination information are important in their search for travel information. As the desire for travel and the need for electronic connectivity grow, it is expected that IT applications will be increasingly important in tourism.

The literature in the field of tourism information technology has matured in the last ten years. A number of publications have helped to define and document the growing field of knowledge. Recent books include Poon (1993), Kasavana and Cahill (1996), Sheldon (1997), Inkpen (1998),

O'Connor (1999), Werthner and Klein (1999) and Buhalis and Minghetti (2001). The importance of the field is further demonstrated by the growth of research publications. The *Journal of Information Technology and Tourism*, started in 1998 as the journal of the International Federation of Information Technology and Tourism (IFITT), is the main refereed publication for research in tourism information technology. The *Journal of Hospitality Information Technology* started in 1999 is the publication for the hospitality technology field and is affiliated with the Hospitality Information Technology Association (HITA) and Hospitality Technology and Finance Professionals (HTFP). Both of these journals are blind reviewed and have published significant contributions to the field. Refereed papers in the field of tourism information research are also published in other generic tourism, computer science and management information system journals, however the volume of such research is limited.

Conferences, seminars, workshops and thinktanks on the topic have occurred at a greater rate in the last ten years than the printed literature. While these have added valuable discussion to the topic, few have generated new knowledge. Many have included informative sessions for industry executives seeking to understand new technologies. Others have focussed on updating attendees on new technologies and future trends. Two exceptions are the two conferences – ENTER: International Conference on Information and Communication Technologies and Tourism (sponsored by IFITT) and HITEC: Hospitality Information Technology (sponsored by HITA) – both of which have a peer review process for research presentations, and publish their conference proceedings. These two conferences are critical venues for the gestation and maturation of ideas in the field.

The success of IT in the tourism industry as noted above is due to the many benefits that it brings to private firms, destinations and travelers. Even though there is a significant cost associated with the installation, maintenance and training for quality computer systems, many short- and long-term economic benefits accrue. These include cost efficiencies in many operational situations such as the reservations function for airlines, the accounting and night audit functions of a hotel, and information retrieval by travel agencies. IT also reduces information and transaction costs for business-to-customer (B2C) and business-to-business (B2B) communications. IT also affects the production function for firms by substituting for human capital in some tasks. Automation of mundane data-processing tasks frees staff to provide more quality service to the customer, and progress to higher-level functions such as supervisory positions or guest service positions. Alternatively human resource expenditures can be diminished.

Large corporations with many branches experience both economies of scale and economies of scope from implementing IT. They typically experience improved communications, centralized record keeping and financial reporting, and vastly improved customer relationship management. Processes such as ordering from suppliers, dealing with customer complaints and preferences, and tracking historical performance are all made more efficient with the use of IT. In addition, the distribution of travel products is facilitated by the internet and the varied computerized marketing channels. The development of strategic alliances and business partners, often at the international level, is another benefit that IT is providing for some travel firms. All sectors of the travel industry are experiencing these benefits to some degree. The airline industry has perhaps been affected most, and as a result significant structural changes have occurred in that sector.

Information and IT has benefits for travelers too. Their access to more information on the destination not only reduces their uncertainty or risk, but also gives them more power in the market transactions that are needed to book travel. The market power of information traditionally resides with the travel intermediaries or the destinations. With accessibility to this information in destination choice and product purchasing at the destination, tourists accrue economic benefits.

The next section will examine the main themes in the tourism IT research literature. Then follows a critical evaluation of the field and suggestions for future directions for exploration.

Overview of main themes
The literature on tourism information technology first focussed on the use of IT to assist private sector firms in processing their internal information, driven by the desire for cost efficiencies and productivity gains. This includes operational systems, and systems for strategic management and decision making. Since large numbers of firms in tourism are small and medium-sized enterprises, research has addressed the special considerations of these enterprises relative to IT. The first part of this section will address these areas. The intangibility, perishability and geographic dispersion of the travel product has caused widespread use of IT and data communications, generating dramatic shifts in the marketing and distribution functions in the travel industry. The second part will address technological applications used in marketing and market research and those providing information and booking capabilities to tourists. The concomitant changes in the distribution systems, the development of travel advising and trip planning systems for consumers, and the use of the internet, intranets and extranets in tourism are further topics in this section.

The last part of the overview of themes will address research on the use of IT by destinations (public sector) to manage and market their destinations. The public sector provision of information through destination management systems, resource management systems, and the applications of mobile technologies are also examined.

Internal information processing at the firm level
In the 1960s and 1970s computers were first used to automate accounting and clerical procedures in hotels, airlines and other travel firms. In the 1980s, more concern and attention was given to the effects of the technology on productivity. The 1990s onward gave more consideration to the use of IT for strategic advantage. The early literature reported on and evaluated the operational aspects of information technology in tourism organizations to assist in commerce and communications. The literature in this theme area often addresses the issue from a sectoral perspective (accommodation, transportation, attractions and so on) and studies refer to the application of technology to specific types of firms in the travel industry.

In many respects the airline sector has been the most aggressive in its use of information technology in enhancing its operations, often providing a model for other sectors. Firm size tends to be larger in the airline sector, explaining their capabilities for research and development and investment in IT. Airline reservation systems, which were developed in the 1960s, formed the basis for many other types of computer reservation systems (CRSs) used in the industry, and developed to become global distribution systems (GDSs). Hotel reservation systems and car rental reservations systems followed the lead of the airlines, and eventually all such systems were connected through networks allowing travel agents and customers to access all reservation systems from a single terminal. Airlines, with their complex pricing structures, also provided leadership in the areas of revenue and yield management which have been used subsequently by other sectors (Gamble and Smith 1986).

The desire to improve operations in the airline industry has given rise to sophisticated computer systems using operations research applications to manage functions such as flight scheduling, crew management, gate assignments and workflow management (Caro et al. 2000). These applications have been shown not only to increase productivity but also to improve customer satisfaction, an important consideration for all tourism firms. Another application of computerization to in-flight catering services demonstrates its potential to streamline similar operations (Baker and Sweeney 1999). Airport operations also use information technology intensively in baggage control, security systems and in the electronic information displays of flight details.

The major operations enhancement research in the hospitality field has dealt with the functionality, application and impacts of property management systems (PMSs) and point-of-sale systems (POSs). PMSs facilitate transaction processing, booking, rooms management, guest accounting and inventory management in hotels, while POSs track order-taking, menu details, and financial and inventory data in restaurants. Much research on this topic can be found in hotel journals such as the *Cornell Hotel and Restaurant Administration Quarterly*, the *Hospitality Research Journal* and the *Journal of Hospitality Management*.

The development of hospitality IT applications is tracked by Baker et al., who studied problems with implementation of IT in hotels and its questionable value in the context of 'the productivity paradox' (1999). The productivity paradox is the concern that computers may not add to the productivity of an organization after record keeping, accounting and report generation contributions have been realized. It has also been suggested that the US lodging industry has focussed its IT applications more on improving employee productivity and enhancing revenues than anything else (Sigauw et al. 2000). There seems to be a consensus in the literature that strategic IT initiatives in the hospitality industry are limited, although different types of properties have been found to utilize IT differently. Chain-affiliated properties, for example, tend to adopt more technology and use it more creatively than do independent hotels.

The increased strategic use of IT, particularly in the area of guest services, increases a hotel's competitive advantage. The use of sophisticated guest history systems in PMSs provides the hotel with the ability to customize and personalize a guest's stay. In-room IT applications to further enhance a guest's stay have grown in recent years, often driven by cost savings for the hotel. In-room electronic bars, in-room security and locking systems, climate control systems and in-room entertainment systems are common applications that can enhance both guest services and guest satisfaction while at the same time reducing costs. Increased guest expectations for faster and more enhanced voice and data networks in their rooms have caused hotels to upgrade their data communication and telecommunication systems. Hotel use of the internet for marketing purposes has expanded, and an interesting benchmarking study of hotel operations on the internet has been published by Woeber (2000).

Cost efficiencies and productivity gains from IT have been documented in almost all sectors of the travel industry, however, since so many firms in tourism are small, medium or micro enterprises which have different resources and different decision variables, the next section will discuss some of the literature addressing this topic.

Special considerations for small and medium-sized enterprises (SMEs)
In many countries, small, micro and medium-sized enterprises constitute the major part of the tourism industry, giving rise to numerous studies

addressing the particular challenges faced by these institutions. In the past, small enterprises have found it difficult to compete with large international firms, since they lack the financial resources for expensive global marketing efforts. IT, however, has provided an equalizing force, giving them access to the same kinds of markets as multinational enterprises. Those SMEs that fail to incorporate IT into their business models are passing up opportunities to enhance their profitability and viability in the global marketplace (Buhalis and Schertler 1999).

A study of SMEs in Wales, UK found that even though usage of IT is reasonably high, it could be improved in quantity and quality of applications used (Main 2002). It is often recommended by researchers that assistance from the public sector destination management organization is needed for training employees in IT and to create networks of small firms. A similar theme is reflected in a study in Australia which suggests that networking tourism SMEs to foster a culture of connectivity would increase the learning and trust between regional Australian SMEs and thereby make them more competitive (Braun 2002).

Studies recommend techniques for small hotels to position themselves on the web effectively (Morrison et al. 1999). Often the web is seen as a substitute for a brochure of the hotel or other travel product. The authors recommend that instead, small hotels be taught how to use the technology to create 'dynamic, interactive relationship marketing tools'. A comparative study of European tourism SMEs found that integration of IT differed by sector, however, marketing applications were found to be more creative and more flexible than other functions (Evans et al. 2000). The authors of this study also recommend that coordination and support from the destination management organization is necessary to assist in the development of IT application in tourism SMEs, and the provision of education and training programs for SME operators by destinations is echoed again by Mistilis and Daniele (2000).

Strategic management and decision making
The use of information technology for decision support and strategic management of tourism enterprises is the focus of more recent research. Technology adoption by firms tends first to be used as a simple substitute for manual processes, followed later by the enlargement of a firm's operations due to cost efficiencies. The next step of IT integration is the use of IT to re-engineer their business processes.

Werthner and Klein (1999) address some of these issues in their book *Information Technology and Tourism: A Challenging Relationship*. In particular they discuss the interrelationship among IT, strategy and organization. How firms can use IT to define their portfolio of products and services, to innovate those products and services, to integrate processes and to create alliances are all examples of the strategic use of IT. The management and re-design of business networks based on the new technologies is discussed as an important strategic direction, as is the use of IT as an enabler of new forms of governance and the replacement of electronic hierarchies by electronic markets. Many low-cost carriers have been able to enter the market competitively due to the new electronic distribution channels that allow consumers to book tickets directly. The use of e-tickets and the streamlining of the reservation procedure by eliminating the travel intermediary have been the basis of their success. The internet has freed airlines and other travel suppliers from travel agent commissions, giving them a lower cost structure. Some airlines are using IT to structure strategic alliances to increase their global reach with other airlines through code sharing and frequent flyer programs, and with other firms in the accommodation or other sectors of the industry. These ideas and other strategies that have been successful for low-cost airlines are discussed in Doganis (2001) and Williams (2002).

Knowledge management requires the use of intelligent systems for maximum decision-making support. Expert systems, knowledge warehouses and data-mining systems are all ways to bring strategic advantage to firms. While they are more costly than less sophisticated computer systems, they bring unique advantages to firms who invest in them by supporting critical decision-making tasks in organizations. These also assist with customer relationship management, a critical function for all tourism enterprises. Some strategic decisions in tourism are spatially related and lend themselves to the use of knowledge management systems based on geographic information systems (GISs). Feick and Hall (2000) show how GISs can be used as a spatial decision support tool for land development planning in tourism. The authors develop a system, which facilitates strategic decisions of land usage, allowing participants from various sectors to designate land parcels appropriate for tourism-related development or for a competing land use. GISs have great promise for assisting strategic destination planning on many levels and is a recommended area for further research.

The travel distribution system, traveler advising and trip planning systems
The use of the internet for travel bookings directly by consumers and also by other travel intermediaries has dramatically and permanently changed the nature of travel distribution channels. The electronic distribution of products in general has caused dis-intermediation, and the travel industry has been affected by this perhaps more than any other industry. GDSs were once the only travel distribution channels until the internet offered an

alternative. In the last decade progressively the internet has become more dominant, giving consumer access to travel inventory. Previously only travel agents had such access using the GDS as their electronic booking and information tool. Travel agents have needed to redefine their services by offering more knowledge to consumers. Subsequently, GDSs have been reconfigured to be compatible with the internet rather than running old software platforms.

An evaluation of electronic distribution channels in the hotel sector using the Delphi technique was undertaken by O'Connor and Frew (2000). They determined four functions of electronic distribution systems and discussed whether each should be part of a system. The four are: (i) information provision, (ii) reservations capabilities, (iii) payment transactions, and (iv) contact with the consumer after the transaction. More systems are incorporating all four aspects as the technology becomes more user-friendly and capable. The same study showed that in the creation of these channels, financial matters were of prime concern, but marketing, operational, strategic and technical concerns also existed.

Many studies have examined consumer choice of distribution systems for travel planning and booking (see, for example, Perdue 1995; Fesenmaier and Jeng 2000; and MacKay and Fesenmaier 2000). The use of the internet rather than a travel agency provides the consumer with more control over the process, however they incur greater information and transaction costs. These need to be offset by price discounts that are often found on the internet. Anckar and Walden (2002) tested the hypothesis that low-complexity travel products are more prone to be self-booked on the internet than highly complex products.

Trip planning takes time and effort. Since dis-intermediation, tourists are researching their own trips and making their own reservations. This is not a costless or easy task and assistance is now being provided in the form of intelligent agents (Godart 1999). Some of the research in this area is to better understand how users think about their travel decisions and formulate their trip queries. TISCover, for example (Dittenbach et al. 2003) is planning to incorporate a trip planning module into their destination management system. Further work in this area investigates how case-based trip planning recommendation systems can assist travelers. This approach recognizes that different travelers have different decision styles and that the software needs to adapt to those decision styles (Fesenmaier et al. 1999). Travelers often experience unsatisfactory searches for travel products due to the mismatch between how they envisage their information search and how the system is programmed to respond to information requests and decisions. This is an area for more research, which if successful could streamline on-line searching for travel information.

In general, travel suppliers use multiple distribution channels to reach travelers. For destinations that are dominated by large tour operators, often the diversification of distribution channels becomes especially important. Vich-I-Martorell (2002) discusses how the internet can create market diversification and reduce the power of the middlemen who may control the success or failure of a destination single-handedly. This is a distinct benefit for developing destinations who wish to maintain control of their destination's development.

The effectiveness of travel websites is dependent on the intelligence contained within them. Electronic customer relationship management requires the use of web mining techniques to perform customer profiling, inquiry routing, e-mail filtering, and on-line auctions. Olmeda and Sheldon (2001) discuss these techniques and the challenges that must be overcome to fully implement them. Increasingly, systems that assist travelers with their planning are designed using data mapping techniques and on-line analytical processing. They often use software called 'case-base querying' to generate travel recommendations (Ricci and Werthner 2002). These systems utilize the Extensible Markup Language (XML) in their architecture. (XML is a simple, flexible language which meets the needs of large-scale electronic publishing and the exchange of a wide variety of data on the web). The creation of an intelligent decision support system for the improvement of tourist satisfaction, and for optimizing national tourism promotion activities is another example of how sophisticated IT models can provide decision support (Klicek 2000).

Marketing and marketing research
Marketing through the internet has brought a shift in the market power of tourism suppliers worldwide. While consumers have also gained from this new form of marketing, perceptions of marketing managers of the effectiveness of the internet as a marketing tool showed that different sectors ranked different features as the most important. Airlines noted that the updating of information was the most important feature of a successful website, whereas other sectors stated that the usefulness of the information was of paramount importance (Jung and Butler 2000).

Woeber and Gretzel (2000) address the use and effectiveness of on-line decision support systems in marketing. They surveyed tourism managers in thirty European countries to examine the factors effecting usage of internet-based marketing decision support systems. Their findings showed the users' perceived ease of use and usefulness of the system as most important. An example of a market analysis application is TourMIS, an on-line hypertext database containing a collection of tourism destination data. It allows users to browse, search, retrieve and analyse the tourism data relevant to the Austrian industry (Woeber 1998). Such systems, however sophisticated, depend on the collection of accurate data. Fesenmaier et al. (1999) argue that the collection of both private and public sector information is critical for thorough market analysis. They created a model integrating the analytical strengths of a marketing intelligence system with an organizational knowledge-creation process.

Effective marketing depends on accessing quality, reliable data on travelers, their behavior and their preferences through market research and survey methodologies. The use of computers to collect survey data is well established and generates significant efficiencies. IT applications can be used in the collection of the data with personal digital assistants (PDAs) and through the internet. PDAs are connected to the computers which receive the travelers' responses from a personal interview, telephone interview or direct input for a computer terminal. Once the data is digitized and stored, the analysis of that data for decision making is possible, using statistical packages such as SPSS or SAS. Dossa and Williams (2001) assess the use of internet surveys for market research in the context of advertisement tracking studies.

Internet, intranets and extranets
The prolific use of the internet for tourism marketing is giving rise to many questions about its effectiveness. The tourism industry is now one of the key users of the internet, using it not only for B2C marketing, but also for B2B purposes. E-purchasing is a common B2B application. Research in this area has examined the success of the internet for travel firms in different sectors, and the significance of the World Wide Web in the distribution channel has been well documented. A typology of websites in the tourism and travel field helps to distinguish the diversity of sites that are available (Pan and Fesenmaier 2000).

Marcussen (2001) suggests a method of tracking trends in travel and tourism services sold on the internet in the European market. Others have predicted usage of the internet for travel bookings (Morrison et al. 2001). Some papers shed light on these questions in different sectors. First, Law and Leung (2002) study the degree to which thirty airlines around the world are using the internet for on-line reservation services. The three regions examined were North America, Europe and the Middle East, and Asia and Australia, and differences were found for airlines in the different regions. The authors assessed the different components of on-line reservation systems, provision of extra benefits, services and facilities, and factors affecting reservation time. A similar study for hotels also exists (O'Connor and Horan 1999), another models e-marketing strategies in Greek hotels (Sigala 2001), and Law et al. (2001) examine the effect of the internet on travel agencies in Hong Kong. An empirical analysis of hotel chain on-line pricing strategies sheds light on the pricing used by major hotel chains (O'Connor 2002). Also benchmarks for website design and marketing by Swiss hotels is covered in Schegg et al. (2002). Similar studies for the remaining industry sectors such as attractions and entertainment, tour operators and wholesalers, ground transportation and cruiselines, would extend this work to more fully understand the internet's impact on all sectors of the industry.

The internet is also an important tool for the public sector in tourism, most notably national and regional tourism offices. Tierney (2001) examines the effectiveness of web advertising for California as a destination. He uses a low-cost, automated, internet-based methodology that extends the usual evaluations of 'hits' and page-viewings. The findings point to a significant level of success of the destination's website on subsequent visitations to California. The results of this study will assist other destinations in maximizing the effectiveness of their electronic marketing. Website evaluation in resort settings using website accessibility, navigation, visual attractiveness and information content has been used by Perdue (2001).

Intranets provide information accessibility to users in a particular tourism firm or organization, and extranets can link users in different organizations who have some similar objective or characteristic, such as a tourism destination. In a study of the use of internet and intranets by visitors and conventions bureaus, Yuan and Fesenmaier (2000) identify ways that such offices can utilize the technologies more effectively. They found that US bureaus are using these technologies only in limited ways such as for communication, customer service and information provision, but are using them to create value networks to expand their functions and competitiveness. The authors encourage the leaders of such organizations to push the more sophisticated use of intranets and internet in their operations. Given the heterogeneity of the tourism industry and the need for increased communication between operators, and between regions in a destination, intranets and extranets offer significant value in this endeavor.

Social and legal issues surface on the internet. Certain traveling groups find the internet a better way to book travel due to the privacy if offers. Poria and Taylor (2001) discuss the internet as a preferable booking tool in that it provides some anonymity and reduction of social risk for groups such as gays and lesbians. The more that the internet is used for commercial transactions, the more likely it is that legal issues emerge. Ismail and Mills (2001) explore contract disputes and contract liability of e-commerce and its impact on the tourism industry. The study recommends policies and actions for travel and tourism e-commerce businesses that will limit contract liability.

Destination management systems
Destinations are finding that policies for information technology, communications and on-line strategies are necessary for the effectiveness and profitability of the tourism destination as a whole. The destination management organization (DMO) is often the focal point for electronic access to information on the destination, and many have adopted IT applications to improve accessibility to their tourism product. Such portals may exist at the national, regional and municipality levels, and in some cases interregional portals such as European Cities are being used (Woeber 2003).

The development of destination management systems (DMSs) which include searchable product databases which are comprehensive and unbiassed, in addition to functions such as enquiry management, reservations management and customer relationship management are increasingly common. DMSs are typically used by all agents in the distribution channel and the consumer. Each user has a different perspective which needs consideration in the DMS design. A study of the effectiveness of a DMS examines the criteria for success from the viewpoints of travel agents, tour operators, investors, consumers, suppliers and the public sector (Buhalis and Spada 2000). Kazasis et al. (2005) suggests the creation of a virtual community where tourists and locals can interact and exchange destination knowledge.

Australia is an example of a country that recognizes the value of a national on-line tourism policy (Sharma et al. 2000). The policy includes five initiatives: (i) to enhance the national data infrastructure, (ii) to develop an on-line resource center, (iii) to develop regional tourism initiatives, (iv) to empower intermediaries and (v) to develop an indigenous tourism on-line strategy. This is deserving of attention by other destinations seeking to incorporate cultural resources into their tourism product.

One of the first, most comprehensive, and most documented DMSs is TISCover in Austria. TISCover not only consists of a comprehensive database of destination products but also has developed sophisticated customer access with e-commerce transactions, access via the web, kiosks and cellular phones. TISCover also uses wireless application protocol (WAP) for mobile access to a destination information system, something that DMOs will need to consider in the future. Tourism suppliers in Austria can directly maintain information on their products on-line, ensuring that information is current and accurate. The value of a comprehensive, unbiassed, current and accurate source of destination information is paramount. The system is also customized for different regions of Austria and is being adapted for use in different countries (Pröll and Retschitzegger 2000).

As DMSs develop and become more comprehensive they are transforming into destination knowledge systems. The need to integrate diverse information in a usable form to manage destinations is the key to competitiveness. The use of knowledge maps to design such systems for a particular destination have been discussed by Pyo (2004).

Mobile technologies

Travelers of all types are the natural market for mobile technologies. Their need to access information while on vacation or a business trip creates a demand for tourism suppliers and destinations to adapt to mobile technologies. Airlines are making data on flight updates accessible to travelers through their mobile phones, providing crucial information that could reduce frustrations of travel delays. Destinations are focussing more on using mobile technologies to provide location-based information to tourists while they are at sites, attractions and facilities at the destination. The same technology can be used to help tourists navigate localities, sites or museums, for example. O'Grady and O'Hare (2002) report on recent developments in the use of wireless and personal navigation technologies for tourism, and recommend how an electronic context-aware tourist guide might operate. Location-based services are discussed by Berger et al. (2003) who explain that mobile services using PDAs, phones or small computers provide four location-based functions of value to travelers. They are: (i) location of persons, objects and places, (ii) routing between them, (iii) search for hotels, restaurants, events and attractions and so on that are in close proximity and (iv) information about traveling conditions.

A recent volume of the *Journal of Information Technology and Tourism* is devoted to the topic of mobile technologies in tourism. The state of the art is covered in the article by Manes (2003), who discusses how ambient intelligence can contribute to these systems. He also gives a comprehensive vision of mobile services in travel and tourism with particular reference to cultural tourism. Krug et al. (2003) studied tourist use of mobile technologies in a Swiss National Park, where 1597 tourists were surveyed. The results show that in this context, safety information is most important, followed by wildlife information, and that information should be provided only on request. Personal privacy and security and control over the information provided on the mobile phone were critical. Given that the traveling public is international, the issue of language barriers with location-based mobile applications must be dealt with. Sharma et al. (2003) present an architecture model and show how it can be combined with a translator web service model.

Evaluation of existing research and issues for further research
A meta-analytic study of the historic trends of peer-reviewed research in the field gives an understanding of the global contributions and research topics

to date (Frew 2000). Frew's work is partially generated from the work of two thinktanks, and the findings show that tourism information technology research has expanded significantly, particularly since 1994, and that it is being done in many countries, with Europe being the most prolific region. Frew also sets forth a research agenda for the field, something previously unattempted and yet very important to the future growth of the field.

The existing literature has mapped out the emerging field of tourism information technology, however there are some critical areas that need further attention by researchers. There has been a predominance of research on the commercial and marketing implications of the technology, leaving other areas untouched. Some of these areas are consumer behavior relative to information, and public sector use of IT for destination management purposes. More robust understanding of consumer behavior with IT could come from the introduction of experimental research of consumer behavior. The use of IT by DMOs reveals a need for tourism organizations to be more flexible and open to change in their visions in the new economy (Gretzel et al. 2000).

Another area worthy of more study by economists is the impact of IT on the industrial and organizational structures in the tourism industry. There is no question that changes are happening rapidly, and are having dramatic impacts on the competitive environment, on the consumer and on the changing nature of travel firms. Barriers to entry and exit are changing, regulations are changing, and competition is becoming co-opetition. These changes have been somewhat documented in the literature, but large-scale studies examining structural changes in the industry are more difficult to perform and perhaps there is a sense that the industry has not yet settled down enough to be measured. A few studies have provided insight into the changes in various sectors (airlines, travel agencies, hotels and so on), however, many sectors are still to be examined as is the industry as a whole. The models and theories from industrial economics could assist in researching these shifts and trends in a rigorous manner. Gretzel et al.'s study examines the organizational changes that can be expected as the web becomes more predominant and the new economy takes hold. Work by Tremblay has set a conceptual framework for this using microeconomic theory (Tremblay 1998).

Another critique is that most research on IT usage tends to focus on applications or issues in the individual country or region in which the researcher works. There are a few exceptions to this, such as studies by Marcussen (2001) who has examined internet use for travel by multiple European countries. More studies examining the comparative adoption of IT systems across international boundaries would add to the global understanding of the topic. Such comparative analysis can be synthesized to generate more conceptual understandings of the field. The differential between developed and developing countries in their use of technology, and models to assist the developing countries would also be of value, recognizing that different political systems and different information and telecommunications environments may lead to different scenarios. This is particularly relevant as discussions of standards for systems and communications become important in the global economy.

An area for further development is the application of IT to issues of environmental protection and cultural sustainability. Tourism today cannot be successful without the consideration of these two issues, and yet the overlay of IT with them has received little attention. There are many potential ways that IT can assist in the development of those goals. The application of global positioning systems (GPSs) and geographic information systems (GISs) has much to offer destinations in regard to the management of natural resources such as national parks, wildlife reserves, culturally and environmentally sensitive areas and so on. More websites are including information of cultures, cultural resources and cultural interpretations of destinations, but it is often demand rather than supply driven. There is, however, a need for more of this type of information and focus in the future. It will require close collaboration between the public sector and the technology vendors, in addition to tourism suppliers. Collaboration will require that the public sector engage in data collection on the environmental and cultural resources and work with the vendors or designers of the systems to create systems that have direct relevant decision-making capability to move the destination further in this direction. Private sector suppliers in the travel industry will also need to collaborate by providing information when needed and collaborating and complying with environmental and cultural policies that may be implemented as a result of such work.

Clearly the cutting edge of the research in tourism information technology is that which examines the use of increasingly intelligent systems. This involves studies on the applications of neural network technologies, intelligent query management, data-mining and data-warehousing systems, multi-media information and virtual reality. When collaboration occurs between the system developers, funding sources and the destinations, the opportunities to further enhance the visitor industry using technology are endless. Firms will benefit economically by applying systems at the operational level by increased efficiency, productivity, customer relationship management, and reach to global markets. At the strategic level they can benefit by becoming more competitive, by developing new products and new market segments, and by creating knowledge warehouses as a basis for strategic decision making. Destinations can benefit in similar ways to firms, but they can also harness technology to facilitate planning and policy making, to improve their transportation and other infrastructure systems, and to improve their sustainability and the overall economic benefit to the destination.

Conclusions

The research discussed in this chapter raises further questions and leaves many signposts for future research in the field. The studies published here represent small but significant steps in the maturation of the field. Joseph Schumpeter has stated that for a field of inquiry to be called a 'discipline' it must provide four kinds of knowledge: (i) empirical data, observations and facts, (ii) theories and paradigms, (iii) ethics, and (iv) history (Mason et al. 1997). This chapter has discussed contributions to the first and fourth kind of knowledge for the tourism information technology field. Some attention has been given to the other two kinds of knowledge but mostly they are left untouched.

It is the challenge of tourism researchers to create all types of knowledge so that the field can truly mature. More theories and paradigms are needed to form strong pillars for the field to move forward. This may require the use of concepts, theories and methods from other disciplines, or the creation of new methodologies within the area of tourism. Tourism is an interdisciplinary field of study, and IT is the realm of computer scientists, management scientists and psychologists to name a few. Cross-fertilization between these disciplines and collaboration across sectors will be necessary to ensure the richest development of research in the field. It is a critical success factor for the tourism industry in general that researchers, educators and practitioners alike collaborate to examine how information technology in all its forms can enhance all aspects of tourism, including the travelers and the host community.

Bibliography

Anckar, Bill and Pirkko Walden (2002), 'Self-booking of high- and low-complexity travel products: exploratory findings', *Information Technology and Tourism*, **4** (3/4),151–65.

Baker, M. and M. Riley (1994), 'New perspectives on the productivity of hotels: some advances and new directions', *International Journal of Hospitality Management*, **13** (4), 297–311.

Baker, Michael, Silvia Sussman and Marisa Meisters (1999), 'The productivity paradox and the hospitality industry', in Buhalis, D. and Schertler, W. (eds), *Information and Communication Technologies in Tourism, Proceedings of the ENTER Conference*, New York: Springer, pp. 300–309.

Baker, Michael and Gerry Sweeney (1999), 'Business process reengineering in the hospitality industry: process improvement in ALPHA flight services', *Information Technology and Tourism*, **2** (1), 45–55.

Baum, Tom (2002), 'Tourism and hospitality in the 21st century', in Lockwood, A. and S. Medlik (eds), *Information Technology and Tourism*, **5** (2), 121–122.

Berger, Stefan, Hans Lehmann and Franz Lehner (2003), 'Location-based services in the tourism industry', *Information Technology and Tourism*, **5** (4), 243–56.

Boger, C. A., L.A. Cai and Li-C. Lin (1999), 'Benchmarking: comparing discounted business rates among lodging companies', *Journal of Hospitality and Tourism Research*, **23** (3), 256–67.

Braun, Patrice (2002), 'Networking tourism SMEs: e-commerce and e-marketing issues in regional Australia', *Information Technology and Tourism*, **5** (1),13–23.

Breiter, D. and S.F. Kline (1995), 'Benchmarking quality management in hotels', *FIU Hospitality Review*, **13** (2), 45.

Buhalis, Dimitrios and W. Schertler (eds) (1999), *Information and Communication Technologies in Tourism*, Vienna: Springer.

Buhalis, Dimitrios and Valeria Minghetti (2001), 'Introduction: information communication technologies, tourism, culture, and art', *Information Technology and Tourism*, **4** (2), 75–6.

Buhalis, Dimitrios and Antonella Spada (2000), 'Destination management systems: criteria for success – an exploratory research', *Information Technology and Tourism*, **3** (1), 41–58.

Caro, Jose L., Antonio Guevara, Andres Aguayo and Sergio Galvez (2000), 'Workflow management applied to information systems in tourism', *Journal of Travel Research*, **39** (2), 220–26.

Dittenbach, M., Dieter Merkl and Helmut Berger (2003), 'A natural language query interface for tourism information', in Frew, A.J., Hitz, M. and O'Connor, P. (eds), *Information and Communication Technologies in Tourism*, Vienna: Springer, pp. 152–62.

Doganis, R. (2001), *Airline Business in the 21st Century*, London: Routledge.

Donaghy, K., U. McMahon and D. McDowell (1995), 'Yield management: an overview', *International Journal of Hospitality Management*, **14** (2), 139–50.

Dossa, Karim B. and Peter Williams (2001), 'Assessing the use of internet surveys in the context of advertisement tracking studies: a case study of tourism Yukon's winter promotion campaign', *Journal of Travel and Tourism Marketing*, **11** (2/3), 39–62.

Durocher, J.F. and N.B. Niman (1993), 'Information technology: management effectiveness and guest services', *Hospitality Research Journal*, **17** (1), 121–31.

Evans, Graeme, Janet Bohrer and Greg Richards (2000), 'Small is beautiful: ICT and tourism SMEs: a comparative European survey', *Information Technology and Tourism*, **3** (3/4), 139–53.

Feick, Robert D. and G. Brent Hall (2000), 'The application of a spatial decision support system to tourism-based land management in small island states', *Journal of Travel Research*, **39** (2), 163–71.

Fesenmaier, Daniel R. and J. Jeng (2000), 'Assessing structure in the pleasure trip planning process', *Tourism Analysis*, **5**, 13–28.

Fesenmaier, Daniel R., A.W. Leppers and Joseph T. O'Leary (1999), 'Developing a knowledge-based tourism marketing information system', *Information Technology and Tourism*, **2** (1), 31–44.

Frew, Andrew J. (2000), 'Information and communications technology research in the travel and tourism domain: perspective and direction', *Journal of Travel Research*, **39** (2), 136–45.

Frew, Andrew J. and Peter O'Connor (1999), 'Destination marketing system strategies in Scotland and Ireland: an approach to assessment', *Information Technology and Tourism*, **2** (1), 3–13.

Gamble, P. and G. Smith (1986), 'Expert front office management by computer', *International Journal of Hospitality Management*, **3**, 109–14.

Godart, Jean-Marc (1999), 'Combinatorial optimization based decision support system for trip planning', in Buhalis, D and Schertler, W. (eds), *Information and Communication Technologies in Tourism, Proceedings of the ENTER Conference*, New York: Springer, pp. 318–27.

Gretzel, Ulrike, Yu-Lan Yuan and Daniel R. Fesenmaier (2000), 'Preparing for the new economy: advertising strategies and change in destination marketing organizations', *Journal of Travel Research*, **39** (2), 146–56.

Holt, Richard (2002), 'Faces of the "New China": a comparison of touristic web sites in the Chinese and English languages', *Information Technology and Tourism*, **5** (2), 105–19.

Inkpen, Gary (1998), *Information Technology for Travel and Tourism*, 2nd edition, New York: Addison-Wesley.

Ismail, Joseph A. and Juline E. Mills (2001), 'Contract disputes in travel and tourism: when the online deal goes bad', *Journal of Travel and Tourism Marketing*, **11** (2/3), 63–82.

Jung, Timothy H. and Richard Butler (2000), 'Perceptions of marketing managers of the effectiveness of the internet in tourism and hospitality', *Information Technology and Tourism*, **3** (3/4), 167–76.

Kasavana, Michael and John Cahill (1996), *Managing Computers in the Hospitality Industry*, Michigan: American Hotel and Motel Association.

Kazasis, F., G. Anestis, N. Moumoutzis and S. Christodoulakis (2005), 'Intelligent information interactions for cultural tourism destinations', in D. Leslie and M. Sigala (eds), *International Cultural Tourism*, London: Butterworth Heinemann.

Klicek, Bozidar (2000), 'Design of a multilevel intelligent decision support system for the improvement of tourist satisfaction', *Information Technology in Tourism*, **3** (3/4), 55–67.

Krug, Katrin, Walter Abderhalden and Ruedi Haller (2003), *User Needs for Location-Based Services in Protected Areas: Case Study Swiss National Park*, **5** (4), 235–42.

Law, Rob, Angela Law and Edmund Wai (2001), 'The impact of the internet on travel agencies in Hong Kong', *Journal of Travel and Tourism Marketing*, **11** (2/3), 105–26.

Law, Rob and Kenith Leung (2002), 'Online airfare reservation services: a study of Asian-based and North American-based travel web sites', *Information Technology and Tourism*, **5** (1), 25–34.

Law, Rob and Rita Leung (2000), 'A study of airlines' online reservation services on the internet', *Journal of Travel Research*, **39** (2), 202–11.

MacKay, K. and D.R. Fesenmaier (2000), 'Travel information search and tourist behavior', *Journal of Travel Research*, **4**, 417–23.

Main, Hillary C. (2002), 'The expansion of technology in small and medium hospitality enterprises with a focus on new technology', *Information Technology and Tourism*, **4** (3/4), 167–74.

Manes, Gianfranco (2003), 'The tetherless tourist: ambient intelligence in travel and tourism', *Information Technology and Tourism*, **5** (4), 211–20.

Marcussen, Carl H. (2001), 'Internet sales of travel and tourism services in the European market 1998–2000: a method of tracking trends by focusing on major online marketers', *Information Technology and Tourism*, **4** (1), 3–14.

Mason, R.O., J.L. McKenney and D.G. Copeland (1997), 'Developing an historical tradition in MIS research', *MIS Quarterly*, **21** (3), 258–75.

Mistilis, Nina and Roberto Daniele (2000), 'Education and Australian government policy: delivering information technology outcomes for tourism businesses?', *Information Technology and Tourism*, **3** (1), 3–14.

Morrison, Alastair M., Su Jing, Joseph T. O'Leary and Liping A. Cai (2001), 'Predicting usage of the internet for travel bookings: an exploratory study', *Information Technology and Tourism*, **4** (1), 15–30.

Morrison, Alastair M., Stephen Taylor, Alison J. Morrison and Allison D. Morrison (1999), 'Marketing small hotels on the world wide web', *Information Technology and Tourism*, **2** (2), 97–113.

O'Connor, Peter (1999), *Electronic Information Distribution in Tourism and Hospitality*, Wallingford, Oxford, UK: CAB International.

O'Connor, Peter (2002), 'An empirical analysis of hotel online pricing strategies', *Information Technology and Tourism-Applications, Methodologies, Techniques*, **5** (2), 65–72.

O'Connor, Peter and Andrew J. Frew (2000), 'Evaluating electronic channels of distribution in the hotel sector: a Delphi study', *Information Technology and Tourism*, **3** (3/4), 177–93.

O'Connor, Peter and Patrick Horan (1999), 'An analysis of web reservation facilities in the top 50 international hotel chains', *International Journal of Hospitality Information Technology*, **1** (1), 77–85.

O'Grady, Michael J. and Gregory M.P. O'Hare (2002), 'Accessing cultural tourist information via a context-sensitive tourist guide', *Information Technology and Tourism*, **5** (1), 35–47.

Olmeda, Ignacio and Pauline J. Sheldon (2001), 'Data mining techniques and applications for tourism internet marketing', *Journal of Travel and Tourism Marketing*, **11** (2/3), 1–20.

Palhares, Guilherme Lohmann (2002), 'Managing airports: an international perspective' in Graham, Anne (ed.), *Information Technology and Tourism*, **5** (2), 122–3.

Pan, Bing and Daniel Fesenmaier (2000), 'A typology of tourism-related web sites: its theoretical background and implications', *Information Technology and Tourism*, **3** (3/4), 155–66.

Pechlaner, Harald and Margit Raich (2002), 'The role of information technology in the information process for cultural products and services in tourism destinations', *Information Technology and Tourism*, **4** (2), 91–106.

Perdue, Richard (1995), 'Traveler preferences for information center attributes and services', *Journal of Travel Research*, **33** (4), 2–7.

Perdue, Richard R. (2001), 'Internet site evaluations: the influence of behavioral experience, existing images, and selected website characteristics', *Journal of Travel and Tourism Marketing*, **11** (2/3), 21–38.

Poon, Auliana, (1993), *Tourism, Technology and Competitive Strategies*, Wallingford, Oxford, UK: CAB International.

Poria, Yaniv and Alex Taylor (2001), ' "I am not afraid to be gay when I'm on the net": minimising social risk for lesbian and gay consumers when using the internet', *Journal of Travel and Tourism Marketing*, **11** (2/3), 127–42.

Pröll, Birgit and Werner Retschitzegger (2000), 'Discovering next generation tourism information systems: a tour on TIScover', *Journal of Travel Research*, **39** (2), 182–91.

Pyo, Sungsoo (2004), 'Knowledge maps for tourism destinations: needs and implications', *Tourism Management*, **25**.

Ricci, Francesco and Hannes Werthner (2002), 'Case base querying for travel planning recommendation', *Information Technology and Tourism*, **4** (3/4), 215–26.

Schegg, Roland, Thomas Steiner, Susanne Frey and Jamie Murphy (2002), 'Benchmarks of web site design and marketing by Swiss hotels', *Information Technology and Tourism*, **5** (2), 73–90.

Sharma, Pramod and Dean Carson (2002), 'Online opportunities and challenges for indigenous cultural tourism in Australia', *Information Technology and Tourism*, **4** (2), 77–90.

Sharma, Pramod, Dean Carson and Terry DeLacy (2000), 'National online tourism policy initiatives for Australia', *Journal of Travel Research*, **39** (2), 157–62.

Sharma, Sushil, Fred L. Kitchens and Phill Miller (2003), 'Overcoming language barriers with flexible services architecture: a tool for travelers', *Information Technology and Tourism*, **5** (4), 203–10.

Sheldon, Pauline J. (1997), *Tourism Information Technology*, Wallingford, Oxford, UK: CAB International.

Sigala, Marianna (2001), 'Modelling e-marketing strategies: internet presence and exploitation of Greek hotels', *Journal of Travel and Tourism Marketing*, **11** (2/3), 83–104.

Siguaw, J.A. and C.A. Enz (1999), 'Best practices in hotel operations', *Cornell Hotel and Restaurant Administration Quarterly*, **40** (6), 42–53.

Siguaw, Judy A., Cathy A. Enz and Karthik Namasivayam (2000), 'Adoption of information technology in US hotels: strategically driven objectives', *Journal of Travel Research*, **39** (2), 192–201.

Tierney, Patrick (2001), 'Internet-based evaluation of tourism web site effectiveness: methodological issues and survey results', *Journal of Travel Research*, **39** (2), 212–19.

Tinnila, Markku (2002), 'Service processes in electronic travel services: a summary', *Information Technology and Tourism*, **4** (3/4), 203–14.

Tremblay, Pascal (1998), 'The economic organization of tourism', *Annals of Tourism Research*, **25** (4), 837–59.

Vich-I-Martorell, G.A. (2002), 'The internet as a marketing tool for tourism in the Balearic islands', *Information Technology and Tourism*, **5** (2), 91–104.

Werthner, Hannes and Stefan Klein (1999), *Information Technology and Tourism: A Challenging Relationship*, New York: Springer.

Williams, G. (2002), *Airline Competition: Deregulation's Mixed Legacy*, London, Ashgate.

Woeber, Karl W. (1998), 'Improving the efficiency of marketing information access and use by tourism organizations', *Information Technology and Tourism*, 1 (inaugural), 45–57.

Woeber, Karl W. (2000), 'Benchmarking hotel operations on the internet: a data envelopment analysis approach', *Information Technology and Tourism*, **3** (3/4), 195–211.

Woeber, Karl W. (2003), 'Information supply in tourism management by marketing decision support systems', *Tourism Management*, **24** (3), 241–55.
Woeber, Karl and Ulrike Gretzel (2000), 'Tourism managers' adoption of marketing decision support systems', *Journal of Travel Research*, **39** (2), 172–81.
Yuan, Yu-Lan and Daniel R. Fesenmaier (2000), 'Preparing for the new tourism economy: the use of the internet and intranet in American convention and visitor bureaus', *Information Technology and Tourism*, **3** (2), 71–85.

19 Destination competitiveness
Geoffrey I. Crouch and J.R. Brent Ritchie

Introduction

Products are a central component of the economics of any industry. In the tourism industry, there are many different types of products. Examples include an airline flight; accommodation in a three-star hotel; entry to the top of the Eiffel Tower; shopping products, crafts and souvenirs; a day at a theme park; a meal in a restaurant; skiing lessons; renting a car; a guided tour of a city; even now a trip into space; and so on – an almost endless list. Each of these are examples of commercial products – mostly services but some involving tangible goods – which are produced or operated by commercial enterprises. But tourists also consume or experience other activities and products as well, such as swimming at a beach; a stroll in a park; a free visit to a public monument or museum; a drive along a scenic coastal road; feeding animals in a national park; or climbing a mountain. These further examples are just as much a part of the tourist's experience as the commercial products listed above. Any trip or vacation, of course, consists of a combination of many of each type of product. Thus, overarching all of these individual commercial and non-commercial goods and services, the tourism destination constitutes the principal element of the tourism product that connects every separate product component to create the overall tourism experience.

The tourist is therefore faced with the choice of selecting from among many possible touristic experiences, each of which revolve around the choice of some destination, or combination of destinations. As the customer – the tourist – must travel to some location to 'consume' such experiences, the location or destination selected therefore represents the principal product unit in the tourism industry. Tourists must primarily make choices between destinations – or more accurately, destination experiences – and secondarily between individual product components such as which airline to fly with, which hotel to stay in, which attractions to visit and so on.

Competition between destinations therefore plays a critical role in shaping the global tourism industry. Some destinations attract many more visitors than others. Some nations such as France, Spain or the United States attract tens of millions of visitors each year. Cities like Paris, New York, Rome, or London also enjoy dominant market shares. And resort regions too, such as the French Riviera, the Colorado Rockies, or the Great Barrier Reef coast and islands in Australia, have economies in which tourism plays a major role. The spatial pattern of tourism is therefore far from uniform, but what explains this distortion? Why do some destinations experience a much higher visitor interest than others? What can tourist destinations do to compete, and to pursue strategies for tourism development that enable them to achieve economic, social and environmental goals? These are important questions for any tourism destination today.

Tourism: an increasingly competitive industry
As noted in *The Economist* (1998, p. 10),

> There may be more tourists to go round, but there is also more competition between destinations as cities, countries and continents latch on to the charms of tourist revenue. . . . Like all consumer products, tourist destinations must persuade their customers that they have some combination of benefits which no one else can offer. Destinations are trying every bit as hard as airlines and hotels to establish themselves as brands, using all the razzmatazz of modern marketing. Every place tries to make the most of what it has got.

This increased competition is evident in a number of indicators. Destinations have moved towards more sophisticated organizational responses. Government departments or national tourism administrations (NTAs); semi-government/private destination management organizations (DMOs) such as convention and visitor bureaux (CVBs), national tourism offices (NTOs), or state/provincial/regional tourism authorities; municipal departments; chambers of commerce; economic development agencies; and so on, with an interest in tourism development have become commonplace. The need to establish cooperative relationships among these various bodies has become critical to successful destination management and marketing (OECD 1998). In terms of marketing and destination promotion, the budgets of these organizations have also increased over the past two decades, and their revenue mix has tended to shift towards increased industry funding (ibid. 1998).

Strategically, destinations have also become more sophisticated with an increased 'emphasis on market research and on analysing the results of promotional activities' (OECD 1998, p. 5). According to Poon (1993): 'The travel and tourism industry is undergoing rapid and radical transformation. Therefore, competitive strategies are more important than ever for the survival and competitiveness of industry players' (p. 24) as tourism transitions from '[o]ld industry practice of mass marketing, standardization, limited choice and inflexible holidays' to a 'greener, more individual, flexible and segmented' (p. 18) approach. Places are now marketed like any other product to attract industry, investment, and residents, as well as tourism. Kotler et al. (1993) describe numerous examples of such 'place' marketing and propose a strategic market planning process to attract investment, industry, and tourism to cities, states and nations.

Destination competitiveness: an overview of research progress
Some destinations appear to be coping with this increased competition quite well, whereas others are struggling. In many cases it is the world's traditional destinations that have awakened to the reality that their share of the tourism market is declining. In certain cases, this reality has been cushioned by the fact that tourism is still growing strongly, albeit more slowly than the international average. In response to these changes, many destinations are seeking solutions to the question of how to become or remain competitive. In doing so, numerous questions often arise. For example, how important are convention facilities; should the airport be expanded; would the construction of a landmark help to enhance the image of the destination by providing it with a recognizable icon; would it be better to concentrate resources on the promotion of the destination; should a hotel room tax be introduced to fund increased destination marketing; should there be more municipal government revenues spent on developing or improving visitor-friendly infrastructure/services; are residents sufficiently visitor friendly; would the hosting of a special event like a cultural festival, World Expo, or Olympic Games help; would efforts to reduce crime have much impact given the media hysteria over isolated events; and so on.

Many questions such as these are being asked but the current state of knowledge provides few answers. However, as destination management and competitiveness is now critically important, more researchers have turned their attention to trying to understand the factors that drive destination competitiveness. We shall briefly overview this research shortly but first we examine *competitiveness* more closely.

What is competitiveness?
The concept of competitiveness in economics and in business management is of critical importance and paramount interest. The origins of our understanding of contemporary economic theory and the nature of competition begins first with Adam Smith who, in 1776, wrote *An Inquiry into the Nature and Causes of the Wealth of Nations*. Smith emphasized the importance of being the lowest-cost producer. He argued that the free market efficiently determined how a country's resources ought to be used in meeting the needs of consumers. However, it was David Ricardo who, when in 1817 he wrote *Principles of Political Economy*, developed the theory of comparative advantage to explain why a country might import a good even

when it is the lowest-cost producer. The theory of comparative advantage is based on differences across countries in their endowments of the factors of production (that is, labour, capital, land and natural resources). Such differences encourage specialization that in turn creates the need for trade.

Despite the many articles and books on economic competitiveness, there seems to be no generally accepted definition. It is perhaps too broad and complex a concept, defying attempts to encapsulate it in universally applicable terms. As noted by Porter (1990, pp. 3–4),

> [S]ome see national competitiveness as a macroeconomic phenomenon . . . Others argue that competitiveness is a function of cheap and abundant labour . . . Another view is that competitiveness depends on possessing bountiful natural resources . . . More recently, many have argued that competitiveness is most strongly influenced by government policy . . . A final popular explanation for national competitiveness is differences in management practices including labour–management relations.

Baker (1987) argues that competitiveness is something more and broader than mere trade statistics. 'Competitiveness – as much a cultural undertaking as an economic or political one – requires changing minds as much as changing policies' (p. 5).

Richardson (1987, p. 61) notes that the travel and tourism sector is 'fully internationally tradeable in the sense that suppliers from any country could compete in these markets in a fully liberalized institutional environment'. As the tourist is required to travel to a destination in order to receive the destination experience (service), factor conditions are important determinants of attractiveness. Porter (1990, p. 256) notes:

> [T]he role of factor conditions in service competition depends on the form of international competition in the particular service industry. In services where the buyer is attracted to a nation (Type 1), factor conditions are usually important to success. For example, tourism depends heavily on climate and geography, and education and health services depend on the training and skill of local personnel.

We would expect therefore, that the theory of comparative advantage, which recognizes spatial variations in endowments of the factors of production, would help to explain the competitiveness of tourist destinations. But Porter has argued:

> A new theory must move beyond the comparative advantage to the competitive advantage of a nation. It must explain why a nation's firms gain competitive advantages in all its forms, not only the limited types of factor-based advantage contemplated in the theory of comparative advantage. Most theories of trade look solely at cost, treating quality and differentiated products in a footnote.

A new theory must reflect a rich conception of competition that includes segmented markets, differentiated products, technology differences, and economies of scale. Quality, features, and new product innovation are central in advanced industries and segments. (p. 20)

To understand the competitiveness of tourist destinations, therefore, it is both appropriate and essential to consider the basic elements of comparative advantage, in addition to the more advanced elements that constitute competitive advantage.

The theory of comparative advantage concerns differences in the endowment of the factors of production which concern naturally occurring as well as created resources. Porter (1990, pp. 74–5) groups the factors of production into five broad categories: human resources, physical resources, knowledge resources, capital resources and infrastructure. In a tourism context it seems appropriate to add historical and cultural resources as an additional category, and to expand the infrastructure category to include tourism superstructure.

Where comparative advantages involve the resources available to a destination, competitive advantages relate to a destination's ability to use these resources effectively over the long term. A destination endowed with a wealth of resources may not be as competitive as a destination lacking in resources, but which is utilizing the little it has much more effectively. By this we mean that a destination which has a tourism vision, shares this vision among all stakeholders, understands its strengths as well as its weaknesses, develops an appropriate marketing strategy, and implements it successfully, may be more competitive than one which has never asked what role tourism is to play in its economic and social development. Porter (1990, p. 83) contends that innovation to offset weaknesses is more likely than innovation to exploit strengths, and he has noted that nations which are factor disadvantaged are often stimulated to find innovative ways of overcoming their comparative weakness by developing competitive strengths.

Overview and evaluation of research progress
The concepts of comparative and competitive advantage therefore provide a theoretically sound basis for the development of a model of destination competitiveness. But no single general trade theory will provide the necessary insight or cover the most appropriate determinants from among the many variables possible. Gray (1989) notes:

[A]ny general model of international trade must encompass an extraordinarily large number of causal variables . . . a single theory of international trade . . . cannot hope to account satisfactorily for all of the kinds of international trade which is undertaken in this world. What is needed, then, is a more flexible body of analysis that will allow studies of specialist sub-categories. (pp. 98–9)

Richardson (1987) expresses a similar view. No 'single theory is likely to be able to encompass all the characteristics which make trade in services such a complex – and such an exciting – domain' (p. 80). A systemic model of destination competitiveness is required. For example, a destination may not possess a dominant position of strength on any particular determinant yet still be highly competitive because its system of factors is unique and difficult to replicate.

Fortunately, in recent years, a number of tourism research scholars have begun to respond to this need for models of competitiveness tailored to the peculiarities of tourism destinations. Poon (1993) for example, suggests that destinations will need to follow four 'key principles' if they are to be competitive; namely, (i) put the environment first, (ii) make tourism a lead sector, (iii) strengthen the distribution channels in the marketplace, and (iv) build a dynamic private sector (p. 24). While these suggestions have merit, one might ask whether there are not other critical competitiveness factors from among the many comparative and competitive advantage dimensions we have so far only touched upon. These four principles are too broad, and general to be managerially useful. A deeper, richer understanding of destination competitiveness is required.

This increased interest in understanding destination competitiveness has spurred a number of destination-specific studies addressing the competitive positions of the United States (Ahmed and Krohn 1990), Sun/Lost City, South Africa (Botha et al. 1999; Kim et al. 2000), Las Vegas (Chon and Mayer 1995), Australia (Dwyer et al. 2003), South Australia (Faulkner et al. 1999), Spain and Turkey (Kozak 2003; Kozak and Rimmington 1999), European cities (Mazanec 1995), Mediterranean resorts (Papatheodorou 2002), Southeast Asia (Pearce 1997), a casino resort (d'Hauteserre 2000) and South Korea (Kim et al. 2001). Other destination-competitiveness research has addressed a variety of other issues including destination positioning (Chacko 1998), destination management systems (Baker et al. 1996), package tours (Taylor 1995), the environment (Hassan 2000; Mihalic 2000), strategic management (Jamal and Getz 1996; Soteriou and Roberts 1998), quality management (Go and Govers 2000), destination marketing (Buhalis 2000) and price competitiveness (Stevens 1992; Tourism Council Australia 1998; Dwyer et al. 2000a, b, c and 2002).

While these research studies suggest that interest in understanding destination competitiveness is high, most of this body of research has not attempted to develop any general models or theories of destination competitiveness. There have, however, been three such efforts to do so. Over an

11-year period, we have been developing a comprehensive, general model of destination competitiveness (Crouch and Ritchie 1994, 1995, 1999; Ritchie and Crouch 1993, 2000a,b; and Ritchie et al. 2001) culminating in our book, *The Competitive Destination: A Sustainable Tourism Perspective* (Ritchie and Crouch 2003). Our model is examined more closely below.

More recently, Dwyer and Kim (2003) and Dwyer et al. (2004a) have contributed to model development. Their model, which is based substantially on the work and model of Crouch and Ritchie, posits that destination competitiveness is a function of endowed resources (comprising natural and heritage resources, and supporting factors), destination management (comprising government and industry), situational conditions and demand.

The third contribution towards model development is by Heath (2003) who, adapting the work of Crouch and Ritchie, and Dwyer and Kim, sought to tailor a model 'from a southern African perspective'. Heath's model comprises 'the foundations that provide an essential base for competitiveness; the cement, which binds and links the respective facets of competitiveness; the building blocks, that are essential to make tourism 'happen'; and the roof (the key success drivers), which comprises the 'people' part of destination competitiveness' (p. 10).

A general conceptual model of destination competitiveness
A conceptual model is a device that provides a useful way of thinking about a complex issue. It is a collection of concepts that together form a 'web of meaning' (Neuman 1994, p. 37) and thereby help to clarify our understanding of, in this case, the factors which affect the competitiveness of a tourist destination. It is a model in that it is a simplified description of a phenomenon which is always more complex than a model suggests. A principle of a good model is parsimony. A parsimonious model is one that seeks to balance the need to maximize explanation but minimize complexity.

A conceptual model can be used for a variety of purposes. It can be used as a basis for research to further test the reliability and validity of the model, or parts of the model, in explaining the actual phenomenon. It can be also used by decision makers to guide the generation of ideas, their analysis, recommendations and implementation. In this regard, it is important to recognize that models are not perfect and should not therefore be used in a 'cook book' fashion. It is always important to check that the basic assumptions and limitations of the model are not violated. Models should not be used to make a decision; they assist decision making but should not be a substitute for the role of the decision maker.

The conceptual model of destination competitiveness presented below is not a predictive or causal model. Rather, its primary purpose is to explain.

Neuman (1994, p. 43) distinguishes between theoretical and ordinary explanations. He notes:

> [A theoretical explanation is] a logical argument that tells why something occurs. It refers to a general rule or principle. These are a researcher's theoretical arguments or connections among concepts. The second type of explanation, ordinary explanation, makes something clear or describes something in a way that illustrates it and makes it intelligible. . . . The two types of explanation can blend together.

We see our model fitting primarily the definition of an ordinary explanation at this stage of our research. The model is relatively abstract in its present form in that it does not lay out specific empirical generalizations. It is best described, using Neuman's typology (p. 51) as a 'theory on a topic' with the topic, in this case, being destination competitiveness. We now provide a brief overview of our model, depicted in Figure 19.1 (see Ritchie and Crouch 2003 for further details). The left- and right-hand sides of the model emphasize the two cornerstones of competitiveness; namely, comparative advantage (consisting of endowed resources) and competitive advantage (consisting of aspects of resource deployment). The main part of the model then illustrates how we see these two cornerstones being operationalized with respect to destination competitiveness.

Destinations operate within an environment. The global (macro) environment consists of a vast array of phenomena which broadly impact all human activities and which are therefore not specific to the travel and tourism industry in their effect. By comparison, the competitive or micro environment is part of the tourism system because it concerns the actions and activities of entities in the tourism system which directly affect the goals of each member of the system whether they be individual companies or a collection of organizations constituting a destination.

The macro environment is global in its scope. Events in one part of the world today can produce consequences for tourist destinations in entirely different regions. Global forces can alter a destination's attractiveness to tourists, shift the pattern of wealth to create new emerging origin markets, adjust the relative costs of travel to different destinations, and disrupt relations between cultures and nations, among many others. These forces present a given destination with a number of special concerns, problems or issues that it must either adapt to, or overcome, if it is to remain competitive. At the same time, these forces provide destinations with a whole new spectrum of opportunities for innovation and market exploitation.

A destination's competitive (micro) environment is made up of organizations, influences and forces that lie within the destination's immediate arena of tourism activities and competition. These close-in elements of the

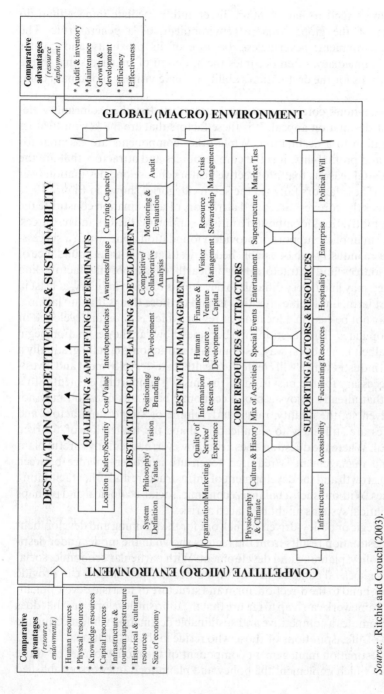

Source: Ritchie and Crouch (2003).

Figure 19.1 General conceptual model of destination competitiveness

environment tend to have a more direct and immediate impact than do elements of the global (macro) environment, as a general rule. The micro environment, nevertheless, because of its proximity and greater sense of immediacy, often occupies the attention of managers due to the ramifications for the destination's ability to serve visitors and remain competitive.

A destination's core resources and attractors describe the primary elements of destination appeal. It is these factors that are the key motivators for visitation to a destination. While other components are essential for success and profitability, it is the core resources and attractors that are the fundamental reasons that prospective visitors choose one destination over another. These factors fall into the seven categories shown in Figure 19.1.

Whereas the core resources and attractors of a destination constitute the primary motivations for inbound tourism, supporting factors and resources, as the term implies, support or provide a foundation upon which a successful tourism industry can be established. A destination with an abundance of core resources and attractors but a dearth of supporting factors and resources, may find it very difficult to develop its tourism industry, at least in the short term, until some attention is paid to those things that are lacking. This may not be easy in a location or region which is poor, undeveloped or underpopulated. The question then becomes, how can the destination begin to use, albeit in a modest way, its abundant attractions to build gradually a tourism industry which will create the wealth, taxes, employment and investment necessary for the provision of the missing supporting elements? In a region that already enjoys a broad economic base, this question may not arise. Even so, the quality, range and volume of supporting factors and resources are still likely to significantly shape the realization of tourism potential. Where the question does arise, however, particularly careful planning and management is required to ensure a proper balance between tourism growth and the development of infrastructure and other facilitating resources. Without such a balance, economic, social, ecological and perhaps even political systems might be placed at risk.

A strategic or policy-driven framework for the planning and development of the destination results from the factors shown in the model under destination policy, planning and development. With particular economic, social and other societal goals as the intended outcome, these factors can provide a guiding hand to the direction, form and structure of tourism development. Such a framework can help to ensure that the tourism development that does occur promotes a competitive and sustainable destination while meeting the quality-of-life aspirations of those who reside in the destination.

The destination management component of the model focuses on those activities which implement the policy and planning framework established under destination policy, planning and development, enhance the appeal of the core resources and attractors, strengthen the quality and effectiveness of the supporting factors and resources, and adapt best to the constraints or opportunities imposed or presented by the qualifying and amplifying determinants. These activities represent the greatest scope for managing a destination's competitiveness as they include programmes, structures, systems and processes which are highly actionable and manageable by individuals, organization and through collective action.

The potential competitiveness of a destination is conditioned or limited by a number of factors which fall outside the scope of the preceding four groups of determinants: core resources and attractors; supporting factors and resources; destination policy, planning and development; and destination management. This final group of factors, which we have called qualifying and amplifying determinants, might alternatively have been labelled 'situational conditioners' because it represents factors whose effect on the competitiveness of a tourist destination is to define its scale, limit or potential. These qualifiers and amplifiers moderate or magnify destination competitiveness by filtering the influence of the other three groups of factors. They may be so important as to represent a ceiling to tourism demand and potential, but are largely beyond the control or influence of the tourism sector alone to do anything about.

Further research and future directions
Destinations have always been an important unit of analysis in tourism development and management. But their importance has never been more acutely realized before, in today's dramatically turbulent and competitive global tourism industry facing the challenges of terrorism, SARS (severe acute respiratory syndrome), an aviation industry on the brink, and other events which have had a seismic impact on the tourism industry (Beirman 2003). The World Tourism Organization has responded by recently holding its First Think Tank on Tourism Destination Management (December 2002):

> [The Think Tank] grew out of the recommendation of WTO Members at the 14th General Assembly, held in Seoul, Korea in September 2001, that Tourism Destination Management should be incorporated into the WTO programme of work and that quality training and education had become increasingly important as a key issue for the competitiveness and success of tourism destinations. With this in mind, it was decided that new programmes should be undertaken in this respect. In light of this recommendation and to facilitate coordination with WTO Members, a WTO Destination Management Task Force was established as an informal, advisory and operational body, and met for the first time in Berlin, March 2002 at ITB. (WTO 2002).

The research and model development summarized in this chapter has contributed to the need for improved frameworks for destination management. But much more research is yet required. A speculative agenda might include the following:

1. Research to examine the relative importance of the factors of destination competitiveness as a function of the competitive environment, target markets, and competitor characteristics. Without this information, destinations will find it difficult to apply these conceptual models.
2. Processes and principles for auditing destination competitiveness and performance. Mounting anecdotal evidence indicates that destination stakeholders are demanding reliable and valid assessments of a destination's competitive position and the suitability of its strategic response.
3. In more specific terms, we require the development of indices, metrics and diagnostic tools for measuring destination competitiveness. It has been said that one cannot manage what one cannot measure. In the industrial world, an index has been developed that purports to capture the competitiveness of the industrial strength of virtually all nations. This index is based on expert opinion within each nation regarding the extent to which a broad range of factors are judged to be effective or desirable. These factors not only include current economic output or performance, but also such input factors such as fiscal policy, business legislation, education levels and quality of the labour market.
4. We further believe it would be very helpful to have a better understanding of the factors that deter the achievement of competitiveness once we know what its determinants are. It seems rather strange that even though we continue to enhance our understanding of the factors that determine destination competitiveness, we somehow seem limited in our ability to achieve it.

The 2002 WTO Think Tank posed the question to participants: 'What are the most critical issues facing destination managers in the next decade?', to which they responded:

1. Knowledge of new trends in tourism demand.
2. The increase of destination competitiveness.
3. The need to establish mechanisms to measure the impact of tourism on the local community.
4. The understanding and management of new technologies.
5. The importance of professionalism in tourism human resources.
6. Sustainable management of the environment.

Item 2 acknowledges the critical importance of destination competitiveness. The other five items are really sub-components of the same issue. Destinations have always sought to understand and improve their competitiveness. In good times, during periods of growth, tourism destinations have been able to prosper with little difficulty. But in these more difficult times, experiencing declining or stagnating global travel and tourism, destinations have had demonstrated the need to take a more serious look at their competitive positions. Research which helps them do so will be critical.

References

Ahmed, Zafar U. and Franklin B. Krohn (1990), 'Reversing the United States' declining competitiveness in the marketing of international tourism: a perspective on future policy', *Journal of Travel Research*, **29** (2), 23–9.

Baker III, James A. (1987), 'Renewing America's competitiveness', in Claude E. Barfield and John H. Makin (eds), *Trade Policy and US Competitiveness*, Washington, DC: American Enterprise Institute for Public Policy Research, pp. 3–10.

Baker, Michael, Claire Hayzelden and Silvia Sussmann (1996), 'Can destination management systems provide competitive advantage? A discussion of the factors affecting the survival and success of destination management systems', *Progress in Tourism and Hospitality Research*, **2**, 1–13.

Beirman, David (2003), *Restoring Tourism Destinations in Crisis: A Strategic Marketing Approach*, Crows Nest, Australia: Allen & Unwin.

Botha, C., J.L. Crompton and Seong-Seop Kim (1999), 'Developing a revised competitive position for Sun/Lost city, South Africa', *Journal of Travel Research*, **37** (4), 341–52.

Buhalis, Dimitrios (2000), 'Marketing the competitive destination of the future', *Tourism Management*, **21** (1), 97–116.

Chacko, Harsha E. (1998), 'Positioning a tourism destination to gain a competitive edge', *Asia Pacific Journal of Tourism Research*, www.hotel-online.com/Neo/Trends/AsiaPacificJournal/PositionDestination.html.

Chon, Kye-Sung and Karl J. Mayer (1995), 'Destination competitiveness models in tourism and their application to Las Vegas', *Journal of Tourism Systems and Quality Management*, **1** (2/3/4), 227–46.

Crouch, Geoffrey I. and J.R. Brent Ritchie (1994), 'Destination competitiveness: exploring foundations for a long-term research program', in Geoffrey Crouch (ed.), *Proceedings of the Administrative Sciences Association of Canada 1994 Annual Conference*, 25–28 June, Halifax, Nova Scotia, **15** (13), pp. 79–88.

Crouch, Geoffrey I. and J.R. Brent Ritchie (1995), 'Destination competitiveness and the role of the tourism enterprise', *Proceedings of the Fourth Annual World Business Congress*, 13–16 July, Istanbul, Turkey, pp. 43–8.

Crouch, Geoffrey I. and J.R. Brent Ritchie (1999), 'Tourism, competitiveness and societal prosperity', *Journal of Business Research*, **44** (3), 137–52.

d'Hauteserre, Anne-Marie (2000), 'Lessons in managed destination competitiveness: the case of Foxwoods casino resort', *Tourism Management*, **21** (1), 23–32.

Dwyer, Larry, Peter Forsyth and Prasada Rao (2000a), 'Price competitiveness of tourism packages to Australia: beyond the, "Big Mac" index', *Asia Pacific Journal of Tourism Research*, **5** (2), 50–56.

Dwyer, Larry, Peter Forsyth and Prasada Rao (2000b), 'Sectoral analysis of destination price competitiveness: an international comparison', *Tourism Analysis*, **5** (1), 1–12.

Dwyer, Larry, Peter Forsyth and Prasada Rao (2000c), 'The price competitiveness of travel and tourism: a comparison of 19 destinations', *Tourism Management*, **21** (1), 9–22.

Dwyer, Larry, Peter Forsyth and Prasada Rao (2002), 'Destination price competitiveness: exchange rate changes vs inflation rates', *Journal of Travel Research*, **40** (February), 340–48.

Dwyer, Larry and Chulwon Kim (2003), 'Destination competitiveness: determinants and indicators', *Current Issues in Tourism*, **6** (5), 369–413.

Dwyer, Larry, Zelko Livaic and Robert Mellor (2003), 'Competitiveness of Australia as a tourist destination', *Journal of Hospitality and Tourism Management*, **10** (1), 60–78.

Dwyer, Larry, Robert Mellor, Zelko Livaic, Deborah Edwards and Chulwon Kim (2004), 'Attributes of destination competitiveness: a factor analysis', *Tourism Analysis*, **9** (1/2), 91–101.

Economist, The (1998), 'Survey: travel and tourism', *The Economist* supplement, 10 January.

Faulkner, Bill, Martin Oppermann and Elizabeth Fredline (1999), 'Destination competitiveness: an exploratory study of South Australia's core attractions', *Journal of Vacation Marketing*, **5** (2), 125–39.

Go, Frank M. and Robert Govers (2000), 'Integrated quality management for tourist destinations: a European perspective on achieving competitiveness', *Tourism Management*, **21** (1), 79–88.

Gray, H. Peter (1989), 'Services and comparative advantage theory', in Herbert Giersch (ed.), *Services in World Economic Growth*, Institut für Weltwirtschaft an der Universität Kiel, pp. 65–103.

Hassan, Salah S. (2000), 'Determinants of market competitiveness in an environmentally sustainable tourism industry', *Journal of Travel Research*, **38** (3), 239–45.

Heath, Ernie (2003), 'Towards a model to enhance destination competitiveness: a Southern African perspective', in Richard W. Braithwaite and Robyn L. Braithwaite *Proceedings of the CAUTHE 2003 Conference*, Coffs Harbour, Australia, 5–8 February Lismore, New South Wales: Southern Cross University.

Jamal, Tazim and Donald Getz (1996), 'Does strategic planning pay? Lessons for destinations from corporate planning experience', *Progress in Tourism and Hospitality Research*, **2**, 59–78.

Kim, C.W., K.T. Choi, Stewart Moore, Larry Dwyer, Bill Faulkner, Robert Mellor and Zelko Livaic (2001), 'Destination competitiveness: development of a model with application to Australia and the Republic of Korea', unpublished report for the Department of Industry, Science and Resources, Australia; the Ministry of Culture and Tourism, Korea; the Korean Tourism Research Institute; the CRC for Sustainable Tourism, Australia; and the Australia-Korea Foundation.

Kim, Seong-Seop, John L. Crompton and Christel Botha (2000), 'Responding to competition: a strategy for Sun/Lost city, South Africa', *Tourism Management*, **21** (1), 33–42.

Kotler, Philip, Donald H. Haider and Irving Rein (1993), *Marketing Places*, New York: Free Press.

Kozak, Metin (2003), 'Measuring competitive destination performance: a study of Spain and Turkey', *Journal of Travel and Tourism Marketing*, **13** (3), 83–110.

Kozak, Metin and Mike Rimmington (1999), 'Measuring tourist destination competitiveness: conceptual considerations and empirical findings', *International Journal of Hospitality Management*, **18**, 273–83.

Mazanec, Josef A. (1995), 'Competition among European tourist cities: a comparative analysis with multidimensional scaling and self-organizing maps', *Tourism Economics*, **1** (3), 283–302.

Mihalic, Tanja (2000), 'Environmental management of a tourist destination: a factor of tourism competitiveness', *Tourism Management*, **21** (1), 65–78.

Neuman, W. Lawrence (1994), *Social Research Methods: Qualitative and Quantitative Approaches*, 2nd edition, Needham Heights, MA: Allyn & Bacon.

Organization for Economic Cooperation and Development (OECD) (1998), 'The changing role of national tourism administrations: findings of the pilot survey', unpublished report, Paris.

Papatheodorou, A. (2002), 'Exploring competitiveness in Mediterranean resorts', *Tourism Economics*, **8** (2), 133–50.

Pearce, Douglas G. (1997), 'Competitive destination analysis in Southeast Asia', *Journal of Travel Research*, **35** (4), 16–24.

Poon, Auliana (1993), *Tourism, Technology and Competitive Strategies*, Wallingford, UK: CAB International.

Porter, Michael E. (1990), *The Competitive Advantage of Nations*, New York: Free Press.
Richardson, John B. (1987), 'A sub-sectoral approach to services' trade theory', in Orio Giarini (ed.), *The Emerging Service Economy*, Oxford, UK: Pergamon, pp. 59–82.
Ritchie, J.R. Brent and Geoffrey I. Crouch (1993), 'Competitiveness in international tourism: a framework for understanding and analysis', *Proceedings of the 43rd Congress of the Association Internationale d'Experts Scientifique du Tourisme*, San Carlos de Bariloche, Argentina, 17–23 October, St Gallen, Switzerland: Association Internationale d'Experts Scientifiques du Tourisme, pp. 23–71.
Ritchie, J.R. Brent and Geoffrey I. Crouch (2000a), 'The competitive destination: a sustainability perspective', *Tourism Management*, **21** (1), 1–7.
Ritchie, J.R. Brent and Geoffrey I. Crouch (2000b), 'Are destination stars born or made: must a competitive destination have star genes?', in Norma P. Nickerson, R. Neil Moisey and Kathleen L. Andereck (eds), *Proceedings of the 31st Annual Travel and Tourism Research Association Conference*, Burbank, California. Boise, Idaho: Travel and Tourism Research Association, 11–14 June, pp. 306–15.
Ritchie, J.R. Brent and Geoffrey I. Crouch (2003), *The Competitive Destination: A Sustainable Tourism Perspective*, Wallingford, Oxon, UK: CAB International.
Ritchie, J.R. Brent, Geoffrey I. Crouch and Simon Hudson (2001), 'Developing operational measures for the components of a destination competitiveness/sustainability model: consumer versus managerial perspectives', *Consumer Psychology of Tourism, Hospitality and Leisure*, 2, New York: CAB International, 1–17.
Soteriou, Evi C. and Chris Roberts (1998), 'The strategic planning process in national tourism organisations', *Journal of Travel Research*, **37** (1), 21–9.
Stevens, Blair F. (1992), 'Price value perceptions of travelers', *Journal of Travel Research*, **31** (2), 41–8.
Taylor, Peter (1995), 'Measuring changes in the relative competitiveness of package tour destinations', *Tourism Economics*, **1** (2), 169–82.
Tourism Council Australia (1998), 'The price competitiveness of Australia as a tourist destination', unpublished report, Woolloomooloo, New South Wales.
World Tourism Organization (2002), 'Executive Report: WTO think tank on destination management – building competitiveness through education, training and research', unpublished report, Madrid, Spain.

20 Tourism destination specialisation
Mondher Sahli

Introduction

Tourism and travel-related services are among the most important tradable sectors. The World Travel & Tourism Council (WTTC) predicts that they will account for 10.3 per cent of world GDP, employ about 234.3 million people worldwide and generate 11.8 per cent of total world export receipts of goods and services in 2006 (WWTC 2006). Furthermore, given that there are now more than 750 million international travellers per year, tourism and travel-related sectors have become dynamic sources of income and a major strategic sector for development in many countries, especially in the global South.

OECD countries still dominate international tourism. The main areas remain Europe and the US, with some new influx from East Asia and the Pacific. Almost half of international tourists come from six OECD countries which are also among the world's top ten tourism earners/spenders. Some of these destinations appear to be coping with increased competition quite well, whereas others are struggling. In many cases it is the world's traditional destinations which have awakened to the reality that their tourism market share is declining. In certain cases this situation has been cushioned by the fact that international tourism is still growing strongly (Crouch and Ritchie 1999).

This chapter examines the concepts of external competitiveness and comparative advantage in terms of its application to tourism destinations. It shows how we arrived at our particular definitions of these concepts and why we believe that they are important in understanding the competitiveness and performance of a destination on the ground plus travel components of the tourism industry (downstream and upstream segments).

We also examine the role of several variables on the tourism comparative advantage in 19 OECD countries. The variables that determine tourism specialisation are: per capita income; real exchange rate; revealed comparative advantage in international passenger transport; the hotel function; and the tourism intensity rate. On the basis of our econometric estimation, it is established that the real exchange rate is one of the key determinants of competitiveness in tourism. This confirms the role of foreign currency holdings (like the real balance effect of Patinkin 1965), that is, money balances held by tourists to undertake travel activity. Intuitively these monetary holdings must respond to changes in exchange rates as the real value of these balances increases (decreases) in response to devaluation (appreciation) of the foreign exchange rate. It is also established that tourism specialisation responds to other economic and social variables as it creates pressures on the natural and cultural environment, and hence on resources, social structures, economic activities and land use.

The database used is from an initial sample of OECD countries (and then from two subgroups) enabling us to carry out regressions on panel data. This method has the distinct advantage of making it possible to combine both the temporal and individual dimensions: each of the two dimensions provides information that the other does not have. This being so, combining these two dimensions is likely to produce results that are both more reliable and more specific than those that would be obtained with other methods using just one of the two dimensions (temporal or spatial).

Competitiveness in tourism

This chapter will begin to examine the concept of competitiveness in terms of its application to tourism destination countries. As a concept in international trade, competitiveness has received widespread interest and attention. Its importance and implications has been the subject of some debate, and there seems to be no generally accepted definition of competitiveness (Crouch and Ritchie 1999; Ritchie and Crouch 2003). The situation is best summed up by Spence and Hazard (1988, p. xvii) as follows:

> The problem of international competitiveness has been defined in highly diverse ways. These definitions (and the proposed solutions to the problem) are partially inconsistent, and thoroughly confusing to most academics, politicians, policy makers, and business managers. There is good reason for this confusion. The collection of problems alluded to as 'competitiveness' is genuinely complex. Disagreements frequently occur not only at the level of empirical effects and of policies, but also in the very definition of the problem. Well-intentioned and reasonable people find themselves talking at cross purposes; sometimes it almost seems they are addressing different subjects.

Regarding traded services, a few researchers have examined the applicability of the theory of international trade and have generally concluded that there is nothing in the theory which intrinsically makes it less applicable to services (Deardorff 1985; Richardson 1987). Free trade in services is therefore a good thing for nations. Nevertheless, Gray (1989) concludes 'that a single theory of international trade . . . cannot hope to account for all of the kinds of international trade which is undertaken in this world. What is needed, then, is a more flexible body of analysis which will allow studies of specialist sub-categories of international trade' (p. 99).

Tourism competitiveness, the focus of this section, provides a basis for starting work on trade in services. It will show how we have arrived at our particular definition of external competitiveness and why we believe it is meaningful and managerially useful when applied to tourist destinations.

Overall external competitiveness: definition and application to tourism
The competitiveness of an industry is a critical determinant of how well it performs in world markets (Crouch and Ritchie 1999; Ritchie and Crouch 2003). The potential for any country's tourism industry to develop will depend substantially on its ability to maintain competitive advantage in its delivery of goods and services to tourists (Dwyer et al. 2000).

This section is the first stage in our investigation of the competitiveness in tourism of those OECD countries for which we have been able to gather the necessary data. We found it useful, in this regard, to know how external competitiveness in tourism is changing and why these changes are occurring. Patterns of changes in demand need to be assessed in the light of changes in the level of commitment, net performance and price competitiveness indices. These indices of overall tourism competitiveness will enable us to see how much more competitive one country is, compared to another, in offering the pattern of goods and services that international tourists purchase. They can also be used to assess a destination's tourism price competitiveness and the relative influences of real exchange rate changes on the indicator of the countries' competitive positions in the tourism industry.

The external competitiveness of a country's tourism industry is defined as that country's competitive ability to retain or increase its market share of tourism export in terms of ground and travel components. It is then a general concept that encompasses price differentials, coupled with exchange rate movements, productivity levels of various components of the tourism industry (transport, accommodation, tour services, restaurants, entertainment and so on) and qualitative factors affecting the attractiveness of a destination. This phenomenon can be illustrated graphically by simultaneous analysis of the degree of commitment to exporting in the tourism industry and of net performance in tourism (see Figure 20.1).

The market shares relating to the various activities are represented on the axes. Import market shares ($PMm_{ij} = M_{ij}/M_{iz}$) are displayed on the abscissa and export market shares[1] ($PMx_{ij} = X_{ij}/X_{iz}$) on the ordinate, where $X_{ij} = $ exports of the product (or service) i by country j, $M_{ij} = $ imports of the product (or service) i by country j, $X_{iz} = $ total exports of i from the reference area and $M_{iz} = $ total imports of i from the reference area. PMm_{ij} (PMx_{ij}) is the import (export) market share of the activity i by country j and PMm_{Aj} (PMx_{Aj}) is the import (export) market share of activity A by country j.

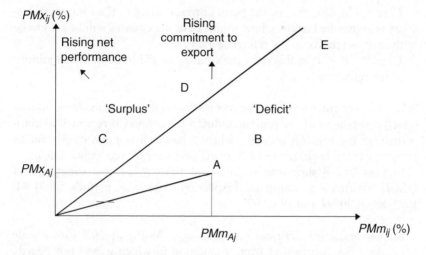

Figure 20.1 Analysis of countries' external competitiveness

Country j is all the more committed to exporting (importing) in the tourism industry t the higher the point representing that industry is located at the top (on the right) of the figure.[2] If all the points representing the various activities in a country j are located on the same horizontal line as the tourism industry, then the commitment to exporting will be the same.

In order to analyse country i's net performance in tourism, it is sufficient to assess its position relative to the first bisector. To that end, it is necessary to calculate the relative coverage ratio, which is written:

$$CR_{tj} = PMx_{tj}/PMm_{tj} = \frac{X_{tj}/X_{tz}}{M_{tj}/M_{tz}} = \frac{X_{tj}/M_{tj}}{X_{tz}/M_{tz}} \qquad (20.1)$$

$$= \text{coverage ratio for country } j\text{'s tourism industry}$$
$$\text{relative to the reference area } z.$$

This ratio is equal to the slope of the right-hand segment linking the origin of the axes to the point representing the tourism industry. There are three possible situations for the CR_{tj}:

Case 1: $CR_{tj} = 1$, that is, if the point representing the tourism industry t is on the bisecting line, country j will be said to be in equilibrium, in the sense that it has the same coverage ratio in this industry as the whole of the reference area z.

Case 2: $CR_{tj} > 1$, that is, the point corresponding to the tourism industry is above the bisecting line; in this case, the country will be said to be in surplus relative to the reference area z.

Case 3: $CR_{tj} < 1$; in this case, the country is said to be in deficit relative to the reference area z.

When can a country be said to be competitive in the combined (ground plus travel) component of the tourism industry? A country is regarded as competitive in the tourism industry when it has a growing commitment to exporting (market share) and a high net performance (coverage ratio).

Figures 20.2–8 show the evolution of the CR_{tj} of two subgroups of OECD destination countries, respectively, for the periods 1980–84, 1985–89, 1990–94 and 1995–97:

- *The major OECD tourist destinations*   As Figure 20.2 shows, only the USA has moved from a situation in which it was not heavily involved in the tourism industry to one in which it is. This finding is consistent with that of Brender and Oliveira-Martins (1984) who note that 'travel flows are the service operations in which the inertia of established positions seems to be greatest', confirming the importance of cultural heritage and family visitation for these countries, which overcome low price competitiveness. The USA's increasing competitiveness in tourism[3] and the relative decline of Italy and the UK are undoubtedly the major factors in the changes that have taken place in tourism in this subgroup. France and Spain, on the other hand, seem to be maintaining their respective positions in the subgroup (see Figures 20.3 and 20.4).
- *The intermediate OECD tourist destinations*   A different guiding principle seems to have emerged in this second subgroup of countries. The overall lack of movement in the hierarchy of the first subsample is replaced here by livelier competition between the countries (see Figure 20.5). Since the early 1980s, countries such as Australia (see Figure 20.6) and, to a lesser extent, Ireland and New Zealand (see Figure 20.7) have become increasingly involved in tourism, while there has been a decline in the external competitiveness of destinations such as Greece, Mexico and Switzerland (see Figure 20.8).

In sum, these findings are evidence of open competition in tourism between these OECD countries. This observation encourages us to investigate the question of competitiveness in tourism and travel components more closely. Let us turn first to the role played by fluctuations in real exchange rates in determining countries' competitiveness.

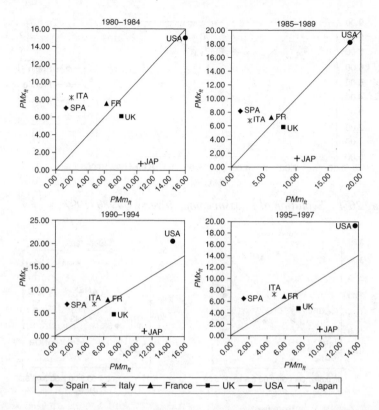

Notes: PMm_{ft}: Import market share in tourism and transport activities of country *f* for the year *t*.
PMx_{ft}: Export market share in tourism and transport activities of country *f* for the year *t*.

Figure 20.2   Competitiveness of the major tourist destination countries

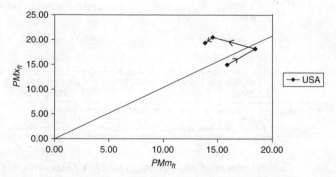

Figure 20.3   Evolution of tourism competitiveness, 1980–1997

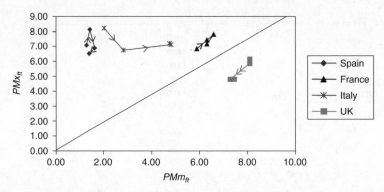

Figure 20.4   Evolution of tourism competitiveness, 1980–1997

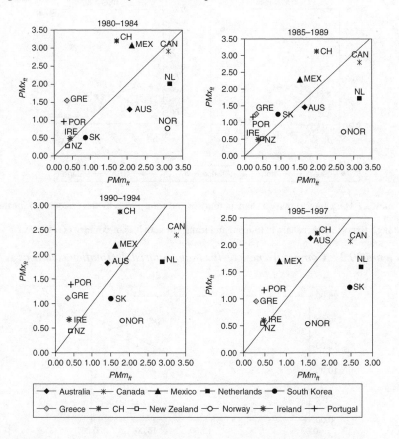

*Figure 20.5   Competiveness of the intermediate OECD tourist
destination countries*

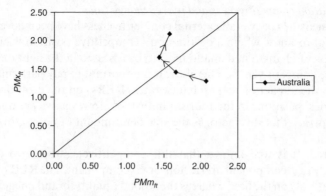

Figure 20.6   Evolution of tourism competitiveness, 1980–1997

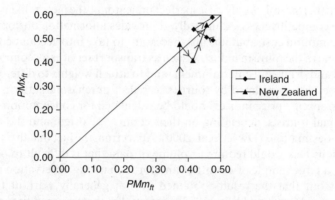

Figure 20.7   Evolution of tourism competitiveness, 1980–1997

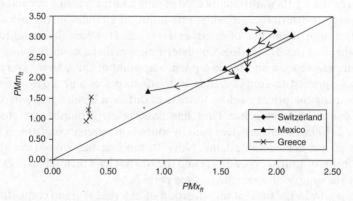

Figure 20.8   Evolution of tourism competitiveness, 1980–1997

Destination competitiveness and real exchange rates
Once measures of overall external competitiveness have been developed, it
is useful to know where a destination's competitive position is changing.
Patterns of changes in demand need to be assessed in the light of changes
in price competitiveness. Therefore, it is important to pay particular attention to the impact of real exchange rates (RERs) on the evolution of the
countries' positions in the tourism industry.[4] However, we are not assuming, a priori, that this factor is the sole determinant of competitiveness in
tourism.

Indeed, it is well known that this competitiveness has two components: a 'price' component and a 'non-price' component. The RER obviously
impacts only on the first, whereas the second (quality, brand image, marketing and so on) probably exerts considerable influence on trade in tourist
services, undoubtedly to an even greater extent than in the case of goods.

Furthermore, it is only an imperfect indicator of the factors likely to affect
price competitiveness. Admittedly, it provides information on comparative
consumption costs, but it is also necessary to take into account costs more
specific to the tourism industry, such as transport services, accommodation,
food and drink and entertainment, and to attach weights to different goods
and services consumed by tourists to reflect purchasing patterns. In addition, specific price indices should be calculated for consumption by international tourists, depending on their country of origin and the nature of
their destinations (Dwyer et al. 2000). Apart from the fact that this extremely
arduous task would require a volume of data that is difficult to obtain for
such a large sample of countries and for such a long observation period, it
turns out that the results obtained do not generally warrant the effort
required. Martin and Witt (1987) confirm that these price indices of tourist
expenditure provide little more information than general consumer price
indices or the RERs traditionally used in international economics and have
attempted to determine exchange rate-adjusted changes in the prices of
identified 'tourist bundles' of goods and services. However, their study does
not go beyond trends and does not determine whether a country is more or
less competitive than another at a particular point of time. To measure the
level, as opposed to simply trends in tourism, prices and cross-sectional
studies using the prices paid by tourists in different countries are needed.
The Economist Intelligence Unit has undertaken a number of studies
(Edwards 1995) based on prices paid by tourists in selected countries. These
studies go into considerable detail. Notwithstanding, they do not incorporate all forms of tourist expenditure and they do not lend themselves to extension of the sample of countries or time periods.[5]

This is why in the present investigation of external tourism competitiveness we shall confine ourselves to using the RER calculated by CEPII. The

advantage of this is that it draws on a comparison of real incomes in the country and abroad that is based on an evaluation in terms of purchasing power parities (PPPs). More precisely, it consists of a comparison of the relationship between GDP in current dollars and GDP in PPP,[6] both for the country in question and the world as a whole:

$$RER_j = 100 * \left(\frac{GDPcur_j / GDPppp_j}{GDPcur_m / GDPppp_m} \right) \qquad (20.2)$$

in which:

RER_j	=	real exchange rate relative to the world;
$GDPcur_j$	=	GDP of country *j* in international value (current international dollars and prices);
$GDPppp_j$	=	GDP of country *j* in volume PPP (constant dollars and international prices);
$GDPcur_m$	=	world GDP in international value (current international dollars and prices);
$GDPppp_m$	=	world GDP in volume PPP (constant international dollars and prices).

Here a rise in RER_j reflects a real appreciation in the currency of country *j*, whereas a fall equates to a depreciation. Table 20.1 shows that during the 1980–97 period there were pronounced fluctuations in the RER, which were themselves the result of various phenomena: appreciation and subsequent depreciation of the dollar, emergence of two blocs of countries in the European Union and so on. The currency fluctuations have had an impact on the indicator of the countries' competitive positions in the tourism industry (see Table 20.2), which is defined as the ratio of the tourism balance in the 'travel' and 'transport of passengers' items of each country's balance of payments to total international trade flows in tourism.

$$POS_{vj} = \frac{X_{vj} - M_{vj}}{\left(\dfrac{X_v + M_v}{2} \right)} \qquad (20.3)$$

where X_{vj} and M_{vj} are the country's earnings from and expenditure on tourism and transport of passengers and X_v and M_v are total international earnings from and expenditure on tourism and transport of passengers.

Examination of the graphs in Figure 20.9 comparing these two ratios (RER_j and POS_{vj}) shows that for most countries they moved in the opposite

Table 20.1   Real exchange rates fluctuations

RER	1980	1981	1982	1983	1984	1985	1986	1987	1988	1989	1990	1991	1992	1993	1994	1995	1996	1997
Australia	123.90	137.52	139.09	137.33	140.38	119.20	107.35	110.42	125.68	135.67	130.67	129.75	119.07	112.48	119.31	116.05	127.14	128.96
Canada	114.62	123.30	134.48	144.84	139.80	137.48	121.49	121.35	128.15	138.30	135.43	137.77	127.06	121.66	113.54	108.25	111.79	115.87
South Korea	72.27	75.69	77.46	78.81	77.21	76.28	69.36	71.05	80.06	90.97	88.31	91.43	87.43	89.99	92.66	95.29	95.85	88.66
Spain	102.0	89.1	88.0	77.4	76.1	77.3	91.8	100.5	105.6	110.3	128.0	130.9	136.3	115.1	111.2	117.2	120.7	111.5
USA	106.4	117.3	128.4	137.7	142.2	148.0	133.6	125.6	122.5	126.6	123.0	124.5	122.6	126.9	126.7	121.1	125.6	134.0
France	138.2	120.3	115.0	111.6	103.3	106.9	128.7	139.0	135.8	129.8	146.1	141.9	148.4	143.1	145.0	153.1	153.5	142.2
Greece	96.2	88.6	94.8	87.9	81.5	78.8	80.5	86.5	89.6	88.7	102.0	103.7	109.4	103.0	105.4	112.3	118.9	118.8
Italy	100.0	89.7	91.0	95.8	91.2	92.0	111.9	124.3	124.2	124.0	142.3	144.2	145.8	120.0	118.4	115.1	129.4	126.0
Ireland	122.5	112.7	118.0	117.5	107.6	111.0	132.6	136.2	135.4	131.7	142.0	137.0	141.9	129.4	129.4	130.2	133.2	135.2
Japan	115.3	123.4	114.7	125.7	127.3	130.2	165.2	175.4	187.2	175.7	159.4	171.4	178.0	205.5	218.8	220.8	192.8	182.7
Mexico	70.2	83.0	59.9	55.0	61.9	63.6	40.8	39.5	44.9	52.0	54.3	60.7	65.0	71.2	69.6	47.1	52.3	62.5
Norway	173.0	168.0	170.1	165.3	155.1	155.8	158.0	168.8	172.0	170.0	181.3	174.7	174.2	157.0	153.9	165.7	172.2	169.1
New Zealand	95.73	98.63	97.26	95.99	86.51	86.64	95.55	109.90	124.27	118.76	113.17	107.96	98.35	101.61	110.70	117.66	127.50	128.58
Netherland	145.5	122.1	124.0	121.6	108.2	107.0	128.0	139.9	136.2	127.3	141.2	137.6	143.6	139.5	142.4	153.4	150.1	138.6
Portugal	61.95	59.26	57.11	52.42	48.81	51.35	62.06	66.03	69.11	70.49	81.56	87.99	100.07	89.00	90.90	99.09	101.43	96.09
UK	126.1	121.5	117.4	110.1	99.6	102.4	106.3	113.2	122.7	119.8	128.8	132.8	132.7	117.8	119.4	117.9	121.7	137.4
Switzerland	153.3	138.3	147.3	150.2	137.1	135.0	167.4	188.8	185.8	169.7	194.0	194.1	195.2	192.0	206.2	225.0	219.6	195.5
Turkey	57.6	56.8	51.2	48.0	43.1	46.6	43.2	41.4	39.7	46.2	55.4	53.6	51.1	54.0	40.4	45.7	46.4	47.3

Note: Reference area: world.

Source: CHELEM.

444

Table 20.2 Evolution of the countries' positions in the tourism industry

POS	1980	1981	1982	1983	1984	1985	1986	1987	1988	1989	1990	1991	1992	1993	1994	1995	1996	1997
Australia	-0.71	-0.69	-0.79	-0.64	-0.82	-0.57	-0.26	-0.04	0.40	-0.10	0.01	0.29	0.28	0.52	0.68	0.77	0.82	0.73
Canada	-0.76	-0.58	-0.66	-1.26	-0.99	-0.89	-0.29	-0.78	-0.88	-1.26	-1.81	-2.03	-1.76	-1.53	-0.92	-0.60	-0.62	-0.64
South Korea	0.02	0.01	-0.14	0.04	0.09	0.16	0.70	0.97	0.98	0.45	0.16	-0.14	-0.17	-0.19	-0.35	-0.32	-0.65	-0.56
Spain	5.81	5.79	6.49	6.42	6.70	6.61	7.92	7.80	7.26	6.22	5.67	5.57	5.59	4.95	5.29	5.57	5.64	5.53
USA	0.18	3.42	2.38	0.28	-2.98	-3.58	-1.00	-0.79	0.99	3.75	4.60	7.57	7.82	8.34	6.98	7.22	7.68	7.85
France	2.26	1.51	1.94	3.12	3.23	3.16	2.41	2.06	2.09	2.94	3.14	3.43	3.78	3.57	3.31	2.97	2.64	2.83
Greece	1.44	1.54	1.22	0.88	0.95	0.98	1.01	1.07	0.85	0.55	0.59	0.60	0.69	0.78	0.84	0.74	0.63	0.61
Ireland	0.00	-0.02	0.01	0.04	0.07	0.11	-0.02	0.01	0.02	0.04	0.12	0.14	0.09	0.12	0.06	0.05	0.07	0.09
Italy	7.14	5.83	6.93	7.74	6.31	6.02	5.16	4.57	3.20	2.42	2.43	2.41	1.32	2.28	3.27	3.68	3.55	3.25
Japan	-4.00	-3.93	-3.56	-3.89	-3.55	-3.41	-4.34	-5.29	-8.11	-9.18	-8.44	-7.89	-7.74	-7.76	-8.24	-8.88	-8.23	-7.13
Mexico	0.14	-0.74	0.48	1.26	1.13	0.64	0.64	0.72	0.44	0.27	0.00	0.06	-0.01	0.20	0.31	0.80	0.89	0.92
Norway	-0.73	-0.85	-1.09	-1.11	-0.91	-1.00	-1.17	-1.13	-1.05	-0.78	-0.83	-0.68	-0.58	-0.51	-0.48	-0.53	-0.57	-0.59
New Zealand	-0.31	-0.27	-0.25	-0.17	-0.09	-0.01	0.04	0.13	0.01	0.03	0.03	0.03	0.04	0.08	0.14	0.27	0.24	0.16
Netherlands	-2.61	-1.67	-1.58	-1.76	-1.35	-1.45	-1.82	-2.02	-1.77	-1.43	-1.27	-1.28	-1.22	-1.18	-1.19	-1.35	-1.25	-1.00
Portugal	0.87	0.79	0.65	0.64	0.71	0.83	0.91	1.05	0.96	1.00	1.06	1.03	0.85	0.72	0.74	0.72	0.63	0.60
UK	0.52	-0.58	-0.83	-0.15	-0.08	0.70	-0.60	-1.01	-1.84	-1.86	-1.50	-1.78	-1.93	-1.75	-2.12	-1.50	-1.53	-1.87
Switzerland	0.80	0.94	0.87	1.12	1.02	0.85	0.84	0.83	0.57	0.50	0.61	0.75	0.67	0.55	0.59	0.54	0.36	0.34
Turkey	0.22	0.28	0.24	0.32	0.26	0.71	0.48	0.63	1.03	0.94	1.07	0.79	0.95	1.01	1.05	1.07	1.09	1.31

Note: Reference area: World.

Source: Own calculations using the CHELEM database (2000).

direction: appreciation of RER_j[7] is usually reflected in a fall in POS_{vj}, and conversely, depreciation of RER_j gives rise to an improvement in POS_{vj}.[8] From this point of view, the real exchange rate certainly emerges as a determinant of price competitiveness in tourism (since depreciation has a positive impact on the country's position in respect of tourism).

In general, the under- or overvaluation of a currency has a fundamental impact on a country's competitiveness. The case of the USA clearly illustrates this phenomenon. The strength of the dollar between 1980 and 1985 led to a collapse of the USA's position in the tourism market. Subsequently, however, when the dollar weakened, the country's position strengthened considerably. This interaction applies to many other countries, including France, Italy, Spain, Switzerland, Austria, Australia, Turkey and Mexico. For all these countries, the analogy with trade in goods is fairly striking.

It should be noted that the change in the competitive position of certain countries, such as the USA, Canada, Australia and New Zealand', is a result not only of currency depreciation but also of the fall in airfares that followed airline deregulation. It is reasonable to assume that in these countries transport costs at the beginning of the period were too high to be ignored. Thus it is the price competitiveness indicator adopted here that is inadequate in this case.

Ultimately, the results of this initial investigation of price competitiveness of a tourist destination are generally satisfactory, with the expected links between RER_j and POS_{vj} emerging clearly, even though there are some exceptions.[9]

Tourism comparative advantage

While there is much literature on the economic impacts of tourism, little attention has, so far, been paid to the topic of tourism comparative advantage. Richardson (1987) notes that the travel and tourism sector is fully and internationally tradable, in the sense that suppliers from any country could compete in these markets in a fully liberalised institutional environment. As the tourist is required to travel to a destination in order to receive the product (service), factor conditions are important determinants of attractiveness. Therefore, the theory of comparative advantage, which recognises spatial variations in endowments of the factors of production, would help to explain the competitiveness of tourist destinations. In this section, we shall:

● examine the countries' specialisation on the ground component of the tourism industry by means of the index of revealed comparative advantage developed by Bela Balassa (1965); and

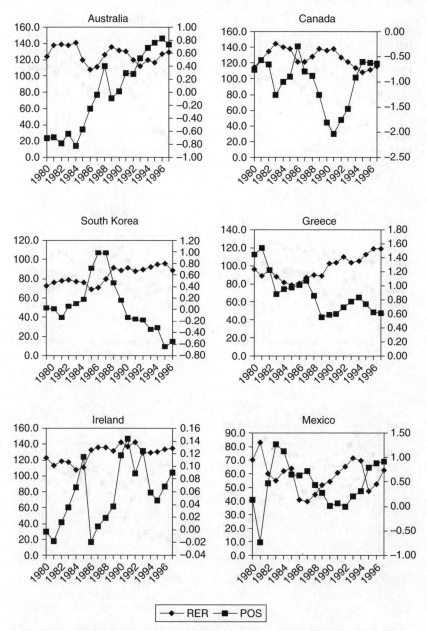

Figure 20.9   Tourism price competitiveness for various OECD destination countries

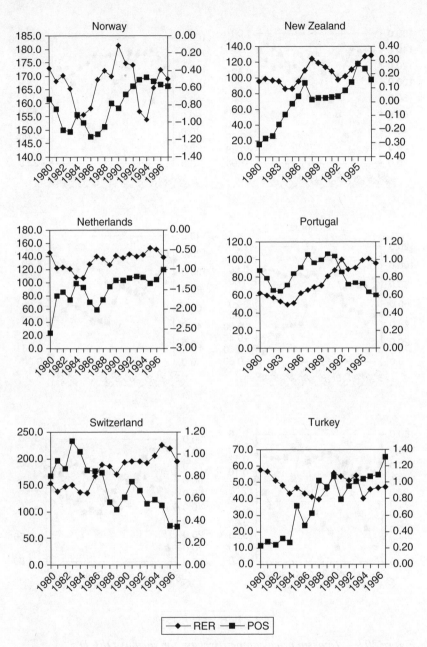

Figure 20.9   (Continued)

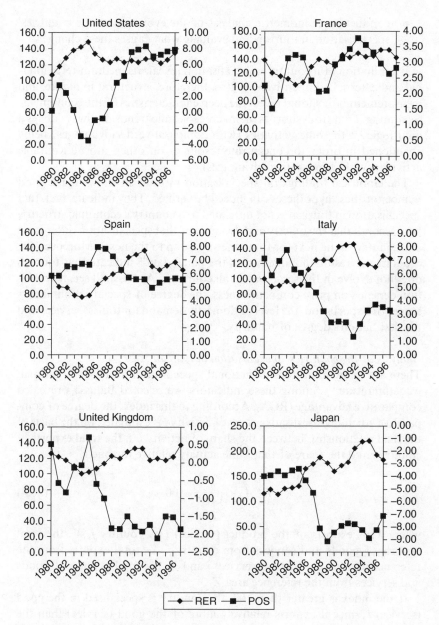

Figure 20.9 (Continued)

- conduct an econometric analysis of the evolution of the countries' specialisation in tourism and evaluate what causes these changes.

Examination of a country's specialisation reveals its medium-term internal and external competitiveness. It is, therefore, structural in nature, and measurement of it should reveal the deep characteristics of the economy by separating it out from short-term macroeconomic trends. It always obeys a dual logic, with some activities (with comparative disadvantages) being abandoned in order to concentrate resources on other, more favourable activities (with comparative advantages).

The empirical findings on specialisation in tourism show that a good number of these hypotheses can indeed be verified. They indicate, first, that specialisation in tourism is not unrelated to a country's economic structure and, second, that the quality and dynamic of that specialisation differ from one country to the next (or from one subgroup to the next). Moreover, the econometric results obtained from the panel data[10] indicate that tourism does not evolve in the same way in all countries. As we shall see, its evolution depends on price competitiveness, the degree of specialisation in passenger transportation, the level of domestic demand for tourist services and the destination's degree of maturity.

Analysis of the countries' specialisation in tourism
There are many indicators of national specialisation in the international trade literature.[11] Among these indicators, we selected Balassa's revealed comparative advantage (RCA). According to this index, the degree of comparative advantage or disadvantage of activity i is estimated on the basis of the dual relationship between the share of activity i in the total exports of country j and the share of that same activity relative to zone z.

$$RCA_{ij} = \frac{X_{ij}/X_j}{X_{iz}/X_z} \cdot 100 \qquad (20.4)$$

where X_{ij} is exports of the product (service) i by country j, X_j the total exports of goods and services from country j, X_{iz} total exports from the reference area of product (or service) i and X_z the total exports of goods and services from the reference area Z.

If the index is greater than 100, the country is specialised in the good (service) i, since it exports relatively more of the good (service) than the reference zone. It therefore has a comparative advantage in that activity. If the index is smaller than 100, the country is not specialised and it therefore has a comparative disadvantage.

Thus this is a method of indirect calculation that can be used to determine the kind of activities in which individual countries have comparative advantages and the degree of advantage or disadvantage associated with each activity.

In both tourism and goods, there are pronounced differences in the degree of specialisation between the countries. The emphasis in this section will be on identifying the forces underlying the comparative advantage of the 'downstream' segments ($RCAD_j$) of the tourism industry such as accommodation, catering and attractions, which are included in the 'travel' item of the balance of payments.

Analysis of Table 20.3 shows that:

- both rich (USA, France, Italy, UK, Australia) and less rich OECD countries (Spain, Portugal, New Zealand, Turkey) are specialised in these 'downstream' segments of the tourism industry, which means that there are several sources of $RCAD_j$ in tourism (international differences in factor endowments,[12] service quality and technological advances);

- the OECD countries that have the highest market shares in travel are not necessarily those that are most specialised in the 'downstream' segments of the tourism industry. For example, the USA, France, Italy, Spain and, to a lesser extent, the UK are in the first rank of world tourism destinations (in terms of foreign exchange earnings from tourism and number of international visitors). Nevertheless, their RCAs on the ground component of the tourism industry are relatively modest compared with other countries with more modest market shares but higher $RCAD_j$ (Greece, Portugal, Turkey, Australia and New Zealand);[13]

- as far as tourism is concerned, France is still an 'intermediate country'. It is not one of the countries with a high manufacturing specialisation, like Japan, nor one of those with a high degree of specialisation in tourism, such as Spain, Portugal or Greece. Its ranking as an 'intermediate tourist destination' is linked to the fact that it has absolute or comparative advantages in tourism relative to certain OECD destinations (Japan, South Korea, Norway, the UK) and comparative disadvantages relative to other, generally less developed countries (Spain, Greece, Australia, Portugal, New Zealand, Turkey);

- Australia and New Zealand seem to be the best-performing tourist destinations in the OECD. On the other hand, Mexico, Ireland, Switzerland and, to a lesser extent, Spain and Italy have seen their RCA dwindle. Airline deregulation seems to have played an important role in the promotion of tourism in the Asia-Pacific region, since

Table 20.3 *Travel-revealed comparative advantage indices*

RCA	1980	1981	1982	1983	1984	1985	1986	1987	1988	1989	1990	1991	1992	1993	1994	1995	1996	1997
Australia	106.4	119.1	117.4	124.1	110.7	102.2	110.4	125.6	154	137.5	142.2	141.3	132.9	143.7	166.3	180.7	182.1	175.4
Canada	81.9	83.5	82.8	81.6	72.2	72.9	78.2	70.7	68.7	69.8	70.9	73.1	63.6	58.1	56.9	58.1	58.7	57.8
South Korea	44.9	44.7	47.3	49.9	48.5	54	74	75.3	80.8	81.9	71.9	57.6	46.8	46.8	46.5	56.2	50.9	46.8
Spain	521.8	494.6	503	484.1	469.6	454.5	498.1	473.8	450.7	407.9	370.7	346	339.4	317.1	311.7	307.5	299.2	294.4
USA	93.4	121.7	125.2	117.3	151.9	151.9	152.6	148.7	142.4	150.3	154.4	156.2	154.3	155.7	150.4	148.7	150.8	146.8
France	129.9	118.6	124.5	130.2	130.2	126.9	112.4	111.4	112.5	122.2	118.4	119	120.5	123.6	126.1	122.3	123.9	124.6
Greece	514.2	505.9	463.3	380.6	403	430.2	443.1	411	382.2	317.5	331.4	295.3	335.3	375.6	418	429	390.6	414.5
Ireland	145.2	129.3	126.5	113.5	98.9	101.9	89.9	86.2	83.8	81.	90.8	88.4	77.2	73.6	74.3	72	71.9	68.5
Iceland	46.2	41.7	54.1	54.6	70.4	74.5	72.9	81.5	96	97.7	120.8	111.8	102.2	106.6	105.1	119.5	106.3	105.1
Italy	221.9	181.9	203.4	215.2	194.2	182	155.36	150.2	137.2	121.1	124.7	138.7	150	152.3	155.2	154.4	149	156.2
Japan	10.5	10	11	11.3	11.1	12	11.9	14.9	17.2	17.7	18.4	15.8	14.2	13.1	12.2	10.5	13.9	14.8
Mexico	341.1	280.3	218.5	208.5	214.8	195.9	216.1	194.7	195.1	199.3	188.9	187.9	166	150.7	139.2	111.4	103.7	101.8
Norway	67.1	66.4	66.3	60.8	55.3	59.1	76.9	77.7	79.9	62.2	55.6	56.3	60.7	61.4	70.1	64.5	55.5	54.1
New Zealand	80.2	88.2	84.7	94	124.9	130.2	155.2	180.1	157.9	156.6	147	143.4	134.2	140.3	163.5	208	205.9	191.6
Netherlands	59.9	57.2	58.3	52.9	52.6	48.4	49.9	49.8	45.9	45.3	43.1	47.7	51.3	48.5	45.8	47.4	46.4	47.6
Portugal	414.5	396.8	346.3	304.5	301.4	310.3	298.1	311.8	295	282.7	275.1	279.1	236.2	267	254	241.1	226.8	230.2
UK	114.1	102.5	100.8	114.1	109.9	113.6	107.3	107	101.5	99.6	98.1	85.9	86.9	88.9	87.6	97.5	90.8	92.2
Switzerland	157.3	154.8	163.7	179.4	162.7	152.5	140	147.6	137.8	129.6	127.5	132.8	122.6	118.1	123.7	123.7	117.6	127.4
Turkey	217	151.5	110.6	121.9	125.1	206.2	169.2	189.8	237.4	246.2	255.6	195.8	226.7	226.2	230.5	218.2	198.5	219.9

Note: Reference area: world.

Source: Own calculations using the CHELEM database (2000).

452

the Asian airlines are highly competitive as a result of their relatively new fleets, good service quality and, above all, lower wage costs.

Econometric analysis of the interface between specialisation and level of development in tourism

Our earlier investigation enabled us to characterise the general framework within which tourist flows take place and to assess the state of competitiveness and specialisation in tourism of certain OECD countries. In particular, it was possible to verify the existence of a link between the evolution of real exchange rates and that of the countries' competitive positions in tourism, as shown by now well-known studies of goods.

The aim of this section is to use some of the findings presented above for an econometric analysis of the evolution of specialisation in tourism.

Specifying the model The econometric analysis undertaken here adopts a different perspective from previous ones and constitutes, to the best of our knowledge, the first attempt to analyse the dynamic of tourism specialisation.[14]

The absence of any theoretical base in this area leads us to adopt a pragmatic approach. The equation tested is not a structural equation derived from a model but was formulated on the basis of an argument based on our earlier findings.

The constitution of a database from an initial sample of OECD countries (and then from two subgroups) enabled us to carry out regressions on panel data. This method has the advantage of making it possible to combine both the temporal and individual dimensions: each of the two dimensions provides information that the other does not have.[15] This being so, combining these two dimensions is likely to produce results that are both more reliable and more specific than those that would be obtained with other methods using just one of the two dimensions (temporal or spatial).

It should be noted that, in practice, the panel data model does not produce interesting results until identifying restrictions reflecting the various hypotheses to be tested are imposed on it. As in any type of regression, these hypotheses relate to the nature of the exogenous variables and the properties of the random term. For each hypothesis about behavioural heterogeneity, there is a corresponding model and method of calculation. The choice of specification depends on the type of economic question that is to be investigated.[16] We shall see how, in our model, the large number of observations enabled us to identify and measure fixed effects, the omission of which could have led to bias in the calculations. However, before examining the results of our calculations, let us first present the equation for the model.

The equation adopted is linear, as it is in many econometric applications, which makes it well suited to econometric analysis of panel data. It is written:

$$RCAD_{jt} = b_1\ SGNP1_{jt} + b_2\ RCAU_{jt} + b_3\ RER_{j(t-1)} +$$
$$b_4\ CHPOPM_{jt} + b_5\ TIRM_{jt} + \alpha_j + \beta_t + U_{jt}. \quad (20.5)$$

All the variables used are double indexed. Index j represents the country, while index t represents the year in question; b_j = structural coefficients; α_j = the specific effect (country dummy); β_t = temporal dummy and U_{jt} = the random error term; $t = 1980, \ldots, 1997$ and $j = 1, \ldots, N$. ($N = 19$ (sample 1); $N = 6$ (subsample 2) and $N = 7$ (subsample 3), see Table 20.4).

The variable to be explained equates to specialisation in the 'downstream' segment of the tourism industry (accommodation–catering– social and cultural activities), which is usually considered labour intensive and 'less progressive' (as defined by the rate at which experience is gained through employing labour – so-called 'learning by doing').[17] This latter assumption may be justified in terms of the importance of services in tourist expenditure and to the fact that, over a long period, productivity growth in tourism has lagged behind that in manufacturing and transport services. In our model, this 'downstream' specialisation is expressed on the basis of Balassa's index of comparative advantages ($RCAD_j$).[18]

The evolution of this specialisation is explained by the following exogenous variables.[19]

Table 20.4 List of countries

	Sample 1		Subsample 2	Subsample 3
	Initial group		Subgroup of Mediterranean tourist countries	Subgroup of North American and Asia-Pacific countries
1. Australia	10.	Italy	1. Spain	1. Australia
2. Canada	11.	Japan	2. France	2. Canada
3. South Korea	12.	Mexico	3. Greece	3. South Korea
4. Spain	13.	Norway	4. Italy	4. USA
5. USA	14.	New Zealand	5. Portugal	5. Japan
6. France	15.	Netherlands	6. Turkey	6. Mexico
7. Greece	16.	Portugal		7. New Zealand
8. Ireland	17.	United Kingdom		
9. Iceland	18.	Switzerland		
	19.	Turkey		

- Income per capita ($SGNP1_j$): gross national product per inhabitant of country j in current dollars). GNP per capita is used because it is a more generic and readily available measurement across different countries, and is widely accepted as being a good indicator of a nation's income (or personal disposable income) and a major economic determinant of domestic and international tourism spending.
- The real exchange rate (RER_j): this is the CEPII real exchange rate relative to the rest of the world. As suggested by the PPP theory, the long-run exchange rate can be a good proxy for the relative cost of living in destination countries. It is argued that potential visitors are well informed on exchange rates but relatively uninformed on general price levels in destination countries. Prior to travel, affordability may therefore be judged by exchange rate movements rather than by shifts in general price levels. In our regressions, this variable is time shifted from one period in order to take account of adjustment lags.
- The revealed comparative advantage in international passenger transport[20] ($RCAU_j$): this is the index of specialisation in the 'upstream' segment of international passenger transport, which is capital intensive in character. This indicator can be used to develop an analysis of specialisation in tourism based on the international segmentation of production.

$$RCAU_j = \frac{X_{ij}/X_j}{X_{iz}/X_z} . 100$$

in which X_{ij} denotes exports of international passenger transport services by country j, X_j the total exports of goods and services from country j, X_{iz} the total exports of international passenger transport services from the reference area and X_z the total exports of real goods and services from the reference area Z.

- The hotel function rate ($CHPOPM_j$): this is a ratio of accommodation supply to host population, which is based on the dual relationship between the number of guest rooms available and the population of country j and that of the reference zone. This simple index can give a fairly good estimate of the relative importance of tourism in country j, because the number of rooms determines the number of people directly employed in this sector. For most international standard hotels, the ratio of rooms to employees range from 0.5 to 2.0, often depending on the availability and cost of labour. A high $CHPOPM_j$ implies that a relatively high proportion of the local population in country j works in the hospitality industry. Hence the higher the hospitality function index, the more important is tourism's role in job creation in the local economy.[21]

$$CHPOPM_j = \frac{Room_j/Population_j}{Room_z/Population_z} * 100$$

- The tourist intensity rate ($TIRM_j$) is defined as the dual relationship between the number of international tourists visiting country j and its permanent population and that of the reference area. This is an indicator of social carrying capacity, which expresses both the level of tolerance on the part of the host population and the quality of the international tourist experience in the host country.

$$TIRM_j = \frac{Tourists_j/Population_j}{Tourists_z/Population_z} * 100$$

Experts generally regard a high tourist intensity rate as indicating that international tourists are dominant and impose their attitudes and culture on the host population. Conversely, a low rate produces the opposite phenomenon, with the visitors deferring to the host population.

These indicators provide a basis for subsequent evaluation of the desirable level of international tourism for OECD countries and estimation of the optimal level of the corresponding supply of hotel rooms.

It is difficult to predict, a priori, the sign of each coefficient because, with the exception of the RER, whose action seems to be clear (non-significant variable or negative sign), and perhaps the evolution of per capita earnings (tendency towards despecialisation), all the other variables may in theory influence specialisation in tourism in one or other direction (see commentary on the results). It is likely that this depends heavily on the characteristics of each country, and particularly on the development of its tourist industry.

Panel regression results   Table 20.5 shows the results of the estimates obtained using the fixed-effects method (*Within*).[22] The test was first conducted on the entire group of 19 countries and then on two subgroups of countries (European countries in the Mediterranean Basin and countries in the Asia-Pacific region and North America). By this means, three samples containing 32 countries in all were obtained.

Despite the reservations that must be expressed with regard to any empirical analysis of international tourism, the results seem to be satisfactory:

Table 20.5   Regression results with panel data***

	Sample 1		Subsample 2		Subsample 3	
*SGNP*1	$0.35 \, 10^{-2}$*	(4.42)	$0.64 \, 10^{-2}$**	(1.79)	$0.55 \, 10^{-2}$*	(5.09)
RCAU	0.09*	(4.83)	0.22*	(3.57)	0.06*	(3.10)
RER (−1)	−0.84*	(−5.23)	−3.55*	(−5.05)	−0.70*	(−3.20)
TIRM	−0.05	(−0.68)	−0.14	(−0.56)	0.51*	(2.08)
CHPOPM	0.07*	(2.34)	0.07	(1.07)	0.04	(0.07)
Adjusted R^2 from WITHIN estimation	0.92		0.89		0.86	
Fisher	79.31		36.95		43.89	
Hausman	27.62		15.89		15.41	
Number of observations	323		102		119	

Note: * Significance level of 5% ; *t*-values in parentheses.
      ** Significance level of 10%.
     *** In the interest of clarity, the temporal dummies are not shown in this table.

taken overall, the variables are significant at the 5 per cent level and only one of the three adjusted coefficients of determination (adjusted R^2) is less than 89 per cent. Furthermore, the results seem to confirm the argument that the influence of the explanatory variables adopted is not the same for all the countries (or subgroups of countries).

In particular, it would seem that for the group as a whole (sample 1) and the subsample of North American and Asia-Pacific countries (subsample 3), the evolution of the specialisation in tourism is positively correlated (albeit weakly) with the level of income per capita GNP (*SGNP*1). This result seems, a priori, paradoxical, since there is a commonly held view that tourism tends to be less technological and skill intensive than other activities. Consequently, it is relatively less developed countries that should be the specialists in tourism. Similarly, from a dynamic perspective, a country that is developing should have a tendency to withdraw from this activity. These two propositions are found wanting in light of the results for the first group (sample 1) and the subgroup of North American and Asia-Pacific countries (subsample 3). Two explanations can be advanced. The first is an extension of recent studies of the implications of long-run specialisation in tourism, which show that even if the potential for productivity growth is poorer in tourist activities than in other sectors, the growth of real incomes may be supported in economies specialising in tourism by a shift of the terms of trade in their favour (see Hazari et al. 2003; Lanza et al. 2003).

Consequently, strong terms-of-trade effects in some instances may induce some switching of specialisation away from manufacturing. The second explanation draws on Linder's representative demand theory (Linder 1961), in which a country's international specialisation is said to depend on the existence of a sufficiently high level of domestic demand. This is especially the case, it would seem, in the countries in subsample 3, since their estimated coefficient of the level of per capita GNP ($SGNP1$) has a positive sign, is statistically significant at the 5 per cent level and has a value greater than that for the initial sample 1 ($0.55 \ 10^{-2} > 0.35 \ 10^{-2}$).

The estimated coefficients of $SGNP1$ suggest that, for these two samples, international demand for tourism seems to supplement demand at national level. In the group of Mediterranean tourist countries (subsample 2), on the other hand, the level of per capita GNP does not seem to influence the countries' level of specialisation in tourism at the 5 per cent level, since the estimated coefficient for $SGNP1$ is not statistically significant. In these countries, domestic demand for tourism seems to have less influence on the evolution of the specialisation in tourism than in the other two samples. From this point of view, it seems quite logical to attribute part of the dynamism of their tourism specialisation to foreign demand from international tourists. Does this mean that, for this subgroup of countries, Linder's theory is not verified at the 5 per cent level? This is what the results seem to indicate.

As far as the estimated coefficients for the index of international specialisation in passenger transport ($RCAU$) are concerned, they are all significant and have a positive sign (albeit with a higher coefficient for countries in subsample 2). We are dealing here with a phenomenon highlighted in our empirical study of the international division of tourism production, since the estimated coefficients suggests that, for these three subgroups, specialisations 'upstream' and 'downstream' of the tourism industry evolve in tandem (see Sahli 1999). Thus these are countries that have vertical specialisation in tourism.

The estimated coefficient of price-competitiveness RER (–1) also proves to be significant in all three cases and has the expected sign (negative): appreciation of the RER has an adverse impact on a country's specialisation in tourism. Furthermore, fluctuations in the real exchange rate seem to play a more important role in the Mediterranean OECD countries. This greater sensitivity to relative prices is certainly indicative of a tourism specialisation based on products that are both more substitutable and exposed to greater competition than those of the countries in subsample 3. This finding corroborates one of our initial hypotheses, namely that travellers are sensitive to relative prices but not indifferent to the nature of the destination. Econometric analysis confirms the initial intuition that there is a general relationship between specialisation in tourism and relative prices but also shows that the strength of this relationship differs depending on the group of countries under consideration.

Regarding the hotel function indicator ($CHPOPM$), the coefficients in all three cases are relatively weakly positive, with only one being statistically significant at the 5 per cent level (initial group). The estimated coefficients for this employment indicator seem to have no effect at all on the tourism specialisation in subgroups 2 and 3 in the 'downstream' segment. Two explanations can be put forward. The first is linked to the relevance of the variable used to evaluate the level of employment. The second follows on from our earlier studies of the technological content of the travel industry (Sahli 1999). For some years now, after all, technological innovation has been a key factor in the travel industry. It is here, therefore, that the origin of some of the comparative advantages in tourism enjoyed by OECD countries should be sought. This argument does not lack supporters, particularly among scholars who see the development of new information technologies as giving rise to a new production cycle that goes hand in hand with a radical change in the tourism production processes and in employment. Thus, major innovations in product and marketing have helped to make the tourism industry more productive, even though this does not always mean it is possible to operate with a smaller workforce, given the importance of the human factor in the delivery of tourist services.

Finally, the results of the estimated coefficients for the tourism intensity rate ($TIRM$), a social variable, are fairly surprising. First, this variable is not significant in two of the three samples analysed (initial group and the Mediterranean countries group). Second, its sign changes (it is negative in the case of the initial sample and of subsample 2 and positive in the case of subsample 3). The estimated coefficient is significant only for the American and Asia-Pacific countries group. Thus, the influence of the social carrying capacity indicator on the evolution of countries' specialisation in tourism seems to be favourable only for countries in this subsample. This is perhaps due to the relatively recent development of international tourism in these countries, particularly compared with the countries in subsample 2. After all, the American and Asia-Pacific countries entered the international tourism market later, which means that the period under investigation was, for them, the expansionary phase for their international tourist industry. In this subsample 3, the number of international tourists does not yet seem to have reached the level beyond which the visitor's pleasure begins to diminish. Thus this empirical finding seems to be consistent with Butler's theory of the life cycle of tourist destinations (Butler 1980) and his famous notion of 'carrying capacity'. In these countries, it appears that the physical carrying capacity has not yet reached its limit and that the effects of the development of tourism on the social relationships between visitors and the visited are still at the initial phases of the Doxey model (euphoria and apathy: Doxey 1975).

On the other hand, for the countries in subsample 2, the estimated coefficient of the social variable is negative (but not significant), which would perhaps indicate that these countries are in the stagnation (or even the declining) phase. This suggests that the number of international tourists is not very far from the last two stages of the Doxey model of host irritation (annoyance and antagonism), which indicates that a level of change to local lifestyles above what is considered acceptable by local people has been reached.

This result leads us to recommend that the authorities in the Mediterranean OECD countries should put a temporary cap on the number of international visitors and therefore restrict the number of permissions issued for the construction of new establishments and even cut back on promotional campaigns abroad. This does not, however, mean that the number of rooms should not be modified. To put it simply, these should be qualitative rather than quantitative in nature (quality drive, further differentiation and so on).

Better specification of the model would have required the introduction of other indicators in order to evaluate the overall dimensions of the tourism/environment interface. Indeed, determining the desirable level of international tourism for a given country is a complex task. This varies from one country to another and is the subject of much debate. According to the literature on the subject, determining the optimal carrying capacity requires consideration of three components: physical capacity, environmental capacity and social capacity.[23] Unfortunately, relevant data encompassing the full spectrum of these three components are unavailable at an international level. Consequently, our analysis of the general relationship between the level of specialisation in tourism and OECD countries' carrying capacity is confined to the social dimension.

Summary and conclusions

Empirical analysis of tourism in OECD countries provides us with a comprehensive overview of two aspects of the various countries' competitiveness.

First, it is shown that a well-known size effect makes the large OECD countries major players in terms of tourism market shares, as for international trade. Short-term competitiveness effects show a certain degree of similarity with trade in goods. Despite the statistical difficulties, the influence of the RER on the countries' positions in the tourism market has been shown. Depreciation stimulates a country's tourism industry by making other destinations more expensive and increasing the competitiveness of the local destination. These results support the notion that the RER is one of the key variables of competitiveness in international tourism.

Second, even if tourism remains to a large extent governed by the existence of certain resources (sea, sun, mountains and cultural heritage), other factors also play an important role. These of course include technological factors, which serve to differentiate the nature of tourism comparative advantages, as well as the social dimension, the destination's degree of maturity, the level of domestic demand for tourism (Linder effect), the price competitiveness and dominance of the transport segment. The econometric analysis of panel data demonstrated the relevance and relative importance of these last factors. Moreover, it revealed that their impact differs depending on the level of development of a country's tourism industry.

Third, tourism specialisation creates pressures on the natural and cultural environment, and hence on resources, social structures, economic activities and land use. It is then in the interest of all players to cooperate in forming the direction of their tourism policies and actions.

Notes

1. Market shares are expressed in value terms, since there are no data on the volume–price distribution in traded services.
2. For a similar representation see the article by d'Ewenczy (1989).
3. Following the period between 1982 and 1987 when the dollar appreciated.
4. See below.
5. For further details, see Dwyer et al. (2000, 2001).
6. GDP expressed in PPP is GDP converted by the PPP exchange rate, that is the rate that equalises the purchasing power of the different national currencies. GDP expressed in PPP measures real purchasing power per head of population.
7. Here it reflects an increase in the prices of tourist services in country j relative to international prices.
8. There are several reasons why this may not always emerge very clearly from examination of the graphs: relatively long response times, statistical difficulties, irrelevance of the indicator used and so on.
9. In these cases, there seems to be a problem, either with the quality of the statistics or the reliability of the indicator used.
10. These tests were conducted on an initial sample of 19 countries and two subgroups, in each case for the 1980–97 period.
11. For a comprehensive survey of these indicators, see Sahli (1999).
12. Factor endowments could be the basic components of the production of tourism products. They correspond to the general factors required for the functioning of the whole economy (human resources, capital and infrastructure resources), and to specific factors to the tourism sector such as certain natural, artistic and cultural heritage.
13. Incidentally, this finding is consistent with that of Peterson who, in his comparison of the market shares in exports of tourist services and the comparative advantages in tourism of countries such as the USA, Greece and Spain, reaches the same conclusion. In his article, he states: 'Thus for all three countries their competitive ability, as measured by the value of their export shares, differed significantly from the pattern of competitiveness highlighted by their RCA indices' (Peterson 1988, p. 362).
14. The existing econometric models of expenditure on and earnings from tourism usually

bring into play two types of variables, some reflecting a 'price effect', the others 'an earn-ings effect'.
15. The large number of observations available to us, and hence the large number of degrees of freedom, also makes it possible to test much more sophisticated hypotheses or models than those that can be tested with small samples.
16. For a detailed study of this question, see Dessus (1996) and Dormont (1989).
17. For further details of this concept, see Lanza et al. (2003).
18. The $RCAD_j$ indicator is based on the 'travel' item. Here, the reference zone is the world as a whole.
19. From a general point of view, our variables are derived from three databases (World Development indicators 1999 from the World Bank, CEPII's CHELEM 2000 database and the World Tourism Organization's statistical yearbooks).
20. This is the indicator of specialisation in international passenger transport, as accounted under the 'services to passengers' heading.
21. This index is the most useful tool for examining tourist activity in countries where most accommodation is in the form of hotels and motels. However, it should be interpreted with caution where there are large spatial variations in the type of accommodation avail-able (camping, campervans and so on).
22. For the econometric estimation, the standard panel technique was used. First of all, we test the significance of group effects with a Fisher-test. So the hypothesis that the country effects are the same is rejected. Second, we use the fixed-effects approach or the random-effects approach. The Hausman test values show that the first one should be used. In this way, the bias derived from the existence of country effects correlated with the explana-tory variables is avoided and the within-group estimator is the only consistent estimator.
23. For further details of these indicators, see: Huan and O'Leary (1999) and Saveriades (2000).

References

Balassa, B. (1965), *Trade Liberalization and Revealed Comparative Advantage*, The Manchester School of Economic and Social Studies, No. 33, May.
Brender, A. and J. Oliveira-Martins (1984), 'Les échanges mondiaux d'invisibles: une mise en perspective statistique', *Economie Prospective Internationale*, **19**, 57–94.
Butler, R.W. (1980), 'The concept of a tourist area cycle evolution: implications for manage-ment resources', *Canadian Geographer*, **XXIV** (1), 5–12.
Crouch, G.I. and J.R.B. Ritchie (1999), 'Competitive tourism destinations: combining the-ories of comparative and competitive advantage', Working paper, Ninth Australian Tourism and Hospitality Research Conference, Adelaide, February.
d'Ewenczy, H. (1989), 'Les échanges internationaux de services (1970–1986): lectures de la spécialisation des grands pays industriels', Institut de Recherches Economiques et Sociales, no. 19, 1st quarter.
Deardorff, A.V. (1984), 'Comparative advantage and international trade in services', Working Paper no. 84441C, University of Western Ontario, Canada.
Deardorff, A.V. (1985), 'Comparative advantage and international trade and investment in services', in Robert M. Stern (ed.), *Trade and Investment in Services: Canada/US Perspectives*, Toronto, Ontario: Ontario Economic Council, pp. 39–82.
Dessus, S. (1996), 'Une brève introduction à l'économétrie des données de panel', Centre d'Études du Développement, Paris: OCDE.
Dormont, B. (1989), *Introduction à l'économétrie des données de panel,* Monographies d'économétrie, Éditions du CNRS, Paris.
Doxey, R. (1975), 'A causation theory of visitor-resident irritants: methodology and research inferences', in *The Impact of Tourism*, Proceedings of the 6th Annual Travel and Tourism Research Association conference, San Diego.
Dwyer, L., P. Forsyth and P. Rao (2000), 'The price competitiveness of travel and tourism: a comparison of 19 destinations', *Tourism Management*, **21**, 9–22.

Dwyer, L., P. Forsyth and P. Rao (2001), 'PPPs and the price competitiveness of international tourism destinations', OECD Seminar on PPPs, January, Washington.

Edwards, A. (1995), 'Asia-Pacific travel forecasts to 2005', Research report, London: Economist Intelligence Unit.

Gray, H.P. (1989), 'Services and comparative advantage theory', in Herbert Giersch (ed.), *Services in World Economic Growth*, Institut Für Weltwirtschaft an der Universität Kiel, pp. 65–103.

Hazari, B., J.J. Nowak and M. Sahli (2003), 'International tourism as a way of importing growth', Proceedings of the International Research Conference on Tourism Modelling and Competitiveness, October, Paphos, Cyprus.

Huan, T.C. and J.T. O'Leary (1999), *Measuring Tourism Performance*, Champaign, IL: Sagamore.

Lanza, A., P. Temple and G. Urga (2003), 'The implications of tourism specialisation in the long run: an economic analysis for 13 OECD economies', *Tourism Management*, **24**, 315–21.

Linder, S.B. (1961), *An Essay on Trade and Transformation*, New York: John Wiley & Sons.

Martin, C.A. and S.F. Witt (1987), 'Tourism forecasting models: choice of appropriate variable to represent tourists' cost of living', *Tourism Management*, **8**, 223–45.

Patinkin, D. (1965), *Money, Interest and Prices*, New York: Harper & Row.

Peterson, J.C. (1988), 'Export shares and revealed comparative advantage: a study of international travel', *Applied Economics*, **20**, 351–65.

Peterson, J.C. and R. Barras (1987), 'Measuring international competiveness in services', *Service Industries Journal*, **7**, 131–42.

Richardson, J.B. (1987), 'A sub-sectoral approach to services' trade theory', in Orio Giarini (ed.), *The Emerging Service Economy*, Oxford: Pergamon, pp. 59–82.

Ritchie, J.R.B. and G.I. Crouch (2003), *The Competitive Destination: A Sustainable Tourism Perspective*, Wallingford, Oxon, UK: CAB International.

Sahli, M. (1999), 'Tourisme et spécialisation internationale', PhD thesis, Université Paris I Panthéon-Sorbonne.

Saveriades, A. (2000), 'Establishing the social tourism carrying capacity for the tourist resorts of the east cost of the republic of Cyprus', *Tourism Management*, **21**, 147–56.

Spence, A.M. and A.H. Hazard (1988), *International Competitiveness*, Cambridge, MA: Ballinger.

WTTC (2006), *World Travel and Tourism Climbing to New Heights*, available at www.wttc.org/2006tsa/pdf/World.pdf.

21 Globalisation
John Fletcher and John Westlake

Introduction

Globalisation is not a single phenomenon – rather it is a collection of forces that tend to change the way that the economic, political and cultural worlds operate. Globalisation is a concept that has been brought to the forefront of politics. From the earliest days when subsistence farming and fishing gave way to market systems there has been an incessant growth in the geographical reach of businesses, people and their culture. The process of globalisation has been accelerating throughout the past century and places and people that were once thought to be inaccessible or unreachable at the beginning of the last century are now an attractive component of the tourism industry.

Globalisation has been referred to as a process in which the geographical distance between economic factors, producers and consumers becomes a factor of diminishing significance as a result of faster and more efficient forms of travel, communication and finance (Robertson 1992). The concentration of capital has served to reinforce the capability of those involved in driving forward the globalisation process. It can be seen as a beneficial process whereby the most efficient use can be made of scarce resources and homogeneity in supply can be achieved irrespective of location. However, it can also be viewed as a predatory process whereby global forces face local economic factors and producers with unfair competitive advantages. Globalisation can be examined from cultural, political and environmental viewpoints. From a cultural point of view globalisation can be seen to lead to a homogenisation of cultures where trekking guides in Nepal can be seen wearing Levi jeans and Rayban sunglasses (Scheyvens 2002); Samoan children wearing Disney T-shirts; hardy Brits enjoying barbecues on the beach (Chavez 2003; Malanes 2003).

Globalisation has political implications in the sense that it reduces the power of the state as policies that encourage free trade and direct foreign investment are adopted. The friction of trade has been mitigated by the adoption of global systems such as the World Trade Organisation (WTO). Initially, the WTO was only concerned with trade in goods (through the General Agreement on Trade and Tariffs GATT) but this has now expanded, like the reach of companies, to encompass trade in services (with the adoption of the General Agreement on Trade in Services GATS).

Combine these events with technological progress that facilitates the rapid and effective transfer of information and the world has the fundamental ingredients for globalisation. There are supporters of globalisation and those that resent its presence, as witnessed by the now customary demonstrations outside the multinational summit meetings.

Globalisation also encompasses the economic driving forces that lead to a small number of travel and tour companies, through a process of vertical integration, taking on immense oligopolistic power and again undermining state control and dominating markets (Anon, Foreign Policy, 2003).

This chapter examines the implications of globalisation for the tourism industry and as such, examines the potential benefits and dangers of this process together with an assessment of the specific sectors within the tourism industry that act as the driving forces of the globalisation process.

The definition of globalisation

The term 'globalisation', like the term 'sustainability', has been a part of the literature for a significant amount of time and yet has only recently become a buzzword of the 1990s and hailed as a new concept (Wood 2000; Fayed and Fletcher 2002).

Globalisation is a topic that has attracted wide-ranging attention from scholars in economics, politics, history, finance and sociology. However, most of the definitions tend to point to the interaction and combined roles of economics, politics and culture. A number of authors have referred to the difficulty involved in trying to arrive at a clear and unambiguous definition of globalisation and without such a definition the implications of globalisation are as varied and far reaching as the definitions (see Wood 2000; Fayed and Fletcher 2002). Whether it is a phenomenon that relates to the growing interactions of countries in world trade, foreign direct investment and the capital markets or whether it relates to the absence of borders and barriers to trade between nations is not as important as the end result.

The World Trade Organisation suggested that globalisation is the product of liberalisation and yet globalisation can be seen to enhance liberalisation, creating a feedback situation (WTO 1999). Liberalisation has afforded opportunities to exploit new technologies. As a political and economic phenomenon, globalisation represents a shift away from a world characterised by distinct national boundaries to one that operates as a global economy. A globalised economy is one where production can take place using international factors and where capital is able to flow freely and instantly between locations. The resulting multinational corporations can wield enormous power, often greater than that of small nations. The capital owners can influence policies, foreign exchange rates and the price of capital on the international markets without ever being identified (Australian Apec Study 2003).

Factors affecting globalisation

There are a number of key drivers that fuel the process of globalisation. These include:

1. *Technological progress.* This brings innovations that facilitate and encourage (directly and/or indirectly) trade between nations. The two most important technological factors that provide the driving force behind economic globalisation are (a) increased specialisation in production, forming one of the principal bases for international trade and (b) advances in communications technology (Greenway 1997 in Fayed and Fletcher 2002). The increased efficiency through economies of large-scale operation provides globally based companies with immense market power and the additional costs normally associated with geographical distance are mitigated by the developments in communication.

2. *Economic changes.* The widespread liberalisation of current and capital account transactions and the development of international financial markets have enhanced the process of globalisation.

3. *Cultural and demographic trends.* Weekly and Aggarwal (1987) assert that there is a strong relationship between demographic developments and the growth of international trade and globalisation. Increasing global population combined with increased flows of information has acted like a catalyst to open up trading opportunities. Further encouragement has come from cultural exposure, through the 'demonstration effect' and via media sources that set in place a move towards homogenisation.

4. *Political stability.* This is a crucial factor in underpinning the willingness and ability of nations to trade. A major characteristic of the post-Second World War era has been the cooperative international efforts to reduce state-imposed barriers to trade such as those implemented through the WTO, that is, GATT and GATS.

The liberalisation of trade and investment has been influenced by the expansion and intensification of regional integration efforts. In fact, it may be suggested that globalisation, internationalisation and regionalisation are together a cyclical process of amorphous dimensions that feed off and consume each other.

Internationalisation, liberalisation and regionalisation

Globalisation and internationalisation are terms that tend to be used interchangeably (see Keller 1996a,b and Mules 2000). Internationalisation is used to refer to the increasing geographical spread of economic activities across national boundaries. In contrast, the globalisation of economic activity is a more advanced and complex form of internationalisation, which implies a degree of functional integration between internationally dispersed economic activities.

Regionalisation has created forces for the liberalisation of trade and investment within the constraints of specific geographical boundaries. It can also be seen to be the initial forerunner of globalisation (Ohmae 1993). However, it can also be argued that regionalisation acts as an obstacle to future movements towards globalisation if one takes the view that regional trade agreements are, in effect, exclusive. The liberalising forces of regionalisation can be witnessed in the processes of developments such as the Uruguay Round and the establishment of the WTO (Fayed and Fletcher 2002). On the other hand, regionalisation as evident in developments such as the EU, can be seen to be geographically exclusive and work against liberalisation and globalisation.

The process of globalisation, and of liberalisation, has clearly been influenced by the expansion and intensification of regional integration efforts (De Rosa 1998) and in turn, the pressures of globalisation bring into play further movements towards regional integration. The existing regional entities move further towards globalisation by the constant pressures to broaden the regions in which they reside. The EU is a good example of expanding regionalisation as trade agreements pave the way towards an ever-expanding membership.

The tourism sector was already more advanced than most in terms of liberalisation before the Uruguay Round that brought GATS into existence and within the GATS the tourism and travel-related sector has been the most popular for commitments of its members. As such, of 127 member states, only eight have not made commitments in the tourism and travel-related sector.

Globalisation and the tourism industry
The growing global significance of tourism is a phenomenon recognised by the WTO with the introduction of the GATS, (albeit imperfectly addressing the needs and demands of tourism).

Technology plays a vital role in making the process of globalisation within the tourism industry feasible. Communication and information are the lifelines of an industry that sells its product on faith and where the service providers are, by definition, geographically dispersed. Consumers, suppliers, intermediaries, governments and researchers are all dependent upon the flow of information that makes the tourism of the twenty-first century a reality. By facilitating the linkages between service providers, tourism information services play a fundamental role in the growing interdependence of markets and production activities across regions and nations (Macleod 1999). In the year 2000, the transportation and travel business accounted for more than 50 per cent of all exports of commercial services (WTO 2001).

Since the 1990s, interest has developed in the liberalisation of services in general and tourism in particular. Unlike trade in goods, the intangibility of services means that barriers to their trade are not normally evident at the borders. The barriers to trade in services tend to be subtler, manifesting themselves in the form of legislation, regulation and administrative practices, which brings with them implications for trade policies. Barriers to trade in services are often less transparent than the tariffs and quotas applied to goods and they are often more difficult to evaluate in terms of their restrictive impact.

There is not always a clear line between a measure that affects trade in services and a barrier to trade in services. What one government may feel is a necessary regulatory measure that is being applied in a non-discriminatory manner, such as those requiring a specific qualification for labour, may in fact constitute a de facto trade barrier in the eyes of a foreign services supplier wishing to operate in this market. This leaves the door open for conflicting trade policies and the potential for unfair protectionist practices.

From the point of view of tourism and product development, globalisation provides a mixed set of blessings. Globalisation can provide the consistency in product standards that help to overcome the uncertainties that generally accompany travel and tourism product quality. Therefore, if a client books a hotel room in a Starwood Hotel in Guam s/he can be confident of the parameters of service likely to be provided. In contrast to this positive aspect, globalisation can result in major international companies dominating overseas markets where local companies do not have the resources and skills to compete. Such events fuel the antagonism that can accompany tourism development through foreign ownership and foreign employment. Although these examples apply to different sides of the tourist coin, both will impact on the development of tourism and the net result is difficult to assess (Garrod 1998).

Clearly globalisation has implications for human resource strategies and treatment. According to Scullion and Starkey (2000), the skill level of the workforce will be a vital element of competition. Managing a workforce within a globalised company requires different human resource strategies from those traditionally associated with nation companies. The distribution of skills and expertise will dictate the location of sectional headquarters and the management of an international workforce with their diverse sets of cultural, ethical and legal implications will present a major challenge (Wahab and Cooper 2001).

The eleventh United Nations Conference on Trade and Development

(UNCTAD 1999) Conference, held in São Paulo, acknowledged the fact that the globalisation process had resulted in as many challenges as it had opportunities and that its global consequences had been quite uneven. However, it was felt that the poorer countries, such as the developing countries in Africa had been 'left on the sidelines' of globalisation. To make matters worse, the poorer countries felt that they were now being disadvantaged not just by the activities of the large industrialised countries but also the major developing countries such as China and India (Teo 2002; UNESCO 1999).

It is not possible within the scope of this chapter to examine the process of globalisation and its implications for every facet of the tourism industry; however, it is important to cover the key elements of the industry. Examples below are drawn from the hospitality, cruise ship and airline sectors.

Globalisation and the hospitality sector
The hospitality sector provides a good example of the constraints of local markets and the consequential need to extend boundaries of the market if the business is to continue expanding. Once a hotel company has expanded to take its optimum share of a local or national market, it is a logical development that it will pursue new markets outside the local area. This can lead to a globalisation strategy where the company can continue to expand and take on new market opportunities. The creation of overcapacity, such as we have seen in the US and UK, leads companies to consolidate their local market positions and to extend into new markets abroad.

The hospitality sector clearly plays an important part in bringing people from different locations and cultures together. It also provides an excellent example of the difficulties facing companies as a result of globalisation. Because, unlike their counterparts in manufacturing, the service industries have to establish a fully operational business in a diverse set of cultural, economic and environmental settings.

Tourism includes not only vacation travel but also business and Meetings, Incentives and Conferences (MICE) tourism, sports and religious travel as well as Visiting Friends and Relatives (VFR) (Hoyer and Naess 2001). Therefore the globalisation of business in general creates an environment that is conducive to the development of a global tourism economy. In addition to the more obvious characteristics associated with globalisation such as communication and travel over distances, conducting business through a variety of currencies, operating with a system of regulations that encompass political, social and environmental issues, the globalised hospitality sector takes advantage of:

1. global marketing programmes;
2. homogenised product and brands;

3.   global delivery to local markets;
4.   cross-border movement of labour and capital to allocate resources efficiently;
5.   cross-border training and support systems; and
6.   international pools of capital resources.

In an industry where the small and medium-sized enterprises (SMEs) dominate, this globalisation brings a stark message to operators within the hospitality sector: adaptation and the forming of alliances are vital to survival. Globalisation has presented just as many challenges to SMEs as it has opportunities. Not only have SMEs had to survive with the competitive pressures brought on by globalisation, they have also had to adjust their mode of operation to take advantage of the developing technological changes that have changed the product and given them access to new markets. To take on board the new technology that will allow them to remain competitive, they have to invest in the labour skills necessary to operate this technology and this has proved to be a challenge for many SMEs. SMEs do not make much use of computer reservation systems at the present point in time. This leaves them reliant upon the more traditional distribution channels via the services of tour operators. If local alliances are formed to enhance the value of Computerized Reservation Systems (CRS) systems to SMEs and the significance of the tour operator is reduced, this will provide local SMEs with a window of opportunity to enhance their profitability (Smeral 1998). Through cooperation and alliances, the SMEs can regain some of their competitive edge within a globalised economy to provide some of the local responsiveness that may be lacking within a global marketplace (Kotabe and Helsen 2000).

For the international hotel companies there is an equally stark message and that is, to be successful in someone else's domestic market will mean adjusting the normal company development model so that it fits into a locally acceptable business environment. The divorce of management and ownership is just one example of a practice that is not fully accepted in some parts of the world. Furthermore, it can be argued that the global companies that are successful will be those that can enjoy the economies of large-scale production while providing their services with a local flavour. This latter point highlights a paradox in the global hospitality business. Global branding, marketing, and reservation systems all exploit the economies that can be achieved by a globalised company. In contrast, to operate successfully in a foreign market requires the level of local control and delivery that can only effectively be achieved by decentralisation. The successful companies will be the ones that can adapt to a truly global management where there is no fixed centre of authority and where the operation has the flexibility to adapt to any of the local circumstances. The effectiveness of such decentralisation has been questioned by some (Klidas 2000).

The larger companies, the international hotel chains, came to the forefront following the Second World War and had their real growth spurt during the 1960s and 1970s. Overbuilding occurred during the 1980s and this caused these companies who were committed to an expansion strategy to look outside of the domestic markets for that growth. From the mid-1990s onwards, the large multinational hotel companies have adjusted to a globalised economy using the development of information technology and electronic business-to-business marketplaces as their platform to exploit market opportunities in the global economy. In 1999, the two largest hotel chains had almost a million rooms between them and the ten largest accounted for almost three million rooms. In terms of their geographical reach, Bass Hotels were operating in almost 100 different countries while Best Western International, Accor and Starwood were all operating in 80 countries or more (IH&RA 2000). A significant part of this globalisation manifests in mergers and acquisitions. See Table 21.1 for examples of such mergers and acquisitions.

Vertical integration is normally the domain of tour operators and airlines where such companies acquire companies that are either forward or backward linkages. Although vertical integration occurs less frequently in the hotel industry, it has occurred as evidenced by the acquisitions of Hyatt and Starwood with Microsoft's Expedia and Carlton and Bass with Wizcom. These examples demonstrate the growing importance of information technology in a globalised economy.

Globalisation and the cruise ship sector
The cruise ship sector has been subject to massive growth in the number of cruise ships and berth capacity since 1988. The number of cruise ships has grown by almost 25 per cent over the period 1988 to 2002 and the number of berths by 50 per cent during that same period (Mintel 2003). This

Table 21.1 Hospitality Sector: mergers and acquisitions

Year	Company acquiring	Company acquired
1999	Hilton	Promus
1998	Bass	Intercontinental
1998	Patriot American	Wyndham
1998	Starwood	Sheraton

Source: Adapted from IH&RA (2000 p. 6).

growth has been encouraged through the promotion of the sector to a wider market segment than the traditional upper and upper middle markets; the media and the *Titanic* movie and the Love Boat series encouraged further popularity; parallel to this, the average age and income of passengers has fallen steadily with the baby boomers now enjoying the cruise sector; and finally, ships are now marketed as destinations in their own right (Wood 2000).

If the mobility of capital and other forms of resources and an inability to easily determine the place of residence of such resources is a sign of globalisation, then the cruise ship industry must be regarded as one of the flagships of the process. Cruise ships represent multinational capital, are serviced by labour from many different countries and are capable of locating themselves anywhere at any time. The cruise ship industry provides some good insight into issues relating to globalisation and the tourism industry. As Wood (2000) points out, one of the best examples of the forces and complexities of globalisation is to be found in the cruise ship industry. The very nature of the industry has facilitated its involvement in the process of globalisation. Global economic restructuring reflects and promotes new forms of the deterritorialisation of capital labour (ibid.). This allows the cruise ship companies to fly Flags of Convenience (FOC) and hence pay little regard for local labour laws, avoid many local taxes and even disregard maritime regulations. The industry also has a pedigree of mergers and acquisitions that is almost as old as the industry itself and this has accelerated the way towards globalisation in the industry.

FOC ship crews are not subject to labour laws of origin countries or those of the employer country. Contracts state that they are subject to the laws of the country in which they are flagged. Labour law for the protection of workers rights are not the norm countries where FOC are issued and where they do exist, they are openly available for modification (ibid.).

The global debate has persuasively argued in favour of free markets rather than restrictive policies and this is a view that has been taken on board by bodies such as the International Monetary Fund (IMF) and the World Bank. The end result has been an economic climate of deregulation and a global supply of migrant labour.

The behaviour and characteristics of labour usage within a globalised world is evident within the cruise ship industry. There is a hierarchical structure of management and staff on ships with ethnic and nationality differences. The companies can use nationality as a marketing tool and change it as and when appropriate within their marketing literature. Wood has likened the treatment of labour under such circumstances as institutional racism! The use of FOC gives the cruise ship companies the ability to draw its labour from the most cost advantageous sources.

The impact of globalisation on the cruise ship sector has led to the increased internationalisation of ownership. For example, the Cunard line, owner of the QE2, changed ownership in 1996 with the sale of Trafalgar House to Kvaerner, the Norwegian Construction Company. In 1998 Cunard was bought by a Carnival Corporation-led consortium and was merged with Seabourn Cruises. A further trend evident within this sector is that with the detachment of the cruise operator from the destination, the positive benefits to destinations are markedly reduced. The purchase of private islands, and detachment from locals, allows the cruise ship companies to avoid feeding money back into the host countries and instead repatriate profits and income to the originating country or to a different country if there are tax advantages in doing so.

The impacts of the companies that exploit their globalised position are such that the living standards of host communities have declined and poverty increased. There is also a danger of displacing tourism activities through cruise ship developments whereby the volume and benefits of land-based tourism suffer at the expense of the cruise industry. This can then put the air-based travel systems in jeopardy due to a decrease in demand (Wackerman 1997).

Globalisation and the airline sector
The airline industry is a key component of the tourism industry and is responsible for 80 per cent of international tourist arrivals in developing countries and 10 per cent of world GDP. The growth in world trade combined with technological and pricing factors have resulted in the airline sector doubling its output in each of the past three decades. This is a growth rate that is almost twice that of global output. The sector can trace its pedigree back to the first quarter of the last century but it is the last sixty years that have seen the airline sector become the kingpin to international travel and tourism.

The major players in the airline industry are based in the industrialised countries. The high fixed-cost nature of the airline industry together with the regulatory structure that controls international aviation has hindered the process of globalisation in this important industry. However, the industry has experienced radical changes to its structure, particularly with respect to the formation of alliances and this has overcome some of the inertia towards globalisation. The processes of globalisation through alliances and liberalisation have helped reshape the airline industry over recent decades, driving carriers to enter new markets and exploit economies of scope and density (Wang et al. 2004). These forces have resulted in deregulation, privatisation and the concentration of the market share into fewer companies. Alliances can take on a variety of guises from those that

Morley (2003) describes as being 'loose' that are essentially based on marketing strategies and functions to 'formal' alliances, which include mergers and joint management of assets. There is a wide range of alternatives within this range.

As the number of alliances increase, companies find that their market share and route network share increase significantly (Wang et al. 2004). Alliances can also have the effect of improving both the efficiency and quality of airline services through the reduced operating costs and greater network flexibility (Morley 2003). However, alliances that involve airlines that were competitors reduces the level of competition and can consequently result in fewer flights and higher fares (ibid.). O'Toole and Walker (2000) identified five significant alliances that have emerged from the multitude of bilateral agreements. These have subsequently been reduced to four with the demise of the Wings alliance (Table 21.2).

The majority of the alliances tend to be in the 'loose' part of the range because they are easier to agree and arrange, and do not possess the risks involved with the more 'formal' alliances where airlines may find that their alliance partners appropriate the use of the assets for their own purposes. Another classification of types of alliances has been put forward by Howarth and Kirsebom (1999) who suggest that they fall into three groups:

1. *Coordination*: a loose form of alliance that involves marketing and sometimes collaboration and sharing of information (for example, Oneworld Alliance).

Table 21.2   Major airline alliances

Alliance	Major members
Star	Air Canada, Air New Zealand, ANA, Asiana Airlines, Austrian, British Midland, LOT Polish, Lufthansa, Scandinavian Airlines, Singapore, Spanair, Thai, United, US Airways, Varig
Oneworld	Aer Lingus, American Airlines, British Airways, Cathay Pacific, Finnair, Iberia, LAN Chile, Qantas
SkyTeam	Aeromexico, Air France, Alitalia, Czech Airlines, Delta, Korean Air
Qualiflyer	Air Europe, Air Littoral, Air Liberte AOM, Balair, Crossair, LOT Polish, LTU , Portugalia, Sabena, Swissair, TAP Portugal, Turkish, Volare
(Dissolved, December 2002)	

Source: O'Toole and Walker (2000), subsequently updated by the author in July 2004.

2. *Sharing*: a half-way house form of alliance that includes the coordination type of collaboration but takes it further to include strategy and operational aspects such as scheduling (for example, Star Alliance).
3. *Unification*: a formal form of alliance involving major equity stakes and the overall control of a unified organisation (for example, the link between Swissair and Sabena within the Qualiflyer Alliance).

Howarth and Kirsebom have suggested that such alliances can reap revenue increases of between 2 and 5 per cent together with cost savings of between 2 and 11 per cent, with the greater benefits being experienced the more formal the alliance (Howarth and Kirsebom 1999, p. 35). Given the potential for such economic benefits it may seem surprising that the vast majority of the alliances are to be found at the loose end of the range (O'Toole and Walker 2000). The explanation for this is found in the difficulties and risks associated with separating and sharing assets and this provides a major hindrance to the move towards real globalisation. The assets and resources of an airline are an essential component of the company. There are, however, inherent problems in devising such a simplistic typology of alliances. Oneworld Alliance has been described as a loose or coordination alliance, yet within it there are some airlines such as British Airways that have equity stakes in Qantas and Iberia, which would suggest that they were part of a more formal alliance.

The type of alliance is important in determining the way in which airlines behave. For example, airlines in loose alliances may still compete in some areas of their operation. Agreements can be made between members of such alliances to share some routes but to compete for others. Formal alliances offer the most attractive returns but these are the most difficult to achieve because of the complexity of mergers, asset sharing, regulatory barriers and differences in corporate cultures. There is also the additional problem of anti-competitive legislation and concerns that can prevent mergers taking place, such as the proposed BA and KLM merger in 2000 (Donne 2000), although KLM and Air France were allowed to merge by the European Commission in 2004.

Morley (2003) provides a different typology of alliances where the distinction is made between complementary and parallel alliances. Complementary alliances take place between airlines that do not have overlapping routes but instead link up through an airport to provide extended routes. This can also include linking international airlines with domestic airlines to provide a more attractive and effective route network. In contrast, a parallel alliance is found where airlines are competitors on routes so that the alliance reduces competition and provides a potential for the alliance to act as a cartel.

Alliances can bring with them enormous benefits to the members. The economies of large-scale operation of marketing, enhanced purchasing power from suppliers, utilisation and finance efficiency through to staff and agency savings. Clearly, the extent and range of such savings will depend upon the nature of the alliance.

There are downsides to airline alliances and these can be quite significant. The customer image of an alliance may only be as good as its worst operating member. This means that an airline that is delivering high quality service may suffer because another member of the alliance is not. Similarly, concerns about the safety of an airline may impact upon other members of the alliance. An example of this can be found in Air France suspending its coordination alliance with Korean Airlines as a result of concerns about the latter's safety record (Morley 2003, p. 38).

In terms of broader movements towards globalisation within the airline industry there have been a number of regional and global initiatives. For instance, the multi-bilateral agreements currently being discussed between the EU and the United States, if successful, will bring 70 per cent of the world's international air traffic within that agreement. The airline sector operates within a network of complex regulations and alliances. Although the regulations are currently changing quickly within a dynamic global setting, there is tremendous resistance and inertia due to the requirements of the infrastructure, the environment and safety. Therefore the movement away from bilateral agreements and towards global agreements is a painfully slow one and fraught with difficulties. Out of the current 3500 bilateral agreements in existence, only just over 50 provide rights to unrestricted market access.

There is evidence that suggests that many of the movements towards liberalisation in the airline industry have been either bilateral or multilateral within a regional context, giving the liberalisation a tinge of exclusivity. The restriction to specific areas means that different rules may apply to those that are not included within the framework of the agreements. The possibility of a truly multilateral liberalisation of the airline sector has been considered within the framework of the GATS process but there has been little movement within this agreement. However, the Uruguay Round that marked the birth of this agreement recognised the difficulties of including all aspects of the airline industry within the schedules and instead opted to include only aircraft repair, maintenance services, selling and marketing air transport services and the computer reservation systems within the scope of GATS. Existing bilateral agreements create hurdles for a wider application of GATS because such alliances would mean that members would have to provide the same level of opportunity to other members of GATS as they do to their bilateral partners (Fayed and Westlake 2002). In effect such alliances would either have to encompass the whole of the GATS membership or cease to operate. Some aspects of the international aviation industry are encompassed in GATS and GATT but there has to be greater inclusion if there is a desire to move towards a global open skies policy.

It has been suggested that in spite of the small proportion of agreements that provide for unrestricted market access, the coverage involved (instigated by the USA), paves the way towards a general open skies policy. However, these impressive indicators may be somewhat misleading in view of the fact that the agreements tend to be limited to market access and not to foreign establishment or foreign direct investment (UNCTAD 1999). For example foreign ownership of US-based airlines is limited to 25 per cent and for EU-based airlines limited to 49 per cent.

The only moves which may be seen to counter global trends and shifts towards consolidation by scheduled carriers, is the rise of low-cost carriers (Lawton 2002). Resulting from and encouraged by deregulation of the airline sector in Europe a new form of business model emerged where service provision is limited and costs are severely reduced and it involves the use of subsidiary airports and in some instances new regional destinations.

The original inspiration for low-cost operation possibly came from the efforts of Texas-based South West Airlines which emerged as a low-cost carrier in the United States as early as the 1970s and their actions were fuelled by deregulation of air transport in North America in the Carter presidential era and as embodied in the Airline Deregulation Act 1978.

Following on from developments in Europe there have been initiatives in Australia with Virgin Blue and Pacific Blue as well as in Asia with the rise of Air Asia and other low-cost providers. There are examples of routes being developed which may be seen to offer hopes for development in economic terms in locations a long way from capital cities and as such these developments are against global trends and may be seen to act as poverty alleviators.

Conclusion and future research

The globalisation of the world economy is a process that has been embraced by tourism which has been a pioneer in terms of both liberalisation and global expansion. Its importance as a service industry makes it vital that the globalisation process is successful not only from an industry and company perspective, but also from the point of view of the destinations and the tourists that consume the services. The process of globalisation means that the multinational corporations have to adjust their management and control systems to be able to enjoy the significant economies of large-scale production that are available, and yet provide sufficient flexibility within their operational structure to allow local delivery of services in a satisfactory manner.

This is true for all aspects of the tourism industry but particularly true for the airlines, the cruise ship companies and the multinational hotel companies.

The plight of SMEs, the most dominant form of business in the tourism industry, is less easily identified. If effective alliances can be formed at the local and regional levels then there are huge opportunities for such businesses to compete in an expanding market. However, globalisation puts enormous pressures on SMEs which are already disadvantaged by being subject to higher unit costs than their multinational counterparts. The challenge for the future is for SMEs to be able to embrace fully the technology that provides them with access to the new markets and to be able to invest in that technology and train their employees in its effective operation.

There is a need for greater understanding of the true costs of globalisation. To some extent those costs can be seen in the transfer of power away from national government control and in favour of multinational corporations. The latter demands that these multinational corporations have to take on a greater sense of responsibility in the operation of their companies if other global objectives are to be achieved, such as the sustainability of the tourism industry.

There is also a greater need to understand the ways that SMEs can not only withstand the pressures of competing in a globalised economy but also take advantage of the enormous economies that can be derived from forming alliances and cooperative systems.

From a human resource management point of view, there are many unanswered questions. These range from issues relating to the concentration of intellectual capital through the human resource policies and practices that will hold the workforce in place, to the issues relating to centralisation or decentralisation (see Becherel and Cooper 2002). In terms of training and education, there are clear signs that globalisation is affecting the way that programmes and curricula are structured. An example of this in tourism is the work undertaken at Bournemouth University on behalf of the World Tourism Organisation to develop a Graduate Tourism Aptitude Test that would be used to specify curricular content that has global understanding and relevance.

References

Australian Apec Study Centre (2003), www.globalisationguide.org, Melbourne: Monash University, 15 August.
Author unknown (2003), 'Measuring globalisation: who's up, who's down?', *Foreign Policy*, **134**, 60–73.
Becherel, L. and C. Cooper (2002), 'The impact of globalisation on human resource management in the tourism sector', *Tourism Recreation Research*, **27** (1), 1–12.
Chavez, R. (2003), 'Globalisation and tourism: deadly mix for indigenous peoples', www.twnside.org.sg/title/chavez-cn.htm, 14 August.

De Rosa, D. (1998), *Regional Integration Arrangements: Static Economic Theory, Quantitative Findings and Policy Guidelines*, Washington, DC: World Bank.

Donne, M. (2000), 'The future of international airline alliances', *Travel and Tourism Analyst*, No. 6, 3–21.

Fayed, H. and J. Fletcher (2002), 'Report: Globalisation of economic activity: issues for tourism', *Tourism Economics*, **8** (2), 207–30.

Fayed, H. and J. Westlake (2002), 'Globalisation of air transport: the challenges of the GATS', *Tourism Economics*, **8** (4), 431–55.

Garrod, B. (1998), 'Are economic globalisation and sustainable development compatible? Business strategy and the role of the multinational enterprise', *International Journal of Sustainable Development*, **1** (1), 43–68.

Howarth, G. and T. Kirsebom (1999), *The Future of Airline Alliances: Current thinking, strategic directions and implications*, Gemini Consulting and Reed Business Information, Sutton.

Hoyer, K. and P. Naess (2001), 'Conference tourism: a problem for the environment, as well as for research?', *Journal of Sustainable Tourism*, **8**, 451–70.

International Hotel & Restaurant Association (IH & RA), (2000), 2nd White Paper on the Hotel Industry, IH & RA, Paris, July.

Keller, P. (1996a), 'Globalisation and tourism', *Tourist Review*, **4**, 6–7.

Keller, P. (1996b), 'Globalisation and tourism', Synthesis of International Association of Scientific Experts in Tourism's 46th World Congress held in Rotorua, New Zealand, 22–28 September.

Klidas, A. (2000), 'Empowering hotel workers across national borders', *Tourism Culture and Communication*, **2** (3), 191–200.

Kotabe, M. and K. Helson (2000), *Global Marketing Management*, 2nd edn, New York: John Wiley & Sons.

Lawton, T. (2002), *Cleared for Take-Off: Structure and Strategy in the Low Fare Airline Business*, Ashgate: Aldershot.

Malanes, M. (2003), 'Tourism killing world's eight wonder', www.twnside.org.sg/title/ mm-cn.htm. 14 August.

Macleod, D. (1999), 'Tourism and the globalisation of a Canary Island', *Journal of the Royal Anthropological Institute*, **5** (3), 443–57.

Mintel (2003), 'Cruises', *Leisure Intelligence*, April, 1–93.

Morley, C.L. (2003), 'Impacts of international airline alliances on tourism', *Tourism Economics*, **9** (1), 31–53.

Mules, T. (2000), 'Globalisation and the economic impacts of tourism', in B. Faulkner, G. Moscardo and E. Laws (eds), *Tourism in the 21st Century: Lessons from Experience*, London: Continuum.

Ohmae, K. (1993), 'The rise of the region state', *Foreign Affairs*, **72** (2), 78–88.

O'Toole, K. and K. Walker (2000), *Alliance Survey, Airline Business*, Reed Business information, July, Sutton, 45–93.

Robertson, R. (1992), *Globalisation, Social theory and Global Culture*, Sage: London

Scheyvens, R. (2002), 'Backpacker tourism and third world development,' *Annals of Tourism Research*, **29** (1), 144–64.

Scullion, H. and K. Starkey (2000), 'In search of the changing role of the corporate human resource function in the international firm', *International Journal of Human Resource Management*, **11** (6), 1061–81.

Smeral, E. (1998), 'The impact of globalisation on small and medium enterprises: new challenges for tourism policies in European countries', *Tourism Management*, **19** (4), 371–80.

Teo, P. (2002), 'Striking a balance for sustainable tourism: implications of the discourse on globalisation', *Journal of Sustainable Tourism*, **10** (6), 459–74.

UNCTAD (1999), 'Globalisation and liberalisation: Development I the face of two powerful currents', Proceedings of the United Nations Conference for Trade and Development, New York.

UNESCO (1999), 'The Globalisation of tourism', *UNESCO Courier*, **52** (7/8), 26–8.

Wackerman, G. (1997), *Transport, Trade, Tourism and the World Economic System*, UNESCO: Oxford.

Wahab, S. and C. Cooper (2001), *Tourism in the Age of Globalisation*, London: Routledge.
Wang, Z.H., M. Evans and L. Turner (2004), 'Effects of strategic alliances on air transport market competition: an empirical analysis', *Tourism Economics*, **10** (1), 23–43.
Weekly, J.K. and R. Aggarwal (1987), *International Business Operating in the Global Economy*, London: Thomson Learning.
Wood, R. (2000), 'Caribbean cruise tourism – globalisation at sea', *Annals of Tourism Research*, **127** (2), 345–70.
World Trade Organisation (WTO) (1999), *World Trade Report*, WTO: Geneva.
World Trade Organisation (WTO) (2001), *World Trade Report*, WTO: Geneva.

Index

ABTA (Association of British Travel Agents) 161
accommodation establishment records 90
ADLM (autoregressive distributed lag model) 93, 105–8
aeronautical revenues 272
African countries 177, 184, 234, 469
AIDS (almost ideal demand system) model 100–102
Air Asia 477
Air Berlin 235
Air China 209
air fares 225–6, 236, 446
　and airline alliances 215–17, 220–21
　and airline mergers 220–21
　deregulation 232–3, 446
　long-haul markets 233–4
　low-cost carriers 234–5
　regulation 228–9
Air France 194, 196, 211, 477
Air New Zealand 219–20, 230
air-package tours, pricing 165–6
air traffic control 239
air travel demand 226, 227
airline alliances 473–7
　benefits 196, 198–9, 212–14
　complementary 193, 213, 215–16, 475
　definition of 198
　disadvantages 213, 477
　and distribution systems 193–4
　economic theories of 216–17
　effect on fares 215–17
　effect on tourism 218–19, 230
　endogamic 193, 195, 200–205
　evolution of 191–207
　exogamic 193, 195, 196, 200–205
　importance of 191–2, 209–11, 212
　mega 203, 205–6
　see also airline sector; alliances
airline sector
　alliances see airline alliances
　charter markets 231–2

code sharing 197, 204, 209, 405
deregulation 191, 232–3, 477
economic regulation 228–9, 231
and globalisation 473–7
government owned 229
and hotel ownership 194
and information technology 402, 405, 408, 411
liberalisation 229, 231–6, 476
and long-haul markets 233–4
low-cost carriers see low-cost carriers (LCCs)
mergers 220–21, 230, 475
passenger levies 241–2
regulations 476
reservation systems 193, 194, 238, 402, 408
and travel agency ownership 244
airline tickets 158, 159
airports 240
　capacity 239–41
　congestion 239
　and information technology 402
　investment in 240–41, 271–3
　operational restrictions 240
　ownership 271–2
　privatisation of 272
　subsidiary 478
alliances 191, 192–3
　complementary 193
　definition of 197–8
　difficulties of 213
　global 192–6
　inter-firm 192–3
　mutual dependency of partners 199–200
　resource profiles 200–202
　see also airline alliances
almost ideal demand system (AIDS) model 100–102
Amadeus 193, 194, 203
American Airlines 193–4
American Society of Travel Agents (ASTA) 157, 158